To Victor, (my history
No...
With love always,
Katie

DISCOVERING AMERICAN HISTORY

ALLAN O. KOWNSLAR · DONALD B. FRIZZLE

HOLT, RINEHART AND WINSTON, INC.
NEW YORK, TORONTO

Acknowledgments

The authors are grateful to the numerous history teachers who offered suggestions and evaluations during the preparation of this book. We especially thank Frances Hendricks, Jesse Carnes, Donald Everett, and Robert Hunter of Trinity University. We thank Richard Brown, Van R. Halsey, and Edmund Traverso of the Committee on the Study of History at Amherst College for their interest and encouragement. We are also grateful to the Amherst Regional School Committee for their support. Finally, we express our appreciation to Susan Nevas for editorial evaluation. We dedicate this book to our patient wives, Marguerite and Kay.

DESIGN: IRVING BARNETT

MAPS: BOB GOLDSTEIN, VIEWPOINT GRAPHICS

ILLUSTRATIONS: DAVID K. STONE

Table of Contents

UNIT V   LIFE AND SOCIETY IN THE YOUNG NATION 1800-1860

UNIT VI THE CIVIL WAR AND ITS AFTERMATH 1860-1877

UNIT VII   THE LAST WEST AND INDUSTRIALISM 1860-1920

THE LAST WEST

I. The Last West: Fact or Fiction?

II. The Last West: The End of a Dream

INDUSTRIALISM

III. A New Era: Industry and the Growth of Wealth

This is not the kind of textbook you are accustomed to reading. In most textbooks the author presents the facts about a given period, such as the period of the American Revolution. He writes a conclusion about what that revolution meant to him. This is not necessarily what the event might mean to you. *Discovering American History* is different in that it is designed to find out what *you* think.

In *Discovering American History,* many of the facts about each era will be presented in selections written during the era. Such writings are known as *original* or *primary sources*. For example, an excerpt from the writings of Columbus is an original source for the period of exploration. You will also learn facts from selections written about a period in later times. These are called *secondary sources*. When a modern historian writes about the world of 1492, his writing is a secondary source.

The facts in the original and secondary sources are *historical evidence*. By using evidence, you will have the opportunity to form your *own* conclusions about the period. This kind of thinking, in which you arrive at conclusions after examining particular ideas and facts, is known as *inductive* thinking. In this book, instead of learning by memorizing other people's conclusions, you will learn inductively. That is, you will learn by forming conclusions based on evidence.

You are not expected to form conclusions from the evidence in the sources immediately. You will need the help of *skills*. Much of the material in this book concentrates on the improvement of your skills. These skills will enable you, for example, to understand the main idea of a selection better, to distinguish between fact and opinion, and to deal with two accounts of an event which do not agree.

As you read this book, you will be introduced to some of the important *themes* in American history. A theme is a proposition or question for discussion or debate. In *Discovering American History* the themes deal with topics such as American characteristics, the role of the frontier, the problem of change in a democratic society, and the effect of ideas on men's actions. You will examine historical evidence in order to come to conclusions about such themes.

At times you will be asked to read what different historians or writers have said about an event or period in history. These writings are *interpretations*. An interpretation is the way one pictures an event. Interpretation is another word for the conclusions you might form from historical evidence. A historian or writer will assemble all the available facts and ideas about an era and record his interpretation of what happened and why it happened. Sometimes you will be asked to compare two such interpretations and to determine the validity of each. You will also be asked to write your own interpretation of a period in history, using the same types of sources that the historian used. Such activities will help you to understand how one writes history and how history itself takes shape. This in turn will help you to use critically the writings of historians —the secondary sources—as you form your own conclusions.

In examining primary sources, there is another point you should keep in mind. Most of what happened in the past was never recorded. All we have today is the fragment set down by observers. But these observers did not tell about everything. They recorded what they thought was important—*their* interpretation. Yet sometimes the material or event that they omitted as unimportant was thought to be very significant by others. Thus two observers might emphasize different things about an event and use different "facts" to describe it.

In this book you will often be asked to form a *hypothesis* and then to test its validity. A hypothesis is an idea that has not been proven but that is assumed to be true for the sake of testing. In other words, a hypothesis is a *tentative,* or temporary, *explanation.* For example, a scientist could assume that the combination of two elements would produce a particular result. But the scientist would have to make experiments in order to determine the validity of his hypothesis. An example of a hypothesis in history is "American democracy is the result of the American encounter with the frontier." This hypothesis would have to be tested against available evidence.

As you begin to think about how you would form a hypothesis or test the validity of one, you might consider:

1. The value of forming and using hypotheses in the study of history.
2. The limitations of the historical evidence available to you.
3. The reliability of the historical evidence available to you.
4. Specific examples that could be used to test the validity of your hypotheses. Suppose, for example, you wanted to find out whether American democracy really is the result of the American encounter with the frontier. You could think first about what makes our country democratic. Then you could try to find out if these features developed due to the influence of the frontier.

One of the main reasons for studying history inductively is that it prepares you to assume the responsibilities of citizenship. One of the major duties of an American citizen is to analyze issues and interpret events intelligently. In a democracy like ours, citizens play a critical role in shaping the future of the nation. It is important for you to carry out this task well.

In an inductive history course, the essence of the study of history is *inquiry,* a quest for understanding. That's what history is all about. Only you can decide how you will use it.

To the Student and the Teacher

Most readings contain introductions that provide background information to the selection that follows. Before some selections you will also find "Points to Consider," which will help to guide your studying. The introductions and "Points to Consider" are printed in brown. Questions that follow the readings are also printed in brown. All source material is printed in black.

Many of the original selections in this book contain irregular spelling and punctuation. This is because they were written before there was any uniform standard for writing the English language. Also, some of the selections were written by British authors whose spelling is somewhat different from American spelling. Unless otherwise specified, spelling and punctuation appear as they do in the source being quoted.

"History" is a tricky word. It has many meanings. At times it is used to refer to the past. At other times it refers to the record of the past that is written in books. At still other times it refers to the investigation of the past. When we say "now John F. Kennedy belongs to history" or "the Middle Ages is history" we do not use the word in the same way Henry Ford did when he said "history is bunk" or that we do when we speak of Bancroft's *History of the United States*. In none of these cases do we mean quite the same thing that we do when we speak of history as a branch of knowledge concerned with recording and explaining past events.

A Note to the Teacher
RICHARD H. BROWN, Director,
Committee on the Study of History

What, then, do we mean when we say that students should study "history"? Do we mean that they should study the past, the way historians do? Or do we mean that they should study what historians have written about the past? Or do we mean, perhaps, that they should study the discipline of history as such, and learn how historians work? Or is it perhaps some combination of the three, or something else altogether?

Tacitly, at least, we have given an answer in the traditional history course. It has been said that students should "learn" what historians have written about the past, as distilled into second- and third-hand accounts by the writers of textbooks. It is, perhaps, the least logical answer of all. The result has been history courses devoid of all meaning or value to students and constituting, all too often, dreary exercises in the memorization of dead and useless "facts"—or alleged facts. Lacking vitality and any clear point to students, these courses have all too often been mere chores to be carried out and put aside. "History" has been a lifeless word—and, to many, a bad one. As a society we lack, perhaps as a result, precisely those qualities of perspective, judgment, and a reasoned temper which a knowledge and love of history should provide.

In our own day there are grounds aplenty for reconsidering what a history course ought to be, and for asking if the traditional answer is adequate. For a decade new courses in mathematics and the sciences have been built on quite a different set of assumptions than those which justify the traditional history course. Almost without exception they are built on the notion that it is an unrewarding and fruitless task for students to try to master, willy-nilly, the conclusions of the scholars. It makes far more sense, the proponents of these courses argue, to ask students to play the role of the scholar, discovering for themselves the relationships which form the basic structure of the discipline, sharing the excitement of inquiry and learning, in the process, methods of inquiry which will serve them through life. If analogy is valid, their assumptions suggest that it might be more appropriate to base a "history" course on a definition of history as either the study of the past or of how historians work or of both. It would be less useful to view history as the writings of historians about the past.

To be sure history is not mathematics, nor is it a science. Theories of education developed for one set of disciplines are apt to apply awkwardly, at best, in another set. That this is so in the present case is attested to by the obvious difficulty of identifying what the "structure" of history is that students should discover. Almost certainly there is, in history, no such thing. What distinguishes history as a discipline is not a series of sets of relationships that explain what has happened to man, but the types of questions the historian asks of his data, the purposes for which he asks them, and the methods he uses in pursuing their answers.

It is precisely these which, as the heart of a history course, might make it something infinitely more valuable in the development of human beings than the traditional course has been. To ask questions of history is to learn a mode of inquiry which can be carried outside the classroom and which will be serviceable for a lifetime. It is to learn to doubt, and to see the relationship between hypothesis, evidence, and proof. It is to learn what a fact is, how one comes by it, and, most importantly of all, how one uses it. It is to learn the limits of generalizations.

Few among the serious proponents of such an approach would argue that this implies for a history course a single method of investigation, or that it implies an exclusive use of "original" sources. Equally few would argue that it means that a student should spend all his time trying to recapitulate for himself all that scholars have found out before him and could tell him if he asked. Nor is it to say that the purpose of a history course should be to train junior historians. History is above all an amateur's discipline. It has no technical tools. Its method is simply logical method. To say that the historian's mode of inquiry should be the heart of a history course is to say simply that what is crucial to learning from history is to ask a genuine question of it, and to let the question guide one's study. The investigation that follows may then proceed inductively at times, deductively at other times. Like the historian the student will doubtless use primary sources—the original evidence of historical truth—as the heart of his investigation; but also like the historian he will read books in the pursuit of his question, and he will listen to people who can tell him something he wants to know.

What is perhaps most appealing about such an approach, and what makes it most appropriate, is that it does not put us in the position of pretending that history as an intellectual discipline is something that it is not. With it we do not confuse history with antiquarianism, or the study and love of the past for its own sake. With it we do not pretend that there is any such thing as the "truth" about history—something to be mastered in successive steps as one grows to adulthood or to scholarly eminence. With it the teacher can level with the student that the pursuit of truth is tough, in history as in anything else; that the process of education is lifelong; and that at best we who are teachers can only invite him to join us.

Ultimately the very nature of history is inquiry. It is this that explains why historians are always writing new "history"—always seeing what happened in a different way—why they never have history "finished." What they are doing, of course, is constantly asking different questions of the past, as their own experience changes. The questions we ask are governed by what we want to know. They grow out of our own lives, and out of the life of the society in which we live. The answers we seek—what we then call "the facts" of history—we seek in order to illumine our own lives, and our own nature. Who can doubt that what we so baldly call *the* facts of history, which we say students should know, are in fact any more than *some* facts which happen to be the answers to questions posed by historians of past generations. Chiefly, in the case of American history, these were nineteenth- and early twentieth-century historians interested primarily in the building of nation-states. And who would argue that there is any value whatever in learning a historical "fact" unless one can use it, functionally, to find out other facts, or, more fundamentally, to find out something about himself or his society?

To see history as inquiry is to see it as something alive and useful. It is also to pose a challenge to what we do, in the name of history, in a school classroom. On the way we meet that challenge rests the future tenability of history as an independent discipline in the school curriculum. On the way we meet it, more importantly, rests our ability as a society to develop precisely those qualities of mind and temper which a proper study of history can give.

unit I
EXPLORATION AND COLONIZATION 1492-1775

The discovery, settlement, and expansion of America form merely one phase in the long and restless movement of mankind on the earth.

CHARLES AND MARY BEARD
THE RISE OF AMERICAN CIVILIZATION, 1933

INTRODUCTION

To understand the beginnings of our nation's history, we need to go back many centuries into the history of Europe. The reason is that Europeans were primarily responsible for the discovery and settlement of our land.

The age of discovery is a striking contrast to earlier eras in European history. From the fifth to the eleventh centuries, a period known as the Middle Ages, Europeans traveled very little. There were some exceptions such as wandering scholars, troubadors (strolling minstrels), and people who made pilgrimages to holy shrines in Europe or even as far as Jerusalem. But the majority of Europeans did not venture far from their homes.

In the Middle Ages travel was difficult and often unsafe. Poor upkeep of roads and bridges made travel dangerous. Thieves abounded along the roads. Travelers also found their journeys interrupted by frequent wars. In the early years of the Middle Ages, tribes of barbarians in search of land for settlement attacked many parts of Europe. When the barbarian invasions subsided and local lords and knights became the recognized leaders of their areas, warfare continued, as each prince sought to subject other lords to his rule.

Life in the Middle Ages was unsettled because there was no national or central authority to unite people under one government. Nations such as France and England had not developed yet. Power was held by many local rulers. Europe had not always been so fragmented. It became that way because of the collapse of a powerful state known as the Roman Empire. The Romans had extended their power from their base in Italy over most of southern and western Europe and as far north as England. People traded and conducted business safely because the strong Roman armies were able to protect them and to hold back the tribes of barbarians clamoring at the borders of the Empire. By the fourth and fifth centuries, however, these outsiders had started to move into the weakening Empire. The strong central authority of the Roman government disappeared, and Roman citizens had to defend themselves from the invading barbarians.

Since nobody was powerful enough to form one central government, thousands of separate kingdoms came into being. People had to depend on the lord of their area to protect them. In turn, they worked on the lord's land and produced most of the food and goods that they and the lord required. This system of local government in which the ruling lord was responsible for defending and policing his own territory is called feudalism. The feudal system helped to stifle travel by narrowing people's horizons. They produced all they needed at home; their lives revolved around the local village and manor.

The only unifying authority in Europe at this time was the Roman Catholic Church. The Latin language and loyalty to the Pope in Rome united church officials. Most people participated in some way in church activities—a church was part of most feudal kingdoms. The lord who ruled a feudal state often allied himself with the Church because he needed its support against his rivals. Also, the Church controlled much land that the ruling noble hoped to control. Thus by uniting the clergy, nobles, and common people, the Church became the one great power of the Middle Ages.

The Church became responsible for the one widespread exception to the medieval custom of staying at home. As the power of the popes increased, their desire to extend their influence and that of the Church expanded. In 1095, Pope Urban II encouraged his followers to form an army for the purpose of capturing Jerusalem from the Moslems. Thousands responded to his call and set off across the Mediterranean Sea. There are many reasons to explain why so many people participated in the Crusades. First, as was mentioned earlier, the practice of making pilgrimages to Jerusalem had existed in Europe for many centuries. Second, Christians had been fighting Moslems for many years to prevent their expansion into Europe. Third, the population increase in Europe made food and jobs less plentiful. People were anxious for a change and a new chance. Fourth, a growing group of merchants, sparked by the new interest in the Middle East and the products they could obtain from there, supported the Crusades in order to expand their trade.

Because of the Crusades, many Europeans traveled farther than they ever had before. But then, in the fifteenth century, Europeans began to strike out across vast oceans to the unknown. This was a far cry from voyaging across the familiar Mediterranean to the Middle East. In the sixteenth and seventeenth centuries, the activity continued, as explorers and colonizers set sail on uncharted waters for strange lands. Why the change?

What inspired Europeans, most of whom had still never ventured farther than the nearest town, to undertake such daring trips? This is one of the principal questions you will be attempting to answer in Unit I. You will consider other problems, too. Part I,

Exploration, contains information on European ideas of the unknown and the New World. As you study this material, you will be asked to think about how men's ideas influence their actions. Also, throughout Part I you will consider the question "What is history?" Part II, Colonization, deals with the Europeans as they arrived and settled in the New World. It shows how they applied their ideas to the problems they encountered here. As you read, your attention will be focused on determining what American values began to emerge from these new situations. In other words, what did the new Americans come to consider important?

To begin our nation's history, then, we turn to fifteenth-century Europe to investigate why Europeans embarked on the dangerous and difficult voyages of exploration and colonization.

Exploration

WHAT IS HISTORY?—AN OPENING DEFINITION

This year you will be studying American history. As a first step, you should think about what history is. Before reading further, and without consulting any source of information other than your own thoughts, define the term *history*. You will be given an opportunity to change your definition later if you so choose.

CATHAYA—China

MANGI AND CIAMPA—Provinces of China, according to a letter Toscanelli wrote Columbus

CAMBALUC—Chinese city of Peking

ZAITON—Chinese city of Changchow, visited by Marco Polo

JAVA—Island off coast of Southeast Asia

CIPANGO—Japan

AZORES—Group of islands off Portugal

ANTILIA—An island described in medieval legends

ST. BRANDAN—A mythical land described in medieval tales

HIBERNIA—Ireland

PALOS—A town in Spain

MADEIRA—Islands off Africa

CANAROS—Islands off Africa

SIERRA LEONE—Region on African coast

---

1. Toscanelli's Map

In the years before 1492, when Columbus was making plans for a westward voyage, he became familiar with many ideas about the unknown world. Among the ideas he encountered were those of an Italian physician and map-maker named Paolo Toscanelli. Toscanelli made the map you see below in 1474. In it he set forth his view that the fabled Indies, which lay *east* of Europe, could be reached by crossing the ocean *west* of Europe. This view was based on the notion that the world was round, a theory held by many learned men of that day. Another current theory was that the world was flat and if one sailed west of Europe, one would reach the edge and fall off into darkness. Columbus accepted the theory that the world was round and used Toscanelli's map to plan his route.

TOSCANELLI'S MAP 1474

I. The Old World Ponders the Unknown

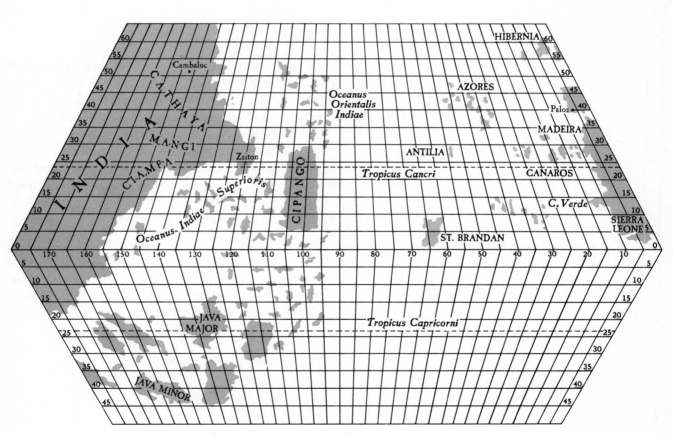

5

1. How does the world as pictured on this map differ from the world as you know it today?

2. How could this map have influenced Columbus in his plans to sail to the Indies? For example:
   What route or routes do you think Columbus would take to get to his destination from Spain? What landmarks would he expect to see? How many miles would he expect the journey to be? How far apart would he expect the landmarks to be?

3. How might plans such as these have affected Columbus' view of what he found?

2. Prester John's Letter

Prester (Priest) John was a legendary Christian leader of the little known lands to the east of Europe. Beginning in the latter part of the twelfth century, letters supposedly written by Prester John and about him were widely circulated in Europe. The story was still popular during Columbus' time. The following reading is a fourteenth-century account of Prester John's description of his empire. Babylon, one of the places referred to in the "Letter," was a Middle Eastern kingdom mentioned in the Bible. The Tower of Babel was a monument in Babylon.

"Prester John's Letter," in **Mandeville's Travels**, edited by Malcolm Letts (London, England: Cambridge University Press for the Hakluyt Society, 1953), Vol. II, pp. 502, 505.

. . . Our magnificence dominates the Three Indias and extends to Further India, where rests the body of St. Thomas the Apostle. It reaches through the desert to the rising sun and continues through the valley of deserted Babylon to the Tower of Babel. . . . Seventy-two provinces, of which some are Christian, are subject to us. . . . We have an abundance of gold, silver, precious stones, elephants . . . camels and dogs. . . . All strangers and pilgrims enjoy our clemency [mercy]. There are no poor among us. Thieves and robbers are not found in our land . . . There is no strife [discord] among us, but our people have an abundance of riches. . . .

[A fountain which is found in the land of Prester John] changes its taste every hour by day and night, and is scarcely three days' journey from Paradise, whence Adam was expelled. Anyone who tastes of this fountain thrice, fasting, will suffer no infirmity thereafter, but remains as [32 years of age] as long as he lives.

1. Columbus was familiar with "Prester John's Letter." How might it have influenced him? Explain your answer.

2. Did you consider all of Prester John's statements in your answer? If not, tell why you think Columbus would have ignored the remaining statements.

3. How did you decide which parts of "Prester John's Letter" would have influenced Columbus? Have you also described how these statements would influence you?

4. Can you make tentative judgments about how people in another time or place felt without studying their ideas thoroughly? Defend your answer with examples from "Prester John's Letter."

3. The Travels of Sir John Mandeville

Sir John Mandeville provided Europeans with another set of ideas about the unfamiliar lands to the east of Europe. Little is known about the life of this English author, who wrote his *Travels* in 1356. However, records show that Mandeville's writings were translated into many European languages during the time of Columbus, and that Mandeville was acquainted with the legends of Prester John.

In one of [these islands] . . . is a manner of folk of great stature, as they were giants, horrible and foul to the sight; and they have but one eye, and that is in midst of the forehead . . . In another isle are foul men of figure without heads, and they have eyes in either shoulder, and their mouths are round shaped like a horseshoe, [in the middle of their chests]. In another isle are men without heads; and their eyes and their mouths are behind their shoulders. . . . In another isle are foul men that have the overlip so great that, when they sleep in the sun, they cover all the visage [face] with that lip. . . .

Mandeville's Travels, edited by Malcolm Letts (London, England: Cambridge University Press for the Hakluyt Society, 1953), Vol. I, pp. 141-142.

1. In what ways do Mandeville's *Travels* and "Prester John's Letter" disagree?

2. Both of these accounts supposedly describe what a traveler would encounter if he journeyed eastward. Why, then, do they disagree?

CONCLUDING EXERCISE

I. Columbus had knowledge of Mandeville's *Travels,* Toscanelli's map, and "Prester John's Letter." When he considered them together, how do you think they influenced him? A hypothesis is an idea that has not been proven but is assumed to be true for the purpose of testing. Is the conclusion you reached a hypothesis or a final explanation of the influence these ideas had on Columbus? Why?

II. Do we think like fourteenth- and fifteenth-century people?

1. What are our "unknowns" today? What are our ideas about them?

2. Do all our ideas about the unknown agree? Why? Why did the writings of Mandeville and "Prester John's Letter" disagree?

3. What is the basis for descriptions of the unknown? For example: Why would anyone think of describing people on other planets as more advanced in science than we, rather than as more backward? Why would "Martians" be pictured with pointed heads or antennae? How do you think fourteenth-century writers chose the particular details they did in writing about the unknown?

4. How do people reading descriptions of the unknown decide whether to reject or accept them? For example: For what reasons do you accept or reject the idea of "flying saucers"? Why might Columbus have accepted or rejected "Prester John's Letter" or Mandeville's *Travels*?

II. The Old World Searches for the Unknown

4. Voyages of Discovery: The Story in Maps

Columbus was only the first of many to embark on explorations late in the fifteenth century. For almost two centuries after 1492, the important European countries sponsored missions of discovery. Spain, one of the first countries to enter the field, understood immediately that there would soon be competition.

After Columbus returned from America, Spain tried to find some way to limit the territorial claims of other nations. At the urging of the Spanish rulers, Pope Alexander VI established the Line of Demarcation in 1493. This line circled the globe, passing through the North and South poles. It was 100 leagues (about 270 miles) west of the Cape Verde Islands. The Pope specified that all future discoveries west of the Line of Demarcation and not held by a Christian prince would belong to Spain.

King John II of Portugal, Spain's main competitor in the exploration of new lands, hoped to establish a settlement more favorable to his country. In 1494, Spain and Portugal negotiated the Treaty of Tordesillas which moved the Line of Demarcation 370 leagues (about 1000 miles) west of the Cape Verde Islands and divided the non-Christian world between the two countries. Spain had exclusive rights to all land west of the Line and Portugal to all land east of the Line.

The three sets of maps that follow show the routes of the explorers who were active in the Age of Discovery, between 1492 and 1682. The maps show voyages for the periods 1492–1506, 1513–1543, and 1553–1682. For each period an additional map has been included to show the expansion of the known world.

Because of space limitations, a few explorers have been omitted, especially some of the minor French explorers of the Great Lakes. The routes shown, however, are representative of the major explorations.

POINTS TO CONSIDER

Patterns you notice in the explorers' routes.

How you might explain these patterns.

What clues these patterns give about the goals of the explorers.

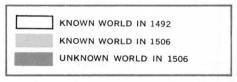

	KNOWN WORLD IN 1492
	KNOWN WORLD IN 1506
	UNKNOWN WORLD IN 1506

EXPANSION OF THE KNOWN WORLD 1492–1506

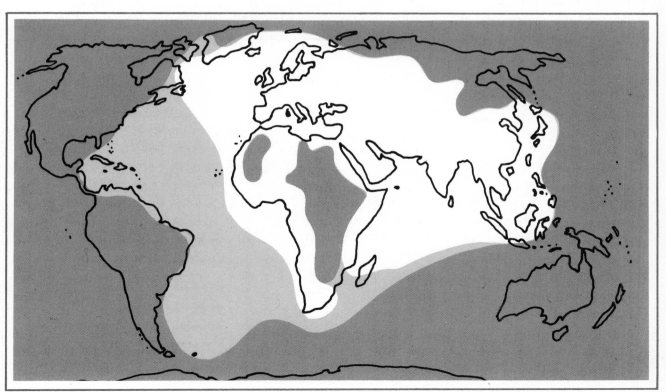

EXPLORATION 1492–1506: COLUMBUS

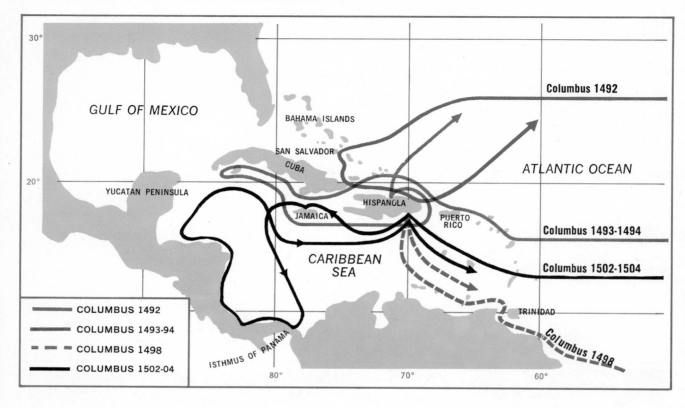

Map legend:
- COLUMBUS 1492
- COLUMBUS 1493-94
- COLUMBUS 1498
- COLUMBUS 1502-04

Map labels: GULF OF MEXICO, BAHAMA ISLANDS, SAN SALVADOR, CUBA, YUCATAN PENINSULA, JAMAICA, HISPANOLA, PUERTO RICO, ATLANTIC OCEAN, CARIBBEAN SEA, TRINIDAD, ISTHMUS OF PANAMA, Columbus 1492, Columbus 1493-1494, Columbus 1502-1504, Columbus 1498

1. In what direction did most of the explorers go between 1492 and 1506? Who were the exceptions?

2. In what area did the most concentrated exploration take place?

3. Does the exploration of the area seem haphazard or systematic? In deciding on your answer, try to reconstruct the order of the explorations. Use the map of Columbus' voyages along with the map of the other explorers.

4. What examples do you find of a man making more than one voyage? What similarities and differences do you see in his routes?

5. What is unusual about Cabral's route?

6. How might you explain the patterns you have just described?

7. What do you think these explorers were seeking?

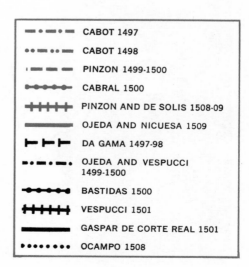

- CABOT 1497
- CABOT 1498
- PINZON 1499-1500
- CABRAL 1500
- PINZON AND DE SOLIS 1508-09
- OJEDA AND NICUESA 1509
- DA GAMA 1497-98
- OJEDA AND VESPUCCI 1499-1500
- BASTIDAS 1500
- VESPUCCI 1501
- GASPAR DE CORTE REAL 1501
- OCAMPO 1508

EXPLORATION 1492–1506: OTHER EXPLORERS

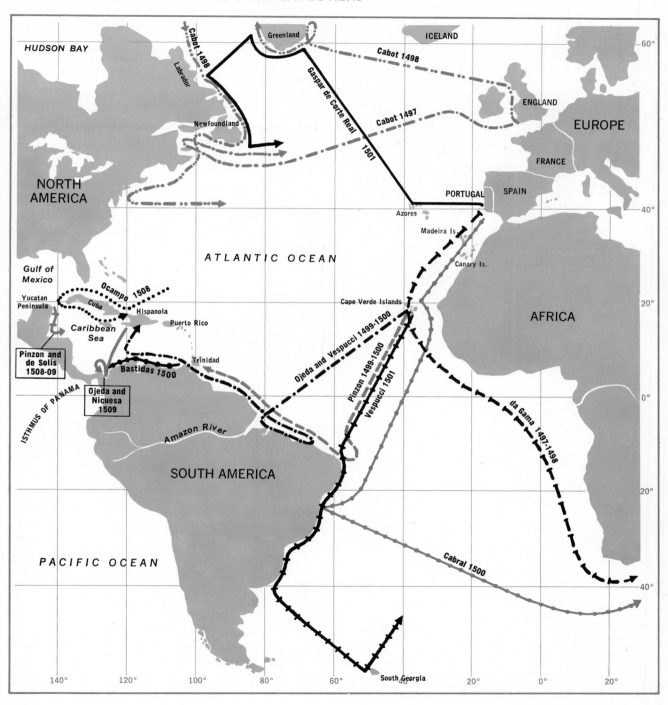

HUDSON BAY

ICELAND

Greenland

Cabot 1498

Cabot 1498

Labrador

Gaspar de Corte Real 1501

ENGLAND

Cabot 1497

EUROPE

Newfoundland

FRANCE

NORTH AMERICA

PORTUGAL   SPAIN

Azores

ATLANTIC OCEAN

Madeira Is.

Gulf of Mexico

Canary Is.

Yucatan Peninsula

Ocampo 1508

Cuba

Cape Verde Islands

AFRICA

Hispanola

Puerto Rico

Caribbean Sea

Ojeda and Vespucci 1499-1500

Pinzon and de Solis 1508-09

Trinidad

Bastidas 1500

Pinzon 1499-1500

Vespucci 1501

ISTHMUS OF PANAMA

Ojeda and Nicuesa 1509

da Gama 1497-1498

Amazon River

SOUTH AMERICA

Cabral 1500

PACIFIC OCEAN

South Georgia

140°   120°   100°   80°   60°   40°   20°   0°   20°

60°

40°

20°

0°

20°

40°

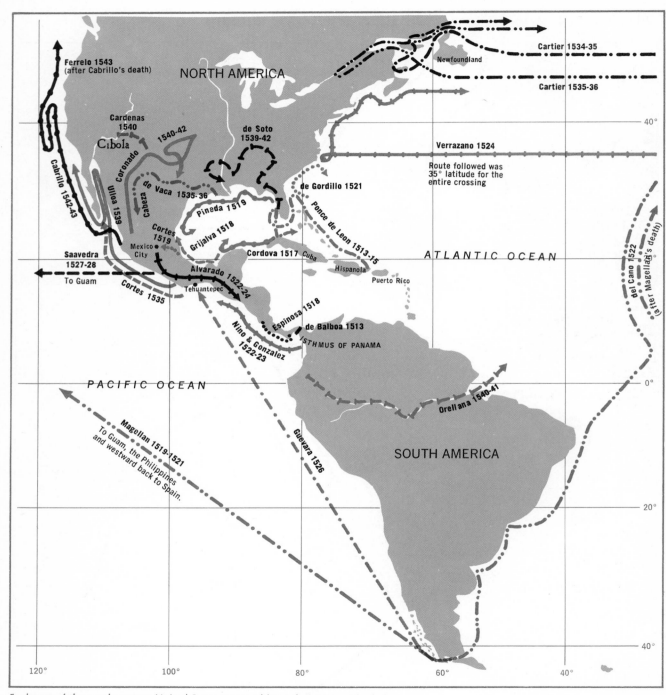

Explorers of the southwestern United States returned from their trips with stories of rich Indian pueblos. The stories gave rise to the legend of the Seven Cities of Cibola, which were supposed to contain great wealth.

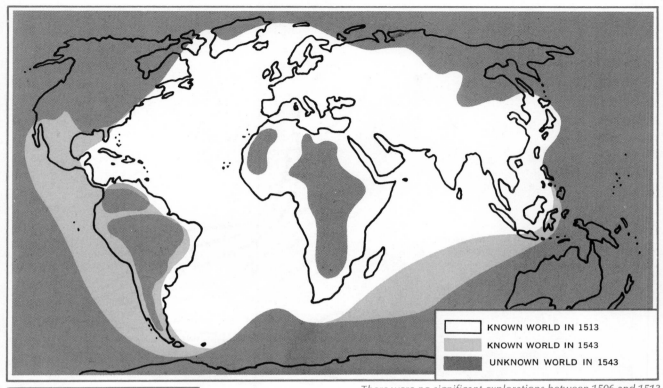

KNOWN WORLD IN 1513

KNOWN WORLD IN 1543

UNKNOWN WORLD IN 1543

There were no significant explorations between 1506 and 1513.

DE BALBOA 1513

ESPINOSA 1518

ALVARADO 1522-24

SAAVEDRA 1527-28

CARTIER 1534-35

CARTIER 1535-36

DE SOTO 1539-42

CABRILLO 1542-43

CORDOVA 1517

GRIJALVA 1518

DE GORDILLO 1521

VERRAZANO 1524

GUEVARA 1526

CABEZA DE VACA 1535-36

ULLOA 1539

CARDENAS 1540

PONCE DE LEON 1513-15

PINEDA 1519

CORTES 1519

MAGELLAN 1519-21

DEL CANO 1522

CORTES 1535

ORELLANA 1540-41

CORONADO 1540-42

1. How does the exploration between 1513 and 1543 differ from what you saw on the first two maps? How is it similar? In forming your answer, think about the same kinds of questions you considered for the earlier maps.

2. Do any of the explorers seem to have influenced each other? How? For example, how did Magellan's voyages influence explorers who came after him? Did the explorers he influenced all go in the same direction?

3. How quickly or slowly does exploration proceed? What period of time elapses before explorers take advantage of information gained from previous explorations?

4. How might you explain the patterns you have just described?

5. Do you think these explorers were looking for the same things the earlier explorers sought?

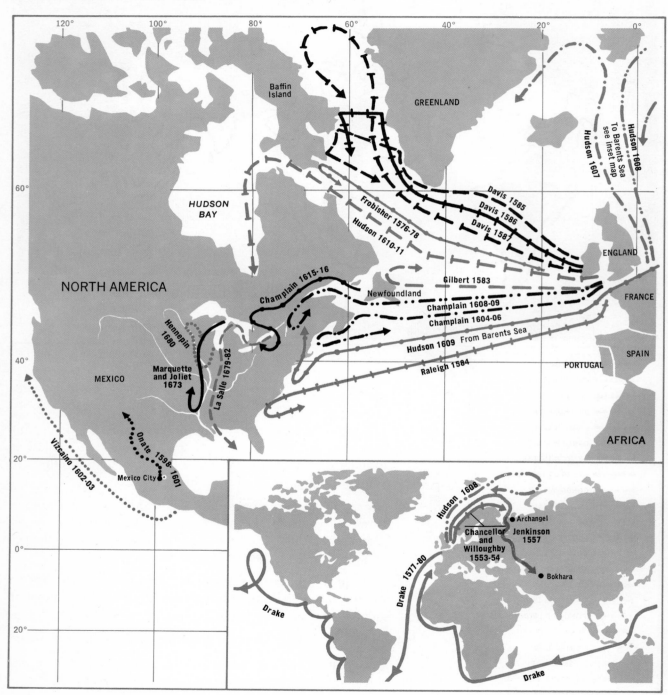

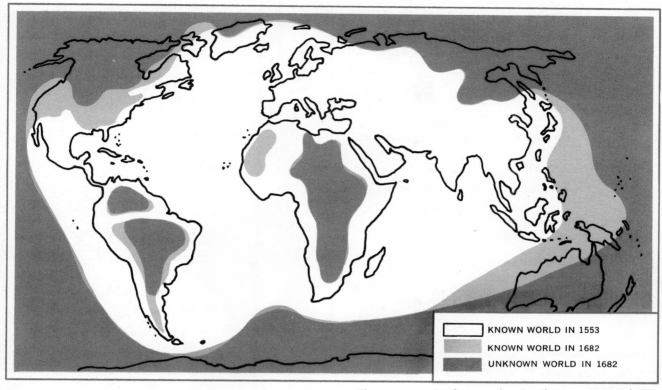

KNOWN WORLD IN 1553

KNOWN WORLD IN 1682

UNKNOWN WORLD IN 1682

There were no significant explorations between 1543 and 1553.

DAVIS 1585

DAVIS 1586

DAVIS 1587

ONATE 1598-1601

CHAMPLAIN 1604-06

CHAMPLAIN 1608-09

CHAMPLAIN 1615-16

MARQUETTE AND JOLIET 1673

CHANCELLOR AND WILLOUGHBY 1553-54

FROBISHER 1576-78

GILBERT 1583

RALEIGH 1584

VIZCAINO 1602-03

DRAKE 1577-80

HUDSON 1607

HUDSON 1608

HUDSON 1609

HUDSON 1610-11

LA SALLE 1679-82

HENNEPIN 1680

---

1. What patterns do you see when you compare this exploration map with the earlier maps? When you compare the routes shown here with each other?

2. How can you explain these patterns?

3. Do you think there has been any change in the goals of the explorers?

5. Explorers: A Chart

A list of facts can tell you much more than it appears to at first glance. One way to make facts speak is to group them in different ways. This chart groups explorers by country and by date. It includes explorers not shown on the maps. Study the chart to see how much you can learn from it about explorations.

SPAIN	PORTUGAL	ENGLAND	FRANCE
	1488 DIAS		
1492–98 COLUMBUS	1497–98 da GAMA	1497-98 JOHN CABOT	
	1498 PEREIRA		
1499–1500 de OJEDA AND VESPUCCI	1499 FERNANDES		
1499–1500 PINZON			
1500 BASTIDAS	1500 GASPAR de CORTE-REAL		
	1500 CABRAL		
	1501 GASPAR de CORTE-REAL		
	1501 *VESPUCCI		
1502–04 COLUMBUS	1502 MIGUEL de CORTE-REAL		
	1505 ALMEIDA		
1508 OCAMPO			
1508–09 PINZON AND de SOLIS			
1509 OJEDA AND NICUESA	1509–15 ALBUQUERQUE	1509 SEBASTIAN CABOT	
1513 de BALBOA	1513 ALVAREZ		
1513–15 PONCE de LEON			
1515–16 de SOLIS			
1517 de CORDOBA AND ALAMINOS	1517 de ANDRADE		
1518 GRIJALVA			
1518 ESPINOSA			
1519 PINEDA			
1519–21 MAGELLAN			
1519–21 CORTES			
1521 de GORDILLO			
1522–23 NINO AND GONZALEZ			
1522–23 DAVILA			
1522–24 ALVARADO			
1526 GUEVARA			
			1524 VERRAZANO
1527–28 SAAVEDRA		1527 MARY GUILDFORD (a ship)	
1528–36 NAVAREZ			
	1530-32 de SOUZA		
1531 PIZARRO			
			1534–41 CARTIER
1535 CORTES			
1535–36 CABEZA de VACA			
1539–42 de SOTO			
1539–42 de NIZA			
1539–43 ALVARADO			
1540–41 ORELLANA			
1540 CARDENAS			
1540–42 CORONADO			
1542–43 CABRILLO	1542 da MOTA		1542–43 de ROBERVAL
		1553 WILLOUGHBY	
		1553–54 CHANCELLOR	
		1557 JENKINSON	
		1576–78 FROBISHER	
		1577–80 DRAKE	
		1583 GILBERT	
		1584 RALEIGH	
		1585–86 DAVIS	
1598–1609 ONATE			
1602–03 VIZCAINO		1602 WEYMOUTH	
			1603–16 CHAMPLAIN
		1605–06 WEYMOUTH	
		1607–11 ** HUDSON	
			1634 NICOLET
			1658–59 RADISSON AND GROSEILLERS
			1665 ALLOUEZ
			1669–70 DOLLIER
			1673 MARQUETTE AND JOLIET
			1679–80 DULUTH
			1679–87 LA SALLE
			1680 HENNEPIN

* In 1501 Vespucci left the service of Spain to sail for Portugal.

**Holland sponsored the voyage made in 1609. However, his 1607, 1608, and 1610 voyages were sponsored by England.

1. Do you recognize any patterns or developments in the exploration of the New World? For example:

   Is there any one nation that dominates the search for the New World in a certain period of time? What else could you say about that nation from the chart?

   What can you say about the relations among different exploring nations at different times?

   What can you say about the exploration activity as a whole?

2. Look back at the maps. Now that you know the nationalities of the explorers, do any new patterns emerge?

3. This chart answers some questions about the explorers. Does it also raise questions? Explain.

4. Could there have been influences on explorers other than the fourteenth- and fifteenth-century ideas you have studied? Does the chart suggest this? Explain your answer.

6. Columbus Reports on a Voyage, 1493

The readings in this section are either direct accounts by the explorers of their own voyages or descriptions of the voyages by contemporaries of the explorers. The selections you will read describe early expeditions of the first half-century of exploration between 1492 and 1543.

Columbus recorded his observations on each of the four voyages he made to the New World. The following letter, which the explorer sent to a nobleman in the court of King Ferdinand and Queen Isabella, contains some of Columbus' ideas about his second voyage.

POINTS TO CONSIDER

The comparison between what Columbus thinks he has discovered and what you know he has found.

How you might explain what Columbus reports about the new area.

Knowing that it will afford you pleasure to learn that I have brought my undertaking to a successful termination, I have decided upon writing you this letter to acquaint you with all the events which have occurred in my voyage, and the discoveries which have resulted from it. Thirty-three days after my departure from Cadiz I reached the Indian sea, [Atlantic Ocean], where I discovered many islands, thickly peopled, of which I took possession without resistance in the name of our most illustrious

III. Tales of the New World

The **Discovery of America, 1492-1584,** edited by Philip F. Alexander (London, England: Cambridge University Press for the Hakluyt Society, 1917), pp. 1-9.

Monarch, by public proclamation and with unfurled banners [flags of Spain]. . . . This said island of Juana [Cuba] is exceedingly fertile, as indeed are all the others; it is surrounded with many bays, spacious, very secure, and surpassing any that I have ever seen; numerous large and healthful rivers intersect it, and it also contains many lofty mountains. All these islands are very beautiful, and distinguished by a diversity [variety] of scenery; they are filled with a great variety of trees of immense height, and which I believe to retain their foliage in all seasons; for when I saw them they were as verdant [green] and luxuriant as they are in Spain in the month of May,—some of them were blossoming, some bearing fruit, and all flourishing in the greatest perfection . . . The nightingale and various birds were singing in countless numbers, and that in November . . . There are besides in the same island of Juana seven or eight kinds of palm trees, which, like all the other trees, herbs, and fruits, considerably surpass ours in height and beauty. The pines are also very handsome, and there are very extensive fields and meadows, a variety of birds, different kinds of honey, and many sorts of metals, but no iron. In that island also which I have before said we named Espanola [Haiti], there are mountains of very great size and beauty, vast plains, groves, and very fruitful fields, admirably adapted for tillage, pasture, and habitation. The convenience and excellence of the harbours in this island, and the abundance of the rivers, so indispensible to the health of man, surpass anything that would be believed by one who had not seen it. The trees, herbage, and fruits of Espanola are very different from those of Juana, and moreover it abounds in various kinds of spices, gold, and other metals . . . [The natives] exhibit great love towards all others in preference to themselves: they also give objects of great value for trifles, and content themselves with very little or nothing in return. I however forbad that these trifles and articles of no value (such as pieces of dishes, plates, and glass, keys, and leather straps) should be given to them, although if they could obtain them, they imagined themselves to be possessed of the most beautiful trinkets in the world. It even happened that a sailor received for a leather strap as much gold as was worth three golden nobles, and for things of more trifling value offered by our men, especially newly-coined blancas [French coins], or any gold coins, the Indians would give whatever the seller required; as, for instance, an ounce and a half or two ounces of gold, or thirty or forty pounds of cotton, with which commodity they were already acquainted. Thus they bartered, like idiots, cotton and gold for fragments of bows, glasses, bottles, and jars;

which I forbad as being unjust, and myself gave them many beautiful and acceptable articles which I had brought with me, taking [nothing] from them in return; I did this in order that I might more easily conciliate them [gain their good will] that they might be led to become Christians, and be inclined to entertain a regard for the King and Queen, our Princes and all Spaniards, and that I might induce them to take an interest in seeking out, and collecting, and delivering to us such things as they possessed in abundance, but which we greatly needed. They practice no kind of idolatry [worship of idols], but have firm belief that all strength and power, and indeed all good things, are in heaven, and that I had descended from thence with these ships and sailors, and under this impression was I received after they had thrown aside their fears . . . [The natives] are still travelling with me, and although they have been with us now for a long time, they continue to entertain the idea that I have descended from heaven . . .

1. Does Columbus reflect any of the fourteenth- and fifteenth-century ideas of the unknown in this account of his second voyage? How do you explain this?

2. Does Columbus reveal any of his reasons for sailing to this area? How can you tell?

7. Vespucci Views the New World, 1504

In 1501, under the flag of Portugal, the Italian explorer Amerigo Vespucci sailed along the eastern coast of South America. The following letter, dated 1504, comes from Vespucci's writings about his discoveries.

On a former occasion I wrote to you at some length concerning my return from those new regions which we found and explored with the fleet, at the cost, and by the command of the Most Serene King of Portugal. And these we may rightly call a new world. Because our ancestors had no knowledge of them, and it will be a matter wholly new to all those who hear about them. For this transcends [surpasses] the view held by our ancients, inasmuch as most of them hold that there is no continent to the south beyond the equator, but only the sea which they named the Atlantic; and if some of them did aver [declare positively] that a continent there was, they denied with abundant argument that

Amerigo Vespucci, **Mundus Novus,** translated by George Tyler Northrup ("Vespucci Reprints, Texts, and Studies," Vol. V [Princeton, New Jersey: Princeton University Press, 1916]), p. 1.

it was a habitable land. But that this their opinion is false and utterly opposed to the truth, this my last voyage has made manifest [obvious] for in those southern parts I have found a continent more densely peopled and abounding in animals than our Europe or Asia or Africa, and, in addition, a climate milder and more delightful than in any other region known to us . . .

1. How does Vespucci's account compare with Columbus' description of the land west of Europe?

2. How is the letter by Vespucci similar or dissimilar to the fourteenth- and fifteenth-century ideas you learned about in Section I?

8. A Later Report by Columbus, 1504

Select Documents Illustrating the Four Voyages of Columbus (London, England: Cambridge University Press for the Hakluyt Society, 1932), Vol. II, pp. 102, 104.

Columbus was on his fourth voyage when he wrote this letter to the Spanish monarchs. The Spanish public, thinking he had found the Indies on his first three trips, waited in vain for the expected cargoes of Indian wealth. Meanwhile, they jealously watched the Portuguese ships, which traveled to India by the route around Africa, as they returned laden with bounty.

When I discovered the Indies, I said that they were the richest dominion that there is in the world. I was speaking of the gold, pearls, precious stones and spices, with the trade and markets in them, and because everything did not appear immediately I was heid up to abuse . . . in this land of Veragua [Nicaragua] I saw greater evidence of gold on the first two days than in Espanola [Haiti] in four years, and that the lands in this district could not be more lovely or better cultivated, nor could the people be more timid . . . Genoese, Venetians, and all who have pearls, precious stones, and other things of value, all carry them to the end of the world in order to exchange them, to turn them into gold. Gold is more excellent. Gold constitutes treasure, and he who possesses it may do what he will in the world, and may so attain as to bring souls to Paradise. . . .

1. What reasons does Columbus give to show that gold is more desirable than other forms of wealth? Do these reasons recall any subjects Columbus discussed in 1493?

2. How does Columbus' description of this discovery compare with his 1493 account?

3. Why does Columbus emphasize gold in this account? Why does he choose to stress certain advantages of gold more than others?

4. Did everyone in your class agree on the answers to question 3? Are different interpretations of Columbus' report equally valid?

9. Peter Martyr Recounts the Explorations of Columbus, 1511

The first written account of the discovery of America was set down by Peter Martyr, an Italian historian who was a chronicler at the court of Spain's King Ferdinand and Queen Isabella. Martyr wrote his book around 1511 and based it on Columbus' original documents.

The following selection is an excerpt from Martyr's book in which he describes Columbus' first voyage to the New World. The spelling of some of the words has been changed to conform with modern usage.

. . . And then other [natives] came, bringing with them stones of gold weighing ten or twelve drams, and they feared not to confess that in the place where they gathered that gold, there were sometimes found stones of gold as big as the head of a child.

The First Three English Books on America, edited by Edward Arber (Birmingham, England: Turnbull & Spears, 1885), p. 74.

A "dram" is ⅛ of an ounce.

1. How does this account compare with Columbus' own account of the gold found on his second voyage?

2. Why do you think Peter Martyr put this emphasis on gold?

10. Friar Marcos de Niza, 1539

Between 1539 and 1542, Marcos de Niza, a Franciscan friar, led an expedition into the area now called New Mexico. He was under the orders of the Viceroy of New Spain (Mexico) who instructed him to find the rich Indian pueblos or Seven Cities of Cibola described by earlier explorers of the area.

In the reading below, de Niza describes his findings. The spelling in this passage has been modernized.

. . . At the end of this desert, I found other Indians which marvelled to see me, because they had no knowledge of any Christians, having no traffic nor conversation with those Indians which I had passed, in regard to the great desert which was between them.

The Journey of Alvar Nunez Cabeza de Vaca, edited by A. F. Bandelier (New York: Barnes & Noble, Inc., 1905), pp. 205-207. Reprinted by permission of the publisher.

These Indians entertained me exceeding courteously, and gave me great store of victuals [food] and sought to touch my garments and called me Hagota, which in their language signifies a man come from heaven . . . In these countries and in all places else by all ways and means possible, I sought information where any Countries were of more Cities and people of civility and understanding, than those which I had found: and I could hear no news of any such: howbeit [nevertheless] they told me, that four or five days journey within the Country, at the foot of the mountains there is a large and mighty plain, wherein they told me, that there were many great Towns, and people clad in cotton: and when I showed them certain metals which I carried with me, to learn what rich metals were in the land, they took the mineral of Gold and told me, that thereof were vessels among the people of the plain, and that they carried certain round green stones hanging at their nostrils, and at their ears, and that they have certain thin plates of that Gold, wherewith they scrape off their sweat, and that the walls of their Temples are covered therewith, and that they use it in all their household vessels. And because this Valley is distant from the Sea-coast, and my instruction was not to leave the coast, I determined to leave the discovery thereof until my return: at which time I might do it more commodiously [properly].

What appears to be Marcos de Niza's major concern in this passage?

11. Raimonde de Soncino Reports on Cabot's First Voyage, 1497

The Duke who ruled Milan, an important Italian state in the fifteenth century, received this letter from his ambassador to London. The letter was dated December 18, 1497, just after John Cabot returned to England. It described Cabot's discoveries.

. . . There is in this kingdom a man of the people, Mr. John Cabot by name, of kindly wit and a most expert mariner. Having observed that the sovereigns first of Portugal and then of Spain had occupied unknown islands, he decided to make a similar acquisition for his Majesty. After obtaining patents [guarantees] that the effective ownership of what he might find should be his, though reserving the rights of the Crown, he committed himself to fortune in a little ship, with eighteen persons. He started from Bristol, a port on the west of this kingdom, passed Ireland, which is still further west, and then bore towards the north, in order

The Cabot Voyages and Bristol Discovery Under Henry VIII, edited by James A. Williamson (London, England: Cambridge University Press for the Hakluyt Society, 1962), pp. 209-210.

to sail to the east, leaving the north on his right hand after some days. After having wandered for some time he at length arrived at the mainland, where he hoisted the royal standard, and took possession for the king here; and after taking certain tokens he returned.

. . . They say that the land is excellent and temperate, and they believe that Brazil wood and silk are native there. They assert [maintain] that the sea there is swarming with fish, which can be taken not only with the net, but in baskets let down with a stone, so that it sinks in the water. . . .

. . . His companions, say that they could bring so many fish that this kingdom would have no further need of Iceland, from which place there comes a very great quantity of the fish called stock-fish [cod and haddock]. But Mr. Cabot has his mind set upon even greater things because he proposes to keep along the coast from the place at which he touched, more and more towards the east, until he reaches an island which he calls Cipango [Japan] situated in the equinoctial [equatorial] region, where he believes that all the spices of the world have their origin, as well as the jewels. He says that on previous occasions he has been to Mecca [a city in the Middle East], whither spices are borne by caravans from distant countries. When he asked those who brought them what was the place of origin of these spices, they answered that they did not know, but that other caravans came with this merchandise to their homes from distant countries, and these again said that the goods had been brought to them from other remote regions. He therefore reasons that these things came from places far away from them, and so on from one to the other, always assuming that the earth is round, it follows as a matter of course [that the real source of these riches must be west of Europe and north of the equator].

. . . Before very long they say that his Majesty will equip some ships, and in addition he will give them all the malefactors [wrongdoers] and they will go to that country and form a colony. By means of this they hope to make London a more important mart [market] for spices than Alexandria.

1. Why was Cabot interested in exploration? What were the goals of this early English voyage of discovery?

2. What does Cabot think he has found?

3. Look again at the map on page 11 that shows Cabot's routes. How would you explain the route of Cabot's second voyage, the one he made in 1498?

Wood from the Brazil tree is used for making red dye.

12. A First-Hand Account of Magellan's Voyage: Antonio Pigafetta, 1526

Ferdinand Magellan sailed from Spain in 1519 in search of a western route to the Moluccas or Spice Islands. His trip took him around the tip of South America and across the Pacific Ocean. In 1521 he discovered the Philippine Islands, where he was killed in battle with the natives. One of his ships continued westward and returned to Spain, thus completing the first voyage around the world.

Among the various accounts of this voyage is one by Antonio Pigafetta, an Italian who sailed with the expedition. The following reading is an excerpt from Pigafetta's writings. The spelling of some words has been modernized.

The First Three English Books on America, edited by Edward Arber (Birmingham, England: Turnbull & Spears, 1885), pp. 251-252.

. . . One day by chance [in Brazil] they spied a man of the stature of a giant, who came dancing and singing and shortly after seemed to cast dust over his head . . . When he saw the captain with certain of his company about him, he was greatly amazed and made signs holding up his hand to heaven, signifying thereby that our men came from thence. This giant was so big that the head of one of our men of mean stature came but to his waist . . . [Other giants appeared] . . . when they saw how they were deceived [and captured] they roared like bulls and cried for their great devil *Setebos* to help them. . . .

1. Does this selection remind you of the fourteenth-century accounts you read?

2. Has observation of the New World changed men's ideas of it?

CONCLUDING EXERCISE

I. Why are the ideas about the New World so much like the old ideas of the unknown?

   1. How do the accounts of the early explorers reflect the ideas in Toscanelli's map, "Prester John's Letter," and Mandeville's *Travels?*

   2. Why did fourteenth- and fifteenth-century men have these ideas about the unknown?

   3. After their voyages, explorers should have known more about the world than Toscanelli, "Prester John," and Mandeville did. Nevertheless, the explorers retained many of the same ideas held by the fourteenth- and fifteenth-century men. How do you explain this?

II. Why did explorers embark on voyages of discovery?

1. Did any of the ideas about the unknown world or the New World influence the actions of the explorers? If so, which ideas were most influential?

2. How do you know which ideas influenced the explorers most? Do any explorers specifically say what they hoped to achieve in the New World?

3. Is your statement about the explorers' motives a hypothesis or a final explanation? Compare this with your statement at the end of Section I of this unit concerning the influence of ideas about the unknown world on Columbus. Is there any difference? Explain.

III. How might the explorers' reports of their discoveries have influenced later explorers?

IV. The New World in Geography

13. Maps of the New World

Sixteenth-century cartographers, or mapmakers, recorded in their drawings what they understood of New World geography. The place names on maps as old as these often differ from the names we use today. One reason is that Europeans used Latin in much of their writing. The word "sea" will always appear in Latin as "mare." The Latin ending "us" will appear on many words. You will be able to tell what many of the names are because they look like modern names. Where it might be difficult to recognize the names, the key will give you the modern terms.

Several of the names will appear with a variety of spellings. Greenland, for example, is "Gruenland" and "Gronelant," while Iceland is "Islandia," "Islanda," and "Island." Many of the names on the original maps have been omitted because they would not help you to see how ideas about world geography changed during the sixteenth century.

POINTS TO CONSIDER

How these maps compare with Toscanelli's fifteenth-century map and with what you know about the voyages of discovery.

JOHANN RUYSCH, 1508

Ruysch was a learned geographer of his day. In 1508 he published this map, which was one of the earliest maps to show any part of the New World. The original map had legends written upon it describing certain characteristics of areas shown. These are listed opposite the map and are designated by capital letters on the map.

A. "Here the ship's compass loses its property, and no vessel with iron on board is able to get away."

B. "This island was entirely burnt in 1456."

C. "The ships of Ferdinand, king of Spain, have come as far as here."

D. "Marco Polo says that 1,400 miles eastward from the port of Zaiton there is a very large island called Cipango, where inhabitants are idolators, and have their own king, and are tributary [subject] to no one. Here is a great abundance of gold and all sorts of gems. But as the islands discovered by the Spaniards occupy this spot, we have not ventured to place this island here, thinking that what the Spaniards call Spagnola (Hispaniola, Hayti) is the same as Cipango, since the things which are described as in Cipango are found in Spagnola, besides the idolatry."

E. "Spanish sailors have come as far as here, and they call this country a New World because of its magnitude, for in truth they have not seen it all nor up to the present time have they gone beyond this point. Wherefore it is here left incomplete, especially as we do not know in what direction it goes."

F. "This region, which by many people is believed to be another world, is inhabited at different points by men and women who go about either quite naked or clad in interwoven twigs adorned with feathers of various hues. They live for the most part in common, with no religion, no king; they carry on wars among themselves perpetually and devour the flesh of human captives. They enjoy a wholesome climate, however, and live to be more than 140 years old. They are seldom sick, and then are cured merely by the roots of herbs. There are lions here, and serpents, and other horrid wild beasts. There are mountains and rivers, and there is the greatest abundance of gold and pearls. The Portuguese have brought from here brazil-wood and quassia [a drug]."

G. "Portuguese mariners have examined this part of the country, and have gone as far as the 50th degree of south latitude without reaching its southern extremity."

1. What does Johann Ruysch include in his map of the world that Toscanelli omitted in 1474?

2. How do you account for these additions?

3. Has Ruysch been scientific in making this map? In other words, has he tried to use all the information available? Has he criticized each piece of information carefully?

"Note B" describes the fate of a small volcanic island that existed in the Middle Ages. It has since disappeared below the surface.

20	240	270	300	330	0	30	60	90	120	150

Circ. Arcticus

A

Islandia

LAPLAND

GOG & MAGOG *Deserta Magna* GRUENLAND

B

NORVEGA

MOSCOVY

CATHAYA

TERRA NOVA I. Baccalauras

Azores

ANGLIA

GERMANIA

M. Casp.

60

MANGI

I. Barbatos

FRANCIA

HISP

ARMENIA

40

CIAMBA Zaiton

C

Antilia Canari

Spagnola

INDIA

Circ. Cancri

20

D

Dominica

LIBYA

ARABIA

Iava Major

E

Circul. Aequin.

AETHIOPIA

0

Iava Minor

F

MUNDUS

20

NOVUS

Circ. Capric.

40

G

60

170	140	110	80	50	20	10	40	70	100	130

GOG AND MAGOG—According to medieval legend, these lands were the source of all evil.

CATHAYA—China

MANGI—Province in China

CIAMBA—Province of China

ZAITON—Chinese city of Changchow

TERRA NOVA—"New Land"

I. BACCALAURAS—Newfoundland

I. BARBATOS—Barbados, island in West Indies

SPAGNOLA—Haiti, island in West Indies

DOMINICA—Island in West Indies

MUNDUS NOVUS—"New World"

ANTILIA—Island described in medieval legend

LIBYA—Old Greek name for North Africa

ARMENIA—An ancient country of Western Asia

27

JOANNES de STOBNICZA, 1512

Joannes de Stobnicza, a Polish geographer, drew this map of the Western hemisphere in 1512. De Stobnicza was able to include Florida on his map because Vespucci had reached it between 1497 and 1498. De Leon's voyage to Florida in 1513 is better known, but only because Vespucci had reported that Florida contained no wealth. Europeans therefore lost interest in the area until de Leon made his trip.

1. How can you explain the differences between the way de Stobnicza and Ruysch showed Central and South America? Did de Stobnicza have more information about these areas?

2. How does de Stobnicza show the position of the New World in relation to the Far East? What could have caused him to take this view?

3. According to this map, what routes are open to an explorer who wishes to journey to the Far East?

JOANNES de STOBNICZA, 1512

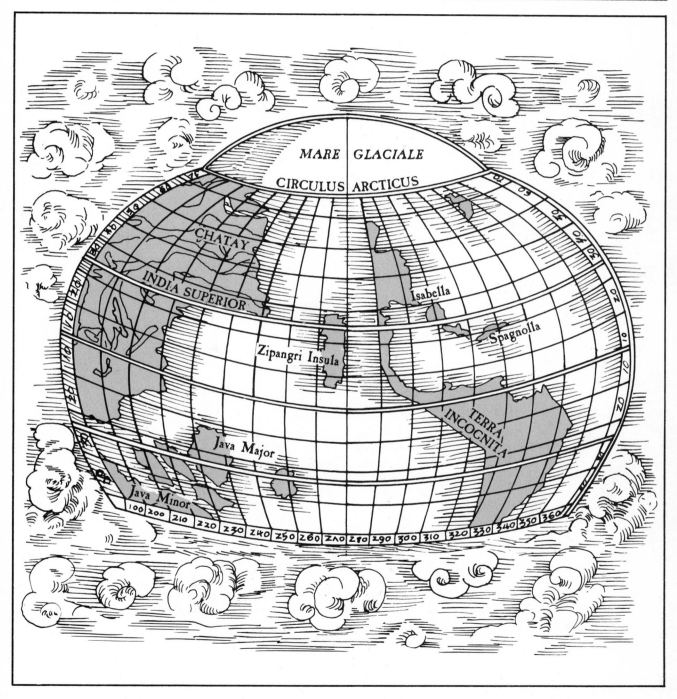

29

ORONTIUS FINAEUS, 1531

The map on the next page is part of the globe sketched in 1531 by Orontius Finaeus, a professor of mathematics at the Royal College of France. The term "America," which Finaeus used, first appeared in 1507 on a map published by Martin Waldseemuller. "America," taken from the name of the explorer Amerigo Vespucci, soon became the accepted name for the New World. However, Waldseemuller applied the name only to the land south of the Equator, since most of Vespucci's explorations were in this area.

1. What information does Finaeus' map have that Ruysch omitted in 1508? How do you account for this?

2. How do you explain the way Finaeus showed the position of America?

3. How might this map influence a prospective explorer?

30

ORONTIUS FINAEUS, 1531

MANGI—Province in China

CAMBALUC—Chinese city of Peking

RIO DE SANTO ESPIRITU ("RIVER OF THE
HOLY SPIRIT")—Mississippi River

BACCALAR—Newfoundland

HISPANIOLA—Haiti

MARE DE SUR—"South Sea"

TEMISTETA—Mexico City

GANGES FL.—River in India

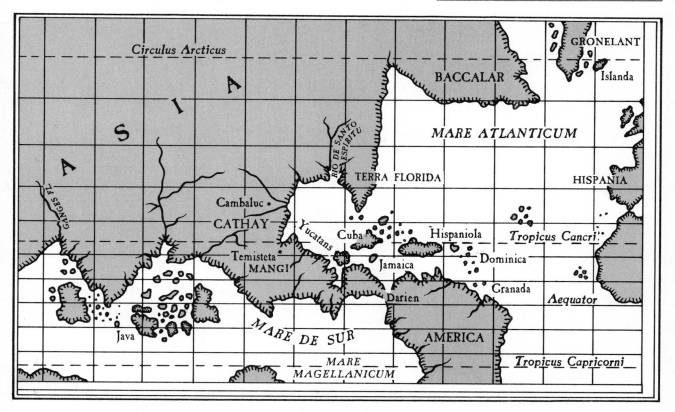

Circulus Arcticus

GRONELANT

BACCALAR

Islanda

A S I A

MARE ATLANTICUM

RIO DE SANTO ESPIRITU

TERRA FLORIDA

HISPANIA

GANGES FL.

Cambaluc

CATHAY

Yucatans

Cuba

Hispaniola

Tropicus Cancri

Temisteta

MANGI

Jamaica

Dominica

Java

Darien

Granada

Aequator

MARE DE SUR

AMERICA

MARE
MAGELLANICUM

Tropicus Capricorni

GERARD MERCATOR, 1541

Mercator was a geographer and mathematician from Belgium. He is most famous for his method of using lines of longitude and latitude to determine distances accurately. Mapmakers had used longitude and latitude before Mercator's time, but none had succeeded in showing the earth's curved surface accurately on a flat map surface.

The map on page 33 was drawn in 1541, before Mercator introduced his method. This 1541 map was, however, the first to show the term "America" on both continents.

1. What is unique about this map as compared with the previous maps?

2. How can you explain the differences?

GERARD MERCATOR, 1541

ISLAND INS

BACCALEARUM

AME

HISPANIA MAJOR

R DEL ESPIRITU SANTO

HISPANIA
NOVA

FLORIDA

CUBA

IUCATANA

HISPANIOLA

BERMUDA

ACORES INS

CANARIE

HESPERIDES INS

TRINITATIS INS

PERU

RICA

A MULTIS
HODIE NOVA
INDIA DICTA

MARE PACIFICUM

SIVE MAGELLANICUM

BACCALEARUM—Newfoundland

HISPANIA MAJOR—Greater Spain

HISPANIA NOVA—New Spain

ACORES INS—Azores

TRINITATIS INS—Island of Trinidad, West Indies

HESPERIDES INS—Islands off the coast of West Africa, south of the Canary Islands. Known today as Cape Verde Islands

A MULTIS HODIE NOVA INDIA DICTA—Today many people call this New India

SIVE MAGELLANICUM—Strait of Magellan

33

SIR HUMPHREY GILBERT, 1576

Sir Humphrey Gilbert, an English navigator, made the following map in 1576 to include in his *Discourse of a Discovery for a New Passage to Cathay*. After Gilbert wrote his *Discourse,* he received permission to explore new lands for the Queen of England.

1. What are the possible routes to the Far East according to Gilbert?

2. How can you account for his views?

SIR HUMPHREY GILBERT, 1576

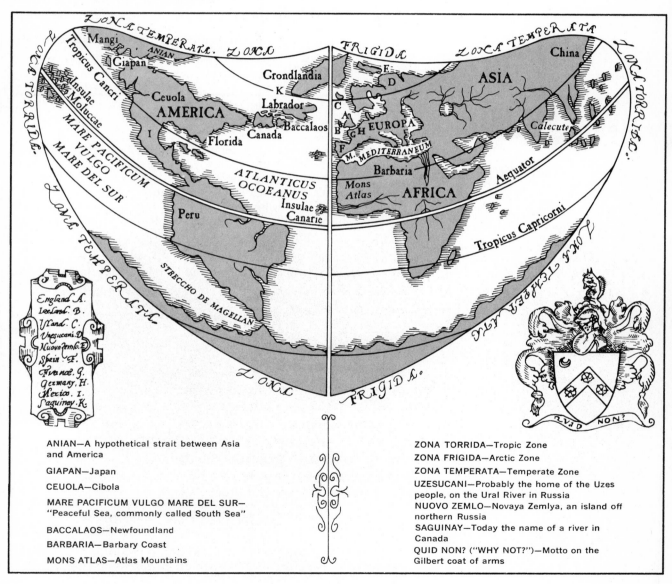

ANIAN—A hypothetical strait between Asia and America

GIAPAN—Japan

CEUOLA—Cibola

MARE PACIFICUM VULGO MARE DEL SUR—
"Peaceful Sea, commonly called South Sea"

BACCALAOS—Newfoundland

BARBARIA—Barbary Coast

MONS ATLAS—Atlas Mountains

ZONA TORRIDA—Tropic Zone

ZONA FRIGIDA—Arctic Zone

ZONA TEMPERATA—Temperate Zone

UZESUCANI—Probably the home of the Uzes people, on the Ural River in Russia

NUOVO ZEMLO—Novaya Zemlya, an island off northern Russia

SAGUINAY—Today the name of a river in Canada

QUID NON? ("WHY NOT?")—Motto on the Gilbert coat of arms

1. How would you describe the development of mapmaking in the sixteenth century?

2. How can you explain this development?

3. Compare these maps with the maps of the explorers' routes on pages 10–14. Where do the explorers seem to have been heading, according to the knowledge *they* had of the world?

4. What, if anything, does this suggest about the motives of the explorers? Was there any change in motives? Do the later explorers seem to have had the same goals as the earlier ones?

5. When you first studied the explorers' routes, how did you explain their direction? Has your explanation changed? Why or why not?

V. Telling the Story

14. Writing History

You have now looked at materials about pre-Columbian views of the unknown world, the major voyages of discovery, tales of the newly explored world, and changing ideas about geography in the sixteenth century. Using this information, make some general statements on the following topics as they relate to the Age of Exploration. Limit each statement to a few complete sentences.

1) What explorers sought.
2) What they found.
3) How changing ideas about the world influenced the voyages.

1. Compare your conclusions with what other members of your class wrote. All of you based your conclusions on facts. Are there, nevertheless, differences among your statements?

2. If so, how do you explain this? For example, how did you arrive at *your* conclusions? What facts did you use? What evidence did your classmates use?

15. A Textbook History of the Age of Exploration

You have already examined some *original sources* on the Age of Exploration. The following reading is a *secondary source*. To review the meaning of these terms see "A Note to the Student."

This reading provides background information for Columbus' discovery of America in 1492 and then describes later explorations. Columbus' voyage in 1492 was discussed in earlier pages which are not included in this selection.

POINTS TO CONSIDER
Compare your conclusions about the Age of Exploration with those in this textbook excerpt.

Early in the fifteenth century, Prince Henry of Portugal took great interest in the training of navigators. He gathered maps, sailing charts, and such writings as he could find on the subject. He also brought in the best experts he could find and opened a school for pilots. He sent trained pilots off on voyages southward along the African coast.

John W. Caughey, John Hope Franklin, and Ernest R. May, **Land of the Free** (New York: Benziger Brothers, Inc., 1966), pp. 23-26.

No direct evidence shows that he hoped that his ships would reach the Spice Islands or Cathay. His interest may have been simply in the science of navigation. His curiosity may have been about what might be found along the African coast.

After Prince Henry's death in 1460, Portuguese mariners pushed the search much farther. Their goal now was India. Bartholomeu Dias came back in 1488 to tell that he had rounded the southern-most tip of Africa, which the king delightedly named the Cape of Good Hope. In 1497 Vasco da Gama took out a fleet to sail this route to India. Two years later, he was back with a meager cargo of eastern goods, but with proof that the round-Africa route really worked. Using it, the Portuguese became the leading European suppliers of spices and silks.

Columbus Determines to Find a Way
Columbus' dream of a western route to the source of these much-wanted goods was bolder thinking. Instead of using a coastal route, he proposed to strike out into an unknown ocean.

As a boy in Genoa, one of the Italian seaports, Columbus had learned about ships, met sailors, and heard much talk of voyages. As a youth and young man, he [often sailed] to the eastern Mediterranean, England, Portugal, and the Madeira Islands.

By the time he was thirty, he was convinced that by sailing west he could reach the fabled Orient, perhaps making good dis-coveries along the way. Lacking the money to hire ships or men, he went from court to court in Portugal, Spain, France, and Eng-land trying to get a backer. In the end, it was the King and Queen of Spain, Isabella more than Ferdinand, who accepted his proposal and his terms.

Upon his return in 1493, Columbus was given a hero's welcome. As he traveled toward court, the curious turned out to see him and the strange things and people that he had brought. The king and queen gave him an immediate audience. He had found lands just as he said he would. Judging by the Indians and the bits of gold, these lands must be very close to the land of spices and silk.

The King of Portugal was enough interested to protest that he had prior right to make such explorations. The Spanish monarchs appealed to the Pope. The Pope drew a line in the Atlantic, leaving the African side to Portugal and the western side to Spain. It was known as the Line of Demarcation. Portugal objected that this line cut too close to Africa. By treaty, Spain agreed to move it to 370 leagues west of the Cape Verde Islands and to extend it around the world to protect Portuguese priority in the Far East.

Columbus Makes Three More Voyages

Meanwhile, Columbus sailed again with a fleet of twenty ships. This time, his landfall [sighting of land] was considerably farther south in the Lesser Antilles. He sailed through these islands, discovering and naming many of them as he went, among them Puerto Rico. Arriving on the north coast of Haiti, he found that the thirty-nine colonists of 1492 had disappeared; presumably the Indians had wiped them out. Columbus established a new station. Hurrying on to Cuba, he followed its coast far enough to reinforce his belief that it was part of the mainland of Asia.

On a third voyage in 1498, Columbus sailed along the southern shore of the Caribbean Sea. Its pearl fishing was the most rewarding activity yet found, but the size of this body of land [South America] was something that he could not fit in with what he believed about Asia and the Spice Islands. Perhaps there was a passage farther west.

Seeking this passage to Asia, Columbus made a fourth voyage in 1502. He found a continuous coastline in Central America and Panama tying on to the Pearl Coast earlier discovered. Meanwhile, other mariners had traced this continental coast much farther to the south. Columbus died in 1504, not knowing quite what to make of this geography.

Explorers for Spain and Portugal pieced together information about the run of that coast all the way down to the Strait of Magellan. Spanish mariners filled in the contours of the Gulf of Mexico. Still other Spaniards, assisted by Sebastian Cabot for England and Giovanni Verrazano for France, outlined the Florida peninsula and the land running on northeastward for many hundreds of miles. By about 1519, it was known that there was a long-drawn-out land barrier across the westward [route, apparently unbroken] from Maine to the Strait of Magellan.

Half a dozen years earlier, Vasco Núñez de Balboa was in charge of a struggling Spanish colony at Panama. Pursued by those to whom he owed money in Haiti, Balboa had escaped by having himself closed in a barrel and stowed on ship with the freight. At Panama, he proved the best leader and, by all odds, the best at getting the help of the Indians. In 1513 he set out to investigate an Indian report of another sea not far to the south. There it was, just as promised! Naming it the South Sea, Balboa claimed this sea and all its shores for Spain.

Magellan Sails Round the World

In 1519 Ferdinand Magellan, a Portuguese who had traded in the East Indies, led a Spanish expedition almost to the tip of South America. He discovered a narrow opening, since called the Strait of Magellan. Passing through, he came out on an ocean which he named the Pacific. Later, it was found to be the same as Balboa's South Sea. Magellan sailed on across the Pacific, a distance four or five times that of Columbus' sail west.

In the Philippines, Magellan was killed. A few of his men then took the ship through the East Indies, across the Indian Ocean, around Africa, and back to Spain. This was the first voyage around the world. The report of this voyage helped to correct ideas about geography. Columbus' west-to-the Orient route, besides being blockaded by land, was now proved to be exceedingly long.

Still another point cleared up by Magellan's voyage was that neither of the continents forming the land barrier from Maine to the Strait of Magellan could be Asia.

The land from the Pearl Coast south had already been named America. Now it could be seen that the land from Panama north, lying so many thousands of miles east of the Philippines and Asia, must be another new continent. Soon the mapmakers would be calling it North America and calling the continent first recognized South America.

Thus far, neither continent had yielded any noteworthy profit to the explorers who had charted its Atlantic frontage.

1. Are there similarities between this history and your statements? Are there differences? How do you explain this?

2. Can you tell from reading this historical account whether it is based on more or less evidence than you have? Do you think this account could be based on *complete* evidence?

3. Is your account a history? Why? Do you learn as much from writing your own account as from reading a textbook history?

16. Extending Ideas

In the introduction to this unit, you learned something about Europe before the Age of Exploration. Now you will read more about European events before 1492.

POINTS TO CONSIDER

How this information could help to explain what happened during the Age of Exploration.

The Crusades, which inspired wave after wave of Europeans to journey to the Middle East between the eleventh and thirteenth centuries, had a great effect on European life. The returning Crusaders set important changes in motion.

One of the changes was economic: the silks, linens, perfumes, spices, sugar, and jewels the Crusaders brought back with them created a demand for luxury goods. Before the Crusades, even nobles lacked such luxuries. In response to the growing demand for luxury items, trade with the Middle East increased rapidly. However, the cost and difficulty of bringing goods to Europe from the Middle East hindered this trade. Most of the journey, first of all, was overland. Overland transport was the slowest way to travel. The poor condition of the roads—where roads existed—added to the caravans' problems. Land travel was dangerous, too, since the caravans were tempting prey for thieves. Finally, it was expensive to outfit and provision a lengthy expedition.

The inconvenience and expense of the route was further aggravated by the many changes of transportation that were necessary. The merchants had to switch their cargo from wagons to ships to camel caravans. In addition, many of the princes through whose territories the traders passed demanded tribute. Because Europeans wanted to expand trade with the East, they began to seek a shorter, easier, and cheaper way of going there.

The Crusades also stirred the curiosity of Europeans. The Crusaders brought back tales of wealth, of strange customs, and of new ways of doing things. Through contact with the Middle East, Europeans first learned to use paper, the magnetic compass, and the kind of numbers we employ today. Like the stories of Marco Polo, an Italian who traveled to China in the thirteenth century, these new ideas fired the European imagination. Europeans began to hunger for more knowledge about the world in general.

Beginning in the fourteenth century, Europe experienced a rebirth of interest in worldly subjects. This became known as the Renaissance. The Crusades were one of the principal factors that helped to cause it. During medieval times scholars had been interested primarily in religious subjects. Now they wished to know how people in foreign countries lived, what happened to a beam of light as it passed through glass, and how to make a clock. The Renaissance drive to explore new ideas and new things —the spirit of inquiry—helped make Europeans want to find a new route to the Far East.

The Renaissance was a period of invention. One of the most influential developments occurred in 1454: the printing of a book with movable type. Prior to that time, all books produced in Europe were handwritten. They took so long to produce that few were available, and those few were so costly that only the very wealthy could afford them. With the invention of the printing press, books, maps, and charts became more plentiful and much cheaper. Since there was a renewed interest in learning at the same time, the reading public grew. This meant that just when discoveries were being made in all fields, more people could learn about new ideas more quickly than ever before.

During the Renaissance, two inventions from earlier times came into widespread use. They were the astrolabe and the magnetic compass, both of great importance to mariners. The astrolabe enabled a sailer to find out how far he was from the equator by measuring the angle between the horizon and the sun or North Star. The magnetic compass made it possible for a seaman to know the direction in which he was sailing. These two tools plus more and better maps and charts made sea voyage much safer.

Toward the latter part of the Renaissance, in the sixteenth century, Europe experienced a great revival of religious feeling. England, Holland, and Germany became champions of Protestantism. Protestantism was a new form of Christianity practiced by people who had separated from the Roman Catholic Church. In part, Protestantism grew out of reaction against medieval religious beliefs and certain common practices of the Catholic Church. The Protestant movement also resulted from the struggle for power between the Pope and the leaders of European states. Partly in response to the challenge of Protestantism, Spain, Portugal, and France became the champions of a revived Roman Catholicism. Intense religious rivalry between the European nations also stimulated the desire to seek new lands. New lands, in terms of religion, meant new people to convert.

As states began to compete over religion, an intense pride in national glory and strength developed. This pride was further stimulated by competition over trade. Because there was such a rapidly expanding market for Middle Eastern goods, there was great opportunity for merchants to become wealthy by selling Eastern goods to Europeans. Each nation wanted its own merchants to lead in this trade. At the outset, however, the advantage was held by the sea-going Italian merchants. Based at the eastern end of the Mediterranean Sea, the Italians were well located to monopolize the new trade. Furthermore, during the Crusades, they had transported Crusaders to the Holy Land and supplied them with goods. Thus, when goods from the East were in great demand, the Italians were already the leaders in transportation to and from the area. A race developed among the other nations to find new routes to the East which would bypass the Mediterranean Sea and take the advantage away from the Italians.

The increase in trade led to a change in the way it was conducted. "Barter," or the exchange of one type of goods for another, was impractical for trading large quantities over long distances. The barter system gave way to the use of gold for buying products. Since gold was highly valued by all European nations, it was readily accepted everywhere in Europe in exchange for goods. Europeans even came to believe that the welfare of a nation was dependent upon the amount of gold it possessed. They thought that the more gold a nation had, the greater would be its power and prosperity. Thus, nations wanted to find lands which might contain a rich supply of gold.

1. Does this information help to confirm your explanations about why the voyages of discovery took place? If so, how?

2. Does it suggest reasons for the explorations that had not occurred to you?

3. Did you use all the information in this unit when you explained the explorations? If there was some data you did not use, can you use it now? Explain.

4. Is there any data that still seems unusable? Try to think of ways this data might help you to explain the events in the Age of Exploration. How could you find out if you are right?

R. A. Skelton, Thomas E. Marston, and George D. Painter, The Vinland Map and the Tartar Relation (New Haven, Conn.: Yale University Press, 1965), pp. 127-143. Copyright © 1965 by Yale University.

17. The Viking Map: Including New Evidence

In the fall of 1965, after eight years of study, a team of researchers from Yale University released a newly found piece of historical evidence about the discovery of the New World. The following map, printed in Europe in 1440, reflects discoveries made early in the eleventh century by the Viking explorer Leif Ericksson and a companion named Bjarni. Some of the less essential original terms on the map have been omitted.

THE VIKING MAP

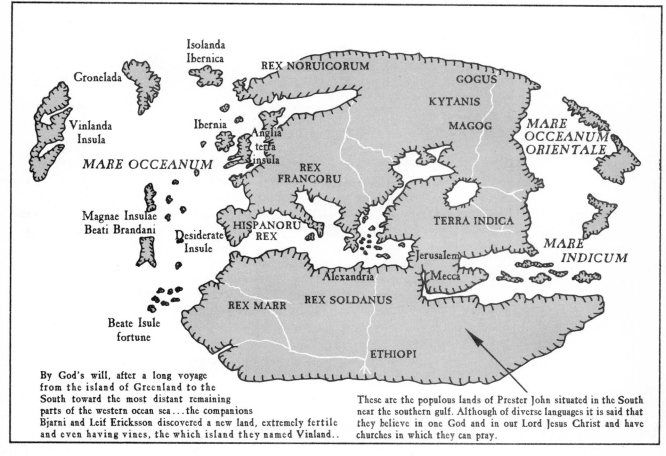

Isolanda
Ibernica

Gronelada

REX NORUICORUM

GOGUS

KYTANIS

MAGOG

MARE
OCCEANUM
ORIENTALE

Vinlanda
Insula

Ibernia

MARE OCCEANUM

Anglia
terra
insula

REX
FRANCORU

Magnae Insulae
Beati Brandani

Desiderate
Insule

HISPANORU
REX

TERRA INDICA

Jerusalem

*MARE
INDICUM*

Mecca

Alexandria

REX SOLDANUS

Beate Isule
fortune

REX MARR

ETHIOPI

By God's will, after a long voyage from the island of Greenland to the South toward the most distant remaining parts of the western ocean sea...the companions Bjarni and Leif Ericksson discovered a new land, extremely fertile and even having vines, the which island they named Vinland..

These are the populous lands of Prester John situated in the South near the southern gulf. Although of diverse languages it is said that they believe in one God and in our Lord Jesus Christ and have churches in which they can pray.

1. What does this map do to the textbook history or to your statements about fourteenth- and fifteenth-century ideas of the world? What does it do to your ideas about the discovery of the New World? Why?

2. Why do you suppose the explorations studied in this unit had so much more impact on world history than the earlier explorations of the Vikings?

3. Why do you think sixteenth-century explorers failed to take the Viking map into account in planning their voyages?

4. Does anything you have learned about European history in Reading 16 suggest answers to questions 2 and 3?

5. Historians will continue to search and study in an attempt to answer the endless stream of questions that history poses. As new evidence is brought to light about a topic, what must be done with conclusions arrived at earlier? What does this tell you about the nature of history?

WHAT IS HISTORY?—A SECOND LOOK

Review your initial definition of history. Does it need some revision or change? Explain.

Do you think it is possible to come to a final conclusion on the definition of history? *If* it is not possible to reach a final conclusion on a subject, is there any point in forming opinions about it or in revising your opinions?

CONCLUDING EXERCISE

"What men believe determines what men do."

Consider this statement as a hypothesis to be tested against the evidence available to you from your study of the Age of Exploration. Review all the material you have studied. Form an opinion about this statement *based* on all the evidence you have so far. Write a summary of your findings showing the evidence you used.

Consider next whether you have *proved* this statement.

Colonization

VI. The People of North America

18. A Map of the American Indians

When explorers and settlers arrived in the newly discovered regions of North America, they met the native inhabitants. By now you can probably guess how these people came to be called "Indians." The origin of Indians is not firmly established. One theory maintains that the Indians came from Asia by way of the Bering Strait, the water passageway between Alaska and Russia, or by way of a land bridge that once connected them. Another matter of debate is how many Indians originally lived in North America. An estimate for the year 1500 places the figure between 1,000,000 and 1,500,000.

The Indians lived in widely scattered areas. There seem to have been few strong ties among tribes. The following map shows the probable locations of Indian tribes around the time of Columbus, the major products on which they relied, and the manner in which the Indians lived. Many Indians lived in villages. Others were nomads who wandered from place to place. Some were semi-nomads, living both a settled and nomadic life.

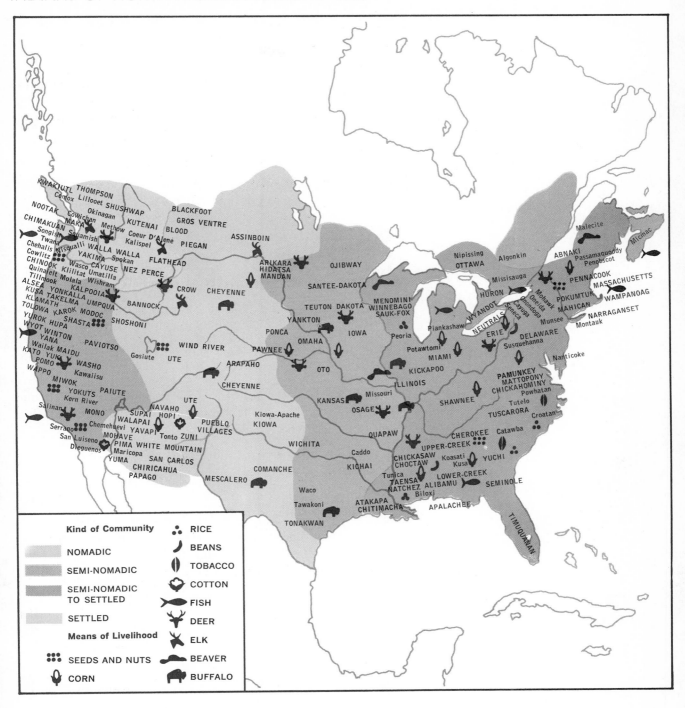

Map legend:

Kind of Community
- NOMADIC
- SEMI-NOMADIC
- SEMI-NOMADIC TO SETTLED
- SETTLED

Means of Livelihood
- SEEDS AND NUTS
- CORN
- RICE
- BEANS
- TOBACCO
- COTTON
- FISH
- DEER
- ELK
- BEAVER
- BUFFALO

1. What does the map on page 45 tell you about the Indians?

2. Which type of community do you think would require the most land? The least? Would a European be likely to recognize each community's right to the land? Why?

3. What would the presence of settlers have meant for the Indians? What would the presence of Indians mean for the settlers? Would they be a help or a problem to each other?

4. What else do you need to know about settlers and Indians to answer questions 2 and 3?

5. According to this map, what influence did Indians have on the United States as you know it today?

19. A Map of the Spanish and French

In the 1500's, 1600's, and 1700's the European powers most active in North America were Spain, France, and England. The map opposite illustrates Spanish and French activities. Only major inland explorers are shown here. For French and Spanish coastal explorers see the maps on pages 12 and 14.

1. What general statements can you make about French and Spanish settlement in the New World? What differences do you observe? What similarities?

   a. How many towns or villages are there? Are they close together or far apart?

   b. What other kinds of settlements are there? Is there any pattern in location?

   c. Does there seem to have been a steady interest in colonization between the 1500's and 1700's, or did most of the colonization take place at certain periods?

2. Look back at the maps of explorers' routes on pages 10–14 and the chart on page 16. What comparisons can you make between French and Spanish explorers? For example, what areas did they explore? When were they active? What were their probable purposes?

3. Can you make any guesses about the major purposes of the French and Spanish efforts in the New World? Do you think that carrying out these purposes would be likely to involve large numbers of people?

SPANISH AND FRENCH
COLONIZATION OF AMERICA

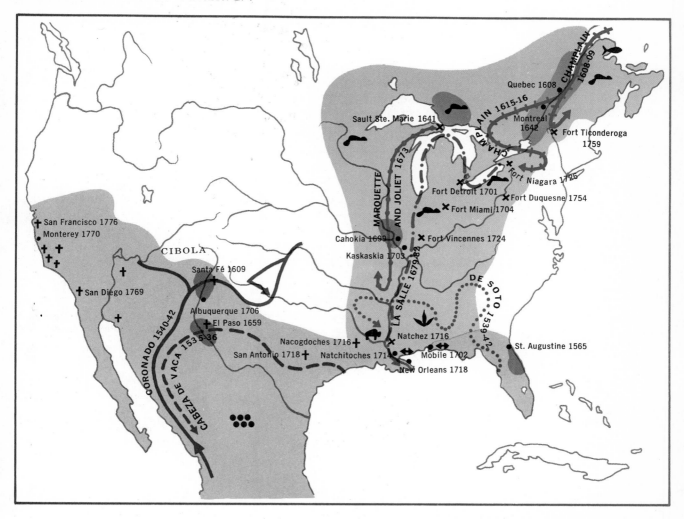

Legend:

Areas of Settlement

- CLAIMED BY SPAIN
- SETTLED BY 1700
- CLAIMED BY FRANCE
- SETTLED BY 1700
- ✝ MISSION
- ✗ FORT
- ↔ TRADING CENTER

Products

- 🐟 FISH
- 🦫 BEAVER FUR
- 🌱 SUGAR
- 🦬 BUFFALO SKINS
- ⚫ GOLD AND SILVER

4. What relation, if any, do you think would exist between the French and Spanish? Between each of the European groups and the Indians? Why?

5. Would relations between colonizers and their neighbors have changed over a period of time?

6. Can you give final answers to questions 3, 4, and 5 by using this map and the chart and the maps on exploration? If not, what other information do you need?

47

20. The English in America: A Chart and a Map

When you studied the explorers and their routes, you saw how a chart could be used along with a map. Here you will again see how a chart can affect ideas based primarily on information from a map. The map on the opposite page is similar to the maps of the Indians, French, and Spanish that you have just examined. The chart gives additional data on English settlements. Because the English settlements became the core of our nation, you will study them in greater depth in the rest of this unit.

POINTS TO CONSIDER

The similarities and differences you observe among the French, Spanish, and English when comparing the maps.

If the chart adds to the points that emerge from the map about English settlement in America. If it confirms or contradicts ideas suggested by the map.

SETTLEMENT OF THE THIRTEEN COLONIES

COLONY	SETTLEMENT	LEADER	DATE	REASON SETTLED
VIRGINIA	JAMESTOWN	JOHN SMITH	1607	TRADE AND PROFITS
MASSACHUSETTS BAY	PLYMOUTH	WILLIAM BRADFORD	1620	RELIGIOUS FREEDOM FOR THE PILGRIMS, WHO WANTED TO SEPARATE FROM THE CHURCH OF ENGLAND
	BOSTON	JOHN WINTHROP	1630	RELIGIOUS FREEDOM FOR THE PURITANS, WHO WANTED TO PURIFY THE ENGLISH CHURCH TRADE AND PROFITS
NEW YORK*	NEW AMSTERDAM	PETER MINUIT (for Holland)	1626	TRADE AND PROFITS
NEW HAMPSHIRE	PORTSMOUTH	JOHN MASON	1630	TO ESCAPE THE STRICT RELIGIOUS AND POLITICAL RULES OF MASSACHUSETTS
CONNECTICUT	HARTFORD	THOMAS HOOKER	1636	TO ESCAPE THE STRICT RELIGIOUS AND POLITICAL RULES OF MASSACHUSETTS MORE LAND
MARYLAND	ST. MARY'S	GEORGE CALVERT	1634	RELIGIOUS FREEDOM FOR CATHOLICS
RHODE ISLAND	PROVIDENCE	ROGER WILLIAMS	1636	TO ESCAPE RELIGIOUS PERSECUTION IN MASSACHUSETTS
DELAWARE†	WILMINGTON	PETER MINUIT‡ (for Sweden)	1638	TRADE AND PROFITS
NORTH CAROLINA	ALBEMARLE COLONY	GROUP OF PROPRIETORS (businessmen)	1653	TRADE AND PROFITS
SOUTH CAROLINA	CHARLESTON	GROUP OF PROPRIETORS	1670	TRADE AND PROFITS
PENNSYLVANIA	PHILADELPHIA	WILLIAM PENN	1682	RELIGIOUS FREEDOM FOR QUAKERS TRADE AND PROFITS
NEW JERSEY	SCATTERED SETTLEMENTS	LORD BERKELEY GEORGE CARTERET	1664	TRADE AND PROFITS
GEORGIA	SAVANNAH	JAMES OGLETHORPE	1733	TRADE AND PROFITS PLACE TO SEND DEBTORS FROM ENGLAND TO KEEP THE SPANISH OUT OF THE ENGLISH COLONIES

* New York, originally named New Netherland by the Dutch, was taken from the Dutch by the English in 1664. Both the colony and its capital were renamed New York.

† Delaware was taken from Sweden by the Dutch in 1655. It was seized by England in 1664.

‡ Peter Minuit was dismissed by the Dutch West India Company in 1631. He entered the Swedish service in 1637.

ENGLISH COLONIZATION OF AMERICA

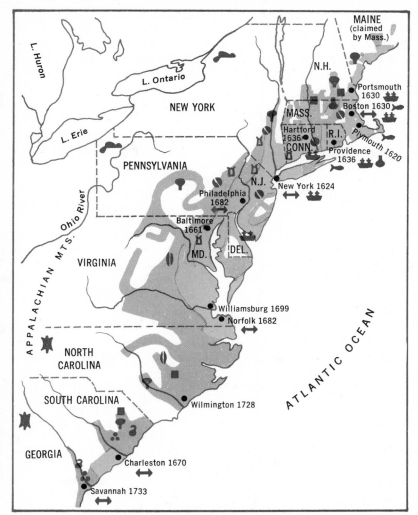

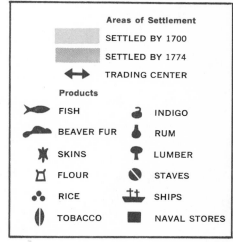

Areas of Settlement

	SETTLED BY 1700
	SETTLED BY 1774
↔	TRADING CENTER

Products

	FISH		INDIGO
	BEAVER FUR		RUM
	SKINS		LUMBER
	FLOUR		STAVES
	RICE		SHIPS
	TOBACCO		NAVAL STORES

1. According to the map, what were the main interests of the English settlers?

2. Do any of the reasons for English colonization indicated on the chart relate to material on the map? Does the chart give reasons *not* suggested by the map?

3. Which reasons for colonization were important in most of the areas where Englishmen settled? What effect would common interests have upon the colonization efforts?

EUROPEANS IN AMERICA: MAKING COMPARISONS

1. What differences do you notice between the English colonies and the French and Spanish colonies?

2. What does this show you about the reasons for colonization? What kind of person do you suppose came to America from England? What did he want? How would he differ from the French or Spanish colonist?

3. What effect do you think the English reasons for colonization would have on English relations with the Indians? Would the English be likely to get along with the Indians better or worse than the French and Spanish?

4. Do you think the English would have any contact with the French and Spanish? If so, would they get along well? Give reasons for your answers.

5. How unified were the interests of the English settlers?

21. A Closer Look at the English Colonies

The territory of the English colonies stretched along the eastern coast of America from Maine to Georgia. The early settlements were mainly near the ocean. As time went on, the colonies gradually extended inland, generally along the more important rivers.

The colonial territory was made up of three regions which differed as to soil, climate, and opportunity. These areas were: New England, comprising Massachusetts, Rhode Island, New Hampshire, and Connecticut; the Middle Colonies—New York, New Jersey, Pennsylvania and Delaware; and the South composed of Maryland, Virginia, North and South Carolina, and Georgia. The following paragraphs explain some of the differences between these areas. The author of this selection, however, emphasizes Maryland, Virginia, and South Carolina in his discussion of conditions in the South. Determine the main characteristics of each area.

The Community

. . . In the main New England was a homogeneous community with the town as the unit of its settlement . . . Unlike the colonists of Maryland, Virginia, and North Carolina, the New Englanders settled in compact, nucleated villages—little congregations of men and women of like minds, socially similar in temperament, clustered closely about the meeting-house, the village green, and the school . . . Wherever the Pilgrim or Puritan found a resting place he set up a form of local life thoroughly characteristic of

Charles McLean Andrews, **The Colonial Period** (London, England: Oxford University Press, 1912), pp. 63-65, 70-72, 90-95.

When something is "homogeneous" all its parts are alike.

For definitions of "Pilgrim" and "Puritan" see pages 57-60.

50

himself and his traditions. He had lived in towns of old England and he had cultivated the soil in the open field, dwelling in close proximity [nearness] to his fellows, owning land in small parcels, and using pasture and woodland in common with his neighbors. In a majority of cases he had come to America not as an isolated individual but as a member of a group or company of Christians covenanted together with God, an indissoluble religious body which became the basis of the town in Massachusetts, Plymouth, and Connecticut. . . .

"Covenanted" means bound together by a pledge.

. . . [The] people of New England deemed themselves supreme lords of their own lands . . . The New Englander held his land either as an outright gift or as his share of territory purchased from a common fund, and his tenure [ownership right], subject only to the higher needs of the community, was for the most part absolute. Imbued [filled] with the idea of religious and political equality for all the "godly men," he endeavored to divide evenly the advantages and burdens of the community by distributing land in small and scattered parcels and by giving every one a share in whatever means of subsistence the town possessed. He forbade accumulation of landed property . . . All undivided land was owned either by the original proprietors or by the town . . .

"Means of subsistence" are means of obtaining food, clothing, and shelter.

A colonial "proprietor" was a person or company that had been granted ownership of land along with the right to govern it.

. . . [Among] the people who settled Virginia there existed no homogeneity, no similarity of origin, customs, experience, political principles, or religious thought.

In making their settlements the Virginia colonists were subject to none of those influences that drew the New Englanders into a close Congregational organization by towns. Very few of the Virginians were either Puritans or Separatists, and those few were bound by no church covenant or plantation compact. Though liberty of religion prevailed, the Church of England was made formally the established church of the colony and its clergy were supported by general taxation. There was but one plan of settlement, that provided by the higher authorities. . . . there was nowhere compactness of life or grouping of colonists. Coming to America with no definite plan of settlement in mind and having no common bond, religious or otherwise, the Virginians felt more readily than the New Englanders the effects of climate, soil, and open country. The heat of the climate, the wide stretches of land, and the ease with which tobacco was cultivated, determined their manner of life, and we find them scattered along the banks of the rivers in private plantations, so far apart as to demand a loose political organization, first of hundreds and eventually of counties.

"Separatists" were people, like the Pilgrims and Quakers, who had separated from the Church of England.

"Hundreds" were English subdivisions of colonies.

51

The system of land distribution was a matter of vital importance in the history of Virginia. In New England the final partition of the soil among the settlers was effected by the colonists themselves according to their own ideas. In Virginia, on the other hand, the company [which had paid for setting up the colony] controlled the entire land system. At first no such thing as private property prevailed. Not until 1614 was any land distributed to colonists, and the little that was given out was burdened with a quit-rent of corn and an obligation to labor for the company one month in the year. Not until 1618 did any general distribution take place. Even then, the acquiring of a title was difficult, and at first the land was largely controlled by the shareholders of the company, two thirds of whom remained in England. Later, any emigrant who paid his own passage money might have fifty acres; but in the main the holdings were large and there were no such minute properties as in New England. It has been estimated that from 1632 to 1650 the average area acquired by grant in Virginia was four hundred and forty-six acres and later grants often rose as high as twenty thousand acres.

The grants steadily increased in size as the years passed, and were held, not in scattered parcels, but in compact masses forming wide and isolated farms. They were cultivated, not by the owner, but by white servants and negroes, neither of whom had any rights [to] the soil. The result of these conditions was social inequality; the country was divided into large plantations; accumulation of property in single hands became a natural and inevitable consequence, and a life essentially aristocratic arose. . . .

The Economy

. . . [The] influence of topography, climate, and staple products [was even more important] in determining the direction that colonial development should take. New England had few rivers and harbors, was broken by small mountain chains, and offered no wide stretching acres or single staple product adapted to plantation life. Virginia and Maryland on the other hand, had great bays and rivers, veritable highways into the heart of the colonies . . . [They had] arable lands stretching from river to river and lying adjunct [next] to great bodies of water like Chesapeake Bay . . . [They also had a] milder climate which led the colonists to seek the easier road to wealth and to scorn the harder pursuits that a colder climate encourages . . . [Virginia and Maryland, therefore,] not only became agricultural, but made one form of agriculture their absorbing interest. . . .[Tobacco became] the only staple that Virginia exported to England, and though Maryland raised fruit and a little grain, bred cattle and trapped fur-bearing animals, her only commodity for export before 1740 was tobacco . . . And even to a greater extent South Carolina with her rice and indigo . . . staked [her] prosperity upon a single commodity . . .

Briefly stated the factors which governed the economic development of the southern, middle, and northern colonies and remained persistent through the colonial era were these. In the south from Maryland to South Carolina manufacturing and commerce were subordinate to agriculture and traffic in furs . . . [The] staple products were carried in the ships of England or of other colonies . . . to England or the Continent [Europe] . . . [In] return the manufactured goods of Europe were brought in large quantities to southern plantations to clothe the people or to furnish their homes. Thus the connection between these colonies and the mother country . . . was a very close one, because the colonies furnished the tobacco, sugar, dye woods, indigo, rice, ginger, and cotton that England needed.

On the other hand the middle and northern colonies furnished none of these things. They had fish and furs for export to England and the Continent and after much urging and granting of bounties [government awards] they shipped a small amount of pitch, tar, turpentine, and hemp, with a few masts for the use of the royal navy. But in the main they did not come into direct contact with England on the export side. The northern and middle colonies raised corn and vegetables and other farm products . . . [They] bred horses, cows, and pigs, they made pipe-staves and clapboards, and built ships, pinks, snows, ketches, schooners, and sloops . . . [They] sent all these articles and products off to the other colonies or to the West Indies. There they received money for their venture or they laid in a stock of sugar, molasses, and rum, some of which was consumed at home, some sent to England in exchange for manufactured goods . . . [Some,] chiefly liquor, they sent to hearten the fishermen off the coast of Newfoundland or to purchase slaves in Africa . . . [The slaves] were in their turn sold to the West Indies for more sugar and molasses, and so the triangular traffic went on. The centres of this trade were Philadelphia, New York, Boston, and especially Newport, the slave emporium [market]. . . .

But the New Englanders were also the great masters of the coasting trade, pedlers at sea as well as on the land, doing a vast business in comparatively small quantities and engaged in a great number of petty [small] domestic exchanges. More than any others among the colonists they were the distributing agents for

"Pipe-staves" are stems of tobacco pipes. "Clapboards" are overlapping boards used in building certain wooden houses. "Pinks," "snows," "ketches," "schooners," and "sloops" are two- and three-masted sailing boats.

"Coasting trade" refers to the practice of sailing along a coast from port to port buying and selling.

53

the produce of the entire colonial seaboard, circulating staples from one end of the coast to another. They were also fishermen, catching their own fish in New England waters or frequenting the harbors of Newfoundland...

From this brief statement it will appear that commerce in the north differed vitally from that of the south. The northern cities became great business communities...With their docks and shipyards, their correspondence with agents in all parts of the world, their warehouses and their offices, these cities became emporia [markets] of trade, of intellectual activity, and scientific ingenuity. On the other hand in the south a strong trading class never came into existence; the planter and the plantation was the seat of business, the bay and the river was the highway to the private wharf where [all the tobacco] was stored. To this wharf...came the vessels twice a year from England bringing foreign goods, letters, and papers to the family on the great plantation...Thus Maryland, Virginia, [and] South Carolina... had no trading and artisan class, no supply of native grown food-stuffs, no diversity of colonial interests. They never developed the trading city...

MAKING AN OUTLINE
The first step in developing your own ideas about a topic in history is to understand what you read. Before you can think about information you must grasp it clearly. One useful technique is to select the main ideas from your reading. See if you can select the main ideas from the selection you have just read.

1. Would the following be a good list of the main ideas from the paragraphs you just read about the New England colonies? Why? Is it accurate? Are all the items important? Does it cover all of the main points? Are the points in the best order?

   NEW ENGLAND COLONIES
   1. The land is mountainous with few rivers and harbors.
   2. The compact, small town was the main type of settlement.
   3. People were much alike in customs and background.
   4. Individuals owned small amounts of land.
   5. There were many different occupations:
      a. Fishing   c. Trade
      b. Farming   d. Small manufacturing

2. Compile your own list of ideas about the Middle Colonies and the colonies of the South. Make sure that you distinguish between the author's main ideas, or *generalizations,* and the *evidence* he uses to support those ideas.

3. Using your lists of ideas, make an outline of the information you have on each area: New England, the Middle Colonies, and the South. Arrange the ideas in the order that shows which ones are most important. Try to set up your outline so that the same topics will be covered for each of the three areas. Can you see how this could be useful?

4. Is there enough information in this selection for you to outline the same topics for each area of the colonies? If not, how could you fill in the blanks?

5. Do you think that Andrews, the author, has presented enough evidence to support his generalizations? Why or why not?

CONCLUDING EXERCISE

Using the information in this section, form a hypothesis about how united the people of the English colonies were likely to be. Take into consideration:
   a. Whether they were likely to have common problems which would require cooperation.
   b. Whether their interests would be similar or different.
   c. Whether their beliefs and attitudes were likely to be the same. Would New Englanders and Southerners, for example, have the same attitudes toward the "common man"? Why or why not?

VII. The People of the Thirteen Colonies

THE NEW ENGLAND COLONIES

22. The Mayflower Compact

During the seventeenth century, many Englishmen were dissatisfied because of the high rate of unemployment, rising prices, and the lack of political and religious freedom. Many fled so that they could live and worship as they pleased.

One such group was the Pilgrims. The Pilgrims were also called Separatists because they wanted to break away or separate from the official state church—the Anglican Church or Church of England. English law required that all citizens belong to the Anglican Church and pay taxes for its support. Pilgrims were persecuted, fined, and sometimes jailed for forming their own religious organizations.

Around 1608, a group of Pilgrims migrated to Holland in search of religious freedom. Although they were permitted to worship as they wished in Holland, they were concerned when they found their children speaking Dutch and losing contact with English culture. They wanted their own church, but they wanted to remain English, too.

The Pilgrims, therefore, decided to go to the New World to establish a "New England." To do this they needed a grant from one of the companies that had been given the right to colonize areas of North America. In 1606, the King had granted this right to two groups of merchants, the London (or Virginia) Company and the Plymouth Company. In return for the royal grant, the companies were to furnish prospective colonists with the provisions and equipment they needed. The merchants who made up the companies hoped to be more than repaid for financing colonies by the profits they could make from trade with the colonists.

The Pilgrims obtained a grant from the London Company to settle on the company's territory south of the Hudson River. But the Pilgrims' ship, the *Mayflower,* was blown off course and landed near Cape Cod. Because they had no charter to establish a colony on this land, they drew up their own substitute—the Mayflower Compact. Certain spellings and symbols in the document have been modernized.

American History Told by Contemporaries, edited by Albert Bushnell Hart (New York: The Macmillan Company, 1897), Vol. I, p. 344.

At this time, Britain claimed lands in France.

In the name of God, Amen. We, whose names are underwritten, the loyal subjects of our dread [awesome] Sovereign Lord King James by the Grace of God, of Great Britain, France, and Ireland, King defender of the faith, etc.

Having undertaken for the glory of God, and the advancement of the christian faith, and the honour of our king and country, a voyage to plant the first colony in the Northern parts of Virginia. Do by these presents, solemnly and mutually, in the presence of God, and one another, covenant [contract] and combine ourselves together into a Civil body politick, for our better ordering and preservation and furtherance of the ends aforesaid; and by Virtue hereof do enact, constitute, and frame such just and equal laws, ordinances, Acts, constitution, and officers, from time to time, as shall be thought most meet [suitable] and convenient for the general good of the Colony; unto which we promise all due submission and obedience. In witness whereof we have hereunto subscribed our names at Cape-Cod the eleventh of November, in the year of the reign of our sovereign Lord King James, of England, France, and Ireland, the eighteenth, and of Scotland, the fifty-fourth, Anno Domini, 1620.

1. According to their own statements, why have the signers of the Mayflower Compact come to the New World? What do they hope to accomplish?

2. What are the main promises made by everyone who signed the Compact?

3. Why did they agree to these promises?

4. Who has set up the "body politick" here? How could this explain the Pilgrims' willingness to make such promises?

5. Do any of the Pilgrims' goals remind you of the explorers' goals?

23. The Puritans

Another group of Englishmen, called Puritans, wanted to purify or simplify some of the practices of the Church of England. Like the Pilgrims, they were persecuted for trying to follow their own beliefs. Like the Pilgrims, they fled to the New World. There they settled the Massachusetts Bay Colony.

The charter for the Massachusetts Bay Colony, first issued by the King to a company of merchants, was soon transferred to the Puritan settlers who were stockholders in this company. However, the majority of colonists had no voice in their government because they did not have the right to vote. Until 1631 only stockholders participated in the government. Then freemen or voters of each town were allowed to elect representatives to the General Court or legislative assembly. But the right to vote and to hold office was limited to men who were members of a church within the colony. This was a severe restriction. The Puritan church was the only one recognized in the colony and only a select few were admitted to church membership. Thus, in 1670, when the colony's population was 25,000, there were only 1,000 freemen.

Within these limits the colonists enjoyed a degree of self-government. The General Court passed all laws necessary for the operation of the colony. It also elected a governor and deputy governor. Until a system of county courts was organized, the legislature even exercised judicial power, which it shared with the governor. Local representatives to the legislature presided over the courts, and all appeals were made to the legislature itself.

In 1691, a royal charter was issued which changed the government of Massachusetts. The charter placed the colony more directly under the control of the King, who now appointed the governor. In addition, a property qualification for voting replaced the religious qualification.

The following selection tells part of the story of the Massachusetts Bay Colony. It tells especially about what the Puritans were like and what they experienced. This account is from a popular American history textbook used one hundred years ago.

G. P. Quackenbos, **Illustrated School History of the United States** (New York: Appleton-Century-Crofts, 1869), pp. 83-85, 105-108.

The Puritans of England, still subjected to various restrictions, continued to seek an asylum in the new world. A grant having been obtained from the Plymouth Company, of a tract bordering on Massachusetts Bay, John En'-di-cott [Endicott] was sent out in 1628 with 100 followers. After exploring the neighborhood, Endicott's party finally settled at a place whose Indian name Naum'-ke-ag [Naumkeag] they changed to Sa'-lem [Salem]. Two hundred more soon followed, some of whom joined the Salem colony, while others founded Charlestown.

Winter, as usual, brought suffering and disease. The following year, those who held the charter transferred it to the colonists themselves, and the change resulted happily. In July, 1630, about 1,500 persons arrived. An independent provincial government was formed, with John Winthrop at its head. Dor'-ches-ter [Dorchester], Rox'-bu-ry [Roxbury], Cambridge . . . and Watertown, were founded; but the greater part settled on a peninsula jutting out into the bay, invited thither by the excellence of its water and the fertility of the land. This peninsula they named Boston, after a city in Lincolnshire, . . . England, from which some of them had come.

The government headed by Winthrop was limited to twelve men who made up the General Court and exercised complete authority over the colonists. The colonists had no voice in their selection.

Shortness of provisions and the severity of the climate caused many deaths during the ensuing [following] winter, and for a season a greater number left the colony than joined it. The following year, affairs assumed a more flourishing aspect; and Boston was visited by various Indian chiefs, who promised peace and friendship.

The law passed in 1631 allowed settlers to vote for the first time. Still, many settlers were dissatisfied because the religious requirement kept them from voting. The religious qualification remained in force until 1664.

In 1631, the General Court passed a law that no man should vote who was not a member of some church in the colony. This greatly reduced the number of [potential] voters, for only a fourth of the adult population were church-members.

The dissatisfaction of the people with this enactment led to earnest discussion and the extension of popular rights. Winthrop was governor for four years, during which the colony became firmly established. A fort was built at Boston; mills were introduced; a coast trade with Virginia and New Amsterdam sprung up; and a ferry was [put into operation] between Boston and Charlestown . . .

Let us glance at the state of society among the Puritans. Their condition, of course, was like that of the English people at this time. Many improvements connected with domestic life were yet unknown, while others had just been introduced. The use of chimneys was becoming common, though opposed by some, who said that smoke improved their health and hardened the timbers of their houses. Wooden dishes and spoons were giving way to pewter ones. Houses of brick and stone were not unfrequent in the old country; but in America boards and unhewn logs were mostly used in building. A poor man in England received but half what he now gets for a day's labor. Rye, barley, and oats, were the common food; and thousands of families hardly knew the taste of meat. The condition of the people in Massachusetts was considerably better than this. After the first few years of scarcity, ordinary industry supplied their wants; and they lived more comfortably and independently than the same class in the old world.

The Puritans of New England had naturally imbibed [absorbed] a strong aversion to the manners and practices of those who had persecuted them. They were opposed to veils, wigs, and long hair, condemned silken hoods and scarfs, required women to restrict the size of their sleeves, and discountenanced [disapproved] all frivolous fashions in dress. They disliked the cross in the British flag, and forbade the observance of Christmas. Comparing themselves to the Israelites of old, who fled from bondage in Egypt to an unknown wilderness, they tried to conform to the laws and customs of the chosen people. Like them, they commenced their Sabbath on Saturday evening, and observed it with the utmost strictness. They took whole sentences from the Bible as names for their children, or called them after Scriptural characters. All religious duties were zealously attended to; prayers and sermons were but little esteemed [valued] unless they were of great length; and the children and servants were regularly catechised [instructed about religious matters]. They were stiff and formal, but at the same time industrious, enterprising, and moral.

The laws of the Puritans condemned all war that was not defensive, and provided penalties for gambling, intemperance, and other immoralities. They forbade the taking of interest on loaned money and punished blasphemy and idolatry with death. Persecuted Christians, of their own faith, who sought refuge among them, were supported for a time at the public expense; but priests and Jesuits were forbidden to set foot within their limits.

"Intemperance" refers here to excessive use of alcoholic beverages.

"Blasphemy" is behavior that shows a lack of respect for God.

"Form" here means ceremony.

Quakers shared with Roman Catholics the hatred of the Puritans. They were first known as a religious body in England in 1644, through the preaching of George Fox. Averse [opposed] to form, the Quakers believed that God communicated directly with the spirits of men, moving them according to His will. They would neither bear arms nor take an oath; they condemned pleasures, forms, and show; they denounced tyranny and abhorred titles. Anxious to propagate [spread] their doctrines, and ready to seal their opinions with their blood, they had turned their eyes to America as a promising field for effort.

In 1656, two Quakeresses arrived at Boston. They were immediately arrested, and after an imprisonment of five weeks expelled from the colony. Laws were passed, forbidding under heavy penalties the introducing or harboring of Quakers in Massachusetts. If one of "the accursed sect" was found within the colony, he was to lose an ear; if he returned, the other was forfeited; and for a third offence his tongue was to be pierced with a red-hot iron.

But the persecuted Quakers gloried in bearing witness to their faith. The severer the laws against them the more they were attracted to Boston. Fines, whippings, and tortures, could not keep them away; and finally the authorities declared that all Quakers found a second time in the colony should be punished with death. Three men and one woman suffered on the scaffold under this law, declaring that they died for conscience' sake. Such horror, however, was excited by these executions, that the cruel law was repealed. After this, Quakers were whipped out of the colony, and the excitement gradually died away.

"Heresy" is belief which contradicts official church doctrine.

Queen Mary, who was Catholic, persecuted the Protestants of England.

It seems strange in this more liberal age that the Puritans should so soon have forgotten their own sufferings, and displayed the same persecuting spirit from which they themselves fled. Their only excuse is to be found in the spirit of the times. Laws for the punishment of heresy existed in every Christian country. In Spain, multitudes had perished at the stake and on the rack.... Even in England, numbers had suffered under Bloody Mary and some of her successors. The Puritans were only carrying out the same intolerant principles. To Roger Williams and his Providence Plantations, to Lord Baltimore and his happy colony on the Chesapeake, belong the honor of first rising superior to the bigotry [intolerance] of their age.

1. Did the Puritans' reasons for coming to the New World have any effect on their actions when they arrived here? How? Can

you explain this? For example, did the Puritan desire to "purify" the English Church affect their behavior in any way?

2. How can you explain the General Court's restriction of voting rights? Was it carrying out any of the Puritans' interests?

3. Some of the Puritans objected to the Court's action on voting. Did you think that this action carried out any of the Puritans' own interests? How do you explain their objections? Compare the ideas the Puritans displayed about government with those the Pilgrims expressed in the Mayflower Compact.

4. How did the Puritan laws affect personal life? Do you feel that government laws should cover personal matters of this kind? Why do you think the Puritans approved of such laws?

5. Is there anything about the New World that might have influenced Puritan actions? You can refer to previous sections of this unit for additional ideas about the conditions Puritans encountered.

A HYPOTHESIS ABOUT PURITANS

Earlier in this unit you were asked to form a hypothesis. Now you will be concerned with testing a hypothesis. You will recall that a hypothesis is not proven but is assumed to be true. After a hypothesis has been formed, it must be tested to determine if it is true or false. For example, a scientist can assume that the combination of two elements will produce a particular result. But the scientist must make tests in order to discover whether his assumption or hypothesis is correct. In history, too, the truth of a hypothesis is determined by testing it against facts or available evidence.

After reading the nineteenth-century textbook selection about the Puritans, you might decide:

"The Puritans were a stern and cruel people."

In order to find out if this hypothesis is valid you could ask, "Is this a true statement?" "If so, how is it true?" "If not, why not?" "What specific information could be used to answer these questions?" "Is additional information necessary to determine if the hypothesis is valid?"

How would *you* answer the previous questions?

Using the information at your disposal, formulate another hypothesis about the Puritans. Then, show how you could determine the validity of your hypothesis.

24. Samuel Sewall: Reviewing a Hypothesis

Samuel Sewall (1652–1730) was a leader of the Massachusetts Bay Colony when the third generation of Puritans were in their prime. He served as an elected member of the lower house of the legislature and was appointed by the governor to be a councilor (member of the upper house of the legislature). The governor also appointed him to be a judge of the courts of Massachusetts. In this period of Massachusetts history, the courts were direct agents of the King. Judges were appointed either directly by the King or by his appointee, the governor.

The reading mentions that Sewall took part in trials of "witches." These were the famous Salem witchcraft trials of the 1690's. Many people believed in the evil power of witches. Fear of this power struck the town of Salem in 1692 and threw it into panic. Several hundred persons were accused of witchcraft and nineteen were hanged. Sewall was one of the judges who tried the witchcraft cases and thus shared responsibility for the condemnation of the nineteen persons.

The following portrait of Sewall is based on his diaries. It was written by Vernon Parrington, a twentieth-century historian whose field was the history of American literature and thought.

Vernon Louis Parrington, **The Colonial Mind** (New York: Harcourt, Brace & World, Inc., 1927), pp. 90-91, 95. Copyright 1927, 1930 by Harcourt, Brace & World, Inc.; renewed 1955 by Vernon L. Parrington, Jr., Louise P. Tucker, Elizabeth P. Thomas. Reprinted by permission of the publisher.

Hooker was a Congregational preacher whose split with the leaders of Massachusetts led to the founding of Connecticut.

"Husbandman," here, means a good manager.

. . . We know Samuel Sewall now and see him as he was. That he was a great man it is impossible to make out; but that he was a small man by no means follows. Behind the formal trappings of magistrate [judge] and councilor, we discover a capable, middle-class soul, honest, simple-hearted, serving himself yet not unmindful of his fellow townsmen, an excellent neighbor and citizen, to whom the strongest appeal of life was the economic. . . . To acquire wealth and honors, to occupy a dignified position among his fellows, was the dominant ambition of his life. With excellent thrift he fixed his young affections upon the only child of a wealthy merchant, the richest heiress in the colony; no penniless "waiting-woman," for Samuel Sewall, such as had contented the unworldly Thomas Hooker. He understood how desirable it is to put money in one's purse; so he made a great alliance and proved himself a shrewd husbandman as well as a kind husband. From commerce and land speculation and money lending and the perquisites [profits] of many offices, he accumulated steadily until his wealth entitled him to be regarded as one of the first citizens of Massachusetts. He did not forget his prudence even in his generosities, but set down carefully in his diary what his benefactions [gifts] cost, that there might be no mistake when he came to make his reckoning with the Lord. He knew his rights and upheld them stoutly; and in the petty quarrels and litigations [legal disputes] in which he found himself involved, he stuck to the letter of the law and usually won his point. He did not misuse his official position to feather his own nest, but what might be got legally from public office he took care to get.

With abundant wealth the path of preferment [advancement] was easy to him. From his election to the privileges of a freeman in 1678, at the age of twenty-six, to the end of a long life, he was continuously engaged in public affairs. He sought office and was not backward in pushing his claims upon a desirable post; and by careful attention to business rather than by exceptional parts [talents], he rose to a place of very great influence in the commonwealth.

. . . When his native kindliness was touched he spoke out frankly. His antislavery tract (*The Selling of Joseph*), slight in extent and somewhat overpraised by historians, was not only much in advance of his time, but it contains one sentence that should not be forgotten, "There is no proportion between twenty pieces of silver and liberty." Equally significant was his stand against capital punishment for counterfeiting. Such acts as the following must also be set down to his credit: "I essay'd June 22 [1716], to prevent Indians and Negroes being Rated with Horses and Hogs; but could not prevail." His native sense of justice was as strong as his kindliness. Who does not know of his confession in regard to the witchcraft persecutions—an act that set all Boston tongues wagging. When he was convinced that he had made a grievous and sorrowful mistake, he rose in the congregation while the minister read his public acknowledgement of that mistake, and his repentance for his share in the unhappy business. Thereafter in commemoration he kept an annual day of prayer and fasting.

"Proportion" means comparison.

1. What is your opinion now of the hypothesis, "The Puritans were a stern and cruel people?" Has it changed? Why? Do you wish to change your own hypothesis? Explain.

2. What do Mr. Sewall's main interests in life seem to be? How do these compare with the interests of the Puritans you read about in the previous selection?

25. The Old Deluder Law

As settlers established themselves along the New England coast and began to spread into the wilderness of western New England, many laws were passed to regulate their lives. Among the laws passed by the General Court of Massachusetts was the Old Deluder Law of 1647. The "Old Deluder" refers to Satan.

What the law tells you about the interests of the people of Massachusetts during this period.

Section 1

The Charter and General Laws of the Colony and Province of Massachusetts Bay (Boston: 1814), p. 186.

It being one chief project of Satan to keep man from the knowledge of the scriptures, . . . [and so] that learning may not be buried in the graves of our forefathers, with the Lord assisting our endeavours:

To "resort," here, means to apply.

It is therefore ordered by this court and authority thereof; that every township within this jurisdiction, after the Lord hath increased them to the number of fifty householders, shall then forthwith appoint one within their towns to teach all such children as shall resort to him to write and read, whose wages shall be paid either by parents or masters of such children, or by the inhabitants in general, by way of supply, as the major part of those that order the prudentials [advisers] of the town shall appoint: provided that those who send their children be not oppressed by paying much more than they can have them taught for in other towns.

Section 2

And it is further ordered, that where any town shall increase to the number of one hundred families or householders, they shall set up a grammar school, the master thereof being able to instruct youth so far as they may be fitted for the university: and if any town neglect the performance hereof above one year, then every such town shall pay five pounds per annum to the [nearest] school till they shall perform this order.

1. What is a law? When laws are made by a group like the General Court, what is their purpose?

2. What does the Old Deluder Law show you that the Massachusetts Bay colonists valued? Why did they feel that the government should have a part in this?

3. Compare the interests revealed in the Old Deluder Law with those you found in the Mayflower Compact and in the account of the Puritans. Are there any similarities? Do you see a pattern emerging that would lead you to make a hypothesis about the people of this area of the colonies? Explain.

26. The Story of Roger Williams

The government and the Puritan Church of Massachusetts Bay Colony were closely interwoven. The laws reflected the ideas and beliefs of the church. Anyone who was not a member of the church had no voice in the government. One of the best-known challengers of this system was Roger Williams, who established the new colony of Rhode Island in 1636. Williams' quarrel with the Puritan authorities is described in the following account by Roger Burlingame, who has written several books about American history.

... [Roger] Williams went to Massachusetts Bay because he had a "call" to it at the time of its founding when there was a shortage of ministers. He was happy to accept, as he belonged to the Puritan band who were being persecuted by Archbishop Laud of the Anglican Church. When he arrived in Boston, however, he was anything but liberal in his views. Almost immediately he accused the Boston church of not being sufficiently separatist and refused its pastorship on the ground that it still clung to the pretense of being a "purified" part of the Church of England.

Roger Burlingame, "Zion in the Forest," **American Heritage,** Vol. VII, no. 4 (1956), pp. 34-36. Reprinted by permission of the publisher.

Laud was the leader of the Church of England.

This was Roger Williams' first offense ... His second was to maintain that the civil government has no right to enforce the first four commandments, all of which were strictly religious injunctions and therefore wholly under the jurisdiction of the church. In other words, he advocated separation of Church and State. As the whole basis of the Massachusetts Bay colony was an identification of Church and State, this seemed like blasphemy and treason.

What power was left to magistrates if they could no longer punish the heinous [hateful] sins of sabbath-breaking, profanity, and the worship of false gods? What would happen to a community in which such criminal conduct could be punished only by excommunication? Would not the pure and holy commonwealth soon be crawling with papists [Roman Catholics], Jews, Quakers and heathen?

But on the heels of this subversion [undermining of beliefs] came the worst pronouncement of all—a dictum which struck at the very foundation of American colonial settlement. This [pronouncement] was no longer religious—except that it favored the very heathen the magistrates feared—it was political, a realm in which, by Williams' own preaching, the clergy had no business!

By this time, ... he had accepted a call to the Plymouth Colony, a community of avowed separatists under the tolerant Governor

William Bradford. Here, perhaps, his early sins might have been forgiven. He had extraordinary magnetism. His gentleness, his kindness to men, women, and children everywhere, and the peculiar charm of his conversation stood in sharp contrast to the fanatic zeal with which he opposed the orthodox dogmas [conventional beliefs]. Bradford thought him "godly and zealous" . . . despite his "strange opinions." But then Roger Williams committed his [worst] "error."

In his spare time at Plymouth he had wandered through the dense forests surrounding the settlements and had come to know and love the Indians. He was one of the very few New England clerics [ministers] who was concerned about the welfare and happiness of the natives. He looked upon them as human beings entitled to certain rights and privileges—not as an inferior race of unredeemable heathen. He even learned certain of the tribal languages. Finally he was so stirred by what he considered the unjust treatment of these aboriginal [native] Americans by the English that his conscience overcame his discretion.

He wrote, then, a treatise maintaining that the English king had no right to give grants and patents to land that belonged to the Indians, and that in doing it James had "told a solemn public lie." Nothing could have been more unfortunate than such a word at that time. New England was already under suspicion among orthodox Englishmen. It seemed to the people of Plymouth and the Bay that such a criticism of royalty might do them great harm in the mother country.

At this time, an attempt was being made in England to revoke the Massachusetts charter.

In July, 1635, therefore, Williams was haled before the General Court [Massachusetts Bay] and charged with his dangerous opinions. In September, when he still refused to recant [revoke his opinions], the sentence of banishment was pronounced against him. . . .

The magistrates did not simply tell him to go. They arranged to seize him at night, put him on a ship, and deport him to England. But Williams had too many friends—people he had captivated by his charm but who did not dare speak out for him—for such a plan to succeed. He was warned and escaped into the trackless wilderness in the dead of winter—a perilous adventure which he could never have carried through without the cooperation of his savage friends of the forest. . . .

An "estuary" is a place where ocean tides meet river currents.

He . . . came, in the spring, to the estuary of Narragansett Bay called Great Salt River [in Rhode Island] and there . . . he arranged with two Indian sachems [chiefs] to buy from them the land for a settlement. He named it Providence in gratitude for his survival; presently he was joined by other exiles and by his own wife and children.

... he set a milestone in the history of the American conscience for which he must be honored while there is still freedom in our land....

No man must be molested for his religion. Whatever faith he might choose, that he must be allowed to hold, be he Jew or Turk or pagan. The magistrates should have no power to intervene in the affairs of any church except in order to keep the civil peace....

From [Providence] the practice spread, slowly through New England, more rapidly through the middle and southern colonies, until at last no American could deny it and the concept was crystallized a century and a half later in the words of the Federal Bill of Rights.

1. What did Roger Williams protest?

2. Why did the Puritans and Pilgrims object to protests on these issues? Does this reveal what was important to them? Why did they go so far as to banish Williams from the colony? What does this do to the impression you have formed of the Massachusetts colonists?

3. How do you account for the actions of those who helped Williams? Does this resemble the behavior of any other Massachusetts colonists about whom you have read? How?

4. What ideas or rules of conduct do you think were most important to Roger Williams? Were these ideas important to any other Massachusetts settlers?

   For example: How did Williams seem to feel people should behave toward government? Did this violate the ideas in the Mayflower Compact?

WHAT ARE VALUES?
1. What does the term "to value" mean?

2. What do you value? How did you decide what your values are? Why do you have these particular values? What difference does it make whether we value anything or not? Explain.

3. Could groups of people like a town or nation have values? Explain.

4. From the evidence in this section, what do you think the colonists of New England valued?

5. Earlier in this unit you tested the hypothesis that man's actions are determined by his beliefs. Does the story of Roger Williams help to verify that idea? Why?

THE MIDDLE COLONIES

27. William Penn: A Letter to the Indians

In the middle of the seventeenth century, the King of England granted a large tract of land to William Penn. The land was payment of an old debt owed to Penn's father, who had recently died. Penn decided to organize a settlement to send to the new colony, which he called Pennsylvania. Before setting out for the colony, Penn sent several messages to the Indians who lived there. The following is one of those letters.

Memoirs of the Historical Society of Pennsylvania (Philadelphia: J. B. Lippincott Company, 1858), Vol. VI, p. 253.

To "traffic" with means to have dealings with.

To "treat," here, means to discuss or negotiate.

The great God that made thee and me, and all the world, incline our hearts to love peace and justice, that we may live friendly together, as becomes the workmanship of the great God. The King of England, who is a great prince, hath, for divers [several] reasons, granted to me a large country in America, which, however, I am willing to enjoy upon friendly terms with thee; and this I will say, that the people who come with me are a just, plain, and honest people, that neither make war upon others, nor fear war from others, because they will be just. I have set up a society of traders in my province, to traffic with thee and thy people, for your commodities, that you may be furnished with that which is good, at reasonable rates; and that society hath ordered their president to treat with thee about a future trade, and have joined with me to send this messenger to thee with certain presents from us, to testify our willingness to have a fair correspondence with thee, and what this agent shall do in our names, we will agree unto. I hope thou wilt kindly receive him, and comply with his desires on our behalf, both with respect to land and trade. The great God be with thee. Amen.

William Penn.

Philip Theodore Lehnman, secretary
London, the 21st day of . . . June 1682.

1. What attitudes and values are reflected in Penn's letter? How do they compare with the values of New England colonists? Which New England colonists does Penn most resemble?

2. Consider the information on Indians of this area on the map on page 45. How would you expect the Pennsylvania Indians to react to Penn's letter? Why? Would this differ from the attitude Indians might have toward colonists in New England? Why?

28. The Trial of Peter Zenger

In 1735, John Peter Zenger, a German immigrant, was charged with seditious libel and brought to trial in the colony of New York. Libel is a written statement that is false and injures someone's reputation. Sedition is the act of encouraging discontent against the government or resistance to authority. Seditious libel is a seditious writing or one that excites discontent against or resistance to the government by exposing government officials to public ridicule. Zenger had published articles in the *New York Weekly Journal* that criticized the governor and government.

New York was a royal colony, controlled directly by the crown. The King appointed the governor and the upper house of the legislative assembly. The governor appointed all judges.

The following is an adaptation of Peter Zenger's own account of the trial. He was defended by Andrew Hamilton, a lawyer from Philadelphia.

[**Clerk of Court:** The people will rise for the Chief Justice. (Pause) The Court of our Lord the King for the Province of New York is now in session.]

Mr. Bradley (Prosecutor): Be it remembered, that Richard Bradley, Esquire, Attorney General of Our Sovereign Lord the King, for the Province of New York, [has been assigned as Prosecutor. I now open the case against] John Peter Zenger, late of the City of New York, Printer. [Mr. Zenger has a reputation as] . . . a seditious Person, and a frequent Printer and Publisher of false news and seditious Libels, . . . [that] wickedly and maliciously . . . [criticize] the Government of Our said Lord the King [and that of the] Province of New York, under the administration of His Excellency [Governor] William Cosby . . . [On] the Twenty eighth Day of January, in the seventh Year of the Reign of Our Sovereign Lord George the second, . . . [Mr. Zenger] did falsely, seditiously and scandalously print and publish, and cause to be printed and published, a certain false, malicious, seditious, scandalous Libel, [in the newspaper entitled], the *New York Weekly Journal* . . .

American History Told by Contemporaries, edited by Albert Bushnell Hart (New York: The Macmillan Company, 1898), Vol. II, pp. 192-199.

The "Attorney General" is the chief law officer of a state or nation. He represents the government in legal disputes.

To "intail" (entail) is to impose. "Posterity" means future generations, or descendants.

[This libel says, and let me read it to you:] . . . "the People of this City and Province [of New York] . . . think as Matters now stand, that their LIBERTIES and PROPERTIES are precarious, and that SLAVERY is like to be intailed on them and their posterity, if some [current governmental practices are not changed] . . . [Evidence collected from many past events reveals a legislature too much affected by the whims of a few of its members] and the Smiles and Frowns of a Governour, . . . WE SEE MENS DEEDS DESTROYED, JUDGES ARBITRARILY DISPLACED, NEW COURTS ERECTED, WITHOUT CONSENT OF THE LEGISLATURE . . . TRYALS [TRIALS] BY JURIES ARE TAKEN AWAY WHEN A GOVERNOR PLEASES, . . . MEN OF KNOWN ESTATES DENYED [DENIED] THEIR VOTES, CONTRARY TO THE RECEIVED PRACTICE. . . . Who is then in that Province . . . [who can] call . . . any Thing his own, or enjoy any Liberty . . . longer than those in the Administration . . . will condescend [yield] to let them do it, for which Reason I have left it, (the Province of New York . . .) as I believe more will."

Zenger went to New Jersey in 1735.

[This kind of writing is a disturbance] of the Peace of the said Province of New York, [and a] Great Scandal of Our said Lord the King, of His Excellency the said Governor, and of all others concerned in the Administration of the Government. . . . Whereupon [as] the said Attorney General of Our said Lord the King, [I bring the charge of seditious libel against John Peter Zenger] . . .

[**Clerk of Court:** How does the Defendant plead to these charges?]

Peter Zenger: To this Information the Defendant has pleaded Not Guilty, and we are ready to prove it . . .

An "information" is a formal statement accusing someone of a crime.

Mr. Andrew Hamilton (Defender): May it please your Honour; I am concerned in this Cause on the Part of Mr. Zenger the Defendant. The Information against my Client was sent me, a few Days before I left Home, with some Instructions to let me know how far I might rely upon the Truth of [the article in the Paper that has just been set forth before you] which are said to be libellous. . . . I cannot think it proper for me (without doing Violence to my own Principles) to deny the Publication of a Complaint, which I think, is the Right of every free-born Subject to make, when the Matters so published can be supported with Truth, and therefore I'll save Mr. Bradley the Trouble of Examining his Witnesses on that Point; and I do (for my Client) confess, that he both printed and published the . . . News Papers set forth in the Information, and I hope in so doing he has committed no Crime . . .

70

Mr. Bradley: The Case before the Court is, whether Mr. Zenger is guilty of Libelling his Excellency the Governor of New York, and indeed the whole Administration of the Government? Mr. Hamilton has confessed the Printing and Publishing, and I think nothing is plainer, than that the Words in the Information are scandalous, and tend to Sedition, and to disquiet [disturb] the Minds of the people of this Province. And if such Papers are not Libels, I think it may be said, there can be no such Thing as a Libel.

Mr. Hamilton: May it please your Honour; I cannot agree with Mr. Bradley: For tho' I freely acknowledge, that there are such Things as Libels, yet I must insist at the same Time, that what my Client is charged with, is not a Libel; and I observed just now, that Mr. Bradley is defining a Libel, made use of the Words scandalous, seditious, and tend to disquiet the People; but (whether with Design or not I will not say) he omitted the Word false.

Mr. Bradley: I think I did not omit the word false: But it has been said already, that it may be a Libel [regardless of whether it is true or not].

Mr. Hamilton: In this I must still differ with Mr. Bradley; . . . We are to be tried upon the Information now before the Court and Jury, and to which we have pleaded Not Guilty, and by it we are charged with printing and publishing, a certain false, malicious, seditious and scandalous Libel. This Word false must have some Meaning, or else how came it there? . . .

Mr. Chief Justice: You cannot be admitted [allowed], Mr. Hamilton, to give the Truth of a Libel in Evidence. A Libel is not to be justified; for it is nevertheless a Libel [whether] it is true [or not].

Mr. Hamilton: I am sorry the Court has so soon resolved upon that Piece of Law; I expected first to have been heard to that Point. I have not in all my reading met with an authority that says we cannot be admitted to give the Truth in Evidence upon an Information for a libel.

Mr. Chief Justice: The Law is clear That you cannot justify a Libel. . . .

Mr. Hamilton: I thank your Honour. Then, Gentlemen of the Jury, it is to you we must now appeal, for Witnesses, to the Truth, of the Facts we have offered, and are denied the Liberty to prove; and let it not seem strange, that I apply my self to you in this Manner, I am warranted [justified] so to do both by Law and Reason. The Last supposes you to be summoned [to serve on this

71

jury], out of the Neighbourhood where the Fact is alledged to be committed; and the Reason of your being taken out of the Neighbourhood is, because you are supposed to have the best Knowledge of the Fact that is to be tried. And were you to find a Verdict against my Client, you must take upon [yourself] to say, the Papers referred to in the Information, and which we acknowledge we printed and published, are false, scandalous and seditious; but of this I can have no Apprehension [worry]. You are Citizens of New-York; you are really what the Law supposes you to be, honest and lawful Men; and, according to my Brief the Facts which we offer to prove were not committed in a Corner; they are notoriously known to be true, and therefore in your Justice lies our Safety. And as we are denied the liberty of giving Evidence, to prove the Truth of what we have published, I will beg Leave to lay it down as a standing Rule in such Cases, That the suppressing of Evidence ought always to be taken for the strongest Evidence; and I hope it will have that weight with you . . .

It is true in Times past that it was a Crime to speak Truth, and in that terrible Court of Star-Chamber, many worthy and brave Men suffered for so doing; and yet even in that Court, and in those bad Times, a great and good Man durst [dared] say, what I hope will not be taken amiss of me to say in this Place, . . . the Practice of Informations for Libels is a Sword in the Hands of a wicked King, . . . to cut down and destroy the innocent; . . .

Mr. Bradley: Pray Mr. Hamilton, have a Care what you say, don't go too far neither, I don't like those Liberties [you take].

Mr. Hamilton: Surely, . . . all Men agree that we are governed by the best of Kings, and I cannot see the Meaning of Mr. Bradley's Caution, my well known Principles, and the Sense I [have] of the Blessings we enjoy under his present Majesty, makes it impossible for me to err, and I hope, even to be suspected, in that Point of Duty to my King. May it please Your Honour, I was saying, that [in spite of] all the Duty and Reverence claimed by Mr. Bradley to Men in Authority, they are not exempt [released] from observing the rules of common Justice, either in their private or publick Capacities; the Laws of our Mother Country know no Exception. . . .

I hope to be pardon'd Sir, for my Zeal upon this occasion: It is an old and wise Caution, that when our Neighbour's House is on Fire, we ought to take Care of our own. For tho', blessed be

A "brief" summarizes the facts of a case and includes the client's main arguments with supporting facts, as well as legal precedents.

The Court of the Star Chamber was an English court of law in the sixteenth and seventeenth centuries. Judgment was made without the benefit of a trial by jury, and torture was often used to obtain confessions.

To "err" means to make a mistake.

72

God, I live in a Government [Pennsylvania] where Liberty is well understood, and freely enjoy'd; yet Experience has shown us all (I'm sure it has to me) that a bad precedent in one Government, is soon set up for an Authority in another, and therefore I cannot but think it mine, and every Honest Man's Duty, that (while we pay all due Obedience to Men in Authority) we ought at the same Time to be upon our guard against Power, wherever we apprehend that it may [affect] ourselves or our Fellow-Subjects.

... I think it my duty, if required to go to the utmost part of the land ... in assisting to quench [put out] the Flame of Prosecutions upon Informations, set on Foot by the Government, to deprive a People of the Right of Remonstrating, (and complaining too), of the arbitrary Attempts of Men in Power. Men who injure and oppress the People under their Administration provoke them to cry out and complain; and then make that very Complaint the Foundation for new Oppressions and Prosecutions. I wish I could say there were no Instances of this Kind. But, to conclude; the Question before the Court and you, Gentlemen of the Jury, is not of small nor private concern, it is not the Cause of a poor Printer, nor of New York alone, which you are now trying; No! It may in its Consequence, affect every Freeman that lives under a British government on the Main of America. It is the best Cause. It is the Cause of Liberty; and I make no Doubt [that] your upright Conduct, this Day, will not only entitle you to the Love and Esteem of your Fellow-Citizens; but every Man, who prefers Freedom to a life of Slavery, will bless and honour You as Men who have baffled the Attempt of Tyranny, and by an impartial and uncorrupt Verdict, [you will] have laid a noble Foundation for securing to ourselves, our Posterity and our Neighbors, That to which Nature and the Laws of our Country have given us a Right—The Liberty—both of exposing and opposing arbitrary Power, ... by speaking and writing Truth. ...

To "remonstrate" means to protest or object.

Mr. Chief Justice: Gentlemen of the Jury. The great Pains Mr. Hamilton has taken, to show how little Regard Juries are to Pay to the opinion of the Judges; ... is done, no doubt, with a Design that you should take but very little Notice of what I may say upon this Occasion. I shall therefore only observe to you that, as the Facts or Words in the Information are confessed: The only Thing that can come in Question before you is, Whether the Words, as set forth in the Information, make a Libel ... But, I shall trouble you no further with any Thing more of my own, but read to you the Words of a learned and upright judge in a Case of like Nature.

"To say that corrupt Officers are appointed to administer Affairs, is certainly a Reflection on the Government. If people should not be called to account for [encouraging] the people [to have] an ill Opinion of the Government, no Government can subsist. For it is necessary for all Governments that the People should have a good Opinion of it. And nothing can be worse to any Government than to [have people attempt to create distrust and dislike of] the Management of it, this has always been looked upon as a Crime, and no Government can be safe without it [being] punished.

Now you are to Consider whether these Words I have read to you do not tend to beget [create] an Ill Opinion of the Administration of the Government? . . ."

[**Clerk of Court:** The Court will rise. The jury may withdraw.]

[A short time later.]

[**Clerk of Court:** The Court will rise for the Chief Justice. (Pause) Has the jury agreed of their verdict? Is John Peter Zenger guilty of printing and publishing the libels mentioned?]

Foreman of the Jury: Not Guilty!

Upon which there were three huzzas [cheers] in the Hall which was crowded with People, and the next Day [Peter Zenger] was discharged from imprisonment.

1. For what is Peter Zenger being tried? Why?

2. Assume you are Peter Zenger. Write a few sentences summarizing your defense.

3. Assume you are the colonial judge. Write a few sentences on your opinion of Peter Zenger's defense.

4. If the judge's opinion were the opinion of our government today, what effect would it have on our life? Explain.

5. Of what value today is the decision of the Peter Zenger case?

6. Do Zenger's behavior and Hamilton's defense of it reflect the ideas in the Mayflower Compact or contradict these ideas? Explain.

29. Benjamin Franklin Comments on His Fortunes

Benjamin Franklin (1706–1790) began his career in printing by working for his brother, who published the *New England Courant* in Boston. He moved to Philadelphia in 1723 with the hope of eventually establishing his own printing business. By 1729 he had acquired an interest in the *Pennsylvania Gazette,* and in 1730 he became its owner and editor. He expanded his publishing interests in 1732 with *Poor Richard's Almanack,* an annual publication of interesting facts, advice, statistics, and witty sayings.

The following readings are taken from *Poor Richard's Almanack* and from Franklin's *Autobiography,* which he began writing in 1771. The *Autobiography* covers fifty-three years of Franklin's life. It is one of Franklin's most famous and important writings, for it gives a good description of colonial life and attitudes.

PREFACE TO POOR RICHARD'S ALMANACK, 1733

Courteous Reader,

I might in this place attempt to gain thy Favour, by declaring that I write Almanacks with no other View than that of the publick Good; but in this I should not be sincere; and Men are now adays too wise to be deceiv'd by Pretences how specious soever. The plain Truth of the Matter is, I am excessive poor, and my Wife, good Woman, is, I tell her, excessive proud; she cannot bear, she says, to sit spinning in her Shift of Tow, while I do nothing but gaze at the Stars; and has threatened more than once to burn all my Books and Rattling-Traps (as she calls my Instruments) if I do not make some profitable Use of them for the Good of my Family. The Printer has offer'd me some considerable share of the Profits, and I have thus begun to comply with my Dame's Desire.

Benjamin Franklin, edited by Chester E. Jorgenson and Frank Luther Mott (American Century Series; New York: Hill and Wang, Inc., 1962), p. 169.

"Specious" means believable on the surface.

A "shift of tow" is a straight, loose undergarment made of coarse linen cloth.

PREFACE TO POOR RICHARD'S ALMANACK, 1734

Courteous Readers,

Your kind and charitable Assistance last Year, in purchasing so large an Impression [a printing] of my Almanacks, has made my Circumstances much more easy in the World, and requires my grateful Acknowledgment. My Wife has been enabled to get a Pot of her own, and is no longer oblig'd to borrow one from a Neighbour; nor have we ever since been without something of our own to put in it. She also got a pair of Shoes, two new Shifts, and a new warm Petticoat; and for my part, I have bought a second-hand Coat, so good, that I am now not asham'd to go to Town or be seen there. These Things have render'd her Temper

Benjamin Franklin, edited by Chester E. Jorgenson and Frank Luther Mott, pp. 172-173.

so much more pacifick [peaceful] than it us'd to be, that I may say, I have slept more, and more quietly within this last Year, than in the three foregoing Years put together. Accept my hearty Thanks therefor, and my sincere Wishes for your Health and Prosperity.

AN EXCERPT FROM FRANKLIN'S AUTOBIOGRAPHY

My business was now continually augmenting [increasing] and my circumstances growing daily easier, my newspaper having become very profitable, as being for a time almost the only one in this and the neighboring provinces. I experienced, too, the truth of the observation, "that after getting the first hundred pounds, it is more easy to get the second," money itself being of a prolific nature.

1. Does Franklin express any values in his prefaces to *Poor Richard*, or do you think he is only making jokes?

2. If Franklin had been addressing his *Almanack* to a group of early Massachusetts Bay Puritans, do you think he would have written prefaces like these? Why or why not? Can you tell anything about the values of his audience from his writing?

3. Does the passage from Franklin's *Autobiography* affect your interpretation of the *Almanack* prefaces? If so, how?

4. Does Franklin resemble any of the New England colonists you read about? If so, whom? Does he resemble any of the other Middle Colonies people you studied?

30. The Albany Plan

As the English colonists moved further and further west, they came into contact with the French military posts, which were strategically placed to control the Ohio Valley and to keep English colonists from settling there. By the early 1750's it was clear that conflict over the settlement of the lands west of the English colonies would lead to war between England and France.

The English colonies presented a weak front when compared with the centralized government of New France with its military posts and friendly relations with most of the Indians. The separate governments of the English colonies seldom acted together. They did not even have a unified plan for defense, for control of the western lands, or for establishing friendly relations with the Indians.

Benjamin Franklin, **The Autobiography of Benjamin Franklin** (New York: Pocket Books, Inc., 1955), p. 134.

"Prolific," here, means having a tendency to increase.

In 1754, delegates from the English colonies met in Albany to strengthen their ties with the Iroquois. The Iroquois, who lived in what is now New York state, were not allied with the French. During the conference, the delegates discussed and adopted a plan of union drawn up by Benjamin Franklin. Part of the plan follows.

AN EXCERPT FROM THE ALBANY PLAN

It is proposed that humble application be made for an act of Parliament of Great Britain, by virtue of which one general government may be formed in America . . . as hereafter follows.

Documents of American History, edited by Henry Steele Commager (New York: Appleton-Century-Crofts, 1962), pp. 43-44.

1. That the said general government be administered by a President-General, to be appointed and supported by the crown; a Grand Council, to be chosen by the representatives of the people of the several Colonies [meeting] in their respective assemblies.

2. . . . members for the Grand Council [shall be chosen] in the following proportion [according to population] . . .

Massachusetts Bay	7
New Hampshire	2
Connecticut	5
Rhode Island	2
New York	4
New Jersey	3
Pennsylvania	6
Maryland	4
Virginia	7
North Carolina	4
South Carolina	4
	48

3. . . . [Grand Council] shall meet for the first time at the city of Philadelphia, being called by the President-General . . .

4. That there shall be a new election of members of the Grand Council every three years . . .

5. That after the first three years, when the proportion of money arising out of each colony to the general treasury can be known, the number of members to be chosen for each Colony shall . . . in all ensuing elections, be regulated by that proportion . . .

6. That the Grand Council shall meet once in every year . . . or as they shall be called to meet . . . by the President-General on any emergency . . .

7. That the Grand Council have power to choose their speaker . . .

8. That the members of the Grand Council shall be allowed for their service ten shillings sterling per diem [for each day] . . .

9. That the assent of the President-General to be requisite [required] to all acts of the Grand Council and that it be his office and duty to cause them to be carried into execution.

10. That the President-General, with the advice of the Grand Council, hold or direct all Indian treaties, . . . and make peace or declare war with Indian nations.

11. That they make such laws as they judge necessary for regulating all Indian trade.

12. That they make all purchases from Indians, . . . of lands not now within the bounds of particular Colonies . . .

13. That they make new settlements of such purchases . . .

14. That they make laws for regulating and governing such new settlements . . .

15. That they raise and pay soldiers and build forts for the defence of any of the Colonies, and equip vessels of force to guard the coasts and protect the trade . . .

16. That for these purposes they have the power to make laws, and lay and levy such general duties, imposts or taxes . . .

21. That laws made by them . . . shall not be repugnant [in opposition], but, agreeable to the laws of England, and shall be transmitted to the King in Council for approbation [approval], . . . and if not disapproved within three years after presentation, to remain in force.

22. That, in case of the death of the President-General, the Speaker of the Grand Council . . . shall succeed . . . till the King's pleasure be known.

1. Refer to page 55 at the end of Section VI, where you formed a tentative hypothesis about the common needs and interests of the English colonists. Does the list of duties assigned to the government in the Albany Plan reflect any of the needs and interests you thought the colonists would have? Does the Albany Plan reflect needs you did not list before?

2. Why was the government given only these duties? What does this tell you about colonial ideas on government?

THE RESPONSE

The Albany Plan was submitted to each of the colonial assemblies and to the King for acceptance. All of the colonies except New York voted against the Plan. In England it received a cold and negative response. Franklin commented in his *Autobiography*, "the assemblies did not adopt it, as they all thought there was too much prerogative in it [power for the King and his appointees] and in England it was judg'd to have too much of the democratic [local rule]."

Does the rejection of the Albany Plan signify any changes in attitude among colonists since the time of the Mayflower Compact? Explain.

A CARTOON

Below is a cartoon drawn by Benjamin Franklin in 1754 to urge adoption of the Albany Plan. It appeared in many colonial newspapers.

JOIN, or DIE.

1. What is Franklin's main idea in this cartoon? Explain.

2. According to this cartoon, how did colonists who favored the Albany Plan feel about union?

CONCLUDING EXERCISE

1. Do you see any similarities between the ideas and actions of Peter Zenger and those of Roger Williams? Are there any similarities between the reactions of the New York and Massachusetts governments toward these men? Any differences? Compare the reactions of the public. How can you explain this?

2. Did the people of the Middle Colonies want the same things as New Englanders? Was there any change of emphasis? How can you explain this? Take into consideration what you learned about the different colonies in Section VI. Consider, too, the effect of the New World on the colonists.

3. How does the attitude toward government in the Middle Colonies compare with what you observed in New England?

THE SOUTHERN COLONIES

31. The Maryland Toleration Act

The colony of Maryland was established in 1634 as a haven for Roman Catholics. Like the Pilgrims and Puritans, Catholics had suffered from religious persecution. Maryland was a proprietary colony, which means that the governor and judges were appointed by the proprietor, the person to whom the charter had been granted. The governor appointed the upper house of the legislature, and the freemen of the colony elected the lower house.

In 1649, when the colony was fifteen years old, its representative assembly passed the Maryland Toleration Act. The reason for the irregular spelling in the law is that before 1755 there was no accepted standard for writing the English language.

American History Told by Contemporaries, edited by Albert Bushnell Hart (New York: The Macmillan Company, 1897), Vol. I, p. 293.

... And whereas the inforcing of the conscience in matters of Religion hath frequently fallen out to be of dangerous Consequences in those commonwealthes where it hath been practised, and for the more quiet and peaceable government of this Province, and the better to preserve mutuall Love and amity amongst the Inhabitants thereof. Be it Therefore ... enacted ... that noe person or [persons] whatsoever within this Province, or the Islands, Ports, Harbors, Creekes, or havens thereunto belonging professing to believe in Jesus Christ, shall from henceforth bee any waies [ways] troubled, Molested or discountenanced [disapproved] for or in respect of his or her religion nor in the free exercise thereof within this Province. . .

1. What is the main point of this law?

2. Why did the colonists in Maryland feel it necessary to have such a law? What does this tell you about their values?

3. How do the values revealed here differ from those of the Massachusetts Bay colonists? Are there any similarities?

32. Slavery

The first Negroes were brought to the colonies in 1619 by the Dutch, who sold them in Jamestown, Virginia, as servants or slaves. During the seventeenth century most colonies had some slaves. By the end of the colonial period, however, slavery had practically disappeared in the North. But northern shippers continued to profit from the slave trade. Rum was shipped from New England to Africa where it was exchanged for slaves. The slaves were then transported to the West Indies where the northern shippers traded them for sugar. The sugar was returned to New England to make more rum.

In the South, the large plantations required many workmen. The planters relied heavily on slave labor, and by the 1750's slavery was firmly established in the South. By the end of the eighteenth century, several hundred thousand Negro slaves lived in the South. To control the slaves, all of the southern colonies enacted special laws or slave codes. Typical of these codes is the following excerpt from a law enacted by South Carolina in 1712.

Whereas the plantations and estates of this province cannot be well and sufficiently managed and brought into use without the labor and service of negroes and other slaves; and forasmuch as the said negroes and other slaves brought unto the people of this province for that purpose are of barbarous, wild, savage natures, and such as renders them wholly unqualified to be governed by the laws, customs, and practices of this province; but that it is absolutely necessary that such other constitutions, laws and orders should in this province be made and enacted for the good regulating and ordering of them, as may restrain the disorders, rapines [lootings], and inhumanity to which they are naturally prone and inclined, and may also tend to the safety and security of the people of this province and their estates, to which purpose.

1. "Be it enacted, [etc.] that all negroes, mulattoes, mestizoes and Indians, which may at any time heretofore have been sold, or are

John Codman Hurd, **The Law of Freedom and Bondage in the United States** (Boston: Little, Brown and Company, 1858), Vol. I, pp. 299-301.

A "mulatto" is a person who is part Negro and part white. A "mestizo" is a person who is part Indian and part European.

now held or taken to be, or hereafter shall be bought and sold for slaves, are hereby declared slaves, and they and their children are hereby made and declared slaves to all intents and purposes, excepting all such negroes, mulattoes, mestizoes, or Indians, which heretofore have been, or hereafter shall be, for some particular merit, made and declared free either by the governor and council of this province, . . . or by their respective owners or masters. . . ."

14. "Whereas divers [several] evil and ill-disposed persons have hitherto attempted to steal away negroes or other slaves, by specious pretence [a deceptive claim] of promising them freedom in another country, against which pernicious [wicked] practice no punishment suitable hath yet been provided," [this law also] provides punishment of the attempt by a fine, [etc.], and makes the act a "felony . . . and the offender shall suffer death accordingly." 15. "That in case any negro or slave shall run from his master or mistress, with intent to go off from this province, in order to deprive his master or mistress of his service, such negro or slave shall, on conviction, suffer death;" [this law also] provides for punishment of slaves enticing other slaves to run away.

1. Who made up the slave population? Why did Southerners think separate laws were necessary for them? What attitudes does this reveal?

2. How did New Englanders and Middle Atlantic colonists regard Indians? What were New Englanders' attitudes toward people with different ideas? Compare this with southern attitudes toward slaves. Are there any similarities? Any differences?

3. Considering southern opinion of the slave population, why did Southerners want slaves at all? What does this reveal about southern values? Did any other colonists display similar values?

4. Why do you think slavery became more important in the South than elsewhere? Consider what you learned in Section VI about the differences between southern colonies and other sections of the country. Does this completely explain why slavery arose in the South? Why?

33. Bacon's Rebellion

In 1619 Virginia voters elected representatives from each county in the colony to form the House of Burgesses. This was the first representative assembly in America. It laid the foundation for representative government in our land.

The House of Burgesses, together with the governor and council (assistants to the governor) who were appointed by the King, governed the colony. The Burgesses had the power to make laws for the colony, but they were subject to the approval of the governor.

During the 1670's the Virginia colonists became dissatisfied with the government. They wanted it to be more responsive to their needs. A revolt resulted. It was led by Nathaniel Bacon, a planter from the western part of the colony.

Though the Virginians loved liberty, they still retained some of the old forms and customs of the English aristocracy. The eldest son inherited the whole of his father's estate; and, as the influence and wealth of the land-owners increased, the dividing line between the higher and lower classes became more distinct. The Virginians were mostly royalists [loyal to the king] and but few republicans [who desired more rule by and for the people] were elected to the new legislature formed after the restoration of Charles II.

The loyal colonists, however, were not treated with [the] favor which they had a right to expect from the home government. Parliament soon ordered that the imports and exports of the colonists should be carried in English vessels alone, and that their chief productions should be shipped only to the mother country. A profitable trade which had sprung up with the West Indies was thus entirely cut off.

The measures of their own legislature were hardly less offensive than those of Parliament. The right of voting was restricted to householders. The forms of the English Church were enforced on all, and a fine of £20 [pounds] was laid on those who [failed to attend] public worship. A special law was passed against Quakers; and Baptists were denounced as "filled with new-fangled conceits [beliefs] of their own heretical invention." The members of this legislature had been elected for two years; but they continued in session without regard to the expiration of their term, and fixed their own salary at 250 pounds of tobacco a day. No public improvements were attempted. Neither roads nor bridges were constructed. Governor Berkeley, whom the long possession of power had made a tyrant, expressed the common sentiment of this royalist legislature, when he said, "I thank God that there are no free schools nor printing, and I hope that we shall not have them these hundred years."

G. P. Quackenbos, **Illustrated School History of the United States** (New York: Appleton-Century-Crofts, 1869), pp. 114-118.

In 1649, after seven years of civil war, the King of England was removed from his throne and beheaded. For the next eleven years, England was governed as a commonwealth. In 1660, the English crown was restored, and Charles II became King.

See Indian map, p. 45.

With such a government the people were justly dissatisfied, and, to add to their troubles, in 1675 an Indian war broke out. The Susquehannas, driven from their abodes [homes] by the Senecas, had fallen back on the Potomac and commenced depredations [attacks] in Maryland. John Washington, great-grandfather of the first president of the United States, hastened to the aid of the settlers. The Indians sent to propose peace; but their ambassadors, in violation of law and justice, were put to death. The savages retaliated by devastating the frontier from the Potomac to the James [rivers], and murdering without mercy all who fell in their power.

The people solicited [petitioned] Gov. Berkeley to take measures for the protection of their lives and property; but he paid no attention to their requests, and the work of death went on unchecked. In 1676, Nathaniel Bacon, who had but recently arrived from England, was urged by the people to lead them against the enemy. The governor would not commission him; but Bacon, moved by the solicitations [pleas] of his friends, declared that if he heard of another murder he would take the field with no commission but his sword. He was shortly afterwards informed that several men had been killed on his own plantation. The brave young leader no longer hesitated. At the head of 57 men, he defeated the Indians, and then turned to meet the tyrannical Berkeley, who was already marching against him. So strongly, however, did the people express their disapprobation [dislike] of the governor's course, that he concluded to abandon it. Concessions were made by Bacon, and he was reinstated in his former position. The old legislature was dissolved, and a new one of totally different principles was elected.

Peace was thus restored, but only for a short time. Bacon and his adherents were still resolved on obtaining the commission which Berkeley had promised but seemed determined to withhold. At last the republican leader appeared before Jamestown with nearly 500 followers, and obtained the governor's signature by force. But no sooner had he marched with his little army against the Indians, than Berkeley, dissolving the legislature, again raised his standard and proclaimed Bacon a rebel. This proceeding gave general offence. Bacon returned, and appealed to the Virginians to overthrow a tyrannical government. The people rose in a body to support their leader, and Berkeley was compelled to flee beyond the Chesapeake.

During the temporary absence of Bacon on an expedition against the Indians, Berkeley once more got possession of Jamestown, but was a second time driven out. To prevent it from falling into his hands, Bacon, before retiring, burned it to the ground. Several patriots applied the torch to their own dwellings. A new statehouse and the oldest church in the Dominion were consumed by the flames.

"Dominion" is a term for a colony that has self-government.

The people of Virginia seemed now to have gained the object for which they had struggled,—a liberal and efficient government,—when their worthy leader was seized with an illness which put an end to his life and their hopes. Though denounced as a traitor in his lifetime by the opponents of popular rights, Bacon has been regarded by posterity as a true friend of the people and a fearless champion of humanity, justice, and liberty.

No one could be found worthy of succeeding Bacon as the leader of the popular party. Berkeley was restored, and with his return began a series of fines, confiscations [seizures], and executions. All that had sided with the "rebels" were cruelly persecuted . . . Twenty-two persons were executed before the vengeance of the . . . governor was satiated [satisfied]. The Assembly at last begged him to abstain from further bloodshed, and he reluctantly yielded to their request.

Berkeley soon after returned to England, where his conduct was severly censured [condemned].

1. Summarize the complaints of the followers of Nathaniel Bacon.

2. Why did Bacon think it necessary to rebel?

3. Are the ideas expressed by Bacon's followers similar to any you discovered in other sections of the colonies? Explain. How do you account for this?

34. Patrick Henry and the House of Burgesses

One of the high points in the history of the House of Burgesses took place on May 29, 1765, when Patrick Henry spoke against the injustice of the English Stamp Act. The English had passed the Stamp Act in 1765 to raise money in the American colonies. The act required that colonists purchase stamps for wills, leases, bills of sale, and all other documents. Without the stamp the documents were not legally binding. The following selection is a fictional account of Patrick Henry's protest against the Stamp Act.

Nardi Reeder Campion, **Patrick Henry, Firebrand of the Revolution** (Boston: Little, Brown and Company, 1961), pp. 77-86. Copyright © 1961 by Nardi Reeder Campion. Slightly adapted.

The House of Burgesses was moved from Jamestown to Williamsburg in 1699.

Patrick Henry had been a member of the House of Burgesses exactly nine days when he rocked that dignified body to its foundations. It happened on Wednesday, May 29, 1765, his twenty-ninth birthday. That date marked a turning point for the delegate from Louisa County and for the crown colony of Virginia. The political climate of Williamsburg was never the same again.

The month-long session of the House was drawing to a close. Many members had already gone home to look after the spring crops. On that warm May day only thirty-nine of the one hundred and sixteen Burgesses gathered for the meeting.

As Patrick strolled along the diagonal path to the capitol he glanced up at the British flag on top of the clock tower. A faint breeze stirred the red and blue Union Jack. He wondered just how strong Virginia's loyalty was to that flag.

Pat stopped a moment to admire the gnarled paper mulberry trees near the capitol. He was never able to ignore the beauties of nature. A richly dressed gentleman in a bottle-green velvet coat stopped beside him. It was Edmund Pendleton, the acknowledged leader of the House. Pendleton was only fifteen years older than Patrick, but his white wig and stately manner made him seem elderly.

"Beautiful morning, eh, Mr. Henry? I've seldom heard a greater variety of bird calls."

"Oh, sir, you should let me take you to the wild woods of Louisa County. There's where the birds abound." Abruptly, Patrick changed the subject. "Sir, will the Stamp Tax be brought up today for discussion?"

"Its passage will be noted. Beyond that, there is little one can do."

"Little one can do? The British force us to pay a tax on every piece of paper used in the colonies, and there is little one can do?"

"The Stamp Tax is now the law of the land, Mr. Henry." Pendleton spoke the words crisply. He bowed formally and departed. It was clear he did not care to discuss the matter with the upstart from Louisa. Like most colonists, Edmund Pendleton felt helpless before the hated Stamp Act. Throughout America there was panic and despair, but little hope that the British government could be resisted. . . .

Patrick hurried through the groups of delegates chatting and laughing in the east wing of the capitol. The man he looked for was not hard to find. He was the tallest man in the room.

"Colonel Washington, at last I've found you!" Pat looked about, then lowered his voice. "Will you help me attack the Stamp Act today?"

"Ah, Mr. Henry, you didn't know that I never speak in public? People accuse me of being active in the field, but silent in the House. I'm afraid it is all too true."

Patrick regarded the tall, muscular man in astonishment. Washington was not handsome, but he was impressive. His large nose, high cheekbones, and alert blue-gray eyes gave him the look of an eagle. Colonel Washington—the hero who had been cited in this very capitol for his "brave and steady behavior" in the French and Indian War—was timid about making a speech. Incredible!

"Some people," Washington continued, "say there is nothing wrong with the Stamp Act. They argue that the tax money will be spent to defend and protect the colonies. Even James Otis and Benjamin Franklin do not object to it."

Benjamin Franklin of Pennsylvania and James Otis of Massachusetts were well known in all the colonies for their patriotism.

"They will," said Henry, narrowing his blue eyes, "but if they don't, I am neither Otis nor Franklin. I am Patrick Henry, Burgess from Louisa County, and I do object. If we need an army we can pay for it ourselves. Colonel, America has never known anything like this before. The Stamp Tax will hit rich and poor, old and young, great and small. Money from every American man, woman, and child will drain into the rich British treasury. And, moreover, no American had a chance to vote on this blasted act. Here is ruthless taxation without the consent of those who are taxed."

"By heaven, Mr. Henry," Washington's voice took on the ring of steel, "I agree with you. I have not the talent to speak on the subject, but I am sure my neighbor and attorney, George Johnston, will do so. He is a man of character and a champion of liberty. I'll speak to him at once . . ."

John Robinson, the genial Speaker of the House, seated himself in his paneled-back chair and called the meeting to order. The Burgesses on the benches before him were an oddly assorted lot. Some were in velvet dress with ruffles and powdered hair. Others wore rough cloth and buckskin. The Tuckahoes, the landed gentry from Tidewater Virginia, took for granted their control of the legislature. True, there were more upcountry members now, but they were inarticulate and lacked leadership. The Tuckahoes had never been seriously challenged.

George Johnston of Fairfax County rose from his seat. "Mr. Speaker, with your permission, sir, I move that the House go into the Committee of the Whole to consider the Stamp Act."

Patrick Henry jumped up. "I second the motion."

There was a slight stir of excitement. Consider the Stamp Act? Could one discuss the pros and cons of a law already passed by the British Parliament?

A vote was taken and the motion carried. The Clerk of the House placed the Speaker's silver mace under the table. Speaker Robinson left his seat and Peyton Randolph, the Attorney General of Virginia, replaced him as presiding officer. Randolph, large and elegant, presided with heavy dignity. It was the Randolph estate, Tuckahoe, that gave the conservative aristocrats their nickname.

Patrick Henry longed to take the floor at once, but he knew it was proper to let the established leaders speak first. A new member must wait his turn. One by one the elegantly dressed gentlemen rose to make tame, dignified comments on the Stamp Act. Lifelong obedience to the king of England kept them from radical thoughts. Virginia had, after all, been an English colony for over one hundred and fifty years. As Patrick listened, he slumped in his seat.

"Let us send another memorial to the King and ask him to reconsider," said Edmund Pendleton.

"May I remind you," said George Wythe, his dark gray eyes snapping, "that Mr. Lee and I drew up resolutions of protest last November, which the king ignored? What attention would he pay to protests made at this late date? Even the Massachusetts patriot, James Otis, says publicly: 'It is our duty humbly and silently to accept the decisions of Parliament.'"

Patrick Henry stared down at his sturdy boots. Virginia could not submit without protest. It was unthinkable. Slowly and thoughtfully he got to his feet. For a few moments he said nothing. He glanced from one member to another. All eyes were fastened on him. Hesitant and awkward, he looked exactly what his drawling accent and plain dress proclaimed him—a member from the country, out of place with men of the world.

88

"Gentlemen," Henry began in a low voice, "the Stamp Tax is going to invade every inch of American life. Picture with me the buckskin bridegroom." Patrick crooked his arm, and with a dreamy expression, took a few steps as though leading a bride down an aisle. Then he turned toward his "bride" and pretended to pull a ring from his pocket. He bent forward, as though he were about to slip the ring on her finger. His pantomime riveted the Burgesses' attention.

"With this ring, I thee—" Pat stopped. A look of dismay spread across his face. "The Stamp!" he cried in mock horror. "I forgot the stamp!" Hastily he pretended to dig a stamp from his pocket, lick it and stick it on an invisible license. Then Pat's fine white teeth flashed a broad smile and he said lovingly, "With this stamp, I thee wed."

Loud laughter rang through the House. Patrick Henry, actor, had captivated his audience. He bowed his head and let the merriment subside. When the room was utterly quiet, Patrick Henry, orator, spoke. His manner was no longer hesitant but self-possessed.

"Gentlemen, the Stamp Act has been forced upon us by a 'sick' king—I understand in Williamsburg it is considered ill-mannered to refer to King George's fits of insanity in plain words—by a 'sick' king, and his weak minister George Grenville. This act is, in my humble opinion, illegal, unconstitutional and unjust."

The Burgesses stirred nervously. What kind of blunt talk was this?

Patrick Henry opened an old law book he held in his hand. "Gentlemen, I have written some resolutions which I respectfully submit to you." With a mounting sense of drama he read aloud the sentences he had jotted on the fly leaf of his book. Not a sound broke the increasing tension in the room.

Patrick had composed seven resolutions. They were simple, clear, defiant.

One—Resolved: That the first settlers in this country brought with them all privileges enjoyed by the people of Great Britain.

Two—Resolved: That these privileges have been confirmed by two royal charters.

Three—Resolved: That self-taxation is the cornerstone of British freedom.

Four—Resolved: That Virginia's right to self-government and self-taxation has been constantly recognized by the kings and the people of Great Britain.

Five—Resolved: That the Virginia assembly has the sole right and power to lay taxes on this colony.

Six—Resolved: That Virginians are not bound to obey any law other than those passed by their own assembly.

Seven—Resolved: That any person who speaks to the contrary shall be considered an enemy of the colony.

Patrick Henry snapped his lawbook shut. He glared around him defiantly, and sat down. All that he had done was to attempt to take the leadership of the colony on the most momentous question of the day.

The stillness that precedes a storm gripped the room. Then a clamor of excitement broke loose. In the words of Thomas Jefferson, who was watching with other students from the doorway, "There followed a most bloody debate." The proud leaders of the House, John Robinson, Peyton Randolph, Edmund Pendleton, George Wythe, and Richard Bland rose one by one to denounce Patrick Henry and his incredible resolutions. In red-faced fury they hurled acid words at him. How dare he place Virginia's lawmaking power above the British Parliament!

Their phrases stung. "The upcountry clown"..."The talkative young actor from Louisa"..."Our buckskin bumpkin orator." The conservatives delivered their bitter insults with exaggerated politeness. Their threats and abuse angered Patrick. Once again he took the floor. Now he was thoroughly aroused. His head was high. His deep-set eyes blazed. His rich voice sent chills through his listeners. As he spoke, Burgesses leaned forward. Their breath came faster, as if they were on a mountain peak. They were listening to one of the world's great orations.

"Caesar had his Brutus," Patrick thundered in conclusion, "Charles the First his Cromwell, and George the Third—"

"Treason!" shouted Speaker Robinson.

"Treason! Treason!" yelled the followers of the king, jumping to their feet.

Henry paused dramatically. For a moment the Burgesses seemed frozen in place. Then with great presence of mind, Patrick finished the sentence and baffled his accusers. Stressing each word, he said slowly, "And George the Third may profit by their example. If this be treason, make the most of it."

. . . The time had come to vote on Henry's radical resolutions. It was clear the delegates from the western part of the colony would follow Henry against the eastern aristocrats . . . The count was taken. Patrick Henry won his resolution—by one vote. Pat looked toward Tom Jefferson in the doorway and saw a broad smile of congratulation spread across his face.

1. What are the basic principles behind Patrick Henry's position? Do these recall ideas other colonists expressed? Explain.

2. Why do you suppose the "Tuckahoes" were slower to oppose royal authority than Patrick Henry's "up-country" followers?

3. Where else in colonial history have you seen instances of colonial support for royal authority? Does there seem to have been any change in the extent of support for the King? If so, can you tell why?

COLONISTS AND GOVERNMENT

1. Compare Patrick Henry with Roger Williams, Peter Zenger, and Nathaniel Bacon.
   a. What do their ideas have in common?
   b. Did you notice any change in the ability of a colonist to criticize his government freely in public?
   c. Did the people's response to such critics change?

2. Did the Virginians seem to feel that Patrick Henry had as great a right to be heard and considered as the Tuckahoes? Judging from this episode, what would you say were the original attitudes of the Virginia colonists toward the importance of the "common man"? Do these attitudes seem to have been changing? Explain.

3. What attitude toward the "common man" was expressed in Andrew Hamilton's speech to the jury in the Peter Zenger trial? What attitude was evident in the behavior of Bacon and his followers? How do ideas about the "common man" seem to be developing in these two cases?

4. How do you explain the attitudes toward the "common man" which you see emerging? What prompted the action of Patrick Henry or of the Zenger jury? What prompted Bacon's action? Might colonial ideas about government or conditions in the New World have had any influence on their actions?

COMPARING THE SECTIONS: DID NATIONAL IDEAS EMERGE?

1. Review the interests and values of New England, the Middle Colonies, and the South. Are these three sections basically different?

2. Review the influence of geography on the three groups of colonies. Do you think that this explains whatever differences you found in their attitudes?

3. How might you explain the similarities that emerge?

PAST AND CURRENT VALUES: ARE THEY RELATED?

One possible hypothesis on the colonial period in American history could be: "America's present values have their roots deep in the colonial experience." Determine what values you consider important in the United States today. Then review the values that seem to be emerging in the colonial period just studied. Is there sufficient evidence to defend this hypothesis? Write out your conclusions.

Time Lines

A time line is a form for placing historical events in chronological order. It helps to show the relationships among events. The following time line of New World Events, for example, shows that the Spanish, French, and English all founded settlements in America early in the seventeenth century. It also shows that after 1609, most of the Spanish activity ceased, that the French were not very active until after 1700, and that British colonial efforts moved swiftly throughout the whole period. Such observations should raise questions in your mind. What are the reasons for these patterns? What do the patterns mean for American history? Do they help to explain any aspects of American history with which you are familiar?

POINTS TO CONSIDER

The new insights into colonial American history that emerge from looking at the time line of Old World Events alone, and looking at European events in connection with the time line of New World Events.

NEW WORLD EVENTS

YEAR	SPANISH	ENGLISH	FRENCH
1607		JAMESTOWN COLONY	
1609	SANTA FE FOUNDED		QUEBEC FOUNDED
1619		FIRST SLAVES BROUGHT TO AMERICA	
		HOUSE OF BURGESSES FORMED	
1620		MAYFLOWER COMPACT	
		PLYMOUTH COLONY	
1630		BOSTON FOUNDED	
1634		ST. MARY'S, MD., FOUNDED	
1636		PROVIDENCE, R.I., FOUNDED	
		HARTFORD, CONN., FOUNDED	
1641			MONTREAL FOUNDED
1643		NEW ENGLAND CONFEDERATION	
1647		OLD DELUDER LAW	
1649		MARYLAND TOLERATION ACT	
1664		DUTCH DRIVEN FROM NEW YORK	
1670		CHARLESTON, S.C., FOUNDED	
1675		KING PHILIP'S WAR BETWEEN INDI-ANS AND NEW ENGLAND SETTLERS	
1676		BACON'S REBELLION	
1682		PHILADELPHIA FOUNDED	LaSALLE EXPLORES MISSISSIPPI RIVER
1689–97		KING WILLIAM'S WAR (WAR OF THE LEAGUE OF AUGS-BURG) BETWEEN THE ENGLISH AND FRENCH	
1692		SALEM WITCHCRAFT TRIALS	
1696		NAVIGATION ACTS	
1699			CAHOKIA FOUNDED
			FORT DETROIT BUILT
1701		QUEEN ANNE'S WAR	
1702–13		(WAR OF THE SPANISH SUCCES-SION) BETWEEN THE ENGLISH AND THE FRENCH	
1703			KASKASKIA FOUNDED
1706	ALBUQUERQUE FOUNDED		
1712		SOUTH CAROLINA LAW ON SLAVERY	
1716			NATCHEZ FOUNDED
1718	SAN ANTONIO FOUNDED		NEW ORLEANS FOUNDED
1724			FORT VINCENNES BUILT
1733		MOLASSES ACT	
		GEORGIA FOUNDED	
1735		PETER ZENGER TRIAL	
1739–42	WAR OF JENKINS' EAR BETWEEN THE SPANISH AND ENGLISH		
1740–48		KING GEORGE'S WAR (WAR OF THE AUSTRIAN SUCCES-SION) BETWEEN THE ENGLISH AND FRENCH	
1754		FORT NECESSITY BUILT	FORT DUQUESNE BUILT
		ALBANY PLAN	
1754–63		FRENCH AND INDIAN WAR (SEVEN YEARS' WAR) BETWEEN THE ENGLISH AND FRENCH	
1755			FORT TICONDEROGA BUILT ENGLISH DEFEATED AT FORT DUQUESNE
1759		QUEBEC AND FORT TICONDEROGA TAKEN FROM FRENCH	
1762	LAND WEST OF MISSISSIPPI RIVER GIVEN SECRETLY TO SPAIN BY FRANCE		
1763		PROCLAMATION LINE	FRANCE LOSES CANADA AND MIDWEST TO ENGLISH

Note: Some wars, such as King William's War, have a second name given in parentheses. This is because many wars of this period had two names—one that related to European events and one to American events.

OLD WORLD EVENTS

YEAR	EUROPE	ENGLAND	FRANCE
1095–1271	THE CRUSADES		
1215		KING JOHN SIGNS THE MAGNA CARTA GUARANTEEING RIGHT TO TRIAL BY JURY AND CONTROL OF TAXES BY THOSE TAXED	
1270–95	MARCO POLO'S TRIP TO THE FAR EAST		
1337–1453		HUNDRED YEARS WAR BETWEEN ENGLAND AND FRANCE	
1456	JOHANN GUTENBERG COMPLETES FIRST BIBLE PRINTED WITH MOVABLE TYPE		
1492	COLUMBUS' FIRST VOYAGE TO NEW WORLD		
1517	MARTIN LUTHER, A GERMAN MONK, CRITICIZES PAPAL RULES; BEGINNING OF PROTESTANTISM		
1534	JOHN CALVIN, FOUNDER OF CALVINISM, PROPOSES RELIGIOUS BASIS FOR CITIZENSHIP IN GENEVA, SWITZERLAND	KING HENRY VIII BECOMES HEAD OF CHURCH IN ENGLAND WHICH HE SEPARATES FROM THE CONTROL OF THE ROMAN CATHOLIC CHURCH	
1555		QUEEN MARY ORDERS PROTESTANTS BURNED IN AN ATTEMPT TO RESTORE CATHOLIC AUTHORITY	
1559		QUEEN ELIZABETH MAKES ANGLICAN CHURCH THE OFFICIAL CHURCH OF ENGLAND	
1560			HUGUENOTS, FRENCH PROTESTANTS, HANGED FOR WORSHIPING APART FROM ESTABLISHED CATHOLIC CHURCH
1588		ENGLISH DESTROY SPANISH ARMADA, A FLEET OF SHIPS SENT AGAINST ENGLAND BY KING OF SPAIN; ENGLAND GAINS CONTROL OF THE SEAS	
1598			EDICT OF NANTES GIVES HUGUENOTS EQUAL POLITICAL RIGHTS WITH CATHOLICS
1642–49		CIVIL WAR; ENDS IN VICTORY OF PURITAN-CONTROLLED PARLIAMENT OVER KING CHARLES I, WHO IS EXECUTED	
1649–60		PURITANS GOVERN COUNTRY	
1660		MONARCHY RESTORED; CHARLES II BECOMES KING	
1685			EDICT OF NANTES REVOKED
1689–97		WAR OF THE LEAGUE OF AUGSBURG	
1702–14		WAR OF THE SPANISH SUCCESSION	
1740–48		WAR OF THE AUSTRIAN SUCCESSION	
1756–63		SEVEN YEARS' WAR	

1. Do you see any developments in English and French history that could relate to those countries' colonization efforts?

2. Review the questions you raised after you studied the chart of explorers in Section II of this unit. Does information in the time line of Old World Events help you to answer any of these questions? Explain.

3. What general conclusions can you draw concerning the relationship between European and American history from the information on these time lines?

BIBLIOGRAPHY

The Age of Exploration

* MILLER, WILLIAM. A NEW HISTORY OF THE UNITED STATES. New York: George Braziller, Inc., 1958. † New York: Dell Publishing Co., Inc.
See especially the sections on Christendom, Islam, the Orient, and ideas of the unknown prior to the voyages of Columbus. The chapter title is "The Four Worlds of the Fifteenth Century."

MORISON, SAMUEL ELIOT. CHRISTOPHER COLUMBUS, MARINER. Boston: Little, Brown and Company, 1955. † New York: Mentor Books.
This is one of the finest biographies of Columbus.

STEFANSSON, VILHJALMUR, Editor. GREAT ADVENTURES AND EXPLORATIONS. New York: The Dial Press, Inc., 1947.
Stefansson uses the original sources that first told about the great explorations. Many of the accounts were written by the explorers themselves.

VAN LOON, HENDRIK WILLEM. THE STORY OF MANKIND. New York: Liveright Publishing Corp., 1951.
Of special interest for a study of the Age of Exploration are the chapters on the Crusades, the medieval city, medieval daily life, medieval trade, the Renaissance, and the great discoveries.

WELCH, RONALD. FERDINAND MAGELLAN. New York: Criterion Books, Inc., 1956.
Welch's book portrays Magellan as a young seaman and as the battle-hardened sea captain in the service of Spain who finds a passage around South America and sails into the uncharted Pacific.

The Colonial Period

ALTSHELER, JOSEPH A. THE SUN OF QUEBEC. New York: Appleton-Century-Crofts, Inc., 1952.
Fictitious story of an adventurous young American, Robert Lennox, who has a narrow escape from Fort Ticonderoga and participates in the capture of Quebec during the French and Indian War.

BENET, STEPHEN V. WESTERN STAR. New York: Holt, Rinehart and Winston, Inc., 1943.
A narrative poem about the heroism displayed in American settlements. The poem traces the adventures of a merchant's apprentice and family who go to New England on the Mayflower.

EATON, JEANETTE. LONE JOURNEY, THE LIFE OF ROGER WILLIAMS. New York: Harcourt, Brace and World, Inc., 1944.
The story of a pioneer in the struggle for freedom of speech and worship.

GALT, TOM. PETER ZENGER, FIGHTER FOR FREEDOM. New York: Crowell-Collier & Macmillan, Inc., 1951.
A famous New York printer goes on trial for libel in 1735. The verdict of the jury establishes freedom of the press in America.

JOHNSTON, MARY. TO HAVE AND TO HOLD. Boston: Houghton Mifflin Company, 1931. † New York: Pocket Books, Inc.
A story of high romance in colonial Virginia. A beautiful woman who escapes from England in a cargo of brides-to-be sent to Virginia marries an expert colonial swordsman. The woman's pursuers are not far behind.

95

* MILLER, ARTHUR. THE CRUCIBLE. New York: Viking Press, 1964. † New York: Bantam Books, Inc.

When the "witches" were condemned to death at Salem in 1692, who was responsible for their deaths? In his drama about the trials, Mr. Miller probes the areas of human conscience and guilt.

SPEARE, ELIZABETH. THE WITCH OF BLACKBIRD POND. Boston: Houghton Mifflin Company, 1958.

Kit, a high-spirited young girl, tries to adjust to life in a strict Puritan town in colonial Connecticut. Intolerant, suspicious people accuse her of witchcraft.

* Denotes more advanced reading.
† Denotes paperback edition.

unit II
THE AMERICAN REVOLUTION 1775-1783

These are the times that try men's souls. The summer soldier and the sunshine patriot will, in this crisis, shrink from the service of their country; but he that stands now deserves the love and thanks of man and woman . . .

THOMAS PAINE
COMMON SENSE, 1776

INTRODUCTION

"When in the Course of human events it becomes necessary for one people to dissolve the political bands which have connected them with one another, and to assume among the Powers of the earth the separate and equal station to which the Laws of Nature and of Nature's God entitle them, a decent respect to the opinions of mankind requires that they should declare the causes which impel them to the separation . . ."

With these words a young Virginia lawyer named Thomas Jefferson dramatized to the world the outbreak of what became the American Revolution. The revolt severed the ties between America and Great Britain—ties that stemmed from Jamestown, Massachusetts Bay, and Plymouth. With the Declaration of Independence of July 4, 1776, the rebelling colonists began to make independence a reality.

The move for independence in 1776 was not a spontaneous one. Resentment of English control existed through much of the colonial period. Colonists were irritated when Great Britain issued the Proclamation of 1763, which prohibited them from moving west of the Appalachians. Southern colonists resented British merchants to whom they were heavily in debt.

Nor was resentment limited only to southerners or to frontiersmen anxious to enter the wilderness. New Englanders were distressed over passage of the Molasses Act of 1733. The Molasses Act attempted to force Americans to trade only at British islands in the West Indies. This upset some of New England's most important sources of income. New England merchants depended heavily on trade with the French, Spanish, and Dutch islands of the West Indies. First of all, these islands, especially the French ones, bought many of New England's products, such as grain, fish, meat, cloth, and lumber. In addition, the non-British islands were important to the *triangular trade*. In the triangular trade, rum was sent from New England to the west coast of Africa. There the rum was exchanged for slaves. The slaves were traded to the West Indies in exchange for sugar, money, or molasses, which were then sent to New England. The molasses was made into rum and the triangular trade began anew. Molasses and sugar were also the main items taken in exchange for the New England products sold directly to the West Indies. According to the Molasses Act, sugar and molasses from the French, Spanish, and Dutch islands could be imported to the colonies only upon payment of a very high duty. The Molasses Act thus threatened to ruin many New England merchants. The act was never strictly enforced, but it made New England merchants fear further limitations on their trade.

Americans were already accustomed to considerable independence. This made it even harder for them to accept British restrictions on their freedom. Although most officials of the colonial governments were appointed by the King and although Great Britain claimed the right to pass all laws regulating American trade, some forms of democracy existed in the colonies prior to 1776. In Virginia, for example, colonists chose delegates to the House of Burgesses, the legislative, or law-making, body. New Englanders elected their own local officials at town meetings. In Rhode Island and Connecticut, colonists even elected their own governors. In the Middle Colonies, local and county officials were selected by the colonists. America's isolation from the Mother Country also contributed to the growth of freedom in the colonies. It was extremely difficult for Great Britain to maintain tight discipline over colonies thousands of miles away. In fact, few of the British laws affecting the trade of the American colonies were strictly enforced. This lack of discipline made the American colonists still more independent.

This unit deals with the movement for independence and especially with what Jefferson described as the "causes which impel . . . separation." The first section of the unit presents several American views of the events that led to revolution: the Declaration of Independence, a nineteenth-century history, some observations on rebel sentiment from the pens of Benjamin Franklin and Thomas Paine, an interview with a veteran of the Revolutionary War, and a recent interpretation by Dumas Malone. The first two readings of this section—a fictional and a first-hand account of the drafting of the Declaration of Independence—will help you to evaluate the Declaration.

The second section of the unit deals with military aspects of the Revolution. Using maps of the battles and descriptions of the soldiers, you will be able to form hypotheses about what happened and why.

Interpretation in history is the theme of the next two sections. How is history formed? How do opinion and fact enter into its formation? How can you distinguish between opinion and fact when you read history? Try to answer these questions as you look at the different versions of the battles at Yorktown and at Lexington and Concord. Then try to answer the questions again as you see how one historian used evidence to describe the trials of the Continental Army and the ordeal at Valley Forge. These

99

two sections will also provide you with new evidence on the military aspects of the Revolution.

In the fifth section of the unit, having had some experience in evaluating historical interpretations, you will take a second look at the causes of the Revolution—this time from the British point of view. You will study America's importance in trade between the British colonies and the Mother Country, the theory of mercantilism which defined the role of colonies within the British Empire, and an account of the Revolution by a modern British historian. See if these documents change your opinions about what caused the Revolution. Decide, too, whether you think the Americans were justified in rebelling.

The final section presents the treaty which formally concluded the war. By reading the treaty you can discover for yourself whether the Americans succeeded in winning their objectives. A library skills section and bibliography are provided for further study or research on the Revolution.

THE ENGLISH–AMERICAN COLONIES, 1776

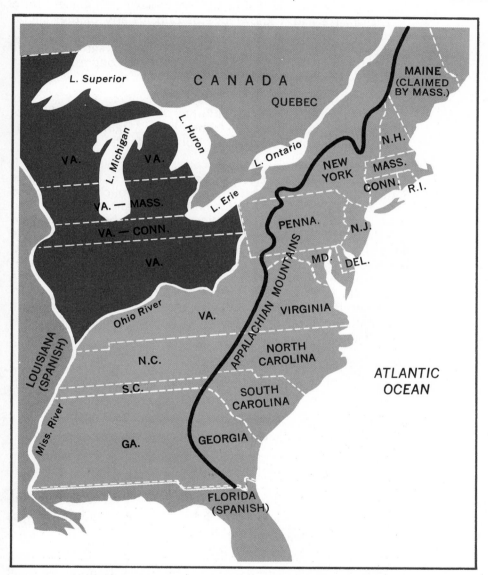

Many of the colonies claimed the land which extended west of their borders to the Mississippi River. Conflicts arose among the colonists over these claims. In 1774, the British passed the Quebec Act to conciliate the French inhabitants in the British colony of Quebec. The act added the land between the Ohio and Mississippi rivers to Quebec at the expense of the American claims.

1. Thomas Jefferson and the Declaration of Independence: A Biographical Account

The late President John F. Kennedy once remarked before an audience comprised of the nation's top scholars that the last time so much talent had assembled under the White House roof was when Thomas Jefferson dined alone. Kennedy's remark tells much about Jefferson. Jefferson was extremely gifted. He read French, Greek, Latin, Spanish, and Anglo-Saxon, an ancient form of English. He had a knowledge of calculus and of the natural sciences. He played the violin and was an architect. As a Virginia planter, he pioneered many studies in scientific agriculture. His library was used to establish the Library of Congress. He was also a lawyer and an authority on education.

Jefferson took an active role in Virginia politics. From 1769 to 1775, he served in the House of Burgesses which met at Williamsburg. In 1775, he was chosen to be one of Virginia's representatives to the Second Continental Congress in Philadelphia.

The First Continental Congress, consisting of delegates from all of the colonies except Georgia, had convened at Philadelphia in September 1774 to protest British colonial policies. It resolved to meet again in May 1775 if American grievances had not been relieved. In April 1775, hostilities broke out between England and the American colonies at Lexington and Concord. When the Second Continental Congress met in May, the delegates attempted to restore harmony with England. At the same time, they provided for the defense of the colonies. Sentiment for a break with England increased as England and the American colonies continued to disagree about how the colonies should be governed. On July 4, 1776, the Second Continental Congress approved the Declaration of Independence.

The passage below tells about Jefferson's role in drafting the Declaration of Independence. The selection is fictional and can be compared with the entry from John Adams' diary which follows it.

POINTS TO CONSIDER

How the author of the fictional account uses fact to create fiction.

What role Jefferson played in drafting the Declaration of Independence.

Clara Ingram Judson, **Thomas Jefferson, Champion of the People** (Chicago: Follett Publishing Company, 1952), pp. 96–102. Copyright © 1952 by Clara Ingram Judson. Reprinted by permission of Follett Publishing Company.

A "chaise" is a light, horse-drawn carriage.

... But in May the time came when he ... [had to] go to Philadelphia. Bob, who had been chosen as Jefferson's body servant at this time, brought the chaise around.

"I wish I were going to Williamsburg," Jefferson said, pausing by the chaise. "I distrust crowds. Real work is done by small groups—but a man must go where duty calls. We'll take the Culpepper road. The mountains will be with me longer."

"You and your mountains," his wife teased him.

"I'd like to carry them to Philadelphia," he retorted, smiling. "It is easier for a man to think straight when he can 'lift up his eyes unto the hills' each morning."

In Philadelphia Jefferson rented rooms from a bricklayer named Graff. Bob unpacked while Jefferson did errands. He had brought with him a drawing for a small writing desk which he wanted his landlord of the year before to make.

"That'll be a neat little desk." Ben Randolph was pleased to be remembered with an order. "I shall make it right away, sir. You'll be wanting it." In a few days Ben brought the writing desk, and Bob put it on the table. It was a handsome thing, though small.

In Congress, Jefferson was put on a Canadian Affairs Committee and given other duties. But he took time to draft a constitution for Virginia. He sent it south by George Wythe when Wythe left for Williamsburg.

On the seventh of June, Richard Henry Lee rose and presented to Congress a resolution which the Virginia assembly had passed and sent to Philadelphia by Lee. At first, men hardly listened; then the room was hushed in startled astonishment. Lee was reading bold words:

"The United colonies are and ought to be free and independent states . . . absolved from all allegiance to the British Crown." This from Virginia was amazing boldness. Men rose, shouting to be heard. The room was in a tumult.

Jefferson listened both to Lee's words and to the shouting. Then he whispered to a colleague, "The middle colonies and South Carolina seem not quite ready yet."

"Better delay the vote rather than risk defeat, eh, Tom?" Someone across the room had the same thought, and a motion was passed to delay action until July first.

The room quieted, and a delegate moved to appoint a committee to prepare a declaration of independence from England. This was not quite as strong as Lee's resolution. It passed; and John Adams of Massachusetts, Roger Sherman, Connecticut, Benjamin Franklin, Pennsylvania, Robert Livingston, New York, and Thomas Jefferson, Virginia, were appointed.

"A nice choice, geographically," someone remarked.

The four who were present came together to arrange a time and place for meeting.

"Dr. Franklin is not well; suppose we meet with him," one said. "We should get at the work at once." So it was agreed that the committee would go to Franklin's house on Bristol Street. They found the statesman sitting in a big chair with his gouty foot propped on a stool. Windows were open; fragrance from his garden drifted in as the men pulled chairs around their host.

"Five is too large a group for the actual work of the writing," Franklin said, after they had talked for a time. "I suggest that one man prepare a draft and then we all go at it."

"That man should be Jefferson," John Adams said quickly.

"Indeed, no!" Jefferson said, flushing. "The matter needs more competence than I possess, sir."

"John is right." Franklin ignored Jefferson's protest. "Virginia has taken the lead; a Virginian should write the paper. The Middle Colonies are not yet ready."

"The work will go better if New England keeps out," Adams remarked. "What with the so-called Boston Tea Party, Bunker Hill, and the writings of Sam Adams, we have the name of being dangerous radicals."

Franklin laughed—then winced with pain.

"You see a British enemy behind every paper, John!"

"But I am right, believe me," Adams insisted. "A Virginian is needed for this work. Jefferson has studied and thought more on the matter than any of us." The others approved his feeling. So Jefferson went to his rooms, opened his new writing desk, sharpened a pen, and laid out paper. Then he began to write. Little Mrs. Graff, sensing important work, tried to protect him from interruptions.

"Mr. Jefferson is busy this morning, sir. Could you leave a message for him?" she would say to callers.

Bob had packed books, but Jefferson did not read. The time for learning from history was ended. Now he must shape the best thinking of past philosophers into a new creed for Americans. Why now? Because the time had come when it was necessary to separate from old ties; when men of a new world should stand alone. He dipped a pen in the inkpot, and his driving thoughts sent it speeding across the paper.

"All men are created equal," he wrote, and paused. Were the people ready for that bold statement? Would they understand that the goal of political equality he stated was quite different from physical, mental, or economic equality [which] no government could promise? Colonials had little education, on the average; but he trusted them to understand. One must have faith and make a beginning. He wrote on.

The document was days in growing. When Jefferson went out to eat, Mrs. Graff slipped in and tidied his room, cherishing every scrap of paper. When he did not leave, she brought him hot soup, nourishing meat, and well-cooked vegetables that he liked. He grew pale. He would not let Bob cut his hair; any fuss fretted him. He wanted only to think and to write.

The final words as he set them down were very simple: "And for the support of this declaration, we mutually pledge to each other our lives, our fortunes, and our sacred honor." There, it was written.

On Friday, the twenty-eighth of June, the declaration was read to the House and ordered put upon the table. On Monday, July first, the earlier Virginia resolution—that the colonies be declared free and independent states—was reopened, debated, and, on the following day, passed.

Then the Declaration of Independence prepared by the committee of five was taken up, and for two days members of Congress argued hotly over this phrase and that. Jefferson sat silent, flushed and miserable. By July fourth, debate had grown acrimonious [bitter]. The heat was frightful, and clouds of flies from the livery stable next door were maddening.

Late in the day the vote was taken; the Declaration was accepted. Jefferson sighed. Cherished sentences had been deleted; the most serious loss was the section against slavery. Perhaps men were not ready for all he had hoped to include. But in the main, the changes were minor.

Jefferson left the turmoil of Congress, and as he walked on a quiet street, phrases from the paper drifted through his mind:

"When in the course of human events it becomes necessary for one people to dissolve the political bands which have connected them with another, and to assume among the powers of the earth the separate and equal station to which the laws of nature and of nature's God entitle them, a decent respect to the opinions of mankind requires that they should declare the causes which impel them to the separation.

"We hold these truths to be self-evident: that all men are created equal; that they are endowed by their Creator with certain unalienable rights, that among these are life, liberty, and the pursuit of happiness; that to secure these rights, governments are instituted among men, deriving their just powers from the consent of the governed . . ."

Suddenly Jefferson was weary. "Perhaps the whole of it is over-long," he thought. "Perhaps those few words are the meat of it and some day the king and his power, the colonies and their wrongs, will be forgotten. Today—or so it seems to me—we have taken a step on the road toward man's freedom. Perhaps July the fourth, 1776, will be a day to remember."

A summer night was falling. A welcome breeze stirred . . .

1. What did Jefferson want the Americans to do in 1776? Does the author suggest why Jefferson wanted America to take this course?

2. Did the Congress appear unanimous in accepting the idea of independence? Did all the points in Jefferson's original draft survive the final vote on the Declaration? Explain.

3. Why was Jefferson given the job of drafting the Declaration of Independence?

4. According to the author, how important was Jefferson in the creation of the Declaration of Independence? How does the author use fact with fiction to illustrate Jefferson's role?

5. After reading this story, does it appear to you that the Declaration of Independence represented ideas held by most Americans or the thoughts of one man?

6. How do Jefferson's beliefs compare with what colonial Americans considered important? Use what you learned in Unit I to answer this question.

2. The Drafting of the Declaration: John Adams' Account

John Adams, too, was on the committee appointed by the Second Continental Congress to draft the Declaration of Independence. Adams had acted in support of justice before 1776. Not only was he a leading spokesman for the American cause, but he was also an ardent defender of individual rights. In 1770, Adams had become defense lawyer for a group of soldiers accused of murdering some Boston citizens. The soldiers, taunted and stoned by a Boston mob, had finally resorted to firing upon the crowd in self-defense. The incident became known as the Boston Massacre. Although Adams believed the British soldiers should not have been stationed in Boston, he believed even more strongly that everyone is entitled to a fair trial.

Adams and Jefferson died the same day, July 4, 1826. Shortly before his death, Adams recorded his version of the formation of the Declaration of Independence.

. . . A meeting we accordingly had, and conned [looked] the paper over. I was delighted with its high tone and the flights of oratory with which it abounded, especially that concerning Negro slavery, which, though I knew his Southern brethren would never suffer to pass in Congress, I certainly never would oppose. There were other expressions which I would not have inserted if I had drawn it up, particularly that which called the King tyrant. I thought this too personal . . . I thought the expression too passionate, and too much like scolding, for so grave and solemn a document; but as Franklin and Sherman were to inspect it afterwards, I thought it would not become me to strike it out. I consented to report it [approve it and pass it on to others], and do not [recall] that I made or suggested a single alteration.

We reported it to the committee of five. It was read, and I do not remember that Franklin or Sherman criticized anything. We were all in haste. Congress was impatient, and the instrument was reported, as I believe, in Jefferson's handwriting, as he first drew it. Congress cut off about a quarter of it, as I expected they would . . .

As you justly observe, there is not an idea in it but what had been hackneyed [made commonplace] in Congress for two years before. The substance of it is contained in the declaration of rights and the violation of those rights in the Journals of Congress in 1774. Indeed, the essence of it is contained in a pamphlet, voted and printed by the town of Boston, before the first Congress met, composed by James Otis . . . and pruned and polished by Samuel Adams.

The Heritage of America, edited by Henry Steele Commager and Allan Nevins (Revised and enlarged edition; Boston: Little, Brown and Company, 1949), p. 151. Copyright 1949 by Henry Steele Commager and Allan Nevins. Reprinted by permission of the publisher.

1. What points does Adams make about Jefferson's part in drafting the Declaration?

2. According to Adams, what was unique about Jefferson's role?

3. How does the Adams account, which is an original source, compare with the fictional account? Do both versions give the same impression about Jefferson's role? About American feelings on independence?

4. To what extent does the Declaration seem to represent American feelings? Do you have the same opinion after reading the Adams diary that you had after reading the fictional account? Explain.

3. The Declaration of Independence

The result of the work done by Jefferson and the committee was the Declaration of Independence of July 4, 1776. That document, which follows, is divided into three parts: (1) a statement of the basic rights of man, (2) a list of American grievances, and (3) a statement of separation. Headings have been added to point out these divisions.

The accusations in the second part were formally leveled against George III. The charges should have been directed against Parliament, the law-making body of Great Britain. Parliament was the real author of the actions that Jefferson listed.

POINTS TO CONSIDER
What the Americans were protesting.

Why the Americans should want to revolt.

In Congress, July 4, 1776,
THE UNANIMOUS DECLARATION OF THE
THIRTEEN UNITED STATES OF
AMERICA

The Basic Rights of Man
When in the Course of human events, it becomes necessary for one people to dissolve the political bands which have connected them with another, and to assume among the Powers of the earth the separate and equal station to which the Laws of Nature and of Nature's God entitle them, a decent respect to the opinions of mankind requires that they should declare the causes which impel them to the separation.

We hold these truths to be self-evident, that all men are created equal, that they are endowed by their Creator with certain unalienable Rights, that among these are Life, Liberty and the pursuit of Happiness. That to secure these rights, Governments are instituted among Men, deriving their just powers from the consent of the governed, That whenever any Form of Government becomes destructive of these ends, it is the Right of the People to alter or to abolish it, and to institute a new Government, laying its foundation on such principles and organizing its powers in such form as to them shall seem most likely to effect their Safety and Happiness. Prudence, indeed, will dictate that Governments long established should not be changed for light and transient [short-lived] causes; and accordingly all experience hath shewn [shown], that mankind are more disposed to suffer, while evils are sufferable, than to right themselves by abolishing the forms to which they are accustomed. But when a long train of abuses and usurpations pursuing invariably the same Object, evinces [reveals] a design to reduce them under absolute Despotism, it is their right, it is their duty to throw off such Government, and to provide new Guards for their future security. Such has been the patient sufferance of these Colonies; and such is now the necessity which constrains them to alter their former Systems of Government.

The List of American Grievances
The history of the present King of Great Britain is a history of repeated injuries and usurpations, all having in direct object the establishment of an absolute Tyranny over these States. To prove this, let Facts be submitted to a candid world.

He has refused his Assent to Laws, the most wholesome and necessary for the public good.

He has forbidden his Governors to pass Laws of immediate and pressing importance, unless suspended in their operation till his Assent should be obtained; and when so suspended, he has utterly neglected to attend to them.

He has refused to pass other Laws for the accommodation of large districts of people, unless those people would relinquish the right of Representation in the Legislature, a right inestimable [priceless] to them and formidable [threatening] to tyrants only.

He has called together legislative bodies at places unusual, uncomfortable, and distant from the depository of their Public Records, for the sole purpose of fatiguing them into compliance with his measures.

He has dissolved Representative Houses repeatedly, for opposing with manly firmness his invasions on the rights of people.

He has refused for a long time, after such dissolutions, to cause others to be elected; whereby the Legislative Powers, incapable of Annihilation [total destruction], have returned to the People at large for their exercise; the State remaining in the mean time exposed to all the dangers of invasion from without, and convulsions within.

He has endeavoured to prevent the population of these States; for that purpose obstructing the Laws for Naturalization of Foreigners; refusing to pass others to encourage their migrations hither, and raising the conditions of new Appropriations of lands.

He has obstructed the Administration of Justice by refusing his Assent to Laws for establishing Judiciary Powers.

"Usurpation" means the illegal seizure and exercise of power.

To "appropriate" land is to take possession of it.

109

He has made Judges dependent on his Will alone, for the tenure of their offices, and the amount and payment of their salaries.

He has erected a multitude of New Offices, and sent hither swarms of Officers to harass our People, and eat out their substance.

He has kept among us, in times of peace, Standing Armies without the Consent of our legislatures.

He has affected to render the Military independent of and superior to the Civil Power.

He has combined with others [Parliament] to subject us to a jurisdiction foreign to our constitutions, and unacknowledged by our laws; giving his Assent to their acts of pretended [so-called] legislation:

For quartering large bodies of armed troops among us:

For protecting them, by a mock Trial, from Punishment for any Murders which they should commit on the Inhabitants of these states:

For cutting off our Trade with all parts of the world:

For imposing taxes on us without our Consent:

For depriving us in many cases, of the benefits of Trial by Jury:

For transporting us beyond Seas to be tried for pretended offences:

For abolishing the free System of English Laws in a neighbouring Province, establishing therein an Arbitary government, and enlarging its Boundaries so as to render it at once an example and fit instrument for introducing the same absolute rule into these Colonies:

For taking away our Charters, abolishing our most valuable Laws, and altering fundamentally the Forms of our Governments:

For suspending our own Legislatures, and declaring themselves invested with Power to legislate for us in all cases whatsoever.

He has abdicated Government here, by declaring us out of his Protection and waging War against us.

He has plundered our seas, ravaged our Coasts, burnt our towns, and destroyed the lives of our people.

He is at this time transporting large armies of foreign mercenaries to compleat [complete] the works of death, desolation and

"Our laws" refers to the laws passed by colonial legislatures.

This passage refers to the Quebec Act passed by the British Parliament in 1774. The act extended the boundaries of Canada to include lands claimed by American colonies, especially Virginia. (See the map on page 101.) It also approved the continued use of French law in Canada. The Quebec Act greatly angered the thirteen colonies.

tyranny, already begun with circumstances of Cruelty and perfidy [treachery] scarcely paralleled in the most barbarous ages, and totally unworthy the Head of a civilized nation.

He has constrained our fellow Citizens taken Captive on the high Seas to bear Arms against their Country, to become the executioners of their friends and Brethren, or to fall themselves by their Hands.

He has excited domestic insurrections amongst us, and has endeavoured to bring on the inhabitants of our frontiers the merciless Indian Savages, whose known rule of warfare is an undistinguished destruction of all ages, sexes, and conditions.

The Statement of Separation

In every stage of these Oppressions We have Petitioned for Redress in the most humble terms: Our repeated Petitions have been answered only by repeated injury. A Prince, whose character is thus marked by every act which may define a Tyrant, is unfit to be the ruler of a free People.

To "petition for redress" means to ask for the removal of grievances.

Nor have We been wanting in attentions to our British brethren. We have warned them from time to time of attempts by their legislature to extend an unwarrantable jurisdiction over us. We have reminded them of the circumstances of our emigration and settlement here. We have appealed to their native justice and magnanimity, and we have conjured [implored] them by the ties of our common kindred to disavow these usurpations, which would inevitably interrupt our connections and correspondence. They too have been deaf to the voice of justice and of consanguinity [common ancestry]. We must, therefore, acquiesce in the necessity which denounces our Separation, and hold them, as we hold the rest of mankind, Enemies in War, in Peace Friends.

We, therefore, the Representatives of the united States of America, in General Congress Assembled, appealing to the Supreme Judge of the world for the rectitude [righteousness] of our intentions, do, in the Name and by Authority of the good People of these Colonies, solemnly publish and declare, That these United Colonies are, and of Right ought to be Free and Independent States; that they are Absolved from all Allegiance to the British Crown, and that all political connection between them and the State of Great Britain is and ought to be totally dissolved; and that, as Free and Independent States, they have full Power to levy War, conclude Peace, contract Alliances, establish Commerce, and to do all other Acts and Things which Independent States may of right do. And for the support of this Declaration,

111

with a firm reliance on the Protection of Divine Providence, we mutually pledge to each other our Lives, our Fortunes and our sacred Honor.

1. In general, what are the charges made against Great Britain in the second part of the Declaration of Independence?

2. How do the specific grievances listed in the second part violate the rights of man or the role of government defined in the first part?

3. What further reasons did the Americans offer for declaring their independence in the third part of the Declaration?

4. John Adams thought that Jefferson's Declaration of Independence was "too passionate." For what reasons might Adams have held this opinion? Now that you have read the Declaration, can you tell whether Adams' opinion was valid? Explain.

THE DECLARATION OF INDEPENDENCE AND COLONIAL IDEAS

1. Does the Declaration of Independence reflect colonial ideas? If so, how?
   a. When you studied the colonial period in Unit I, you learned about what early Americans wanted for themselves, what role they thought government should play in their lives, and how they thought government should be organized. What statements in the Declaration of Independence reflect these ideas?
   b. Are there any ideas in the Declaration that you did *not* encounter when you read about colonial America? If so, how do the new ideas relate to the ones you have already studied?

2. Does the newness or oldness of the ideas in the Declaration of Independence have anything to do with what caused the Revolution? Would people be more influenced by an idea they had believed for one hundred years than by an idea they had held for ten years? Defend your answer.

WHAT CAUSED THE REVOLUTION? —FORMING A HYPOTHESIS

Review what was said about hypotheses in the Student's Introduction to this book. What hypothesis can you now form about causes of the American Revolution? You will be able to revise your hypothesis later if you deem it necessary.

4. The Road to Revolution: A Nineteenth-Century Account

The Declaration of Independence is a primary or original source for the study of the American Revolution. Now you will examine a secondary source, an American history textbook written in 1857 by G. P. Quackenbos. The following passages describe some of the events that led to the American Revolution. These selections appear under headings such as "Taxation Without Representation" which have been added to the original material to make it clearer.

POINTS TO CONSIDER

The events that were most important in causing the American Revolution.

The difference between fact and opinion. Begin by defining the two terms, and then look for passages that show whether the author was pro- or anti-British.

Taxation Without Representation The people of America were descendants of men who had fled from oppression, and braved the hardships of the wilderness for the blessings of civil and religious liberty. They had endured incredible sufferings, and through their own unaided industry had at last prospered and grown strong. When poor and feeble, they had been neglected by the mother country; as soon as they became worth governing, Britain had sent them governors; and now that they were growing rich, she sought to increase her revenue by taxing them. A pretext was not wanting. Heavy expenses had been incurred by the home government for the protection of the colonies in the French and Indian War; and these it was claimed, should be reimbursed [repaid]. The commanders sent over had been generally incompetent, and much of their success was due to the colonial troops and officers who served under them; yet the Americans would not have objected to contributing their share, had they been allowed a voice in laying the tax or directing how it should be appropriated. Having no representatives in Parliament, however, they claimed that Parliament had no right to tax them. The ministers of George II had not only asserted the right, but exercised it, by laying duties on various imported articles. The question was freely discussed throughout America, and everywhere a unanimous voice rose from the people that taxation without representation was unjust and intolerable. The law [Molasses Act of 1733] imposing the obnoxious duties was declared unconstitutional and oppressive. In New England it was constantly evaded, by secretly conveying the taxable articles ashore and concealing them from the collectors. To put a stop

George Payne Quackenbos, **Illustrated School History of the United States and the Adjacent Parts of America** (New York: Appleton-Century-Crofts, 1857), pp. 188–204.

For a description of the Molasses Act, see page 98.

to this practice, at the accession of George III in 1760, edicts were issued commanding all sheriffs and constables to aid the collectors, when called upon, in breaking open and searching cellars, houses, or vessels, that were suspected of containing concealed goods.

Salem was the first place in which it was attempted to enforce this law. The inhabitants denied the right of officers to force their dwellings, and the Supreme Court directed that the question should be argued at Boston. The people were represented by James O-tis [Otis], an eloquent and able lawyer, who had been advocate-general [chief government lawyer] for the crown, but resigned his office rather than enforce an unconstitutional law. Otis' speech on this question produced a thrilling effect on the vast concourse [audience] that heard it. It was the ablest defense of popular rights yet put forth, and confirmed the patriots of Massachusetts in their resolution to resist, even by force of arms.

At the south, too, the same spirit was rife [current]. In Virginia, the Church of England was established by law, and its ministers had been voted an annual salary of 16,000 pounds of tobacco each. In 1758 a year of scarcity, with the view of relieving the people, it was enacted by the colonial legislature that the salaries of the clergy, as well as other public dues, might be paid in cash, each pound of tobacco being rated at two pence, which was below its real value. The clergy resisted, and the king refused to sign the act. Several years passed, and in 1763 the clergy brought a suit for damages. The cause of the people was in the hands of Patrick Henry.

This distinguished man was born in Virginia, in 1736. A lover of nature, he had preferred rural pleasures and solitary forest rambles to his books, and had grown up with a mind strong but not cultivated, and an education varied rather than profound.

He had tried mercantile pursuits and farming without success, and at last, turning his attention to the law, was licensed after six weeks' study. He had reached the age of twenty-seven without distinction; and now he stood in the old Hanover courthouse, before the most learned of the colony, the triumphant clergy smiling at his awkwardness, and many an anxious eye bent on him in the crowded audience.

The commencement of his speech made little impression; but, as the young orator warmed with his subject, his eye lighted up with genius, his figure became erect, his expression grand, his action bold, his voice commanding, his words impassioned, his arguments irresistible. Men looked at each other in surprise,

Today an English "pence" and an American penny have the same value. In the eighteenth century a pence or any other coin bought far more than it does today. In other words, it was worth more. However, it is hard to fix the exact value of colonial money in modern terms.

then, fascinated, drank in with eyes and ears, in death-like silence, the eloquence of the gifted speaker. The clergy shrank in alarm from his scathing sarcasm; and the jury, under the spell of his glowing appeals, returned a verdict of *one penny damages*. The people shouted with delight at their unexpected triumph, and bore their gallant champion from the court-house on their shoulders.

Meanwhile the British ministry, no longer guided by the liberal counsels of Pitt, pushed through Parliament a bill [Sugar Act of 1764], which laid an impost [tax] on wines, increased the duty on sugar [and molasses], and provided for the more rigid enforcement of the regulations for collecting the revenue. Even before the passage of this bill was announced, the principle it involved was condemned in the strongest terms in a town-meeting at Boston. Samuel Adams, a stout-hearted patriot, who had already proved that taxation and representation were inseparable, protested in the name of the people against the assumption by Parliament of powers fatal to liberty and inconsistent with the right to which every Briton was born.

The Sugar Act renewed the policy of the Molasses Act of 1733. It taxed products imported from outside the British Empire.

The Stamp Act   In 1765, the famous Stamp Act was passed. It had long been contemplated by the enemies of America, but no British statesman, up to this time, had ventured to urge its passage. According to its provisions, no deed, bond, note, lease, contract, or other legal document, was valid, without a stamp, costing, according to the nature of the instrument, from 3 pence to £6 [pounds]. Every newspaper, pamphlet, [etc.,] was also required to bear a stamp, costing from a half-penny to 4 pence; and on each advertisement they contained a duty of two shillings was imposed. The passage of this act seemed to sound the knell [death] of freedom in America. "The sun of liberty is set," wrote Franklin to Charles Thompson, the future secretary of Congress; "the Americans must light the lamps of industry and economy." "Be assured," was his friend's answer, "we shall light the torches of a very different character." Such was the general feeling of the colonists—war, rather than submission to injustice.

"Instrument," here, refers to the documents mentioned earlier.

Today an English "pound" is worth $2.40 in American money. A "shilling" (twelve English pence) is worth 12¢.

The House of Burgesses of Virginia was in session when the news arrived. Odious [hateful] as the measure was, there was danger in opposing it, and no one durst [dared] introduce the subject. Patrick Henry was the youngest member. After waiting in vain for older men to lead the way, he hastily drew up on the blank leaf of an old law-book five resolutions, which in strong terms asserted the rights of the colonies, and denied the authority of Parliament to impose taxes upon them. The reading of these

resolutions produced unbounded consternation in the House. The Speaker and many of the members were royalists, and a protracted [long] and violent debate followed. But the eloquence of Henry bore down all opposition. Indignant at the attempt to inthrall [enslave] his country, the fearless orator, in the midst of an impassioned harangue, exclaimed, "Caesar had his Brutus, Charles I his Cromwell, and George III . . ." "Treason!" shouted the Speaker. "Treason! Treason!" was heard in different parts of the House. "And George III," repeated Henry, with flashing eye and unfaltering voice, "may profit by their example. If that be treason, make the most of it." Again the young mountaineer triumphed. The resolutions were carried. They were circulated throughout the colonies, and everywhere excited the same determined spirit that they breathed.

Among those who listened to the inspiring words of Patrick Henry on this occasion, was a young Virginian, destined to play no unimportant part in his country's history. It was Thomas Jefferson, then a student twenty-two years old. Standing in the lobby, he heard the whole discussion. The words of the eloquent patriot found an abiding echo in his heart, and awakened there the sentiment which directed all his future conduct—that "resistance to tyrants is obedience to God."

The indignation of the people at the passage of the Stamp Act was not confined to Virginia. Similar resolutions to those of Patrick Henry were passed in New York, Massachusetts, and elsewhere. Early in October, 1765, delegates from nine colonies assembled at New York, and drew up a declaration of their grievances and rights. A petition embodying their views was forwarded to both king and Parliament.

The Act was to go into effect on the first of November, and the excitement became intense as the day approached. Those who were appointed to sell the stamps were burned in effigy, and compelled to resign or quit the country. On the arrival of stamps at the seaport towns, the flags were placed at half-mast, muffled bells were tolled, and the citizens walked the streets attired in mourning. In New York, ten boxes of stamps were destroyed by the people, and the merchants resolved to import nothing from the mother country till the offensive act was repealed. The business men of Philadelphia and Boston followed this example. In the latter city, a handbill was posted at the corners, warning the person who should first distribute or use stamped sheets to take care of his property and person. A paper was issued, bearing for its device a snake, on the head of which were the letters N. E. (New England), while the body was divided into several pieces, marked with the initials of the other colonies. The motto, *Join or die*, explained its meaning. In New Hampshire, on the morning of the eventful day, the bells tolled, and the people assembled as if for a funeral procession. A coffin bearing the name of LIBERTY was borne to a grave on the shoulders of eight persons, to the sound of minute-guns. A funeral oration was pronounced, and the coffin was lowered into the grave. Suddenly signs of life appeared. It was raised to the surface, and now bore the inscription LIBERTY REVIVED. Enthusiastic shouts from the multitude, and the triumphant sound of drums and trumpets, greeted the resurrection. . . .

"Minute-guns" were cannons discharged at intervals of a minute.

In March, Parliament gave way to the determined spirit of the Americans by repealing the odious act, though it reasserted its rights [in the Declaratory Act] "to bind the colonies in all cases whatsoever."

The Townshend Acts   Harmony might now have been restored, had not the enemies of America, mortified at their recent defeat, succeeded in passing through Parliament an act [Townshend Acts, 1767] for imposing a duty on all tea, glass, paper, and painters' colors, imported into the colonies. At the same time, officers were appointed to enforce the Acts of Navigation and Trade, and the authority of the Assembly of New York, which had refused to quarter British troops at the expense of the colony, was suspended till it should comply with the requisitions [demands] of Parliament.

The Acts of Navigation and Trade (1650–1767), which included the Molasses Act and the Sugar Act, regulated trade within the British Empire to the benefit of the Mother Country. See page 172.

The Quartering of Troops   This injudicious [unwise] course again aroused the indignation of the colonists, which was increased in the fall of 1768 by the announcement that Parliament had determined to send several regiments to Boston, to reduce the people to submission. A day of fasting and prayer was appointed. Town-meetings and a general convention of delegates from all parts of the province were held at [Faneuil] Hall, at which the course of the home [British] government was freely denounced. On the 1st of October, the troops landed. The council refused to furnish them quarters, and it was with difficulty that accommodations were procured for them, even at the expense of the crown. When the next General Court [legislative assembly] met, an armed force was found stationed in the hall. Otis and others protested against so tyrannical an attempt to overawe the members; and, when the governor called on the House to pay for the quartering of the troops, they firmly refused to do so.

The governors of the colonies at this time were in the [service] of

"Extortion," here, refers to the offense committed by an officer who uses his position to take money which does not belong to him.

the king, and constantly tried to extend their authority at the expense of the people. Their subordinates followed their example, and sought to enrich themselves by all kinds of extortion. . . .

The Boston Massacre The soldiers brought over for the extinction of liberty, imbibing [adopting] the spirit of their masters, conducted themselves so offensively that difficulties with the inhabitants constantly occurred. In New York, early in 1770, they cut down a liberty-pole which had stood three years in the Park. An affray [dispute] followed, in which the people had the advantage, and a new pole was erected in the upper part of the city. In Boston, the excesses of the soldiers, and the injustice of their officers in screening them from punishment, gave the people just grounds for complaint. A collision between the troops and the citizens (in March, 1770) was the natural result. Three of the latter were killed, and several wounded. This event was called "the Boston Massacre." It produced the deepest excitement, and fatally widened the existing breach. The townsmen, with Samuel Adams at their head, insisted on the immediate withdrawal of the troops, and their commander was obliged to remove them to the neighboring fort.

The Boston Tea Party . . . The merchants of America adhered to their resolution not to import British commodities, and the effect began to be felt across the Atlantic. An appeal was made to Parliament by London merchants; and, in 1770, Lord North having become prime minister, the offensive duty was removed from every article except tea, on which it was retained, to show that Parliament still claimed the right. It was against this alleged right, however, and not the tax itself, that the Americans had contended [struggled]; and they were by no means satisfied with such tardy and partial concession. The use of tea was voluntarily laid aside; and, to insure united action, the friends of liberty (now known as Whigs, in contradistinction to the Tories, or advocates of Parliamentary taxation) established committees of correspondence in various colonies.

"Committees of correspondence" were organized by several colonies to spread news through the colonies. In the absence of any central government, the committees provided a way for leaders to communicate with each other and to inform colonists of their opinions.

No orders being received from America, tea rapidly accumulated in the English warehouses. The duty before laid on its exportation [was] now removed [Tea Act, 1773], with the view of lowering the price, and thus inducing the colonists to purchase it in spite of the import tax. Cargoes were sent to different American ports, but the result showed that the spirit of the colonies was not yet understood. At New York and Philadelphia, the ships, prevented from landing their cargoes, were sent back as they came. At Charleston, the tea was stored in damp cellars, where it was spoiled. At

Boston, the captains would have complied with the demands of the citizens and returned to London, but the governor and custom-house officers withheld their permission. Finding the authorities determined to force the tea upon them, the people settled the question themselves. Several thousand men assembled in town-meeting on the 16th of December, 1773, a day memorable in history. Fearless speeches were made by Adams, Quincy, and others; at the close of which, an hour after dark, a war-whoop was raised, and about fifty persons disguised as Indians, were seen to pass the door in the direction of the wharf where the three tea-ships were moored. The vessels were boarded; and the contents of 340 chests of tea were emptied into the water. No resistance was offered, and all the proceedings were conducted in the most orderly manner, in the presence of a vast concourse [audience].

As the party [was] returning, they passed a house at which Admiral Montague was spending the evening. Raising the window, the admiral cried, "Well, boys, you've had a fine night for your Indian caper. But, mind, you've got to pay the fiddler yet." "Oh! never mind," replied one of the leaders, "never mind, squire! just come out here, if you please, and we'll settle the bill in two minutes!" The admiral preferred letting the bill stand, and quickly shut down the window.

This bold act provoked Parliament to pass the "Boston Port Bill," which forbade the masters of vessels to take in or discharge cargoes in that harbor. The Virginia House of Burgesses was in session when the news of this retaliatory measure was received; a protest against it was at once entered on their journal. Governor Dunmore, to show his disapproval of their action, the next day dissolved the House. They separated, but only to meet elsewhere and pass strong resolutions, declaring an attack on one colony an attack on all, and recommending a general congress for the purpose of deciding on some common course. Similar resolutions were passed in Massachusetts, and by common consent it was ordered that a congress of delegates from all the colonies should meet at Philadelphia in September....

The Final Steps Toward War   On the 5th of September, 1774, the Continental Congress met at Carpenter's Hall, Philadelphia. Fifty-three delegates appeared, the ablest men of America, representing every colony but Georgia. It was a solemn meeting, for it involved the destiny of America. Adams was there, and Washington, Richard Henry Lee, of Virginia, and Patrick Henry, never deaf to his country's call. There was but one voice in the assembly, one feeling—never to submit. A petition was addressed to the obstinate king, whose infatuated course was flinging the brightest jewel from his crown; and appeal was made to the people of Great Britain; but preparations for the worst were not forgotten.

Despite the efforts of the British General Gage, the Assembly of Massachusetts met in October, 1774. John Hancock, a graduate of Harvard and one of the ablest statesmen of the Revolution, was elected president. Active preparations were made for the war, which it now required little sagacity [keenness] to foresee. Measures were taken for organizing the militia. Officers were appointed, and a committee of safety was empowered to call the citizens together whenever circumstances required. The people, too, did their part. There was no shrinking from the impending struggle. The anniversary of "the Boston massacre" was solemnly celebrated in that city; on which occasion Dr. Joseph Warren, ...setting the threats of British officials at defiance, stirred the deepest sympathies and strongest passions of an immense audience. . . .

In March, 1775, the Virginia legislature again assembled. Patrick Henry, the great orator of the Revolution, was a member. Believing war inevitable, he introduced resolutions providing for the organization of a republican army, and in their support delivered a memorable speech whose electrical effect can now hardly be imagined, though it will never be read without emotion. "I know not what course others may take," said he, after kindling the spirits of those who listened with his burning eloquence, "but for me, give me liberty or give me death."

The struggle was at hand. An appeal to the God of battles alone was left. . . .

. . . An act of Parliament, passed in February, 1775, declared that a rebellion existed in Massachusetts, and that an additional force should be sent over to Boston. About 3,000 British troops were already there. Boston Neck, which connected the peninsula on which the rebellious town was built with the mainland, had been fortified by Gage, and a line of sentinels stationed there cut off the inhabitants from communication with the surrounding country. The patriots, however, had secretly conveyed their cannon, as well as a quantity of powder and cartridges, out of the city, [by] concealing them in loads of manure with which they passed the guard unsuspected. Their principal depot was at Concord, about eighteen miles northwest of Boston. Of this Gage was aware; and he resolved to send a strong detachment thither, to destroy their stores and secure the persons of Hancock and Samuel Adams, whom he supposed to be in that vicinity. Arrangements were made with the greatest secrecy; and on the 18th of April, 1775, an hour before midnight, 800 men, under Lieutenant-colonel Smith, set out for Concord.

1. Which events does Quackenbos seem to think were most important in leading to the Revolution?

2. How could the events described by Quackenbos be used to support the grievances listed in the second part of the Declaration of Independence? Which grievances in particular would the Quackenbos account confirm? Does the Quackenbos account support the claims in the third part of the Declaration?

3. According to Quackenbos, what liberties were the Americans attempting to protect? Do you get the same view of what caused the Revolution from Quackenbos that you got from the Declaration of Independence?

4. How does Quackenbos show whether he was pro- or anti-British? How would Quackenbos' feelings about the British affect his interpretation of the events that led to independence?

5. Has the Quackenbos selection confirmed your interpretation of what caused the Revolution? Has it changed your interpretation in any way? Explain.

5. Trade and Taxes: A Dialogue by Benjamin Franklin

Benjamin Franklin began his career as a printer. He soon became known for his wit, which he displayed in his *Poor Richard's Almanack,* a collection of miscellaneous facts about many subjects. Franklin also won renown as a statesman. In 1754, he argued for the acceptance of the Albany Plan, a scheme for colonial defense against the French and their Indian allies. Though the colonists did not accept the Albany Plan, Franklin was a recognized leader in the drive for closer cooperation among the colonies. As Americans became irritated with British rule, Franklin assumed a leading role in America's movement toward independence. In 1766, he wrote the following dialogue or conversation to dramatize the colonial cause.

POINTS TO CONSIDER

The main points made by Franklin.

How he illustrates possible causes of the Revolution.

Q. What is your Name, and Place of abode?
A. Franklin, of Philadelphia.

American History Told by Contemporaries, edited by Albert Bushnell Hart (New York: The Macmillan Company, 1898), Vol. II, pp. 407–411.

The purpose of the stamp tax was to raise money for the quartering of troops in America. While all the colonies had to pay the tax, the troops were stationed only in certain areas, mainly in the East. Many colonists resented the necessity of supporting troops which were not even protecting them from such threats as Indian attacks.

Q. Do the [American people] pay any considerable taxes among themselves?

A. Certainly many, and very heavy taxes.

Q. What are the present taxes in Pennsylvania, laid by the laws of the colony?

A. There are taxes on all estates real and personal, a poll tax, a tax on all offices, professions, trades and businesses, according to their profits; an excise upon all wine, rum, and other spirits; and a duty of ten pounds per head on all [slaves] imported, with some other duties. . . .

Q. Are not the Colonies, from their circumstances, very able to pay the stamp-duty?

A. In my opinion, there is not gold and silver enough in the colonies to pay the stamp duty for one year.

Q. Don't you know that the money arising from the stamps was all to be laid out in America?

A. I know it is appropriated by the act to the American service; but it will be spent in the conquered colonies, where the soldiers are, not in the Colonies that pay it. . . .

Q. What may be the amount of one year's imports into Pennsylvania from Britain?

A. I have been informed that our merchants compute the imports from Britain to be above 500,000 Pounds.

Q. What may be the amount of the produce of your province exported to Britain?

A. It must be small, as we produce little that is wanted in Britain. I suppose it cannot exceed 40,000 Pounds.

Q. How then do you pay the balance [of 460,000 Pounds]?

A. The balance is paid by our produce carried to the West-Indies, and sold in our own islands, or to the French, [Spaniards], Danes and Dutch; by the same carried to other colonies in North-America, as to New-England, Nova-Scotia, Newfoundland, Carolina and Georgia; by the same carried to different parts of Europe, as Spain, Portugal and Italy . . .

The trade patterns Franklin describes here were typical not only of Pennsylvania but of all the American colonies.

Q. Do not you think the people of America would submit to pay the stamp duty if it was moderated?

A. No, never, unless compelled by force of arms . . .

Q. What was the temper of America towards Great Britain before the year 1763?

A. The best in the world. They submitted willingly to the government of the Crown, and paid, in all their courts, obedience to acts of parliament . . . They were led by a thread. They had not only a respect, but an affection, for Great Britain, for its

At the end of the French and Indian War in 1763, the British faced a large debt and the continued expense of supporting an army in America. To raise money, Parliament turned to internal taxes such as the stamp tax. Internal taxes were paid directly to the government. Colonists resented them more than external taxes, or taxes on imports. External taxes were paid indirectly, as part of the price of the goods.

laws, its customs and manners, and even a fondness for its fashions, that greatly increased the commerce. Natives of Britain were always treated with particular regard; to be an Old England-man was, of itself, a character of some respect, and gave a kind of rank among us.

Q. And what is their temper now?

A. O, very much altered.

Q. Did you ever hear the authority of parliament to make laws for America questioned till lately?

A. The authority of parliament was allowed to be valid in all laws, except such as should lay internal taxes. It was never disputed in laying duties to regulate commerce.

Q. If the stamp-act should be repealed, would it induce the assemblies of America to acknowledge the rights of parliament to tax them, and would they erase their resolutions?

A. No, never.

Q. Is there no means of obliging them to erase those resolutions?

A. None that I know of; they will never do it unless compelled by force of arms.

Q. Is there no power on earth that can force them to erase them?

A. No power, how great soever, can force men to change their opinions . . .

Q. Would it be most for the interest of Great-Britain, to employ the hands of Virginia in tobacco, or in manufactures?

A. In tobacco to be sure.

Q. What used to be the pride of the Americans?

A. To indulge in the fashions and manufactures of G. Britain.

Q. What is now their pride?

A. To wear their old clothes over again, till they can make new ones.

"Their resolutions" refers to the resolutions issued by the Stamp Act Congress in 1765. This congress, composed of representatives from nine of the colonies, denied the right of Parliament to tax the colonies.

1. For what reasons did Americans object to paying internal taxes?

2. Franklin states that Pennsylvanians bought much more from the British than they sold to the Mother Country. The colonists made up the difference by selling goods to countries other than Great Britain. Why do you think Franklin brings out this point?

3. Why does Franklin ask whether Great Britain would prefer that Virginia produce tobacco or manufactures?

4. How does Franklin seem to view the relationship between Britain and America? Do you think this is the same view the British had?

5. What does Franklin specifically refer to when he says, "No power, how great soever, can force men to change their opinions"?

6. Does Franklin support the interpretation of the Revolution that Quackenbos offered? Explain.

6. A Selection from *Common Sense* by Thomas Paine

Thomas Paine came to Philadelphia from England in 1774. He was a journalist who was interested in the American movement toward independence. While men like Thomas Jefferson and John Adams appealed to the wealthy classes, Paine wrote for the masses, who had less formal education. The passage quoted here is from his pamphlet, *Common Sense,* which was written in 1776. This spirited call to arms was widely read and became a favorite of the American rebels.

Free Government in the Making, edited by Alpheus Thomas Mason (New York: Oxford University Press, 1949), pp. 137–141.

... Volumes have been written on the subject of the struggle between England and America. Men of all ranks have embarked in the controversy, from different motives, and with various designs; but all have been [useless], and the period of debate is closed. Arms, as the last resource, must decide the contest ... I have heard it asserted by some, that as America hath flourished under her former connexion [connection] with Great Britain, the same connexion is necessary towards her future happiness, and will always have the same effect ... I answer roundly, that America would have flourished as much, and probably much more, had no European power had any thing to do with her. The articles of commerce [foodstuffs] by which she hath enriched herself, are the necessaries of life, and will always have a market while eating is the custom of Europe. ...

We have boasted the protection of Great Britain, without considering, that her motive was *interest* not *attachment;* and that she did not protect us from *our enemies* on *our account,* but from *her enemies* on *her own account* ...

But Britain is the parent country, say some. Then the more shame upon her conduct. Even brutes do not devour their young, nor savages make war upon their families; ... Europe, and not England, is the parent country of America. This new world hath been the asylum for the persecuted lovers of civil and religious liberty from every part of Europe. ...

Small islands not capable of protecting themselves, are the proper objects for kingdoms to take under their care; but there is something absurd, in supposing a continent [America] to be . . . governed by an island [Great Britain]. In no instance hath nature made the satellite larger than its primary planet; and as England and America, with respect to each other, [reverse] the common order of nature, it is evident that they belong to different systems: England to Europe—America to itself . . . In short, independence is the only *bond* that can tie and keep us together. . . . The mercantile and reasonable part of England, will be still with us; because, peace, *with* trade is preferable to war, *without* it. . . .

1. Does Paine believe that it was America's destiny to remain in the British Empire or to stand alone? Why?

2. According to Paine, why was Great Britain interested in America? Is there anything in the Franklin reading that could support Paine's opinion?

3. What does Paine think of Great Britain's right to rule America? Why?

4. Does Paine suggest any *new* reasons for the Revolution?

5. Paine was trying to stir the emotions of the colonists when he wrote this piece. Does this affect his accuracy? In the light of everything you have read about the colonial period and the American Revolution, decide whether Paine's statements seem true.

7. A Veteran and a Historian View the Revolution

The following readings are explanations of why the Americans rebelled in 1775. The first reading is an interview with Captain Levi Preston, a veteran of the Revolutionary War. Mellen Chamberlain, a Massachusetts state legislator, judge, and later Head Librarian of the Boston Public Library, interviewed Captain Preston in 1842. He wanted to know why Preston, a farmer, fought the British at Concord in 1775.

The second reading is an excerpt from a book published in 1954 by Dumas Malone, a noted American historian and authority on Thomas Jefferson. As you read this selection, remember that, like the nineteenth-century account by Quackenbos you read earlier, it is an interpretation.

AN INTERVIEW WITH CAPTAIN PRESTON

. . . "Captain Preston, why did you go to the Concord Fight, the 19th of April, 1775?" The old man, bowed beneath the weight of years, raised himself upright, and turning to me said: "Why

Mellen Chamberlain, **John Adams: The Statesman of the American Revolution, with Other Essays and Addresses Historical and Literary** (Boston: Houghton Mifflin Company, 1898), pp. 248–249.

did I go?" "Yes," I replied; "my histories tell me that you men of the Revolution took up arms against 'intolerable oppressions.' " "What were they? Oppressions? I didn't feel them." "What, were you not oppressed by the Stamp Act?" "I never saw one of those stamps, . . . I am certain I never paid a penny for one of them." "Well, what then about the tea-tax?" "Tea-tax! I never drank a drop of the stuff; the boys threw it all overboard." "Then I suppose you had been reading Harrington or Sidney and Locke about the eternal principles of liberty." "Never heard of 'em. We read only the Bible, the Catechism, Watts's Psalms and Hymns, and the Almanack." "Well, then what was the matter? and what did you mean in going to fight?" "Young man, what we meant in going for those redcoats was this: we always had governed ourselves, and we always meant to. They didn't mean we should."

These men were English writers on the nature of government.

Dumas Malone, Hirst Milhollen, and Milton Caplan, **The Story of the Declaration of Independence** (New York: Oxford University Press, 1954), pp. 5–6, 8. Copyright 1954 by Oxford University Press, Inc. Reprinted by permission.

A MODERN INTERPRETATION OF THE REVOLUTION

. . . [As] John Adams reminded his old friend Thomas Jefferson when both of them were aged, the real revolution occurred in 'the minds of the people' before the clash of arms. He set . . . its beginnings in 1760—the year that George III became King, . . .

Now that we can look back at this revolution through the generations, it seems to have started long before that. It began in the spirit of liberty which was brought by the colonists to the remote shores of a fresh continent and was nourished by the relatively independent lives they lived here. The Americans would hardly have sought full freedom if they had not previously enjoyed a high degree of personal and political liberty and had not already become habituated [accustomed] to local self-government. In New England towns and in Southern counties, in the Massachusetts General Court and the Virginia House of Burgesses, colonial Americans had grown accustomed to the control of their own lives and the management of their own affairs. Occasionally they had suffered from despotic royal governors, but rarely was there a question of their rights and privileges and immunities as freeborn Englishmen.

In the far-flung British Empire the colonies were subordinate to the mother country and were expected to contribute to her welfare, but the imperial tie rested lightly on most Americans and they were far from subservient [slavish] in spirit. A visitor among the polite planters of Virginia toward the end of the French and Indian War, while noting that they were characteristically a generous and loyal people, had this to say about their public character: "They are haughty and jealous of their liberties, and can scarcely bear . . . being controlled by any superior power."

The simplest explanation of the revolt of the Americans is that they had attained such maturity and self-reliance by the end of the successful British struggle against the French that they resented the degree of control which the mother country sought to impose upon them in the postwar period; . . . On the other hand the mother country, showing a not uncommon parental blindness to increased maturity, had sought for her own purposes to impose fresh restrictions at just the time that the colonists saw little further need for her protection. Thus she had precipitated [brought on] a crisis.

The fateful quarrel began when the home government, bearing the burdens and facing the problems of an enlarged empire, sought to gain increased revenue from the colonies—which were in fact major beneficiaries of the great victory over the French. First the British officials attempted to gain better enforcement of the existing trade laws. Then, directly and indirectly, they sought to tax the colonies. Meeting resistance at every turn, they finally attacked the colonial governments themselves. In the course of the dispute, colonial leaders such as Benjamin Franklin, John Adams, Thomas Jefferson, and James Wilson of Pennsylvania proposed what amounted to a dominion status, but the British statesmanship of the era was incapable of rising to the occasion as it did in the case of Canada in the next century. Because of official stupidity and the mulish stubbornness of King George III himself, the issue finally became one between freedom and coercion, and it was in the name of political liberty and personal rights that the Americans took up their arms.

> The "beneficiaries" of an event are those who profit from it.

> Under "dominion status" a country governs itself with its own constitution and military force, but remains loyal to the mother country's king.

1. Why did Captain Preston fight in 1775?

2. What does Malone think caused the Americans to revolt? What evidence does he use to support his interpretation?

3. How do Preston's views and Malone's interpretation of the Revolution differ from the interpretation suggested by the Declaration of Independence?

CONCLUDING EXERCISE

1. On what main points in readings 4–7 do all the authors agree? Does the Declaration of Independence also stress these points?

2. Review your hypothesis about what you thought caused the American Revolution. Does it need revision? Explain.

3. How does each author, including Thomas Jefferson, interpret the American attitude toward Great Britain?

4. What evidence does each author use to back his views?

5. Do these interpretations of American attitudes toward Britain disagree? If so, on what points? What does this do to your hypothesis about what caused the Revolution?

II. Why Did America Win?— Military Aspects of the Revolution

8. American and British Soldiers: Contemporary Portraits

Why did America win the war for independence? Was there some difference between British and American troops that gave Americans an advantage? Were other factors responsible for the victory? Try to answer these questions as you study this section.

The portraits below are both by British artists. "The American Rifle Men" appeared in *The Gentlemen's and London Magazine* in March 1776. The portrait of British recruits, engraved in 1780, is by W. H. Banbury.

ENGLISH RECRUITS FOR AMERICA

NEW YORK PUBLIC LIBRARY, PRINT DIVISION

128

THE METROPOLITAN MUSEUM OF ART, BEQUEST OF CHARLES ALLEN MUNN, 1924

1. What is your impression of the soldiers from these two pictures?

2. How accurate do you suppose these pictures are? Why? Is there likely to be any difference between the two in accuracy? Why?

3. According to these portraits, did one side have better fighting men than the other?

129

9. More Recent Views of the Soldiers

The American Heritage Book of the Revolution (New York: American Heritage Publishing Co., Inc., 1958), p. 154. Reprinted by permission of the publisher.

A "militia" is a group of citizens enrolled as a regular army for a period of training. They are called into active service only in an emergency.

The American Soldier   America's success in the Revolutionary War is all the more remarkable when it is considered that the contest was essentially one between a collection of inexperienced amateurs and an army of trained professionals. With a distrust of standing armies which has lasted into the twentieth century, the Americans . . . relied on militia for their defense, supplemented with volunteers for special emergencies. The colonial tradition was of short service for a single campaign—a habit which plagued George Washington until the end of the war.

Many Americans had been exposed to the rudiments of drill at militia "training days," others had seen combat against French or Indians; but Washington's first army was, as he observed, "a multitude of people . . . under very little discipline, order or government." The men, he said, "regarded an officer no more than a broomstick." Uniforms were almost nonexistent, ammunition scarce, weapons of every conceivable quality and type (since they belonged to the men who carried them), and the essentials of drill and camp routine almost unknown.

The American Heritage Book of the Revolution, p. 171.

The British Soldier   In the eighteenth century, British regiments were raised by a favored officer or gentleman who was paid by the Crown for each soldier he enlisted. Commissions [certificates of military rank] in his command were sold to such other officers or gentlemen who could afford them. . . . [Common] soldiers were recruited by the formula: "By lies they lured them, by liquor they tempted them, and when they were dead drunk they forced a shilling [signifying enlistment] into their fists." Unreliable the system may have been, but it brought into the army tough, hardened, and often desperate men who made good soldiers.

An English regiment had ten companies—eight for line duty, one of light infantry, and a grenadier [grenade-throwing] company. The elite grenadiers were picked for strength and courage, and given detached duty or posts of honor in battle. [The] fast light infantry was used for reconnaissance or skirmishing.

"Detached duty" is military service away from one's assigned group. "Reconnaissance" is finding out the enemy's positions.

Uniforms, patterned after German models, were highly ornamental and often impractical. Scarlet coats had colored linings, facings, piping, lace, and brass or pewter buttons. Stiff collars and high leather stocks restricted movement of the head, and none of the awkward hats had a visor or brim to shield the eyes. To wash his white breeches, powder his hair, and clean brightwork and belts often took the British soldier three hours a day, but this was part of the discipline that made him so reliable in battle . . .

The British army ... had its problems. Since commissions in infantry and cavalry regiments were purchased, the quality of officers was generally low. In this era of precise linear tactics, some authorities felt that it took as long as five years to make an accomplished soldier of a recruit. ... [That] task fell on a fine but inadequate cadre of noncommissioned professionals. All too often the men they had to work with were the worst elements of British society, recruited from jails and slums.

"Precise linear tactics" refers to the method, widely used during this period, by which soldiers, standing and kneeling shoulder to shoulder in a line three deep, fired their weapons.

A "cadre" is a small, well-trained group.

1. What impressions of American and British soldiers do you get from these descriptions? How do these compare with the impressions you received from the contemporary pictures?

2. Judging from these descriptions, who had the best soldiers?

3. How accurate do you think the portraits are? Are the pictures more or less correct than you had suspected?

4. If you were to look at a similar set of soldiers' portraits from a different war, how could you use them to learn about the soldiers? Assume that you would have no other information.

10. American Problems: The Diary of an Officer

The American rebels won their war for independence, but only with great sacrifice. The following excerpt from the *Journals of Major Samuel Shaw* indicates the typical conditions under which American soldiers fought. Shaw describes a mutiny of the Pennsylvania line which he witnessed in January 1781.

POINTS TO CONSIDER
How the soldiers' attitudes might have hampered the American attempt to defeat the British.
How the account by Major Shaw compares with the previous description of the American soldier.

... The accumulated distresses of the army have ... produced most dreadful effects. The noncommissioned officers and privates of the Pennsylvania line, stationed at Morristown, have mutinied, broken up their cantonments, and in a body are marching to Philadelphia, to demand redress of their grievances from Congress.

The Heritage of America, edited by Henry Steele Commager and Allan Nevins (Revised and enlarged edition; Boston: Little, Brown and Company, 1949), pp. 177–178. Copyright 1949 by Henry Steele Commager and Allan Nevins. Reprinted by permission of the publisher.

The particulars of this revolt, as nearly as I have been able to collect them, are as follows. On the 1st instant, the whole line, except three regiments, by a signal given for that purpose, turned out under arms, without their officers, and declared for a redress of grievances. General Wayne and the officers did everything that

"Instant" means of the present month.

131

could be expected to quell the tumult, but in vain. Numbers of them were wounded, and one (a captain) killed. The three regiments above mentioned paraded under their officers, but, being called on by the others to join, threatened with death in case of refusal, and actually fired on, they complied. They then seized upon the fieldpieces, and forcing the artillerymen, who had not yet joined them, to do it instantly under penalty of being every man bayoneted, the mutiny became general.

Besides the many and complicated injuries arising from the want of clothing, pay, and provision which the army at large have for so long a time groaned under, there was one circumstance peculiarly aggravating to the soldiers of the Pennsylvania line, and which conduced [contributed] not a little to hasten the catastrophe. A deputation from the state had arrived in camp a few days before, with six hundred half joes [Portuguese gold coins], to be given three to each man as a bounty to such of the six-months levies [drafted soldiers], whose times were then expired, as would enlist again for the war. This was too much for veterans who had borne the burden of the day to put up with. They made it the principal article of grievance, and told their officers they neither could nor would be any longer abused; that they were determined, at every hazard, to march in a body to Congress and obtain redress. On General Wayne's cocking his pistols there were a hundred bayonets at his breast. "We love you, we respect you," said they, "but you're a dead man if you fire," and added: "Do not mistake us; we are not going to the enemy; on the contrary, were they now to come out, you should see us fight under your orders with as much resolution and alacrity [energy] as ever." They began their march that night, and the next day General Wayne forwarded after them provisions, to prevent the otherwise inevitable deprecation which would be made on private property . . .

"Deprecation," here, means looting or stealing.

1. What problems faced the Americans?

2. Does the remark by Thomas Paine that introduces this unit apply to the Shaw account? Explain.

3. How could the problems Major Shaw describes influence the outcome of the war?

11. The Progress of the War: Five Maps

The following maps show the progress of the war as it moved over the American countryside between 1775 and 1781. The conflict spread from the Northeast to the Middle Atlantic area, upper

New York, the Ohio Valley, and the South. As you look at each map:

1. Reconstruct the events. The first event is marked with a star. Follow the movements of the troops from battle to battle. Notice new troops coming in from other directions.

2. Try to determine the reasons for the troop movements. Were they offensive, that is, directed at gaining control of a certain area? Were they defensive, that is, intended to stop the enemy?

3. Decide how successful each army was. Did it succeed in gaining control of the territory it wanted or in stopping the enemy?

4. See if you can find reasons for British or American successes.

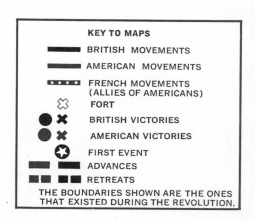

THE WAR BEGINS IN THE NORTHEAST, 1775–1776

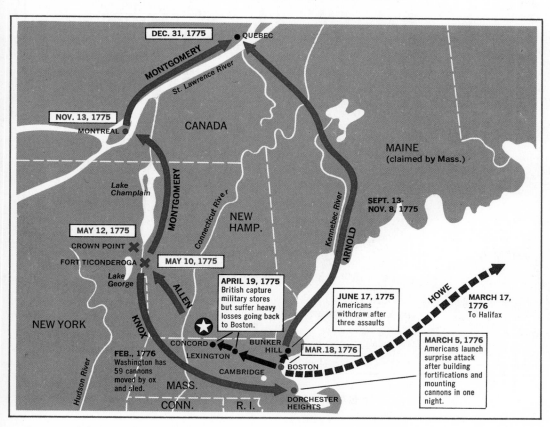

At the start of the war, the British occupied Boston, from which they launched their assaults on Lexington, Concord, and Bunker Hill. Washington arrived in Cambridge to form the Continental Army on July 3, 1775.

1. How would you describe American efforts in 1775 and 1776? What explanations can you offer for this?

2. What has happened to the British position?

WAR IN THE MIDDLE ATLANTIC REGION, 1776–1778

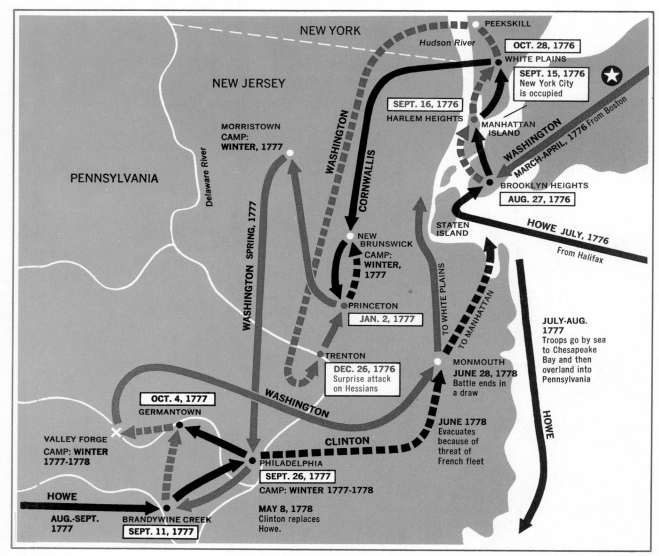

Philadelphia was originally occupied by the Americans. Thus, when Washington passed through Philadelphia in the summer of 1777, it was under American control.

1. What observations can you make about Washington's movements in this area? Can you suggest some explanations for his actions?

2. For the British, what was the outcome of these two years of fighting?

WAR IN UPPER NEW YORK, 1777

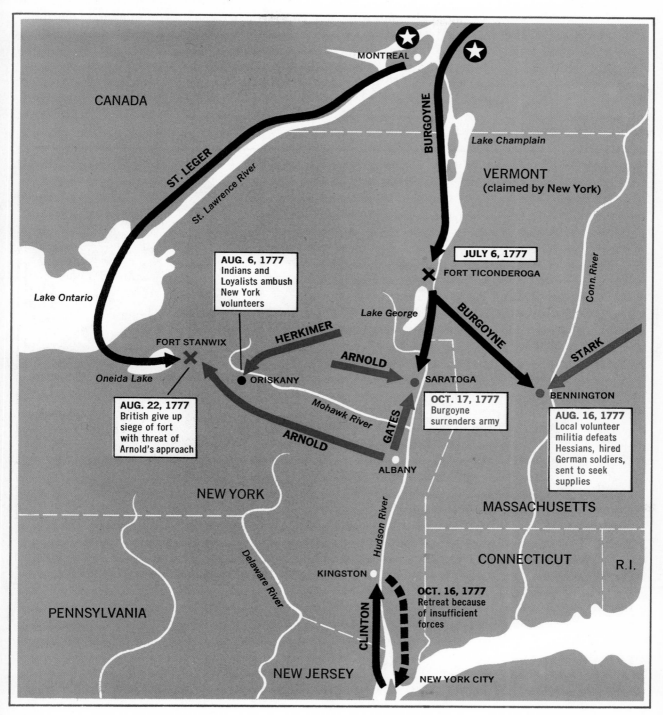

CANADA

St. Lawrence River

ST. LEGER

MONTREAL

BURGOYNE

Lake Champlain

VERMONT
(claimed by New York)

Lake Ontario

JULY 6, 1777
FORT TICONDEROGA

Conn. River

FORT STANWIX

HERKIMER

AUG. 6, 1777
Indians and
Loyalists ambush
New York
volunteers

Lake George

ARNOLD

BURGOYNE

STARK

Oneida Lake

ORISKANY

SARATOGA

BENNINGTON

AUG. 22, 1777
British give up
siege of fort
with threat of
Arnold's approach

Mohawk River

GATES

OCT. 17, 1777
Burgoyne
surrenders army

AUG. 16, 1777
Local volunteer
militia defeats
Hessians, hired
German soldiers,
sent to seek
supplies

ARNOLD

ALBANY

NEW YORK

Hudson River

MASSACHUSETTS

CONNECTICUT

R.I.

Delaware River

KINGSTON

OCT. 16, 1777
Retreat because
of insufficient
forces

PENNSYLVANIA

CLINTON

NEW JERSEY

NEW YORK CITY

1. What was the British plan of attack? What was the aim of this plan? How can you explain the results?

2. The French allied themselves with the Americans after the defeat of General Burgoyne. Why do you think the French did not join the Americans earlier in the war? What does this show about the importance of these battles?

3. How would you describe the British success thus far in the war? Is this what you might have expected? Explain.

WAR IN THE OHIO VALLEY, 1778–1779

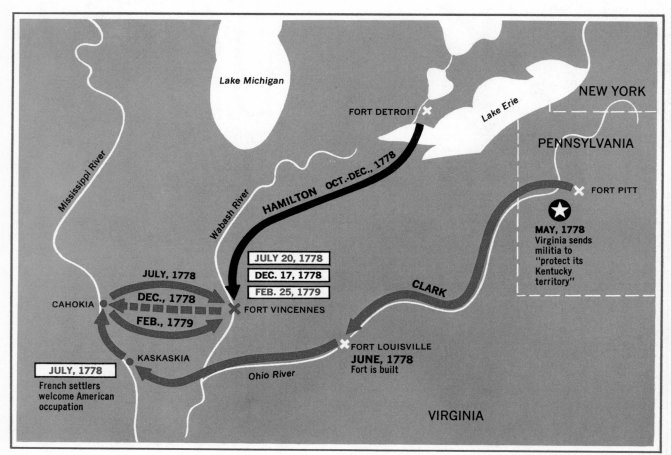

The western boundaries shown here for Virginia, Pennsylvania, and New York are the ones established by the Quebec Act of 1774. (See page 101.)

1. Why do you think Virginia sent troops into the Ohio Valley? Review the map of the colonies and territories on page 101.

2. What value could Virginia's move have had for the American cause?

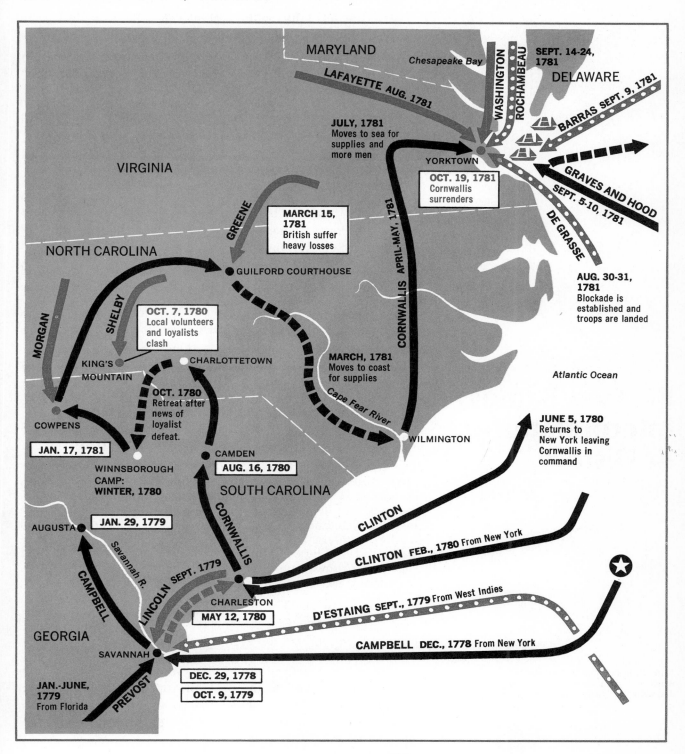

MARYLAND

Chesapeake Bay

SEPT. 14-24, 1781

DELAWARE

WASHINGTON

ROCHAMBEAU

LAFAYETTE AUG. 1781

BARRAS SEPT. 9, 1781

JULY, 1781
Moves to sea for supplies and more men

YORKTOWN

OCT. 19, 1781
Cornwallis surrenders

GRAVES AND HOOD

SEPT. 5-10, 1781

DE GRASSE

VIRGINIA

GREENE

CORNWALLIS APRIL-MAY, 1781

MARCH 15, 1781
British suffer heavy losses

AUG. 30-31, 1781
Blockade is established and troops are landed

Atlantic Ocean

NORTH CAROLINA

GUILFORD COURTHOUSE

MORGAN

SHELBY

OCT. 7, 1780
Local volunteers and loyalists clash

CHARLOTTETOWN

KING'S MOUNTAIN

MARCH, 1781
Moves to coast for supplies

Cape Fear River

OCT. 1780
Retreat after news of loyalist defeat.

COWPENS

JAN. 17, 1781

WINNSBOROUGH CAMP: WINTER, 1780

CAMDEN

AUG. 16, 1780

WILMINGTON

JUNE 5, 1780
Returns to New York leaving Cornwallis in command

SOUTH CAROLINA

AUGUSTA

JAN. 29, 1779

CORNWALLIS

Savannah R.

CAMPBELL

LINCOLN SEPT. 1779

CLINTON

CLINTON FEB., 1780 From New York

CHARLESTON

MAY 12, 1780

D'ESTAING SEPT., 1779 From West Indies

GEORGIA

SAVANNAH

CAMPBELL DEC., 1778 From New York

JAN.-JUNE 1779
From Florida

PREVOST

DEC. 29, 1778

OCT. 9, 1779

1. How would you explain British movements in this area? How does the need for supplies influence their activities? Why must the British acquire supplies in this manner?

2. When the Americans were victorious against Cornwallis in North and South Carolina, what kind of tactics did they use? Why did they employ these tactics?

3. How valuable were the French to the Americans during this stage of the war?

CONCLUDING EXERCISE

1. How could you use the portraits and descriptions of the soldiers, the account by Major Shaw, and the interview with Captain Preston when forming conclusions about the military aspects of the Revolution?

2. What did the American armies accomplish between 1775 and 1781? What makes the American achievements exceptional?

3. What general conclusions can you now form about the military aspects of the Revolution? How can you explain the American victory in the war?

III. Two Battles: Interpretation in History

American History Told by Contemporaries, edited by Albert Bushnell Hart (New York: The Macmillan Company, 1898), Vol. II, pp. 615–618.

YORKTOWN AND LEXINGTON-CONCORD: CONTEMPORARY VIEWS

12. Cornwallis Reports the Battle at Yorktown

The final military actions of the war occurred at Yorktown, Virginia. There the American forces under George Washington's command defeated the British army under Cornwallis. Cornwallis, realizing that his forces were surrounded, surrendered to Washington on October 19, 1781. In the following selections, you will read two different interpretations of this event—one by Cornwallis and one by Washington. Both men were writing to their superiors, Cornwallis to the supreme commander of British forces in America and Washington to Congress.

POINTS TO CONSIDER
What type of men Cornwallis and Washington seemed to be. How each interpreted the events at Yorktown.

. . . I have the mortification to inform your Excellency that I have been forced to give up the posts of York and Gloucester, and to surrender the troops under my command, by capitulation, on the 19th instant, as prisoners of war to the combined forces of America and France.

I never saw this post in a very fashionable light, but when I found I was to be attacked in it in so unprepared a state, by so powerful an army and artillery, nothing but the hopes of relief would have induced me to attempt its defence, for I would either have endeavoured to escape to New York by rapid marches from the Gloucester side, immediately on the arrival of General Washington's troops at Williamsburg, or I would, notwithstanding the disparity [inequality] of numbers, have attacked them in the open field, where it might have been just possible that fortune would have favoured the gallantry of the handful of troops under my command, but being assured by your Excellency's letters that every possible means would be tried by the navy and army to relieve us, I could not think myself at liberty to venture upon either of those desperate attempts; therefore, after remaining for two days in a strong position in front of this place in hopes of being attacked, upon observing that the enemy were taking measures which could not fail of turning my left flank in a short time, and receiving on the second evening your letter of the 24th of September, informing me that the relief would sail about the 5th of October, I withdrew within the works on the night of the 29th of September, hoping by the labour and firmness of the soldiers to protract the defence until you could arrive. Everything was to be expected from the spirit of the troops, but every disadvantage attended their labour, as the works were to be continued under the enemy's fire, and our stock of intrenching tools, which did not much exceed 400 when we began to work in the latter end of August, was now much diminished.

The enemy broke ground on the night of the 30th, and constructed on that night, and the two following days and nights, two redoubts, which with some works that had belonged to our outward position, occupied a gorge between two creeks or ravines, which come from the river on each side of the town. On the night of the 6th of October they made their first parallel, extending from its right on the river, to a deep ravine on the left, nearly opposite to the centre of this place, and embracing our whole left at a distance of 600 yards. Having perfected this parallel, their batteries opened on the evening of the 9th against our left, and other batteries fired at the same time against a redoubt advanced over the creek upon our right, and defended by about 120 men of the 23rd Regiment and marines, who maintained that post with uncommon gallantry. The fire continued incessant from heavy cannon and from mortars and howitzers throwing shells from 8 to 16 inches, until all our guns on the left were silenced, our work much damaged, and our loss of men consid-

A "redoubt" is a small defensive stronghold.

"Sorties" are troops sent suddenly from a defensive position to attack or harass the enemy. An "embrasure" is an opening in a wall through which cannons are fired.

erable. On the night of the 11th they began their second parallel, about 300 yards nearer to us. The troops being much weakened by sickness, as well as by the fire of the besiegers, and observing that the enemy had not only secured their flanks, but proceeded in every respect with the utmost regularity and caution, I could not venture so large sorties as to hope from them any considerable effect, but otherwise, I did everything in my power to interrupt this work by opening new embrasures for guns and keeping up a constant fire from all the howitzers and small mortars [two types of cannon] that we could man. On the evening of the 14th they assaulted and carried two redoubts that had been advanced about 300 yards for the purpose of delaying their approaches, and covering our left flank, and during the night included them in their second parallel, on which they continued to work with the utmost exertion. Being perfectly sensible that our works could not stand many hours after the opening of the batteries of that parallel, we not only continued a constant fire with all our mortars and every gun that could be brought to bear upon it, but a little before daybreak on the morning of the 16th, I ordered a sortie of about 350 men, under the direction of Lieut.-Colonel Abercrombie, to attack two batteries which appeared to be in the greatest forwardness, and to spike [disable] the guns. A detachment of Guards with the 80th company of Grenadiers, under the command of Lieut.-Colonel Lake, attacked the one, and one of light infantry, under the command of Major Armstrong, attacked the other, and both succeeded in forcing the redoubts that covered them, spiking 11 guns, and killing or wounding about 100 of the French troops, who had the guard of that part of the trenches, and with little loss on our side. This action, though extremely honourable to the officers and soldiers who executed it, proved of little public advantage, for the cannon having been spiked in a hurry, were soon rendered fit for service again, and before dark the whole parallel and batteries appeared to be nearly complete. At this time we knew that there was no part of the whole front attacked on which we could show a single gun, and our shells were nearly expended [used up]. I, therefore, had only to choose between preparing to surrender next day, or endeavouring to get off with the greatest part of the troops, and I determined to attempt the latter. . . . In this situation, with my little force divided, the enemy's batteries opened at daybreak. The passage between this place and Gloucester was much exposed, but the boats having now returned, they were ordered to bring back the troops that had passed during the night, and they joined us in the forenoon without much loss. Our works, in the mean time, were going to ruin, and not having been able to strengthen them by an abattis [a defensive barrier], nor in any other manner but a slight fraizing [low barricade], which the enemy's artillery were demolishing wherever they fired, my opinion entirely coincided with that of the engineer and principal officers of the army, that they were in many places assailable in the forenoon, and that by the continuance of the same fire for a few hours longer, they would be in such a state as to render it desperate, with our numbers, to attempt to maintain them. We at that time could not fire a single gun; only one 8-inch and little more than 100 Cohorn [mortar] shells remained. A diversion by the French ships of war that lay at the mouth of York River was to be expected. Our numbers had been diminished by the enemy's fire, but particularly by sickness, and the strength and spirits of those in the works were much exhausted, by the fatigue of constant watching and unremitting duty. Under all these circumstances, I thought it would have been wanton [merciless] and inhuman to the last degree to sacrifice the lives of this small body of gallant soldiers, who had never behaved with so much fidelity and courage, by exposing them to an assault which, from the numbers and precautions of the enemy, could not fail to succeed. I therefore proposed to capitulate; and I have the honour to enclose to your Excellency the copy of the correspondence between General Washington and me on that subject and the terms of capitulation agreed upon. I sincerely lament that better could not be obtained, but I have neglected nothing in my power to alleviate the misfortune and distress of both officers and soldiers. The men are well clothed and provided with necessaries, and I trust will be regularly supplied by the means of the officers that are permitted to remain with them. The treatment, in general, that we have received from the enemy since our surrender has been perfectly good and proper, but the kindness and attention that has been shown to us by the French officers in particular—their delicate sensibility of our situation—their generous and pressing offer of money, both public and private, to any amount—has really gone beyond what I can possibly describe, and will, I hope, make an impression on every British officer, whenever the fortune of war should put any of them into our power.

1. According to Cornwallis, what caused the British defeat at Yorktown?

2. In defeat, what was his attitude toward the Americans and French?

13. Washington Reports on Yorktown

The Writings of George Washington from the Original Manuscript Sources 1745–1799, edited by John C. Fitzpatrick (Washington, D.C.: United States Government Printing Office, 1937), Vol. XXIII, pp. 241–242.

"Reducing an army" means forcing it to surrender.

Head Quarters near York, October 19, 1781.

To the President of Congress.

Sir:

I have the honor to inform Congress, that a Reduction of the British Army under the Command of Lord Cornwallis, is most happily effected. The unremitting [tireless] Ardor which actuated [moved] every Officer and Soldier in the combined Army on this Occasion, has principally led to this Important Event, at an earlier period than my most sanguine [optimistic] Hopes had induced me to expect. . . .

I should be wanting in the feelings of Gratitude, did I not mention on this Occasion, with the warmest Sense of Acknowledgements, the very chearfull [cheerful] and able Assistance, which I have received in the Course of our Operations, from his Excellency the Count de Rochambeau [a French commander], and all his Officers of every Rank, in their respective Capacities. Nothing could equal this Zeal of our Allies, but the emulating Spirit of the American Officers, whose Ardor would not suffer their Exertions to be exceeded.

The very uncommon Degree of Duty and Fatigue which the Nature of the Service required from the Officers of Engineers and Artillery of both Armies, obliges me to mention the Obligations I am under to the Commanding and other Officers of those Corps.

I wish it was in my Power to express to Congress, how much I feel myself indebted to The Count de Grasse [the French admiral] and the Officers of the Fleet under his Command for the distinguished Aid and Support which have been afforded by them; between whom, and the Army, the most happy Concurrence of Sentiments and Views have subsisted . . .

1. What feelings does Washington express when he writes about the British defeat at Yorktown?

2. Do Cornwallis and Washington agree on the reasons for the outcome of the battle? Explain.

3. What other comparisons can you make? How can you explain them?

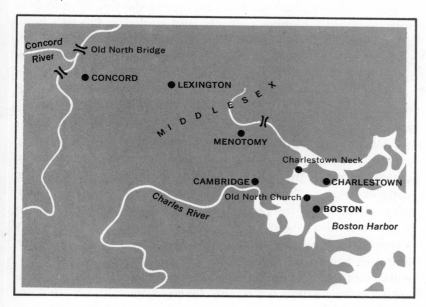

14. Lexington and Concord: An Account from the *Salem Gazette*

The opening event of the American Revolution occurred on April 19, 1775, when American colonists and British soldiers clashed at Lexington and Concord in Massachusetts. Here are two versions of the battles that appeared in newspapers in 1775. The American account is from the *Salem* (Massachusetts) *Gazette*. The British account appeared in the *London Gazette*.

In the 1700's, writers often italicized proper nouns. Where such italics occurred in the following two articles, they have been omitted.

POINTS TO CONSIDER

How each newspaper deals with the conflicts.

If the accounts interpret the battles or if they only report the facts.

. . . Last Wednesday the 19th of April, the Troops of His Britannick Majesty commenced hostilities upon the people of this Province, attended with circumstances of cruelty, not less brutal than what our venerable ancestors received from the vilest Savages of the wilderness. The particulars relative to this interesting event, by which we are involved in all the horrours of a civil war, we have endeavoured to collect as well as the present confused state of affairs will admit.

American History Told by Contemporaries, edited by Albert Bushnell Hart (New York: The Macmillan Company, 1898), Vol. II, pp. 546–548.

On Tuesday evening a detachment from the Army, consisting, it is said, of eight or nine hundred men, commanded by Lieutenant Colonel Smith, embarked at the bottom of the Common in Boston, on board a number of boats, and landed at Phipps's farm, a little way up Charles River, from whence they proceeded with silence and expedition on their way to Concord, about eighteen miles from Boston. The people were soon alarmed, and began to assemble in several Towns, before daylight, in order to watch the motion of the Troops. At Lexington, six miles below Concord, a company of Militia, of about one hundred men, mustered near the Meeting-House; the Troops came in sight of them just before sunrise; and running within a few rods of them, the Commanding Officer accosted the Militia in words to this effect: "Disperse, you rebels—... throw down your arms and disperse"; upon which the Troops huzzaed [cheered], and immediately one or two officers discharged their pistols, which were instantaneously followed by the firing of four or five of the soldiers and then there seemed to be a general discharge from the whole body: eight of our men were killed, and nine wounded. In a few minutes after this action the enemy renewed their march for Concord; at which place they destroyed several Carriages, Carriage Wheels, and about twenty barrels of Flour, all belonging to the Province. Here about one hundred and fifty men going towards a bridge, of which the enemy were in possession, the latter fired and killed two of our men, who then returned the fire, and obliged the enemy to retreat back to Lexington, where they met Lord Percy, with a large reinforcement, with two pieces of cannon. The enemy now having a body of about eighteen hundred men, made a halt, picked up many of their dead, and took care of their wounded. At Menotomy, a few of our men attacked a party of twelve of the enemy, (carrying stores and provisions to the Troops,) killed one of them, wounded several, made the rest prisoners, and took possession of all their arms, [etc.], without any loss on our side. The enemy having halted one or two hours at Lexington, found it necessary to make a second retreat, carrying with them many of their dead and wounded, who they put into chaises and on horses that they found standing in the road. They continued their retreat from Lexington to Charlestown with great precipitation [haste]; and notwithstanding their field-pieces, our people continued the pursuit, firing at them till they got to Charlestown Neck, (which they reached a little after sunset,) over which the enemy passed, proceeded up Bunker's Hill, and soon afterwards went into the Town, under the protection of the Somerset Man-Of-War of sixty-four guns.

In Lexington the enemy set fire to Deacon Joseph Loring's house and barn, Mrs. Mullikin's house and shop, and Mr. Joshua Bond's house and shop, which were all consumed. They also set fire to several other houses, but our people extinguished the flames. They pillaged almost every house they passed by breaking and destroying doors, windows, glasses, [etc.], and carrying off clothing and other valuable effects. It appeared to be their design to burn and destroy all before them; and nothing but our vigorous pursuit prevented their infernal purposes from being put in execution. But the savage barbarity exercised upon the bodies of our unfortunate brethren who fell, is almost incredible; not contented with shooting down the unarmed, aged, and infirm, they disregarded the cries of the wounded, killing them without mercy, and mangling their bodies in the most shocking manner.

We have the pleasure to say, that, notwithstanding the highest provocations given by the enemy, not one instance of cruelty, that we have heard of was committed by our victorious Militia; but, listening to the merciful dictates of the Christian religion, "they breathed higher sentiments of humanity."

The consternation of the people of Charlestown, when our enemies were entering the Town, is inexpressible; the Troops however behaved tolerably civil, and the people have since nearly all left the Town.

The following is a List of the Provincials who were killed and wounded: [49 killed; 34 wounded; 5 missing.] . . .

Mr. James Howard and one of the Regulars discharged their pieces at the same instant, and each killed the other . . .

The publick most sincerely sympathize with the friends and relations of our deceased brethren, who gloriously sacrificed their lives in fighting for the liberties of their Country. By their noble and intrepid conduct, in helping to defeat the forces of an ungrateful tyrant, they have endeared their memories to the present generation, who will transmit their names to posterity with the highest honour.

1. How does the author of the article reveal his opinions?

2. In describing the battle of Lexington and Concord, how does the author of this article portray the British? Did Washington express opinions like this about the British at Yorktown? How might you explain this?

3. What effect might this article have on American readers in 1775? How could this news story influence the war?

American History Told by Contemporaries, edited by Albert Bushnell Hart (New York: The Macmillan Company, 1898), Vol. II, pp. 548–550.

15. An Account from the *London Gazette*

. . . Lieutenant Nunn, of the Navy, arrived this morning at Lord Dartmouth's [Secretary of State for the Colonies], and brought letters from General Gage, Lord Percy, and Lieutenant-Colonel Smith, containing the following particulars of what passed on the nineteenth of April last between a detachment of the King's Troops in the Province of Massachusetts-Bay, and several parties of rebel Provincials, viz:

General Gage having received intelligence of a quantity of military stores being collected at Concord, for the avowed [declared] purpose of supplying a body of troops to act in opposition to His Majesty's Government, detached, on the eighteenth of April at night, the Grenadiers of his Army, and the Light-Infantry, under the command of Lieutenant-Colonel Smith, of the Tenth Regiment, and Major Pitcairn, of the Marines, with orders to destroy the said stores; and the next morning eight Companies of the Fourth, the same number of the Twenty-Third and Forty-Ninth, and some Marines, marched under the command of Lord Percy, to support the other detachment.

Lieutenant-Colonel Smith finding, after he had advanced some miles on his march, that the country had been alarmed by the firing of guns and ringing of bells, despatched six Companies of Light-Infantry, in order to secure two bridges on different roads beyond Concord, who, upon their arrival at Lexington, found a body of the country people under arms, on a green close to the road; and upon the King's Troops marching up to them in order to inquire the reason of their being so assembled, they went off in great confusion, and several guns were fired upon the King's Troops from behind a stone wall, and also from the meeting-house and other houses, by which one man was wounded, and Major Pitcairn's horse shot in two places. In consequence of this attack by the rebels, the troops returned the fire and killed several of them. After which the detachment marched on to Concord without any thing further happening, where they effected the purpose for which they were sent, having knocked off the trunnions [pivots] of three pieces of iron ordnance [cannon], burnt some new gun carriages and a great number of carriage-wheels, and thrown into the river a considerable quantity of flour, gunpowder, musket-balls, and other articles. Whilst this service was performing, great numbers of the rebels assembled in many parts, and a considerable body of them attacked the Light-Infantry, posted at one of the bridges, on which an action ensued [followed], and some few were killed and wounded.

On the return of the Troops from Concord, they were very much annoyed, and had several men killed and wounded by the rebels firing from behind walls, ditches, trees, and other ambushes; but the brigade under the command of Lord Percy, having joined them at Lexington with two pieces of cannon, the rebels were for a while dispersed; but as soon as the troops resumed their march, they began to fire upon them from behind stone walls and houses, and kept up in that manner a scattering fire during the whole of their march of fifteen miles, by which means several were killed and wounded; and such was the cruelty and barbarity of the rebels, that they scalped and cut off the ears of some of the wounded who fell into their hands.

It is not known what numbers of the rebels were killed and wounded, but it is supposed that their loss was considerable.

General Gage says that too much praise cannot be given to Lord Percy for his remarkable activity during the whole day; and that Lieutenant-Colonel Smith and Major Pitcairn did everything that men could do, as did all the officers in general, and that the men behaved with their usual intrepidity [bravery].

Return of the Commission, Non-commission Officers, and Rank and File, killed, wounded, prisoners, and missing, on the 19th of April, 1775. . . .

Total: One Lieutenant-Colonel killed; two Lieutenant-Colonels wounded; two Captains wounded; nine Lieutenants wounded; one Lieutenant missing; two Ensigns wounded; one Sergeant killed, four wounded, two missing; one Drummer killed, one wounded; one sixty-two rank and file killed, one hundred and fifty-seven wounded, and twenty-four missing. . . .

1. How does the author of the *London Gazette* article reveal his opinions?

2. How are the Americans portrayed in the *London Gazette* article? How does this view of Americans differ from the general temper of Cornwallis' account of Yorktown? Can you explain the differences between the two?

3. What aspects of the article would anger Britons? How could this influence the war?

COMPARING TWO ACCOUNTS: WHAT HAPPENED AT LEXINGTON AND CONCORD?

Reconstruct the story of the battles at Lexington and Concord from the evidence found in the American and British versions.

When or if you find that the two versions disagree on a point, choose the version you regard as the most valid. Be able to defend your reconstructed story. In other words, what really happened at Lexington and Concord? As a guide:

1. Determine the points on which the two versions *agree*.

2. Determine what points were made by one version but omitted by the other.

3. Determine the points on which the two versions *disagree*.

4. If the two versions disagree on a point, decide, on the basis of your limited evidence, a) the cause for the disagreement, and b) which account is probably the most valid account.

For example:

Points of agreement.	Points omitted by one source.
1.	1.
2.	2.
3.	3.

Points of disagreement.

American version	*British version*
1.	1.
2.	2.
3.	3.

Decisions as to which is the most *valid* and *why*.

1.

2.

3.

LEXINGTON AND CONCORD: CHANGING INTERPRETATIONS

16. Paintings of the Battle at Lexington

Many people have recorded the British and American encounter at Lexington in picture form. Some examples are included here.

POINTS TO CONSIDER

How the illustrations compare with the written accounts of the conflict.

Which illustration seems to be the most accurate.

A 1775 VERSION

Ralph Earl, a Connecticut militiaman, drew this picture a few weeks after the battle. Amos Doolittle later made an engraving from Earl's illustration.

A VERSION FROM THE 1830'S

This representation of the battle at Lexington is an engraving by J. Baker.

149

AN 1855 VERSION

Hammat Billings, the artist who painted this scene, was an illustrator and architect from Massachusetts.

AN 1886 VERSION

In the latter part of the nineteenth century, Henry Sandham painted this picture of the battle.

1. How do the four pictures differ?

2. In each of the four battle pictures, what is your impression of the American role? Of the British role?

3. Does the British cartoon of the American soldier (at the beginning of Section II) correspond with what each of the four paintings of the battle at Lexington shows? How can you explain this?

4. How do the four illustrations compare with the written accounts from the *Salem Gazette* and *London Gazette*?

5. How can the illustrations of the battle at Lexington be called interpretations?

17. An 1857 American Interpretation: G. P. Quackenbos

American and British writers, as well as artists, continued to depict the battles of Lexington and Concord long after the Revolution had ended. The readings that follow present some of their interpretations. The first account is from a popular American history book of the mid-nineteenth century. It appeared just two years after Hammatt Billings' painting of the battle at Lexington.

POINTS TO CONSIDER

How each of the following versions compares with the reports from the *Salem Gazette* and *London Gazette*.

If any patterns emerge from these comparisons.

How the interpretations of Lexington and Concord have changed over the years.

Before five the next morning, the British advanced guard, commanded by Major Pitcairn, reached Lexington . . . ten miles from Boston, on the Concord road. On the green, a body of minutemen, hastily gathered and poorly equipped, were ready to receive them. "Disperse, ye rebels," cried the British leader. The Americans stood their ground: Pitcairn discharged his pistol at them, and a volley from his men followed. A few shots were returned; but the Americans gave way, with a loss of 7 men. The main body now came up, and the march was resumed for Concord. They arrived there at seven. The inhabitants had received news of the intended movement about midnight, and had conveyed part of the arms and ammunition to a place of safety. The rest was destroyed. Meantime a large body of minute-men had assembled, and a skirmish took place, which resulted in the loss of several on both sides, and the retreat of the British from a bridge which they had seized.

George Payne Quackenbos, **Illustrated School History of the United States and the Adjacent Parts of America** (New York: Appleton-Century-Crofts, 1857), pp. 204–205.

The work of destruction having been completed, the British began to return. This was the signal for the brave yeomanry of the surrounding country. Posting themselves in houses, and behind sheds, trees, and fences on the roadside, they poured in an unremitting [steady] and deadly fire on the retreating army. Even boys and old men hastened to strike a blow for their country. Thus for miles the British marched, their officers falling and their ranks thinning under a continuous fire which they were unable to return with effect. Colonel Smith was severely wounded, and his men, sinking under fatigue and discouraged by their losses, were in danger of being entirely cut off, when they were met, eleven miles from Boston, by a timely reënforcement of 1,000 men under Lord Percy. Received by their comrades in a hollow square, they threw themselves on the ground, and were allowed a short rest to fit them for the balance of the march.

The patriots, notwithstanding Lord Percy's field-pieces, continued the pursuit to Charlestown. Here the disastrous retreat terminated, the British having lost 65 killed, 180 wounded, and 28 taken prisoners. On the opposite side, 59 were killed, 39 wounded, and 5 missing. The first battle of the Revolution was fought, and its result was not such as to discourage the colonists.

At this early period were commenced those acts of savage cruelty which too often disgraced the British troops in the course of the war. Percy allowed his men to plunder and fire a number of houses on the route. In one of these a woman was lying sick, and her child had taken refuge under the bed. The former was barbarously dragged out of the house, and one of the marauders, seeing the boy's foot protrude, wantonly [mercilessly] pinned it to the floor with his bayonet. No groan escaped the little hero; but the merciless soldiers reduced the house to ashes and hurried on to other outrages.

1. What are the author's feelings toward the British?

2. What comparisons can you make between this account and the American one of 1775?

18. A Poet's Interpretation in 1863: Henry Wadsworth Longfellow

In 1863 Henry Wadsworth Longfellow, an American poet, completed his *Tales of a Wayside Inn*. One of the poems in this collection, "Paul Revere's Ride," became a popular favorite.

Listen, my children, and you shall hear
Of the midnight ride of Paul Revere,
On the eighteenth of April, in Seventy-five;
Hardly a man is now alive
Who remembers that famous day and year.

He said to his friend, "If the British march
By land or sea from the town to-night,
Hang a lantern aloft in the belfry arch
Of the North Church tower as a signal light,—
One, if by land, and two, if by sea;
And I on the opposite shore will be,
Ready to ride and spread the alarm
Through every Middlesex village and farm,
For the country folk to be up and to arm."

Then he said "Good night." and with muffled oar
Silently rowed to the Charlestown shore,
Just as the moon rose over the bay,
Where swinging wide at her moorings lay
The Somerset, British man-of-war;
A phantom ship, with each mast and spar
Across the moon like a prison bar,
And a huge black hulk, that was magnified
By its own reflection on the tide. . . .

Then he climbed the tower of the Old North Church,
By the wooden stairs, with stealthy tread,
To the belfry-chamber overhead,
And startled the pigeons from their perch
On the somber rafters, that round him made
Masses and moving shapes of shade,—
By the trembling ladder, steep and tall,
To the highest window in the wall,
Where he paused to listen and look down
A moment on the roofs of the town,
And the moonlight flowing over all. . . .

Meanwhile, impatient to mount and ride,
Booted and spurred, with a heavy stride
On the opposite shore walked Paul Revere.
Now he patted his horse's side,
Now gazed at the landscape far and near,
Then, impetuous, stamped the earth,
And turned and tightened his saddle-girth;
But mostly he watched with eager search
The belfry-tower of the Old North Church,
As it rose above the graves on the hill,

The Poetical Works of Henry Wadsworth Longfellow
(Household Edition; Boston: Houghton Mifflin
Company, 1884), pp. 235–237.

"He" refers to Paul Revere's friend.

"Spectral" means ghostly.

Lonely and spectral and somber and still.
And lo! as he looks, on the belfry's height
A glimmer, and then a gleam of light!
He springs to the saddle, the bridle he turns,
But lingers and gazes, till full on his sight
A second lamp in the belfry burns! . . .

It was one by the village clock,
When he galloped into Lexington.
He saw the gilded weathercock
Swim in the moonlight as he passed,
And the meeting-house windows, blank and bare,
Gaze at him with a spectral glare,
As if they already stood aghast
At the bloody work they would look upon.

It was two by the village clock,
When he came to the bridge in Concord town.
He heard the bleating of the flock,
And the twitter of birds among the trees,
And felt the breath of the morning breeze
Blowing over the meadows brown.
And one was safe and asleep in his bed
Who at the bridge would be first to fall,
Who that day would be lying dead,
Pierced by a British musket-ball.

You know the rest. In the books you have read,
How the British Regulars fired and fled,—
How the farmers gave them ball for ball,
From behind each fence and farmyard wall,
Chasing the redcoats down the lane,
Then crossing the fields to emerge again
Under the trees at the turn of the road,
And only pausing to fire and load.
So through the night rode Paul Revere;
And so through the night went his cry of alarm
To every Middlesex village and farm,—
A cry of defiance, and not of fear,
A voice in the darkness, a knock at the door,
And a word that shall echo forevermore!
For, borne on the night-wind of the Past,
Through all our history, to the last,
In the hour of darkness and peril and need,
The people will waken and listen to hear
The hurrying hoof-beats of that steed,
And the midnight message of Paul Revere.

1. What is the central event of Longfellow's poem?

2. How does this version compare with selections from the *Salem Gazette* and the mid-nineteenth-century American textbook that you read?

19. An Evaluation of "Paul Revere's Ride": Esther Forbes

Esther Forbes is one of the leading biographers of Paul Revere. In the following selection, she presents her views on "Paul Revere's Ride."

The idea that Paul Revere was the only rider out that night was so picturesquely implanted in the American mind by Longfellow in 1863 [that] there was a natural reaction when it was learned he was by no means out alone. Although Joseph Warren officially sent out from Boston but two men—William Dawes and Paul Revere—at least three others noticed something was afoot that day in town and in a mild way did spread the alarm. These are Ebenezer Dorr, Joseph Hall, and Solomon Brown. Brown lived in Lexington, and on his way home from market noticed the little advance guard of British officers. His news resulted in the guard stationed that night about the Clark parsonage, and he and Sanderson and Loring were asked to go on to Concord and tell them there what he had seen—not that the British were marching by the hundreds, but that officers were abroad. All three of these men were picked up by Major Mitchell and were among the 'countrymen' Revere mentioned as having been collected in the pasture before he himself was caught. Richard Devens had tried to get word through to Lexington as soon as the lanterns had been shown on Christ's spire. This man also seems to have been picked up, for no word of an actual expedition had come to Lexington until Paul Revere arrived. Although Longfellow made several historical mistakes, in one thing he was right. If there was room for but one man in the limits of his poem, Revere was the one to choose. He had already ridden thousands of miles as an official express [messenger]. His reputation and name were well known to his friends and even enemies—like Governor Wentworth, Major Mitchell, and the two other British soldiers, Sutherland and Pope. It was he who had arranged about the signals from the spire and had already (the Sunday before) warned Concord [that] they might be attacked and [that] it was time to begin hiding supplies.

Esther Forbes, **Paul Revere and the World He Lived In** (Boston: Houghton Mifflin Company, 1942), pp. 475, 482–483.

Wentworth was the loyalist governor of New Hampshire.

155

His part was much more active than Dawes', and (what with slipping past the *Somerset* and getting through the officers on 'Charlestown Common') much more adventurous. Neither man got to Concord. Revere was captured and Dawes fell off his horse, but by then the alarm was so general someone else would be sure to get word in time. This happened to be Doctor Prescott, for riders were setting off in all directions as soon as they heard Paul Revere's warning, at first, second, or third hand, that the British had marched. By breakfast (one notes) Private Howe found so many men on this errand that claiming to be a patriot express was the best alibi a British spy could offer . . .

The 'Tales of the Wayside Inn' was published in 1863—when the pressure of the Civil War had created a demand for popular heroes. The story of his [Revere's] gallant ride filled a need. How much was known about it before that time? The earliest biographical sketch I have found of him (except the obituary notices) is in the *New England Magazine* (1832)—fourteen years after his death. The unknown author seems to have known him personally . . . He speaks of him as a 'messanger' and quotes almost completely his own account of the nineteenth of April as it had already been published by the Massachusetts Historical Society . . .

. . . the first known attempt to put this ride into romantic form [was] by 'Eb. Stiles,' written in 1795. In 1835, Joseph Warren's sister wrote a child's life of General Warren. It is a dialogue between a mother, 'Mrs. M.,' and her two children, whose well-timed questions help Mama tell her story. Mrs. M. says, 'Col Revere was one of his messangers. I think he was sent to Lexington'; and she describes his escape from the British officers on Charlestown Neck. 'I think he was a brave man, do not you, Mama?' says the priggish [stuffy] little William. 'I fear I should have turned back when I saw the soldiers coming.' 'Mrs. M.: ''He certainly was a very brave man. . . .'' '

Dixon Wecter [a modern historian] in commenting on the sudden burst of Paul Revere's fame, says: 'Silver made by Revere grew rapidly in value, until a good piece fetched $5,000; it was rumored that the late J. P. Morgan offered Mrs. Marston Perry $100,000 for Revere's famous "Sons of Liberty" punch bowl. His engravings and caricatures were cherished. The folk mind, upon learning that Paul Revere made false teeth and that George Washington wore false teeth, invented the well-known statement that Revere made a set of dentures for the master of Mt. Vernon.'

1. According to Esther Forbes, was Longfellow's account of Revere's ride inaccurate?

2. How does Esther Forbes explain Longfellow's use of Paul Revere in the poem?

20. Twentieth-Century American Views: Three Versions

American interpretations of Lexington and Concord have continued into the twentieth century. The next three versions appeared in 1905, 1917, and 1959. George Elliott Howard, a scholar who specialized in the period 1763–1775, wrote the first account. The other two are from American history textbooks which have enjoyed popularity.

POINTS TO CONSIDER
How these selections compare with the earlier American versions.
How and why Paul Revere appears in each selection.

A 1905 AMERICAN VERSION

Gage now determined to send a secret expedition to destroy the magazines at Concord, a village eighteen miles northwest of Boston. To accomplish this task, on the night of April 18 Lieutenant Colonel Smith set out with eight hundred men. The secret was not well kept, and William Dawes and Paul Revere were despatched to give the alarm. About daylight the troops reached Lexington, a small town twelve miles from Boston. On the common near the church sixty or seventy of the "minutemen" under Captain Parker were drawn up. According to evidence which American historians have usually accepted as conclusive, Major Pitcairn commanded the provincials to lay down their arms and disperse. When the order was not promptly obeyed, the regulars began firing, and soon eight of the Americans lay dead or dying upon the green while ten others were wounded. After the battle the provincial congress of Massachusetts ordered depositions [testimony] to be taken and a narrative prepared, with a view to fixing the responsibility for the commencement of hostilities. Of the sixty-two eye-witnesses, many of them members of Captain Parker's company, who testified regarding the fight at Lexington, all but one swore that the British began firing at the command of an officer before the minutemen had made any resistance. Nevertheless, such ex parte [one-sided] evidence, from the very nature of the circumstances, is not decisive. Incidentally, its weakness is in part disclosed by a British soldier who deposed [testified] that he took

George Elliott Howard, **Preliminaries of the American Revolution 1763–1775** (New York: Harper & Row, Publishers, 1905), pp. 307–309.

part in the action, "but which party fired first, I cannot exactly say, as our troops rushed on shouting, and huzzaing [cheering], previous to the firing, which was continued . . . so long as any of the provincials were to be seen." Moreover, Major Pitcairn— an honorable man, not at all likely unprovoked to order a murderous assault upon peaceful citizens—"insisted upon it to the day of his death, that the colonists fired first; and that he commanded not to fire, and endeavoured to stay and stop the firing after it began." At any rate, the real responsibility for this fatal affray [fight] mounts higher than Captain Parker or Major Pitcairn, and rests squarely on the shoulders of the statesmen whose fatuous [foolish] policy had created these dangerous conditions.

From Lexington the British marched on to Concord, where a guard placed by them at the Old North Bridge fired on a body of provincials who approached. The fire was returned, and several men were killed and wounded on each side.

Meanwhile the country was aroused; and when about noon— after destroying such stores as he could find—Colonel Smith began the return march, he found his troops menaced in flank and rear by the provincials, who had gathered from many towns. From the shelter of rocks, trees, and fences, during a retreat of six miles to Lexington, an irregular but deadly fire was poured in. The regulars showed no lack of courage, but they were without necessary supplies and fought at a terrible disadvantage. At Lexington they were nearly exhausted, and probably must soon have surrendered had they not here been received in a hollow square by a strong force under Lord Percy. . . .

After a short rest, Percy, who now had about eighteen hundred men in his command, began the retreat. At once the Americans renewed the attack, and the fight did not cease until at nightfall the harassed troops found shelter in Charlestown. . . . On this day the Americans lost about ninety men and the British three times as many.

1. How does this later account compare with the 1857 textbook version?

2. What differences in attitude do you find? How can you explain this?

3. How can you determine if your explanation is correct?

A 1917 AMERICAN VERSION

On the night of the eighteenth of April Gage sent troops to seize the powder which the provincials had collected at Concord, and at the same time to arrest the "traitors," John Hancock and Samuel Adams, who had taken refuge with parson Jonas Clark of Lexington. But the ardent Boston patriot, Paul Revere, had learned of the expedition, and galloping ahead of the British troops, he roused the farmers on the way and warned the refugees. When the van [advancing unit] of the British column reached Lexington, they found a little company of "minutemen" (militia ready to fight at a minute's notice) drawn up on the village green under Captain Parker. The British major Pitcairn ordered "the rebels" to disperse. Then came a volley of musket shots, apparently without the major's orders, and the British marched on, leaving eight minutemen dead or dying on the green. Reaching Concord, Pitcairn's troops were checked at "the rude bridge that arched the flood," and soon began the long retreat toward Boston, harassed by a deadly fire from behind stone walls and apple trees. Lord Percy, with the main column, met the exhausted troops just below Lexington Green and conducted them safely within the British lines. The colonial militia, aroused for miles around, closed in upon Boston 16,000 strong and held Gage besieged in his capitol.

David Saville Muzzey, **An American History** (Boston: Ginn and Company, 1917), pp. 124–125.

A 1959 AMERICAN VERSION

General Gage, the commander of the British forces in Massachusetts, learned that the Patriots had stored their military supplies at Concord, about eighteen miles from Boston. Since he had three thousand men, he decided to capture the supplies and at the same time arrest John Hancock and Samuel Adams, who were in Lexington, a small town on the way to Concord.

On April 18, 1775, General Gage sent eight hundred of his soldiers under cover of darkness across the Charles River to a point where they could begin their march to Concord. He thought that his plans were secret, but some Patriots knew what was going on. As the British crossed the river, two lighted lanterns appeared in the tower of the Old North Church in Boston. To Paul Revere, a great Boston patriot who had been waiting with his horse, this was the signal that the British were on the move.

Revere had made arrangements for the lanterns to be placed there if the British started coming. One lantern meant that they would march the longer way overland; two lanterns meant that they would cross the river and take a shorter route.

Rebekah R. Liebman and Gertrude A. Young, **The Growth of America** (Third edition; Englewood Cliffs, N.J.: Prentice-Hall, Inc., 1966), pp. 120–121, 123. First published in 1959. © 1966 by Prentice-Hall, Inc. Reprinted by permission.

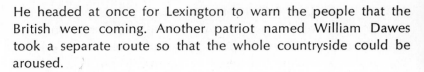

He headed at once for Lexington to warn the people that the British were coming. Another patriot named William Dawes took a separate route so that the whole countryside could be aroused.

Paul Revere was captured by a small force of men, but enough people were told so that at dawn when the British arrived at Lexington, they found about eighty Minute Men ready for battle on the village green, a small park in the center of the village. Meanwhile, John Hancock and Samuel Adams had been warned in time to make their escape.

Captain Parker, leader of the Minute Men, heard the British commander demanding that the Patriots lay down their arms and said to his men, "Don't fire unless fired on, but if they mean to have a war, let it begin here."

Where the first shot came from, no one knows; but when it happened, the British fired. Seven Americans were killed. Realizing that he was far outnumbered, Captain Parker ordered his men to withdraw; and the British continued on their way to Concord.

Here the story was different. The British were turned back by a larger group of Americans. As they retreated, the Minute Men kept up a constant firing on them from behind rocks, trees, houses, and fences along the road until by the time they reached Boston they had lost nearly 300 men, either killed or wounded. Had the British managed to stay in Concord their trip would have been a complete failure, for the ammunition which they had been sent to capture had been moved to another place.

1. When comparing the American versions beginning with the 1775 account from the *Salem Gazette,* what variations do you find in the story of Lexington and Concord? For example, is the American version of 1959 the same as that of 1775? How does each account deal with the events?

2. How did American interpretation of the events at Lexington and Concord change during the century between 1857 and 1959?

3. After 1865 the United States and Great Britain became more friendly. By 1917 the two countries were close allies. They have remained so to the present. What influence could this have had on the interpretation of the battles of Lexington and Concord? Can you find any possible examples of this effect?

21. British Views: Three Versions

The following readings are taken from popular British histories written in 1871, 1886, and 1954. In each instance, the excerpt appearing here is the author's complete description of the events at Lexington and Concord.

AN 1871 BRITISH VERSION

...an engagement at Lexington took place, near Boston, April 19, 1775. In this affair the English lost 273 soldiers, and the Americans about forty or fifty....

Amelia B. Edwards, **A Summary of English History** (London, England: George Routledge and Sons, 1871), p. 74.

AN 1886 BRITISH VERSION

The struggle opened with a skirmish between a party of English troops and a detachment of militia at Lexington...

J. R. Green, **A Short History of the English People** (New York: Harper & Row, Publishers, 1886), p. 742.

A 1954 BRITISH VERSION

...only one end of the dispute [between England and America] was possible: a decision by brute force.

On April 19, 1775, the first shots were fired in a skirmish at Lexington, between the British troops in Boston, and the militiamen who had long been drilling under the orders of the Massachusetts Assembly. The dismemberment of the Commonwealth [of the British Empire] by civil war had begun.

Ramsay Muir, **A Short History of the British Commonwealth** (Eighth edition; London, England: George Philip and Son Ltd., 1954), Vol. II, p. 50. Reprinted by permission of the publisher.

1. Review the selection from the *London Gazette*. Since that report, what has happened to the British interpretations of events at Lexington and Concord?

2. How do these three excerpts from British histories compare with those from American sources? How can you explain the similarities or differences?

A SECOND LOOK: WHAT HAPPENED AT LEXINGTON AND CONCORD?

1. Review your account, based on the two 1775 versions, of what you thought happened at Lexington and Concord. What would cause you to revise or change your original story?

2. How would you now reconstruct the story of what happened at Lexington and Concord?

3. Lexington and Concord provoked the Americans to take up arms against the British. When news of the battle of Lexington and Concord spread through the colonies, Americans volunteered for militia companies. A large group of militiamen surrounded Boston. The Second Continental Congress soon

designated these militiamen to be the Continental Army, and requested more troops from the colonies. Do you regard the events in your reconstructed story of Lexington and Concord as ample reason for the Americans to fight against British rule?

JUDGING INTERPRETATIONS

1. Why do you think each author interpreted the battles as he did?

   a. Why does Longfellow make Paul Revere the main figure in his account?

   b. Why do the American accounts of 1857 and 1905 give different versions of British behavior?

   c. Why does the American version of 1959 differ from the *Salem Gazette* account? Why do the 1954 British version and the *London Gazette* differ?

   d. Might similar influences have shaped the other versions of the battles?

   e. What other factors might influence the way men interpret history?

2. How can you find out what an author's point of view is?

3. If you want to find out the truth about an event, are interpretations of any value or are they simply misleading?

4. Do you think it is possible to tell about an event without interpreting it?

5. How could knowing the reasons for an interpretation help you to use it? Illustrate your answer with examples from the readings in this section.

IV. The War in Midstream: A Case Study in the Writing of History

22. Washington's Problems in 1776: Claude Halstead Van Tyne

The excerpts in the next two readings are taken from the work of Claude Halstead Van Tyne, a well-known American historian. Van Tyne tells about some of the problems Washington faced after the Revolution began. Like all historians, Van Tyne had to do research into *original sources* before he could write his history. By comparing the two excerpts with the sources on which they are based, you will have the opportunity to see how one scholar used evidence to write history.

The evidence Van Tyne used to write the following account was taken from the *Writings of George Washington*. Van Tyne acknowledged his use of this source in his footnotes. Writers often use footnotes to show the sources that support their statements.

VAN TYNE'S PARAGRAPH

After the retreat from Long Island Washington wrote letter after letter to Congress telling how poor was his faith in militia. The defeat "has dispirited too great a proportion of our troops," he lamented. "The militia . . . are discouraged, intractable, [stubborn] and impatient to return." Great numbers had gone off, "almost by whole regiments, by half ones, and by companies at a time." Their example of course, infected the rest of the army. "To place any dependence upon militia is assuredly resting on a broken staff," Washington declared, and he added that he would subscribe on oath that they had been hurtful rather than serviceable. No dependence could be put on them or other troops, he assured Congress, than those enlisted and embodied for a longer period than the regulation then allowed. A permanent standing army was needed.

Claude Halstead Van Tyne, **The American Nation: A History** (New York: Harper & Row, Publishers, 1905), Vol. IX, p. 119.

SOME OF THE SOURCES HE USED

1. Letter of Washington to the President of the Congress, New York, September 2, 1776. . . . Our situation is truly distressing. The check our detachment sustained on the 27th . . . has dispirited too great a proportion of our troops and filled their minds with apprehension and despair. The militia, instead of calling forth their utmost efforts to a brave and manly opposition in order to repair our losses, are dismayed, intractable, and impatient to return. Great numbers of them have gone off; in some instances, almost by whole regiments, by half ones, and by companies at a time . . . no dependence could be put in a militia, or other troops than those enlisted and embodied for a longer period than our regulations heretofore have prescribed. I am persuaded, and as fully convinced as I am of any one fact that has happened, that our liberties must of necessity be greatly hazarded, if not entirely lost, if their defence is left to any but a permanent standing army; . . . Men, who have been free and subject to no control, cannot be reduced to order in an instant; and the privileges and exemptions, they claim and will have, influence the conduct of others; and the aid derived from them is nearly counterbalanced by the disorder, irregularity, and confusion they occasion [cause].

The Writings of George Washington, edited by Worthington Chauncey Ford (New York: G. P. Putnam's Sons, 1889), Vol. IV, pp. 379–380.

2. Letter of September 22, 1776. . . . The Dependence, which the Congress have placed upon the militia, has already greatly in-

The Writings of George Washington, edited by Worthington Chauncey Ford, Vol. IV, p. 429.

jured, and I fear will totally ruin our cause. Being subject to no [control] themselves, they introduce disorder among the troops, whom you have attempted to discipline, while the change in their living brings on sickness; this makes them Impatient to get home, which spreads universally, and introduces abominable [loathsome] desertions. . . .

The Writings of George Washington, edited by Worthington Chauncey Ford, Vol. IV, p. 443.

3. Letter of September 24, 1776. . . . To place any dependence upon militia is assuredly resting upon a broken staff. Men just dragged from the tender scenes of domestic life, unaccustomed to the din of arms, totally unacquainted with every kind of military skill, ([and at the same time lacking] confidence in themselves, when opposed to troops regularly trained, disciplined, and appointed, superior in knowledge and superior in arms,) . . . [are] timid and ready to fly from their own shadows. . . .

4. Letter of September 30, 1776. . . . I assured [Congress] that the longer they delayed raising a standing army, the more difficult and chargeable [costly] would they find it to get one, and that, at the same time that the militia would answer no valuable purpose, the frequent calling them in would be attended with an expense, that they could have no conception of. . . .

The Writings of George Washington, edited by Worthington Chauncey Ford, Vol. IV, p. 457.

1. How did Van Tyne use the original sources to write his paragraph? Did he simply copy the documents in his own history? Explain.

2. According to the Van Tyne account, what was Washington's main military concern?

3. Why would this factor disturb Washington in September, 1776?

4. How does Washington's attitude as seen in these readings differ from his attitude at Yorktown?

23. Washington at Valley Forge, 1777: Van Tyne

In the following paragraph, Van Tyne describes Washington's ordeal at Valley Forge during the winter of 1777. Below the paragraph are four sources Van Tyne might have used.

POINTS TO CONSIDER
Which of the possible sources shown Van Tyne probably used to write this paragraph.

VAN TYNE'S PARAGRAPH
When, in December, 1777, Washington retired to Valley Forge, his army entered upon a most trying winter encampment. The

Claude Halstead Van Tyne, The American Nation: A History (New York: Harper & Row, Publishers, 1905), Vol. IX, pp. 236–237.

attempt of Congress to make of the commissary department a democratic institution had utterly ruined its effectiveness. Unfit men filled the offices of the department, and responsibility rested nowhere. While "hogsheads [large barrels] of shoes, stockings and clothing were lying at different places on the roads, ... perishing for want of teams" or teamsters, nearly three thousand men in Washington's army were unfit for duty because they were barefoot and otherwise naked. Steuben wrote that the men were literally [unclothed, some in the most terrible shape]. Hundreds of horses starved to death. Men yoked to the provision wagons like oxen brought meagre relief to starving comrades, who lay in huts or wigwams of twisted boughs. At evening the cry would go up along the soldiers' huts, "No meat, no meat."

Steuben was a German officer who served with the American forces as Inspector General.

SOURCES VAN TYNE COULD HAVE USED

1. Letter of Washington to the President of Congress, Valley Forge, December 23, 1777. ... The soap, vinegar, and other articles allowed by Congress, we see none of, nor have we seen them, I believe, since the battle of Brandywine [September 11, 1777]. The first, indeed, we have now little occasion for; few men having more than one shirt, many only the moiety [half of] one, and some none at all. In addition to which, as a proof of the little benefit received from a clothier-general, and as a further proof of the inability of an army, under the circumstances of this, to perform the common duties of soldiers, ... we have, by a field-return [count] this day made, no less than two-thousand eight hundred and ninety-eight men now in camp unfit for duty, because they are barefoot and otherwise [unclothed]. ...

The Writings of George Washington, edited by Worthington Chauncey Ford (New York: G. P. Putnam's Sons, 1889), Vol. VI, p. 260.

2. An Account of Life at Valley Forge by Doctor Albigence Waldo, a Surgeon from Connecticut, Dec. 21, 1777.—Preparations made for hutts. Provision Scarce. Mr. Ellis went homeward —sent a Letter to my Wife. Heartily wish myself at home—my Skin and eyes are almost spoil'd with continual smoke.

A general cry thro' the Camp this Evening among the Soldiers— "No meat!—No meat."—the Distant vales Echo'd back the melancholly sound—"No meat! No meat." Imitating the noise of Crows & Owls, also, made a part of the confused Musick.

American History Told by Contemporaries, edited by Albert Bushnell Hart (New York: The Macmillan Company, 1898), Vol. II, p. 570.

3. Letter of Washington, August 4, 1775. I am now, Sir, in strict confidence, to acquaint you, that our necessities in the articles of powder and lead are so great, as to require an immediate supply. I must earnestly entreat, you will fall upon some measures to forward every pound of each in the colony, which can possibly be spared. ...

The Writings of George Washington, edited by Worthington Chauncey Ford, Vol. III, p. 54.

Friedrich Kapp, **The Life of Frederick William Von Steuben** (New York: Mason Brothers, 1859), pp. 117–118.

4. From the Life of Steuben. "The arms at Valley Forge were in a horrible condition, covered with rust, half of them without bayonets, many from which a single shot could not be fired. The pouches [small bags for ammunition] were quite as bad as the arms. A great many of the men had tin boxes instead of pouches, others had cow-horns; and muskets, carbines, fowling-pieces, and rifles were to be seen in the same company.

"The description of the dress is most easily given. The men were literally naked, some of them in the [most terrible condition]. The officers who had coats, had them of every color and make. I saw officers, at a grand parade of Valley Forge, mounting guard in a sort of dressing-gown, made of an old blanket . . ."

1. Which of the sources did Van Tyne investigate to write the paragraph about Valley Forge? How did he use these sources?

2. What does Van Tyne emphasize about Valley Forge?

3. According to the Van Tyne account, what military problems concerned Washington? Did Washington have particular cause to be worried about such problems in 1777?

4. How would you use the two paragraphs by Van Tyne to form conclusions about military aspects of the Revolution?

MILITARY ASPECTS OF THE REVOLUTION: ANOTHER LOOK
Review the descriptions of the soldiers, the story about Captain Preston, the account by Major Samuel Shaw, the interpretations of Lexington and Concord, the observations by Cornwallis and Washington at Yorktown, the two paragraphs by Van Tyne, and the maps of the war.

1. In each of the narratives, what appears to be the spirit of the American army? How can you account for that spirit?

2. What conclusions can you now form about the military aspects of the American Revolution?
   For example, what can you tell about the problems or advantages of each side in acquisition of supplies, discipline of troops, soldiers' level of training, and numerical strength? Can you think of any factors not mentioned in this list that would help or hinder an army? What have you learned about the advantages of each side in these matters?

3. How can you use these comparisons to explain what happened in the American Revolution?

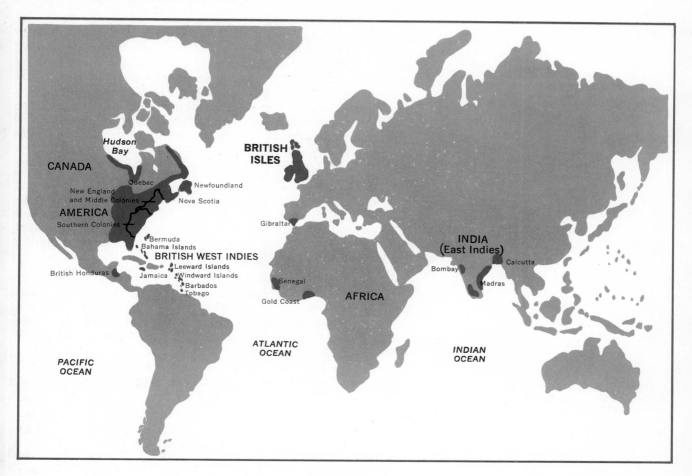

Map labels:
Hudson Bay
BRITISH ISLES
CANADA
Quebec
Newfoundland
New England and Middle Colonies
Nova Scotia
AMERICA
Southern Colonies
Gibraltar
Bermuda
Bahama Islands
BRITISH WEST INDIES
INDIA (East Indies)
British Honduras
Leeward Islands
Jamaica
Windward Islands
Bombay
Calcutta
Senegal
Madras
Barbados
Tobago
AFRICA
Gold Coast
ATLANTIC OCEAN
INDIAN OCEAN
PACIFIC OCEAN

24. Trade in the British Empire: America's Role

Earlier in this unit, you examined the causes of the Revolution from the American point of view. Now you are about to look at the British side of the story. As you may recall, many of the American protests centered around Britain's economic policies. Americans, at least from the time of the Molasses Act in 1733, often complained that British taxes and trade regulations threatened their prosperity, their freedom, or both. Why, then, did the British make such laws? Why did they sometimes try to enforce the laws, and at other times retreat in the face of American anger? Why, finally, did Britain go to the effort and expense of trying to quell the American rebellion? Another course would have been to let the troublesome colony go its own way.

One way to begin answering these questions is to find out how important America was to Britain. Since it was economic policies

V. Causes of the Revolution: British Views

that provided the focus for many American complaints, let us look first at the importance of America in Britain's colonial economy. The charts below will help you to decide how vital the thirteen American colonies were as trade partners for Britain. The first chart shows what percentage of all the goods sent by the major British colonies to the Mother Country was sent by each of the colonies. The second chart is a comparison of each colony's role as a market for British goods: it shows how much the Mother Country exported to each one. The two charts are based on a report to King George III by the British Trade Commissioner, Sir Charles Whitmore. In the report he gave the value of the products that passed between Britain and the colonies from 1697 to 1773. We have used the figures for four representative years before the Revolution.

The next two charts are based in part on the same report to the Crown. They show what products Britain obtained from her colonies, and what products the colonies purchased from Great Britain. Asterisks indicate the most important products where the relative importance of the items is known.

The slaves mentioned in the list of British imports from Africa are not accounted for in the percentage figures for British imports from Africa. The reason is that the slaves were not important in Britain itself, but rather in British colonies like the West Indies. There they worked at growing crops like sugar, which Britain bought in large amounts.

Sir Charles Whitworth, **State of the Trade of Great Britain in Its Imports and Exports Progressively for the Year 1697** (London, England: publisher unknown, 1776), pp. *xvii–xviii, xxi–xxii, xlii–lii, lv–lx, lxii–lxv*, 64, 69, 74, 77.

PER CENT OF BRITISH COLONIAL IMPORTS FROM

AREA	1760	1765	1770	1773
AMERICA (TOTAL)	17.0	24.2	17.5	23.8
NEW ENGLAND AND MIDDLE COLONIES	(1.8)	(4.7)	(4.2)	(4.1)
SOUTHERN COLONIES	(15.2)	(19.5)	(13.3)	(19.7)
BRITISH WEST INDIES	41.5	42.2	46.0	39.4
EAST INDIES	39.8	30.6	33.4	33.6
AFRICA	.9	1.0	1.2	1.2
CANADA*	.8	2.0	1.9	2.0

PER CENT OF BRITISH COLONIAL EXPORTS TO

AREA	1760	1765	1770	1773
AMERICA (TOTAL)	47.1	42.1	37.8	38.8
NEW ENGLAND AND MIDDLE COLONIES	(32.2)	(25.9)	(19.7)	(24.5)
SOUTHERN COLONIES	(14.9)	(16.2)	(17.1)	(14.3)
BRITISH WEST INDIES	22.6	20.6	22.3	22.9
EAST INDIES	20.9	19.8	21.2	16.7
AFRICA	6.2	10.2	11.2	13.1
CANADA*	3.2	7.3	7.5	8.5

* Trade with Canada increased after 1763 because Britain acquired more territory in Canada after the French and Indian War.

GREAT BRITAIN'S IMPORTS FROM

NEW ENGLAND AND THE MIDDLE COLONIES	SOUTHERN COLONIES	BRITISH WEST INDIES	EAST INDIES	AFRICA	CANADA
*Naval supplies: MASTS YARDS	*Naval supplies: PITCH TAR TURPENTINE LUMBER WAX	*SUGAR *RUM *MOLASSES COCOA GINGER COTTON GUMS DRUGS	*RAW SILK *COTTON CLOTH *SPICES TEA GOLD DIAMONDS ARRACK (an alcoholic drink) PORCELAIN-WARE DRUGS	*GOLD *SLAVES (for the Br. West Indies & America) DRUGS GUMS IVORY ELEPHANT TEETH	FURS FISH
PIG AND BAR IRON	*RICE *INDIGO *TOBACCO COTTON RAW SILK SKINS OLIVES				
FOODSTUFFS					

GREAT BRITAIN'S EXPORTS TO

NEW ENGLAND AND THE MIDDLE COLONIES‡	SOUTHERN COLONIES‡	BRITISH WEST INDIES	EAST INDIES	AFRICA	CANADA
British manufactures: FARM IMPLEMENTS FURNITURE NAILS GLASS LOCKS HINGES CUTLERY	British manufactures: LINENS WOOLEN CLOTH FURNITURE HARDWARE	British manufactures: UTENSILS MEDICINES SOAP BEER REFINED SUGAR INDIGO	*BULLION (bars of gold used to pay for imports)	British manufactures: GUNS GUNPOWDER BULLETS HARDWARE BUGLES	British manufactures: GUNS GUNPOWDER WOOLEN AND LINEN CLOTH HATCHETS KETTLES
Indian goods: SILK TEA SPICES		Cloth: (Br. or Indian): COTTONS LINENS WOOLENS SILKS	British manufactures: WOOLEN CLOTH HARDWARE LEAD QUICK-SILVER	SPIRITS (alcoholic drinks) INDIAN CLOTH TOBACCO GROCERIES INDIA WOODS IRON	SPIRITS TOBACCO
		Metals: COPPER TIN LEAD			
		FISH STARCH BOOKS LEATHER GRINDSTONES			

* Most important products.
‡ Products listed are those that passed through the ports in each area.

1. From which colony did Britain import, or buy, the most products? What were the second and third largest sources of imports?

2. To which colony did Britain export, or sell, the most goods? Which colonies were Britain's second and third largest markets?

3. Of the thirteen American colonies, were the Southern Colonies or New England and the Middle Colonies more important as a market for British products? Which area was more important in supplying goods to Britain?

4. In general, what kinds of goods did the colonies send to the Mother Country? What kinds of goods did Britain send to the colonies?

5. What specific products seemed to be Britain's most important imports from the colonies? In determining your answer, remember which colonies sold the most goods to Britain.

6. What seemed to be Britain's most important exports to the colonies?

7. How would you summarize the importance of the American colonies to Britain, as compared with Britain's other colonies?

8. How do your conclusions compare with the statements of Benjamin Franklin and Thomas Paine? (See pages 121 and 124.)

25. Mercantilism

The seventeenth and eighteenth centuries were a time of empire-building. England, like France, the Netherlands, and Spain, entered the race for new colonies. The basic idea behind that race was called mercantilism.

Mercantilism is an economic system under which the national government regulates the economy. The goal of the regulation is to gain wealth and power for the nation. In the seventeenth and eighteenth centuries, the major way mercantilists tried to gain wealth and power was by achieving a *favorable balance of trade*. A country is said to have a favorable balance of trade when it exports, or sells, more of its products than it imports, or buys, from other nations. By selling more goods than it has to buy, a country should be able to accumulate money. Thus, a favorable balance of trade should bring national wealth. The wealth, in turn, should bring power, by enabling the government to pay for an army and navy.

A nation that practiced mercantilism wanted wealth and power for two major reasons. One was simply to make the country more prosperous. The other was to enable the country to hold its own among rival nations. The armies and navies paid for by trade profits were expected to defend the nation against foreign competition.

Commercial rivalry was one of the most important sources of friction. To the mercantilist, there was a fixed amount of trade in the world. A nation that wanted to enlarge its share of trade, therefore, had to do so at the expense of other nations. In fact, as European nations sought to expand their foreign trade, they came into conflict with one another. They expected this, and consciously engaged in a race with one another. Thus, to support merchants far from home, a nation needed a strong navy. It also needed a strong army, because trade rivalries often erupted into European wars.

Another source of friction was religion. The bitter religious struggles of the sixteenth century spilled over into the seventeenth century. Finally, there was political rivalry. Each European nation was afraid to allow any of its neighbors to become too powerful. Some wars were fought to maintain what came to be called the "balance of power."

Many European nations thus viewed mercantile policy as crucial to their well-being. Maintaining a favorable balance of trade, the keystone of mercantilism, was considered an urgent need. To the mercantilist one of the best ways to achieve a favorable balance of trade was to acquire colonies. A colony could provide the nation with the finished goods and raw materials it lacked, thus reducing the need to purchase these supplies from other countries. To put it another way, the colony could help the nation to become self-sufficient. A colony could also help the mother country to increase its exports, by providing a market for the nation's products. In addition, colonies sometimes supplied goods that the mother country could sell to other nations, again enhancing the balance of trade. England, for example, was able to increase trade with Russia by selling goods like sugar and tobacco obtained from the English colonies.

In addition to acquiring colonies, mercantile nations tried to achieve a favorable trade balance in other ways. Government-sponsored merchant companies sought trade agreements with rulers of distant countries who might supply needed goods at favorable prices. They sought permission, also, to sell their nation's goods in these untapped foreign markets.

At home, European governments attempted to encourage the development of agriculture and manufacturing. The more a country could produce on its own, the less it would need to purchase from abroad and the more it would have to sell. Tariffs, or taxes on foreign goods coming into the country, were set up to protect the nation's industries from foreign competition. If foreign goods could be made to cost more than home-produced goods, people would buy the products of their own country.

International rivalries provided an additional reason for trying to produce as many goods as possible at home or in one's colonies. Not only did such a policy promote national wealth, but it helped insure national security, too. In time of war, a self-sufficient nation would not have to depend on foreign countries for supplies.

The attempt to expand foreign trade implied one other policy. In order to make the long sea voyages that were necessary, and to transport merchandise to and from distant ports, a country needed many large trading ships. It needed, in other words, a merchant marine. Colonies were useful partly because they stimulated the development of a merchant marine.

To guarantee that mercantile principles would be followed, many European countries passed national laws to regulate trade. Many of these laws governed trade with the colonies. England, for example, passed laws known as the Navigation Acts. One of the Navigation Acts, passed in 1660, required the colonies to sell certain products only to England. The products listed were ones that England needed. Another of the Navigation Acts helped to make sure that the colonists would buy goods from England. This act required most goods imported to the colonies from Europe to pass through England first. In England, duties were charged on the European goods which raised their prices above the prices of British products. Still another Navigation Act specified that all trade within the British Empire had to be carried in British ships. This helped Britain to develop a strong merchant marine.

The most important commercial rivalry of the seventeenth and eighteenth centuries was the contest between Britain and France. Because these two nations had been able to back their commercial ventures with powerful armies and navies, they had taken the lead in world trade. The two principal areas of competition between these trade giants were India and North America. Between 1756 and 1763, Britain fought France in the Seven Years' War. (The portion of the war that took place in North America was called the French and Indian War.) Britain emerged from the struggle victorious. This victory gave her control of India and North America and made her mistress of the seas. With France eliminated as a threat to the British Empire, England looked forward to a period of even greater wealth and power, based on trade with her colonies.

1. What does this description of mercantilism add to your understanding of why America was important to Britain?

2. Why do you think Britain passed the Molasses Act of 1733? Why do you think Britain passed the Sugar Act of 1764? (See pages 98 and 115.)

3. As described on page 114, the colonists resisted measures to enforce the Molasses Act. They also resisted the Sugar Act. If you were a mercantilist, how would you view this resistance? What would you think was at stake?

4. Quackenbos, the nineteenth-century American historian, noted that merchants of New York, Boston, and Philadelphia agreed not to import British goods until the Stamp Act was repealed. How would a mercantilist view this action?

5. After Parliament repealed the Stamp Act, it still insisted on the right "to bind the colonies in all cases whatsoever." Then, in 1770, when the Townshend Acts were repealed, a tax on tea was kept in order to show that Parliament still had the right to tax the colonies. (See pages 117 and 118.) If you were a mercantilist, would you feel that this was an important principle? Why or why not?

6. Which would be more important to a British mercantilist: keeping American customers friendly to Britain, or asserting Britain's right to make laws within her colonial empire?

7. At this point, what would you say caused the war between Britain and America from the British point of view?

26. A Modern British Interpretation of the Revolution: Ramsay Muir

The following account of the American Revolution is by Ramsay Muir, a modern British historian. Before reading the account, you might wish to review previous material about the right of Parliament to tax colonies, the Stamp Act, the Tea Tax, and the Declaration of Independence, since Muir deals with each of these topics. In the Muir account, headings such as "The Right of Taxation" have been added.

Ramsay Muir, **A Short History of the British Commonwealth** (Eighth edition; London, England: George Philip and Son Ltd., 1954), Vol. II, pp. 38–48, 51–53, 55–56, 59. Reprinted by permission of the publisher.

POINTS TO CONSIDER

If your previous ideas about what caused the Revolution need revision.

If the Americans were justified in revolting.

The importance of interpretation in history.

... There was some soreness on both sides. But the main point was that just because the colonies were, by the gift of the mother-country, almost the freest societies in the world, they were bound to strive for the completion of their own political liberties ...

The Right of Taxation   Closely connected with this question was the further question whether the British Parliament had the right to legislate for or to tax the colonies over the heads of their assemblies. ... There could be little doubt that such a right existed; if it did not exist, there was no common legislative authority for the whole empire. ... But it is essential to remember that apart from the British Government and Parliament there was no common authority for the thirteen colonies. They were so much attached to their local independence that they had refused to have anything to do with the scheme of federation [the Albany Plan] which had been drawn up by their own representatives in 1754. ...

Trade Problems   The problem of trade relationships was not less difficult. Ever since 1660 the unity of the British Empire had mainly depended upon the ties of trade, and upon the maintenance of a uniform system of trading regulations. The main principles of the system [known as mercantilism] were: (1) that inter-imperial trade should be carried only in British or colonial ships; (2) that some of the most important products of the colonies should be exported only to Britain, which thus became, for these goods, the market for the rest of the world; (3) that goods from other countries should only be imported to the colonies through Britain, where dues were levied upon them; and (4) that colonial produce should have a monopoly or a strong preference in British markets.

It has often been said that this system was conceived wholly in the interests of the mother-country. But that is not a just view. The aim of the system was to promote the prosperity of all the members of the Commonwealth by encouraging them to play their parts in a carefully planned economic system. It is certain that the colonies had derived great advantages from the system in some ways, though they may have suffered in others. The limitation of imperial trade to British and colonial ships had fostered the growth of a very active shipping trade in New England. The dues levied on foreign goods destined for the colonies were generally refunded, except in the case of goods which directly competed with British goods. The facts that colonial tobacco, coffee, sugar and rice had a monopoly of the British market . . . formed a solid compensation for the limitation of the export of certain articles to Britain . . .

. . . A very active trade had sprung up between the New England colonies and the French West Indian Islands, to which corn, cattle, and other produce were exported in exchange for molasses and sugar. This trade, which was entirely legal until 1733, provided an outlet for some of the principal products of the northern colonies. In the interests of the British West Indian Islands, Walpole had endeavoured to put an end to it by the Molasses Act of 1733, which imposed prohibitive duties on foreign sugar imported into any of the British lands—a prohibition which of course applied to Britain equally with the colonies. From the first the New Englanders had defied this law, and had carried on so vigorous a smuggling trade with the French West Indies that the Act had been almost a dead letter . . .

Robert Walpole was Prime Minister of England from 1721 to 1742.

Colonial Security   But it was the problem of colonial defence that seemed most urgent in 1763. The war just ended had left Britain burdened with a debt so colossal in the eyes of that generation that many financiers, and among them George Grenville, believed that there was an imminent danger of national bankruptcy. This debt had been mainly incurred in defending the colonies from a very grave peril; and in the struggle against this peril the colonists themselves had, in the judgment of most Englishmen, been extraordinarily backward. They had refused to take common action. Most of the individual colonies had been strangely reluctant to provide either men or money, even when the enemy was pressing on their borders. . . . Moreover, the continued security of the colonies against the real danger of a renewed French attack depended wholly upon the supremacy of the British fleet, which formed a heavy burden on Britain, and towards which the colonies made no contribution whatsoever.

George Grenville was Prime Minister of England from 1763 to 1765.

. . . For the safety of the whole group, and for the policing of the new territory, it seemed to be necessary to maintain a small permanent British force, the annual cost of which was estimated at £350,000 [pounds]. Even if the colonists were not to be asked to make any contribution to the burden of debt which had largely been incurred on their behalf, or to the cost of the fleet which safeguarded them from a possible French attack (and nobody proposed that they should be asked for money for these purposes), it seemed reasonable that they should be called upon to defray the cost of the small force maintained for their protection, and rendered necessary in part by their own refusal to adopt any adequate means for self-defence.

This at any rate was how the situation appeared to George Grenville and his colleagues when, on the conclusion of peace, they addressed themselves to the colonial problem. In the forefront of their minds were two questions: first, colonial defence and the organization of the new territories; secondly, the notorious and wholesale evasion of the trade laws, more particularly of the Molasses Act. They cannot fairly be blamed for their failure to see, what none of their contemporaries either in England or in America perceived, that the old colonial system had in fact broken down, and needed to be radically reconstructed on the basis of a great enlargement of colonial autonomy, combined with some system of co-operation for common needs.

. . . [Grenville] altered the character of the Molasses Act. In place of the prohibitive duties imposed by that Act, which would, if the Act had been observed, have destroyed the trade between New England and the French West Indies, he substituted moderate duties, which allowed the trade to be carried on legitimately, and might be expected to yield some revenue towards the cost of colonial defence. Grenville, in short, made an honest and intelligent attempt to revise and improve the old trade system, having in view the prosperity of the colonies as well as that of Britain . . .

The Stamp Act   The stricter enforcement of the trade laws, and the revised scale of dues, were expected to bring in some revenue, which would form a contribution towards the cost of colonial defence and the administration of the new territories. But the total yield (of which a large part would be paid by the West Indies) would be only sufficient to supply about one-seventh of the estimated outlay. How was the balance to be got? The colonists generally recognized that it was fair that this outlay should be met by themselves. But the colonists would not combine to tax themselves in common; and they had always failed to make fair contributions individually. The only alternative was that a tax should be imposed by the authority of the imperial Parliament, and this course had been urged by some of the colonial Governors, and by some of the agents appointed by the colonists to represent them in England. Grenville accordingly proposed that stamps should be required for certain documents

—a form of taxation as unoppressive and as easily levied as could readily be devised. He made this proposal in 1764, but allowed a year for the colonists to put forward any alternative proposals. None were suggested. Accordingly, in 1765, the famous Stamp Act was passed, practically without opposition, through the British Parliament. . . . The Act provided that every penny so raised should be spent on colonial defence. Its yield was only estimated at £100,000, part of which would be paid by the West Indies, so that more than half the cost of the local defence of the colonies, as well as the whole cost of the navy and and the whole burden of the debt, would still fall upon the British exchequer [treasury]. It cannot be pretended that there was anything tyrannical or oppressive in these proposals, or that £100,000 would form an unreasonably heavy burden upon the thirteen thriving settlements . . .

The passage of the Stamp Act produced a wholly unexpected outcry in America—an outcry which was certainly intensified, and perhaps mainly caused, by the unpopularity of the strict enforcement of the trade laws. The colonial leaders everywhere repudiated [rejected] the right of the British Parliament to impose direct taxation upon them; 'no taxation without representation' became their cry . . .

. . . The Act simply could not be enforced. What was more, the colonists began to enter into agreements to boycott British goods; and British merchants at home, seeing their trade threatened, began to clamour for the repeal of the Act.

Evidently the Act had to be repealed. Evidently the British taxpayer would have to go on bearing the whole burden of colonial defence. The weak and short-lived Whig ministry which succeeded Grenville repealed the Act (1766) . . . And the clamour in America died down. But with the repeal was coupled a Declaratory Act, asserting the power of the British Parliament to impose laws or taxes on the colonies. This unqualified assertion of principle played into the hands of that section of colonial opinion, as yet small, but full of vigour, which was aiming at complete independence, though it did not yet venture to say so. . . .

The Tea Tax   The Whig ministry was succeeded by Lord Chatham's ministry; and Lord Chatham was the proclaimed friend of the colonies, their idol during the late war [the French and Indian War]. Surely his Government might be expected to face the issue? . . . In 1767 . . . Parliament readily accepted, a series of new duties on tea and other goods imported into America [the Townshend Acts].

The colonial protest was as vigorous as before. According to the words of the Act itself, the new duties were imposed for the purpose of raising revenue, not for the purpose of regulating trade. . . . In most of the colonies non-importation agreements for the boycotting of British trade were widely adhered to. Massachusetts, as always, took the lead in resistance; its Assembly sent out a letter inviting all the other colonies to combine; and being thereupon dissolved by the Governor, it continued to sit as a convention, and to organise and guide public feeling, in open defiance of the regular Government. So dangerous was the temper of Boston that in 1768 two regiments were sent from Halifax to be quartered in the town. But the townsmen refused to find quarters for them; and a town's meeting, on the . . . pretext of a possible French invasion, requested all citizens to equip themselves with arms. The inevitable friction which followed between the excited townspeople and the harassed troops led, not unnaturally, to an affray [fight] (1770), in which three people were killed. The episode was denounced as the Boston Massacre, and became the theme of anniversary orations on the brutal tyranny of the mother-country.

In the [face] of these difficulties, and lest worse should come, the British Government decided that it was necessary to give way. In March, 1770, all the duties were withdrawn except that on tea; and the retention of the duty on tea was only decided by a majority of one in the cabinet . . . But the leaders in the colonies, at any rate in Massachusetts, were not only determined to have no compromise, they were becoming daily bolder in the assertion of principles which were essentially inconsistent with the maintenance of any part of the old ties. . . .

. . . During the five years from 1769 to 1773 . . . the leaders of the resistance found it impossible to keep the popular excitement at the pitch which it had reached in 1765 and in 1768: for when all was said, an addition of 3d. in the pound to the duty on tea (which formed the whole of the British oppression) was not in itself a very obvious sign of slavery, and it was hard for the ordinary man to keep himself in a passion, year after year, on such a matter. But in 1773 an event happened which quite unexpectedly fanned the flames again.

. . . Lord North introduced an Act [the Tea Tax] permitting the East India Company to export its tea direct to America. Hitherto

Halifax is in Nova Scotia.

"3d." is three pence in the English system.

it had been sent through England, where it had paid a duty of 1s. [1 shilling], the additional Townshend duty of 3d. being levied at the American customs-houses. Now it was pay the 3d. only; the Americans would get their tea cheaper than before Townshend's time, and cheaper than it could be got in England. In reality this marked a complete victory for the Americans. But their leaders did not so regard it. They looked upon it as [a] . . . trick to persuade their followers to buy the taxed article; but they feared that many would do so. Consignments [shipments] of tea were sent under the new rules to four American ports. At three of them the vendors were peaceably persuaded to withdraw the tea from sale. But at Boston a town-meeting was summoned, to declare that this was 'the last, worst, and most destructive measure of Government,' and that those who landed the tea would be 'treated as wretches unworthy to live.' No one proposed to force the people of Boston to buy the tea; they were free to let it rot in the warehouses, as the people of Charleston did. But this was not enough. On December 16, 1773, a band of men, in the darkness of night, and carefully disguised as Red Indians, boarded the ships, and threw the property of the East India Company into the harbour.

The Boston tea riot was a deliberate defiance of the laws; it was proof that the regular Government was powerless in the city. When the news reached England it produced a fierce outburst of anger. It made reconciliation almost impossible, as perhaps it was intended to do; for it is significant that in this same autumn of 1773 Samuel Adams, the real leader of the Bostonians, had published three letters in a Boston paper openly advocating independence. In March 1774 Lord North introduced a series of penal [punitive] measures. One of these closed the port of Boston, and removed the customhouse to Salem until compensation should have been paid for the tea. Another, having in view the difficulty of enforcing obedience to the laws, vested in the Crown the appointment of all judicial officers, and made it possible to bring offenders to England for trial. But the most important of these enactments was one which cancelled the charter of Massachusetts and revised its system of government. This strange folly [foolish act] had the most dire effects. It was the first act of the British Government which seemed to afford real and solid evidence that its aim was the destruction of American liberty. It drove the colonists to unite. It played into the hands of those, hitherto a small minority, who desired, and had been working for, independence. . . .

A Civil War The eight years' war which opened with the skirmish of Lexington forms one of the saddest episodes in the history

of the British Commonwealth. It was a very cruel civil war, not only because Britons and Americans came from the same stock and cherished the same ideals, but because both Britons and Americans were painfully divided among themselves. In Britain, indeed, a majority had no doubts about the justice of the British cause; but the minority included some of the noblest living Englishmen ... who regarded the revolting colonists not as enemies, but as fellow-citizens upholding a cause dear to themselves. In America, on the other hand, there were thousands of loyalist Tories in every colony, even in New England; and among these were included many who had strongly opposed the Stamp Act and the tea duty, but who shrank from the prospect of breaking up the unity of the empire ...

The fact that the war was a civil war, marked by all the heartbreaking hesitations and divisions which civil war involves, explains many aspects [that would] otherwise be unintelligible. It explains in part the half-heartedness ... with which the struggle was conducted on the British side, by generals who hated the work they had to do. ... It explains the inadequate support of which Washington bitterly complained, and the constant difficulty of recruiting and provisioning the American armies ... A long comradeship of nearly two centuries, recently sealed by the efforts and triumphs of a great war [the French and Indian War], could not be broken up without terrible suffering and grave doubts on both sides.

The fact that so many of the colonists were either half-hearted or favoured the British cause ought of itself almost to have ensured the success of British arms, and would have done so if this advantage had been skillfully used. Indeed, at the outset all the advantages seemed to be on the British side, and there was a general expectation that victory would be quickly and easily secured. The colonists were mutually jealous, and had not learnt to act together. Their Congress, hastily improvised, had no effective control over the country as a whole, and no efficient administrative system; its members spent their time in arguing and quarrelling, and gave no steady support to their commanders in the field. Communications between the long straggling line of colonies were extremely bad; they had in the past been mainly conducted by sea, and the British fleet held the seas ...

The Colonial Cause   Two things alone gave any hope of success to the colonial cause. The first was the fighting quality of the colonial troops. Though the men were undisciplined, and prone [likely] to leave the standards on the least provocation, they showed themselves to be splendid fighting men, staunch, cool,

180

and courageous; and though they were at a disadvantage in regular operations, they were very skillful in irregular warfare. But the second and the greatest factor of success was the personality of the great leader, George Washington, who was appointed to the chief command at the opening of the struggle, and held it to the end in face of infinite [endless] difficulty and misrepresentation. He was not a man of brilliant inspirations or dazzling adventures; perhaps he was not even a general of the first rank. But he was a man ... resolute in action, patient in adversity, sound in judgment, endowed with a masculine intelligence which could grasp the real essentials of a situation and could look at even the most unpleasant facts squarely and honestly, without blinking what he did not like, utterly trustworthy, completely devoted to the cause he had adopted, undismayed when things were darkest. To him alone it was due that against all the odds, and in face of infinite difficulties, the American cause tided over the interval until the power of France was ready to come to its aid.

On the British side there was no man of this quality, or of anything like this quality.... the real control of policy was wielded by the King, and though he was brave, tenacious, and industrious, George III had no touch of genius ...

The Declaration of Independence ... On July 4, 1776, [the Americans] issued a Declaration of Independence, in which they renounced their allegiance to the British Crown, and proclaimed to the world the separate existence of the United States of America as a sovereign Power.

The Declaration of Independence was one of the most momentous documents in the history of the world. It not only broke into fragments the British Commonwealth as it had hitherto existed; it not only launched upon history a very great new State of unlimited potentialities; it began a new era in human history, the era of democratic revolution.... The new State began its history with a declaration that all men are born equal, and have an inalienable right to liberty. This was, indeed, only a general statement, with no practical effects. It did not make any difference to the rights or to the laws of the American people, which remained in all essentials the rights and the laws which they had derived from Britain; nor did those among the signatories [signers] of this pronouncement who were slave-owners, as many of them were, even think of applying their principles by giving to their slaves the 'inalienable right' of liberty.... But it was a new thing in human history that a great State should thus choose as

181

the motto of the first chapter in its history a proclamation of universal human rights as the ideal to be aimed at.

This preamble was followed by eighteen articles of charge against Britain and her King, to justify the renunciation of allegiance. Not one of them would to-day be accepted, without large qualifications, as a statement of historical fact . . . But even so, it was a new and great thing in the world's history that a group of communities should claim, as a matter of right, the power to sever ancient ties and cast off their allegiance solely on the grounds of alleged breaches of right and justice. We may feel that in the heat of a great crisis the indictment [accusation] was unfairly laid, and yet also feel that was a fine thing that it should have been laid at all. . . .

A Conspiracy There is something of high comedy in the spectacle of two absolute monarchies [France and Spain], two colonial Powers which had never allowed the slightest semblance of self-governing rights to their own colonies, coming forward to protect the British colonies against the tyranny of the mother-country which had granted them, as a matter of course, self-governing rights wider than any other country in the world enjoyed. But it was not the freedom of the colonies which France and Spain desired; it was the downfall and ruin of Britain. And therefore from the moment of the French declaration of war, the struggle changed its character. It became no longer a civil strife among the divided peoples of a group of free communities; it became, for Britain, a struggle of life and death against ancient enemies, now for the first time effectively combined: a struggle in which no aid was to be looked for in any quarter; a struggle, therefore, which called, and did not call in vain, for the dogged and obstinate courage which refuses to admit or to be disheartened by failure.

1. Look again at the material in this section. Had America fulfilled the British expectations for a colony?

2. How can you explain British action in each of the events Muir describes? For example:
   Muir doesn't explain why the British were willing to pay for the fleet, much of the permanent force for America, and the whole debt from the French and Indian War. Why do you think the British were willing to assume these expenses?
   Muir describes the Molasses Act as hurting New England's trade. According to Muir, what was the purpose of the Molasses Act? What theory justified such an act?

Why do you think the British response to American complaints against such tax laws was to withdraw or modify them?

3. What were the British trying to protect in America?

4. Why does Muir think the Americans rebelled? Does he approve or disapprove of the reason for their rebellion?

5. Does Muir think the Americans were *justified* in rebelling? Explain.

6. How would you summarize Muir's view of the causes of the Revolution?

7. To what factors does Muir attribute the American victory?

**THE BRITISH VIEW OF THE REVOLUTION:
AN EVALUATION**

1. Review what the rebelling Americans wanted to protect and what actions of the British they objected to. How does this compare with the British position?

2. Over what issues did the Americans and British clash most often? Why?

3. Do you think the Americans were justified in revolting? Why or why not?

4. Review your hypothesis about what you thought caused the American Revolution. What do you now interpret as the cause or causes of the American Revolution? Tell why you have changed or retained your hypothesis.

---

27. The Treaty of Paris, 1783

A treaty is an agreement between two or more independent states. It is the result of negotiations, or discussions, between the representatives of each power. Once the treaty has been signed by the representatives, it generally must be sent to each nation for ratification (approval) by the nation's government. In the United States a treaty is ratified if the Senate approves it by a two-thirds majority vote.

A treaty is often complicated and difficult to read. However, treaties usually follow a recognizable pattern.

1. A preamble is a statement of purpose or intent at the beginning of the treaty. The preamble often sets forth general agreements between the powers. It may also list the names and positions of the men representing each power.

VI. The Peace Treaty: Assessing Results

2. The main body of a treaty is divided into articles. Each of these covers an item on which the representatives have agreed.

3. The last article states when and where the treaty was settled. The signatures of the participating representatives follow it.

Below is the Treaty of Peace that ended the Revolutionary War. It was signed by the United States and Great Britain in Paris on September 3, 1783.

Read the treaty. Then briefly state the main ideas in a form like that given below:

Treaty of Paris, 1783

Preamble:

Article I:

Article II:

Article III:

Article IV:

Article V:

Article VI:

Article VII:

Article VIII:

Article IX:

Article X:

POINTS TO CONSIDER

If the peace treaty was a *just one*.

Which agreements would *most* please the Americans.

Which agreements would displease *some* Americans.

If the Americans accomplished what they fought for.

In the name of the most Holy & undivided Trinity.

It having pleased the divine Providence to dispose the Hearts of the most Serene and most Potent Prince George the third, by the Grace of God, King of Great Britain, France & Ireland, Defender of the Faith, Duke of Brunswick and Lunebourg, Arch Treasurer, and Prince Elector of the Holy Roman Empire . . . and of the United States of America, to forget all past Misunderstandings and Differences that have unhappily interrupted the good Correspondence and Friendship which they mutually wish to restore; and to establish such a beneficial and satisfactory Intercourse between the two Countries upon the Ground of reciprocal [corresponding] Advantages and mutual Convenience

Treaties and Other International Acts of the United States of America, edited by Hunter Miller (Washington, D.C.: United States Government Printing Office, 1931), Vol. II, pp. 151–156.

The preamble of this treaty is all in one sentence.

as may promote and secure to both perpetual Peace & Harmony, and having for this desirable End already said the Foundation of Peace & Reconciliation by the Provisional Articles signed at Paris on the 30th of Nov. 1782. by the Commissioners empower'd on each Part, which Articles were agreed to be inserted in and to constitute the Treaty of Peace proposed to be concluded between the Crown of Great Britain and the said United States, but which Treaty was not to be concluded until Terms of Peace should be agreed upon between Great Britain & France, And his Britannic Majesty should be ready to conclude such Treaty accordingly: and the Treaty between Great Britain & France having since been concluded, His Britannic Majesty & the United States of America in Order to carry into full Effect the Provisional Articles abovementioned, according to the Tenor [substance] thereof, have constituted & appointed, that is to say His Britannic Majesty on his Part, David Hartley Esq., Member of the Parliament of Great Britain; and the said United States on their Part, John Adams Esq., late [formerly] a Commissioner of the United States of America at the Court of Versailles, late Delegate in Congress from the State of Massachusetts and Chief Justice of the said State, and Minister Plenipotentiary [ambassador] of the said United States to their High Mightinesses the States General of the United Netherlands; Benjamin Franklin Esq., late Delegate in Congress from the State of Pennsylvania, President of the Convention of the said State, and Minister Plenipotentiary from the United States of America at the Court of Versailles; John Jay Esq., late President of Congress and Chief Justice of the State of New-York & Minister Plenipotentiary from the said United States at the Court of Madrid; to be the Plenipotentiaries for the concluding and signing the Present Definitive Treaty; who after having reciprocally [mutually] communicated their respective full Powers have agreed upon and confirmed the following Articles.

When diplomats meet they exchange credentials which show that they are authorized to act for their governments or heads of state.

Article 1 His Britannic Majesty acknowledges the said United States, viz. New Hampshire Massachusetts Bay, Rhode-Island & Providence Plantations, Connecticut, New York, New Jersey, Pennsylvania, Delaware, Maryland, Virginia, North Carolina, South Carolina & Georgia, to be free sovereign & Independent States; that he treats with them as such, and for himself his Heirs & Successors relinquishes all Claims to the Government Propriety & Territorial Rights of the same & every Part thereof.

[Article 2 established the boundary lines of the new United States as shown on the following map. The map also shows areas of North America that other countries claimed in 1783. However, the Treaty of Paris was not concerned with these areas. Compare this map with the map at the beginning of the unit which shows the American colonies prior to the Revolution.]

NORTH AMERICA IN 1783

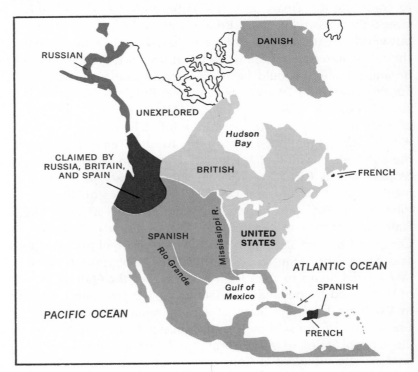

Article 3   It is agreed that the People of the United States shall continue to enjoy unmolested the Right to take Fish of every kind on the Grand Bank and on all the other Banks of New-foundland, also in the Gulph [Gulf] of St. Lawrence, and at all other Places in the Sea where the Inhabitants of both Countries used at any time heretofore to fish. And also that the Inhabitants of the United States shall have Liberty to take Fish of every Kind on such Part of the Coast of New-foundland as British Fishermen shall use, (but not to dry or cure the same on that Island) And also on the Coasts Bays & Creeks of all other of his Britannic Majesty's Dominions in America, and that the American Fishermen shall have Liberty to dry and cure Fish in any of the unsettled Bays Harbours and Creeks of Nova Scotia, Magdalen Islands, and Labrador, so long as the same shall remain unsettled but so soon as the same or either of them shall be settled, it

186

shall not be lawful for the said Fishermen to dry or cure fish at such Settlement, without a previous Agreement for that purpose from the Inhabitants, Proprietors or Possessors of the Ground.

Article 4 It is agreed that Creditors on either side shall meet with no lawful Impediment [obstacle] to the Recovery of the full Value in Sterling Money of all bona fide [genuine] Debts heretofore contracted.

Article 5 It is agreed that the Congress shall earnestly recommend it to the Legislatures of the respective States to provide for the Restitution [return] of all Estates, Rights and Properties which have been confiscated [seized] belonging to real British Subjects; and also of the Estates Rights and Properties of Persons resident in Districts in the Possession of his Majesty's Arms, and who have not borne Arms against the said United States. And that Persons of any other Description shall have free Liberty to go to any Part or Parts of any of the thirteen United States and therein to remain twelve Months unmolested in their Endeavours to obtain the Restitution of such of their Estates Rights & Properties as may have been confiscated. And that Congress shall also earnestly recommend to the several States, a Reconsideration and Revision of all Acts or Laws regarding the Premises, so as to render the said Laws or Acts perfectly consistent, not only with Justice and Equity, but with that Spirit of Conciliation, which, on the Return of the Blessings of Peace should universally prevail. And that Congress shall also earnestly recommend to the several States, that the Estates, Rights and Properties of such last mentioned Persons shall be restored to them, they refunding to any Persons who may be now in Possession, the Bona fide Price (where any has been given) which such Persons may have paid on purchasing any of the said Lands, Rights or Properties, since the Confiscation.

And it is agreed that all Persons who have any Interest in confiscated Lands, either by Debts, Marriage Settlements, or otherwise, shall meet with no lawful Impediment in the Prosecution of their just Rights.

Article 6 That there shall be no future Confiscations made nor any Prosecutions commenc'd against any Person or Persons for or by Reason of the Part, which he or they may have taken in the present War, and that no Person shall on that Account suffer any future Loss or Damage, either in his Person, Liberty or Property; and that those who may be in Confinement on such Charges at the Time of the Ratification of the Treaty in America shall be

187

immediately set at Liberty, and the Prosecutions so commenced be discontinued.

Article 7   There shall be a firm and perpetual Peace between his Britannic Majesty and the said States and between the Subjects of the one, and the Citizens of the other, wherefore all Hostilities both by Sea and Land shall from henceforth cease: All Prisoners on both Sides shall be set at Liberty, and his Britannic Majesty shall with all convenient speed, and without causing any Destruction, or carrying away any Negroes or other Property of the American Inhabitants, withdraw all his Armies, Garrisons & Fleets from the said United States, and from every Port, Place and Harbour within the same; leaving in all Fortifications the American Artillery that may be therein: And shall also Order & cause all Archives [collection of documents], Records, Deeds & Papers belonging to any of the said States, or their Citizens, which in the Course of the War may have fallen into the Hands of his Officers, to be forthwith restored and deliver'd to the proper States and Persons to whom they belong.

Article 8   The Navigation of the River Mississippi, from its source to the Ocean shall for ever remain free and open to the Subjects of Great Britain and the Citizens of the United States.

Article 9   In Case it should so happen that any Place or Territory belonging to Great Britain or to the United States should have been conquer'd by the Arms of either from the other before the Arrival of the said Provisional Articles in America it is agreed that the same shall be restored without Difficulty and without requiring any Compensation.

Article 10   The solemn Ratifications of the present Treaty expedited [dispatched] in good & due Form shall be exchanged between the contracting Parties in the Space of Six Months or sooner if possible to be computed from the Day of the Signature of the present Treaty. In Witness whereof we the undersigned their Ministers Plenipotentiary have in their Name and in Virtue of our Full Powers signed with our Hands the Present Definitive Treaty, and caused the Seals of our Arms to be affix'd thereto.

Done at Paris, this third Day of September, In the Year of our Lord one thousand seven hundred & eighty three

D Hartley   *John Adams*   *B Franklin*   *John Jay*

TIME LINE

EVENTS IN AMERICA

EVENTS IN BRITAIN

1727 GEORGE II BECOMES KING OF ENGLAND.

1733 THE MOLASSES ACT IS PASSED BY PARLIAMENT.

1756 THE FRENCH AND INDIAN WAR BEGINS. (IN EUROPE IT WAS CALLED THE SEVEN YEARS' WAR.)

1756 THE SEVEN YEARS' WAR BEGINS.

1760 GEORGE III BECOMES KING OF ENGLAND.

1763 THE SEVEN YEARS' WAR ENDS.

1763 THE FRENCH AND INDIAN WAR ENDS.

1763 THE PROCLAMATION OF 1763 CLAIMS FORMER FRENCH LANDS WEST OF THE APPALACHIANS FOR BRITAIN, AND FORBIDS AMERICANS TO SETTLE THERE.

1764 THE SUGAR ACT IS PASSED.

1765 THE STAMP ACT CONGRESS MEETS TO PROTEST THE TAXING POLICIES OF GREAT BRITAIN.

1765 THE QUARTERING ACT REQUIRES COLONISTS TO PROVIDE FOOD AND LODGING FOR BRITISH SOLDIERS STATIONED IN AMERICA.

1765 THE STAMP ACT IS PASSED.

1766 THE STAMP ACT IS REPEALED.

1766 THE DECLARATORY ACT IS PASSED. IT ASSERTS PARLIAMENT'S RIGHT TO MAKE LAWS ON ANY SUBJECT.

1767 THE TOWNSHEND ACTS ARE PASSED. TO ENFORCE THEM, PARLIAMENT APPROVES THE USE OF "WRITS OF ASSISTANCE," WHICH PERMIT OFFICIALS TO SEARCH ANY BUILDING OR SHIP AT ANY TIME WITHOUT STATING THEIR PURPOSE.

1767 NEW YORK REFUSES TO PROVIDE LODGING FOR SOLDIERS SENT TO ENFORCE THE TOWNSHEND ACTS.

1767 PARLIAMENT SUSPENDS THE NEW YORK ASSEMBLY.

1768 THE MASSACHUSETTS ASSEMBLY DENOUNCES THE TOWNSHEND ACTS. THE ASSEMBLIES OF NEW HAMPSHIRE, NEW JERSEY, CONNECTICUT, AND VIRGINIA SUPPORT MASSACHUSETTS.

1768 BRITISH OFFICIALS DISSOLVE THE MASSACHUSETTS ASSEMBLY. BRITISH TROOPS ARE STATIONED IN BOSTON.

1769 TWELVE OF THE THIRTEEN COLONIES OPPOSE THE TOWNSHEND ACTS BY REFUSING TO IMPORT BRITISH GOODS.

1770 THE BOSTON MASSACRE.

1770 THE TOWNSHEND ACTS ARE REPEALED, BUT A TAX ON TEA IS RETAINED.

1772 MASSACHUSETTS ORGANIZES A COMMITTEE OF CORRESPONDENCE. OTHER COLONIES FOLLOW SUIT.

1773 THE BOSTON TEA PARTY.

1773 THE TEA ACT IS PASSED, LOWERING THE PRICE OF TEA.

1774 THE FIRST CONTINENTAL CONGRESS CONVENES.

1774 THE INTOLERABLE ACTS ARE PASSED. THESE ACTS CLOSE THE PORT OF BOSTON, SUSPEND MASSACHUSETTS' CHARTER AND ITS RIGHT TO HOLD TOWN MEETINGS, RENEW THE QUARTERING ACT, AND ALLOW BRITISH OFFICIALS CHARGED WITH CRIMES IN MASSACHUSETTS TO BE TRIED IN ENGLAND.

1774 THE QUEBEC ACT ENLARGES CANADA AT THE EXPENSE OF MASSACHUSETTS', CONNECTICUT'S AND VIRGINIA'S CLAIMS TO WESTERN LANDS.

1775 WAR BEGINS WITH THE BATTLES OF LEXINGTON AND CONCORD.

1776 THE SECOND CONTINENTAL CONGRESS CONVENES. IT ISSUES THE DECLARATION OF INDEPENDENCE.

1778 FRANCE BECOMES THE UNITED STATES' ALLY.

1781 THE FINAL VICTORY AT YORKTOWN.

1783 THE PEACE TREATY: INDEPENDENCE IS ACHIEVED.

1783 THE PEACE TREATY: BRITAIN SURRENDERS HER AMERICAN COLONIES.

---

1. What events do you regard as major turning points in the American Revolution?
2. What events preceded or followed each of these turning points?
3. How did the happenings preceding or following each of these events help make them turning points?

For Additional Information: Use of the Library

At this point you should have encountered some questions for which the answer was not immediately available. No one source in history contains *all* the answers. In fact, in studying history, perhaps some questions have no *final* answers. But many questions do have an answer.

Consult your library for additional information on the American Revolution, *for any topic or subject of interest to you,* or when you wish to locate an answer to a question of any kind.

The Card Catalog

Use the *card catalog* in order to locate a particular book or source of information.

For example, to find information on the American Revolution look for:

1. American Revolution.
2. Colonial History.
3. Declaration of Independence.
4. England—History.
5. Great Britain—History.
6. Patriotism—Patriots.
7. United States—History.

Or, look under biographical sketches such as those of George Washington, Thomas Jefferson, Alexander Hamilton, John Adams, John Hancock, George III, or Samuel Adams.

Under the Dewey decimal system of book classifications, history and biography are in the 900–999 group, and social science and government are in the 300–399 group.

A particular book you want could be listed three different ways in the card catalog: by author, by book title, or by subject.

For example, note the account you read on the formation of the Declaration of Independence by Clara I. Judson. It would be listed in the card catalog as

AUTHOR CARD

CALL
NUMBER   AUTHOR
923   Judson, Clara I.
J26j   TITLE   Thomas Jefferson, Champion
        of the People. Follette. c 1952

```
Thomas Jefferson, Champion of the People.
923
J26j
Judson, Clara I.
Thomas Jefferson, Champion of the People.
Follette. c 1952
```

```
                    THOMAS JEFFERSON—BIOGRAPHY
923
J26j
Judson, Clara I.
Thomas Jefferson, Champion of the People.
Follette. c 1952
```

Reference Books

If you wish to determine the validity of a historical fact or event or simply want to search for new information on a topic, the following works of references in American history are of value:

The Album of American History

The Atlas of American History

The Dictionary of American Biography

The Dictionary of American History

The Encyclopedia of American History

Historical Statistics of the United States: Colonial Times to the Present

Periodicals

For periodical material, consult the READERS' GUIDE TO PERI-ODICAL LITERATURE. For example, a source of information in the READERS' GUIDE on the Declaration of Independence would read: Our Declaration is still a rallying cry. H. S. Commager. il N Y Times Mag p5—Jl 2 '61. This means that the *title* of the article is "Our Declaration is Still a Rallying Cry." The *author* is Henry S. Commager. "Il" means the article is illustrated. The *periodical* is the NEW YORK TIMES MAGAZINE. The *information* is on page 5. The *date* the article appeared in the NEW YORK TIMES MAGAZINE is July 2, 1961.

What would the following mean as they are listed in the READERS' GUIDE under United States history?

1. Mercantilism and American trade. G. Langdon. Our Hist 42:321–6 Je '62.

2. Seven who set our destiny; the Founding Fathers. R. B. Morris. il N Y Times Mag p9 F 19 '61.

3. Then and there the child Independence was born. R. B. Morris. il Am Heritage 13:36–9 F '62.

Textbooks

If the previous information does not prove satisfactory, consult a standard American history book for further guidance. Look for your topic, event, or person in the *index* or the *table of contents* of that book. Good hunting!

BIBLIOGRAPHY

BOYD, JAMES. DRUMS. New York: Charles Scribner's Sons, 1936.
  The fictional story of a North Carolina lad who meets John Paul Jones and takes an active part in the Revolution.

*COOPER, JAMES FENIMORE. THE SPY. New York: Dodd, Mead & Co., 1949; †New York: Dolphin Books, 1961.
  A fictional account of a spy employed by George Washington.

EDMONDS, WALTER D. DRUMS ALONG THE MOHAWK. Boston: Little, Brown and Company, 1936; †New York: Bantam Books, Inc., 1963.
  Historical fiction that tells about the hardships of frontier settlers in the Mohawk Valley during the Revolution.

FORBES, ESTHER. JOHNNY TREMAIN. Boston: Houghton Mifflin Company, 1943; †Boston: Houghton Mifflin Company, 1965.
  A novel set in Boston during the Revolution.

PAGE, ELIZABETH. TREE OF LIBERTY. New York: Holt, Rinehart and Winston, Inc., 1939.
  Historical fiction that describes the roles of Thomas Jefferson, John Adams, Alexander Hamilton, Aaron Burr, and George Washington in creating a new nation.

*TURNBULL, AGNES S. DAY MUST DAWN. New York: The Macmillan Company, 1942.
  A novel about the position of the Loyalists during the Revolution.

* Denotes more advanced reading.
‡ Denotes paperback edition.

unit III
FORGING
A NATION: LAW
AND LEADERSHIP 1783-1800

But know, ye favor'd race, one potent head
Must rule your states, and strike your foes with dread,
The finance regulate, the trade control
Live through the empire, and accord the whole.

THE HARTFORD WITS, 1786
FEDERALIST POETS

INTRODUCTION

"Thirteen sovereignties pulling against each other . . . will bring ruin on the whole; whereas [an] energitic constitution . . . might restore us to that degree of respectability . . . to which we had a fair claim . . . [in 1783]."

George Washington expressed these convictions in 1786. He was one of many who saw how little the thirteen states cooperated with each other and how jealous each was of its independence. His letter emphasized the need for a stronger central government.

From 1781 to 1788, the central government of the United States was based on the Articles of Confederation. The Articles were the *constitution* which the United States adopted after declaring its independence. A constitution is a document that tells how a government is to be organized. It defines the powers of the government and the rights of the people. For a new nation desperately in need of unity, the Articles did little to help. When Washington called for an "energitic constitution," he was reacting to the weaknesses of the Articles. The following are among the weaknesses commonly associated with the Articles.

1. The state legislatures controlled Congress. Congress consisted of only one house, in which the delegates were chosen annually by the states. The states also paid the delegates and could recall them at any time. Each state had one vote.
2. There was no independent executive or president to enforce acts of Congress. When Congress was in recess, a Committee of the States made up of one delegate from each state carried on the functions of the government.
3. There was no national court system. State courts enforced the laws passed by Congress.
4. Congress had no power to levy, or collect, taxes.
5. Congress could not regulate trade between the states or with foreign nations.
6. The approval of nine of the thirteen states was necessary for Congress to carry out many of the functions that had been delegated to it. Congress could not enter into treaties, borrow or coin money, or decide the size of the armed forces without the consent of nine states.
7. Congress could not force obedience to its laws or to the Articles of Confederation. States assumed powers specifically assigned to Congress. For example, states negotiated with foreign governments and established their own currency and post offices.
8. Consent of all the states was needed to amend or change the Articles of Confederation.

194

The deficiencies of the Articles were not the only problems confronting the United States in 1787. Even though Great Britain, France, Russia, Sweden, Spain, and Denmark had recognized American independence, it was still not clear whether independence could be maintained. One problem was the inability of the government to pay the war debt. The war with Great Britain had cost the United States $135 million, and America still owed $40 million to foreign governments and unpaid soldiers. Congress was not even able to pay the interest on the debt. Many states repeatedly refused to pay their share of the national debt. If a state decided not to send money to the national government, the government was powerless to act. Lack of union at home prevented the United States from being respected abroad. It was all too obvious that the power of the national government was slight.

The condition of the country was distressing for other reasons, too. The United States had hoped for an immediate immigration from Europe and a proportionate increase in the value of American lands. In this, it was disappointed. Business was in a state of depression and many businesses closed. Meanwhile, the people were taxed heavily for the support of state governments. In some places, such as western Massachusetts, rebellion threatened.

In January 1786, the legislature of Virginia called for a convention of state delegates to regulate the commercial relations of the country. In the following September, delegates from five states met at Annapolis, Maryland. The delegates decided that there ought to be a general meeting of all states to solve the whole range of problems confronting the nation. They recommended that Congress call a general convention. In May 1787, representatives from all the states, except Rhode Island, assembled in Philadelphia. The Constitutional Convention began its work.

The makers of the Constitution designed a *federal* form of government. A federal government is one in which a number of states join together to form a union. Each state, as it enters the union, agrees to give up some of its powers to the central government.

Try to imagine what it would be like if, instead of fifty states, we had fifty separate countries. What would life be like if Connecticut, Georgia, and Oregon were all independent nations? Does the idea appeal to you?

Today the United States is a strong, unified country. It is easy to assume that this was a natural, inevitable development. But there were many suggestions at the Constitutional Convention of ways to organize the government. Not all of them led to a strong federal union. Nor was the Constitution adopted by all Americans quickly and easily. There was hesitation, misgiving, and even bitter opposition. Nor, once adopted, did federal government in the United States seem sure to survive. The first years of federal rule were plagued by dangerous tensions.

This unit deals with the drama surrounding the first crucial years of the federal union. It begins with an examination of the issues involved in the drafting and acceptance of the Constitution. The unit continues with a study of the problems faced by Presidents Washington and Adams in the years 1789-1801.

Before studying the Constitution, you will read descriptions of some of the Convention delegates and a skit based on the major issues discussed at the Convention. As you form ideas about what kind of men wrote the Constitution and what kind of rules they desired for governing their society, you will understand better why the Constitution took the shape it did. Throughout your study of the Constitution you will deal with *values*. A value is an idea about what is good or important.

The Constitution was submitted to the states for *ratification*, or acceptance. Each state called a convention to decide whether or not to ratify it. You will look at two case studies of ratification, the debates and issues in Massachusetts and in Virginia. Massachusetts was a leader within the northern group of states, and Virginia within the southern.

In the second part of this unit, you will consider the problems of the first two leaders of the nation, Presidents Washington and Adams. You will be able to compare the problems they faced with the problems which made it difficult to write an acceptable Constitution. You will be asked to identify what Washington's and Adams' most important problems were and to judge whether or not these men were good leaders. You will also consider what, in general, makes a man a good leader and a good President.

The unit concludes with a study of the distinction between fact and myth. Here you will examine the original version of the story of George Washington and the cherry tree, along with later comments about the story.

As you study this formative era in American history, keep in mind the central problem of the unit: What made it possible for this nation to survive when many forces threatened to pull it apart? What held the nation together through the crisis period?

Forging a Nation: Law

1. The Delegates to the Convention: Contemporary Portraits

Major William Pierce was a delegate from Georgia to the Constitutional Convention. While attending the Convention, he recorded his impressions of the delegates assembled at Philadelphia in 1787. This reading contains some of his descriptions.

POINTS TO CONSIDER

The kind of men described by Pierce.

How their traits might affect the formation of a government.

From Massachusetts.

Mr. [Nathaniel] Gorham is a Merchant in Boston, high in reputation, and much in the esteem of his Country-men. He is a Man of very good sense, but not much improved in his education. . . . He has been President of Congress, and three years a Member of that Body. Mr. Gorham is about 46 years of age. . .

From Connecticut.

Mr. [Roger] Sherman . . . is an able politician, and extremely artful in accomplishing any particular object; —it is remarked that he seldom fails. I am told he sits on the Bench in Connecticut, and is very correct in the discharge of his Judicial functions. In the early part of his life he was a Shoe-maker; —but . . . turned Almanack maker, and so progressed upwards to a Judge. He has been several years a Member of Congress. . . . He is about 60.

From New York.

. . . [Colonel Alexander] Hamilton is deservedly celebrated for his talents. He is a practitioner of the Law, and reputed to be a finished Scholar. . . . He is about 33 years old . . .

From Pennsylvania.

. . . Dr. [Benjamin] Franklin is well known to be the greatest [philosopher] of the present age. . . It is certain that he does not shine much in public Council—he is no Speaker, nor does he seem to let politics engage his attention. He is, however, a most extraordinary Man, and tells a story in a style more engaging than anything I ever heard. . . . He is 82 years old, and possesses an activity of mind equal to a youth of 25 years of age. . . .

I. Making a Constitution: Values and Government

Charles C. Tansill, **Documents Illustrative of the Formation of the Union of the American States** (Washington, D.C.: United States Government Printing Office, 1929), pp. 96–98, 100–101, 105–107.

"Congress" refers here to the Congress established by the Articles of Confederation.

Mr. [James] Wilson ranks among the foremost in legal and political knowledge. . . . He is well acquainted with Man, and understands all . . . that influences him. Government seems to have been his peculiar Study, all the political institutions of the World he knows in detail . . . He is about 45 years old.

From Virginia.

Mr. [James] Madison is a character who has long been in public life; and what is very remarkable, every Person seems to acknowledge his greatness. He blends together the profound politician, with the Scholar. . . . [Affairs] of the United States, he perhaps, has the most correct knowledge of, of any Man in the Union. He has been twice a Member of Congress, and was always thought one of the ablest Members that ever sat in that Council. Mr. Madison is about 37 years of age, a Gentleman of great modesty . . .

From South Carolina.

Mr. [Charles] Cotesworth Pinckney is a Gentleman of Family and fortune in his own State. He has received the advantage of a liberal education, and possesses a very extensive degree of legal knowledge. . . . Mr. Pinckney was an Officer of high rank in the American Army, and served with great reputation through the War. He is now about 40 years of age.

1. How would you describe the delegates to the Constitutional Convention? For example, were they qualified to write a Constitution? What experiences had they had with government? What was the economic class or standing of the delegates?

2. How could the characteristics and experiences of the delegates affect their writing of the Constitution?

2. "To Form a More Perfect Union": A Play

The following skit is based on the records of the Constitutional Convention. In it you will encounter the main arguments made by key members of the Convention. Whenever an argument is presented for the first time, a marginal note refers you to a major weakness of the Articles of Confederation. The numbers in the notes correspond to the numbers used to list the weaknesses of the Articles of Confederation in the Introduction. (See p. 194.)

POINTS TO CONSIDER

What the delegates saw as their major responsibility.

The points on which the delegates agreed or disagreed.

What values the delegates revealed.

Scene: The Constitutional Convention of 1787

Time: May 25–September 17, 1787

Place: Independence Hall, Philadelphia

Characters: George Washington, President of the Convention; Edmund Randolph, Delegate from Virginia; William Paterson, Delegate from New Jersey; Charles C. Pinckney, Delegate from South Carolina; Alexander Hamilton, Delegate from New York; and Dr. William Samuel Johnson, Delegate from Connecticut.

Washington: On this day of May 25, 1787, Friday, a quorum being present, I call this convention to order. Each of you realizes why we are here. Briefly, our purpose is to revise and strengthen the Articles of Confederation and thereby form a more perfect union of our states. If we do not succeed in achieving that goal, I fear for the unity of our new born nation. Let us refer to the first order of business. As President of this meeting I will now recognize those who wish to debate the first order of business—that of the nature of the legislative branch of the national government.

Randolph: Mr. President.

Washington: The Chair recognizes Mr. Edmund Randolph, Governor of Virginia.

Randolph: Mr. President, the Virginia delegation, under the capable leadership of Mr. James Madison, has come to the conclusion that the Articles of Confederation, with only the minor revisions contemplated by many of the delegates present here today, would still be unsuitable. Therefore, we advocate a complete overhauling of the Articles, and if necessary to meet the needs of the country, even the adoption of a new form of government.

Washington: What you say is interesting, but somewhat radical. We are here to revise the Articles; not to adopt a new document. Nevertheless, please explain your proposal.

Randolph: Thank you. As representatives of the largest state of this Confederation, we of the Virginia delegation think that a Congress should be composed of two houses. Representation in the lower house would be based on population, and representatives would be popularly elected. A second house of Congress, a Senate, would consist of delegates who had been nominated by the state legislatures and then elected by the lower house of Congress. The number of representatives for each state would be based on money contributions or, more importantly, on the free population of the state.

Paterson: Mr. President.

Copyright 1967 by Allan O. Kownslar. Based on a) Charles C. Tansill, **Documents Illustrative of the Formation of the Union of the American States** (Washington, D.C.: United States Government Printing Office, 1927), especially the notes made by James Madison; and on b) John H. Ferguson and Dean E. McHenry, **The American Federal Government** (Third edition; New York: McGraw-Hill, Inc., 1953), pp. 45–48.

A "quorum" is the number of members that must be present in order to conduct business.

1. State legislatures controlled Congress; Congress consisted of only one house; delegates were chosen annually by the state legislatures; each state had one vote.

Washington: The Chair recognizes Mr. William Paterson of New Jersey.

Paterson: Mr. President, I hesitate to interrupt or disagree with Mr. Randolph and his large-state plan; but we of the small states would be at a distinct disadvantage if the Virginia plan were adopted. For example, if the plan were accepted, Virginia would have about sixteen representatives in Congress; while New Jersey, or Delaware, or Rhode Island, would have only two or three. Thus, Virginia could out-vote all of the smaller states combined. We advocate the adoption of a plan in which Congress would consist of only one house. Delegates would be chosen by the state legislatures, and each state would have only one vote. Nor should this one house be allowed to become too powerful. It must not have the power to collect taxes. The states should do that. Congress should be allowed to act only when a state does not collect the taxes due to the national government. Therefore, we argue that we will not enter into a union which would impair the identity and equality of the smaller states.

Pinckney: Mr. President.

Washington: The Chair recognizes Mr. Charles C. Pinckney of South Carolina.

Pinckney: Mr. President, I cannot agree with Mr. Paterson in his advocacy of a one-house legislature. What we need is a two-house body. A larger house, the House of Delegates, would be elected by the people. The number of delegates from each state would be based on the population of each state. Members of the smaller house, the Senate, would be elected by the House of Delegates. Each delegate and senator would have one vote. In this way the smaller and larger states would achieve a satisfactory representation in Congress.

Johnson: Mr. President.

Washington: The Chair recognizes Dr. William Samuel Johnson, Delegate from Connecticut.

Johnson: Thank you, Mr. President. This controversy will be endless so long as gentlemen differ on the grounds of their arguments. Those on one side consider the states as districts of people composing one political society. Those on the other consider them as so many separate and distinct political societies. In some respects the states are to be considered in their political capacity, and in others as districts of individual citizens. The two ideas, instead of being opposed to each other, ought to be combined—

200

in one branch of Congress the people ought to be represented, and in the other, the states. Thank you for your patience.

Pinckney: Dr. Johnson, you have aptly summarized my basic argument. I thank you. However, I still wish to argue another point which is very dear to the interests of the six slave-holding states. If we accept the two-house plan, should slaves be counted when determining the number of representatives each state should have? And, should slaves be counted when setting state quotas for direct taxes? The southern states favor the counting of slaves when deciding representation. The delegates from the northern commercial and industrial states do not. Yet the northerners want slaves counted when it comes to allocating [distributing] quotas for direct taxes. I realize that there is a basic conflict of interest over these issues. We of the South suggest, then, that perhaps slaves could be counted as three-fifths of a person both in determining representation in Congress and in apportioning taxes. Thank you, Mr. President.

Hamilton: Mr. President, may I say a few words?

Washington: The Chair recognizes Mr. Alexander Hamilton of New York.

Hamilton: Mr. President and Delegates. I realize that many people, and indeed, some of you present here today, regard me as a supporter of the aristocracy or upper class. That does not bother me as much at the present time as does the fate of our newly won independence. I think we should have a two-house legislature. One house should be an assembly elected by the people on the basis of population. Each representative should serve for a term of three years. A second house should be called the Senate. Senators should be elected for life terms by electors chosen by the people. The Senate should be able to declare war, for example, and to approve treaties and appointments. Congress should be very strong and stable. Thus, it should have the power to pass all laws deemed necessary for the common defense and the general welfare of this union. I urge you to consider these proposals seriously. The fate of our country hinges on them. Thank you.

Washington: Are there any more comments to be made on the role of the legislative branch of the national government?

Randolph: Mr. President.

Washington: The Chair recognizes Mr. Randolph.

Randolph: Mr. President, if I may, at this point I would like to open debate on the role of the executive branch of government.

1. State legislatures controlled Congress; Congress consisted of only one house; delegates were chosen annually by the state legislatures; each state had one vote.

6. Approval of nine states was necessary for Congress to carry out many functions.

Washington: The Chair has no objections. Proceed, Mr. Randolph.

Randolph: Thank you. We have seen, during the last war, the excesses a monarch could commit. Therefore, I urge the adoption of a plan in which a single executive is chosen by Congress for one term only. To have an executive serve longer would only invite a dictatorship or establishment of another monarch. The chief executive, or President, should be given the power to execute the laws. A weak executive would be a repetition of government under the Articles.

Paterson: Mr. President.

Washington: The Chair recognizes Mr. Paterson.

Paterson: I can agree with Mr. Randolph on restricting the executive term, but there is too much danger in having just one executive. We need a plural executive so that no one man can obtain too much power. I also think a plural executive branch should have appointive powers and be given the right to direct military operations. We do not want the armed forces ever to be in a position to run the affairs of the country. Our country is based on the right of civilians to govern themselves.

Pinckney: Mr. President.

Washington: The Chair recognizes Mr. Pinckney.

Pinckney: I might add that the executive should be chosen annually by Congress. This would eliminate the possibility that any one man or group of men would remain in office too long. It would also prevent the executive from establishing himself as a monarch.

Hamilton: Mr. President.

Washington: The Chair recognizes Mr. Hamilton.

Hamilton: We desperately need a strong President. He should be allowed to veto laws of Congress when deemed necessary, to fully execute all laws, to declare war, to make treaties and appointments, and to grant pardons. For the President to perform these duties, he should be elected not for one year, or four, or even ten, but for life—and elected by electors chosen by the people of each state. That is all I wanted to add.

Randolph: Since we have been considering the legislative and executive branches of government, I suggest we now examine the role to be assumed by the judicial branch.

Washington: If there are no objections, and I see none, then you may proceed, Mr. Randolph.

Randolph: Thank you. If we are to have strong executive and legislative branches of the government, then the judiciary must be so, too. Any government, to be strong, must also be balanced, whereby each branch acts as a check upon the others. I therefore urge the convention to establish a Supreme Court and inferior courts. The judges of each should be appointed by Congress for life. If judges are not appointed for life then they can hardly be independent. A judge appointed for a short term would often be tempted to favor that group which had the power to reappoint him.

Hamilton: Mr. President, may I interrupt again?

Washington: Yes, Mr. Hamilton.

Hamilton: Almost all of us agree on the validity of appointing judges for life. We also think that we desperately need a court system which will protect *life, liberty,* and *property.* But, the question is, a judiciary appointed by whom? Mr. Randolph wants Congress to appoint judges as he favors a strong legislative branch. I, however, disagree. I think the President should appoint judges to the Supreme Court. But his appointments should be approved by the Senate. This also provides a balance of power in the national government. Moreover, as our expanding society grows more complex, we will need additional inferior courts. Thus, I suggest that Congress institute lower courts in each state.

Randolph: It seems we differ mainly on who should appoint the judiciary, Mr. Hamilton. That can be settled later. I would like to open discussion on a final point—that of federal-state relations in general.

Washington: Proceed, Mr. Randolph.

Randolph: Thank you. As it is now apparent that we shall inevitably adopt a new system of government, I believe that the new federal government should be granted the power to admit new states as well as to guarantee them a republican form of government. Moreover, the federal government should be able to outlaw any state act which is incompatible with the Union. In addition, the federal government should be empowered to use force against any state which fails to fulfill its duty. Only in this way can we avoid having another government like the one we have had under the Articles of Confederation.

Pinckney: Mr. President.

Washington: The Chair recognizes Mr. Pinckney.

Pinckney: I want to propose that states be prohibited from keeping troops of war, entering into compacts, establishing their own

3. No national court system.

3. No national court system.

7. Congress could not force obedience to its laws or to the Articles.

7. States assumed powers assigned to Congress.

coinage, and having their own post offices. These powers should be left to the national government so as to achieve uniformity. I would also suggest that all state laws first be approved by the federal legislature before becoming effective. This would eliminate conflicting state laws such as Mr. Randolph mentioned, or any which conflicted with the laws of the national government.

Hamilton: Mr. President.

Washington: Yes, Mr. Hamilton.

7. Congress could not force obedience to its laws or to the Articles.

Hamilton: I agree that no state law which stands in contradiction to those of the federal government should be allowed to remain in force. I suggest that when such a situation does arise, a special court should hear the controversy. I also propose that all the governors of the states be appointed by the federal government. The governors would have the right to veto state legislation. These proposals would permit the development of a stronger federal government which would provide more stability for our growing industries and commerce. Thank you.

5. Congress could not regulate trade.

Washington: In this assembled convention we have heard many arguments on numerous plans of government. Since we have certainly departed from our original purpose of simply amending the Articles, and if I may be allowed some liberty to speak, there are some other points I would like to present at this time.

I have taken note of the following points during my observations of the proceedings. Particularly, there are the problems related to commerce and slave-trading. If they are not solved, there will ultimately be serious conflicts of interest. The delegates from New England and the Middle States are interested in manufacturing, trade, and shipping. They want the central government to have adequate powers to protect and regulate interstate and foreign commerce. The delegates from the South fear that such power in the hands of the central government will lead to prohibitions against importing slaves. The southerners also fear that a government with such powers will enact laws and treaties favoring the manufacturing interests of the North. If our Union is to remain stable, these problems must be solved with good will, by peaceful compromise, and in the name of national unity. We must bear this in mind at all times if we are to survive. And not only to survive, but to thrive. That being said, this session is now adjourned so that the appointed committees may perform their appropriate duties.

5. Congress could not regulate trade.

1. What did the delegates to the Constitutional Convention see as their major responsibility? Why?

2. Did the delegates agree at all about the form the new government should take? If so, on which points?

3. On which points did the delegates disagree, when they discussed the new government? How can you explain the different positions they took?

4. A value, you will recall, is an idea that a person or society holds about what is important. What values did the delegates to the Convention reveal? What values lay behind their agreements and disagreements about the shape of the proposed government? Do these values reflect their major purpose or other aims?

5. Did all the delegates express the same values? Explain.

6. Can you explain any of the delegates' views by using information from Unit I?

7. Judging from what you learned about colonial Americans in Units I and II, would you have expected them to be more or less unified than they appear in this debate?

3. The Constitution of the United States of America

The following reading consists of the Preamble and Articles I, II, III, IV, and VI of the Constitution. Article V, which contains provisions for amending the Constitution, and Article VII, which covers ratification procedure, appear in Sections II and III of this unit. The version of the Constitution presented here is the one that emerged from the Constitutional Convention. Later changes have not been incorporated. Marginal notes again refer to the weaknesses of the Articles of Confederation as listed in the Introduction. Titles, such as the "The Legislature" and "The Executive," have been added at the beginning of each article.

The following are definitions of some legal terms which you will find in the Constitution.

Letters of marque and reprisal are special licenses to raid enemy ships given by a government to private individuals.

A *writ of habeas corpus* is an order demanding that a prisoner be brought before a court at a certain time and place. This is to protect a person from arrest and imprisonment when there is not sufficient evidence to try him.

A *bill of attainder* is a special act of a legislature to punish a person who has not been tried by a court.

An *ex post facto law* is a law passed after an act has been committed. It punishes a person for violating the law even though at the time the act was committed there was no rule against it.

POINTS TO CONSIDER

What topics are covered in each article. In Article I, for example, which deals with the legislature, the topics include the method of election for members of Congress and limitations on the powers of Congress.

What weaknesses of the Articles of Confederation each article attempts to eliminate. Whether the weaknesses *will* be eliminated by these provisions.

What common values, if any, the delegates to the Constitutional Convention seemed to have. Whether any of the provisions in the Constitution reflect these values, and if so, how.

Whether any provisions in the Constitution appear to be *compromises*. A compromise is a settlement by which each of two or more opposing sides gives up some demands. The different sides do not necessarily sacrifice their basic principles or beliefs.

Preamble.   We the people of the United States, in Order to form a more perfect Union, establish Justice, insure domestic Tranquility [peacefulness], provide for the common defence, promote the general Welfare, and secure the Blessings of Liberty to ourselves and our Posterity, do ordain and establish this CONSTITUTION for the United States of America.

Article I The Legislature

Section 1.   All legislative Powers herein granted shall be vested in a Congress of the United States, which shall consist of a Senate and House of Representatives.

1. Congress consisted of only one house.

Section 2.   The House of Representatives shall be composed of Members chosen every second Year by the People of the several States, and the Electors in each State shall have the Qualifications requisite [necessary] for Electors of the most numerous Branch of the State Legislature.

1. Delegates were chosen annually by the state legislatures.

No Person shall be a Representative who shall not have attained to the Age of twenty-five Years, and been seven Years a Citizen of the United States, and who shall not, when elected, be an Inhabitant of that State in which he shall be chosen.

Representatives and direct Taxes shall be apportioned among the several States which may be included within this Union, according to their respective Numbers, which shall be determined by adding to the whole Number of free Persons, including those bound to Service for a Term of Years, and excluding Indians not taxed, three fifths of all other Persons. The actual Enumeration shall be made within three Years after the first Meeting of the Congress of the United States, and within every subsequent Term of ten Years, in such Manner as they shall by Law direct. The Number of Representatives shall not exceed one for every thirty Thousand, but each State shall have at Least one Representative; and until such enumeration shall be made, the State of New Hampshire shall be entitled to chuse [choose] three, Massachusetts eight, Rhode-Island and Providence Plantations one, Connecticut five, New-York six, New Jersey four, Pennsylvania eight, Delaware one, Maryland six, Virginia ten, North Carolina five, South Carolina five, and Georgia three.

When vacancies happen in the Representation from any State, the Executive Authority thereof shall issue Writs of Election to fill such Vacancies.

The House of Representatives shall chuse their Speaker and other Officers; and shall have the sole Power of Impeachment.

Section 3. The Senate of the United States shall be composed of two Senators from each State, chosen by the Legislature thereof, for six Years; and each Senator shall have one Vote.

1. Delegates were chosen annually by the state legislature.

Immediately after they shall be assembled in Consequence of the first Election, they shall be divided as equally as may be into three Classes. The Seats of the Senators of the first Class shall be vacated at the Expiration of the second Year, of the second Class at the Expiration of the fourth Year, and of the third Class at the Expiration of the sixth Year, so that one third may be chosen every second Year; and if Vacancies happen by Resignation, or otherwise, during the Recess of the Legislature of any State, the Executive thereof may make temporary Appointments until the next Meeting of the Legislature, which shall then fill such Vacancies.

No Person shall be a Senator who shall not have attained to the Age of thirty Years, and been nine Years a Citizen of the United States, and who shall not, when elected, be an Inhabitant of that State for which he shall be chosen.

The Vice President of the United States shall be President of the Senate, but shall have no Vote, unless they be equally divided.

The Senate shall chuse their other Officers, and also a President pro tempore, in the Absence of the Vice President, or when he shall exercise the Office of President of the United States.

A "pro tempore" officer is one who serves temporarily, as a substitute for another.

The Senate shall have the sole Power to try all Impeachments. When sitting for that Purpose, they shall be on Oath or Affirmation. When the President of the United States is tried, the Chief Justice shall preside: And no Person shall be convicted without the Concurrence [agreement] of two thirds of the Members present.

Judgment in Cases of Impeachment shall not extend further than to removal from Office, and disqualification to hold and enjoy any Office of honor, Trust or Profit under the United States: but the Party convicted shall nevertheless be liable and subject to Indictment, Trial, Judgment and Punishment, according to Law.

Section 4. The Times, Places and Manner of holding Elections for Senators and Representatives, shall be prescribed in each State by the Legislature thereof; but the Congress may at any time by Law make or alter such Regulations, except as to the Places of chusing Senators.

The Congress shall assemble at least once in every Year, and such Meeting shall be on the first Monday in December, unless they shall by Law appoint a different Day.

Section 5. Each House shall be the Judge of the Elections, Returns and Qualifications of its own Members, and a Majority of each shall constitute a Quorum to do Business; but a smaller Number may adjourn from day to day, and may be authorized to compel the Attendance of absent Members, in such Manner, and under such Penalties as each House may provide.

Each House may determine the Rules of its Proceedings, punish its Members for disorderly Behavior, and, with the Concurrence of two thirds, expel a Member.

Each House shall keep a Journal of its Proceedings, and from time to time publish the same, excepting such Parts as may in their Judgment require Secrecy; and the Yeas and Nays of the Members of either House on any question shall, at the Desire of one fifth of those present, be entered on the Journal.

Neither House, during the Session of Congress, shall, without the Consent of the other, adjourn for more than three days, nor to any other Place than that in which the two Houses shall be sitting.

Section 6. The Senators and Representatives shall receive a Compensation for their Services, to be ascertained [determined] by Law, and paid out of the Treasury of the United States. They shall in all Cases, except Treason, Felony and Breach of the Peace, be privileged from Arrest during their Attendance at the Session of their respective Houses, and in going to and returning from the same; and for any Speech or Debate in either House, they shall not be questioned in any other place.

1. Delegates were paid by the state legislature.

No Senator or Representative shall, during the time for which he was elected, be appointed to any civil Office under the authority of the United States, which shall have been created, or the Emoluments [salary] whereof shall have been encreased during such time; and no Person holding any Office under the United States, shall be a Member of either House during his Continuance in Office.

Section 7. All Bills for raising Revenue shall originate in the House of Representatives; but the Senate may propose or concur with Amendments as on other Bills.

Every Bill which shall have passed the House of Representatives and the Senate, shall, before it become a Law, be presented to the President of the United States; if he approve he shall sign it, but if not he shall return it, with his Objections to that House in which it shall have originated, who shall enter the Objections at large on their Journal, and proceed to reconsider it. If after such Reconsideration two thirds of that House shall agree to pass the Bill, it shall be sent, together with the Objections, to the other House, by which it shall likewise be reconsidered, and if approved by two thirds of that House, it shall become a Law. But in all such Cases the Votes of both Houses shall be determined by Yeas and Nays, and the Names of the Persons voting for and against the Bill shall be entered on the Journal of each House respectively. If any Bill shall not be returned by the President within ten Days (Sundays excepted) after it shall have been presented to him, the Same shall be a Law, in like Manner as if he had signed it, unless the Congress by their Adjournment prevent its Return, in which Case it shall not be a Law.

2. No independent executive.

Every Order, Resolution, or Vote to which the Concurrence of the Senate and House of Representatives may be necessary (except on a question of Adjournment) shall be presented to the President of the United States; and before the Same shall take Effect, shall be approved by him, or being disapproved by him, shall be repassed by two thirds of the Senate and House of Representatives, according to the Rules and Limitations prescribed in the Case of a bill.

2. No independent executive.

Section 8. The Congress shall have Power

To lay and collect Taxes, Duties, Imposts and Excises to pay the Debts and provide for the common Defence and general Welfare of the United States; but all Duties, Imposts and excises shall be uniform throughout the United States;

4. Congress had no power to lay or collect taxes.

5. Congress could not regulate trade.

To borrow Money on the Credit of the United States;

To regulate Commerce with foreign Nations, and among the several States, and with the Indian Tribes;

To establish an uniform Rule of Naturalization, and uniform Laws on the subject of Bankruptcies throughout the United States;

To coin Money, regulate the Value thereof, and of foreign Coin, and fix the Standard of Weights and Measures;

To provide for the Punishment of counterfeiting the Securities and current Coin of the United States;

To establish Post Offices and post Roads;

To promote the Progress of Science and useful Arts, by securing for limited Times to Authors and Inventors the exclusive Right to their respective Writings and Discoveries;

To constitute Tribunals inferior to the supreme Court;

To define and Punish Piracies and Felonies committed on the high Seas, and Offences against the Law of Nations;

To declare War, grant Letters of Marque and Reprisal, and make Rules concerning Captures on Land and Water;

To raise and support Armies, but no Appropriation of Money to that Use shall be for a longer Term than two Years;

To provide and maintain a Navy;

To make Rules for the Government and Regulation of the land and naval Forces;

7. Congress could not force obedience to its laws or to the Articles.

To provide for calling forth the Militia to execute the Laws of the Union, suppress Insurrections and repel Invasions;

To provide for organizing, arming, and disciplining, the Militia, and for governing such Part of them as may be employed in the Service of the United States, reserving to the States respectively, the Appointment of the Officers, and the Authority of training the Militia according to the discipline prescribed by Congress;

To exercise exclusive Legislation in all Cases whatsoever, over such District (not exceeding ten Miles square) as may, by Cession [grant] of particular States, and the Acceptance of Congress, become the Seat of the Government of the United States, and to exercise like Authority over all Places purchased by the Consent of the Legislature of the State in which the Same shall be, for the Erection of Forts, Magazines, Arsenals, dock-Yards, and other needful Buildings;—And

To make all Laws which shall be necessary and proper for carrying into Execution the foregoing Powers, and all other Powers vested by this Constitution in the Government of the United States, or in any Department or Officer thereof.

6. Approval of nine states necessary for Congress to carry out many functions.

Section 9. The Migration or Importation of such Persons as any of the States now existing shall think proper to admit, shall not be prohibited by the Congress prior to the Year one thousand eight hundred and eight, but a Tax or Duty may be imposed on such Importation, not exceeding ten dollars for each Person.

The Privilege of the Writ of Habeas Corpus shall not be suspended, unless when in Cases of Rebellion or Invasion the public Safety may require it.

No Bill of Attainder or ex post facto Law shall be passed.

No Capitation, or other direct, Tax shall be laid, unless in Proportion to the Census or Enumeration herein before directed to be taken.

"Capitation" is a direct tax placed upon each person, like a poll tax.

No Tax or Duty shall be laid on Articles exported from any State.

5. Congress could not regulate trade.

No Preference shall be given by any Regulation of Commerce or Revenue to the Ports of one State over those of another: nor shall Vessels bound to, or from, one State, be obliged to enter, clear, or pay Duties in another.

No Money shall be drawn from the Treasury, but in Consequence of Appropriations made by Law; and a regular Statement and Account of the Receipts and Expenditures of all public Money shall be published from time to time.

No Title of Nobility shall be granted by the United States: And no Person holding any Office of Profit or Trust under them, shall, without the Consent of the Congress, accept of any present, Emolument, Office, or Title of any kind whatever, from any King, Prince, or foreign State.

Section 10. No State shall enter into any Treaty, Alliance, or Confederation; grant Letters of Marque and Reprisal; coin Money; emit [issue] Bills of Credit; make any Thing but gold and silver Coin a Tender in [the means for] Payment of Debts; pass any Bill of Attainder, ex post facto Law, or Law impairing the Obligation of Contracts, or grant any Title of Nobility.

7. States assumed powers assigned to Congress.

No State shall, without the Consent of the Congress, lay any Imposts or Duties on Imports or Exports, except what may be absolutely necessary for executing its inspection Laws: and the net Produce of all Duties and Imposts, laid by any State on Imports

5. Congress could not regulate trade.

or Exports, shall be for the Use of the Treasury of the United States; and all such Laws shall be subject to the Revision and Controul [Control] of the Congress.

No State shall, without the Consent of Congress, lay any Duty of Tonnage, keep Troops, or Ships of War in time of Peace, enter into any Agreement or Compact with another State, or with a foreign Power, or engage in War, unless actually invaded, or in such imminent Danger as will not admit of Delay.

Article II The Executive

Section 1. The executive Power shall be vested in a President of the United States of America. He shall hold his Office during the Term of four Years, and, together with the Vice President, chosen for the same Term, be elected, as follows

Each State shall appoint, in such Manner as the Legislature thereof may direct, a Number of Electors, equal to the whole Number of Senators and Representatives to which the State may be entitled in the Congress: but no Senator or Representative, or Person holding an Office of Trust or Profit under the United States, shall be appointed an Elector.

The electors shall meet in their respective States, and vote by ballot for two Persons, of whom one at least shall not be an Inhabitant of the same State with themselves. And they shall make a List of all the Persons voted for, and of the Number of Votes for each; which List they shall sign and certify, and transmit sealed to the Seat of the Government of the United States, directed to the President of the Senate. The President of the Senate shall, in the Presence of the Senate and House of Representatives, open all the Certificates, and the Votes shall then be counted. The Person having the greatest Number of Votes shall be the President, if such Number be a Majority of the whole Number of Electors appointed; and if there be more than one who have such Majority and have an equal Number of Votes, then the House of Representatives shall immediately chuse by Ballot one of them for President; and if no person have a Majority, then from the five highest on the List the said House shall in like Manner chuse the President. But in chusing the President, the Votes shall be taken by States, the Representation from each State having one Vote; A quorum for this Purpose shall consist of a Member of Members from two-thirds of the States, and a Majority of all the States shall be necessary to a Choice. In every Case, after the Choice of the President, the person having the greatest Number of Votes of the Electors shall be the Vice President.

But if there should remain two or more who have equal Votes, the Senate shall chuse from them by Ballot the Vice-President.

The Congress may determine the Time of chusing the Electors, and the Day on which they shall give their Votes; which Day shall be the same throughout the United States.

No person except a natural born Citizen, or a Citizen of the United States, at the time of the Adoption of this Constitution, shall be eligible to the Office of President; neither shall any Person be eligible to that Office who shall not have attained to the Age of thirty-five Years, and been fourteen Years a Resident within the United States.

In Case of the Removal of the President from Office, or of his Death, Resignation, or Inability to discharge the Powers and Duties of the said Office, the same shall devolve on [pass to] the Vice President, and the Congress may by Law provide for the Case of Removal, Death, Resignation, or Inability, both of the President and Vice President, declaring what Officer shall then act as President, and such Officer shall act accordingly, until the Disability be removed, or a President shall be elected.

The President shall, at stated Times, receive for his Services, a Compensation, which shall neither be encreased [increased] nor diminished during the Period of [for] which he shall have been elected, and he shall not receive within that Period any other Emolument from the United States, or any of them.

Before he enter on the Execution of his Office, he shall take the following Oath or Affirmation:—"I do solemnly swear (or affirm) that I will faithfully execute the Office of President of the United States, and will to the best of my Ability, preserve, protect and defend the Constitution of the United States."

Section 2.   The President shall be Commander in Chief of the Army and Navy of the United States, and of the Militia of the several States, when called into the actual Service of the United States; he may require the Opinion, in writing, of the principal Officer in each of the executive Departments, upon any Subject relating to the Duties of their respective Offices, and he shall have Power to grant Reprieves and Pardons for Offences against the United States, except in Cases of Impeachment.

He shall have Power, by and with the Advice and Consent of the Senate, to make Treaties, provided two thirds of the Senators present concur; and he shall nominate, and by and with the Advice and Consent of the Senate, shall appoint Ambassadors, other public Ministers and Consuls, Judges of the supreme Court, and

213

all other Officers of the United States, whose Appointments are not herein otherwise provided for, and which shall be established by Law: but the Congress may by Law vest the Appointment of such inferior Officers, as they think proper, in the President alone, in the Courts of Law, or in the Heads of Departments.

The President shall have Power to fill up all Vacancies that may happen during the Recess of the Senate, by granting Commissions which shall expire at the End of their next Session.

Section 3. He shall from time to time give to the Congress Information of the State of the Union, and recommend to their Consideration such Measures as he shall judge necessary and expedient [advisable]; he may, on extraordinary Occasions, convene both Houses, or either of them, and in Case of Disagreement between them, with Respect to the Time of Adjournment, he may adjourn them to such Time as he shall think proper; he shall receive Ambassadors and other public Ministers; he shall take Care that the Laws be faithfully executed, and shall Commission all the Officers of the United States.

Section 4. The President, Vice President and all civil Officers of the United States shall be removed from Office on Impeachment for, and Conviction of, Treason, Bribery, or other high Crimes and Misdemeanors.

Article III The Judiciary

Section 1. The judicial Power of the United States, shall be vested in one supreme Court, and in such inferior Courts as the Congress may from time to time ordain and establish. The Judges, both of the supreme and inferior Courts, shall hold their Offices during Good Behavior, and shall at stated Times, receive for their Services, a Compensation, which shall not be diminished during their Continuance in Office.

Section 2. The judicial Power shall extend to all Cases, in Law and Equity, arising under this Constitution, the Laws of the United States, and Treaties made, or which shall be made, under their Authority;—to all Cases affecting Ambassadors, other public Ministers and Consuls;—to all Cases of admiralty and maritime Jurisdiction;—to Controversies to which the United States shall be a Party;—to Controversies between two or more States;—between a State and Citizens of another State;—between Citizens of different States,—between Citizens of the same State claiming Lands under Grants of different States, and between a State, or the Citizens thereof, and foreign States, Citizens or Subjects.

3. No national court system.

A court of equity has special rules. These rules are concerned with the fairness of a decision rather than with the exact meaning of the law.

214

In all Cases affecting Ambassadors, other public Ministers and Consuls, and those in which a State shall be Party, the supreme Court shall have original Jurisdiction. In all the other Cases before mentioned, the supreme Court shall have appellate Jurisdiction, both as to Law and Fact, with such Exceptions, and under such Regulations as Congress shall make.

The Trial of all Crimes, except in Cases of Impeachment, shall be by Jury; and such Trial shall be held in the State where the said Crimes shall have been committed; but when not committed within any State, the Trial shall be at such Place or Places as the Congress may by Law have directed.

Section 3. Treason against the United States, shall consist only in levying War against them, or in adhering to [supporting] their Enemies, giving them Aid and Comfort. No Person shall be convicted of Treason unless on the Testimony of two Witnesses to the same overt Act, or on Confession in open Court.

The Congress shall have Power to declare the Punishment of Treason, but no Attainder of Treason shall work Corruption of Blood, or Forfeiture except during the Life of the Person attained.

> "Appellate jurisdiction" means that a court, such as the Supreme Court, has the right to hear cases that have been tried in courts below it. Cases from lower courts are appealed to higher courts for review.

> "No attainder of treason shall work corruption of blood" means that punishment for treason will not affect a convicted person's descendants.

Article IV The States

Section 1. Full Faith and Credit shall be given in each State to the public Acts, Records, and judicial Proceedings of every other State. And the Congress may by general Laws prescribe the Manner in which such Acts, Records and Proceedings shall be proved, and the Effect thereof.

Section 2. The Citizens of each State shall be entitled to all Privileges and Immunities of Citizens in the several States.

A person charged in any State with Treason, Felony, or other Crime, who shall flee from Justice, and be found in another State, shall on Demand of the executive Authority of the State from which he fled, be delivered up to be removed to the State having Jurisdiction of the Crime.

No Person held to Service or Labour in one State, under the Laws thereof, escaping into another, shall, in Consequence of any Law or Regulation therein, be discharged from such Service or Labour, but shall be delivered up on Claim of the Party to whom such Service or Labour may be due.

Section 3. New States may be admitted by the Congress into this Union; but no new State shall be formed or erected within the Jurisdiction of any other State; nor any State be formed by the

Junction of two or more States, or Parts of States, without the Consent of the Legislatures of the States concerned as well as of the Congress.

The Congress shall have Power to dispose of and make all needful Rules and Regulations respecting the Territory or other Property belonging to the United States; and nothing in this Constitution shall be so construed as to Prejudice any Claims of the United States, or of any particular State.

Section 4.   The United States shall guarantee to every State in this Union a Republican Form of Government, and shall protect each of them against Invasion; and on Application of the Legislature, or of the Executive (when the Legislature cannot be convened) against domestic Violence.

Article VI National Supremacy

All Debts contracted and Engagements entered into, before the Adoption of this Constitution, shall be as valid against the United States under this Constitution, as under the Confederation.

7. Congress could not force obedience to its laws or the Articles.

This Constitution, and the Laws of the United States which shall be made in Pursuance thereof; and all Treaties made, or which shall be made, under the Authority of the United States, shall be the supreme Law of the Land; and the Judges in every State shall be bound thereby, any Thing in the Constitution or Laws of any State to the Contrary notwithstanding.

The Senators and Representatives before mentioned, and the Members of the several State Legislatures, and all executives and judicial Officers, both of the United States and of the several States, shall be bound by Oath or Affirmation, to support this Constitution; but no religious Test shall ever be required as a Qualification to any Office or public Trust under the United States.

APPLYING IDEAS: INSTITUTIONS, VALUES, AND COMPROMISES

Institutions and Values

An *institution* is an established law, a custom, a system, a practice, or a set of rules by which people live.

How does the Constitution, as an institution, reflect some of the *values* of the delegates? For example, how do the following phrases or values from the Preamble apply to the parts of the Constitution listed below them?

216

1. "to form a more perfect Union"

2. "establish Justice"

3. "insure domestic Tranquility"

4. "provide for the common defence"

5. "promote the general Welfare"

6. "secure the Blessings of Liberty"

a. "All legislative Powers herein granted shall be vested in a Congress of the United States..."

b. Article I, Section 8.

c. "The Privilege of the Writ of Habeas Corpus shall not be suspended, unless when in Cases of Rebellion or Invasion the public Safety may require it."

d. "No Tax or Duty shall be laid on Articles exported from any State."

e. "No State shall... coin Money; emit Bills of Credit; make any Thing but gold and silver Coin a Tender in Payment of Debts; pass any Bill of Attainer, ex post facto Law, or Law impairing the Obligation of Contracts..."

f. "The executive Power shall be vested in a President..."

g. "Before he enter on the Execution of his Office, he [the President] shall take the following Oath or Affirmation:—'I do solemnly swear (or affirm) that I will faithfully execute the Office of President of the United States, and will to the best of my Ability, preserve, protect and defend the Constitution...'"

h. "The President shall be Commander in Chief of the Army and Navy... and of the Militia of the several States, when called into the actual Service of the United States..."

i. "He [the President] shall from time to time give to the Congress Information of the State of the Union, and recommend to their Consideration such Measures as he shall judge necessary and expedient..."

j. Article III and Article IV.

k. "All Debts contracted and Engagements entered into, before the Adoption of this Constitution, shall be as valid against the United States under this Constitution, as under the [Articles of] Confederation."

l. "This Constitution... shall be the supreme Law of the Land..."

217

Compromises

Using the previous material in this unit, consider the following:

1. Is any of the following a compromise in the Constitution?

   (a) the basis of representation in Congress, (b) the power of the President, (c) the method of selecting judges, (d) the power of the states.

2. What other compromises can you suggest?

3. How much of the Constitution seems to consist of compromises between conflicting interests?

4. Assuming that the delegates to the Constitutional Convention felt strongly about their opinions, why do you think they agreed to make these compromises?

5. Should they have made such compromises? Why or why not?

6. Is compromising a good way to settle disagreements? Is it a good method only in certain cases? Explain.

II. Winning Assent: The Battle for Ratification

THE STATES VOTE

4. How the States Voted: A Chart

Article VII of the proposed Constitution stated that "The Ratification of the Conventions of nine States, shall be sufficient for the Establishment of this Constitution between the States so ratifying the Same." The following chart shows the results of ratification.

STATE	DATE OF VOTE	FOR	AGAINST
1. DELAWARE	DECEMBER 7, 1787	30	0
2. PENNSYLVANIA	DECEMBER 12, 1787	46	23
3. NEW JERSEY	DECEMBER 18, 1787	38	0
4. GEORGIA	JANUARY 2, 1788	26	0
5. CONNECTICUT	JANUARY 9, 1788	128	40
6. MASSACHUSETTS	FEBRUARY 6, 1788	187	168
7. MARYLAND	APRIL 28, 1788	63	11
8. SOUTH CAROLINA	MAY 23, 1788	149	73
9. NEW HAMPSHIRE	JUNE 21, 1788	57	47
10. VIRGINIA	JUNE 25, 1788	89	79
11. NEW YORK	JULY 26, 1788	30	27
12. NORTH CAROLINA	NOVEMBER 21, 1789	194	77
13. RHODE ISLAND	MAY 29, 1790	34	32

1. To what extent did each state favor ratification?

2. In which states was the vote on ratification the closest?

3. Does this chart give you any other ideas about ratification?

218

5. How the Votes Were Divided: A Map

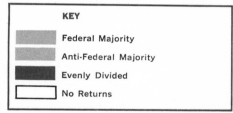

KEY

Federal Majority

Anti-Federal Majority

Evenly Divided

No Returns

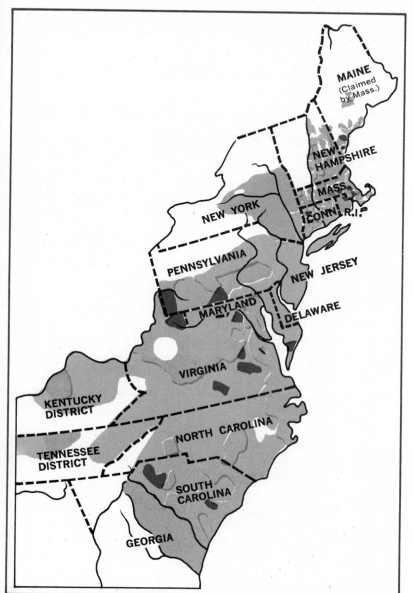

1. How does the map compare with the chart?

2. Generally, how did the coastal areas vote?

3. What other patterns of support and opposition to the Constitution do you find?

4. How might you explain these patterns?

FORMING A HYPOTHESIS

Review what was said about forming a hypothesis in the Note to the Student. What hypothesis can you form about ratification?

THE ISSUES IN MASSACHUSETTS

6. The Massachusetts Vote: A Chart and a Map

Analysis of the Massachusetts Vote on the Constitution

COUNTIES	DELEGATES FOR	DELEGATES AGAINST	PRIMARY ECONOMIC INTEREST
BARNSTABLE	7	2	MERCHANT-SHIPPING
BERKSHIRE	7	15	AGRICULTURAL
BRISTOL	10	12	AGRICULTURAL
DUKES	2	0	FISHING
ESSEX	38	6	MERCHANT-SHIPPING
HAMPSHIRE	19	33	AGRICULTURAL
MIDDLESEX	17	25	AGRICULTURAL
PLYMOUTH	21	6	MERCHANT-SHIPPING
SUFFOLK	34	5	MERCHANT
WORCESTER	7	43	AGRICULTURAL
OTHER COUNTIES*	25	21	
TOTALS	187	168	

*Includes Nantucket Island and counties in Maine.

Orin Grant Libby, "The Geographical Distribution of the Vote of the Thirteen States on the Constitution, 1787–1788," **Bulletin of the University of Wisconsin,** Vol. 1, no. 1 (1894), pp. 106–107.

According to this chart, to what extent does the vote on ratification in Massachusetts reflect a clash of economic interests?

THE VOTE IN MASSACHUSETTS COUNTIES,* 1788

KEY

- Federal Majority
- Anti-Federal Majority
- Evenly Divided
- No Returns

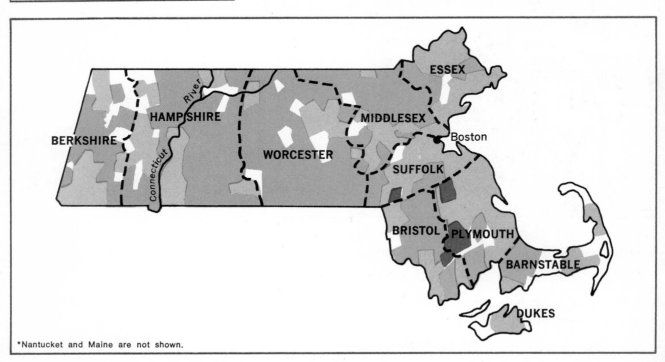

*Nantucket and Maine are not shown.

1. What does the map add to your knowledge about the ratification vote in Massachusetts?

2. Does the map suggest any explanation for the division of votes within counties?

3. Does the map strengthen or weaken your impression of an economic clash?

7. Background to the Vote: Shays' Rebellion

Daniel Shays, a Revolutionary War officer, led a rebellion against the Massachusetts government in 1786. The rebellion and its causes are described in the following selection. Richard Hofstadter, one of the authors of this account, is a well-known interpreter of American history.

POINTS TO CONSIDER
The connection between Shays' Rebellion and the vote on ratification in Massachusetts.

[Immediately after the Revolution, the established small farmer in the older sections of the country did well.] His market for cash crops remained lively, at least so long as British, French, and American forces needed his stores and supplies. . . . By 1785, however, the foreign troops had withdrawn, the American army had been disbanded, and the farmer's market shrank. War-time creditors began to press the farmers for back interest. To make matters worse, the state legislatures began to raise taxes and to demand that they be paid in specie [coin], so that the states themselves could pay the back interest on their Revolutionary debts. Stunned by this bitter reversal of fortune, the farmers and the small retailers who depended on them cried out for relief. As in colonial times, they agitated for the states to issue paper money that would serve as legal tender in the payment of all debts, public and private; and they demanded that the states enact . . . laws that would postpone the foreclosure of farms on which mortgage payments were in arrears [overdue]. . . .

An articulate rebel, Captain Shays became a spokesman for his neighbors when the western counties became increasingly agitated over their worsening economic straits [distress]. Some of these counties were too poor to afford to send delegates to the legislature in far-off Boston; and in some of the towns no men were to be found who could meet the property qualifications to sit in the General Court. In effect, the farmers, most of them veterans of the Revolution, were deprived of any voice in the state government, and the nabobs [men of great wealth] of Boston and

Richard Hofstadter, William Miller, Daniel Aaron, **The American Republic** (Englewood Cliffs, N.J.: Prentice-Hall, Inc., 1959), Vol. I, pp. 222–225. © 1959. Reprinted by permission of Prentice-Hall, Inc.

"Legal tender" is currency which by law must be accepted for payment of debts.

If a farm is "mortgaged," the farmer is paying for it in installments, or parts. He usually makes these payments to a bank or loan company. Until the farm is completely paid for, the bank or loan company owns it, and has the right to "foreclose" on the mortgage if the farmer fails to make a payment. "To foreclose" means to take over the property unless the entire remaining cost is paid immediately.

An "articulate" person is one who expresses himself clearly and effectively.

The commercial interests of the port towns backed laws that required the farmers to pay more than their share of taxes. One estimate is that, after 1780, the farmer paid a third of his income in taxes.

other port towns were quick to take advantage of this agrarian weakness. To make their protests heard, the farmers resorted to the time-honored device of county conventions. Here men from neighboring towns would gather at the county seats on a basis of personal equality and give voice to their political feelings by means of published resolutions and petitions to the legislature. [But] the legislature adjourned in July, 1786, having ignored the petitions of the disfranchised . . . [soon] more and more county conventions were called in all parts of the state.

Under the leadership of ex-officers like Shays . . . the members [of the conventions] were warned to "abstain from all mobs and unlawful assemblies until a constitutional method of redress can be obtained." But popular discontent soon overrode these cautions and hotheads took advantage of the seething situation to organize riotous mobs. Their targets were civil courts where foreclosure proceedings by the hundreds were scheduled; having succeeded in forcing the suspension of many of these courts, they also attacked the criminal courts to prevent the trial of rioters. Finally, when federal arsenals were menaced, the government no longer could postpone action. . . . [Moderate] leaders were forced to put themselves at the head of the mobs if only to restrain them from greater violence. Somehow Shays [rose] to the leadership of the whole movement. . . . Fighting between Shays' forces and Lincoln's continued from mid-January to the end of February, 1787, when the Rebellion finally was crushed and Shays fled to Vermont. . . .

General Benjamin Lincoln led the militia which was sent to put down Shays' Rebellion.

1. Who participated in Shays' Rebellion?

2. What basic grievances did they wish to remedy?

3. Why did they resort to armed rebellion?

4. How does the situation described above compare with the vote on ratification in Massachusetts?

5. Does this situation *explain* the vote in Massachusetts?

8. Some Opponents of the Constitution

The following arguments are typical of the objections to the Constitution in Massachusetts. The arguments were made by delegates to the convention which was called to vote on ratification.

AMOS SINGLETARY, WORCESTER COUNTY

. . . We contended with Great Britain, some said, for a three-penny duty on tea; but it was not that—it was because they claimed a

Debates and Proceedings in the Convention of the Commonwealth of Massachusetts, Held in the Year 1788 (Boston: William White, Printer to the Commonwealth, 1856), pp. 202–203.

right to tax us and bind us in all cases whatever. And does not this Constitution do the same? Does it not take away all we have, all our property? Does it not lay *all* taxes, duties, imposts and excises? And what more have we to give? They tell us Congress [will be able to] collect all the money they want by impost. I say there has always been a difficulty about impost. Whenever the general court [state legislature] was agoing to lay an impost, they would tell us it was more than trade could bear, that it hurt the fair trader, and encouraged smuggling; and there will always be the same objection—they won't be able to raise money enough by impost, and then they will lay it on the land, and take all we have got. These lawyers, and men of learning, and moneyed men, that talk so finely, and gloss over matters so smoothly, to make us, poor illiterate people, swallow down the pill, expect to get into Congress themselves; they expect to be the managers of this Constitution, and get all the power and all the money into their own hands, and then they will swallow up all us little folks, like the great leviathan [sea monster], Mr. President; yes, just as the whale swallowed up Jonah. This is what I am afraid of . . .

"Impost" here refers to a tax on imports. An "excise" tax is a tax on goods produced and used within a country, such as a tax on liquor.

1. What group do you think Singletary represents? Why?

2. What does Singletary appear to fear most?

3. Did the events of the post-war years in Massachusetts provide any basis for Singletary's fears? Explain.

GENERAL THOMPSON, LINCOLN COUNTY

—Sir, the question is, whether congress shall have power. . . . This section ["provide for the common defense, promote the general welfare"] I look upon . . . [as] big with mischiefs. Congress will have power to keep standing armies. The great Mr. Pitt says, standing armies are dangerous—keep your militia in order. . . . We are able to stand our own ground against a foreign power—they cannot starve us out, they cannot bring their ships on the land; we are a nation of healthy and strong men—our land is fertile, and we are increasing in numbers. . . . Let us amend the old confederation. Why not give congress power only to regulate trade? Some say, that those we owe will fall upon us; but . . . the balance of power in the old countries will not permit it—the other nations will protect us. . . . [Where] is the bill of rights which shall check the power of this congress, which shall say, *thus far shall ye come, and no farther*. The safety of the people depends on a bill of rights. . . . There are some parts of this constitution which I cannot digest; and, sir, shall we swallow a large bone for the sake of a little meat? Some say swallow the whole now, and pick out the

The Debates, Resolutions, and Other Proceedings in Convention, on the Adoption of the Federal Constitution, edited by Jonathan Elliot (Washington, D.C.:Jonathan Elliot, 1827), Vol. I, pp. 93–94.

Lincoln County, located in southern Maine, is not shown on the map of Massachusetts counties. Some of the economic interests of Maine at this time were lumbering, fishing, and shipbuilding.

Massachusetts adopted a Bill of Rights in 1780. It prevented the state government from restricting or interfering with individual liberties, such as freedom of the press and religion.

bone afterwards. But I say, let us pick off the meat, and throw the bone away.

1. Does Thompson seem to represent a particular group?

2. What is Thompson's basic objection to the Constitution?

3. What do you think Thompson means when he says, "The safety of the people depends on a bill of rights"? Can you think of situations that could illustrate his point?

4. As voiced in these speeches, what were the major objections to the Constitution in Massachusetts?

5. What connection do you now see between the vote on ratification and Shays' Rebellion?

9. Some Supporters of the Constitution

The delegates to the Massachusetts convention heard many speeches like those of Singletary and Thompson. They also listened to speeches like the ones that follow, which are typical of the "pro" side of the Massachusetts debate.

James Bowdoin was the governor responsible for crushing Shays' Rebellion. Thomas Dawes, Jr., another champion of the Constitution, was a resident of Boston, which was part of Suffolk County.

Debates and Proceedings in the Convention of the Commonwealth of Massachusetts, Held in the Year 1788 (Boston: William White, Printer to the Commonwealth, 1856), pp. 156–159.

THOMAS DAWES, JR., SUFFOLK COUNTY

... In the States southward of the Delaware, it is agreed, that three-fourths of the produce are exported, and three-fourths of the returns are made, in British bottoms [ships]. . . . [The profit from this trade] is money which belongs to the New England States, because we can furnish the ships as well as, and much better than, the British. . . . We are independent of each other, but we are slaves to Europe. . . . Congress has no authority to withhold advantages from foreigners, in order to obtain advantages from them. . . .

Our manufactures are another great subject, which has received no encouragement . . . and . . . never can by any authority in the Confederation. . . . Has Congress been able, by national laws, to prevent the importation of such foreign commodities as are made from such raw materials as we ourselves raise? . . . If we wish to encourage our own manufactures—to preserve our own commerce—to raise the value of our own lands—we must give Congress the powers in question.

1. What are Dawes' two arguments for the Constitution?

2. What do these arguments have in common?

224

JAMES BOWDOIN, GOVERNOR OF MASSACHUSETTS

... [If] we attend to our trade, as it is at present, we shall find, that the miserable state of it is owing to a ... want of power in Congress. Other nations prohibit our vessels from entering their ports, or lay heavy duties on our exports carried thither; and we have no retaliating or regulating power over their vessels and exports to prevent it. Hence, a decrease of our commerce and navigation, and the duties and revenue arising from them. Hence, an insufficient demand for the produce of our lands, and the consequent discouragement of agriculture. Hence, the inability to pay debts, and particularly taxes, which by that decrease are enhanced [increased]. And hence, as the necessary result of all these, the emigration of our inhabitants. If it be asked, how are these evils, and others that might be mentioned, to be remedied? The answer is short, by giving congress adequate and proper power. ...

The Debates, Resolutions, and Other Proceedings in Convention, on the Adoption of the Federal Constitution, edited by Jonathan Elliot (Washington, D.C.: Jonathan Elliot, 1827), Vol. I, p. 96.

Bowdoin referred to one of the same facts that Singletary mentioned: the increase in taxes in Massachusetts. Both men felt that such high taxes were harmful. Why did Singletary think the Constitution would aggravate the problem while Bowdoin thought the Constitution would solve it?

JONATHAN SMITH, BERKSHIRE COUNTY

... I am a plain man and get my living by the plough. I am not used to speak in public, but I beg your leave to say a few words to my brother plough-joggers in this house. ...

Debates and Proceedings in the Convention of the Commonwealth of Massachusetts, Held in the Year 1788, pp. 203–205.

We are by this Constitution allowed to send ten members to Congress. Have we not more than that number fit to go? I dare say, if we pick out ten, we shall have another ten left, and I hope ten times ten—and will not these be a check upon those that go? Will they go to Congress and abuse their power, and do mischief, when they know that they must return and look the other ten in the face, and be called to account for their conduct? Some gentlemen think that our liberty and property are not safe in the hands of moneyed men, and men of learning. I am not of that mind.

Brother farmers, let us suppose a case now: Suppose you had a farm of fifty acres, and your title was disputed, and there was a farm of five thousand acres joined to you, that belonged to a man of learning, and his title was involved in the same difficulty; would not you be glad to have him for your friend, rather than to stand alone in the dispute? Well, the case is the same; these lawyers, these moneyed men, these men of learning, are all embarked in the same cause with us, and we must all swim or sink together; and shall we throw the Constitution overboard because

it does not please us alike? Suppose two or three of you had been at the pains to break up a piece of rough land, and sow it with wheat; would you let it lie waste, because you could not agree what sort of a fence to make? Would it not be better to put up a fence that did not please every one's fancy, rather than not fence it at all, or keep disputing about it, until the wild beasts came in and devoured it. Some gentlemen say—don't be in a hurry, take time to consider, and don't take a leap in the dark. I say—take things in time, gather fruit when it is ripe. There is a time to sow, and a time to reap. We sowed our seed when we sent men to the Federal Convention; now is the harvest, now is the time to reap the fruit of our labor, and if we don't do it now, I am afraid we never shall have another opportunity.

1. According to these speeches, what were the principal arguments for ratification of the Constitution in Massachusetts?

2. To what extent was the conflict over ratification based on a clash of economic interests?

WHAT WERE THE ISSUES IN MASSACHUSETTS?
1. Did Singletary and Thompson express values different from those embodied in the Constitution? If not, why did the two Massachusetts men oppose the Constitution?

2. According to the map and chart, what conflict was behind the basic disagreement over ratification in Massachusetts?

3. For dealing with the topic of ratification in Massachusetts, what are the limitations of the map and the chart?

THE ISSUES IN VIRGINIA

10. Foes of the Constitution: Patrick Henry

In the Massachusetts debates over the Constitution, many delegates stepped forward to voice their opinions. Generally, each man who spoke offered all of his views at once. In Virginia, the discussion proceeded differently. During most of the convention, only a few men occupied the floor. These men were the leaders of public opinion in Virginia: they included Patrick Henry and George Mason, against the Constitution, and James Madison and Edmund Randolph, in favor of it. The discussion was a very orderly one. Issues were taken up one by one, point by point. The next four readings are selections from speeches of leaders at the Virginia convention. The arguments presented here reflect the issues emphasized in the Virginia debates.

The first excerpt is from a speech by Patrick Henry. Henry originally came from the western part of Virginia, where he had been a farmer. He is remembered for his opposition to Britain before the Revolution and for his statement, "Give me liberty or give me death!"

... [Under the proposed Constitution] if your American chief be a man of ambition and abilities, how easy it is for him to render himself absolute! ... The president, in the field at the head of his army, can prescribe the terms on which he shall reign master, so far that it will puzzle [be a problem for] any American ever to get his neck from under the galling yoke. ...

What can be more defective than the clause [Article I, Section 4 of the Constitution] concerning the elections? The controul given congress over the time, place, and manner of holding elections, will totally destroy the end [purpose] of suffrage. The elections may be held at one place, and the most inconvenient in the state; or they may be at remote distances from those who have a right of suffrage; hence nine out of ten must either not vote at all, or vote for strangers; ... The proceedings in the northern conclave will be hidden from the yeomanry [farmers] of this country. [For the Congressmen] are not to publish what parts they think require secrecy: they *may* think, and *will think*, the whole requires it.

The Debates, Resolutions, and Other Proceedings in Convention, on the Adoption of the Federal Constitution, edited by Jonathan Elliot (Washington, D.C.: Jonathan Elliot, 1827), Vol. II, pp. 71–72.

The "northern conclave" refers to Congress, which would be meeting in the North. A "conclave" is a secret council.

1. What different arguments does Henry make?

2. What, in general, does Henry fear?

3. Do his arguments remind you of any of the issues in Massachusetts? Explain.

4. Henry thought that Congress would keep its proceedings secret. What group of people, in particular, did he think this secrecy would hurt?

11. Foes of the Constitution: George Mason

George Mason, along with Patrick Henry, led the fight in Virginia against ratification of the Constitution. Mason owned a large plantation in eastern Virginia. In 1776, he wrote Virginia's Declaration of Rights, which became the basis for the first ten amendments to the Constitution.

One of Mason's main arguments against the Constitution was that it would work against the interests of southern planters. The Constitution stated that a majority in Congress could make trade laws. The North contained more states and more people than the South, and would have a majority of the votes. Since shipping was one of the biggest businesses in the North, northerners wanted to pass laws to discourage the use of foreign ships. The planters of the South were accustomed to hiring foreign ships to transport their crops. These planters were afraid they would have to pay higher freight charges if they were forced to use northern ships. In protesting against the power the North would have in Congress, Mason echoed a fear also expressed by Patrick Henry. The following excerpts summarize two of Mason's other principal objections to the Constitution.

The Debates, Resolutions, and Other Proceedings in Convention, on the Adoption of the Federal Constitution, edited by Jonathan Elliot (Washington, D.C.: Jonathan Elliot, 1827), Vol. II, pp. 208–209.

When the people of Virginia formed their government, they reserved certain great powers in the bill of rights. They would not trust their own citizens, who had a similarity of interest with themselves, and who had frequent and intimate communication with them . . . with the exercise of those great powers reserved in the bill of rights. Do we not by this system give up a great part of the rights, reserved by the bill of rights, to those who have no fellow-feeling for the people—to a government where the representatives will have no communication with the people?

[In addition, under this Constitution taxes will] be laid upon us by those who have no information of our situation, and by a government where the wealthy are only represented. . . .

1. What are Mason's objections to the Constitution?

2. Do you see any connections between Mason's arguments and the fears expressed by Patrick Henry?

3. Do you think that Mason represented one group or a broad range of interests?

4. How do the objections to the Constitution voiced in Virginia compare with the ones voiced in Massachusetts?

12. Champions of the Constitution: James Madison

James Madison, a plantation owner in eastern Virginia, represented his state at the Constitutional Convention. As one author of a collection of essays called *The Federalist*, Madison was a major spokesman for ratification. He made the following arguments at the Virginia convention.

. . . If any dangerous and unnecessary powers be given to the general legislature, let them be plainly demonstrated . . .

. . . Sir, by this government, powers are not given to any particular set of men, they are in the hands of the people; delegated to their representatives chosen for short terms; to representatives responsible to the people, and whose situation is perfectly similar to their own: as long as this is the case we have no danger to apprehend [fear]. . . .

[Those] who wish to become federal representatives, must depend on . . . that class of men who will be the most popular in their counties, who generally represent the people in the state governments . . . It is almost certain, therefore, that the deliberations of the members of the federal house of representatives, will be directed to the interests of the people of America. As to the other branch, the senators will be appointed by the legislatures, and though elected for six years, I do not conceive [think] they will so soon forget the source from whence they derive their political existence. . . .

[Direct] taxation is . . . generally objected to [but it] can be of little advantage to those in power, to raise money in a manner oppressive to the people. . . .

The Debates, Resolutions, and Other Proceedings in Convention, on the Adoption of the Federal Constitution, edited by Jonathan Elliot (Washington, D.C.: Jonathan Elliot, 1827), Vol. II, pp. 90, 92–93, 95–97.

A "direct tax" is one that is paid directly to the government, such as a land tax.

1. Which of Patrick Henry's arguments, if any, did Madison answer in these excerpts? *How* did Madison answer Henry?

2. Which of Patrick Henry's points did Madison leave unanswered here? Judging from what he said on the other points, how do you think he would have answered Henry?

3. Did Madison answer any of George Mason's objections? If so, how?

13. Champions of the Constitution: Edmund Randolph

Edmund Randolph, who came from a family of prominent lawyers, was elected governor of Virginia in 1786. The following year, he represented his state at the Constitutional Convention. At the end of the Convention, Randolph refused to sign the completed Constitution. He feared that under the Constitution the United States would become a monarchy rather than a republic. He thought that the Constitution gave the President too much power, and that he could remain in office indefinitely. However, when ratification was discussed in Virginia, Randolph reversed his position and argued strongly for the acceptance of the Constitution.

But we are now enquiring particularly, whether Virginia . . . can exist without the Union. A hard question, perhaps, after what has been said. I will venture, however, to say, she cannot. . . . [She] is

The Debates, Resolutions, and Other Proceedings in Convention, on the Adoption of the Federal Constitution, edited by Jonathan Elliot (Washington, D.C.: Jonathan Elliot, 1827), Vol. II, pp. 30–31, 108–109.

very accessible: the large capacious [roomy] bay of Chesapeake, which is but too excellently adapted for the admission of enemies, renders her very vulnerable. . . . This being her situation by sea, let us look at land. . . . Cast your eyes to the western country, that is inhabited by cruel savages, your natural enemies; besides their natural propensity [tendency] to barbarity, they may be excited by the gold of foreign enemies to commit the most horrid ravages on your people. Our great increasing population is one remedy to this evil; but being scattered thinly over so extensive a country, how difficult is it to collect their strength, or defend the country. . . . There is another circumstance which renders us more vulnerable. Are we not weakened by the population of those whom we hold in slavery? The day may come when they may make impression upon [attack] us. . . . Manufactures and military stores may afford relief to a country exposed: Have we these at present? . . . If we shall be separated from the union, shall our chance of having these be greater? . . .

. . . My idea is, that we should go hand in hand with Massachusetts; adopt it [the Constitution] first, and then propose amendments [changes] . . . By union alone can we . . . exist: by no other means can we be happy. . . . By previous adoption, the union will be preserved: by insisting on alterations previous to our adoption, the union may be lost . . .

Under the Articles of Confederation, the national government depended on the state governments for its money.

. . . Is it necessary that the legislative power of the United States should be authorized to levy taxes? . . . Money is the nerves—the life and soul of a government. . . . Wars cannot be carried on without a full and uncontrolled . . . power to raise money in the most eligible [acceptable] manner. Nay, Sir, government cannot be administered in time of peace without this power.

1. Randolph originally disapproved of the Constitution, and then decided to back it. What reasons do the previous arguments give for his change of mind? What seemed to be *most* important to Randolph?

2. How do Randolph's and Madison's arguments differ?

3. What do Madison and Randolph argue for? Are these things that will help all Virginians equally, or just one special group?

THE ISSUES IN VIRGINIA

1. What were the major points made by the opponents of the Constitution in Virginia?

2. Did Madison and Randolph answer *all* of these points? If not, which ones did they neglect?

230

3. Did Madison or Randolph introduce any subjects that had not been emphasized by the opposition?

4. Do class interests seem to have played an important part in the Virginia convention called to ratify the Constitution?

5. In summary, what would you say were the important issues in the Virginia ratifying convention?

6. Are these the same issues that the map on page 219 suggests? If there is any disagreement, what could account for it?

7. How can you tell which issues are most important in determining a vote? For example, which issues do you think would have the greatest influence on the final vote: those discussed by both sides, or those mentioned by only one side? What other questions might you ask about the speeches in the debate? Would reading all the speeches be enough to determine what influenced the vote? Explain.

MAKING JUDGMENTS

1. Is there any difference between the major issues over ratification in the Massachusetts and Virginia conventions? Explain.

2. To what extent could you use Massachusetts and Virginia to predict what the issues were in the rest of the country?

3. What hypothesis can you now form about the reasons the Constitution was opposed or supported? How does this compare with the hypothesis you formed after studying the map and chart on pages 218 and 219?

4. What values do the arguments about the Constitution reflect? How do the values of the opponents to the Constitution compare with those of its supporters?

5. If you had lived in this country in 1787, would you have supported the Constitution? Why or why not?

---

14. Article V of the Constitution

The Congress, whenever two thirds of both Houses shall deem it necessary, shall propose Amendments to this Constitution, or, on the Application of the Legislatures of two thirds of the several States, shall call a Convention for proposing Amendments, which, in either Case, shall be valid to all Intents and Purposes, as Part of this Constitution, when ratified by the Legislatures of three fourths of the several States, or by Conventions in three fourths

III. The Constitution Faces Challenges

thereof, as the one or the other Mode of Ratification may be proposed by the Congress; Provided that no Amendment which may be made prior to the Year One thousand eight hundred and eight shall in any Manner affect the first and fourth Clauses in the Ninth Section of the First Article; and that no State, without its Consent, shall be deprived of its equal Suffrage in the Senate.

1. What does Article V of the Constitution make possible?

2. Does Article V make this difficult or easy to accomplish? Do you think it makes it *too* difficult or *too* easy? Tell why.

3. Do you think that the framers of the Constitution were wise to include such a clause? Explain your opinion.

15. The First Ten Amendments

As you have noted, a major objection to adoption of the Constitution was that it contained no "bill of rights." Although many state constitutions included provisions which protected individual liberties against action by state governments, the federal Constitution contained nothing to prevent the federal government from restricting or interfering with many liberties. In 1791, ten amendments to the Constitution were adopted. They became known as the Bill of Rights and fulfilled a pledge made by supporters of the Constitution to those who opposed the extension of federal power.

Article I. Congress shall make no law respecting an establishment of religion, or prohibiting the free exercise thereof; or abridging the freedom of speech, or of the press; or the right of the people peaceably to assemble, and to petition the Government for a redress [remedy] of grievances.

Article II. A well regulated Militia being necessary to the security of a free State, the right of the people to keep and bear Arms, shall not be infringed.

Article III. No Soldier shall, in time of peace be quartered in any house, without the consent of the Owner, nor in time of war, but in a manner to be prescribed by law.

Article IV. The right of the people to be secure in their persons, houses, papers, and effects, against unreasonable searches and seizures, shall not be violated, and no Warrants shall issue, but upon probable cause, supported by Oath or affirmation, and particularly describing the place to be searched, and the persons or things to be seized.

Article V. No person shall be held to answer for a capital, or otherwise infamous crime, unless on a presentment or indictment of a Grand Jury, except in cases arising in the land or naval forces, or in the Militia, when in actual service in time of War or in public danger; nor shall any person be subject for the same offence to be twice put in jeopardy of [in danger of losing] life or limb; nor shall be compelled in any Criminal Case to be a witness against himself, nor be deprived of life, liberty, or property, without due process of law; nor shall private property be taken for public use, without just compensation.

A "capital" crime is punishable by death; "infamous" crimes are punishable by long jail sentences, fines, loss of citizenship. "Presentments" and "indictments" are forms of accusation.

Article VI. In all criminal prosecutions, the accused shall enjoy the right to a speedy and public trial, by an impartial jury of the State and district wherein the crime shall have been committed, which district shall have been previously ascertained [defined] by law, and to be informed of the nature and cause of the accusation; to be confronted with the witnesses against him; to have compulsory [guaranteed] process for obtaining Witnesses in his favor, and to have the Assistance of Counsel for his defence.

Article VII. In suits at common law, where the value in controversy shall exceed twenty dollars, the right of trial by jury shall be preserved, and no fact tried by a jury shall be otherwise re-examined in any Court of the United States, than according to the rules of the common law.

Article VIII. Excessive bail shall not be required, nor excessive fines imposed, nor cruel and unusual punishments inflicted.

Article IX. The enumeration in the Constitution, of certain rights, shall not be construed [interpreted] to deny or disparage others retained by the people.

Article X. The powers not delegated to the United States by the Constitution, nor prohibited by it to the States, are reserved to the States respectively, or to the people.

1. What liberties did the Bill of Rights secure?

2. What values are reflected in the Bill of Rights? Are they representative of any one particular group's point of view?

3. Review your list of the values held by those who objected to the Constitution and those who supported the Constitution. How do you think each group would have felt about the Bill of Rights? Do you think each group would have been satisfied or dissatisfied with the Bill of Rights? Why?

4. What effect do you think the values of a society have upon the institutions it establishes?

16. State vs. Federal Rights

In 1793, two South Carolina citizens sued the state of Georgia for payment of a debt. They were heirs of an Englishman named Alexander Chisholm, to whom Georgia owed money. The case became known as *Chisholm v. Georgia*.

The federal Supreme Court ordered the state of Georgia to appear as defendant in the case. The Court was carrying out the provisions of Article III, Section 2 of the Constitution, which stated that a controversy between a state and citizens of another state were to be tried in a federal court. Georgia denied the right of the Court to hear the case and refused to appear. The Supreme Court then ruled that Georgia was to pay the debt.

The Georgia House of Representatives refused to allow payment of the debt, on the grounds that the Supreme Court had no right to interfere with the affairs of the state of Georgia. The Supreme Court did not pursue the issue any further.

There was a strong feeling in other states that the Chisholm case established a dangerous principle. If one state could be sued in a federal court, it was feared that the sovereignty of all the states was threatened.

1. How would Patrick Henry or George Mason have felt about the example set by *Chisholm v. Georgia?* What would they have probably suggested as a solution?

2. What would James Madison or Edmund Randolph have suggested as a solution?

17. The Eleventh Amendment, 1798

The Judicial power of the United States shall not be construed to extend to any suit in law or equity, commenced or prosecuted against one of the United States by Citizens of another State, or by Citizens or Subjects of any Foreign State.

1. Considering opponents of the Constitution like Mason and Henry as one group, and supporters of the Constitution like Madison and Randolph as another, which side would have been pleased with the Eleventh Amendment? Why?

2. Review the first eleven amendments to the Constitution. Does it appear that the federal government was becoming what Mason, Henry, or Thompson feared? Explain.

18. The Emergence of American Political Parties

Article II, Section 1 of the Constitution provides that the President and Vice-President are to be selected by an *electoral college* composed of electors from each state. A state has as many electors as it has senators and representatives in Congress. Instead of voting directly for President, the voters in each state cast their ballots for a group of electors who support a particular candidate. Afterwards, the electors meet to elect the President and Vice-President.

Originally there was no distinction between the candidates for President and Vice-President. All candidates appeared on the same list. Each elector voted for two candidates. The man with the highest number of votes became President, and the one with the second highest number became Vice-President.

In 1789, in the first Presidential election, the sixty-nine electors unanimously selected George Washington to be President. John Adams, with thirty-four votes, was chosen Vice-President. There were no political rallies, speeches, or campaigns in this election. One reason for this is that in 1789 there were no political parties. The Constitution did not provide for political parties, and political parties had not yet been formed. A political party comes into being when a group of people who believe in the same basic ideas or goals join together and form an organization. The purpose of the organization is to gain control of the government. In the United States, a political party obtains control of the government by getting its candidates elected as lawmakers and public officials.

When Washington became President, he appointed Thomas Jefferson and Alexander Hamilton to be two of his advisers. Jefferson and Hamilton had different views about the nature of government. Hamilton had little faith in the common man's ability to govern. Partly because of this view, Hamilton wanted a strong central government. He, therefore, favored a loose or broad interpretation of the Constitution, so that the powers of the federal government would not be limited to those specifically mentioned in the Constitution. Jefferson, on the other hand, believed in the wisdom of the common man. He believed that government should be strongest at the state and local levels. He, therefore, wanted a strict or narrow interpretation of the Constitution in order to restrict the power of the federal government. Those who supported Hamilton and his ideas formed the Federalist party. The supporters of Jefferson organized the Democratic-Republican party, also known as the Republican party.

235

In the election of 1792, political parties entered the contest. Both Federalists and Republicans supported Washington, and he was unanimously elected again. Adams, with seventy-seven electoral votes, was also re-elected. But George Clinton, governor of New York, received fifty votes. The Republicans had supported Clinton in an attempt to prevent Adams' re-election to the Vice-Presidency.

With Washington's refusal to run for a third term, the two new parties struggled for control of the Presidency in the election of 1796. The Federalist candidates were John Adams and Thomas Pinckney. The Republicans ran Thomas Jefferson and Aaron Burr. It was expected that the electors would elect either both Federalist candidates or both Republican candidates. But when the votes were counted, Adams became President, with seventy-one votes; and Jefferson, with sixty-eight votes, became Vice-President. Thus, the nation had a Federalist President and a Republican Vice-President. After 1796, the electors adopted the practice of voting only for the candidates of their own party.

In 1800, Adams and Jefferson again opposed each other for the Presidency. Aaron Burr was the Republican candidate for Vice-President. Charles C. Pinckney was on the ticket with Adams. The electoral vote for President was:

Candidate	Political Party	Electoral Votes
Thomas Jefferson	Republican	73
Aaron Burr	Republican	73
John Adams	Federalist	65
Charles C. Pinckney	Federalist	64
John Jay	Federalist	1

When a tie occurred in the Presidential vote, only the House of Representatives could decide who would become President. The Federalists controlled the House—they had sixty-four seats to forty-two for the Republicans. The House finally chose Jefferson because Alexander Hamilton, who preferred Jefferson over Burr, used his influence to win votes for Jefferson. Burr then became Vice-President.

1. Why did political parties emerge in the United States?

2. What would have displeased the Federalists or the Republicans in the election of 1796 and 1800?

3. Is there anything wrong with having a President and Vice-President from two different political parties?

4. When an election is decided in the House of Representatives, is there anything wrong with having members of one party select the President or Vice-President from candidates of another political party?

5. What happened to Article II, Section 1 of the Constitution when it was put into practice? Why did this happen? When problems like this arise, what should be done?

19. The Twelfth Amendment, 1804

Approved in 1804, the Twelfth Amendment to the Constitution stated:

The Electors shall meet in their respective states, and vote by ballot for President and Vice-President, one of whom, at least, shall not be an inhabitant of the same state with themselves; they shall name in their ballots the person voted for as President, and in distinct ballots the person voted for as Vice-President, and they shall make distinct lists of all persons voted for as President, and of all persons voted for as Vice-President, and of the number of votes for each, which lists they shall sign and certify, and transmit sealed to the seat of the government of the United States, directed to the President of the Senate; —The President of the Senate shall, in presence of the Senate and House of Representatives, open all the certificates and the votes shall then be counted; —The person having the greatest number of votes for President, shall be the President, if such number be a majority of the whole number of Electors appointed; and if no person have such majority, then from the persons having the highest numbers not exceeding three on the list of those voted for as President, the House of Representatives shall choose immediately, by ballot, the President. But in choosing the President, the votes shall be taken by states, the representation from each state having one vote; a quorum for this purpose shall consist of a member or members from two-thirds of the states, and a majority of all the states shall be necessary to a choice. And if the House of Representatives shall not choose a President whenever the right of choice shall devolve upon them, before the fourth day of March next following, then the Vice-President shall act as President, as in the case of the death or other constitutional disability of the President. The person having the greatest number of votes as Vice-President, shall be the Vice-President, if such number be a majority of the whole number of Electors appointed, and if no person have a majority, then from the two highest numbers on the list, the Senate shall

237

choose the Vice-President; a quorum for the purpose shall consist of two-thirds of the whole number of Senators, and a majority of the whole number shall be necessary to a choice. But no person constitutionally ineligible to the office of President shall be eligible to that of Vice-President of the United States.

1. How can you explain the adoption of the Twelfth Amendment?

2. Why wasn't the Twelfth Amendment part of the original Constitution? Why do you suppose this amendment wasn't adopted until 1804?

ARTICLE V AND THE NEW NATION

If Article V had not been part of the Constitution, what do you think would have been the outcome of the problems that were solved by the first twelve amendments to the Constitution? What role, then, did Article V play in the country's history between 1787 and 1804?

CONFLICTS AND LAW

Our Fundamental Law: The Constitution

Although state and local laws vary from place to place, all of them must agree with the Constitution. Any state or local law which violates the Constitution can be declared invalid in the federal courts. Thus the Constitution provides our fundamental law.

1. Articles I–VII of the Constitution spell out specific laws. What is the connection between those laws and the values expressed in the Preamble to the Constitution? Review your concluding study of the Constitution, on pages 216–218, in answering this question.

2. Do you agree with the values set forth in the Preamble to the Constitution? Do your classmates agree with them? Take a poll in your class to determine which values each student feels are the *most* important ones. Are there any differences in your answers?

3. Do you think that the values expressed in the Preamble to the Constitution have been fully realized in American life today? Explain.

Conflicts over the Constitution

A conflict is a disagreement or argument. Conflicts can involve as few as two people, or they can divide an entire nation. There are even conflicts which leap national barriers and involve large parts of the world. You can probably think of many examples.

Your study of the Constitution included several situations that involved conflicts. In particular, there were disagreements over how to write the Constitution and whether to ratify it. Why were there such conflicts? Hadn't the United States just emerged from a revolution in which Americans joined together to fight for the same principles? Didn't all Americans believe in the values expressed in the Declaration of Independence? Didn't they believe in the values expressed in the Preamble to the Constitution?

Review the conflicts you have just studied. Try to determine whether both sides in each conflict endorsed the basic American values set forth in the Preamble. If so, how can you explain their disagreement? For example:

1. In the Virginia arguments over whether to ratify the Constitution, why did Patrick Henry oppose the Constitution? How did James Madison meet his arguments? Was Madison more devoted to the principles of the Preamble than Henry?

2. Edmund Randolph supported the Constitution in the Virginia convention. He had opposed it earlier. What values lay behind his two positions? Which values were closer to the spirit of the Preamble?

3. In Massachusetts, was Dawes, who supported the Constitution, more faithful to the ideas of the Preamble than Singletary?

Resolving Conflicts

1. When the Constitution was adopted, people like Amos Singletary were overruled. Suppose that you were Singletary, and you felt that the government was controlled by people who would act against your interests. How could you resolve your conflict with the leaders and your disapproval of the way the government was structured? What action would be in your best interest? Would there be any advantage in agreeing to live peacefully under the Constitution?

2. What are some of the important public issues in the United States today? Are there different groups who seek opposing solutions to these problems? What methods might each group use to get its way? Would violating the law ever be in a group's best interest? Why or why not?

Forging a Nation: Leadership

A PRESIDENT TAKES THE HELM

20. Public Expectations

George Washington, the nation's first President, had a distinguished career even before he assumed the country's highest elective office. He frequently took time from his duties as a prosperous Virginia planter to serve the public. He was a colonel for the British in the French and Indian War, commander of the American forces during the American Revolution, and President of the Constitutional Convention.

In the next two selections you will read what Washington himself wrote as he witnessed the problems and events of his age. The first reading is a letter from Washington to Edward Rutledge, a signer of the Declaration of Independence and a legislator from South Carolina. The letter was written in New York in 1789. New York was the first seat of the national government. In 1790 the government moved to Philadelphia. Washington, D.C., became the permanent capital in 1800.

POINTS TO CONSIDER
Washington's role as a leader.

The Writings of George Washington from the Original Manuscript Sources 1745–1799, edited by John C. Fitzpatrick (Washington, D.C.: United States Government Printing Office, 1940), Vol. XXX, pp. 308–309.

To "concenter" means to draw into a common center.

"Induced" means persuaded. To "apprehend" means to fear.

"Issue," here, means outcome.

. . . When I had judged . . . that it was my duty to embark again on the tempestuous and uncertain Ocean of public life, I gave up all expectations of private happiness in this world. You know, my dear friend, I had concentered all my schemes, all my wishes, within the narrow circle of domestic enjoyment. Though I flatter myself the world will do me the justice to believe, that, at my time of life and in my circumstances, nothing but a conviction of duty could have induced me to depart from my resolution of remaining in retirement; yet I greatly apprehend that my Countrymen will expect too much from me. I fear, if the issue of public measures should not corrispond [correspond] with their . . . expectations, they will turn the extravagant (and I may say undue) praises which they are heaping upon me at this moment, into equally extravagant (though I will fondly hope unmerited) censures [criticism] . . . I feel, in the execution of the duties of my arduous [difficult] Office, how much I shall stand in need of the . . . aid of every friend to myself, of every friend to the Revolution, and of every lover of good Government. . . .

21. America's Prospects

Washington wrote the following letter to Philip Schuyler, a senator from New York. In it he confided his view on the future of America. The letter was written on May 9, 1789.

. . . An honest zeal [enthusiasm] and an unremitting attention to the interest of United America is all that I dare promise.

The good dispositions which seem at present to pervade every class of people afford reason for your observation that the clouds which have long darkened our political hemisphere are now dispersing, and that America will soon feel the effects of her natural advantages. That invisible hand which has so often interposed [intervened] to save our Country from impending destruction, seems in no instance to have been more remarkably excited than in that of disposing the people of this extensive Continent to adopt, in a peaceable manner, a Constitution, which if well administered, bids fair to make America a happy nation.

The Writings of George Washington from the Original Manuscript Sources 1745–1799, edited by John C. Fitzpatrick (Washington, D.C.: United States Government Printing Office, 1940), Vol. XXX, p. 317.

To "pervade" is to spread through.

1. How would you define the word "leader"?

2. In his letter to Edward Rutledge, what characteristics did Washington exhibit?

3. Can someone with those characteristics be a good leader?

4. In his letter to Philip Schuyler, what is Washington's attitude toward his new duty? What did he think about the future of the young United States?

5. How could these attitudes affect his performance as a leader?

A CABINET DISPUTE

22. Alexander Hamilton's Opinion of Thomas Jefferson

In Section III you learned that Alexander Hamilton supported a stronger and more active federal government than Thomas Jefferson and that this conflict gave rise to the first political parties in America. The conflict between Hamilton and Jefferson became apparent many years earlier, however. As members of Washington's Cabinet, or advisory council, they disagreed from the start on how to govern the new nation.

The Constitution did not set up a cabinet, but it did give the President power to make appointments that had not been provided for specifically. Washington used this power to appoint men to advise and assist him. The first Cabinet consisted of the Attorney General, or chief legal adviser, and the secretaries of State, Treasury, and War. Hamilton was Secretary of the Treasury, and Jefferson was Secretary of State.

During Washington's first term of office, the political disagreements between Hamilton and Jefferson were focused on the financial policies developed by Hamilton. Among the measures Hamilton proposed were the following:

1. *Payment by the federal government of the national debt.* The debt, which was inherited from the previous national government, was to be repaid so that foreign nations would respect us and trust us to pay back future loans. Repaying the debt would also encourage people to buy bonds, by inspiring confidence that the government would pay them back. Bonds are certificates that a government issues in exchange for money. The government promises that the money plus interest will eventually be repaid.

2. *Payment by the federal government of state debts incurred during the Revolution.* The purpose of this measure was to encourage those who had lent money to look to the federal government for payment rather than to the state governments.

3. *Enactment of a tariff.* A tariff would help pay the federal and state debts and protect the infant industries of America from foreign competition.

4. *Establishment of a national bank.* This would serve as a safe place for the deposit of funds by both individuals and the government, and would provide the country with a sound, uniform currency. The bank would loan money to businessmen and thus encourage the development of industry. It would also handle the payment of public debts for the Treasury and pay the salaries of public officials.

Hamilton's policies tended to increase the power of the federal government and to encourage the development of industry, commerce, and shipping. The establishment of the national bank also helped enlarge the powers of Congress. The Constitution did not specifically delegate to Congress the power to establish a national bank, but Hamilton argued that this power was implied in the powers that were granted to Congress. He favored a "loose construction" or broad interpretation of the Constitution.

Jefferson consistently opposed Hamilton's programs. In the following letter to a friend in Virginia, Hamilton revealed his reaction to this opposition. Hamilton also referred to James Madison, who was closely associated with Jefferson and was identified with his political beliefs.

Philadelphia, May 26, 1792.

... I became ... convinced of the following truth, "that Mr. Madison, *co-operating with Mr. Jefferson, is at the head of a faction* [party], *decidedly hostile to me, and my administration;*

American History Told by Contemporaries, edited by Albert Bushnell Hart (New York: The Macmillan Company, 1900), Vol. XXX, pp. 289–292.

and actuated [motivated] *by views, in my judgment, subversive of the principles of good government, and dangerous to the Union, peace and happiness of the country."*. . . In various conversations with *foreigners,* as well as citizens, he [Jefferson] has thrown censure on my principles of government, and on my measures of administration . . . Another circumstance has contributed to widening the breach. 'Tis evident, beyond a question, from every moment, that Mr. Jefferson aims, with ardent [intense] desire, at the Presidential chair . . .

By "foreigners" Hamilton meant primarily Frenchmen. Since Jefferson had been Minister to France, he had many associations with the French.

23. Jefferson's View of Hamilton

Jefferson believed in giving as much power as possible to the states and in developing agriculture more than industry. He felt that the centralization of financial power advocated by Hamilton would increase federal power at the expense of the states. He felt, too, that Hamilton's program aided the commercial interests but ignored the agricultural interests. Jefferson also opposed Hamilton's proposed national bank on constitutional grounds. Because he wished to limit federal power, Jefferson advocated a "strict," or narrow, interpretation of the Constitution. Thus, he maintained that the establishment of a national bank was unconstitutional because it was not among the powers specifically delegated to Congress. In the following letter to Washington, Jefferson expressed his sentiments toward Hamilton.

Philadelphia, May 23, 1792.

American History Told by Contemporaries, edited by Albert Bushnell Hart (New York: The Macmillan Company, 1900), Vol. III, p. 287.

. . . The ultimate object of [Hamilton's program] is to prepare the way for a change, from the present republican form of government, to that of a monarchy, of which the English constitution is the model, [and to produce] in the future a king, lords & commons, or whatever else those who direct it may chuse [choose] . . .

24. Washington Advises Jefferson and Hamilton

LETTER FROM WASHINGTON TO JEFFERSON, 1792

. . . I regret, deeply regret, the difference in opinions which have arisen, and divided you and another principal officer of the Government [Hamilton]; and wish, devoutly [sincerely], there could be an accommodation of them by mutual yieldings.

A Measure of this sort would produce harmony, and consequent good in our public Councils; the contrary will, inevitably, introduce confusion, and serious mischiefs; and for what? because mankind cannot think alike, but would adopt different means to attain the same end. For I will frankly, and solemnly declare that,

The Writings of George Washington from the Original Manuscript Sources 1745–1799, edited by John C. Fitzpatrick (Washington, D.C.: United States Government Printing Office, 1940), Vol. XXXII, pp. 132–133.

I believe the views of both of you [Hamilton and Jefferson] are pure, and well meant; and that experience alone will decide [who is right] . . .

LETTER FROM WASHINGTON TO HAMILTON, 1792

. . . Differences in political opinion are as unavoidable as, to a certain point, they may, perhaps, be necessary; but it is exceedingly to be regretted that subjects cannot be discussed with temper on the one hand, or decisions submitted to without having the motives [distorted by the other party. Here] we find that men of abilities, zealous patriots, having the same *general* objects in view, and the same upright intentions to prosecute them, will not exercise more charity in deciding on the opinions and actions of one another. . . . Having premised [stated] these things, I would fain [gladly] hope that liberal allowance will be made for the political opinions of each other; and instead of those wounding suspicions, and irritating charges . . . that there might be mutual forbearances [restraints] . . . *on all sides.* Without these I do not see how the Reins of government are to be managed, or how the Union of the States can be much longer preserved.

1. What were the main issues over which Jefferson and Hamilton disagreed?

2. How would you characterize the Jefferson and Hamilton letters? Are there any similarities between their statements?

3. Why was Washington so concerned about the conflict between the two men?

4. What role did Washington play in the dispute?

The Writings of George Washington from the Original Manuscript Sources 1745–1799, edited by John C. Fitzpatrick, Vol. XXXII, pp. 185–186.

THE PRESIDENT AND THE LAW

25. The Whiskey Tax

In 1791, Congress approved one of Hamilton's most unpopular financial measures—an excise tax on whiskey. An excise tax is a tax on goods produced and used within a country. Hamilton felt the tax was necessary to raise revenue and to extend the authority of the federal government over the western farmers.

Many of the inhabitants of the western part of Pennsylvania, Maryland, Virginia, the Carolinas, and Georgia were extremely dissatisfied with the tax. It placed a heavy burden on backwoods farmers for whom whiskey was the most important source of money. These farmers were unable to realize a profit from the sale of their major surplus, which was grain. Due to poor roads and the high cost of shipment, it was too expensive to transport a bulky product like grain to eastern markets. Therefore, the farmers used the surplus grain to make whiskey. Whiskey occupied less space and thus was easier to transport.

Opposition to the excise tax was particularly strong in four Pennsylvania counties west of the Allegheny Mountains. In 1792, mass meetings were held to protest the tax. A convention in Pittsburgh denounced the tax and stated that collection of it would be obstructed. On September 29, Washington proclaimed that the tax would be enforced.

Discontent over the enforcement of the excise tax resulted in what has become known as the "Whiskey Rebellion." In 1794, over two thousand men protesting against the tax threatened Pittsburgh. When the governor of Pennsylvania did not act to stop the disorder, Washington ordered fifteen thousand militiamen from Virginia, Maryland, New Jersey, and Pennsylvania into the area. Upon their arrival, the rebels fled and the troops restored order.

When Washington first learned about the unrest in Pennsylvania in 1792, he wrote to Hamilton.

The last post [mail] brought me your letter of the 1st instant, with the enclosures respecting the disorderly conduct of the Inhabitants of the Western Survey of the District of Pennsylvania, in opposing the execution of what is called the Excise Law; and of the insults which have been offered by some of them to the Officers who have been appointed to collect the duties on distilled spirits . . .

Such conduct of *any* of the Citizen of the United States, under *any* circumstances that can well be conceived, would be exceedingly reprehensible [blameworthy]; but when it comes from a part of the Community for whose protection the money arising from the Tax was principally designed, it is truly unaccountable, and the spirit of it much to be regretted. . . . It is my duty to see the Laws executed: to permit them to be trampled upon with impunity [without punishment] would be repugnant to it; nor can the Government longer remain a passive spectator of the contempt with which they are treated. . . .

The Writings of George Washington from the Original Manuscript Sources 1745–1799, edited by John C. Fitzpatrick (Washington, D.C.: United States Government Printing Office, 1940), Vol. XXXII, pp. 143–144.

"Instant" means of the present month.

During this period, there were several Indian attacks upon frontier settlements.

1. What problem did Washington face here?

2. Review what you learned about the problems that arose over the ratification of the Constitution. How does the protest and rebellion against the tax on whiskey relate to those problems?

3. According to this letter, what consideration determined Washington's action?

4. Do you think Washington acted wisely?

RELATIONS WITH FRANCE

26. The French Revolution Begins

In the summer of 1789, France witnessed the beginning of a democratic revolution against the abuses of the French government. Washington wrote to the Comte de Rochambeau, a French general who had aided the Americans in their revolution against Great Britain, to express his interest in what was happening in France.

The Writings of George Washington from the Original Manuscript Sources 1745–1799, edited by John C. Fitzpatrick (Washington, D.C.: United States Government Printing Office, 1940), Vol. XXX, p. 437.

... The political affairs of the United States are in so pleasing a train as to promote respectability to their government, and happiness to our Citizens. The opposition offered [to federal power] ... has in a great measure subsided, and there is every reason to predict political harmony and individual happiness to the States and Citizens of confederated America.

The Revolution, announced by the intelligence from France, must be interesting to the nations of the world in general, and is certainly of the greatest importance to the country in which it has happened. I am persuaded I express the sentiments of my fellow-citizens, when I offer an earnest prayer, that it may terminate [end] in the permanent honor and happiness of your government and people. ...

1. Judging from Washington's letter, what kind of relations did America have with France in 1789? What in the letter suggests this?

2. Why do you think French-American relations were this way?

3. What did Washington forecast for the United States? On what did he base his predictions? What does this reveal about Washington's concerns?

27. The Question of Neutrality

On February 1, 1793, France declared war on England. The war placed America in an awkward position. Since 1778 the United

States had honored a treaty of alliance with France. The treaty provided that the United States would assist France in the defense of her West Indian colonies. If the United States abided by the treaty, she would become an ally of France and an enemy of England. Fortunately for the United States, France did not ask for American defense of the West Indies. But on April 18, 1793, Washington did not know if France would request aid from the United States. In a letter to the Cabinet, he expressed his views on the problem of French-English relations.

[Partial List of] Questions Submitted to the Cabinet by the President

Question I. Shall a proclamation issue for the purpose of preventing interferences of the Citizens of the United States in the War between France and Great Britain...? Shall it contain a declaration of Neutrality or not? What shall it contain?

[Question] II. Shall a Minister from the Republic of France be received?

[Question] III. If received shall it be absolutely or with qualifications; and if with qualifications, of what kind?

[Question] IV. Are the United States obliged by good faith to consider the Treaties heretofore made with France as applying to the present situation of the parties[?] May they either renounce them, or hold them suspended 'till the Government of France shall be *established*[?]

The Writings of George Washington from the Original Manuscript Sources 1745–1799, edited by John C. Fitzpatrick (Washington, D.C.: United States Government Printing Office, 1940), Vol. XXXII, p. 419.

1. By the questions he asked, what position did Washington seem to want the United States to take in the war between France and Great Britain?

2. Would you have expected him to encourage this position? Why?

3. Why do you think he suggested such a policy?

4. Can you explain why Washington felt it was necessary to question the Cabinet about his ideas?

28. The Proclamation of Neutrality

The war between England and France threatened to involve the United States. Washington responded by issuing the following proclamation on April 22, 1793.

Whereas it appears that a state of war exists between Austria, Prussia, Sardinia, Great Britain, and the United Netherlands, on

The Writings of George Washington from the Original Manuscript Sources 1745–1799, edited by John C. Fitzpatrick (Washington, D.C.: United States Government Printing Office, 1940), Vol. XXX, p. 430.

the one part, and France on the other; and the duty and interest of the United States require, that they should with sincerity and good faith adopt and pursue a conduct friendly and impartial towards the belligerent [warring] powers:

I have therefore thought fit by these presents [writings], to declare the disposition [desire] of the United States to observe the conduct aforesaid towards those powers [mentioned above] . . . and to exhort [urge] and warn the citizens of the United States carefully to avoid all acts and proceedings whatsoever, which may in any manner tend to contravene [violate] such disposition.

And I do hereby make known, that whosoever of the citizens of the United States shall render himself liable to punishment or forfeiture [loss] under the law of nations, by committing, aiding, or abetting [encouraging] hostilities against any of the said powers, or by carrying to any of them, those articles which are deemed contraband [forbidden] by the modern usage of nations, will not receive the protection of the United States against such punishment. . . .

1. What specifically was Washington trying to prevent?

2. Do you think that this was likely to occur? Why?

3. Does Washington give any reasons why he thought such an outcome would violate the "duty and interest of the United States"? Can you think of any reasons?

4. What sources would you have to investigate in order to understand why Washington pursued this policy?

5. Can you think of any arguments against Washington's policy?

29. Citizen Genêt

In the beginning the French Revolution had enlisted the sympathy of most Americans. Many believed that the American example had inspired the French to revolt. Names of places in America that referred to royalty were changed. For example, Royal Exchange Alley in Boston became Equality Lane. However, the establishment of the French Republic in 1792, in place of the monarchy, and the subsequent execution of King Louis XVI, his Queen, Marie Antoinette, and many of the King's loyal followers, sharply divided American opinion.

American views on the French Revolution split along the lines of the political parties forming around Jefferson and Hamilton. Hamiltonians believed that the Revolution would lead to the end of law, order, and justice. To them the new French Republic merely substituted the tyranny of the masses for the tyranny of the legal rulers. To the Jeffersonians, the French Revolution was the issue of 1776 all over again—a revolt against an oppressive government. Many Jeffersonians, including Jefferson himself, did not approve of the executions, but did favor the downfall of the French monarchy. They hoped that Frenchmen would establish a democratic republic in its place.

When France declared war on Great Britain in 1793, the breach between the two groups widened. Hamiltonians, or Federalists, naturally sympathized with the British, the Jeffersonians or Republicans with the French. The two groups disagreed on how the United States should act toward Great Britain and France.

In the midst of this dispute, the French government sent Citizen Edmond C. Genêt to the United States as its foreign minister. Genêt landed at Charleston, South Carolina, and then traveled to Philadelphia. He took the back-country route to Philadelphia. Most of the people in this region were small farmers who favored the democratic, pro-French beliefs of the Republicans over the aristocratic, pro-British views of the Federalists. While traveling to Philadelphia, Genêt was warmly greeted by crowds of people.

Genêt attempted to gain popular support for the French Revolution and the French cause against Great Britain. He tried to organize expeditions against British and Spanish territories. He had the *Little Sarah,* a captured British ship, loaded at Philadelphia with arms and supplies for France. Before Washington could stop him, Genêt sent the ship out to war on British commerce. All this was done in defiance of the Proclamation of Neutrality.

Washington did not approve of Genêt's military activities in behalf of the French. He refused to heed Genêt's demands for United States support of France. When informed of Washington's decision, Genêt threatened to appeal to the American people. He believed he could gain the support of the people over the government because of the warm reception he had received and because of the pro-French feelings of the Republicans. However, the Cabinet met and unanimously demanded the recall of Genêt. Even Jefferson felt that Genêt had become too extreme in his actions. Genêt was removed from the French foreign service.

Washington discussed the Genêt incident in the following letters. He wrote the first letter to Jefferson while Genêt was having the *Little Sarah* fitted for her voyage. The second letter, to Richard Henry Lee, a former senator from Virginia, was written prior to Genêt's recall by the French government.

LETTER TO THOMAS JEFFERSON

After I had read the Papers put into my hands by you, requiring "instant attention," and before a messenger could reach your Office, you had left town.

The Writings of George Washington from the Original Manuscript Sources 1745–1799, edited by John C. Fitzpatrick (Washington, D.C.: United States Government Printing Office, 1940), Vol. XXXIII, p. 4.

What is to be done in the case of the Little Sarah, now [on the Delaware River]? Is the Minister of the French Republic [Genêt] to set the Acts of this Government at defiance, *with impunity?* and then threaten the Executive with an appeal to the People. What must the World think of such conduct, and of the Governm[en]t of the U. States in submitting to it?

These are serious questions. Circumstances press for decision, and as you have had time to consider them (upon me they come unexpected) I wish to know your opinion upon them, even before tomorrow, for the vessel may then be gone.

LETTER TO RICHARD HENRY LEE

The specimens you have seen of [Mr. Genêt's] sentiments and conduct in the Gazettes [newspapers] form a small part of the aggregate [total]; but you can Judge from these to what test the temper of the Executive has been put in its various transactions with this Gentleman. It is probable, that the whole will be exhibited to public view in the course of the next session of Congress ... The best that can be said of this agent [Genêt] is, that he is entirely unfit for the Mission on which he is employed, unless, contrary to the express and unequivocal [clear] declaration of his Country [France] it is meant to involve ours in all the horrors of a European War....

1. According to his letters, why was Washington disturbed about Genêt's behavior? Do you think Washington was wise to be concerned over this? Explain.

2. Can you think of other reasons why Genêt's actions would have alarmed the President?

3. Was Washington wise to let the Cabinet decide how to deal with Genêt? Explain.

RELATIONS WITH GREAT BRITAIN AND SPAIN

30. Troubles with Great Britain

In 1794, the American government was troubled by various British policies. One irritation was that Great Britain still maintained forts in the Great Lakes region eleven years after she had promised to give them up in the Treaty of Paris of 1783. Many Americans regarded the forts as a threat to their security. The British posts also obstructed western settlement and made it possible for the British to control the fur trade. In addition, America was bothered by Britain's interference in the trade of neutral na-

The Writings of George Washington from the Original Manuscript Sources 1745–1799, edited by John C. Fitzpatrick, Vol. XXXIII, p. 138.

tions. As a result of her war with France, Great Britain seized American ships bound for Europe on the pretense that they were loaded with goods for France. American sailors on the seized ships were forced to serve on British ships. This practice was known as impressment. America also disliked the restrictions on American trade with the British West Indies.

Washington sent John Jay, Chief Justice of the Supreme Court, to England to negotiate a treaty. Washington instructed Jay to ask Great Britain to abandon her western outposts, to halt the seizure of American ships, and to grant America better commercial privileges in the British West Indies. Washington's feelings regarding Jay's mission are recorded in letters he wrote to his Secretary of State and to Jay.

LETTER TO THE SECRETARY OF STATE

"My objects are, to prevent a war," Washington wrote the Secretary of State, "if justice can be obtained by fair and strong representations . . . of the injuries which this country has sustained from Great Britain in various ways," injuries which "leave very unfavorable impressions of their friendship, and little to expect from their justice."

Samuel Eliot Morison and Henry Steele Commager, **The Growth of the American Republic** (Fourth edition; New York: Oxford University Press, 1950), Vol. I, p. 356. Reprinted by permission.

LETTER TO JAY

Philadelphia, August 30, 1794.

. . . [For] there does not remain a doubt in the mind of any well informed person in this country (not shut against conviction) that all the difficulties we encounter with the Indians, their hostilities, the murders of helpless women and innocent children along our frontiers, results from the conduct of the Agents of Great Britain in this Country. In vain is it then for its Administration *in Britain* to disavow [deny] having given orders which will warrant such conduct, whilst [while] their Agents go unpunished. . . . whilst they keep in a state of irritation the tribes who are hostile to us, and are instigating [encouraging] those who know little of us, or we of them, to unite in the War against us . . .

The Writings of George Washington from the Original Manuscript Sources 1745–1799, edited by John C. Fitzpatrick (Washington, D.C.: United States Government Printing Office, 1940), Vol. XXXIII, pp. 484–485.

Can it be expected I ask, so long as these [wrongs] are known in the United States, or at least firmly believed, and suffered with impunity [without punishment] by [from] G. Britain, that there ever will, or can be any cordiality [warmth] between the two Countries? I answer NO! and I will undertake, without the gift of prophecy, to predict, that it will be impossible to keep this Country in a state of amity [friendship] with G. Britain long if the Posts are not surrendered. . . .

"Prophecy" is the ability to foresee the future.

31. The Jay Treaty

In the Jay Treaty, England agreed to abandon her western outposts in America. The United States also won the right to participate in trade with the British East and West Indies. Our entry into the West Indian trade was hedged with restrictions, however. American claims against the British for seizure of American ships were referred to a commission for settlement.

The treaty contained no provisions for several issues of concern to the United States. Nothing was included that would prohibit future seizures of American ships. Neither the impressment of American seamen nor British efforts to encourage Indian attacks against American frontier settlers was mentioned.

The treaty did not solve the most serious problems, and the concessions made by the British were minor ones. The United States could have tried to satisfy its grievances by declaring war on Britain. War would have put a halt to trade with other nations, however. Without trade, the United States government would have been very poor indeed. Under Hamilton's program, customs were the major source of income for the government. Because the British knew this, it would have been very difficult for Jay to obtain a better treaty. The American public was indignant over the terms of the treaty. Copies of the treaty were burned, and flags were lowered to half-mast. Republicans attacked the treaty as a sellout by the Federalists, Hamilton and Jay, to the British.

With such strong public reaction against the treaty, Washington was under pressure to abandon the treaty by not carrying out the final steps of ratification. However, after much thought, Washington decided to complete the ratification process.

The Writings of George Washington from the Original Manuscript Sources 1745–1799, edited by John C. Fitzpatrick (Washington, D.C.: United States Government Printing Office, 1940), Vol. XXXIV, p. 244.

Mount Vernon, July 22, 1795.

To the Secretary of State.

... My opinion respecting [Jay's] treaty, is the same now that it was: namely, not favorable to it, but that it is better to ratify it in the manner the Senate have advised ... than to suffer matters to remain as they are, unsettled....

1. What problems with Britain did the Jay Treaty settle? Which ones did it leave unsettled?

2. Did Washington have any alternatives besides signing the Jay Treaty or going to war with Britain?

3. Why do you think Washington accepted the Jay Treaty?

4. Do you think Washington made the right decision? Explain.

5. Was it courageous or weak of Washington to accept the treaty? Tell why.

32. The Pinckney Treaty

In 1795, Thomas Pinckney, the American minister, concluded a treaty with Spain. Spain agreed to allow free navigation of the Mississippi River and to let American shippers deposit goods at New Orleans. This meant that the American frontiersman could send his goods down the Mississippi. He also had the right to transfer goods from riverboats to oceangoing vessels at New Orleans. The frontier settler now had an outlet for bulky products like grain, which were difficult to transport overland. Spain also agreed to a settlement of the northern boundary of Florida and promised to restrain Indian raids from Florida.

The issues that the Pinckney Treaty settled had long been problems between the United States and Florida. Jay had tried to settle these problems with Spain ten years earlier, but the Spaniards were unreceptive until they learned of the Jay Treaty. Then, fearing an alliance between Britain and the United States, they decided to safeguard their American possessions by improving relations with the United States.

Following approval of the treaty, Washington wrote to Pinckney.

Philadelphia, March 5, 1796.

The Writings of George Washington from the Original Manuscript Sources 1745–1799, edited by John C. Fitzpatrick (Washington, D.C.: United States Government Printing Office, 1940), Vol. XXXII, p. 485.

The ship Favourite, by which these dispatches are sent, having been delayed much longer in this Port than was expected, affords me an opportunity of informing you, that the Spanish Treaty arrived here on the 22d. [of last month]; that it was laid before the Senate . . . and that on the 3d. instant, the Ratification of it was advised and consented to by an unanimous vote of that body. Hence you may form an opinion of the general approbation [approval] of your negotiation. . . .

1. What importance did the Pinckney Treaty have for the United States? Do you think that the issues it settled were critical ones? Why or why not?

2. What does Washington's letter to Pinckney show about his attitude toward the treaty?

3. Would the President's attitude to a treaty affect its passage?

4. Based on the information in the introduction and in the letter, do you think that Washington deserves any credit for the Pinckney Treaty?

5. Can you think of ways Washington might have helped the treaty that are not mentioned? Where might you find out whether your hypotheses are correct?

WASHINGTON'S FOREIGN POLICY

1. What were the reasons for Washington's policy toward France?

2. Washington was sterner and more insistent in his policy toward France than in his policy toward Britain. Can you think of any reasons to explain this? Do you think that his policy toward Britain was weak or unwise?

3. How does Washington's approval of the Pinckney Treaty compare with the rest of his foreign policy?

4. What was the main goal of Washington's foreign policy toward both France and England? According to Washington's correspondence and official dispatches, why did he pursue this policy? Can you think of other reasons why Washington might have followed this policy? What other sources could you investigate to find the reasons for Washington's actions?

VISIONS TO GUIDE THE FUTURE

33. A Letter to Patrick Henry

The political dissension between Jefferson and Hamilton rocked Washington's Cabinet. Jefferson resigned from his position in December 1793. He was replaced by Edmund Randolph, who resigned in 1795. In his search for a new Secretary of State, Washington tried to persuade Patrick Henry to assume the office. The President wrote to Henry and expressed his feeling about the proper course for the nation. When Washington wrote the letter, only two years remained of his second and last Presidential term.

The Writings of George Washington from the Original Manuscript Sources 1745–1799, edited by John C. Fitzpatrick (Washington, D.C.: United States Government Printing Office, 1940), Vol. XXXIV, p. 335.

. . . In a word, I want an *American* character, that the powers of Europe may be convinced we act for *ourselves* and not for *others;* this in my judgment, is the only way to be respected abroad and happy at home and not by becoming the partizans [supporters] of Great Britain or France, create dissentions, disturb the public tranquillity, and destroy, perhaps for ever the cement [which] binds the Union.

1. What course does Washington recommend here for the United States?

2. Does this letter add to your knowledge of the aims behind Washington's foreign policy? Explain.

3. To Washington, what was the main danger of foreign alliance?

254

34. The Farewell Address

On retiring from public office, the first President left some advice for the new country.

. . . The name of American, which belongs to you, in your national capacity, must always exalt [raise] the just pride of Patriotism, more than any appellation [name] derived from local discriminations. With slight shades of difference, you have the Same Religeon, Manners, Habits and political Principles. You have in a common cause fought and triumphed together. The independence and liberty you possess are the work of joint councils, and joint efforts; of common dangers, sufferings and successes.

. . . Respect for [the government's] authority, compliance with its laws, [acceptance of] its measures are duties . . . of true liberty. The basis of our political systems is the right of the people to make and to alter their Constitutions of Government. But the Constitution which at any time exists, 'till changed by an explicit [clear] and authentic act of the whole People, is sacredly obligatory [binding] upon all. The very idea of the power and the right of the People to establish Government presupposes [assumes] the duty of every Individual to obey the established Government.

The Great rule of conduct for us, in regard to foreign Nations is in extending our commercial relations to have with them as little *political* connections as possible. So far as we have already formed engagements let them be fulfilled, with perfect good faith. Here let us stop. . . .

The Writings of George Washington from the Original Manuscript Sources 1745–1799, edited by John C. Fitzpatrick (Washington, D.C.: United States Government Printing Office, 1940), Vol. XXXV, pp. 219–220, 233–234.

1. What points does Washington make here in his parting public address to the country? Why do you think he emphasizes these topics?

2. Is it possible to find one underlying concern here, or does Washington reveal several different concerns in his address? Compare the Farewell Address with the letter to Patrick Henry.

FORMING A JUDGMENT

1. What concerned Washington most? Was there any difference between his basic concerns in domestic and foreign affairs? Explain.

2. Why was Washington so concerned about these matters? Do you think he correctly identified the most important problems he faced?

3. Did Washington handle his problems well? Was he coura-geous? Wise? Effective?

4. Review the purposes of the United States government as set forth in the Preamble to the Constitution. Then review the President's role in carrying out these purposes. Did Washington use the powers he was given effectively?

5. How do the writings of a man help you to judge his role in history? Do you need other information? If so, what kinds of information would be helpful to you in testing your ideas about Washington?

6. How would you form a judgment about other Presidents or other kinds of leaders? List the questions you would ask in order to make your evaluation. Keep these questions in mind as you study John Adams.

V. Interpreting John Adams

35. Thoughts of John Adams

John Adams, second President of the United States, had long been active in the affairs of the nation. He had been a delegate to the Continental Congress that met during the revolutionary period, a member of the committee which drafted the Declaration of Independence, the main author of the Massachusetts Constitution of 1780, and Vice-President under George Washington from 1789 to 1797. When he was elected President in 1797, Adams became the leader of the Federalist party.

Recorded below are some of Adams' thoughts at different points in his career. Other selections in this section deal with events during Adams' administration (1797–1801).

POINTS TO CONSIDER
Whether Adams was a good leader.
Whether he was a good President.

In his *Novangelus: Or A History of the Dispute with America,* Adams recalled how he felt in 1774 during the movement toward American independence.

The Works of John Adams, edited by Charles Francis Adams (Boston: Little, Brown and Company, 1851), Vol. IV, p. 8.

. . . Swim or sink, live or die, survive or perish with my country, was my unalterable determination.

In January 1776, in an essay entitled "Thoughts on Government," Adams wrote:

The Works of John Adams, edited by Charles Francis Adams, Vol. IV, pp. 193–194.

. . . [The] form of government which communicates . . . happiness, to the greatest number of persons, and in the greatest degree is the best . . .

Fear is the foundation of most governments; but it is so sordid [foul] and brutal a passion, and renders [makes] men . . . so stupid and miserable, that Americans will not be likely to approve of any political institution which is founded on it.

In June 1790, Adams wrote in a letter:

I am so well satisfied of my own principles, that I think them as eternal and unchangeable as the earth and its inhabitants.

The Works of John Adams, edited by Charles Francis Adams, Vol. IX, p. 568.

Immediately after becoming President, Adams wrote:

I have it much at heart to settle all disputes with France, and nothing shall be wanting on my part to accomplish it, excepting a violation of our faith and a sacrifice of our honor. But old as I am, war is, even to me, less dreadful than iniquity [injustice] or deserved disgrace. . . .

American History Told by Contemporaries, edited by Albert Bushnell Hart (New York: The Macmillan Company, 1900), Vol. III, pp. 300–301.

1. Judging from the statements made by Adams, what sort of a man does he appear to have been?

2. Do you think a man like this would make a good leader? Do you think, in particular, he would make a good President?

36. Problems with France: The XYZ Affair

The negotiation and ratification of the Jay Treaty angered the French government. To retaliate, the French announced that they would treat neutral nations in the same manner as England—they too would search and seize American ships. In December 1796, the French refused to receive the new United States minister to France, Charles C. Pinckney. This action broke diplomatic ties between the two countries.

When Adams became President, he wanted to improve relations between the United States and France. To accomplish this, he appointed, in May 1797, a commission to France composed of Charles C. Pinckney, John Marshall, and Elbridge Gerry. Upon their arrival in Paris, Talleyrand, the French foreign minister, sent three of his agents to meet them. These agents became known as X, Y, and Z. They soon disclosed that the United States would have to give the French money before negotiations could begin between America and France. The Americans were out-raged, and Marshall and Pinckney, both Federalists, immediately left the country. Gerry, a pro-French Republican, stayed on but was eventually recalled by the American government.

As soon as the American public learned that the French had asked

for a bribe, there was a popular reaction against France. The excitement increased when Adams submitted the X Y Z correspondence to Congress. Thousands of copies of these documents were distributed at public expense. The American people clamored for war. The slogan, "Millions for defense but not one cent for tribute," became popular.

Congress responded to the demands of the public by authorizing the capture of French armed ships and by suspending trade with France. Congress also declared that the treaty of alliance with France was no longer in effect.

For the next two years, 1798–1800, France and the United States were involved in an undeclared naval war. Hamilton and many of the Federalists favored the outbreak of full hostilities with France and encouraged Adams to issue an immediate declaration of war. However, Adams preferred to let France make the first move in order to give America time to strengthen her national defenses.

France, too, wanted to avoid a full-scale war with America. Talleyrand made it known that he would receive a new United States minister with respect. Upon learning this, Adams decided to ignore the urgings of members of his own party who pleaded with him to engage France in a total war. In February 1799, without consulting his Cabinet, Adams nominated William Vans Murray to be minister to France. This meant that if Murray went to France there would probably be no war.

The Hamiltonian wing of the Federalists was extremely critical of Adams' action. They favored a war against France because it would permit the Federalists to strengthen their hold on the national government and to discredit the Jeffersonian Republicans. But Adams had decided that war must be avoided. The new nation was not prepared for war. A full-scale war with France could only make the United States more dependent on England. Moreover, although there was much public support for war, the nation was by no means unified in its views on war. Republicans and even some Federalists opposed war with France.

Despite pressure from leaders of the Federalist party, Adams held to his decision to send a minister to France. He made one minor concession to the pleadings of the Federalists. Instead of naming a single minister, he appointed a commission of three.

The negotiations of the commission resulted in the Convention of 1800, in which France agreed to cancel its treaty of alliance with the United States if the United States would drop its financial claims against France. The United States had demanded that France pay $20 million for her seizures of American ships.

Adams' handling of the French crisis created a split in the Federalist party. Adams was defeated by Jefferson in the election of 1800, and the Federalists never regained control of the national government.

1. What was Adams' role in dealing with France? What steps did Adams take as the crisis with France developed?

2. In deciding how to deal with France, what did Adams seem to consider important? Did his concerns change while he was in office, or was his policy consistent?

3. Did Washington face any foreign problems similar to the ones Adams faced? Explain.

4. Did Washington and Adams have the same ideas about what was important for the United States in foreign relations?

5. What position did the majority of the Federalists take on France? What was the Republican position? Does Adams' policy seem to have been affected by pressures from either party? Did Washington face similar party pressures? How did he react?

6. From the way Adams handled the crisis with France, what impression do you get of his character or personality?

7. Do you think Adams' stand could have affected the way the President's prestige or power was viewed? If so, how? If not, why not? How might Adams' policy have influenced the prestige of the new nation?

8. Was Adams' policy in the best interests of the nation? Why or why not?

37. The Alien and Sedition Acts

During Adams' Presidency the Federalists were concerned about the fact that most of the Europeans who migrated to America joined the Republican party. Most of these foreigners, or aliens, were inspired by the political ideals of the French Revolution, and many of them became publicists for the Republican party. Their writings sharply criticized the Federalists.

The threat of war with France intensified the hostile feelings of the Federalists toward the aliens. In addition, some French immigrants were suspected of engaging in espionage. To impose restrictions on aliens and to repress political opposition, a Federalist-controlled Congress passed the Alien and Sedition Acts in 1798. Adams agreed to the acts.

259

You will recall from your study of Peter Zenger that sedition is the act of encouraging discontent against the government or resistance to authority. The main provisions of the Alien and Sedition Acts were as follows:

1. The period of residence required for a foreigner to become a citizen and to qualify to vote was extended from five years to fourteen years.

2. If an alien was regarded as dangerous to the public peace, the President could order him to leave the country.

3. Persons who published anything that was "false, scandalous and malicious" and that brought dishonor to the government, Congress, or the President, could be fined and imprisoned.

Many of the provisions of the Alien and Sedition Acts were not enforced or even used extensively. Only twenty-five persons were prosecuted under the third provision of the laws mentioned above. Out of these twenty-five prosecutions only ten were convicted; but all of those convicted were Republican editors and printers..

The Republicans attacked the Alien and Sedition Acts as unconstitutional. Thomas Jefferson and James Madison secretly drafted resolutions which the legislatures of Kentucky and Virginia adopted. In these resolutions, known as the Kentucky and Virginia Resolutions, Jefferson and Madison maintained that, in passing the Alien and Sedition Acts, Congress had exceeded its powers. However, neither Kentucky nor Virginia took action to obstruct the Alien and Sedition Acts.

The Republicans made opposition to the Alien and Sedition Acts a major part of their platform in the election of 1800. Public displeasure over the Federalists' passage of the acts contributed to Adams' defeat in his bid for re-election in 1800.

The readings below will help you to understand Adams' attitude toward the Alien and Sedition Acts. The first selection is from one of Adams' letters to Timothy Pickering, Secretary of State from 1795 to 1800. Adams refers to the *Aurora,* which was a newspaper published in Philadelphia. It was the Republicans' most powerful voice. Adams also mentions William Duane, editor of the *Aurora,* and William Rawle, United States attorney for Pennsylvania. The second selection is taken from a history of the period. This excerpt draws heavily on Adams' own statements.

LETTER TO PICKERING, 1799

. . . Is there any thing evil in the regions of actuality or possibility, that the Aurora has not suggested of me? You may depend upon it, I disdain [scorn] to attempt a vindication [defense] of myself against any lies of the Aurora . . . If Mr. Rawle does not think this

The Works of John Adams, edited by Charles Francis Adams (Boston: Little, Brown and Company, 1854), Vol. IX, p. 5.

paper libellous, he is not fit for his office; and if he does not prosecute it, he will not do his duty.

The matchless effrontery [offensive boldness] of this Duane merits the execution of the alien law. . . .

A SELECTION FROM A HISTORY BY MANNING J. DAUER

. . . [One] of Adams' remarks of this . . . period is . . . "I ought not forget the worst enemy we have:—That obloquy, which you have observed . . . leads to divisions, sedition, civil war, and military despotism.". . .

To the citizens of Franklin, North Carolina, he declared: "It was indeed high time for the friends of government and good order to exert themselves, and declare their opinions, or in a short time, there might have remained, neither government nor order." Becoming even more specific, he stated to the citizens of Baltimore City and County: "Republics are always divided in opinion concerning forms of governments, and plans and details of administration—these divisions are generally harmless, [and] often salutary [beneficial] . . . except when foreign nations interfere and by their arts and agents excite . . . them into parties and factions: such interference and influence must be resisted and exterminated or it will end in America, as it did anciently in Greece, and in our own time in Europe, in our total distruction as a republican government, and independent power." Further as early as 1797 he had stated to the citizens of Boston: "Although many of our worthy Citizens may flatter themselves that calumnies [malicious lies] . . . against the Constituted Authorities will not make a dangerous impression upon a public opinion formed with so much . . . intelligence . . . yet I cannot but be of the opinion, that the profligate [immoral] spirit of falsehood and malignity [viciousness], which has appeared in some, and the unguarded disposition of others, to encourage it, are serious evils, and bear a threatening aspect upon the Union of the States, their Constitution of Government, and the moral character of the Nation."

1. In his letter to Pickering, why did Adams seem to favor the Alien and Sedition Acts?

2. According to Adams' public statements, why were criticisms of the nation dangerous? Why, then, would the Alien and Sedition Acts be desirable?

3. Can you think of any other reasons why Adams might have considered the Alien and Sedition Acts vital to national interests at this time?

A written statement that is "libellous" is false and injures someone's reputation.

Manning J. Dauer, **The Adams Federalists** (Baltimore: The Johns Hopkins Press, 1953), pp. 160–161.

"Obloquy" is strong and destructive criticism.

4. According to Adams' public statements, what was he trying to protect? Did Washington ever try to protect the same thing? Did he face problems similar to those which moved Adams to support the Alien and Sedition Acts? If so, how would you compare the way Washington met these problems with Adams' action?

5. What political pressures did Adams face in this situation?

6. What do you think was the major reason for Adams' support of the Alien and Sedition Acts? Do you think there were other reasons, too?

7. How would you describe Adams' policy here? Was he a good leader?

8. Do you think the information here is complete enough to make a final judgment about Adams' action? If not, what more would you need to know?

EVALUATING A PRESIDENT

1. How does Adams' role in relations with France compare with his endorsement of the Alien and Sedition Acts? How can you explain the similarities or differences in the actions he took on these two issues?

2. How would you appraise Adams as a President? What standards are you using to make your appraisal? In other words, what is your idea of a good President?

3. Did making comparisons between Adams' ideas and experiences and those of Washington help you to evaluate Adams? If so, how? If not, why not?

4. If you wanted to evaluate the leadership of our President today, would it be helpful to compare him with Washington? Would it be useful to compare him with some other President? Explain.

5. Define the terms "fact" and "opinion." In your appraisal of John Adams how much is fact and how much is opinion? On what facts did you base your opinion?

38. Historians Interpret Adams: Personality and Political Ideas

The following are interpretations by prominent American historians of John Adams as a President. The three selections in this reading emphasize Adams' personality and political beliefs. The two selections in the next reading focus on Adams' accomplishments. Before reading these appraisals, review your own judgments about Adams.

POINTS TO CONSIDER

Why each author views Adams as he does.

How each of the historians uses "fact" and "opinion."

How each historian's view of Adams compares with your view.

What traits make an individual a good President.

JOHN SPENCER BASSETT, 1906

No president of the United States ever desired a prosperous and peaceful administration more than John Adams, and none ever fell further short of his wishes. [Benjamin] Franklin said of him that he was always honest, often great, and sometimes mad. He himself . . . described his own personality better than another could do it. "I have never," he said, "sacrificed my judgment to kings, ministers, nor people, and I never will. When either shall see as I do, I shall rejoice in their protection, aid, and honor: but I see no prospect that either will ever think as I do, and therefore I shall never be a favorite with either." He was tactless, immovable, honest, patriotic, and fearless. He was not a party leader, and knew not how to arouse the enthusiasm of his supporters. He probably saved the country from war, which the [Hamiltonian] Federalists would have precipitated. He did not wreck his party, but he contributed towards its destruction. His part in that operation was a passive one. . . .

John Spencer Bassett, **The Federalist System** (New York: Harper & Row, Publishers, 1906), pp. 204–205.

GILBERT CHINARD, 1929

. . . [John Adams] was not a party man or party leader. The irritable, impulsive, patriotic, peevish old New Englander was too individualistic to belong to any party; he was not the man either to rally the hesitating, to uphold the vacillating [doubting], or to encourage and educate the blind. Curiously enough, he has found very few defenders. Severely treated by the friends of Jefferson, he has not been spared by the admirers of Hamilton. He stands alone, one of the most complicated and contradictory figures in American History—a pure patriot, whose patriotic work is almost forgotten, a catholic [well-rounded] spirit who loved to play with ideas and paradoxes [contradictions], a contrary mind, but in my opinion more widely read than any of his American contemporaries, not excepting Jefferson. . . .

Gilbert Chinard, **Thomas Jefferson: The Apostle of Americanism** (Second edition, revised; Ann Arbor Paperback; Ann Arbor: The University of Michigan Press, 1957), p. 323. Copyright 1929 by Gilbert Chinard. Reprinted by permission of Little, Brown and Company.

SAMUEL ELIOT MORISON AND HENRY STEELE COMMAGER, 1937

. . . In no sense a democrat, he regarded Jefferson's belief in the common man's innate virtue as sentimental nonsense . . .

Samuel Eliot Morison and Henry Steele Commager, **The Growth of the American Republic** (New York: Oxford University Press, 1937), Vol. I, p. 275. Reprinted by permission.

THE EFFECT OF PERSONALITY

1. How do Bassett and Chinard portray Adams' personality? Do they agree?

2. Does Bassett seem to feel that Adams' personality helped or hindered him in his role as President? How does this compare with Chinard's opinion?

3. Is it important for a President to be a good party leader? Why or why not? Should he be able to resist party pressures? What personal traits would these abilities require?

4. Does Adams' action in supporting the Alien and Sedition Acts seem to reflect his personality? Does his role in relations with France reflect his personality?

5. Review the statement about war which Adams made at the time of his inauguration (page 257). How does this statement compare with Adams' policy toward France? Does this comparison suggest anything new about Adams' personality? Does it suggest traits you would have expected to find or ones that surprise you?

6. Do you think that a personality like Adams' is an asset or a handicap to a President? What personal qualities do you think would be most desirable in a President? Explain your answers.

THE EFFECT OF POLITICAL IDEAS

1. What political idea do Morison and Commager attribute to Adams? Do the other two historians support this interpretation? Explain.

2. Do you think there was any connection between Adams' personality and his political philosophy? Explain.

3. Review the statement Adams made in his essay, "Thoughts on Government," quoted on pages 256–257. How does this compare with your impression of Adams' political philosophy?

4. Were Adams' policies consistent with his political beliefs?

5. Do you think it is helpful or important for a President to have a carefully worked out political philosophy? Why or why not?

6. What was Chinard's overall opinion of Adams? What factors did Chinard seem to consider important? Do you think that these are important factors?

7. In the material you have read, is there any evidence to support Chinard's statement that Adams was a "complicated and contradictory figure"?

39. Historians Interpret Adams: Achievements

The next two selections emphasize Adams' foreign policy, but evaluate it in relation to his other policies. Keep in mind the questions with which you approached the previous interpretations of Adams. In addition, think about the following:

POINTS TO CONSIDER

The importance of Adams' foreign policy to the welfare of the country during this period.

The relative importance of the many other issues that faced Adams.

Whether Adams' most significant decisions were basically wise or unwise.

What factors each historian felt were responsible for Adams' wise or unwise decisions.

What else you would need to know in order to judge Adams' policies.

PAGE SMITH, 1962

... The standard mode [fashion] has been to dismiss the Adams years as unfortunate ones, sandwiched in somehow between two great Presidents—Washington and Jefferson—and doomed to failure because of Adams' bad temper and inability to get along with his subordinates. ...

... addressing ourselves to the particular question of Adams' stature as a President, it might be well to ask how the success of an administration had best be measured. Here one would assume the answer to be: by its accomplishments. According to this standard, it is possible to argue that Adams' administration deserves high marks. In the first place, he came to the presidency at one of the most critical periods in the nation's history. Only Washington's enormous prestige had prevented very serious divisions in Congress and in the country. The success of the new experiment represented by the federal constitution was so far from being assured that many thoughtful and devoted patriots despaired of its future. The country was on the verge of a ruinous war which, had it taken place, might well have resulted in domestic conflict and disunion. ... When [Adams] brought his administration to a close, there existed a small but effective navy, [a strengthened] army, a solvent treasury, and above all peace. ...

But the urgencies of the hour, not the abstract propositions and measuring sticks of historians, are the standard of successful leadership and here it seems clear enough that Adams' policy, or perhaps it should be said Adams' character, served his country well. Of the rightness of his basic policy—to make the country

Page Smith, **John Adams** (Garden City, New York: Doubleday & Company, Inc., 1962), Vol. II, pp. 1058–1059. Copyright © 1962 by Page Smith. Reprinted by permission of Doubleday & Company, Inc.

A "solvent" treasury is one that is not in debt.

strong while continuing to negotiate for peace—there can be little question.

THOMAS A. BAILEY, 1966

Thomas A. Bailey, **Presidential Greatness: The Image and the Man from George Washington to the Present** (Des Moines, Iowa: Meredith Press, 1966), pp. 269–271. Copyright 1966 by Thomas A. Bailey. Reprinted by permission of Appleton-Century-Crofts.

John Adams, temperamentally unfitted to be President, is over-generously rated a Near Great by [one school of] experts. In some respects he was a flat failure.

We have been thrown off the track by his undeniably valuable services to the Republic during the Revolutionary years, by the magic name of one of America's most distinguished families, and above all by his "courageous" handling of the X Y Z crisis with France in 1798. He dramatically opted for [chose] peace in the teeth of violent opposition from the Hamiltonian wing of his own Federalist party, and he later suggested for his epitaph: "Here lies John Adams, who took upon himself the responsibility of peace with France in the year 1800."

Adams' management of the French crisis has been extravagantly overpraised. The masterly policy of George Washington and the other Founding Fathers was to remain neutral and stall for time while our weak and divided nation grew strong and our birthrate fought our battles for us. When we had attained sufficient strength, we could stand up to the major powers of Europe. But Adams, swept off his feet by the anti-French hysteria of 1798, led the nation to the brink of hostilities—an early exercise in "brink-manship"—and then recoiled when he looked over the edge of the abyss. His enthusiasm for war further cooled when he perceived that Alexander Hamilton, his scheming and ambitious rival, was seeking to milk the maximum military glory from it. Adams finally decided, with George Washington approving, to do what he should have done in the first place: patch up the ridiculous quarrel with France.

"Birthrate," here, refers to an increase in population.

If an outfielder badly misjudges a fly ball and then makes a desperate shoestring catch, we cheer him wildly while forgetting that if he had played his position properly, there would have been no need for heroics. It took considerable courage for Adams to plump for peace while the warhawk wing of his own party was clamoring for war. But it took perhaps more courage to go to war, with a large element in the country—probably a majority—clamoring against it. Adams may even have concluded that his political fortunes would be best promoted by giving the country the peace that it so urgently needed. In any event, we do not ordinarily praise men for doing their plain duty after having departed so irrationally from its path.

Obstinate, opinionated, vain, ill-tempered, impatient, and lacking in sound judgement, Adams was additionally a poor administrator. He could hardly fail to be when, as an absentee-landlord President, he spent one year out of his four at home in Massachusetts. His Cabinet was not so much a cabinet as a cabal. He was not alert enough at the outset to perceive that it was plotting against him and conniving [scheming] with Hamilton. He favored the notorious Alien and Sedition Laws, which were an alarming assault on free speech and other civil liberties. He left his Federalist Party disrupted and badly demoralized, never to regain control of the national administration. He himself was defeated for re-election, though narrowly. All this does not add up to a highly effective presidency.

On the other hand, Adams demonstrated that the country could muddle along after a fashion without the towering Washington, whom he had the misfortune to follow. . . . As for the notorious Alien and Sedition Acts, they were precautionary crisis measures passed during an undeclared war which was expected to widen momentarily into a full-dress conflict. In this context they do not seem either so hysterical or so tyrannical. And it should be remembered that the record of other war-crisis Presidents on civil-rights—Lincoln, Wilson, Franklin Roosevelt—is not one of the proudest chapters in American history. Even so, I would seriously question the Near Great ranking by the experts and rate John Adams, if a rating is called for, no higher than Below Average.

1. Why does Smith consider Adams' policy towards France a wise one?

2. What qualities or talents does he consider responsible for Adams' action?

3. According to Smith, was foreign policy a crucial issue in this period? Why or why not?

4. What does Smith feel were the most important measures of a President's greatness?

5. Bailey's judgment of Adams disagrees sharply with Smith's assessments. Why? Do they differ about what happened during Adams' administration?

6. How do these historians' assessments of Adams compare with your view? Do you wish to change your judgment? Why or why not?

An "opinionated" person refuses to change his opinions.

A "cabal" is a secretive group which works for a sinister purpose.

7. What factors do you now consider most important in judging a President? Can you think of any important factors that none of these selections has discussed?

8. Refer to the list of questions you made up when evaluating George Washington. How does your list compare with the factors you have just mentioned? Does your list of questions have to be expanded? Can your list be used to evaluate different kinds of leaders? Are there some questions on your list that are more important than others?

FACTS AND OPINIONS IN HISTORY

1. What parts of the appraisals by the preceding historians are facts and what parts are opinions?

2. How did each author use facts to form an opinion?

3. If you had to write a history of the Washington and Adams administrations, how would you evaluate both men; and in your evaluation how would you make use of fact and opinion? Why should both fact and opinion be included?

4. What can you now conclude about the writing of history?

RELATING THE FIRST YEARS OF THE NATION TO THE PRESENT

1. In this unit you have been concerned with the formation and ratification of the federal Constitution. You also studied some of the major events that occurred during the first twelve years of the Constitution's operation. What conclusions can you form about:
   a. The success of this experiment in government during the years you have studied.
   b. The emergence and effect of American political parties.
   c. The role of the President during this period.

2. What are your ideas on the role of government today?

3. What do you think about political parties today?

4. What current ideas about the role of government and political parties emerged from the period 1787–1800?

5. What were the major contributions of these years?

40. The Original Cherry Tree Story

Mason Locke Weems was a minister of the Church of England. He left the ministry to become a book peddler and a writer. Around 1800, he wrote a biography of George Washington entitled *The Life of George Washington: With Curious Anecdotes, Equally Honorable to Himself, and Exemplary to His Young Countrymen.*

Weems' book was very popular and went through many editions. In the fifth edition, published in 1806, Weems related, for the first time, the story about George Washington and the cherry tree. The following group of readings, beginning with Weems' story, explores the question of whether the cherry tree tale is myth or fact. The Weems selection is from an 1832 printing of his book.

POINTS TO CONSIDER
What a myth is and how to separate myth from fact.
How historical evidence could help to make this distinction.
The role of interpretation in history.

Some idea of Mr. Washington's plan of education . . . may be collected from the following anecdote [story], related to me twenty years ago by an aged lady, who was a distant relative, and, when a girl, spent much of her time in the family. . . .

"When George," she said, "was about six years old, he was made the wealthy master of a *hatchet!* of which, like most little boys, he was immoderately fond; and was constantly going about chopping every thing that came in his way. One day, in the garden, where he often amused himself hacking his mother's pea-sticks, he unluckily tried the edge of his hatchet on the body of a beautiful young English cherry-tree, which he barked so terribly, that I don't believe the tree ever got the better of it. The next morning the old gentleman, finding out what had befallen his tree, which, by the by, was a great favorite, came into the house; and with much warmth asked for the mischievous author, declaring at the same time, that he would not have taken five guineas [$22.00] for his tree. Nobody could tell him anything about it. Presently George and his hatchet make their appearance. "George," said his father, "do you know who killed that beautiful little cherry tree yonder in the garden?" This was a *tough question;* and George staggered under it for a moment; but quickly recovered himself: and looking at his father, with the sweet face of youth brightened with the inexpressive charm of all-conquering truth, he bravely cried out, "I can't tell a lie, Pa; you know I can't tell a lie. I did cut it with my hatchet."—Run to my arms, you dearest boy, cried his father in transports [joy], run to my arms; glad am I, George, that you killed my tree; for you have

Mason Locke Weems, **The Life of George Washington** (Philadelphia: Joseph Allen, 1832), pp. 11, 13–14.

A tree that has been "barked" has been stripped of its bark.

269

paid me for it a thousand fold. Such an act of heroism in my son is more worth than a thousand trees, though blossomed with silver, and their fruits of purest gold."

1. What is the main point made by Weems?

2. On what evidence did Weems base his story of the cherry tree?

41. A Scholar Attacks the Story

William Bryan studied references to Washington in American literature. He made the following comments about Weems' book.

William Alfred Bryan, **George Washington in American Literature 1775–1865** (New York: Columbia University Press, 1952), pp. 95–96. Reprinted by permission.

. . . Weems "enlivened" his story with several anecdotes of his hero's boyhood. Some, like the cherry-tree story, are dramatic scenes in which two characters converse. . . .

The most serious charge against [Weems], of course, concerns his . . . portrayal of Washington as a boy and youth. The boy of the cherry tree story . . . may be somewhat like young Weems, who early felt he was called to the ministry; certainly he is not young Washington.

1. What is the *main point* made by Bryan?

2. On what evidence did Bryan base his opinion?

42. Myth or Fact?

An Associated Press release of September 30, 1964, speculated:

Associated Press, September, 1964. Slightly adapted. Reprinted by permission.

Did George Washington really cut down his father's cherry tree?

There are still the very young (and maybe some of the not-so-young) who would like to know how this story started, and if it is true. One of these . . . wrote House Democratic Leader Carl Albert.

Albert turned to the Library of Congress, and this is what he found: "Parson Weems," the indefatigable [tireless] Mason Locke Weems, appears to have been the first to chronicle the tales in print. Weems, a prolific author of "moral tracts," once preached at Pohick Church, in whose parish lay Mount Vernon. . . .

A "prolific" author produces works in great numbers.

Historians have laughed at [the cherry tree] story on the virtue of truth as a myth, but is it? The . . . Library of Congress turned up this curious fact:

In 1899, Richard T. H. Halsey in his book, "Pictures of Early New York on Dark Blue Staffordshire Pottery," made a discovery:

An earthen mug, made in Germany between 1770 and 1790, was decorated with a quaint illustration of the cherry tree story. A youth dressed of the continental period was depicted [shown] standing near a felled tree. A large hatchet, the letters "G.W." and the numerals "1776" also appeared.

Does this mean the story had been current long before Weems flourished [was active]? Was it spread across the Atlantic in Revolutionary times? And does it add more authenticity [truth] to the tale?

John T. Rogers of the Library of Congress . . . can only say:

Who can tell? But why not believe it?

DISTINGUISHING BETWEEN MYTH AND FACT IN HISTORY

1. What is the main point of the Associated Press article?

2. What new evidence or interpretation does the Associated Press article provide about the cherry tree story? Does this material favor Weems' version or cast doubt on it? Explain. How does it affect the Bryan account?

3. Using *only* the Bryan account, can you state that the Weems version is *not* accurate? Why or why not?

4. Using only the new evidence from the Associated Press article, can you state that the Weems version is historically accurate? Why or why not?

5. Is an interpretation of history something that cannot change? Use the cherry tree story as an example.

6. Can answers always be found to problems in history? Can you definitely prove, for example, that Washington did *not* cut down the cherry tree? Is the Weems story a *myth* or a presentation of *fact*? Explain your answers.

BIBLIOGRAPHY

EATON, JEANETTE. LEADER BY DESTINY: GEORGE WASHINGTON, MAN AND PATRIOT. New York: Harcourt, Brace & World, Inc., 1938.
The author gives an insight into the gradual development of Washington's thinking during the period of his rise to leadership.

FOSTER, GENEVIEVE. GEORGE WASHINGTON'S WORLD. New York: Charles Scribner's Sons, 1941.
Foster's biography of Washington also includes an account of events and people, both in America and in the rest of the world, during Washington's lifetime, 1732–1799.

KUMMER, FREDERICK A. TORCH OF LIBERTY. New York: Holt, Rinehart and Winston, Inc., 1941.

> The theme of this group of dramatically told episodes is man's struggle for freedom. The account of the Alien and Sedition Acts of 1789 is of special interest.

*RUTLAND, ROBERT A. THE BIRTH OF THE BILL OF RIGHTS. Chapel Hill, N.C.: University of North Carolina Press, 1955. † New York: Collier Books, 1962.

> This work, on the historical and political background of the first ten amendments to the Constitution, provides a discussion of how the final version of the Bill of Rights differed from early expectations.

WILKIE, KATHARINE E. FATHER OF THE CONSTITUTION: JAMES MADISON. New York: Julian Messner, 1963.

> The role of Madison in the Constitutional Convention and the reasons for his actions are the focal points of this biography.

* Denotes more advanced reading.
† Denotes paperback edition.

TIME LINE

	AMERICAN DEVELOPMENTS		FOREIGN DEVELOPMENTS
1781	ARTICLES OF CONFEDERATION RATIFIED.		
1783	PEACE TREATY WITH GREAT BRITAIN.		
1786	ANNAPOLIS CONVENTION ASKS CONGRESS TO CALL A MEETING TO STUDY WEAKNESSES IN ARTICLES OF CONFEDERATION.		
1786–87	SHAYS' REBELLION.		
1787	CONSTITUTIONAL CONVENTION.		
1788	NINE STATES RATIFY THE CONSTITUTION.		
1789	GEORGE WASHINGTON ELECTED PRESIDENT.	1789	FRENCH REVOLUTION BEGINS.
1789	ALL THIRTEEN STATES RATIFY THE CONSTITUTION.		
1790	HAMILTON INTRODUCES HIS FINANCIAL PROGRAM.		
1791	THE BILL OF RIGHTS, THE FIRST TEN AMENDMENTS TO THE CONSTITUTION, IS ADOPTED.		
1792	GEORGE WASHINGTON RE-ELECTED PRESIDENT.	1792	FRANCE IS PROCLAIMED A REPUBLIC.
1793	PROCLAMATION OF NEUTRALITY.	1793	FRENCH REVOLUTIONISTS EXECUTE KING LOUIS XVI.
1793	CITIZEN GENêT AFFAIR.	1793–1800	ENGLAND, ALONG WITH OTHER EUROPEAN COUNTRIES, AT WAR WITH FRANCE.
		1793	ENGLAND FIRST INTERFERES WITH AMERICAN SHIPPING.
1794	WHISKEY REBELLION.	1793–94	GREAT BRITAIN REFUSES TO GIVE UP HER WESTERN OUTPOST IN AMERICA.
1795	JAY TREATY.		
1795	PINCKNEY TREATY.		
1796	JOHN ADAMS ELECTED PRESIDENT.		
1797–98	XYZ AFFAIR.	1797	FRANCE BEGINS ATTACKS ON AMERICAN COMMERCE.
1798	ELEVENTH AMENDMENT ADOPTED.	1798	NAPOLEON TAKES OVER FRENCH GOVERNMENT.
1798	ALIEN AND SEDITION ACTS PASSED.		
1798	KENTUCKY AND VIRGINIA RESOLUTIONS.	1798–1800	UNDECLARED NAVAL WAR BETWEEN FRANCE AND AMERICA.
		1800	FRANCO-AMERICAN TREATY OF ALLIANCE OF 1778 ABOLISHED.
1801	THOMAS JEFFERSON ELECTED PRESIDENT.		
1804	TWELFTH AMENDMENT RATIFIED.		

unit IV
THE NATION GROWS AND CHANGES 1800-1854

Westward the course of empire takes its way . . .   BISHOP BERKELEY
*VERSES ON THE PROSPECT OF PLANTING ARTS
AND LEARNING IN AMERICA, 1726*

INTRODUCTION

Stephen Vincent Benét, **America** (New York: Holt, Rinehart and Winston, Inc., 1944), pp. 62-63. Copyright 1944 by Rosemary Carr Benét. Reprinted by permission of Brandt & Brandt.

"And, meanwhile, [America] grew.

It grew by leaps and bounds—it stretched out to the west and the south and the northwest. To use an American phrase, it grew like nothing on earth. The Thirteen States, so long penned in behind the mountain wall of the Appalachians, suddenly spread and ran and overflowed like quicksilver. By 1821, eleven more states had entered the Union—Vermont, Mississippi, Alabama, Illinois, Indiana, Kentucky, Tennessee, Louisiana, Maine, Missouri, Ohio. Men and women packed up their goods and loaded them on wagons and moved a thousand miles, with their children, their few and cherished possessions, their slips of rosebushes and apple seedlings, their Bibles, their books and their guns—to find a new home in the rich and dangerous western lands. They floated down the rivers in flatboats, they fought Indian tribes and the weather, they starved and suffered and planted themselves in the land. Single men, adventurous men, drifted out to the frontier, following some impulse that haunted their hearts like the call of the wild geese. Immigrants from Europe, Danes, Swedes, Germans, Irishmen, suddenly found themselves, after a long and trying voyage that should have been hardship enough, starting out overland to follow the sun in its course for days and days till, at last, after many days, they reached an empty prairie, and fed the beasts that had brought them there and out of logs or sod, made their first American house."

Between 1787 and the 1850's, the spirit of expansion gripped the nation. Stephen Vincent Benét could have been describing Daniel Boone in the 1700's or the California gold prospectors in 1849. Tens of thousands of Americans went west in this period. Why? Why did we acquire the frontier lands that lured them? These are some of the questions this unit explores.

The unit also raises questions about how much change took place during this period and whether the change was a result of growth. In particular, it concentrates on changes that have to do with government. First, did democracy grow? If so, did it grow because of the frontier? In the year 1800 the Federalist party gave way to the Democratic-Republican, or Democratic party. Did this mean that the "common man" had attained power?

The second question concerns government change, too. The Federalists had tried to build a strong national, or federal government. They had tried to make the federal government stronger than the state governments. They also favored a broad interpretation of the Constitution, so that the federal government could have as much

274

power as it needed. Did the end of the Federalist party mean the end of these policies? Would the new Democrats, who believed in giving the ordinary citizen as much responsibility as possible, try to decentralize the government?

The unit begins with the story of American expansion. Here you will be called upon to identify the methods that the United States used in acquiring new lands, and to decide whether our methods changed between 1803 and 1853. The first section also contains information about the westward expansion of our population. The final selections indicate what the new lands cost the United States and how much was known about one area of the west at the time it was acquired. Taken together, this material can provide the basis for some tentative ideas about why Americans wanted the western lands.

The second part of the unit deals with the reasons for expansion. By comparing the arguments of leaders who favored expansion and statements by pioneers who went west, you will be able to form an opinion about why the United States acquired its vast new lands. You will also read speeches by political leaders who opposed expansion. Their comments about the motives behind expansionist policy will give you further insight into the problem.

At the outset of the third section, you will consider what democracy is and what promotes it. Then you will read the thesis of a famous historian, Frederick Jackson Turner, about the relationship between the frontier and the growth of American democracy. The rest of the section consists of materials relating to the practice of democracy in the first half of the nineteenth century. These materials will enable you to test Turner's idea.

You will study, for example, methods of choosing candidates for elections and changes in suffrage qualifications. You will compare the practice of democracy in the eastern part of the country and in the western part. You will compare the election campaigns of 1832 and 1840. The materials you will examine include paintings, posters, statistics, speeches, songs, and personal recollections about campaigns.

In the last section you will study the Presidencies of Thomas Jefferson (1801-1809) and Andrew Jackson (1829-1837). When these men were elected, the elections were considered revolutions. People thought Jefferson and Jackson would behave very differently from the Federalist Presidents, Washington and Adams. You will analyze a few of Jefferson's and Jackson's most important decisions to see whether or not they pursued new policies. You will also be asked to think about why the two Presidents followed the policies they did. As a point of departure, to help you recall what Federalist policies were like, you will study the major Supreme Court decisions handed down when John Marshall was Chief Justice. Marshall, a Federalist, led the Court between 1800 and 1835. His ideas about federal power were like those of Washington and Adams.

How crucial were the events of 1800-1850 for the United States today? To help you answer this question, you might consider throughout the unit how our history would differ if the United States stopped at the Appalachian Mountains or the Mississippi River.

NEW LANDS: THE STORY IN WORDS AND MAPS

I. The Nation Grows Westward

1. The Northwest Territory: A Beginning

This section is about the growth of the thirteen original states into a nation that spans a continent. The story includes the acquisition of territory by the federal government and the growth of the nation in terms of population.

Expansion occurred quickly. Except for the addition of Alaska and Hawaii as states in 1959, the United States has had its present boundaries since 1853. The American Revolution ended in 1783. Thus it took just seventy years for the United States to reach almost full growth. The Northwest Territory, acquired at the end of the Revolution, was one of the earliest additions to the country.

POINTS TO CONSIDER

Which areas the United States obtained from 1803 to 1853.

The reasons for westward expansion.

The methods used by the United States to acquire new territory.

The first step in the growth of the United States was the Treaty of Paris of 1783. Before the American Revolution, in 1774, Britain had given the area between the Ohio and Mississippi rivers to the colony of Quebec, in Canada. Even earlier, in 1763, Britain had forbidden colonists to settle west of the Appalachian Mountains. By the terms of the Treaty of Paris, the western boundary of the United States was extended to the Mississippi River. All the land east of the Mississippi River, from the Great Lakes south to Florida, became part of the United States.

Part of the area granted to America by the Treaty of Paris was known as the Northwest Territory. This was the land north of the Ohio River and east of the Mississippi River, the same area that Britain had once given to Quebec. The Northwest Territory was the object of much of the earliest westward expansion. To regulate the development of the area and to define its relationship to the rest of the country, Congress passed the Northwest Ordinance in 1787. Following are some of the provisions of the Ordinance.

1. The territory was to be governed by a governor, a secretary, and three judges appointed by Congress.

2. When the territory had 5,000 free male inhabitants over 21 years of age, the settlers could elect a legislature. The legislature could send a delegate to the United States Congress, but the delegate could not vote.

3. When any part of the territory reached a population of 60,000 free inhabitants, the people could write a constitution and apply to Congress for statehood. All states admitted by this process were to be considered equal in all respects with the older states.

4. Inhabitants of the territory were guaranteed freedom of religion and the civil liberties mentioned in the Bill of Rights. Slavery was prohibited. Public support of education was encouraged.

THE UNITED STATES IN 1783

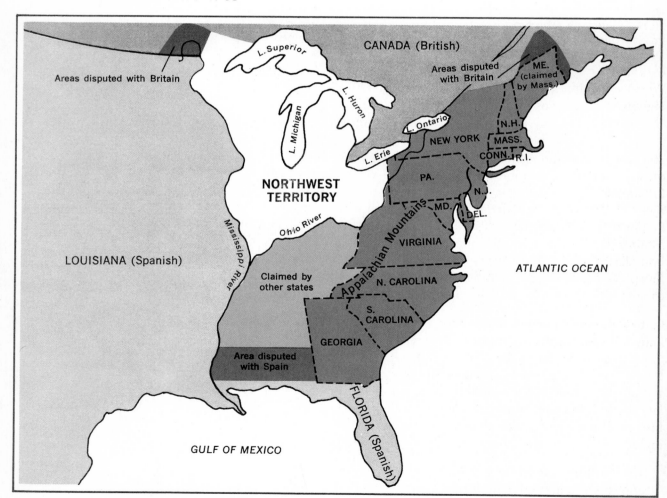

1. How did the United States come to acquire the Northwest Territory?

2. What do the provisions of the Northwest Ordinance show about the attitude of the United States government toward new territories?

3. How could the United States benefit from its acquisition of the Northwest Territory from Great Britain?

4. According to this map, what were the obstacles to further expansion?

5. Recall what you know about the problems that Washington and Adams faced. Review, too, the situation of the United States at the end of Adams' administration. Do you think that President Jefferson, who succeeded Adams, would have wished to tackle the obstacles to expansion?

2. The Louisiana Purchase

The Northwest Territory was part of the spoils of the Revolutionary War. It was added to the country before the real wave of expansion began. In 1803, President Thomas Jefferson bought the Louisiana Territory, a vast area west of the Mississippi River. This move marked the beginning of fifty years of deliberate land acquisition. During the first half of the nineteenth century, expansion became an important policy of the United States government.

Jefferson purchased Louisiana from France. The previous map shows that Spain owned this area. Spain had acquired the Louisiana Territory from France in 1762. However, in 1800 Spain returned the territory to France, under the terms of a secret treaty. At the time, Napoleon, the French ruler, wanted Louisiana so that France could rebuild her colonial empire in North America. Three years later, Napoleon abandoned his plans for a North American empire and offered to sell Louisiana to the United States. Jefferson accepted the offer.

The following map shows the territory that the United States purchased in 1803. Included on the map are the routes of several explorers. After the purchase of the Louisiana Territory, Jefferson sent Meriwether Lewis and William Clark to explore the area. Their journeys took them through Louisiana and on to the Pacific Ocean between the years 1804 and 1806. Between 1805 and 1807, Zebulon Pike also explored Louisiana. He conducted two expeditions through the territory.

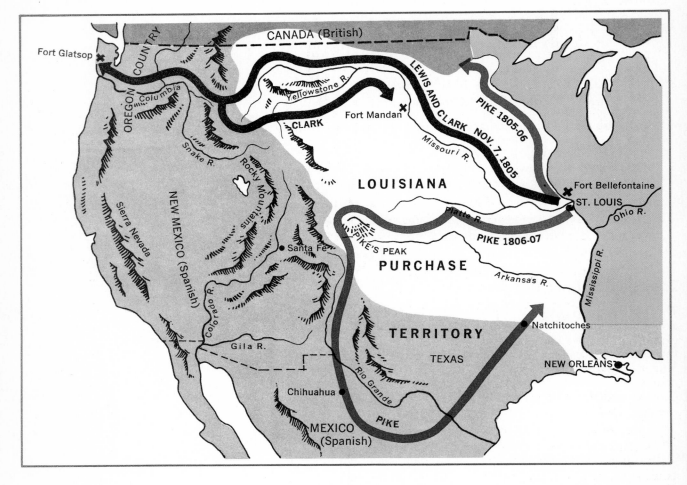

1. What did the United States acquire in the Louisiana Purchase?

2. Compare the thirteen original colonies with the Northwest Territory and the Louisiana Purchase. Can you tell anything about the significance of the two acquisitions?

3. Why do you think Jefferson wanted to buy Louisiana?

3. Florida and the Boundaries of Louisiana

The boundaries of the Louisiana Purchase were not clearly defined. The Gulf of Mexico was established as the southern limit of the Louisiana Territory and the Mississippi River as the eastern limit. In the west, however, it was not clear whether the Louisiana Purchase included Texas, which was claimed by Spain. In the north, the boundary that separated Louisiana and British North

280

America was also unclear. Furthermore, some American leaders claimed that the Louisiana Purchase included western Florida. It was not known whether Spain had given Florida back to France along with Louisiana.

Disputes developed because of the poorly defined boundaries. At the same time, there was pressure in the United States to take all of Canada from the British and all of Florida from the Spaniards. These two problems—the borders of Louisiana and the fate of Canada and Florida—were settled by treaties with Britain and Spain. The events leading to the treaties occurred during the Presidencies of James Madison (1809–1817) and James Monroe (1817–1825).

THE WAR OF 1812 AND TREATIES WITH BRITAIN

In 1812, the United States and Britain went to war for the second time in less than fifty years. The United States declared the war. This country claimed that, despite American protests, Britain had continued to violate the United States' rights as a neutral nation on the high seas. It was true that Britain had violated American rights repeatedly. During their struggles with France, the British had boarded American ships to search for deserters from the British Navy. Many American sailors had been seized, under the pretext that they were British, and forced to serve on British ships. By the time the war started, however, Britain had ceased this practice and had promised not to resume it.

The United States had several other reasons for going to war with Britain. One was the Indian attacks on settlers in the northern frontier regions. These attacks often originated in Canada. British Canadians were suspected of encouraging the Indians. In addition, northern farmers wished to expand into the fertile, wooded country north of the border. The Canadian fur trade was another tempting prize. At the same time, southern frontier farmers favored war with Britain. They, too, wanted to expand. They looked to Spanish Florida as a place to establish new farms. Since Spain was an ally of Britain, war with Britain would provide an excuse to seize Florida. Frontier farmers also favored seizing Florida as a way to cut off an important source of Indian attacks. In addition, southerners hoped to end Florida's role as a refuge for runaway slaves. The men in Congress who favored war with Britain in order to take Canada and Florida were known as "War Hawks."

The war itself was inconclusive. Neither side won a decisive victory. The Treaty of Ghent, which ended the war, did not settle the major conflicts between the United States and Great Britain. But the treaty did provide for the appointment of a com-

281

mission to settle certain boundary disputes. This provision established an important principle: the peaceful negotiation of disagreements. Thus, the boundary with Canada was settled by negotiation rather than by armed combat.

Two treaties were important in the settlement of the boundary with Canada. The Rush-Bagot Agreement, drafted in 1817, provided for disarmament on the Great Lakes and Lake Champlain. The Convention of 1818 established the border with Canada. It extended along the 49th parallel, from the Lake of the Woods, which is above the present state of Minnesota, to the Rocky Mountains. This meant that the United States no longer claimed land north of the line and that Great Britain relinquished her claim to land south of the line. Another part of the 1818 treaty provided for joint American and British occupation of the Oregon country.

THE ADAMS-ONÍS AGREEMENT WITH SPAIN

In 1819, the United States signed a treaty with Spain. The treaty was negotiated for this country by John Quincy Adams, the Secretary of State. The Spanish representative was Don Luis de Onís, the Spanish minister to the United States. The treaty settled the Spanish-American conflicts over who owned Florida and Texas.

A series of American actions in Florida forced Spain to give up part of her claims. In 1810, American settlers in western Florida revolted. President Madison proclaimed United States possession of the area and authorized occupation of it. In 1813, the United States seized the Spanish fort at Mobile and occupied the region around it. Spain was unable to halt American expansion into western Florida because she was busy combatting revolutions in her Latin American colonies. In 1818, Andrew Jackson pursued a group of Indians into Spanish territory and seized forts in eastern Florida. Spain, realizing that the loss of Florida was inevitable, decided to sell it.

By the terms of the Adams-Onís Treaty, the United States acquired eastern Florida, and Spain renounced her claims to western Florida and the Oregon country. The treaty also defined the western limits of the Louisiana Purchase. The United States gave up its claim to Texas and agreed to pay the claims that American citizens had made against the Spanish government. These claims were for damage done to American shipping during the undeclared war with France and Spain from 1798 to 1800. The claims totaled $5 million.

BOUNDARY CHANGES, 1810–1819

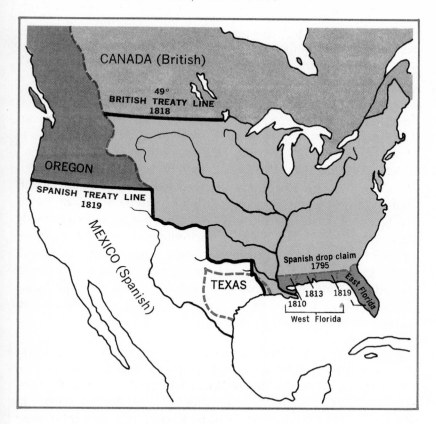

1. What did the United States acquire through the 1818 and 1819 treaties?

2. What did the United States give up in those treaties?

3. How did the United States acquire the land it received from Britain in 1818? Do you suppose that the War of 1812 helped America to get this territory? Why or why not? How could you check your answer?

4. How did the United States get the territory it acquired from Spain in 1819? Do you suppose that the War of 1812 influenced the settlement?

5. Compare the way the United States acquired land in 1818 and 1819 with the way it gained possession of the Louisiana Territory.

6. How did American policy in the War of 1812 differ from the foreign policies of Washington and Adams? Why do you think American policy changed?

283

4. Texas and the Mexican Cession

When the United States purchased Louisiana from France in 1803, it also claimed the territory of Texas. The United States renounced this claim in the Adams-Onís Treaty of 1819. Americans were permitted to settle in Texas, however, and by 1845 Texas had entered the Union. Three years later, the United States also acquired the territory between Texas and the Pacific Ocean. This area is generally known as the Mexican Cession. The narrative that follows tells how Texas and the Mexican Cession became part of the United States.

TEXAS ENTERS THE UNION

In 1820, the Spanish authorities granted an American citizen named Moses Austin the right to bring a limited number of colonists to Texas. Austin died shortly thereafter, but his son, Stephen F. Austin, carried on with his plans for settlement. In 1821, the people of Mexico revolted against Spanish rule. Texas now came under the control of the new Mexican government. The Mexican attitude was more favorable to American settlers than the Spanish attitude had been. Soon many Americans were moving to Texas to live and work.

Friction quickly developed between the American colonizers and the Mexicans. The Texas settlers began to resent Mexican rule. Many things disturbed the Texans. First, the Mexican authorities opposed slavery. Many Texans wanted to use slaves for work in the cotton fields. Second, the Texans wanted more control of their local government than the Mexican authorities would permit. Third, the Mexican government required that all settlers adopt the Roman Catholic faith and become citizens of Mexico. Most of the settlers were Protestants who considered themselves American citizens living in a foreign land. Finally, in 1830, the Mexican government, fearful of the rising number of Americans in Texas, prohibited further settlement of Texas by United States citizens.

Armed clashes between the Texans and Mexicans occurred in 1835. The dictator of Mexico, Santa Anna, responded by abolishing all local rights. Then, in February 1836, he marched to San Antonio to beseige the Alamo, a mission held by the Texans. The Mexicans overran the Alamo killing all of the defenders. The famous frontiersmen Davy Crocket and Jim Bowie were among the victims.

On March 2, 1836, the Texans declared their independence and established the Lone Star Republic. Sam Houston was named commander of the Texan army.

The small Texan army fared poorly against the more numerous Mexican troops. However, in April 1836, the Texans defeated the Mexican army decisively at San Jacinto. Santa Anna was captured and forced to sign a treaty in which he promised to secure Mexican recognition of Texas. Both he and the Mexican government later rejected the treaty.

The Texans formed a government and elected Sam Houston president. They sent a representative to Washington to seek recognition of their independence and admission to the Union.

Opposition to the admission of Texas soon developed. Since Mexico still claimed Texas, many Americans believed that the annexation of Texas would bring about war with Mexico. Also, since Texas permitted slavery, many northerners feared that its admission would strengthen the position of the southern states in Congress.

By the early 1840's, the question of Texas' admission into the Union was an important issue. In April 1844, the United States and Texas signed a treaty which provided for United States annexation of Texas. President Tyler submitted the treaty to the Senate with a message in which he argued for annexation. He believed that the annexation of Texas was in the best interests of the nation. The Constitution, you will recall, requires that treaties be approved by two thirds of the Senate. On June 8, 1844, the Senate rejected annexation by a vote of thirty five to sixteen.

The question of the annexation of Texas became an important factor in the Presidential election of 1844. The major political parties of this period were the Democrats and the Whigs. James K. Polk, the Democratic candidate, ran on an expansionist platform which called for the annexation of Texas. Henry Clay, the Whig candidate, feared war with Mexico. He opposed immediate annexation. Polk won the election. The popular vote was close, however. Out of almost 3,700,000 votes, Polk won by a margin of only 38,000.

In March 1845, before Polk took office, President Tyler made a bold move. He recommended that the treaty providing for the annexation of Texas be accepted by a joint resolution of Congress. Passage of a joint resolution requires only a majority vote of both houses of Congress. Thus, the two-thirds vote of the Senate needed for the ratification of a treaty was bypassed. Congress approved the resolution, and Tyler signed it only three days before he left office. Following Texas' approval of annexation, Texas was admitted to the Union. United States annexation of Texas

285

angered the Mexican government. Mexico broke off diplomatic relations with the United States.

TEXAS BOUNDARIES AND THE MEXICAN CESSION

Now that Texas was part of the country, President Polk was anxious to extend the boundaries of the United States from Texas to the Pacific Ocean. This territory, too, was a source of friction between the United States and Mexico. Many Americans had settled in the Mexican province of California. The American settlers objected to Mexican rule, and the Mexican government opposed American settlement of the area.

Polk also wanted to define the Texas boundaries more clearly. When Texas achieved its independence from Mexico, the new Texas government claimed that its boundaries extended as far south as the Rio Grande. Mexico had always regarded the Nueces River as Texas' southern boundary. When Texas became a part of the United States, Polk felt he should settle the boundary problem. Mexico, however, was not interested in discussing boundaries. Mexico had never recognized the independence or statehood of Texas in the first place.

President Polk hoped to settle these questions with Mexico by peaceful means. In November 1845, he appointed John Slidell minister to Mexico. Slidell was instructed to negotiate the Texas boundary and to purchase New Mexico and California. But the Mexican government refused to receive Slidell.

Upon learning of Slidell's rejection, Polk ordered General Zachary Taylor to move his troops from the Nueces River to the north bank of the Rio Grande. Following Slidell's return to Washington on May 8, 1846, Polk discussed the Mexican crisis with his Cabinet. Polk maintained that there were ample reasons for sending a war message to Congress. In the midst of these discussions, Polk received a report from General Taylor of a skirmish between the Mexican and American forces. Polk sent a war message to Congress on May 11. Two days later, Congress declared war.

The war with Mexico lasted until 1848. The Treaty of Guadalupe Hidalgo was signed on February 2, 1848. Under the terms of the treaty, Mexico recognized the American claim to Texas as far south as the Rio Grande and ceded the territories of New Mexico and California to the United States. The treaty also fixed the boundary between Mexico and the United States. In return, the United States paid Mexico $15 million. The United States also agreed to assume the claims of American citizens against the Mexican government. These claims, for damage to American property during the Mexican War of Independence, amounted to approximately $3.25 million.

TEXAS AND THE MEXICAN CESSION

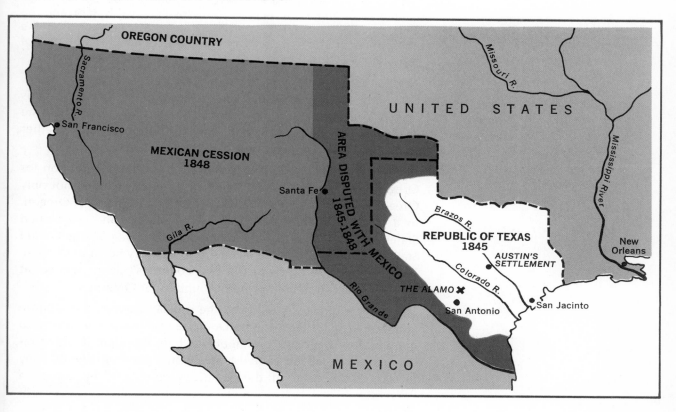

1. What were the major steps in the entrance of Texas into the Union? How did we acquire the area known as the Mexican Cession?

2. On what basis did Congress assume the right to annex Texas? Did we have any legal title to the area?

3. Why do you think Tyler and Polk were willing to risk war over Texas?

4. Why do you suppose Mexico was willing to fight for Texas? Why would Mexico refuse to give up Texas when it was threatened, as Spain gave up Florida?

5. What would you say were the most important factors in the United States' acquisition of Texas and the Mexican Cession?

6. How does this compare with earlier land acquisitions? How might you explain the similarities or differences?

5. Oregon

The Oregon Territory, a vast area in the northwest corner of the country, included the present states of Washington, Oregon, and Idaho, parts of Montana and Wyoming, and about half of British Columbia. In the early 1800's, Spain, Russia, Great Britain, and the United States claimed this territory. In 1846, one year after the annexation of Texas, most of the Oregon country became part of the United States. The story of this acquisition follows.

The first European power to drop its claim to Oregon was Spain. Spain renounced her stake in Oregon in 1819, in the Adams-Onís Treaty. You may wish to review the reasons why Spain became willing to negotiate about her American interests, and whether Spain received compensation for Oregon. (See page 282.)

The next European power to withdraw from the competition for Oregon was Russia. Russia's claims in America included not only Oregon, but also much of the Pacific coastal area north of Oregon. In a treaty negotiated in 1824 between Russia and the United States, Russia agreed to give up her claims to Oregon. The United States in return renounced all claims to territory north of Oregon. The dividing line between the two countries' claims was set at 54° 40′, which was the northern boundary of Oregon.

The treaty with Russia followed the proclamation of the Monroe Doctrine in 1823. The Monroe Doctrine was an announcement to the world of American foreign policy. In it, President James Monroe declared that the United States would view unfavorably any further colonization of the American continents by European powers.

By 1824, only Great Britain and the United States claimed Oregon. You will recall that, in the Convention of 1818 (see p. 282), Great Britain and the United States agreed to joint occupation of the territory. The two countries later specified that this agreement could be terminated by either country on one year's notice.

Meanwhile, British and American settlers moved into the area. Both the British and the Americans established fur-trading companies. However, by the 1820's a British organization, the Hudson's Bay Company, controlled most of the trade in Oregon.

American settlement of Oregon was insignificant at first. In 1842, however, a large number of Americans, victims of the so-called "Oregon fever," set off across the plains on the Oregon Trail. Nearly all of the American immigrants settled south of the Columbia River in the fertile Willamette Valley. By 1845, there were approximately five thousand Americans south of the river, compared to about seven hundred British settlers north of the river.

In the campaign of 1844, James K. Polk, the Democratic Presidential candidate, called for the "reoccupation" of Oregon. You will remember that Polk also called for the annexation of Texas in 1844. By joining the two issues, he helped make both of them more popular. Many northerners opposed the admission of Texas to the Union because it would become a slave state. Southerners, in turn, objected to Oregon's admission to the United States because Oregon would be free territory. Joining the two questions made each more acceptable to the other side.

Although committed to the acquisition of Oregon, Polk hoped to achieve his objective through negotiation. In July 1845, Polk's Secretary of State informed the British minister in Washington that the United States would agree to divide the Oregon country at the 49th parallel. The British minister rejected the offer.

Polk now believed he was justified in reasserting America's claim to all of the Oregon country. He maintained that if war resulted, the United States could not be blamed for starting it. In his annual message to Congress, in December 1845, Polk claimed all of Oregon and recommended that the United States give Great Britain the one year's notice required for ending joint occupation. Polk's message was favorably received. Congress passed a resolution in April 1845 that gave the President power to terminate joint occupation.

While Congress debated the resolution to end joint occupation, it appeared that the United States and Great Britain were headed for war. However, the leaders of the British government decided to offer concessions to the United States. They felt it was essential to avoid war because of the domestic problems Britain was facing at the time, and because of the close economic ties between Great Britain and the United States. British manufacturers depended on America as a market for their goods and as a supplier of raw cotton.

When the British government was notified of the intention of the United States to terminate joint occupation, British officials suggested that the two countries establish a boundary along the 49th parallel. This proposal was submitted to Washington on June 6, 1846. Polk was convinced that it should be rejected. However, his Cabinet urged him to submit the proposed treaty to the Senate for its advice before he took action on it himself. In this way, Polk and his administration would escape responsibility for accepting or rejecting the British offer. Polk accepted the Cabinet's suggestion and sent the treaty to the Senate. Two factors that influenced his decision were the outbreak of hostilities with Mexico, in May

1846, and naval preparations by the British. The Senate advised acceptance of the treaty and ratified it on June 15, 1846.

The peaceful settlement of the Oregon boundary was a compromise. The United States and Great Britain both lost territory they had previously claimed. The United States abandoned her demand that the boundary be fixed along 54°40′. However, America gained territory north of the Columbia River that had barely been settled by Americans.

THE OREGON COUNTRY IN 1846

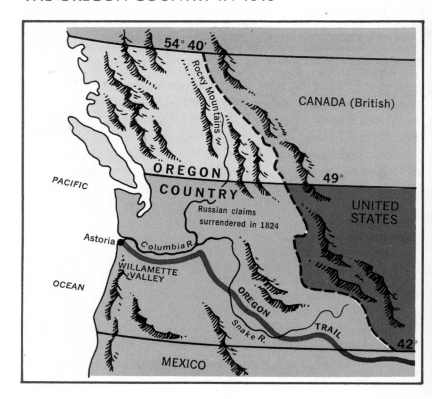

1. How did the United States become one of the two powers claiming Oregon? Why do you think Russia and Spain decided to surrender their claims? Why do you think Britain agreed to share occupation of Oregon with the United States? Consider all the events described in this section before you give your answers.

2. Mexico fought for Texas and the area included in the Mexican Cession. Why would Britain refuse to fight for Oregon? In your answer consider the reasons mentioned in the above account and the other events described in this section.

3. What do you think were the most important factors in our acquisition of Oregon?

4. Compare the reasons for our success in acquiring Oregon with the reasons for success in gaining other territories. What changes have there been since 1803? How would you explain these changes?

5. Between 1815 and 1825, the Czar, or King, of Russia was concerned with reforming the Russian government. Because of dissatisfaction with the Czar's policies, a revolt against the government occurred in 1825. How do you think this could have influenced Russian policy in Oregon? How did revolutions in Spain's Latin American colonies affect Spanish policy in Florida? What other kinds of European affairs could have affected the policies of European countries toward their American lands?

6. In question 4, how did you explain the changes in the way the United States acquired territory? What questions might you ask about European history to test your explanation?

6. Rounding Out the Nation

THE WEBSTER-ASHBURTON TREATY

The boundary between Maine and Canada established by the Treaty of Paris of 1783 was unclear. In time, disputes over the boundary flared up between Great Britain and the United States. In 1827, the two countries agreed to submit the issues in question to the King of the Netherlands. The boundary he suggested was a compromise, but the Senate, by a margin of one vote, refused to accept his settlement of the boundary.

In 1842, with new administrations in control of the British and American governments, negotiations for settling the differences between the two countries were resumed. Daniel Webster, then Secretary of State under President John Tyler, and Lord Ashburton, the British special envoy, met in Washington. They formulated the Webster-Ashburton Treaty, which was approved by the Senate in August 1842.

The Webster-Ashburton Treaty established the boundary between the United States and Canada at its present line. The United States received about 7,000 of the 12,000 square miles of the disputed territory. An important factor that influenced the negotiations was the discovery of a map, supposedly drawn in 1782, that supported

British claims to all of the disputed territory. The treaty also established the boundary line from the frontiers of Vermont and New York to the Lake of the Woods. The United States gained about 6,500 square miles in the settlement of this boundary.

THE GADSDEN PURCHASE

With the exception of Alaska, the United States reached her present continental boundaries in 1853 with the acquisition of some territory from Mexico. Even after the Treaty of Guadalupe Hidalgo in 1848, questions about the boundary with Mexico remained. James Gadsden was named by the United States government to negotiate a settlement. A treaty was approved in which the United States purchased a strip of land from Mexico for $10 million. The territory, located south of the Gila River, became known as the Gadsden Purchase. This area, which is now part of Arizona and New Mexico, was regarded as a desirable location for a southern railroad route to California. The southern boundary of the Gadsden Purchase is the present-day boundary with Mexico.

▦ AREA DISPUTED WITH BRITAIN		

TERRITORIAL GROWTH OF THE UNITED STATES

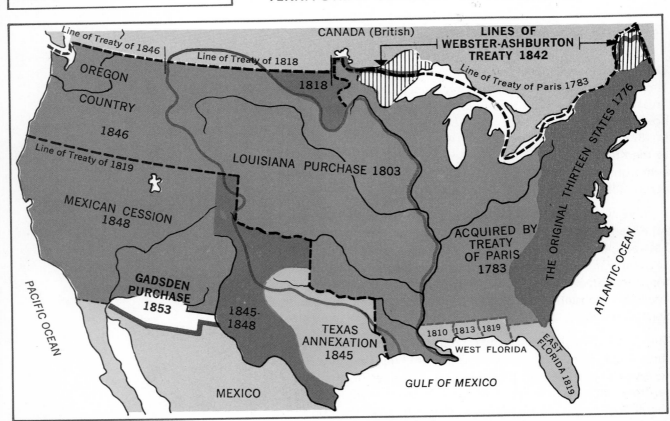

1. What did the United States give up in the Webster-Ashburton Treaty? What did we gain?

2. Why do you think we were able to win these territorial grants so peacefully? How do the reasons for our gains under the Webster-Ashburton Treaty compare with the reasons for our earlier gains from Britain?

3. What did we gain by the Gadsden Purchase?

4. Contrast the method by which we obtained the Gila River Valley from Mexico with the way we acquired Texas and the Mexican Cession. How might you explain the differences?

SEVENTY YEARS OF EXPANSION: HOW WAS IT DONE?
1. What happened to the area of the United States between 1783 and 1853?

2. How did we acquire the different territories that were added to the United States? Did any trend develop in the way these areas were acquired?

3. Were there any changes in American foreign policy between the time of Washington and 1853? Were there any changes in the way other nations behaved toward the United States?

4. How might you explain whatever trends or changes you have noticed?

5. What information is lacking about the territorial growth of the United States?

ANOTHER KIND OF EXPANSION

7. Observers of the Westward Movement

Up to this point, you have been concerned with the United States' vast increase in territory. Now, you will examine another kind of expansion—the movement of people to the West.

The following selections present the impressions of three men who viewed the American westward movement as it happened. The first account is by Morris Birkbeck, an Englishman who started on a westward journey to Illinois in 1817. In it, he describes the advance of settlers into Pennsylvania. The second account is taken from the writings of Francis Parkman, a leading nineteenth-century American historian. It is an excerpt from his description of a journey to Oregon in 1846. The trip was so exhausting that it left him a semi-invalid for the rest of his life. The third report, by a Baltimore journalist, describes conditions in Texas in 1844. It appeared in a newspaper article, under the section dealing with foreign affairs.

WESTERN PENNSYLVANIA: MORRIS BIRKBECK

Morris Birkbeck, **Notes on a Journey in America, from the Coast of Virginia to the Territory of Illinois** (London, England: James Ridgeway, 1818), pp. 30-32, 35-36.

So here we are, nine in number, one hundred and thirty miles of mountain country between us and Pittsburg. We learn that the stages which pass daily from Philadelphia and Baltimore are generally full, and that there are now many persons at Baltimore waiting for places. No vehicles of any kind are to be hired, and here we must stay or *walk* off: the latter we prefer; and separating each our bundle, from the little that we have of travelling stores, we are about to undertake our mountainous pilgrimage; accepting the alternative most cheerfully, after the dreadful shaking of the last hundred miles by stage. . . .

We have now fairly turned our backs on the old world and find ourselves in the very stream of emigration. Old America seems to be breaking up, and moving westward. We are seldom out of sight, as we travel on this grand track, towards the Ohio [River], of family groups, behind and before us, some with a view to a particular spot, close to a brother, perhaps, or a friend, who has gone before, and reported well of the country. Many like ourselves, when they arrive in the wilderness, will find no lodge prepared for them.

. . . The condition of the people of America is so different from aught [anything] that we in Europe have an opportunity of observing, that it would be difficult to convey an adequate notion of their character.

They are great travellers; and in general, better acquainted with the vast expanse of country, spreading over their eighteen states, (of which Virginia alone nearly equals Great Britain in extent), than the English with their little island.

They are also a migrating people; and even when in prosperous circumstances, can contemplate a change of situation, which under our old establishments and fixed habits, none, but the most enterprising, would venture upon, when urged by adversity [misfortune].

To give an idea of the internal movements of this vast hive, about 12,000 waggons passed between Baltimore and Philadelphia, in the last year, with from four to six horses, carrying from thirty-five to forty cwt [hundredweight]. The cost of carriage is about seven

294

dollars per cwt, from Philadelphia to Pittsburg, and the money paid for the conveyance of goods on this road, exceeds £300,000 [pounds] sterling. Add to these the numerous stages loaded to the utmost, and the innumerable travellers on horseback, on foot, and in light waggons, and you have before you a scene of bustle and business, extending over a space of three hundred miles, which is truly wonderful.

OREGON: FRANCIS PARKMAN

Last Spring, 1846, was a busy season in the city of St. Louis. Not only were emigrants from every part of the country preparing for the journey to Oregon and California, but an unusual number of traders were making ready their wagons and outfits for Santa Fé. The hotels were crowded, and the gunsmiths and saddlers were kept constantly at work in providing arms and equipments for the different parties of travellers. Steamboats were leaving the levee [landing place] and passing up the Missouri, crowded with passengers on their way to the frontier. . . .

The passengers on board the "Radnor" corresponded with her freight. In her cabin were Santa Fé traders, gamblers, speculators, and adventurers of various descriptions, and her steerage was crowded with Oregon emigrants, "mountain men," negroes, and a party of Kanzas [Kansas] Indians, who had been on a visit to St. Louis. . . .

In five or six days we began to see signs of the great western movement that was taking place. Parties of emigrants, with their tents and wagons, were encamped on open spots near the bank, on their way to the common rendezvous at Independence. On a rainy day, near sunset, we reached the landing of this place, which is some miles from the river, on the extreme frontier of Missouri. The scene was characteristic, for here were represented at one view the most remarkable features of this wild and enterprising region. On the muddy shore stood some thirty or forty dark slavish-looking Spaniards, gazing stupidly out from beneath their broad hats. They were attached to one of the Santa Fé companies, whose wagons were crowded together on the banks above. In the midst of these, crouching over a smouldering fire, was a group of Indians, belonging to a remote Mexican tribe. One or two French hunters from the mountains, with their long hair and buck-skin dresses were looking at the boat; and seated on a log close at hand were three men, with rifles lying across their knees. The fore-most of these, a tall, strong figure, with a clear blue eye and an open, intelligent face, might very well represent that race of rest-less and intrepid [fearless] pioneers whose axes and rifles have

In 1817, $7.00 was worth much more than it is worth today. A pair of shoes cost only $1.28, a quart of milk 4¢, and a pound of butter 22¢. £300,000 was worth about $1.5 million.

Francis Parkman, **The Oregon Trail: Sketches of Prairie and Rocky-Mountain Life** (Eighth edition; Boston: Little, Brown and Company, 1883), pp. 1-3, 5-6.

The "steerage" is the deck where passengers paying the lowest fares used to ride.

295

opened a path from the Alleghanies [Alleghenies] to the western prairies. He was on his way to Oregon, probably a more congenial field [pleasant area] to him than any that now remained on this side of the great plains. . . .

. . . The emigrants, for whom our friends professed such contempt, were encamped on the prairie about eight or ten miles distant [away], to the number of a thousand or more, and new parties were constantly passing out from Independence to join them. They were in great confusion, holding meetings, passing resolutions, and drawing up regulations, but unable to unite in the choice of leaders to conduct them across the prairie. Being at leisure one day, I rode over to Independence. The town was crowded. A multitude of shops had sprung up to furnish the emigrants and Santa Fé traders with necessaries for their journey; and there was an incessant hammering and banging from a dozen blacksmiths' sheds, where the heavy wagons were being repaired, and the horses and oxen shod. The streets were thronged with men, horses, and mules. While I was in the town, a train of emigrant wagons from Illinois passed through, to join the camp on the prairie, and stopped in the principal street. A multitude of healthy children's faces were peeping out from under the covers of the wagons. Here and there a buxom [plump] damsel was seated on horseback, holding over her sunburnt face an old umbrella or a parasol, once gaudy enough, but now miserably faded. The men, very sober-looking countrymen, stood about their oxen; and as I passed I noticed three old fellows, who, with their long whips in their hands, were zealously [eagerly] discussing the doctrine of regeneration. The emigrants, however, are not all of this stamp. Among them are some of the vilest outcasts in the country. I have often perplexed myself to divine [guess] the various motives that give impulse to this migration; but whatever they may be, whether an insane hope of a better condition in life, or a desire of shaking off restraints of law and society, or mere restlessness, certain it is, that multitudes bitterly repent [regret] the journey, and, after they have reached the land of promise, are happy enough to escape from it.

The "doctrine of regeneration" is a religious belief which maintains that salvation is granted to only a few select individuals.

Niles' National Register, Dec. 28, 1844, p. 257.

TEXAS: A JOURNALIST

Two gentlemen from Missouri, who have just arrived, for the purpose of selecting a location to move to, state, they counted all the emigrant wagons as they passed between Fayetteville, Arkansas, and Doaksville, some coming, and some returning from the Trinity [Texas] country. There were 225 wagons coming, and

75 returning. As they met on the road, the faint hearted, who were going back, would tell of their difficulties, which were all embraced in the want of provisions, arising from the want of means to get them, with the addition [comment] that those who turn back from a good work always make, namely, that everybody that started with them was doing, or about to do likewise—which was untrue. But they stopped none—they deterred none. Those whose faces were turned hitherward, kept on; and being warned of the high price of corn on Trinity [River], will generally wait till spring, before they go there, spending the winter where the corn is cheaper and easier obtained. Even now, as we write, four wagons are passing the office from Green County, Illinois, with "Polk Dallas, Oregon and Texas," painted on the covers. These intend going direct to the forks of Trinity.

1. What are the major impressions you get about the westward movement from these three accounts?

2. Do any of the three writers try to explain what they have observed? If so, how?

3. Can you think of any possible explanations for what is described here?

4. What are the limitations of reports like these as sources of information about the westward movement? What are the values of such reports?

8. New States, 1790–1861

Under the Constitution, a territory which is part of an existing state can enter the Union as an independent state only with the original state's consent. Except for this provision, Congress can admit new states by any procedure it chooses.

The procedure by which new states were created usually began when a territory presented a petition to Congress asking for statehood. If Congress approved the petition, it passed an "enabling act" that authorized the territory to prepare a state constitution. If the constitution was acceptable to Congress, Congress passed a joint resolution declaring the territory to be a state. The President then had to approve the resolution and issue a proclamation of statehood.

The map on the next page shows the states that were admitted to the Union between 1790 and 1861. The date that appears with each state name is the date of the state's admission into the United States.

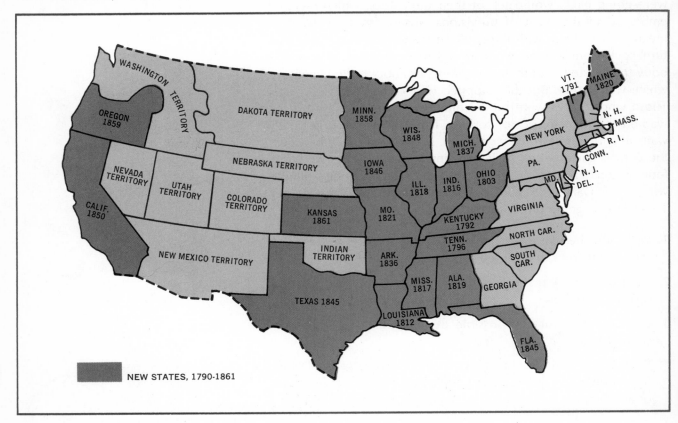

NEW STATES, 1790-1861

ORDER OF ENTRY INTO THE UNION
1791—VERMONT
1792—KENTUCKY
1796—TENNESSEE
1803—OHIO
1812—LOUISIANA
1816—INDIANA
1817—MISSISSIPPI
1818—ILLINOIS
1819—ALABAMA
1820—MAINE
1821—MISSOURI
1836—ARKANSAS
1837—MICHIGAN
1845—FLORIDA
1845—TEXAS
1846—IOWA
1848—WISCONSIN
1850—CALIFORNIA
1858—MINNESOTA
1859—OREGON
1861—KANSAS

1. How does the entry of new states into the Union compare with America's acquisition of territory?

2. Does it appear from this comparison that many Americans were anxious to move to the West? Explain.

9. The Distribution of Population: Four Maps

1790

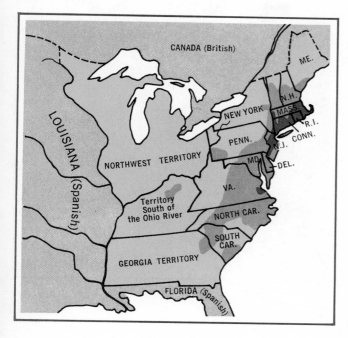

1800

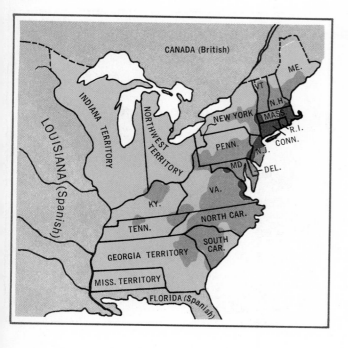

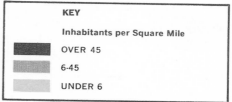

KEY

Inhabitants per Square Mile

OVER 45

6-45

UNDER 6

1830

KEY

Inhabitants per Square Mile

OVER 45

6-45

UNDER 6

1840

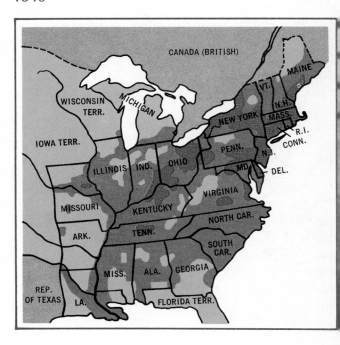

300

1. What do these maps tell you about the distribution of population in the United States between 1790 and 1840? What changes in population distribution show up? Do they follow any pattern?

2. What events do you think might have caused these population changes?

3. How does the information in these maps add to what you learned from the first-hand accounts of people who observed or took part in the western movement? to what you learned from the map of new states?

10. Population Changes: Harold Underwood Faulkner

Harold Underwood Faulkner, a modern historian, specialized in American economic and social history. This selection from one of his books presents a description of the changes in population from 1790 to 1850.

. . . The population of the Old Northwest (Ohio, Indiana, Illinois, Michigan, Wisconsin), which at the opening of the Revolution was composed of but a few thousand French, by 1810 numbered 272,324, and by 1860 amounted to 6,926,884. Indiana was admitted into the Union in 1816, Illinois in 1818, and Michigan in 1837. By 1830 Ohio had over one million people, more than Massachusetts and Connecticut combined. Indiana in the decade 1810 to 1820 grew from 24,000 to 147,000. That this increase in population seriously drained the East is seen by the fact that Virginia and Massachusetts during the decade 1820 to 1830 remained almost stationary while the western states grew at a rate of 100 to 150 per cent. Chicago, a mere fur-trading station in 1830, increased to over 100,000 by 1860; Cleveland, with only 6070 in 1840, numbered 43,000 in 1860. . . .

. . . In 1790 over 94 per cent lived on the Atlantic slope of the thirteen original colonies, with less than a quarter of a million west of the Alleghenies. By 1820 the proportion had distinctly changed. The census of that year showed about 73 per cent living on the Atlantic slope and 27 per cent west of the mountains. The southern group of states was still the most populous, but New York could boast of the greatest population of any single state. The population beyond the mountains now outnumbered that of New England. During the decade 1810 to 1820 New York added

Harold Underwood Faulkner, **American Economic History** (Seventh edition; New York: Harper & Row, Publishers, 1954), pp. 182, 287-288. Copyright © 1960 by Harold Underwood Faulkner. Reprinted by permission of the publishers. Abridged.

413,000 to her numbers, more than any other state; Ohio came next, with 351,000. But the ratio of increase had been greatest in the new western states; one eastern state, Delaware, had remained practically stationary. In the thirty years from 1790 to 1820 the seaboard states had contributed almost two and one half millions to the population of the West.

The Census of 1850 revealed that almost half of the population (45 per cent) now lived west of the Alleghenies. Professor Channing has pointed out that in the thirty years from 1820 to 1850 the number of inhabitants of the region west of the Appalachians more than doubled while the population of the seaboard states, notwithstanding the immigration from Europe, failed to double . . . [It] seems probable, he believes, that during these three decades the East contributed at least four million to the population of the West.

The South furnished the largest proportion of this western migration. Two-fifths of the inhabitants of South Carolina, one-third of those of Virginia and North Carolina, and nearly one-quarter of those of Georgia emigrated west of the mountains to form almost the entire population of the Old Southwest and the predominating element in the Old Northwest. A continual stream of New Englanders moved toward the west, sometimes pausing for a generation in Vermont or western New York, but in most cases pushing on eventually to the new country and giving a distinct New England tone to the northern tier [row] of counties in Ohio and Indiana. There was also a large movement from the middle states into the Northwest, in actual numbers greater than that from New England.

1. Does this description provide information that you could not have gotten by a close study of the four population maps? If so, what?

2. Does Faulkner confirm any of the ideas about population changes that the maps gave you?

3. What are some of the major differences between the United States in 1790 and in 1850?

4. How did the settlers seem to react to the acquisition of new lands?

5. What information is still lacking in the full story of westward expansion?

THE BARGAIN

11. The Costs of Expansion

EVENT	TOTAL OF ALL UNITED STATES GOVERNMENT EXPENDITURES IN THE YEAR(S) OF THE EVENT	AMOUNT SPENT ON THE EVENT	NUMBER OF SQUARE MILES ACQUIRED	COST PER SQUARE MILE OF TERRITORY	COST IN BATTLE DEATHS
LOUISIANA PURCHASE, 1803	$ 7,852,000	$15,000,000*	827,192	$ 18.00	——
WAR OF 1812 (PARTLY INSPIRED BY DESIGNS ON FLORIDA AND CANADA)	$ 20,281,000	$ 2,000,000	——	——	2260
ADAMS-ONÍS AGREEMENT, 1819	$ 21,464,000	$ 5,000,000	71,003	$ 70.00	——
MEXICAN WAR, 1846–48, AND TREATY OF GUADALUPE HIDALGO, 1848	$130,425,000 ——	$97,500,000 $18,250,000	—— 1,193,063	—— $ 10.54	1721 ——
GADSDEN PURCHASE, 1853	$ 48,184,000	$10,000,000	29,640	$337.00	——

*Two million dollars were appropriated for the first payment. The remaining thirteen million dollars were paid over a period of years.

1. What do these figures tell you about expansion?

2. What did Morris Birkbeck add to this topic?

3. What costs of expansion might there have been other than the ones shown here?

THE STORY OF AMERICAN EXPANSION

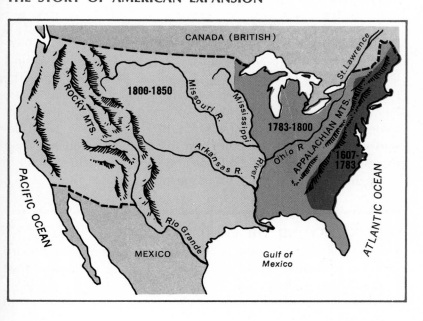

What developments does the map on the previous page summarize? Relate what you know of the story behind this map.

12. What Did We Get?

American officials knew very little about what lay west of the Mississippi River in 1800. Most of the area was unexplored. This lack of knowledge was a major reason why President Thomas Jefferson sent Meriwether Lewis and William Clark on their expedition in 1804. Zebulon Pike, in his explorations from 1805 to 1807, also surveyed areas previously unexplored by Americans.

Now that he had Louisiana, a host of questions pecked at Jefferson's restless brain. He had no information about the vast territory except fantastic tales of trappers. He wanted factual answers. He knew that in 1792 the Boston skipper Robert Gray had sailed his ship up the Columbia River and seen the edge of the Oregon country. Now Jefferson wanted this region explored overland. And Congress, by voting money to extend American trading posts with the Indians up the Missouri River, gave him the opportunity.

He would send a corps of exploration to the new Northwest, headed by his secretary, Meriwether Lewis. Then 29, Lewis had first seriously thought of exploring the Far West when he was 18. As his associate, Lewis chose a man born to distinguish himself: red-headed William Clark, younger brother of George Rogers Clark, a hero of the Revolution....

Jefferson drew up their instructions: to find the source of the Missouri, to cross the mountain barriers, to reach the Pacific. Waterfalls, rapids and islands were to be located; weather, animal life, minerals were to be noted, as well as the kinds of furs. The President wanted to know about Indians and their customs, and he wanted specimens: the hides of strange creatures, perhaps some mammoth bones. These were the specifics. The grand design was even more sweeping: to discover the overland water route to the Pacific, to challenge the British fur trade, to fill in every possible blank place on the map.

Margaret L. Coit, **The Growing Year** ("The Life History of the United States," Vol. III [New York: Time Inc., 1963]), p. 79.

LOOKING BEYOND THE EVENTS

1. If you had been an American citizen at the time of westward expansion, what would you have thought of each successive acquisition of land? Remember the costs of the acquisition, what was known about the territory, and the method used to acquire it.

2. How can you account for the number of pioneers who were willing to go west? Do you think that the information pioneers had about the new lands could have attracted them in any particular way?

SOME LEADERS SPEAK FOR EXPANSION

II. The Forces Behind Expansion

13. James Madison, 1785

In the previous section, you were concerned with the tremendous territorial growth of the United States. You saw how the new nation acquired more and more land until it spanned the continent from the Atlantic to the Pacific oceans. Now you are going to examine some of the forces behind this growth. You will read opinions on expansion held by government leaders of the period as well as the comments of western pioneers. In this way you will become familiar with the spirit of the era and will gain additional insight into some of the reasons behind the country's growth.

The first group of readings represents the views of leaders who favored expansion. One such leader was James Madison, who was to become President in 1809. On March 20, 1785, Madison wrote a letter to the Marquis de Lafayette, a French general who had fought for the United States in the American Revolution. The following excerpt from Madison's letter shows his reaction to Spain's refusal to permit Americans to deposit goods at New Orleans. The Treaty of Paris of 1783 had given the United States the right to use the river. The Spanish, however, claimed the land west of the Mississippi, and they believed that they had exclusive control over the waterway.

POINTS TO CONSIDER
How the feelings of national leaders could have contributed to expansion.

The various reasons they gave for expansion.

Nature has given the use of the Mississippi to those who may settle on its waters [along its shores], as she gave to the United States their independence.

1. According to Madison, who owned the western lands?

2. What was the source of their rights?

3. How could such beliefs influence expansion?

The Writings of James Madison: Comprising His Public Papers and His Private Correspondence, Including Numerous Letters and Documents Now for the First Time Printed, edited by Gaillard Hunt (New York and London, England: G. P. Putnam's Sons, 1901), Vol. II, pp. 121-22.

14. President Thomas Jefferson, 1801

The following excerpt is from a letter that Thomas Jefferson wrote to James Monroe on November 24, 1801. Monroe participated in the negotiations for Louisiana in 1803.

The Writings of Thomas Jefferson, 1801-1806, edited by Paul Leicester Ford (New York and London, England: G. P. Putnam's Sons, 1897), Vol. VIII, p. 105.

... However our present interests may restrain us within our own limits, it is impossible not to look forward to distant times, when our rapid multiplication will expand itself beyond those limits, & cover the whole northern, if not the southern continent, with a people speaking the same language, governed in similar forms, & by similar laws ...

15. Senator John Breckenridge, 1803

Senator John Breckenridge of Kentucky approved of Jefferson's decision to purchase Louisiana. Breckenridge later became Jefferson's Attorney General.

The Shaping of American Diplomacy, edited by William Appleman Williams (Chicago: Rand McNally & Company, 1956), p. 99. Reprinted by permission of the publisher.

A "republic" is a government controlled by voting citizens.

This ... is an old and hackneyed doctrine; that a Republic ought not to be too extensive. ... Is the Goddess of Liberty restrained by water courses? Is she governed by geographical limits? Is her dominion on this continent confined to the east side of the Mississippi? So far from believing in the doctrine that a Republic ought to be confined within narrow limits, I believe, on the contrary, that the more extensive its dominion the more safe and more durable it will be. In proportion to the number of hands [to which] you entrust the precious blessings of a free government, in the same proportion do you multiply the chances for their preservation. ...

1. Against what belief is Breckenridge arguing?

2. What belief is he supporting?

16. The Monroe Doctrine, 1823

On December 2, 1823, President James Monroe delivered his annual message to Congress. Parts of his speech later became known as the Monroe Doctrine. This declaration was an announcement to the world of United States foreign policy.

At the time, the country was united strongly behind Monroe. Following the War of 1812, a wave of patriotism had swept the country. When Monroe, a Democratic-Republican, was elected in 1816, he received 183 electoral votes. Rufus King, the Federalist candidate, received only 34. In 1820, Monroe received all but one of the electoral votes. This overwhelming victory for the Democratic-Republicans destroyed the Federalist party. The period from 1817 to 1825 was called the "Era of Good Feelings."

Monroe announced his famous Doctrine partly in reply to a proposal made by the head of the British foreign office, George Canning. Canning wanted the United States to join with Great Britain in telling European powers to stay out of South America. Many of Spain's South American colonies had rebelled and formed republics. Britain was afraid that other European nations would help Spain recapture the lost colonies.

Monroe, like Canning, did not want European powers in South America. But Monroe did not want England involved in the affairs of the New World, either. He felt, therefore, that the United States should act alone in this matter. Monroe had still other reasons for proclaiming the Monroe Doctrine. He feared that England had designs on Cuba and that Russia was attempting to gain control of the disputed territory in the Pacific Northwest. Russia had established a fort just north of San Francisco in 1812, and then, in 1821, had tried to regulate the activity of ships of other nations along the Pacific coast.

One of the main points of the Monroe Doctrine was made in the following passage.

... [The] American continents, by the free and independent condition which they have assumed and maintain, are henceforth not to be considered as subjects for future colonization by any European powers....

Documents of American History, edited by Henry Steele Commager (Seventh edition; New York: Appleton-Century-Crofts, 1963), p. 236.

1. What was the size of the United States at the time the Doctrine was proclaimed?

2. By proclaiming the Doctrine, what did Monroe imply about the position of the United States concerning the rest of America?

3. What does this have to do with expansion?

4. Summarize the reasons for the Monroe Doctrine. What, basically, did Monroe fear?

5. Review the United States' acquisition of territory between 1803 and 1853. Could fears similar to those that prompted proclamation of the Monroe Doctrine have inspired any of the acquisitions? If so, which acquisitions?

17. Senator George McDuffie, 1844

Before he became a senator, George McDuffie served as governor of South Carolina. In the 1840's, about fifty per cent of the state's population were slaves. McDuffie presented the following argument about slavery in a speech to the Senate on May 23, 1844. This argument was used by many congressmen from slave-holding states.

Congressional Globe, 28th Congress, 1st Session, Appendix, pp. 531-532.

I never, till now, fully realized the truth and justice of [James] Monroe's declaration [of 1823], that no European power must ever be permitted to establish a colony on this continent. The more I reflect on the subject the more I am convinced that the interests, both of Europe and of this country, require that that declaration shall be maintained. . . . [Should] Great Britain permanently secure the control of Texas, it will be . . . inconsistent with the interest of every portion of the United States . . .

[The slave] population in the United States cannot be diminished, but must be increased. Now, if we shall annex Texas, it will operate as a safety-valve to let off the superabundant [excess] slave population from among us; and will, at the same time, improve their condition. They will be more happy, and we all shall be more secure. . . .

1. How does McDuffie apply the Monroe Doctrine to the situation in Texas?

2. What other reason for expansion does McDuffie give? Do you think this argument made Congress more or less likely to adopt an expansionist policy? Why?

18. Senator Sidney Breese, 1844

Sidney Breese was a Democratic senator from Illinois. He favored the annexation of Texas and the war with Mexico. On June 3, 1844, he made the following statements in a speech before the Senate.

Congressional Globe, 28th Congress, 1st Session, Appendix, p. 543.

The soil and climate of Texas are very desirable, and her productions rich and varied. Constituting, as she will, a planting state, a producer of our great staple—cotton—and of one of the great necessaries of life—sugar,—she will, united with us, greatly augment [increase] her power of production, and add largely to the number of consumers of the bread-stuffs and provisions we in the West raise in such abundance, and for which it is an object to open new markets, so that [profitable] prices for our labor can be obtained. To the manufacturing industry of the North, additional purchasers of their beautiful and necessary fabrics will be found in constantly increasing numbers, giving to their shipping interest also additional and profitable employment. . . .

19. President John Tyler, 1844

On April 22, 1844, a treaty providing for the annexation of Texas was submitted to the Senate for ratification. The treaty was accompanied by the following message from President John Tyler. Although Tyler urged the Senate to permit the annexation, the Senate rejected the treaty.

To *the Senate of the United States:*
... [Texas] has been settled principally by persons from the United States ... who carried with them into the wilderness ... the laws, customs, and political and domestic institutions of their native land. They are deeply indoctrinated in all the principles of civil liberty, and will bring along with them in the act of re-association [a] devotion to our Union and a firm and inflexible resolution to assist in maintaining the public liberty ... [Texas itself] is of incalculable value in an agricultural commercial point of view. To a soil of inexhaustible fertility it unites a genial [pleasant] and healthy climate, and is destined at a day not distant to make large contributions to the commerce of the world. ...

... I repeat, the Executive [branch of the government] saw Texas in a state of almost hopeless exhaustion, and the question was narrowed down to the simple proposition whether the United States should accept the boon [benefit] of annexation upon fair and even liberal terms, or, by refusing to do so, force Texas to seek refuge in the arms of some other power [France or Great Britain] ... through a treaty of alliance ... which might virtually make her ... dependent upon it for all future time. ...

A Compilation of the Messages and Papers of the Presidents, 1789-1897, edited by James D. Richardson (Washington, D.C.: United States Government Printing Office, 1897), Vol. IV, pp. 308, 312.

20. Senator Thomas Hart Benton, 1844

Thomas Hart Benton was one of the most outspoken advocates of westward expansion. As a senator from Missouri, he delivered this speech to Congress in 1844.

After twenty-five years, the American population has begun to extend itself to the Oregon. Some hundreds went a few years ago; a thousand went last year; two thousand are now setting out from the frontiers of Missouri; tens of thousands are meditating [thinking about] the adventure. I say to them all, Go on! the Government will follow you, and will give you protection and land ... let the emigrants rely upon it. It is the genius of our people to go ahead, and it is the practice of our Government to follow, and eventually to protect and reward the bold pioneers who open the

Abridgement of the Debates of Congress, From 1789 to 1856, edited by Thomas Hart Benton (New York: Appleton-Century-Crofts, 1861), Vol. XV, pp. 141-142.

way to new countries, and subdue the wilderness for their country. They will get protection, both civil, military and naval; for a Government will be established for them, and ships of war will visit their coast, and enter their river. Lands will be granted to them; land to the father and to the mother; land to the young men and the young women over eighteen; land to all the children. . . .

Let the emigrants go on, and carry their rifles. We want thirty thousand rifles in the valley of the Oregon; they will make all quiet there, in the event of a war with Great Britain for the dominion of that country. The war, if it comes, will not be topical [local]; it will not be confined to Oregon; but will embrace the possession of the two powers throughout the globe. Thirty thousand rifles on the Oregon will annihilate [wipe out] the Hudson Bay Company, drive them off our continent, quiet their Indians, and protect the American interests in the remote regions of the upper Missouri, the Platte, and the Arkansas [rivers], and in all the vast region of the Rocky Mountains.

Besides the recovery of the country lost, or jeoparded [endangered] by our diplomacy of 1818, the settlers in Oregon will also recover and open for us *the North American road to India!* This road lies through the South Pass and the mouth of the Oregon; and as soon as the settlements are made, our portion of the North American continent will immediately commence its Asiatic trade on this new and national route. This great question I explored some years ago, and only refer to it now to give a glimpse of the brilliant destiny which awaits the population of the Oregon valley.

1. Compare Benton's statements with those made by Breese and President Tyler. In what ways do the viewpoints of the three men resemble one another?

2. How could you characterize the difference in spirit between Benton's views and the opinions of Breese and Tyler?

21. President James K. Polk, 1845

In his inaugural address of March 4, 1845, President Polk reaffirmed his position on expansion.

To Texas the reunion is important, because the strong protecting arm of our Government would be extended over her, and the vast resources of her fertile soil and genial climate would be speedily

Inaugural Addresses of the Presidents of the United States (Washington, D.C.: United States Government Printing Office, 1961), pp. 96-97.

developed, while the safety of New Orleans and of our whole southwestern frontier against hostile aggression, as well as the interests of the whole Union, would be promoted by it. . . .

. . . As our population has expanded, the Union has been cemented and strengthened. As our boundaries have been enlarged and our agricultural population has been spread over a large surface, our . . . system [of government] has acquired additional strength and security. It may well be doubted whether it would not be in greater danger of overthrow if our present population were confined to the comparatively narrow limits of the original thirteen States than it is now that they are sparsely settled over a more expanded territory. . . . [I believe] that our system may be safely extended to the utmost bounds of our territorial limits, and that as it shall be extended the bonds of our Union, so far from being weakened, will become stronger.

None can fail to see the danger to our safety and future peace if Texas remains an independent state or becomes an ally or dependency of some foreign nation more powerful than herself. . . .

1. Which of Polk's statements echo those made by some of the other leaders?

2. What new points does he make?

3. Compare the statements of the expansionists of the 1840's with the policies defined in the Monroe Doctrine. In what way do the expansionist statements and the Monroe Doctrine reflect the same kind of thinking?

22. William Gilpin, 1846

William Gilpin was an enthusiastic advocate of our country's westward expansion. In the 1840's, he accompanied an expedition, led by the famous American explorer John Charles Frémont, to the Rocky Mountains and Nevada country. Gilpin became the first territorial governor of Colorado.

The *untransacted* [yet-to-be-accomplished] destiny of the American people is to subdue the continent—to rush over this vast field to the Pacific Ocean—to animate the many hundred millions of its people, and to cheer them upward . . . —to agitate these herculean [powerful] masses—to establish a new order in human affairs—to set free the enslaved—to regenerate superannuated

William Gilpin, **Mission of the North American People, Geographical, Social and Political** (Philadelphia: J. B. Lippincott Company, 1873), p. 124.

311

[old] nations—...to stir up the sleep of a hundred centuries—to teach old nations a new civilization—to confirm the destiny of the human race—to carry the career of mankind to its culminating point—to cause a stagnant people to be reborn—to perfect science—to emblazon history with the conquest of peace—to shed a new and resplendent glory upon mankind—to unite the world in one social family—to dissolve the spell of tyranny and exalt charity—to absolve the curse that weighs down humanity, and to shed blessings round the world!

WHY DID THE LEADERS FAVOR EXPANSION?

1. Compare Gilpin's declaration with the first part of Benton's statement. How are the ideas in the two readings alike? How do they differ?

2. What reasons do the leaders offer in justifying American expansion?

3. Which reasons appear most often?

MANIFEST DESTINY

23. An 1845 Editorial: John Louis O'Sullivan

John Louis O'Sullivan was the editor of a popular expansionist newspaper, the Democratic Review. O'Sullivan is generally given credit for coining the term "manifest destiny." This expression was often used by expansionists in the late 1840's. The following passage is from an editorial entitled "Annexation" which O'Sullivan wrote in 1845.

John Louis O'Sullivan, "Annexation," **Democratic Review**, Vol. XVII (1845), p. 5.

[Concerning] this question of the reception of Texas into the Union ... it surely is to be found [that] other nations have undertaken to intrude themselves into it, between us and the proper parties to the case, in a spirit of hostile interference against us, for the avowed object of thwarting our policy and hampering our power, limiting our greatness and checking the fulfilment of our manifest destiny to overspread the continent allotted by Providence for the free development of our yearly multiplying millions.

What did O'Sullivan mean when he used the term "manifest destiny"?

24. An 1872 Painting: John Gast

THE IDEA OF A MANIFEST DESTINY

COURTESY OF AMERICAN HERITAGE PUBLISHING CO.

MANIFEST DESTINY: AN EVALUATION

1. What was manifest destiny?

2. What points can you make about the painting on manifest destiny?

3. What developments between 1803 and 1853 would further illustrate or verify the painting's interpretation?

4. Do the selection by O'Sullivan and the painting by Gast give the impression that American expansion was inevitable? If so, how?

5. You have read statements by a number of expansionist leaders. Do any of these statements reveal a belief in manifest destiny? If so, which ones? Did the idea of a manifest destiny exist before O'Sullivan described it?

WHY PIONEERS WENT WEST

25. A Frenchman Comments, 1786

Westward expansion came about because senators and Presidents decided to buy, seize, or bargain for huge parcels of the continent. It came about because of the actions of thousands of ordinary citizens—the pioneers. Why did the pioneers go west? Clues may be found in the statements of the pioneers themselves, in the remarks of foreign observers, and in information about events that happened in the nineteenth century. The readings which follow here will introduce you to some of those materials.

The motives of one major group of pioneers are not discussed in the readings. This group is the Mormons, a religious sect formed in 1830. Because of persecution, the Mormons were forced to migrate from New York to Illinois and then to Utah. They finally found refuge on the shores of the Great Salt Lake, where they established a permanent settlement in 1847.

Earlier in this unit you read reports about the people involved in the westward movement. Harold Underwood Faulkner also commented on the makeup of the pioneer groups: "Just who went west during the first half of the nineteenth century is by no means as clear as might be supposed. The results of the most recent research indicate that the movement was essentially one of farmers and their children rather than one of city laborers." As you read the following selections, keep in mind Faulkner's remark and what you read earlier.

The Marquis de Chastellux was a French officer who served in the American Revolution. In 1786, he recorded his observations about how the American frontier was settled. Part of his report appears below.

POINTS TO CONSIDER

Why the pioneers went west.

How their reasons compare with the ones offered by the nation's leaders.

American History Told by Contemporaries, edited by Albert Bushnell Hart (New York: The Macmillan Company, 1898), Vol. II, p. 392.

At that time, twenty-five pounds sterling was worth about $111.00.

. . . The following is the manner of proceeding in these improvements, or new settlements. Any man who is able to procure a capital of five or six hundred livres of our money, or about twenty-five pounds sterling, and who has strength and inclination to work, may go into the woods and purchase a portion of one hundred and fifty or two hundred acres of land, which seldom costs him more than a dollar or four shillings and six-pence an acre, a small part of which only he pays in ready money. There he conducts a cow, some pigs, or a full sow, and two indifferent [medium quality] horses which do not cost him more than four guineas each. To these precautions he adds that of having a provision of flour and cyder [cider]. . . .

26. Noah Smithwick Goes to Texas

The following selection is from the records of Noah Smithwick. He was a blacksmith who decided to migrate to Texas in the 1820's.

What the discovery of gold was to California, the colonization act of 1825 was to Texas. In the following year Sterling C. Robinson, who had obtained a grant for a colony, for each hundred families of which he was to receive a bonus of 23,025 acres of land, went up into Kentucky recruiting. The glowing terms in which he talked of the advantages to be gained by emigrating were well calculated to further his scheme. To every head of a family, if a farmer, was promised 177 acres of farming land and 4428 acres of pasture land for stock; colonists to be exempt from taxation six years from date of settlement, with the privilege of importing, duty free, everything they might desire for themselves and families; an abundance of game, wild horses, cattle, turkeys, buffalo; deer and antelope by the drove. The woods abounded in bee trees, wild grapes, plums, cherries, persimmons, haws, and dewberries, while walnuts, hickory nuts, and pecans were abundant along the watercourses. The climate was so mild that houses were not essential; neither was an abundance of clothing or bedding, buffalo robes and bearskins supplying all that was needed for the latter and buckskin the former. Corn in quantity was to be had for the planting. In short, *there* the primitive curse was set at defiance. Mexican soldiers were stationed on the frontier to keep the Indians in check.

Of the hardships and privations, the ever-increasing danger from the growing dissatisfaction of the Indians, upon whose hunting grounds the whites were steadily encroaching, and the almost certainty of an ultimate war with Mexico, Robinson was discreetly silent. Viewed from that distance, the prospect was certainly flattering, and it should not occasion surprise that men with large families were induced to migrate thither with the hope of securing homes for themselves and children.

The Heritage of America, edited by Henry Steele Commager and Allan Nevins (Revised and enlarged edition; Boston: Little, Brown and Company, 1949), pp. 589-590. Copyright 1949 by Henry Steele Commager and Allan Nevins. Reprinted by permission of the publisher.

In 1825, the Mexican government passed an act that encouraged Americans to settle in Texas.

A "persimmon" is a soft, sweet, bright red fruit; "haws" and "dewberries" are types of wild berries.

315

27. A Missionary Writes About the Mississippi Valley

Timothy Flint, a missionary in the Mississippi Valley from 1816 to 1826, wrote about pioneer life in that region.

The Heritage of America, edited by Henry Steele Commager and Allan Nevins (Revised and enlarged edition; Boston: Little, Brown and Company, 1949), p. 267. Copyright 1949 by Henry Steele Commager and Allan Nevins. Reprinted by permission of the publisher.

A "freeholder," here, is a person who owns his land, instead of renting it or working it for a portion of the crops.

. . . But the backwoodsman of the west, as I have seen him, is generally an amiable and virtuous man. His general motive for coming here is to be a freeholder, to have plenty of rich land, and to be able to settle his children about him. It is a most virtuous motive. And I fully believe that nine in ten of the emigrants have come here with no other motive. . . .

28. Recruiting Oregon Settlers

Hall J. Kelley, a New England schoolmaster, went on several expeditions to the West. He also organized a society to promote migration to Oregon. His many writings helped to encourage the mass migration to Oregon in the 1840's. The following passages originally appeared in the September 25, 1832, issue of the *American Traveller,* a periodical published in Boston.

The Call of the Columbia, Iron Men and Saints Take the Oregon Trail, edited by Archer Butler (The Stewart Commission of Colorado College and the Denver Public Library, 1934), pp. 59-60, 63. Reprinted by permission of the Denver Public Library.

Each man and each youth, over 14 years of age, will receive 200 acres of land. Each unmarried female, over 14 years, will likewise receive 200 acres. Every individual above that age, will be required to pay $50, for which sum he will be carried to Oregon, and receive a right to 200 acres of land. Children will pay a less sum, and receive no land. Emigrants will furnish their own bedding and small stores. Other freight will be taken in vessels round Cape Horn, at $2 a barrel. Farmers and mechanics will carry their tools, and such materials as they may immediately want. As small a quantity of baggage as possible must be carried by the overland expedition. . . .

The local position of that country; its physical appearance and productions; its qualities of soil and climate, suggest, not only the practicability [possibility] of founding a colony in it; but the consequent beneficial results to our Republic; and the many valuable blessings it might be made to yield to the settlers, and to their posterity. . . . It is the object of these remarks to notice some of the advantages, which would inevitably accrue [come] to the government of the United States, from a colonization of that country.

First. The occupancy of it, by three thousand of the active sons of American freedom, would secure it from the possession of another nation, and from augmenting the power and physical resources of an enemy. It might save that and this country, from the disastrous consequences of a foreign and corrupt population; and benefit mankind by a race of people, whose past lives, affording the most honourable testimony of their characters, would be a pledge for their future conduct, and a full indemnity [payment] for all expenses incurred in their behalf.

1. Which of Kelley's reasons for going west are like the reasons given by Chastellux, Smithwick, and Flint?

2. What additional reasons does Kelley think people had for going west?

29. The California '49ers

When James W. Marshall discovered gold at Sutter's Mill in California in 1848, neither he nor Johann Sutter realized that a gold rush would follow. Thousands of people the world over caught "gold fever" and left for California. In his *Early Recollections of the Mines,* J. H. Carson describes the frantic and exciting days of the rush of the '49ers to California.

Each day now added thousands to our population, all of whom came intent on making fortunes in a few days and then leaving the country; many came on speculating expeditions; property of every description ran up to rates that set the world to wondering. In San Francisco, in particular, lots and buildings changed hands at rates unknown before in the annals of trade.

But to return to the diggings. This swarm of human beings laid cold the bright calculations of the old diggers of 1848. [In 1848 the diggers] had found gold at every step and looked on the supply as inexhaustible . . . [They thought] that for years to come . . . few would be here and . . . our rich harvest would continue . . . Men who would work could get from one to five hundred dollars per day, and in confidence of this good fortune continuing, these heavy earnings were foolishly spent in drinking and gaming, purchasing fine horses, and dressing in gaudy Indian style. Honesty was the ruling passion of '48. If an *hombre* got broke, he asked the first one he met to lend him such amount as he wanted until he could "dig her out." The loans were always made and always paid according to promise. . . .

But this honesty, so universal in '48, was not to be found in the crowds that daily thickened around us in '49. Hordes of pickpockets, robbers, thieves, and swindlers were mixed with men who had come with honest intentions. These rascals had lived all

The Heritage of America, edited by Henry Steele Commager and Allan Nevins (Revised and enlarged edition; Boston: Little, Brown and Company, 1949), pp. 560-562. Copyright 1949 by Henry Steele Commager and Allan Nevins. Reprinted by permission of the publisher.

their lives by sleight of hand, and it was evident that they had not come to California with gold rings on their white, soft hands for the purpose of wielding the pick and pan in obtaining their wishes. Murders, thefts, and heavy robberies soon became the order of the day. A panic seized that portion of the diggers who had never before been out of sight of "marm's chimbly" and who went cringing about in fear, though most of them presented the appearance of traveling armories; yet it was evident they wouldn't shoot. But men were to be found who had ridden the elephant of this world all their lives and well knew the course we had to pursue under the change of affairs. Whipping on the bare back, cutting off ears, and hanging soon became matters of as frequent occurrence as those of robbery, theft, and murder.

An armory is a place where weapons are kept.

30. Events and Conditions in the Early 1800's

So far, you have read statements by observers of the westward movement and by participants in it. Now let us turn to the background of the period.

POINTS TO CONSIDER

How the events and conditions listed below could help explain why pioneers went west.

How these events and conditions could relate to the specific statements by pioneers that you have read.

The use of background information in exploring a historical problem.

1. By the early 1800's, much of the tobacco-growing soil in Virginia and North Carolina was exhausted, incapable of bearing good crops.
2. Because of the invention of the cotton gin in 1793, more cotton could be processed, and the number of cotton plantations increased.
3. In 1811, William Henry Harrison broke the power of the Indians in a large portion of the old Northwest by defeating an Indian chief named Tecumseh at the Battle of Tippecanoe in Indiana.
4. In 1814, Andrew Jackskon won an important military victory at Horseshoe Bend, Alabama, over the Indians of the old Southwest.
5. During the administration of President James Monroe (1817–1825), the price of government lands decreased from $2.00 to $1.25 per acre.
6. American commerce and industry began to grow during Monroe's administration.

318

7. During Monroe's Presidency, better roads and canals were built to link the East with the West.

8. Prior to 1812, immigration from Europe was about 5,000 a year. Between 1812 and 1830, about 500,000 European immigrants came to the United States, or an average of almost 28,000 people each year.

9. In 1837, there were many business and farm failures.

WESTWARD EXPANSION: WHY?

1. Review the selections by Birkbeck and Parkman, on pages 294 and 295, and the newspaper account of 1844, on page 296. What reasons does each offer to explain *why* people would want to go west?

2. What reasons do Chastellux, Smithwick, Flint, Kelley, and Carson offer to explain why people moved west?

3. Considering all these selections, what were the main reasons people moved westward?

4. How do the reasons given by the settlers compare with those offered by the leaders?

5. What reasons for westward expansion does the background information suggest? How might it relate to the specific statements you have studied?

6. Do you think that the events and conditions of the early 1800's could completely explain expansion? Why or why not? Give reasons for your answer.

THE OPPOSITION SPEAKS

31. Joshua Giddings on Texas

The statements made by opponents of expansion also help to reveal the forces behind expansion. The next group of readings is taken from speeches made by Whig congressmen who opposed America's expansionist policy in the 1840's.

Joshua Giddings was a Whig congressman from Ohio. In the following excerpt, he refers to one of the issues that began to divide the country as the Era of Good Feelings drew to a close. This issue was the *tariff* question. A tariff is a tax placed on imported foreign goods. The purpose of a tariff is to raise the price of the foreign product, and thereby encourage people to buy the

319

product made at home. In the mid-1820's, as northern manufacturing began to expand, the tariff became a serious problem. The northern manufacturers wanted a high tariff to protect them from European competition. The southerners, who preferred to buy the cheaper European goods, wanted *free trade,* or low tariff rates.

By the late 1820's, North and South were also divided over federal policy on the sale of government-owned western land. The South supported the sale of western land in large tracts at low prices. The North called for limited sale of western land at high prices. By 1830, the northern manufacturing interests controlled their states' delegations to Congress. The manufacturers sought to discourage population movement to the West because they wanted to have plenty of workers available for their factories.

POINTS TO CONSIDER

Which ideas and interest groups were aligned against expansion. What the opponents of expansion add to your ideas about the expansionists.

Joshua R. Giddings, **Speeches in Congress** (Boston: John P. Jewett and Company; Cleveland, Ohio: Jewett, Proctor and Worthington, 1835), pp. 104-105.

[Our] population at the North has increased so much faster than it has in the slave States, that under the late census the North and West hold the balance of political power . . . But let us admit Texas, and we shall place the balance of power in the hands of the Texans. They, with the southern States, will control the policy and the destiny of this nation; our tariff will then be held at the will of the Texan advocates of free trade. Are our friends of the North prepared to deliver over this policy to the people of Texas? Are the liberty-loving democrats of Pennsylvania ready to give up the tariff? To strike off all protection from the articles of iron and coal and other productions of that State, in order to purchase a slave-market for their neighbors, who, in the words of Thomas Jefferson Randolph, "breed men for the market like oxen for the shambles [slaughterhouse]?"

1. According to Giddings, what would be the most important outcome of admitting Texas to the Union?

2. How does Giddings say this would harm the North? Can you think of other ways in which it might harm northern interests?

3. Why do you suppose that Giddings, a westerner, opposed expansion into Texas? Are there any clues in his speech?

4. Who do you think would *support* admitting Texas to the Union? Why? Use the information in the introduction to this reading and your knowledge of conditions in the early 1800's to help answer this question.

320

32. John Hardin on Texas

Representative John Hardin of Illinois was a member of the Whig party. He was later killed during the Mexican War.

... But if we adopt Texas, and with it that spirit of national aggrandisement and unlimited ambition which has been advanced by some gentlemen, and especially by my colleague [Mr. Stephen A. Douglas] when he said that he wished to see all foreign nations driven from this continent, and our dominion only bounded by the ocean, I feel it imperative [necessary] ... to inquire what is to be the result of such a policy ...

... It is very convenient for us, and therefore we must make war upon England, and take from her Canada, Nova Scotia, and New Brunswick. After we have fairly thrashed that puny power and reannexed all the country north of us to Baffin's Bay and the Frozen Ocean, we will turn our warlike eyes to Cuba, which is the key of the Gulf of Mexico; and as that would be very convenient for us, we would forthwith demolish the dominion of Spain in that fertile island. That would be another opportunity, which should not be neglected, of "extending the area of freedom," by adding the vast numbers of slaves which abound in that island to the limited number in our southern States. Such a reannexation of the island to the continent would doubtless soothe the expansive patriotism of sundry [various] overburdened patriots.

Congressional Globe, 28th Congress, 2nd Session, Appendix, pp. 275-76.

33. Daniel Webster on Texas

Daniel Webster was a Whig senator from Massachusetts. When he battled the expansionists of 1845, he was carrying on a fight he had begun in 1812. At that time, he had opposed the "War Hawks" who advocated war with England. (See pages 281–282.) Webster had represented northern commercial interests, who feared that war with Britain would hurt shipping and trade. In 1845, Webster spoke against annexing Texas. The following passages are excerpts from one of his speeches.

... In the first place, I have, on the deepest reflection, long ago come to the conclusion, that it was of very dangerous tendency and doubtful consequences to enlarge the boundaries of this Government, or the territories over which our laws are now established. There must be some limit to the extent of our territory, if we would make our institutions permanent. And in this permanency lives the great subject of all my political efforts, the paramount object of my political regard. The Government is very likely to be endangered, in my opinion, by a further enlargement of its already vast territorial surface.

Abridgement of the Debates of Congress, From 1789 to 1856, edited by Thomas Hart Benton (New York: Appleton-Century-Crofts, 1861), Vol. XV, pp. 296-297.

This argument was also used in 1803 by those who opposed the purchase of Louisiana.

In the next place, I have always wished that this country should exhibit to the nations of the earth the example of a great, rich, and powerful Republic, which is not possessed by a spirit of aggrandizement. It is an example, I think, due from us to the world, in favor of the character of republican government....

...I never could, and never can, persuade myself to be in favor of the admission of other States into the Union as slave States, with the inequalities which were allowed and accorded to the slaveholding States then in existence by the constitution....

1. Does Webster oppose expansion into Texas for any of the reasons expressed by Giddings and Hardin?

2. What additional arguments does he make?

3. Do you think Webster might have opposed expansion for any reasons that do not appear in this excerpt? Explain.

4. What were probably the most important arguments against annexing Texas?

5. What do Giddings, Hardin, and Webster suggest about the interests and spirit of those who wanted to annex Texas?

34. Joshua Bell on Oregon

On February 4, 1846, Representative Joshua Bell, a Whig from Kentucky, argued against acquiring Oregon. The following comment is part of his speech.

Congressional Globe, 29th Congress, 1st Session, Appendix, p. 270.

... [The] history of the world, from the earliest establishment of empires among men, proves, that when contiguous [neighboring] territory is necessary to the general, political, or commercial welfare of a particular people, and they have the power to take and keep it, its acquisition becomes a matter of "manifest destiny"; it is not always right, for it is sometimes the "manifest destiny" of nations to do wrong.

1. Does Bell seem to recognize that some of the expansionists' arguments are valid? If so, which ones?

2. Why, then, does Bell oppose expansion?

35. Thomas Corwin on the Mexican War

Senator Thomas Corwin, a Whig from Ohio, gave the following speech before the Senate on February 11, 1847. At this time the

United States and Mexico were at war. Because of his opposition to this war, Corwin destroyed his chances for future political advancement.

Sir, look at this pretense of want of room. With twenty millions of people, you have about one thousand millions of acres of land, inviting settlement by every conceivable argument, bringing [the cost of land] down to a quarter of a dollar an acre, and allowing every man to squat where he pleases. But the Senator from Michigan says we will be two hundred millions in a few years, and we want room. If I were a Mexican I would tell you, "Have you not room in your own country to bury your dead men? If you come into mine, we will greet you with bloody hands, and welcome you to hospitable graves."

Why, says the chairman of this Committee on Foreign Relations, it is the most reasonable thing in the world! We ought to have the Bay of San Francisco. Why? Because it is the best harbor on the Pacific! It has been my fortune, Mr. President, to have practiced a good deal in criminal courts in the course of my life, but I have never yet heard a thief, arraigned for [charged with] stealing a horse, plead that it was the best horse that he could find in the country! We want California. What for? Why, says the Senator from Michigan, we will have it; and the Senator from South Carolina, with a very mistaken view, I think, of policy, says you can't keep our people from going there. I don't desire to prevent them. Let them go and seek their happiness in whatever country or clime [climate] it pleases them.

...But you still say you want room for your people. This has been the plea of every robber chief from Nimrod to the present hour. . . .

American History Told by Contemporaries, edited by Albert Bushnell Hart (New York: The Macmillan Company, 1901), Vol. IV, pp. 25-26.

A REEXAMINATION OF THE REASONS FOR EXPANSION

1. Why does Corwin object to expansion? Why did Bell object?

2. Are some of the objections to expansion in Texas, Oregon, and the Southwest similar? Explain.

3. What specific arguments for expansion are Bell and Corwin answering?

4. What do Bell and Corwin feel are the real forces behind expansion? How do they describe the *spirit* of the expansionists?

5. Have the five Whig congressmen given you new ideas about the forces behind expansion? If so, what?

1. How can you account for expansionism in the first half of the nineteenth century?

2. How did American expansionism affect the country as a whole in the first half of the nineteenth century?

3. If you had lived in the United States between 1800 and 1850, would you have favored expansion? Why or why not?

III. Democracy and the Frontier

WHAT MAKES DEMOCRACY?

What is democracy?

What is an attitude?

Do some attitudes promote democracy more than others?

What would make one society more democratic than another?

What is a standard? What standards would you use to measure how democratic a society is?

THE INFLUENCE OF THE FRONTIER

36. The Turner Thesis

At a meeting of the American Historical Association in 1893, Frederick Jackson Turner delivered a paper entitled "The Significance of the Frontier in American History." His interpretation of the effect of the frontier on American democracy had a tremendous influence on American historical writing. The following selection by Turner appeared in the *Atlantic Monthly* in 1903.

Frederick Jackson Turner, **The Frontier in American History** (New York: Holt, Rinehart and Winston, 1962), pp. 247-248, 259-260, 266. Copyright 1920 by Frederick Jackson Turner. Copyright 1948 by Caroline M. S. Turner. Reprinted by permission of the publisher.

In 1676, Nathanial Bacon, a planter from the western part of the colony, led a rebellion against the colonial government. See pages 82-85.

From the beginning of the settlement of America, the frontier regions have exercised a steady influence toward democracy. In Virginia, to take an example, it can be traced as early as the period of Bacon's Rebellion, a hundred years before our Declaration of Independence. The small landholders, seeing that their powers were steadily passing into the hands of the wealthy planters who controlled Church and State and lands, rose in revolt. A generation later, in the governorship of Alexander Spotswood, we find a contest between the frontier settlers and the property-holding classes of the coast. The democracy with which Spotswood had to struggle, and of which he so bitterly complained, was a democracy made up of small landholders, of the newer immigrants, and of indented servants, who at the expiration of their time of servitude passed into the interior to take up lands and engage in pioneer farming. . . .

In each colony this region was in conflict with the dominant classes of the coast. It constituted a quasi-revolutionary [rebellious] area before the days of the Revolution, and it formed the basis on which the Democratic party was afterwards established. It was, therefore, in the West, as it was in the period before the Declaration of Independence, that the struggle for democratic development first revealed itself, and in that area the essential ideas of American democracy had already appeared. Through the period of the Revolution and of the Confederation a similar contest can be noted. On the frontier of New England, along the western border of Pennsylvania, Virginia, and the Carolinas, and in the communities beyond the Allegheny Mountains, there arose a demand of the frontier settlers for independent statehood based on democratic provisions. There is a strain of fierceness in their energetic petitions demanding self-government under the theory that . . . people have the right to establish their own political institutions in an area which they have won from the wilderness. . . .

Most important of all has been the fact that an area of free land has continually lain on the western border of the settled area of the United States. . . . These free lands promoted individualism, economic equality, freedom to rise, democracy. Men would not accept inferior wages and a permanent position of social subordination [inferiority] when this promised land of freedom and equality was theirs for the taking. Who would rest content under oppressive legislative conditions when with a slight effort he might reach a land wherein [he could] become a co-worker in the building of free cities and free States on the lines of his own ideal? In a word, then, free lands meant free opportunities. Their existence has differentiated the American democracy from the democracies which have preceded it . . .

. . . American democracy is fundamentally the outcome of the experiences of the American people in dealing with the West. Western democracy through the whole of its earlier period tended to the production of a society of which the most distinctive fact was the freedom of the individual to rise under conditions of social mobility . . . [The ambition of this society has been] the liberty and well-being of the masses . . .

1. According to Turner, what effects did the frontier have on the attitudes of people?

"Indented" or "indentured" servants were bound by contract to serve their masters for a stated number of years.

"Social mobility" exists in societies where it is easy to improve one's social standing. If social status is permanently fixed by family, wealth, occupation, race, or religion, there is little social mobility.

2. How do you suppose such attitudes could promote democracy?

3. What examples does Turner use to illustrate his ideas? Do you think these examples prove his point?

WHO REALLY VOTED?

37. Suffrage Qualifications, 1775-1828

The following chart shows the progress different states made toward removing restrictions on voting during the period 1775–1828. The first three columns show states which placed religious, tax, or property restrictions on voting. The last column shows states which had removed all such requirements. The chart does not deal with restrictions on women and Negro voters, because such restrictions did not start to disappear until well after 1828. All of the southern states and most of the northern ones only permitted white males to vote.

The date in parentheses after a state's name is the year when the state entered the Union. The date of entry into the Union is given for all states other than the original thirteen. In the last two columns, the states are listed according to the order in which they revised their requirements.

SUFFRAGE QUALIFICATIONS, 1775–1828

YEAR	* RELIGIOUS REQUIREMENTS	* PROPERTY REQUIREMENTS	* TAX REQUIREMENTS	* NO RELIGIOUS, PROPERTY, OR REQUIREMENTS
1775	MASSACHUSETTS NEW YORK MARYLAND VIRGINIA SOUTH CAROLINA	NEW HAMPSHIRE MASSACHUSETTS RHODE ISLAND CONNECTICUT NEW YORK NEW JERSEY DELAWARE MARYLAND VIRGINIA NORTH CAROLINA SOUTH CAROLINA GEORGIA	PENNSYLVANIA	
1790		Massachusetts Rhode Island Connecticut New York New Jersey Delaware Maryland Virginia North Carolina	Pennsylvania SOUTH CAROLINA NEW HAMPSHIRE GEORGIA	

* States listed for the first time are printed in capital letters.

326

YEAR	RELIGIOUS	PROPERTY	TAX	NO RELIGIOUS, PROPERTY, OR TAX
1800		Massachusetts Rhode Island Connecticut New York New Jersey Maryland Virginia North Carolina TENNESSEE (1796)	Pennsylvania South Carolina DELAWARE	VERMONT (1791) KENTUCKY (1792) NEW HAMPSHIRE GEORGIA
1815		Massachusetts Rhode Island Connecticut New York New Jersey Virginia North Carolina Tennessee	Pennsylvania Delaware OHIO (1803) LOUISIANA (1812)	Vermont Kentucky New Hampshire Georgia SOUTH CAROLINA MARYLAND
1828		Rhode Island New Jersey Virginia North Carolina Tennessee	Pennsylvania Delaware Ohio Louisiana CONNECTICUT MISSISSIPPI (1817) MASSACHUSETTS	Vermont Kentucky New Hampshire Georgia South Carolina Maryland INDIANA (1816) ILLINOIS (1818) ALABAMA (1819) MAINE (1820) NEW YORK MISSOURI (1821)

1. According to this chart, did democracy grow between 1775 and 1828?

2. Compare this chart with the map of new states on page 298. What conclusions can you draw?

3. How would Turner explain a tendency for states to remove more and more restrictions on voting?

4. Does this chart support such an explanation? Why or why not?

5. Does this chart contain all of the information needed to test such an explanation?

38. The National Nominating Convention

The Constitution does not specify how candidates for the Presidency and Vice-Presidency are to be nominated. When political parties began to sponsor candidates, the party leaders developed their own methods for the selection of candidates. They decided to call together the members of their party who were serving in Congress. Legislators met in secret congressional meetings, or caucuses, to select candidates for federal offices. The people had no voice in the procedure.

327

As more men obtained the right to vote, they demanded a role in the selection of candidates. By 1832, the major political parties nominated candidates by means of national conventions. This method of choosing candidates is still used today. Under this system, local members of each political party send delegates to county conventions to nominate candidates for county offices. Some delegates from the county conventions are then sent to state conventions to nominate candidates for state and congressional offices. The state conventions, in turn, send delegates to national conventions to nominate Presidential and Vice-Presidential candidates.

1. According to this account, what development caused the national nominating convention to replace the caucus?

2. Was this development, in turn, influenced by the frontier? Explain your answer.

3. Does the change to the national nominating convention seem to bear out Turner's thesis? If so, how? If not, why not?

CONCLUDING EXERCISE

1. Did democracy grow from 1775 to 1832?

2. Was the growth of democracy in this period the result of the frontier?

3. By what standards have you been measuring the growth of democracy? Are these standards a sufficient measurement for democracy?

THE NEW DEMOCRACY

39. The Workingman

Reforms in voting requirements, in selection of Presidential electors, and in procedures for nominating Presidential candidates began a new era in American democracy. The symbol of this era is Andrew Jackson, who was first elected in 1828, and then again in 1832. In fact, the period of Jackson's two terms in office, from 1828 to 1836, is often referred to as the period of "Jacksonian democracy."

The term "Jacksonian democracy" refers partly to the way Jackson governed. The spoils system is one example of his ideas.

Under this system, Jackson removed his political opponents from public office and replaced them with people who had supported him. Jackson felt that this was more democratic because it allowed more men to participate in the government. He saw no need to leave the same people in office for a long time, because he felt that one man could serve the public as well as another.

"Jacksonian democracy" also refers to the fact that Jackson represented the new voters. The "new democracy" meant that a new group of people had gained political power. These people elected Jackson. The election of 1828, when Jackson was swept into office, was the first election in which voting reforms were strongly felt. By then, twelve out of twenty-four states had given the vote to all white male citizens. Another seven had abolished property requirements and only required the payment of a tax.

So far, you have been testing Turner's thesis by seeing whether the areas that promoted the democratic reforms were frontier areas. In the next three readings, you will question Turner's thesis from another point of view. What *people* were behind the growth of democracy? Are they the kind of people Turner described? One way to consider these questions is to look at the people who demanded voting reforms. Another way is to look at the people who voted for Jackson. Often they were the same. But in any case, the people who backed Jackson were important in their own right. If they had not exercised their new voting privilege, democracy would not have grown.

POINTS TO CONSIDER

Which groups of people demanded the right to vote.

Which groups of people backed Jackson.

What these people wanted.

Whether these people, who promoted the growth of democracy, were the kind of people Turner described.

... The growth of the factory system increased the number of workmen who could scarcely hope to amass [acquire] enough property to be able to vote, and who yet stood more in need of the protection of the state than any other class. To obtain desired legislation they must have a voice on election day. Designing politicians, themselves often risen from the masses, saw in a widened electorate the chance for personal advancement that under the old régime they might have waited for in vain. Each potential party boss was a noisy and effective advocate of the principle that the people must have the right to rule. One after another the citadels of aristocracy fell before the attack, until by the time the election of 1828 was held three of the original states, New Hampshire, Maryland, and Connecticut, had abolished all property qualifications for voting, while two others, Massachusetts and New York, had made them only nominal.

John D. Hicks, **The Federal Union** (Second edition; Boston: Houghton Mifflin Company, 1952), pp. 363-364. Reprinted by permission of the publisher.

Something that is "nominal" exists in name only.

Thus by 1828 the masses in a good majority of the states had the ballot, and, what is even more significant, they had acquired the will to use it. In Pennsylvania, for example, only forty-seven thousand votes were cast in the election of 1824, whereas with no changes of consequence [importance] in the election laws one hundred and fifty thousand votes were cast in 1828.

1. After you studied the chart on page 326, what explanation did you give for the change in voting requirements by 1828?

2. Has this reading changed your explanation? Why or why not?

3. Does your explanation now support or contradict Turner's thesis?

40. The Small Capitalist

The next two selections focus on the forces that brought Jackson to office in 1828 and 1832. The following account is an interpretation by the American historian, Richard Hofstadter. In this excerpt, Hofstadter discusses the small manufacturers and skilled craftsmen, many of whom supported Jackson for the Presidency.

Richard Hofstadter, **The American Political Tradition and the Men Who Made It** (New York: Alfred A. Knopf, 1959), pp. 55-56, 58. Copyright 1948 by Alfred A. Knopf, Inc. Reprinted by permission of the publisher.

These people were capitalists. That is, they had invested their money in setting up businesses. Their wealth was in the form of *capital,* or the equipment and supplies they used for producing goods. Through business, they hoped to increase their wealth. They were small capitalists, because they had small businesses.

In the Jacksonian period the democratic upsurge was closely linked to the ambitions of the small capitalist.

To understand Jacksonian democracy it is necessary to recreate the social complexion of the United States in the 1830's. Although industrialism had begun to take root, this was still a nation of farms and small towns, which in 1830 found only one of every fifteen citizens living in cities of over 8,000. Outside the South, a sweeping majority of the people were independent property-owners. Factories had been growing in some areas, but industry was not yet concentrated in the factory system; much production was carried out in little units in which the employer was like a master craftsman supervising his apprentices. . . . [The] hope of growing more prosperous remained intensely alive in the breast of the small manufacturer and the skilled craftsman.

The "spirit of enterprise" is the willingness to do something that is hard or risky.

The flowering of manufacturing in the East, the rapid settlement of the West, gave to the spirit of enterprise a large measure of fulfillment. The typical American was an expectant [hopeful] capitalist, a hardworking, ambitious person for whom enterprise was a kind of religion, and everywhere he found conditions that encouraged him to extend himself. . . .

The prevalent method of granting corporation charters in the states was a source of enormous resentment. The states [with exceptions] did not have general laws governing incorporation. Since banks and other profit-making businesses that wished to incorporate had to apply to state legislatures for individual acts of incorporation, the way was left open for favoritism and corruption. Very often the corporation charters granted by the legislatures were, or were construed to be, monopolies. Men whose capital [wealth] or influence was too small to gain charters from the lawmakers were barred from such profitable [businesses] as banks, bridges, railroads, turnpikes, and ferries. The practice was looked upon as an artificial closure [closing] of opportunity . . .

. . . An enterpriser of middling success . . . [Jackson himself] could spontaneously see things from the standpoint of the typical American who was eager for advancement in the democratic game of competition—the master mechanic who aspired to open his own shop, the planter or farmer who speculated in land, the lawyer who hoped to be a judge, the local politician who wanted to go to Congress, the grocer who would be a merchant. He had entered the scramble himself in a variety of lines, as a professional man, a merchant, a land speculator, a planter, an officeholder, and a military chieftain. He understood . . . the aspiring citizen's hatred of privilege. . . .

1. According to Hofstadter, what did the small capitalist want? What developments had shaped his interests?

2. Suppose that a legislature were to grant a company the only corporation charter in a certain line of business. How could this make the company a monopoly?

3. Why would a small capitalist dislike this?

4. Hofstadter asserts that the small capitalist was one of the main forces behind Jackson. He says that small capitalists were found in all parts of the country, and not just in the West. Does this disprove Turner's thesis? Explain.

41. The Bank Issue

The Bank of the United States was first chartered in 1791 during Washington's administration. One fifth of the stock, or ownership shares, belonged to the government. The rest of the stock

A "corporation" is a business with the legal rights of an individual. For example, a corporation can borrow money. This is an important privilege. It is often necessary to pay for expensive construction and equipment in order to start a business. Borrowing is also useful for expanding or improving a business. In order to become a corporation, a company must acquire a permit, or charter.

A "monopoly" is a business that has no rivals. It is the only business in an area that supplies a certain product or service. With no company to undersell it, a monopoly can easily charge high prices.

was held by private companies and individuals. All government funds were deposited in the bank. The bank issued paper money and also lent funds to both the government and individuals. After the bank's charter expired, the second Bank of the United States was established in 1816.

President Andrew Jackson attacked the bank. Supporters of the bank decided to bring the issue to a head. They urged the president of the bank, Nicholas Biddle, to apply for renewal of the bank's charter in 1832. This was four years before the charter was due to expire. Biddle agreed, and the bank's supporters pushed the recharter bill through Congress. They hoped that Jackson would veto it. A Presidential veto would make the bank a major issue in the election of 1832. Jackson did not let his opponents down. He vetoed the bill and delivered a message which strongly denounced the bank.

The crucial issue of the 1832 election was the question of the bank. Henry Clay, who was an ardent supporter of the national bank, ran against Jackson. Jackson won an overwhelming victory. The major issues regarding the Bank of the United States focused on the following points.

Control by the wealthy. The majority of the bank's stockholders were wealthy individuals who lived either in the Atlantic seaboard states, from Massachusetts to Maryland, or in Europe. There were few stockholders from the area west of the Appalachian Mountains. Like the stockholders of any business, the bank's stockholders shared the profits made by the federal bank. They also had a voice in deciding what the bank did. Many people thought that the wealthy stockholders ran the bank for their own profit. They felt it was wrong for the government to support such an institution.

Ability to influence legislators. The bank often lent money to Congressmen. Out of 261 Congressmen, 52 borrowed money from the bank in 1830, and 59 in 1831. Opponents of the bank charged that such practices allowed it to influence legislation.

Difficulty in obtaining credit. Farmers, wage earners, and small businessmen opposed the bank because it would not lend them money. Before the bank would lend money to someone, it required that he give adequate security in money or goods to insure payment of the loan. Often, people were unable to provide the necessary security and were denied the funds they needed. Supporters of the bank pointed out that it was a sound business practice not to lend money without adequate assurance that the money would be repaid.

The national bank also prevented many state banks from issuing paper money unless they had an equal amount of gold or silver. Such backing guaranteed the worth of the paper money. This limited the amount of cash available and, thus, the number of loans which state banks could make to small capitalists. The small capitalist resented the power of the national bank to cut off easy loans at the state as well as at the national level. He felt that the power of the national bank over the state banks was evidence that the national bank was a monopoly. The small capitalist also believed that the bank was run by people who had obtained monopoly privileges in business for themselves. This made him even more resentful.

Low value of the dollar. Labor had a special grievance against the bank. The cost of living was getting higher and higher. Every year the same products cost a little more. This meant that the dollar bought less and less. The value of the worker's paycheck was becoming lower. In effect, the worker was deprived of part of his pay. Although the bank was not responsible, the worker blamed the bank for the low value of his paycheck.

The following excerpt from one of Jackson's speeches presents his ideas about the bank.

POINTS TO CONSIDER
Who would have voted for Jackson in 1832, and why.

... The result of the ill-advised legislation which established this great monopoly [the bank] was to concentrate the whole moneyed power of the Union, with its boundless means of corruption and its numerous dependents, under the direction and command of one acknowledged head [the bank] ...

... [If] you [the common people] had not conquered [in this election], the Government would have passed from the hands of the many to the hands of the few, and this organized money power from its secret conclave [meeting place] would have dictated the choice of your highest officers and compelled you to make peace or war, as best suited their own wishes. ...

... The agricultural, the mechanical, and the laboring classes have little or no share in the direction of the great moneyed corporations, and from their habits and the nature of their pursuits they are incapable of forming extensive combinations to act together with united force. ...

... The planter, the farmer, the mechanic, and the laborer ... form the great body of the people of the United States; they are the bone and sinew of the country—men who love liberty and desire nothing but equal rights and equal laws, and who, moreover, hold the great mass of our national wealth ... But with overwhelming numbers and wealth on their side they are in constant danger of losing their fair influence in the Government, and with difficulty maintain their just rights against the incessant efforts daily made to encroach [infringe] upon them. The mischief springs from the power which the moneyed interest derives from

Sources of the American Republic: A Documentary History of Politics, Society, and Thought, edited by Marvin Meyers, Alexander Kern, John Cawelti (Chicago: Scott, Foresman and Company, 1960), Vol. I, pp. 343-344. Reprinted by permission of the publisher.

a paper currency which they are able to control . . . [a power] employed . . . for their benefit; and unless you become more watchful in your States and check this spirit of monopoly and thirst for exclusive privileges you will in the end find that the most important powers of Government have been given or bartered away, and the control over your dearest interests has passed into the hands of these corporations. . . .

1. What was Jackson's main reason for opposing the bank? What did he feel the bank threatened?

2. What groups would have endorsed Jackson's stand on the bank issue? Why?

3. Review the effects Turner said the frontier had on the American people. Does Jackson's overwhelming victory in 1832 illustrate these effects? Remember that the bank was the major issue in the 1832 election.

CONCLUDING EXERCISE

1. Considering everything you have read so far, would you say that democracy grew between 1800 and 1832? Why?

2. Were the changes you noticed caused by the frontier?

3. Do you think Turner's thesis has been proved? Why or why not?

THE COMMON MAN AND GOVERNMENT

42. A Cartoon Version, 1844

"The common man" is a term frequently employed by historians. It refers to the average citizens as opposed to the minority of individuals with more wealth or education. The following cartoon expresses one attitude toward the growth of universal suffrage and the entry of the common man into politics. The cartoonist has used "Jefferson House" to symbolize Thomas Jefferson's belief in man's ability to govern himself. "Unionists," "Spartans," "Butt Enders," and "Indomitables" were political factions active in 1844.

1. According to the artist, what is the result of the political power of the common man?

2. Does he feel that it results in the growth of democracy?

3. What is the artist criticizing? If it exists, is he right to criticize?

43. An Eyewitness Account of Andrew Jackson's First Inauguration

Thousands of people traveled to Washington for Jackson's first inauguration. The new President held open house in the White House where western frontiersmen mixed with Washington society. The inaugural celebration became a symbol of the common man's attainment of political power. The author of the following selection quotes an eyewitness account of the inauguration.

"No one who was at Washington at the time of General Jackson's inauguration is likely to forget that period to the day of his death. To us, who had witnessed the quiet and orderly period of the Adams' administration, it seemed as if half the nation had rushed at once into the Capital. It was like the inundation [flood] of the northern barbarians into Rome, save that the tumultuous tide came in from a different point of the compass. The West and the South seemed to have precipitated [thrown] themselves upon the North and overwhelmed it. On that memorable occasion you might tell a 'Jackson man' almost far as you could see him. Their every motion seemed to cry out 'victory!' Strange faces

James Parton, **Life of Andrew Jackson** (New York: Mason Brothers, 1861), Vol. III, pp. 169-170.

When the Roman Empire grew weak, tribes of barbarians within and outside of the Empire, invaded Italy and set themselves up as its rulers.

335

"Praetorian band" refers to the Praetorian Guard, the bodyguard of the Roman emperors.

filled every public place, and every face seemed to bear defiance on its brow. It appeared to me that every Jackson editor in the country was on the spot. They swarmed, especially in the lobbies of the House, an expectant host [eagerly waiting crowd], a sort of Praetorian band, which, having borne in upon their shields their idolized leader, claimed the reward of the hard-fought contest. His quarters were assailed, surrounded, hemmed in, so that it was an achievement to get into his presence. On the morning of the inauguration, the vicinity of the Capitol was like a great agitated sea; every avenue to the fateful spot was blocked up with people, in so much that the legitimate [official] procession which accompanied the President-elect could scarce make its way to the eastern portico [porch], where the ceremony was to be performed. To repress [hold back] the crowd in front, a ship's cable was stretched across about two-thirds of the way up the long flight of steps by which the Capitol is approached on that side, but it seemed, at times, as if even this would scarce prove sufficient to restrain the eagerness of the multitude, every man of whom seemed bent on the glory of shaking the President's hand. Never can I forget the spectacle which presented itself on every side, nor the electrifying moment when the eager, expectant eyes of that vast and motley [varied] multitude caught sight of the tall and imposing form of their adored leader, as he came forth between the columns of the portico, the color of the whole mass changed, as if by miracle; all hats were off at once, and the dark tint which usually pervades a mixed map of men was turned, as by a magic wand, into the bright hue of the ten thousand upturned and exultant human faces, radiant with sudden joy. The peal of shouting that arose rent the air, and seemed to shake the very ground. But when the Chief Justice took his place and commenced the brief ceremony of administering the oath of office, it quickly sank into comparative silence; and as the new President proceeded to read his inaugural address, the stillness gradually increased; but all efforts to hear him, beyond a brief space immediately around [him], were utterly vain."

Mr. [Daniel] Webster, in his serio-comic manner, remarks: "I never saw such a crowd here before. Persons have come five hundred miles to see General Jackson, *and they really seem to think the country is rescued from some dreadful danger!*"

1. Why did people like Jackson?

2. How does this description of the inauguration compare with the cartoon? Does the inauguration scene bear out the criticism of the cartoonist?

3. Do you think that what is shown by the inauguration scene is good or bad for democracy? Why?

44. Some Portraits of Jackson

The next three selections present unfavorable views of Jackson. The first reading focuses on an event that occurred early in Jackson's career. The last two selections concern the election of 1828.

AN EARLY VIEW OF JACKSON

Of all of [President] Jefferson's appointments and refusals to appoint [during the years 1801–1809], one shows a lack of political insight which, considering [that] the man in error was Jefferson, is curious, to say the least. Among the men who have ever attained great distinction in American politics, no one would seem to come nearer to Jefferson than Andrew Jackson. Yet Andrew Jackson was one of the few ardent Republicans whom Jefferson absolutely refused to appoint to office. The issue arose in 1804, when the time was come to make arrangements for the government of a portion of the Louisiana purchase. The two senators from Tennessee and that state's four representatives united in recommending Jackson for the position of governor of Orleans territory. Jefferson, however, seems to have disliked the displays of temper which made Jackson popular with other classes in the community. He is said to have pronounced him a "dangerous man." This declaration was made many years later. We have no clew [clue] as to what were Jefferson's reasons for not appointing Jackson in 1804, except a letter written by William Henderson. In this letter Henderson says that he has been acquainted with Jackson for several years, and views him as a man of violent passion. At that moment, he declared, Jackson was being sued for assault and battery, and in a few days would surely be indicted for [charged with] a breach of the peace. "Were it not for those despotic [dictatorial] principles," wrote Henderson, "he might be a useful man."

Edward Channing, **The Jeffersonian System 1801-1811** (New York: Harper & Row, Publishers, 1906), pp. 19-20. Copyright 1906 by Harper & Brothers; renewed 1934 by Alice Channing. Reprinted by permission of the publishers. Slightly adapted.

"Republicans" refers to the political party that formed around Thomas Jefferson. It was originally called the Democratic-Republican party. By the 1830's, it was known as the Democratic party.

CAMPAIGN PORTRAITS IN 1828

. . . During the rest of the year, the country rang with the names of JACKSON and CALHOUN, ADAMS, and RUSH. The contest, during this final year, became one of personalities chiefly. Against Mr. Adams, every possible change was rung upon Bargain and Corruption. He was accused of federalism, of haughtiness, of selfishness, of extravagant expenditures, and, O, crime of crimes! of polluting the White House, that sacred abode of purity and

James Parton, **Life of Andrew Jackson** (New York: Mason Brothers, 1861), Vol. III, pp. 140-141.

To "ring every change," here, means to give all the possible variations on the themes unfavorable to Adams. Jackson's supporters accused Adams of having made a corrupt bargain in 1824, in order to win the Presidency away from Jackson. (See note on page 330.)

wisdom, with a billiard table! Mr. Adams' son and secretary had actually bought, out of his allowance, a billiard table, and set it up in an apartment of the presidential mansion. . . . It was charged him [Adams], that the East Room, in which his excellent mother had hung clothes to dry, was now furnished with such appalling extravagance, that country members were quite overcome at the spectacle . . .

General Jackson was accused of every crime, offense, and impropriety [improper action] that man was ever known to be guilty of. His whole life was subject to the severest scrutiny. Every one of his duels, fights, and quarrels was narrated at length. . . . The eleven military executions which he had ordered, beginning with John Woods and ending with Arbuthnot and Ambrister, were all recounted. John Binns, of Philadelphia, issued a series of hand bills, each bearing the outline of a coffin-lid, upon which was printed an inscription recording the death of one of these victims. Campaign papers were first started this year. One entitled, *We the People,* and another called the *Anti-Jackson Expositor,* were particularly prominent. . . .

AN 1828 CAMPAIGN POSTER

During the War of 1812, Jackson executed several militiamen who had panicked in battle. Then, in 1818, Jackson invaded Florida and executed two British citizens, Robert Arbuthnot and Alexander Ambrister, for inciting Indian attacks against settlers.

The caption that appeared with this poster was: "Jackson is to be President and you will be HANGED." Jackson's opponents used this type of campaign poster widely.

1. What kind of man did Jackson's opponents think he was? If their views were right, how could he have become President?

2. What kind of issues and practices entered into the political campaign of 1828? Why do you suppose this sort of thing happened?

45. Morison and Commager Interpret the Election of 1828

Samuel Eliot Morison and Henry Steele Commager, both noted American historians, give the following analysis of Andrew Jackson's election in 1828.

POINTS TO CONSIDER

What reasons Hofstadter and Hicks gave for the coming of "Jacksonian democracy."

How the interpretation offered by Morison and Commager compares with the interpretations of Hofstadter and Hicks.

... But in the last instance it was classes rather than sections that elected Jackson: the Southern hunters and backwoods farmers whom he had led to glory; the Northern democracy [laborers], tired of respectable, gentlemanly promotions from cabinet to White House. They cared little for policies, but much for personality, and they voted for Jackson because he was their sort of man. After all, the most sophisticated among us often have no better reason for voting as we do than had the American democracy of 1828, in exalting a man of their own sort, uneducated, intolerant, yet professing the immortal principles of Thomas Jefferson. ...

Samuel Eliot Morison and Henry Steele Commager, **The Growth of the American Republic** (Revised and enlarged edition; New York: Oxford University Press, 1950), Vol. I, p. 469. Reprinted by permission of the publisher.

All Presidents elected from 1800 to 1828 had held positions in the Cabinet prior to their election.

CONCLUDING EXERCISE

1. Did the expanded role of the common man in government mean that democracy had grown? Explain.

2. What standards are you using to measure democracy here? Are they the same standards you used on page 324? If not, which standards are more important measurements of democracy? Why?

3. Was the common man's entry into politics the result of the frontier? Could his behavior be attributed to the frontier?

46. Davy Crockett Runs for Office

The next group of readings concerns political campaigns in the East and West in the 1820's and 1830's. During this period, frontiersmen became more active in government. Davy Crockett represented Tennessee in the House of Representatives from 1827 to 1831, and from 1833 to 1835. The following selection is an account of his 1821 campaign for a seat in the Tennessee House of Representatives. The account is from Crockett's supposed autobiography, published in 1834. The book was probably written by someone else, but it accurately portrays Crockett's style and many adventures.

The Heritage of America, edited by Henry Steele Commager and Allan Nevins (Revised and enlarged edition; Boston: Little Brown and Company, 1949), pp. 263-266. Copyright 1939, 1949 by Henry Steele Commager and Allan Nevins. Reprinted by permission of Little, Brown and Company.

I just now began to take a rise [in social standing], as in a little time I was asked to offer for the Legislature in the counties of Lawrence and Heckman.

I offered my name in the month of February, and started about the first of March with a drove of horses to the lower part of the state of North Carolina. This was in the year 1821, and I was gone upwards of three months. I returned and set out electioneering, which was a bran-fire new business to me. It now became necessary that I should tell the people something about the government, and an eternal sight of other things that I knowed nothing more about than I did about Latin and law and such things as that. I have said before that in those days none of us called General Jackson the government, nor did he seem in as fair way to become so as I do now; but I knowed so little about it that if anyone had told me he was "the government," I should have believed it, for I had never read even a newspaper in my life, or anything else, on the subject. But over all my difficulties, it seems to me I was born for luck, though it would be hard for any one to guess what sort. I will, however, explain that hereafter.

I went first into Heckman County to see what I could do among the people as a candidate. Here they told me that they wanted to move their town nearer to the center of the county, and I must come out in favor of it. There's no devil if I knowed what this meant, or how the town was to be moved; and so I kept dark, going on the identical same plan that I now find is called noncommital. About this time there was a great squirrel hunt on Duck River, which was among my people. They were to hunt two

A "noncommittal" person is one who refuses to say definitely what he will do.

days, then to meet and count the scalps and have a big barbecue, and what might be called a tiptop country frolic. The dinner, and a general treat, was all to be paid for by the party having taken the fewest scalps. I joined one side, taking the place of one of the hunters, and got a gun ready for the hunt. I killed a great many squirrels, and when we counted scalps, my party was victorious.

The party had everything to eat and drink that could be furnished in so new a country, and much fun and good humor prevailed. But before the regular frolic commenced, I mean the dancing, I was called on to make a speech as a candidate . . .

A public document I had never seen, nor did I know there were any such things; and how to begin I couldn't tell. I made many apologies and tried to get off, for I knowed I had a man to run against who could speak prime [very well], and I knowed too that I wa'n't able to shuffle and cut with him. He was there, and knowing my ignorance as well as I did myself, he also urged me to make a speech. The truth is, he thought my being a candidate was a mere matter of sport, and didn't think for a moment that he was in any danger from an ignorant backwoods bear hunter. But I found I couldn't get off, and so I determined just to go ahead, and leave it to chance what I should say. I got up and told the people I reckoned they knowed what I come for, but if not, I could tell them. I had come for their votes, and if they didn't watch mighty close, I'd get them too. But the worst of all was, that I couldn't tell them anything about government. I tried to speak about something, and I cared very little what, until I choked up as bad as if my mouth had been jammed and crammed chock-full of dry mush. There the people stood, listening all the while, with their eyes, mouths, and [ears] open to catch every word I would speak.

"To shuffle and cut" with someone means to keep up with him.

At last I told them I was like a fellow I had heard of not long before. He was beating on the head of an empty barrel near the roadside when a traveler who was passing along asked him what he was doing that for. The fellow replied that there was some cider in that barrel a few days before and he was trying to see if there was any then, but if there was, he couldn't get at it. I told them that there had been a little bit of speech in me awhile ago, but I believed I couldn't get it out. They all roared out in a mighty laugh and I told some other anecdotes, equally amusing to them; and believing I had them in a first-rate way, I quit and got down, thanking the people for their attention. But I took care to remark that I was as dry as a powder horn and that I

341

thought it was time for us to wet our whistles a little; and so I put off to the liquor stand and was followed by the greater part of the crowd.

I felt certain this was necessary, for I knowed my competitor could open government matters to them as easy as he pleased. He had, however, mighty few left to hear him as I continued with the crowd, now and then taking a horn [full of liquor] and telling good-humored stories till he was done speaking. I found I was good for the votes at the hunt, and when we broke up, I went on to the town of Vernon, which was the same they wanted me to move. Here they pressed me again on the subject, and I found I could get either party by agreeing with them. But I told them I didn't know whether it would be right or not, and so couldn't promise either way.

. . . [The] barbecue was on a Saturday, and the candidates for governor and for Congress as well as my competitor and myself all attended.

The thought of having to make a speech made my knees feel mighty weak and set my heart to fluttering almost as bad as my first love scrape with the Quaker's niece. But as good luck would have it, these big candidates spoke nearly all day, and when they quit, the people were worn out with fatigue, which afforded me a good apology for not discussing the government. But I listened mighty close to them, and was learning pretty fast about political matters. When they were all done, I got up and told some laughable story and quit. I found I was safe in those parts, and so I went home and didn't go back again till after the election was over. But to cut this matter short, I was elected, doubling my competitor and nine votes over.

A short time after this, I was in Pulaski [Tennessee], where I met with Colonel [James K.] Polk, now a member of Congress from Tennessee. He was at that time a member elected to the [state] Legislature as well as myself, and in a large company he said to me, "Well, Colonel, I suppose we shall have a radical change of the judiciary at the next session of the Legislature." "Very likely, sir," says I, and I put out [talked] quicker, for I was afraid some one would ask me what the judiciary was; and if I knowed I wish I may be shot. I don't indeed believe I had ever before heard that there was any such thing in all nature, but still I was not willing that the people there should know how ignorant I was about it.

When the time for meeting of the Legislature arrived, I went on, and before I had been there long, I could have told what the judiciary was, and what the government was too; and many other things that I had known nothing about before.

47. The Election of 1832 in the East

Andrew Jackson ran for re-election in 1832. In the same year, Davy Crockett campaigned for his third term in the House of Representatives. The next two readings describe the atmosphere of Jackson's campaign. The first selection presents a Frenchman's impression of some election practices. The other is a story which originally appeared in *Harper's Magazine* in 1832. It typifies what many of the common men thought of Andrew Jackson.

POLITICAL PARADES IN PHILADELPHIA AND NEW YORK

The [Democratic] party made great use of pictures, processions, and hickory poles. M. Chevalier, a French gentleman then traveling in the United States, gives an amusing account of the Jackson processions. They were so frequent that the traveler was led to suppose them one of the institutions of the country. "Besides the camp-meetings," he says, "the political processions are the only things in this country which bear any resemblance to festivals. . . . I stopped involuntarily at the sight of the gigantic hickory poles which made their solemn entry on eight wheels, for the purpose of being planted by the democracy on the eve of the election. I remember one of these poles, with its top still crowned with green foliage, which came on to the sound of fifes and drums, and was preceded by ranks of democrats, bearing no other badge than a twig of the sacred tree in their hats. It was drawn by eight horses, decorated with ribbons and mottoes. Astride on the tree itself were a dozen Jackson men . . . waving flags with an air of anticipated triumph, and shouting '*Hurra for Jackson!*'

"But this entry of the hickory was but a by-matter compared with the procession I witnessed in New York. It was nearly a mile long. The democrats marched in good order, to the glare of torches; the banners were more numerous than I had ever seen them in any religious festival; all were in transparency, on account of the darkness. On some were inscribed the names of the democratic societies or sections: *Democratic young men of the ninth* or *eleventh ward*; others bore imprecations [curses] against the Bank of the United States; *Nick Biddle* and *Old Nick* here figured largely. Then some portraits of General Jackson afoot and on horseback; there was one in the uniform of a general, and another in the person of the Tennessee farmer, with the famous hickory cane in his hand. Those of Washington

James Parton, **Life of Andrew Jackson** (New York: Mason Brothers, 1861), Vol. III, pp. 424-426.

"Camp-meetings" refers to religious meetings held on the frontier.

Jackson's nickname was "Old Hickory."

343

and Jefferson, surrounded with democratic mottoes, were mingled with emblems in all tastes and of all colors. Among these figured an eagle, not a painting, but a real, live eagle, tied by the legs, surrounded by a wreath of leaves, and hoisted upon a pole, after the manner of the Roman standards. . . . From further than the eye could reach, came marching on the democrats. I was struck with the resemblance of their air [appearance] to the train [procession] that escorts the religious ceremonies in Mexico . . . The American standard-bearers were as grave as the Mexican Indians who bore the sacred tapers [candles]. The democratic procession . . . had its halting-places; it stopped before the houses of the Jackson men to fill the air with cheers, and halted at the doors of the leaders of the Opposition [the Henry Clay men], to give three, six, or nine groans. If these scenes were to find a painter, they would be admired at a distance, not less than the triumphs and sacrificial pomps [ceremonies] which the ancients [Greeks and Romans] have left us delineated in marble and brass; for they are not mere grotesques . . . they belong to history, they partake of the grand; they are the episodes of a wondrous epic which will bequeath a lasting memory to posterity [future generations], that of the coming of democracy."

James Parton, **Life of Andrew Jackson,** Vol. III, p. 426. Slightly adapted.

A NEW YORKER SPEAKS ABOUT JACKSON

During General Jackson's second presidential campaign there flourished at the Quarantine Ground, Staten Island, an honest old fellow, a baker by trade, and a staunch democrat withal. One evening a political meeting was held at a small tavern . . . Our good friend, and several other residents at the Quarantine, attended the meeting. Among them was old Dr. H., who was a noted wag [joker], and it occurred to him that if a speech could be got out of the old baker it would be exceedingly amusing. Accordingly, he called on him for an address.

"No, no," said the baker; "I can make bread, but I can't make speeches."

The suggestion, however, had excited the audience, and the old man was at length compelled to make the effort. So, rising in his seat, he said:

"Feller-citizens: it is well known to you all that when John Quincy Adams was President, the Emperor of Brazil seized several of our ships, and wouldn't let 'em come home. So, President Adams wrote him a letter, and a very *purty* letter it was, too—for to give him his due, he knew how to write, if he didn't know anything else. So the Emperor he got the letter, and, after he had read it, he asked who this Adams was? and his head men told him he was President of the United States: 'Well, well' says the Emperor, 'he wants me to send them ships home, but I won't do it; for it is quite plain to me that a man who can write so beautiful, don't know anything about fighting; so the ships must stay where they are.' Well," continued the baker, "by-and-by Ginral [General] Jackson got to be President, and he wrote a letter to the Emperor, and it was something like this:

" 'You Emperor, send them ships home right away. Andrew Jackson.'

"Well, the Emperor got that letter too, and after he had read it, he laughed, and said . . . 'Who is this Jackson? 'Peers to me I've heerd of him before.' 'We'll tell you,' said his head men, 'who he is. He is the New Orleans Jackson.' 'What!' said the Emperor, 'the New Orleans Jackson: That's quite another matter. If this man don't write so beautiful, he knows how to fight; so send them ships home right away.' And it was done."

Jackson's defeat of the British at New Orleans was an outstanding American military victory of the War of 1812.

CONCLUDING EXERCISE

1. On what basis did some voters choose candidates?

2. What type of practices characterized the campaigns discussed in the preceding readings? How can you explain these developments?

3. Do you think the artist who drew the 1844 cartoon was right? (See page 335.)

4. Was democracy practiced differently in the East than in the West? Explain.

5. Were the changes in democracy due to the frontier?

THE ELECTION OF 1840

48. Whig Campaign Songs

The various factions opposed to Andrew Jackson combined, in 1834, to form a new political party, the Whigs. Despite the new coalition, Martin Van Buren, the Democratic candidate was elected President in 1836. The Whigs decided, therefore, to wage a strong campaign in the next election.

The Whig candidate for President in 1840 was William Henry Harrison, a military hero of the Indian wars and the War of 1812. His running mate was John Tyler. The Democrats nominated Van Buren for a second term.

This time the Whigs won the election. Harrison polled 234 electoral votes to Van Buren's 60. A month after he assumed office, however, Harrison died of pneumonia. John Tyler, the Vice-President, then assumed the nation's highest office.

The Whigs used songs and pictures in place of a party platform, which is a list of the party's opinions on issues. The documents in the next two readings show how the Whigs went about getting popular support for their candidates. The following selections are two songs that were often sung during the campaign.

POINTS TO CONSIDER

The tactics used by the Whigs.

Why they used such tactics.

How their tactics compare with the ones used in the Democrats' campaigns for Jackson in 1828 and 1832.

Samuel Eliot Morison and Henry Steele Commager, **The Growth of the American Republic** (New York: Oxford University Press, 1937), Vol. I, pp. 452-453.

Harrison was famous for his victory over the Indians at the Battle of Tippecanoe in 1811.

AN 1840 WHIG CAMPAIGN SONG

What has caused this great commotion, motion, motion
Our country through?
—It is the ball a-rolling on for
... Tippecanoe and Tyler too:—
Tippecanoe and Tyler too.
And with them we'll beat little Van, Van, Van,
Oh! Van is a used-up man.

Samuel Eliot Morison and Henry Steele Commager, **The Growth of the American Republic**, Vol. I, p. 452.

ANOTHER WHIG SONG OF 1840

Let Van from his coolers of silver drink wine,
And lounge on his cushioned settee.
Our man on his buckeye bench can recline,
Content with hard cider is he,
The iron-armed soldier, the true hearted soldier,
The gallant old soldier of Tippecanoe.

49. Whig Campaign Illustrations

The Whigs also used pictures and posters in the campaign. The topic of many of these illustrations was Harrison's home in North Bend, Ohio. Examples of these pictures appear below. The first drawing is from the cover of an almanac. The man handing out the cider is Harrison. Van Buren is behind the cider keg. Andrew Jackson is standing beside the doorway of the log cabin.

POINTS TO CONSIDER

Why the Whigs used such posters.

How the campaign illustrations compare with the picture of Harrison's home.

AN ALMANAC COVER

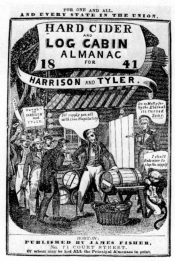

AMERICAN ANTIQUARIAN SOCIETY

AN ANNOUNCEMENT FOR A POLITICAL RALLY

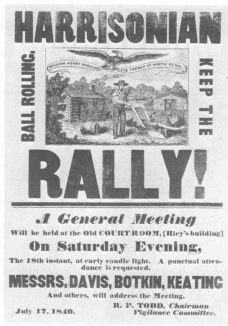

THE GRANGER COLLECTION

347

HARRISON'S ACTUAL HOME

NEW YORK PUBLIC LIBRARY

1. What was there about Jackson that appealed to the voters in 1828 and 1832?

2. What did the Whigs emphasize about Harrison in 1840?

3. What kind of tactics did they use? What explanation can you make for this?

4. A leading journal of the Democratic party in 1840 declared, "We have taught them [the Whigs] how to conquer us." Is there any truth in this statement?

REVIEWING A HYPOTHESIS: WAS TURNER RIGHT?

1. Was the growth of democracy in the first half of the nineteenth century a result of American experience on the frontier?

2. On the whole, do you think that the frontier strengthened or weakened American democracy?

IV. Federalists to Democrats: A Revolution?

A FEDERALIST BECOMES CHIEF JUSTICE

50. John Marshall and the Supreme Court, 1800-1835

The year 1800 marked the beginning of a new era. In that year, with the election of Thomas Jefferson to the Presidency, Federalist control of the national government ended. The Federalist party gave way to the Democratic-Republican party, whose members were known simply as Republicans. By the 1830's, the same political party was called the Democratic party.

From 1789 to 1800, the Federalist leaders—President George Washington, President John Adams, and Secretary of the Treasury Alexander Hamilton—mapped out a set of policies designed to put the young nation on its feet. These policies aimed at creating a strong and active federal government. In order to give the federal government as much power as possible, the Federalists favored what can be considered a broad, or loose, interpretation of the Constitution.

The Federalist tradition was put to the test in 1800, when the Democratic-Republicans gained control of the government. What would happen to relations between the national government and the states under the new party? What would happen to interpretation of the Constitution? Would the Democratic-Republicans seek to restrict the power of the federal government? In this section, you will examine these questions by looking at some of the actions of two Presidents who furthered the principles of the Democratic-Republican party. Both Thomas Jefferson, who came to office in 1801, and Andrew Jackson, who assumed the Presidency in 1829, were considered revolutionary when they were elected. You will have the opportunity to consider just how revolutionary they were, and in what ways.

Before we turn to Jefferson and Jackson, however, let us take a glimpse at a Federalist who survived the eclipse of his party. John Marshall's time as Chief Justice of the Supreme Court from 1801 to 1835 spanned the administrations of both Jefferson and Jackson. Born on the Virginia frontier in 1755, Marshall served the nation in many ways before he became Chief Justice. He was a soldier in the American Revolution, a member of the Virginia legislature, a congressman, and, briefly, Secretary of State under John Adams. It was Adams who appointed Marshall to the Supreme Court.

By studying Marshall's handling of the cases that came before him, you will be able to review what Federalist policies meant in practice. You can then compare Marshall's policies on states' rights and interpretation of the Constitution with the policies of Jefferson and Jackson.

Marbury v. Madison, 1803. When Jefferson was elected President in 1800, the Republicans gained control of both the executive and legislative branches of the government. Although the election was in December 1800, the Republicans did not take office until March 4, 1801. During this period, the Federalists took steps to strengthen their hold on the judicial branch of the government. Congress passed the Judiciary Act of 1801 which increased the number of federal judges, marshals, attorneys, and clerks. President Adams appointed Federalists to fill these new positions.

William Marbury was one of Adams' appointees. The *Marbury v. Madison* case resulted when Jefferson ordered his Secretary of State, James Madison, to withhold Marbury's appointment. Marbury sued Madison and carried the case to the Supreme Court.

In deciding this case, Chief Justice Marshall declared unconstitutional the congressional act on which Marbury's claim to his appointment was founded. This was the first time the Supreme Court canceled an act of Congress. With this ruling, Marshall established the doctrine of *judicial review*. Judicial review means that when a court is deciding a case, it may review acts of the legislature applying to the case to determine whether they violate the Constitution.

United States v. Judge Peters, 1809. The Supreme Court held that a state legislature could not nullify or set aside a judgment or order of a federal court.

Trustees of Dartmouth College v. Woodward, 1819. Woodward represented the state of New Hampshire, which wanted to cancel the charter incorporating Dartmouth College. The Court reasoned that the college's charter was a *contract*. New Hampshire did not have the right to nullify a valid contract between the state and private individuals.

McCulloch v. Maryland, 1819. Maryland levied a tax against the Baltimore branch of the Bank of the United States. The bank refused to pay the tax. Marshall ruled that a state could not tax the federally sponsored bank. He also stated that Congress had *implied* powers to charter the bank.

Cohens v. Virginia, 1821. The Court held that in a case involving federal law or rights, a decision by a state court was subject to review by the Supreme Court.

Gibbons v. Ogden, 1823. This case involved a monopoly granted by the legislature of New York for operating steamboats on state waters. The Court invalidated the grant. Marshall declared that a state could not interfere with the authority of Congress to regulate interstate commerce.

1. Review Article III of the Constitution. What in that article gave the Supreme Court the power or right to make the decisions you have just studied? Where in the Constitution can you find specific mention of these rights or, the specific powers stated by the Supreme Court in its decision? For ex-

ample, what part of the Constitution gave Congress the right to charter a bank? How can you explain this?

2. How did Marshall make the Constitution *flexible?*

3. How did he continue the policies established by Alexander Hamilton and the Federalists?

THOMAS JEFFERSON: A DEMOCRAT BECOMES PRESIDENT

51. The Election of 1800: How the Nation Voted

Thomas Jefferson was elected President in 1800. Few men selected for the nation's highest office have been so well qualified as Jefferson. He wrote the Declaration of Independence, served as ambassador to France and as Washington's Secretary of State, founded the Democratic-Republican party, and was Vice-President under John Adams.

Jefferson came to the Presidency with well-defined ideas on the role and purpose of government. He distrusted powerful central government and advocated a strict, or narrow, interpretation of the Constitution. He thought the farmers' interests should be favored over industrial and commercial interests. Jefferson was a *democrat:* he had confidence in the ability of the people to govern themselves. He believed that every man should receive some formal education so that he could participate better in his government. Jefferson's views on government were in opposition to Alexander Hamilton's Federalist policies.

The two maps on the next page illustrate the extent of Jefferson's victory in 1800. The following reading will show some Federalist attitudes toward his election. The maps show the popular and electoral votes received by Jefferson and Adams. The electoral votes received by Aaron Burr, the Democratic-Republican candidate for Vice-President, are not shown. Burr got as many electoral votes as Jefferson and became Jefferson's rival for the Presidency. This happened because electors could vote for two candidates and because there were no separate ballots for President and Vice-President. The election had to be decided by the House of Representatives.

Later, to prevent a repetition of the situation, a Constitutional amendment was passed. (See the material on the Twelfth Amendment on pages 237–238). Burr's votes are omitted here because they do not affect the basic issue: the comparative strength of Jefferson and Adams.

THE POPULAR VOTE

THE ELECTORAL VOTE

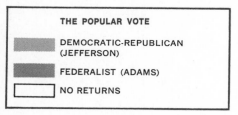

THE POPULAR VOTE

DEMOCRATIC-REPUBLICAN (JEFFERSON)

FEDERALIST (ADAMS)

NO RETURNS

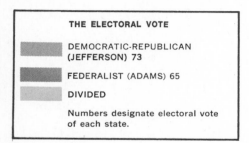

THE ELECTORAL VOTE

DEMOCRATIC-REPUBLICAN (JEFFERSON) 73

FEDERALIST (ADAMS) 65

DIVIDED

Numbers designate electoral vote of each state.

1. What points can you make about the popular vote and electoral vote of 1800? For example, what parts of the country supported Jefferson? What groups do you think supported him? How large was his margin of victory?

2. Jefferson won the New York electoral vote by a margin of 300 popular votes. What would have happened if he had obtained just 301 less votes there?

52. The Election of 1800: Federalist Reactions

Upon Thomas Jefferson's inauguration to the Presidency in 1801, a Boston Federalist newspaper called the *Columbian Centinel* printed an inscription for a monument to the Federalist party. The cartoon that follows the inscription shows another Federalist reaction to Jefferson.

A TRIBUTE TO FEDERALISM FOR ITS "FUNERAL"

MONUMENTAL INSCRIPTION.
"That life is long which answers Life's great end"
YESTERDAY EXPIRED,
Deeply regretted by MILLIONS of grateful Americans
And by *all* GOOD MEN,
The FEDERAL ADMINISTRATION
Of the
GOVERNMENT of the *United States:*
Animated by
A WASHINGTON, an ADAMS;—a
HAMILTON . . . .
Its death was occasioned by the
Secret Arts, and Open Violence,
Of Foreign and Domestic Demagogues:
Notwithstanding its whole Life
Was devoted to the Performance of every Duty
to promote
The UNION, CREDIT, PEACE, PROSPERITY, HONOR. . . .
In one word,
It found AMERICA *disunited, poor, insolvent,*
weak, discontented, and *wretched.*
It hath left HER
United, wealthy, respectable, strong,
happy and prosperous.
Let the faithful Historian, in after times,
say these things of its Successor, if it can.
And yet—notwithstanding all these services and
blessings there are found
Many, very many, weak, degenerate Sons,
who lost to virtue, to gratitude,
and patriotism,
Openly exult, that this Administration
is no more.
And that
The "Sun of Federalism is set for ever."
"Oh shame where is thy blush?"
As one Tribute of Gratitude in these Times,
This MONUMENT
Of the Talents and Services of the deceased;
is raised by

March 4th, 1801.   THE CENTINEL.

American History Told by Contemporaries, edited by Albert Bushnell Hart (New York: The Macmillan Company, 1900), Vol. III, pp. 339-340, 343.

A "demagogue" is a leader who appeals to the emotions rather than to the intellect of a crowd.

A CARTOON VIEW OF THOMAS JEFFERSON

MAD TOM in A RAGE

1. According to the *Centinel,* what did the Federalist administrations of George Washington and John Adams mean to America?

2. According to the Federalist cartoon of Jefferson, what would happen as a result of his election? How does that agree with the tone of the *Centinel*'s inscription for the Federalist party?

3. Judging from the inscription and the cartoon, what would you expect of Jefferson as a President? How would you expect Jefferson to act as President if you judged him on his ideas? Consider Jefferson's ideas about democracy, the role of the federal government, interpretation of the Constitution, and other mattters.

4. Thomas Jefferson's election was known as the "Revolution of 1800." Does it seem to be an accurate description?

53. The Louisiana Purchase

Thomas Jefferson served as President from 1801 to 1809. During Jefferson's second administration, Great Britain and France were at war. The two countries interfered with American trade, established blockades that kept American ships from their destinations, and seized American ships and sailors. These practices eventually led to the War of 1812 between the United States and Great Britain.

During most of Jefferson's first administration, however, Great Britain and France were at peace. Peace in Europe permitted Jefferson to pursue policies which might have been impossible otherwise. For example, Jefferson was able to reduce the size and expenditures of the army and navy. Trade with foreign countries flourished, and the amount of money collected from taxes on imports increased. As a result of reduced expenditures and additional revenue from trade, Jefferson was able to cut taxes. He eliminated internal taxes, or taxes paid directly to the government on goods produced and used within the country. Jefferson announced a treasury reserve of $6 million.

A major achievement of Jefferson's first term was the purchase of the Louisiana Territory from France. Jefferson wanted the western frontiersmen to have free use of the Mississippi River and the port of New Orleans. Moreover, Jefferson believed that the presence of an aggressive foreign power, such as France, on the American border posed a threat to the United States. He feared that the United States would be forced to rely on Great Britain to offset France's power in America.

In the next reading, a noted American historian, Edward Channing, describes the negotiations between the United States and France for the purchase of Louisiana.

Until 1763 Louisiana lived a life of its own, removed from the influence of the outer world, except so far as it was French. In 1763, however, Louisiana was handed over by France to Spain to make good the loss which the latter had sustained in coming to her aid in the tremendous contest with [England]. After a delay of some years, and then with a good deal of difficulty, the Spaniards took possession of their new colony . . .

[By 1800 Napoleon of France decided he must have Louisiana. To get it he offered Spain] an Italian kingdom of at least one million inhabitants . . . The territory selected [in Italy] was Tuscany . . . For [Tuscany] Spain retroceded [gave back] Louisiana to France . . . This treaty was signed at San Ildefonso on October 1, 1800 . . .

The secret of the retrocession of Louisiana was well kept. The first mention of it, in Jefferson's correspondence, was eight months later (May 26, 1801). On that day he wrote to [James] Monroe that "there is considerable reason to apprehend [fear] that Spain cedes Louisiana and the Floridas to France. . . ."

The first step in the prosecution of the French plans for rebuilding an American colonial empire was the reconquest of Santo Domingo. That island would serve as a sort of stepping-stone between France and Louisiana; moreover, Louisiana would provide a [source] of supplies for the laborers of the island. On November

Edward Channing, **The Jeffersonian System 1801-1811** (New York: Harper & Row Publishers, 1906), pp. 51, 59-61, 67-75.

France and England opposed each other in the French and Indian War, 1756-1763.

The 1800 agreement ended an undeclared naval war between the United States and France, which had gone on between 1798 and 1800.

France once ruled the island of Santo Domingo. However, the islanders revolted under the leadership of Toussaint L'Ouverture and gained their independence.

22, 1801, Leclerc, Napoleon's brother-in-law, sailed from Brest [France] for Santo Domingo with ten thousand soldiers. His object was truly stated by Robert R. Livingston, the new American minister at Paris, to be in the first instance Santo Domingo, and then, if Toussaint made no opposition, to proceed to Louisiana.

Fortunately for the United States, not only Toussaint, but half a million Santo Domingo negroes . . . opposed the French, and their efforts to destroy the invading French army were most relentlessly seconded [aided] by the yellow fever. Ten months later, September, 1802, Leclerc wrote to his brother-in-law and master that of the 28,000 men who, up to that time, had been sent to Santo Domingo, 4,000 remained fit for service. In order to enable him to conquer the island, 12,000 men should be sent to him without losing a day, to be followed by 5,000 more in the next summer. Instead of subduing the Santo Domingans, re-establishing slavery and France's colonial empire in America, General Leclerc himself died within a month of writing this letter. . . .

Meantime, affairs had been moving rapidly in France . . . Napoleon, irritated by the constant failure in Santo Domingo, suddenly turned in anger and loathing from colonial enterprises. With one of those abrupt face-abouts which he may have learned at the military school, he now seemed to be as [eager] to rid himself of Louisiana as he had been anxious a few months earlier to secure it. Louisiana was of no use without Santo Domingo, and Santo Domingo could not be conquered with any means at his command. . . . Napoleon's prestige had been injured by the many disasters to French arms in Santo Domingo; it must be regained by one or more brilliant strokes at home. Besides, Louisiana could not be held for a moment in case of war, if the United States alone should undertake its seizure. Still less could it be held if the American people, in conjunction [together] with the British fleet and nation, should undertake its conquest. Besides, Napoleon, with a Frenchman's idea of things maritime, dreaded—or detested would perhaps be the better word—the sea-power of Great Britain. In the cession of Louisiana to the United States his prophetic eye, peering far into the future, saw the young republic become a world-power, alone among nations able to lower the pride of the Mistress of the Seas [Britain]. It would be well, however, to make as much money out of the matter as possible. . . .

[Negotiations dragged on until suddenly] on Monday, April 11, 1803 . . . Talleyrand [Napoleon's chief minister] startled Livingston by asking him whether the United States wished to have the whole of Louisiana? Livingston said No; that the United States had in mind only New Orleans and the Floridas; but he thought, in addition, that France might very well sell Louisiana above the Arkansas [River], as that region was of no use to her. Talleyrand replied by the observation that without New Orleans Louisiana itself would be of no use to France, and wanted to know what the United States would give for the whole thing? Livingston replied that it was a subject he had not thought of, but that he supposed that the Americans would not object to twenty millions of francs, provided France paid the claims of the citizens of the United States for French spoliations [damages] since the period covered by [an 1800 agreement]. Talleyrand replied that this sum was too little. Livingston closed the interview by saying that he would think the matter over, that [James] Monroe would reach Paris within a short time and that the two of them would then make a further offer. . . . Finally, the negotiators settled on the sum of eighty millions of francs, sixty of them to go to France direct, the rest to be paid by the United States to American citizens in the settlement of claims against France—fifteen million dollars in all. Such was the price paid for an empire, the western half of the most valuable river valley on the surface of the earth.

It took three weeks to put all the various matters into shape. Monroe was formally received by Napoleon on May 1, and on May 2 the treaty of cession was actually signed. After Livingston set his name to the great act, he rose and . . . said, "We have lived long, but this is the noblest work of our lives." What Livingston said was true, for without the Louisiana purchase the United States would not have grown into the strong nation which it has since become. To Napoleon, also, the cession seemed full of promise: [He noted,] "Sixty millions for an occupation that will not last perhaps a day."

The most curious thing about the Louisiana purchase, however, is to be found in the fact to which Napoleon alluded, that France was able to hand over to the United States an imperial domain which was not in her possession and which, indeed, she had no right to sell to the United States. In the first place, Napoleon had promised the Spaniards that France would not [sell or trade off] Louisiana, that if she did not occupy it herself she would restore the province to Spain. In the second place, it cannot be said that Napoleon had ever fulfilled the condition [to give Tuscany to Spain] on which Louisiana had been retroceded to France. Finally, the constitution of the French republic forbade the executive by his own power to dispose of the dominions of France. The measure of credit which can attach to Livingston and Monroe, to Jefferson and Madison, is not hard to see. Diplomatically, they had achieved nothing; Louisiana had been thrown into their hands through no efforts of theirs. Great credit is due to them, never-

"To allude" to something means to refer to it.

James Madison was Jefferson's Secretary of State.

theless, because, when the fate of the United States hung in the balance, they took the responsibility of paying money, millions of dollars, which they had no authority to expend in the purchase of the country which they had no authority to buy....

When the news of the purchase of Louisiana for fifteen million dollars reached the United States, Jefferson was thunderstruck. It was not the expenditure of the money which troubled him, it was not the acquisition of an empire which disturbed his mind, it was the constitutional aspect which annoyed him, but which, curiously enough, did not in the least trouble his strict-constructionist adherents [followers] in Kentucky and Tennessee.

For years Jefferson and his followers had been talking about the necessity of interpreting the Constitution with greatest strictness. But where in that instrument could they find power expressly delegated to the central government to acquire territory? That troubled Jefferson, because he felt that what he was doing was for the good of the nation, and that the nation would ratify his act, and in so doing would make the Constitution so much blank paper. But this seemed to be the only thing that could be done.... Jefferson felt that he would not be disavowed ... that the nation would confirm his act, and by an amendment to the Constitution at once justify him and strengthen that instrument.

Acting on this general idea, the President drew up amendments to the Constitution.... Between August 12 and August 18, however, two letters came from Robert R. Livingston, advising the administration to make the greatest despatch [haste], as Napoleon might change his mind at any moment. Jefferson thereupon sat himself down and wrote ... that the less said about the constitutional difficulties the better, and that whatever was done would better be done in silence. Early in September, Jefferson received a letter from one of his steadiest and ablest supporters, Wilson Cary Nicholas ... Nicholas wrote that the Constitution did not in any way confine the Congress of the United States, in the admission of new states, to what was at that time the territory of the United States; it only said that new states could not be formed out of old ones without the consent of the state to be dismembered. Nor did Nicholas see anything in the Constitution that limited the treaty-making power....

So the treaty [for the Louisiana Purchase] was ratified and the Jeffersonian theory of strict construction was abandoned in the house of its friends [Jefferson and his supporters].

1. Where in the Constitution does it specifically state that the federal government can purchase new territory?

Article II, Section 2 of the Constitution states that the President "shall have power, by and with the advice and consent of the Senate, to make Treaties, provided two-thirds of the Senators present concur . . ."

358

2. Why did Jefferson want to have the Constitution amended before he purchased Louisiana?

3. What part of the Constitution did Jefferson finally use to support his purchase of Louisiana?

4. In using that part of the Constitution, did Jefferson apply a broad or a strict interpretation of the Constitution? Explain.

5. How did the purchase of Louisiana disagree with Jefferson's ideas about how the Constitution should be interpreted?

6. What were the events that led to Napoleon's decision to sell Louisiana?

7. If you were Jefferson, how would you view these events once you learned about them? Why?

54. Jefferson's Second Inaugural Address

In his second inaugural address, on March 4, 1805, Thomas Jefferson again made his thoughts about Louisiana known.

. . . I know that the acquisition of Louisiana has been disapproved by some from a candid apprehension [sincere worry] that the enlargement of our territory would endanger its union. But who can limit [define] the extent to which the federative principle may operate effectively? The larger our association the less will it be shaken by local passions; and in any view is it not better that the opposite bank of the Mississippi should be settled by our own brethren and children than by strangers of another family? With which should we be most likely to live in harmony and friendly intercourse [contact]?

Inaugural Addresses of the Presidents of the United States (Washington, D.C.: United States Government Printing Office, 1961), p. 18.

The "federative principle" is the principle of organizing a group of self-governing individuals or territories into a union, or federation.

1. Review the letter that Jefferson wrote to James Monroe on November 24, 1801 (see page 306). What is the main point that Jefferson makes?

2. Jefferson's decision to send James Monroe to France to aid Livingston in the purchase of Louisiana and his decision to send Lewis and Clark on their expedition were made only seven days apart. The decisions preceded Senate approval of the treaty for the purchase of Louisiana. How do these decisions, along with Jefferson's letter to Monroe in 1801, show Jefferson's feelings about the area west of the Mississippi?

3. In his second inaugural address, how does Jefferson justify his decision to buy Louisiana? Which of these reasons do you think was most important in his decision?

4. Review the selection on page 304. Does this help you to evaluate Jefferson's reasons for wanting Louisiana? If so, how? If not, why not?

5. In summary, why do you think Jefferson acted against his original ideas about how the Constitution should be interpreted?

JEFFERSON AS PRESIDENT

1. What would Alexander Hamilton and John Marshall have thought about Jefferson's new interpretation of the Constitution? Why?

2. George Washington and John Adams acted with the interests of the nation in mind. What did they think were the United States' major interests? How does this compare with Jefferson's motives for purchasing Louisiana?

3. How would you evaluate Jefferson as a President?

4. How does the following statement by Jefferson apply to his actions during the purchase of Louisiana? "Nothing then is unchangeable but the inherent and unalienable rights of man."

ANDREW JACKSON: ANOTHER DEMOCRAT AS PRESIDENT

55. The Tariff Issue

Like the election of Thomas Jefferson in 1800, the election of Andrew Jackson in 1828 was considered a revolution. Jackson's assumption of the Presidency symbolized the common people's entry into political power. In contrast to earlier Presidents, Jackson had been born into poverty. He was the first frontiersman to sit in the White House.

Many southern planters, small farmers, and city workers supported Jackson in the election of 1828. He received the electoral votes of all the western and southern states. Although few issues had been developed in the campaign of 1828 and people had not been able to discover what Jackson really stood for, most people expected him to favor the interests of the little man, the West, and the South.

Before Jackson became President, Congress passed the Tariff Act of 1828. A tariff is a tax on goods imported into a country. Many southerners opposed the tariff because they felt it favored the manufacturing interests. South Carolina passed a series of eight resolutions calling the tariff unjust and unconstitutional. Georgia, Mississippi, and Virginia soon passed similar measures.

The legality of the tariff became the subject of much debate and dispute. Jackson, in 1830, affirmed the constitutionality of the Tariff of 1828, but recommended tariff revisions.

Congress enacted a new tariff law in 1832 which was somewhat milder than the previous one. But the act still angered many southerners. Another crisis developed over the tariff.

The following selection, from a biography of Andrew Jackson by Clara I. Judson, begins with a discussion of events in 1830 and continues with an account of the 1832 issues.

POINTS TO CONSIDER

The interests of the groups involved in the struggle over the tariff.

Why Jackson acted on this issue and how he acted.

Whether Jackson's action promoted the kind of revolution that was expected of him.

Jackson kept a watchful eye on Congress as it went to work. A trusted friend was present at every session, and the President never went to bed until he had listened to the report of the day's actions. So he was not really surprised when . . . [a] knotty problem . . . [the] tariff, came up.

Clara I. Judson, **Andrew Jackson: Frontier Statesman** (Chicago: Follett Publishing Company, 1954), pp. 202-206, 214-216. Copyright © 1954. Reprinted by permission of the publisher.

That word, tariff, was often seen in newspapers. But many citizens hardly bothered to understand that it meant a tax, a "duty," to be paid on goods brought into the country. Tariff had been started to get money for the young nation, and to make foreign goods more expensive than American. This was called "protecting home industry." But *how much tariff to charge* was a problem. A man's opinion depended on where he lived.

English goods were generally cheaper than goods from the Northeast.

New Englanders wanted a high tariff.

"How can factories make money when Americans buy cheap things made abroad?" they asked. "Slap on a high duty and make people buy home goods."

Southerners disagreed. They sold cotton abroad, bought things overseas, and had very few factories of their own.

"Why should we pay a high duty?" they asked. "We don't need protection. We like to trade abroad. Let northerners do as they please. We'll have a low tariff."

Unexpectedly a bill about another matter brought the dispute into the open. This bill proposed to restrict land sales in the west. Westerners wanted settlers so they were against the bill. Easterners wanted to check the movement west so they were for the bill.

Southerners were quick to turn the dispute to help their tariff problem. They declared that no section of the nation had a right to impose a law on any other section. A state could do as it wanted, regardless of federal law, because a state was more important than the union of states.

Daniel Webster, a New Englander, chanced to enter the Senate chamber one day as Senator [Robert Y.] Hayne of South Carolina was ending an impassioned speech favoring states' rights. On the spur of the moment, Webster took the floor and talked on the side of a strong union—and against states' rights. He closed with a bold challenge to Hayne to rally.

Hayne accepted the chance to explain his views.

On the 21st of January, 1830, the galleries were packed when the southern orator rose to make his speech. Many people had not studied the arguments for and against states' rights. Now they listened intently as Hayne spoke of the problems of Kentucky and Virginia in 1798, and of New England, when she opposed the war of 1812 and threatened to secede [leave the Union].

"Is the federal government to be the judge of its own power?" Hayne cried. "Is it without limitations? High tariff would ruin the South!" He spoke well as he answered his own questions.

Five days later the chamber was again crowded when Daniel Webster replied. He was a tall, dignified man; many thought him the most brilliant speaker of his time.

"The Constitution by the will of the people is the supreme law of the land," he said. "It must be obeyed or changed." His audience listened intently through the four hours of his speech. He told them that the Constitution had created a supreme court; it, not the states, should decide what laws were right. He ended with ringing words:

"While the union lasts we have high prospects spread out before us, for us and for our children. Hayne says, 'liberty first and union afterward.' I speak another sentiment, dear to every American heart—Liberty AND union, now and forever."

These brilliant speeches were reprinted in newspapers over the nation. They were read by thousands—in colleges, in homes, in debating societies, in rural groups, in Gentry's crossroads store in southern Indiana. There a young clerk, Abe Lincoln, got the paper and read both addresses to men gathered to hear the news. Like many other Americans, they had given no thought to the meaning of their Constitution; now they did.

Kentucky and Virginia passed resolutions in 1798 declaring that the states had the power to judge and override federal acts.

Through February and March of 1830, talk surged in Washington. The mystery no one could solve was, "Which side is the President on?" Both factions claimed him.

April came, and with it the annual birthday banquet in honor of Thomas Jefferson, who had died four years earlier. South Carolinans had charge of the affair, and they made sure that the speakers and the toasts would favor states' rights. Of course the President would speak.

"Have you any idea what he'll say?" a committeeman asked.

"Oh, he's for states' rights. I know that."

"But do you? Can you prove it? Can you quote him?"

No, they could not prove; they could not quote. The President had been very silent.

The guests gathered. The dinner was served. The time for speeches and toasts drew near. The President sat silent and thoughtful. He was introduced—and for seconds he did not move. Then he unfolded his long legs and stood tall before them. He lifted a glass, cast his eyes around the hushed room—and spoke fateful words:

"Our federal union, it must be preserved!"

Men gasped. Calhoun leaped to his feet and tried to save the day for the south.

"The union, next to liberty, most dear! May we all remember that it can only be preserved by respecting the rights of states and distributing equally the benefits and burthens [burdens] of the union."

Calhoun meant well. But too many words are never as effective as a few. Jackson's terse, honest statement would be remembered; in it he had boldly dealt states' rights a staggering blow. . . .

In the midst of the bank fight [in 1832], Jackson was warned that the problem of states' rights was stirring again.

"We ought to go down to South Carolina and settle that idea once and for all!" the President exclaimed angrily.

Many citizens certainly would have approved drastic action when it was known that the South Carolina delegation in Congress voted to nullify federal laws. The President was furious.

"This act doesn't prove anything!" Men in a conference group at the White House tried to soothe him. "It's just talk."

363

"Oh, I let them talk and threaten to their heart's content," the President retorted. "Free speech is not treason."

"But just let them *act!*" he roared angrily. "If *one* drop of blood is shed in defiance of the law of the United States, I'll hang the first man of them that I can get my hands on to the first tree that I can find!"

His vivid warning was not heeded—and the campaign went on, a bitter battle with words for American votes.

Henry Clay was the presidential nominee of the National-Republican party—which soon was to be known as the Whigs. Van Buren was running with Jackson for the Democrat-Republicans; in this campaign the double word was dropped, and Jackson followers called themselves Democrats. Americans watched the contest anxiously as the fateful day of voting drew near.

The voters spoke decisively; they gave Jackson 219 electoral votes and Clay 49.

The President took [his election] as a mandate to act. He ordered General Scott to keep southern forts ready, and he had the navy stay near Charleston. Then he waited.

During this period, General Sam Dale, who had been a messenger at the battle of New Orleans, called on the President. They talked of those exciting days and then of present trouble and the danger to the union. As the President walked to the door with his guest, puffing vigorously at his pipe, he said: "If this thing goes on, Sam, our country will be like a bag of meal tied in the middle and open at both ends. Pick it up, and the meal will run out. I have to tie up that bag!"

"I hope things will turn out all right, Sir," Dale said.

"They shall go right!" Jackson shouted, and threw his pipe onto the floor violently. The clay pipe broke with a shattering sound. Dale grinned. The general hadn't changed.

The act nullified the tariffs of 1828 and 1832 and prohibited the collection of duties within the state.

After the election South Carolina passed a Nullification Act. Jackson decided to write a proclamation to the people, giving his ideas about this dangerous act. He had faith that they would understand him and make known their approval. He drove his pen furiously over the paper, tossing sheet after sheet to the floor to dry.

Edward Livingston was Jackson's Secretary of State from 1831 to 1833.

"There! That's what I want to say! The Union must be preserved, without blood if this is possible," he told Livingston. "Fix it so it sounds right."

Livingston gave the paper a bit of scholarly polish, but the ideas were Jackson's. The most vital phrases were put in bold type when the editors printed it in the news:

"I consider the power to annul a law of the United States, assumed by one state, incompatible with the existence of the Union, contradicted expressly by the letter of the Constitution, unauthorized by the spirit, inconsistent with every principle on which it was founded, and destructive of the great objective for which it was formed."

A large part of the nation was aroused by this defense of its pride and dignity. Excitement was so great that Jackson's second inauguration was hardly noticed. There was no reception; he was far too busy. As the speeches and newspaper articles continued, both sides hoped that the dispute would be resolved by a conclusive victory.

In Jackson's next message to Congress he reported the excellent state of the nation's finances. Debt was about paid; soon the treasury would have a surplus. High tariff was not needed for income, and so duties were gradually reduced.

Peace came with this compromise. Both sides claimed victory. The North said that federal law was upheld. The South said that tariff had come down; they would obey federal law—but on their own terms. The final solution was shrouded in the mists of the future.

1. What was the issue in the debate between Daniel Webster and Robert Hayne?

2. Why was this an important issue in 1830?

3. If you were a southerner or a westerner in 1830, would you object to a tariff on English goods? Why?

4. What would probably have happened if a majority of states had acted as South Carolina did in declaring the tariffs of Congress null and void?

5. Assume that you are a citizen in 1830. You are convinced that failure to uphold a federal law will throw the Union into a situation similar to the one that existed under the Articles of Confederation, when the states had more power than the central government. You believe that it is essential to preserve the Union. What would you do about South Carolina and the tariff?

6. What attitude did Jackson take on the tariff issue?

7. Why do you think he took such a position?

8. Which people who voted for Jackson in 1828 would have been displeased with his stand on the tariff?

9. Does Jackson, in his stand on the tariff, remind you of any other President? Explain.

56. Jackson's Second Inaugural Address

Inaugural Addresses of the Presidents of the United States (Washington, D.C.: United States Government Printing Office, 1961), pp. 58-59.

In the domestic policy of this Government there are two objects which especially deserve the attention of the people and their representatives, and which have been and will continue to be the subjects of my increasing solicitude [concern]. They are the preservation of the rights of the several States and the integrity of the Union. . . .

My experience in public concerns and the observation of a life somewhat advanced confirm the opinions . . . that the destruction of our State governments or the annihilation of their control over the local concerns of the people would lead directly to revolution and anarchy, and finally to despotism and military domination. . . . [My] countrymen will ever find me ready to exercise my constitutional powers in arresting measures which may directly or indirectly encroach [intrude] upon the rights of the States or tend to consolidate all political power in the General Government. But of equal, and, indeed, of incalculable, importance is the union of these States, and the sacred duty of all to contribute to its preservation by a liberal support of the General Government in the exercise of its just powers. . . . Without union our independence and liberty would never have been achieved; without union they never can be maintained. Divided into twenty-four, or even a smaller number, of separate communities, we shall see our internal trade burdened with numberless restraints and exactions; communication between distant points and sections obstructed or cut off; our sons made soldiers to deluge [flood] with blood the fields they now till [plow] in peace; the mass of our people borne down and impoverished by taxes to support armies and navies, and military leaders at the head of their victorious legions becoming our lawgivers and judges. The loss of liberty, of all good government, of peace, plenty, and happiness, must inevitably follow a dissolution of the Union. In supporting it, therefore, we support all that is dear to the freeman . . .

A REVOLUTION?

1. In his second inaugural address, what seems to be most important to Jackson? Why does that seem vital to him?

2. What would Alexander Hamilton and John Marshall have thought of Jackson's stand on the tariff issue?

3. In comparing what seemed vital to Washington and Adams with what seemed important to Jefferson and Jackson, what trend emerges?

4. Was there really a "revolution" in 1800 or in 1828? Give reasons for your answer.

5. In their actions concerning the Louisiana Purchase and the tariff issue, do you think Jefferson and Jackson were good Presidents? Why or why not?

6. Should a President of the United States carry out revolutionary policies? Should there be any limit on this?

GROWTH AND CHANGE

Between the end of the American Revolution and 1853, the United States more than tripled in size. Did this dramatic development fundamentally change our nation? In answering this question, you might think about the following:

1. What changes took place in the United States after 1800? What did not change?

2. What would our country be like today if it consisted of only the original thirteen states? What would our country be like if it were confined to the area east of the Mississippi River?

BIBLIOGRAPHY

BENET, STEPHEN V. THE DEVIL AND DANIEL WEBSTER. New York: Holt, Rinehart and Winston, Inc., 1937.
Benet spins an amusing tale about a battle of wits between the devil and Daniel Webster over the soul of a poor New Hampshire farmer.

CATHER, WILLA. DEATH COMES FOR THE ARCHBISHOP. New York: Alfred A. Knopf, Inc., 1927.
The main character of this famous novel is a French priest who dedicates himself to working among the New Mexican Indians during the mid-1800's.

GUTHRIE, ALFRED B. THE BIG SKY. Revised edition; Boston: Houghton Mifflin Company, 1950.† Sentry edition; Boston: Houghton Mifflin Company, 1965.
The author presents a realistic picture of the brutal lives of the trappers and mountain men of the West.

GUTHRIE, ALFRED B. THE WAY WEST. Boston: Houghton Mifflin Company, 1949. New York: Pocket Books, Inc., 1964.
The theme of this novel is the problems and hardships involved in a wagon train's journey from Independence, Missouri, to Oregon.

KJELGAARD, JAMES A. THE LOST WAGON. New York: Dodd, Mead & Co., 1955. This is a fictional account of the problems one family faced as they traveled by wagon and mule to find a new home in the West.

WELLMAN, PAUL I. MAGNIFICENT DESTINY. Garden City, New York: Doubleday & Company, Inc., 1962.
The story opens in 1813 when Andrew Jackson was forty-six and Sam Houston was twenty. From that date until Jackson's death in 1843, their careers were intertwined.

† Denotes paperback edition.

TIME LINE

1787	THE NORTHWEST ORDINANCE.
1800	THOMAS JEFFERSON ELECTED PRESIDENT.
1801	JOHN MARSHALL APPOINTED CHIEF JUSTICE OF THE SUPREME COURT.
1803	THE LOUISIANA PURCHASE.
1804–06	LEWIS AND CLARK EXPEDITION.
1804	JEFFERSON RE-ELECTED PRESIDENT.
1805–07	PIKE'S EXPEDITIONS.
1808	JAMES MADISON ELECTED PRESIDENT.
1810	ANNEXATION OF WEST FLORIDA.
1812	THE WAR OF 1812 BEGINS.
1815	THE TREATY OF GHENT ENDS THE WAR OF 1812.
1816	JAMES MONROE ELECTED PRESIDENT.
1817	RUSH-BAGOT AGREEMENT.
1818	CONVENTION OF 1818.
1819	THE ADAMS-ONÍS AGREEMENT.
1820	MONROE RE-ELECTED PRESIDENT.
1823	THE MONROE DOCTRINE.
1824	JOHN QUINCY ADAMS ELECTED PRESIDENT.
1828	TARIFF ACT.
1828	ANDREW JACKSON ELECTED PRESIDENT.
1830	WEBSTER-HAYNE DEBATE.
1832	TARIFF ACT.
1832	NULLIFICATION CONTROVERSY.
1832	JACKSON VETOES THE BILL TO RECHARTER THE BANK OF THE UNITED STATES.
1832	JACKSON RE-ELECTED PRESIDENT.
1834	FORMATION OF THE WHIG PARTY.
1835	JOHN MARSHALL LEAVES THE SUPREME COURT.
1836	THE TEXAS REVOLUTION.
1836	MARTIN VAN BUREN ELECTED PRESIDENT.
1840	WILLIAM HENRY HARRISON ELECTED PRESIDENT.
1841	HARRISON DIES; JOHN TYLER BECOMES PRESIDENT.
1842	THE WEBSTER-ASHBURTON AGREEMENT.
1844	JAMES K. POLK ELECTED PRESIDENT.
1845	TEXAS ANNEXED TO THE UNION.
1846	THE OREGON SETTLEMENT.
1846	THE MEXICAN WAR BEGINS.
1848	THE TREATY OF GUADALUPE HIDALGO ENDS THE MEXICAN WAR.
1848	GOLD DISCOVERED IN CALIFORNIA.
1848	ZACHARY TAYLOR ELECTED PRESIDENT.
1850	TAYLOR DIES; MILLARD FILLMORE BECOMES PRESIDENT.
1852	FRANKLIN PIERCE ELECTED PRESIDENT.
1853	THE GADSDEN PURCHASE.

unit V
LIFE AND SOCIETY
IN THE
YOUNG NATION 1800-1860

America, with thee life's better,
  Thou art free from our old Europe's faults; . . .
No ruined castles fetter . . . no useless tradition,
  No purposeless strife,
Hinder the fruition
  Of thy pulsing life.

JOHANN WOLFGANG VON GOETHE
WILHELM MEISTER'S WANDERING YEARS, 1827

INTRODUCTION

Between 1783 and 1860, the United States grew at a rapid rate. From thirteen colonies concentrated on the Atlantic seaboard, the country expanded until it reached the shores of the Pacific Ocean. The Mississippi Valley was added in 1803, Florida in 1819, Oregon in 1846, and most of the Southwest in 1848. During this period, Americans achieved independence and won three wars. They found markets for their abundant farm products and laid the basis for the growth of industry. Americans also built a stable democratic government.

Such were the military, economic, and political achievements of the American people. But what were the people like? What were the beliefs and social customs that influenced their actions?

The national origins of America's population were changing. A large percentage of the people in America were British during the seventeenth and eighteenth centuries. Then, toward the end of the eighteenth century, large groups of Scotch-Irish came to the Appalachian frontier regions. From 1830 to 1850, the Irish made up almost 50 per cent of the immigrants who came to America. The Irish often settled in the eastern seaboard cities. They provided much of the manual labor that went into construction of the nation's canals and railroads. By the 1850's large numbers of Germans, Dutch, Belgians, and Scandinavians were coming to the United States. These people went west and settled in Wisconsin, Ohio, Missouri, and Texas.

J. Hector St. John de Crèvecoeur, a Frenchman who migrated to America before the Revolution, remarked that Americans "are a mixture of English, Scotch, Irish, French, Dutch, Germans, and Swedes. From this promiscous [mixed] breed, that race now called Americans have risen." Crèvecoeur felt, however, that the uniqueness of America went deeper than national origins. "What is the American, this new man?" he asked. Crèvecoeur's question is the main theme of this unit and one you will be asked to answer. As you read about Americans during the years 1800-1860, your principal task will be to decide what they were like.

The pioneer was one of the most important representatives of early America. As you learned in Unit IV, large numbers of people moved west during the early nineteenth century. Whereas only 6 per cent of Americans lived west of the Allegheny Mountains in 1790, by 1820 these westerners accounted for 27 per cent of the population. Forty-five per cent of the population lived west of the

Alleghenies by 1850. The unit, therefore, begins with a study of the pioneer. In the first section, you will have an opportunity to study what the West was like and what problems it presented to the settler. You will be able to form ideas about what kind of person was attracted to such an adventure and how the conditions he met further shaped his personality. You will start by looking at maps and pictures which will show characteristics of the land along the various routes to the West. You will be asked to speculate on the difficulties travelers might encounter, and on the advantages or disadvantages of settling in different areas. Then, as you read actual accounts by frontiersmen about their experiences, you will be able to verify your findings. You may discover frontier problems you did not anticipate.

In addition to showing the problems that pioneers faced, the frontier accounts will reveal how pioneers solved their problems. All of these materials will give you hints about the hopes, fears, and personal characteristics of the pioneers.

The second section of the unit is not directly about people. Instead, it shows what transportation was like in early nineteenth century America and how it changed. It also tells about some of the major inventions of the period. You will be asked to relate this material to your ideas about pioneers.

The next part of the unit deals with people other than pioneers. Here you will have the opportunity to read about life in different parts of the country between the years 1800 and 1860. You will see American life first through the eyes of Americans and then of foreign observers. In order to form a total picture of the early American, you will have to think about how to judge and use these different accounts.

Two other kinds of sources are presented to give you insight into the American character. First, you will read reports about developments that captured the imagination of nineteenth-century Americans. You will be asked to consider what this shows about American traits. Then, at the end of the unit, you will find several examples of frontier folklore, both stories and folk songs. The folklore may reflect some of the strains in the American personality which you had detected earlier. It may also reveal aspects of the American which were not as apparent in more formal writings.

Before you begin this unit, you might stop and think about what Americans are like today. Then you will be able to judge how much we have—or haven't—changed.

A LOOK AT THE LAND

1. A Map Overview

In the 1600's, the early settlers on American soil faced and solved numerous problems. In spite of many obstacles, Americans pushed westward so that by the 1840's they had crossed the continent. The first two readings in this section contain maps and pictures of the continent that the pioneers encountered. The maps in this reading show the early routes to the West, the nation's topography or physical characteristics, original soil and forest regions, and annual rainfall. Later you will read accounts actually written by pioneers.

POINTS TO CONSIDER

The problems that pioneers might encounter as they moved west.

The advantages or disadvantages of moving to different areas of the country.

I. Problems of Americans on the Frontier

The date that appears with the name of each route shows when the route first came into use. However, the route was often incomplete at that time.

LAND ROUTES TO THE WEST

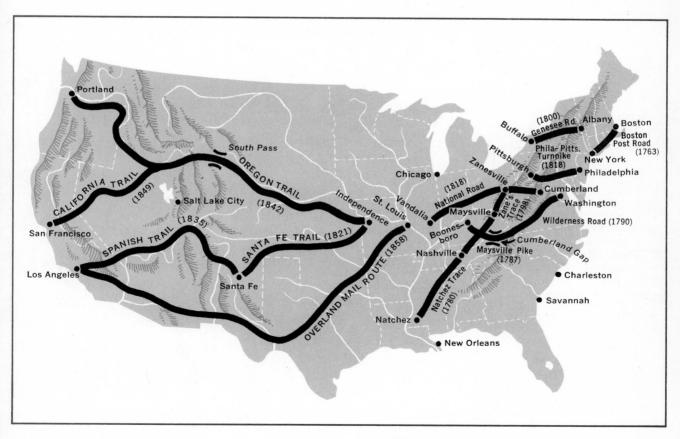

TOPOGRAPHY OF THE UNITED STATES

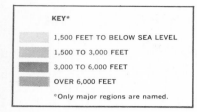

KEY*

1,500 FEET TO BELOW SEA LEVEL

1,500 TO 3,000 FEET

3,000 TO 6,000 FEET

OVER 6,000 FEET

*Only major regions are named.

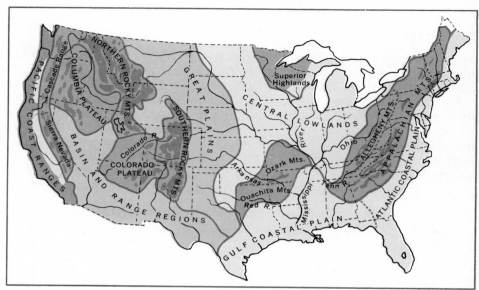

ORIGINAL SOIL REGIONS OF THE UNITED STATES

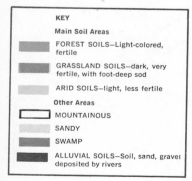

KEY

Main Soil Areas

FOREST SOILS—Light-colored, fertile

GRASSLAND SOILS—dark, very fertile, with foot-deep sod

ARID SOILS—light, less fertile

Other Areas

MOUNTAINOUS

SANDY

SWAMP

ALLUVIAL SOILS—Soil, sand, gravel deposited by rivers

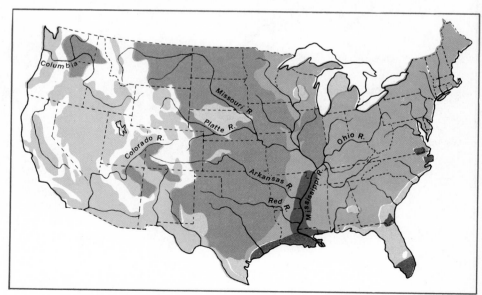

ANNUAL RAINFALL OF THE UNITED STATES

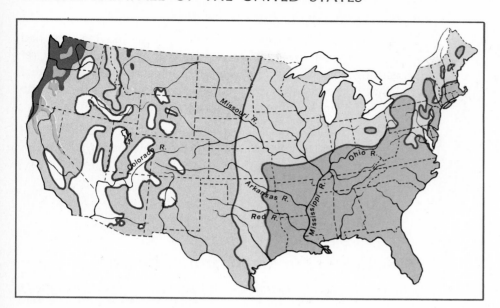

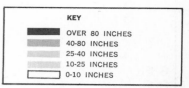

KEY
- OVER 80 INCHES
- 40-80 INCHES
- 25-40 INCHES
- 10-25 INCHES
- 0-10 INCHES

ORIGINAL FORESTS OF THE UNITED STATES

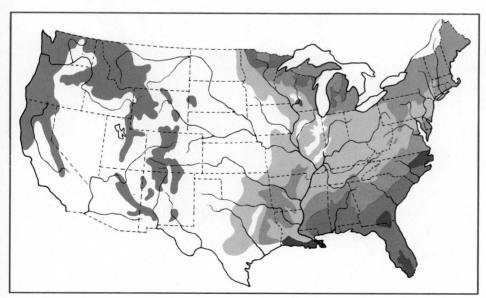

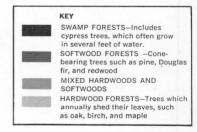

KEY

SWAMP FORESTS—Includes cypress trees, which often grow in several feet of water.

SOFTWOOD FORESTS —Cone-bearing trees such as pine, Douglas fir, and redwood

MIXED HARDWOODS AND SOFTWOODS

HARDWOOD FORESTS—Trees which annually shed their leaves, such as oak, birch, and maple

1. What advantages and disadvantages do you think the settlers might have had as they moved west?

2. What problems do you see that the people moving west had to encounter? What tentative conclusions can you draw regarding the ways these people overcame their problems? What is the basis for your conclusions? What information do you need in addition to the information on the maps?

3. Look at the map of Indian tribes on page 45 of Unit I. What does this add to your ideas about the problems or advantages pioneers might have as they crossed or settled different areas?

2. Scenes of the American Landscape

The following pictures will give you an idea of what the pioneers found as they moved into different areas of the country. The map will show you the area illustrated in each picture.

LOCATION OF AREAS SHOWN IN THE PICTURES

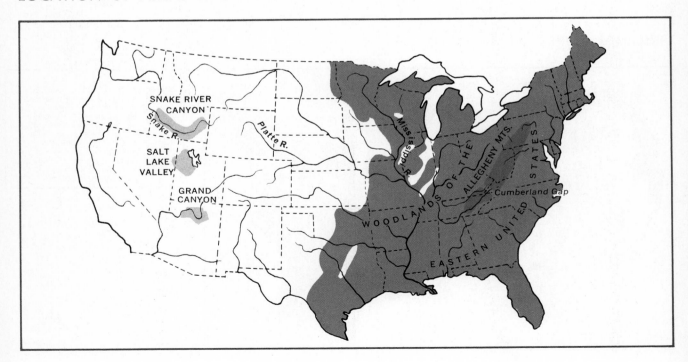

THE ALLEGHENY MOUNTAINS

A sketch made about 1845 of Cumberland Gap, the passage through the Allegheny Mountains.

THE UPPER MISSISSIPPI RIVER

Jonathan Carver traveled through the Great Lakes region and then west to the Minnesota area. This drawing of the Mississippi River was included in his Travels Through the Interior Parts of America in the Years 1766, 1767, & 1768.

AREA NEAR THE PLATTE RIVER

The area of the Platte River in Nebraska is shown in this photograph.

A CANYON IN THE NORTHWEST

The canyon in this photograph is on the Snake River, between Idaho and Oregon.

THE GRAND CANYON

A picture of the Grand Canyon by a member of an 1858 expedition into the area.

PLAINS OF THE SOUTHWEST

The land in this photograph is located in the Southwest near the Oklahoma and Texas border.

THE SALT LAKE VALLEY

This view of the Salt Lake Valley in Utah was drawn by an Englishman who traveled to this area with the Mormons in 1853.

1. Do any of these views of the American landscape suggest additional problems that the settlers might encounter as they moved west?

2. Do these pictures verify ideas you formed when studying the preceding maps? How?

PERSONAL NARRATIVES OF THE WESTWARD MOVEMENT

3. The Pilgrims Come to Plymouth, 1620

You will now have the chance to test your ideas about pioneer problems against the reports of the pioneers themselves. In Unit IV you studied the reasons why people went west. Keep this in mind as you read the following personal stories.

The first two accounts are from the writings of William Bradford, leader of the Pilgrims when they landed at Plymouth. The Pilgrims originally left England in 1608 to go to Holland. Then, in 1620, they migrated to America. When the Pilgrims came west from England to America, the frontier was the shore of the eastern seaboard. In the first selection, Bradford tells why the Pilgrims left Holland. In the second, he discusses the New World. In both accounts, the spelling appears as it does in the source being quoted.

POINTS TO CONSIDER

The problems settlers encountered.

How they began to solve their problems.

What common experiences settlers from various areas of the country had.

What the settlers were like and why.

REASONS FOR LEAVING HOLLAND

After they had lived in this citie [in Holland] about some 11. or 12. years . . . they began to incline to this conclusion, of remooval to some other place. . . . First, they saw and found by experience the hardnes of the place and countrie [Holland] to be such . . . [that] some preferred and chose the prisons in England, rather [than] this libertie in Holland, with these afflictions. But it was thought that if a better and easier place of living could be had, it would . . . take away these discouragements. . . .

[Secondly,] . . . according to the devine proverb, that a wise man seeth the plague when it cometh, and hideth him selfe . . . so they like skillfull and beaten [experienced] souldiers were fearfull either to be intrapped or surrounded by their enimies . . . and therefor thought it better to dislodge . . . [while there was time] to some

Bradford's History of the Plymouth Plantation, edited by William J. Davis (New York: Charles Scribner's Sons, 1908), pp. 44-49, 171-172.

Holland, a Spanish possession, repeatedly fought to gain its independence. A truce established in 1609 between Holland and Spain was to end in April 1621. The Pilgrims feared the outbreak of war and the coming of the Spanish.

place of better advanage and less danger, if any such could be found. Thirdly . . . many of their children . . . were, often times, so oppressed with their hevie labours, that [they] . . . became decreped [worn out] in their early youth . . . But . . . of all sorowes most heavie to be borne, was that many of their children . . . [through] the great licentiousness [unchecked freedom] of youth in that countrie, and the manifold [many] temptations of the place, were drawne away by evill examples into extravagante and dangerous courses . . . departing from their parents. Some became souldiers, others tooke upon them farr viages [voyages] by sea, and other some worse courses, tending to . . . the danger of their soules, to the great greefe [grief] of their parents and dishonour of God. . . .

"Extravagant," here, means outside the bounds of good conduct.

Lastly, (and which was not least), a great hope and inward zeall [desire] they had of laying some good foundation . . . for . . . advancing the gospell of the kingdom of Christ in those remote parts of the world . . .

The place they had thoughts on was some of those vast and unpeopled countries of America, which are frutfull [fruitful] and fitt for habitation . . . wher ther are only salvage [savage] and brutish men, which range up and downe, little otherwise [than] the wild beasts . . . Some . . . out of their fears, objected . . . [that this plan was] subjecte to many . . . dangers; as, besids the casulties [accidents] of the seas (which none can be freed from) the length of the vioage [voyage] was such, as the weake bodys of women and other persons worne out with age and traville [travel] (as many of them were) could never be able to endure. . . .

It was answered, that . . . the dangers were great, but not desperate; the difficulties were many, but not invincible. . . . [All] of them, through the help of God, by fortitude and patience, might either be borne, or overcome. . . . They lived hear [here] but as men in exile, and in a poore condition; and as great miseries might possible befale [befall] them in this place, for the 12. years of truce were now out, and ther was nothing but beating of drumes, and preparing for warr, the events wherof are allway [always] uncertaine. The Spaniard might prove as cruell as the salvages of America, and the famine and pestelence [plague] as sore hear as ther, and their libertie less . . .

An "invincible" difficulty has no solution.

THE NEW WORLD
The countrie is anoyed with foxes and woules [wolves].

. . . So are many other good countries too; but poyson [poison], traps, and other such means will help to destroy them. . . .

383

The people are much anoyed with muskeetoes.

. . . They are too delicate and unfitte to begine new-plantations . . . [if they] cannot enduer [endure] the biting of a muskeeto; we would wish such to keepe at home till at least they be muskeeto proofe. Yet this place is as free as any, and experience teacheth that the more the land is tild [tilled], and the woods cut downe, the fewer ther will be, and in the end scarse any at all.

1. What problems did the Pilgrims face in coming to the New World?

2. Why were they willing to face these problems?

3. What kind of people do the Pilgrims seem to have been?

4. Cooperstown, New York, 1789

Judge William Cooper, who had obtained title to a large tract of land in upper New York, started a settlement there in 1789. He described his experiences in *Guide in the Wilderness,* from which the following excerpt is taken.

In 1785 I visited the rough and hilly country of Otsego, where there existed not an inhabitant, nor any trace of a road; I was alone three hundred miles from home, without bread, meat, or food of any kind; fire and fishing tackle were my only means of subsistence. I caught trout in the brook, and roasted them on the ashes [coals]. My horse fed on the grass that grew by the edge of the waters. I laid me down to sleep in my watch coat, nothing but the melancholy wilderness around me. In this way I explored the country, formed my plans of future settlement, and meditated upon the spot where a place of trade or a village should afterwards be established.

In May, 1786, I opened the sales of forty thousand acres, which, in sixteen days, were all taken up by the poorest order of men. I soon after established a store and went to live among them, and continued to do so till 1790, when I brought on my family. For the ensuing [next] four years the scarcity of provisions was a serious calamity; the country was mountainous, and there were neither roads nor bridges.

But the greatest discouragement was in the extreme poverty of the people, none of whom had the means of clearing more than a small spot in the midst of the thick and lofty woods, so that their grain grew chiefly in the shade; their maize did not ripen; their wheat was blasted [withered by disease], and the little they

The Heritage of America, edited by Henry Steele Commager and Allan Nevins (Boston: Little, Brown and Company, 1949), pp. 256-257. Copyright 1939, 1949 by Henry Steele Commager and Allan Nevins. Reprinted by permission of the publisher.

did gather they had no mill to grind within twenty miles distance; not one in twenty had a horse, and the way lay through rapid streams, across swamps, or over bogs. They had neither provisions to take with them, nor money to purchase them; nor if they had, were any to be found on their way. If the father of a family went abroad to labor for bread, it cost him three times its value before he could bring it home, and all the business on his farm stood still till his return.

I resided among them, and saw too clearly how bad their condition was. I erected a store house and during each winter filled it with large quantities of grain, purchased in distant places. I procured [obtained] from my friend Henry Drinker a credit for a large quantity of sugar kettles; he also lent me some potash kettles, which we conveyed as we best could, sometimes by partial roads on sleighs, and sometimes over the ice. By this means I established potash works among the settlers and made them debtor for their bread and laboring utensils. I also gave them credit for their maple sugar and potash, at a price that would bear transportation, and the first year after the adoption of this plan I collected in one mass forty-three hogsheads of sugar and three hundred barrels of pot- and pearlash, worth about nine thousand dollars. This kept the people together and at home, and the country soon assumed a new face.

Potash, when refined, is used in manufacturing soap and glass.

A "hogshead" is a large cask that holds 63 to 140 gallons.

I had not funds of my own sufficient for the opening of new roads, but I collected the people at convenient seasons, and by joint efforts we were able to throw bridges over the deep streams, and to make, in the cheapest manner, such roads as suited our then humble purposes.

1. Why did the settlers of Cooperstown have such a hard time making a living at first?

2. How were their problems solved?

5. Migrants to Kentucky, 1792

Following the American Revolution, Gilbert Imlay moved west to Kentucky. He became a surveyor and a recognized authority on that area of the frontier. The following reading is his description of routes into the territory. Refer to the map of westward routes to locate places mentioned in this selection (see p. 373).

The distance from Philadelphia by land to Kentucky is between seven and eight hundred miles; from Baltimore nearly seven hundred; nearly six hundred from Alexandria; and upwards of

Gilbert Imlay, **A Description of the Western Territory of North America** (Dublin, Ireland: William Jones, 1793), pp. 146-148.

five hundred from Richmond. The roads and accomodations are tolerably good to the borders of the Wilderness; through which it is hardly possible for a carriage to pass, great part of the way being over high and steep hills, upon the banks of the rivers and along defiles [narrow passes], which in some places seem to threaten you at every step with danger. This is the only route the people coming from the upper parts of Virginia and North Carolina can take at present to get into the country; the gap of Cumberland mountain being the only place it can be passed without the greatest difficulty. The opening [of navigation on] the Tenasee [Tennessee River] will afford a convenient communication with the Mississippi. The Wilderness, which was formerly two hundred miles through, without a single habitation, is reduced from the settlement of Powel's Valley [in northeastern Tennessee], to nearly one half of that distance; and it is to be expected that in a few years more . . . the remainder of the distance will afford settlements for the accomodation of people travelling that route; when a good road may be made quite to Kentucky. The canals [that are being cut] on the Potowmac [Potomac River] and the removal of the obstructions in Cheat River, will render the passage from Alexandria, or the federal city [Washington] to the Ohio, both cheap and easy.

1. What difficulties for pioneers does Imlay describe?

2. What developments are easing these difficulties?

6. The Louisiana Frontier, 1816–1826

Timothy Flint went to the Mississippi River Valley as a missionary in 1816. Disappointed and discouraged by disease, he returned to New England to write about the West. You read some of his writings earlier, in Unit IV.

. . . When we look round these immense regions, and consider that I have been in settlements three hundred miles from any court of justice, when we look at the position of the men, and the state of things, the wonder is, that so few outrages and murders occur. The gentlemen of the towns, even here [in Louisiana], speak often with a certain contempt and horror of the backwoodsmen. . . . It is true there are gamblers, and gougers [swindlers], and outlaws; but there are fewer of them, than from the nature of things, and the character of the age and the world, we ought to expect. . . . You find, in truth, that [the backwoodsman] has vices and barbarisms [uncivilized habits], peculiar to his situation. His manners are rough. He wears, it may be, a long beard. He has a great

The Cheat River flows from northwest Virginia into Pennsylvania.

Timothy Flint, **Recollections of the Last Ten Years . . . in the Valley of the Mississippi** (Boston: Cummings, Hilliard, and Company, 1826), pp. 175-177.

quantity of bear or deer skins wrought into [used in] his household establishment, his furniture, and dress. He carries a knife, or a dirk [dagger] in his bosom, and when in the woods has a rifle on his back, and a pack of dogs at his heels. An Atlantic stranger, transferred directly from one of our cities to his door, would recoil from [an encounter] with him. But remember, that his rifle and his dogs are among his chief means of support and profit. Remember, that all his first days here were passed in dread of the savages. Remember, that he still encounters them, still meets bears and panthers. Enter his door, and tell him you are benighted, and wish the shelter of his cabin for the night. The welcome is indeed seemingly ungracious: "I reckon you can stay," or "I suppose we must let you stay." But this apparent ungraciousness is the harbinger [forerunner] of every kindness that he can bestow, and every comfort that his cabin can afford. Good coffee, corn bread and butter, venison [deer meat], pork, wild and tame fowls are set before you. His wife, timid, silent, reserved, but constantly attentive to your comfort, does not sit at the table with you, but like the wives of the patriarchs, stands and attends [waits] on you. You are shown to the best bed which the house can offer. When this kind of hospitality has been afforded you as long as you choose to stay, and when you depart, and speak about your bill, you are most commonly told with some slight mark of resentment, that they do not keep tavern. Even the flaxen-headed urchins will turn away from your money.

A person who is "benighted" is overtaken by nightfall.

1. According to Flint, what are frontiersmen like?

2. How does Flint think their behavior has been influenced by the frontier?

7. On the Oregon Trail, 1843

Jesse Applegate traveled the Oregon Trail in 1843 with a group of emigrants. He owned a large herd of cows that was being driven west with the wagon train. In the following excerpt, Applegate describes the group's movement along the Platte River.

It is four o'clock A.M.; the sentinels on duty have discharged their rifles—the signal that the hours of sleep are over . . . Sixty men start from the corral, spreading as they make [move] through the vast herd of cattle and horses that make a semicircle around the encampment, the most distant perhaps two miles away.

The herders pass to the extreme verge [edge] and carefully examine for trails beyond, to see that none of the animals have strayed or been stolen during the night. This morning no trails

W. J. Ghent, **The Road to Oregon** (New York: Tudor Publishing Company, 1934), pp. 73-76. Reprinted by permission of the publisher.

led beyond the outside animals in sight, and by 5 o'clock the herders begin to contract [reduce] the great, moving circle, and the well-trained animals move slowly towards camp, clipping here and there a thistle or a tempting bunch of grass on the way. In about an hour, five thousand animals are close up to the encampment, and the teamsters are busy selecting their teams and driving them inside the corral to be yoked. The corral is a circle one hundred yards deep, formed with wagons connected strongly with each other; the wagon in the rear being connected with the wagon in front by its tongue and ox chains. It is a strong barrier that the most vicious ox cannot break, and in case of an attack of the Sioux would be no contemptible intrenchment [protection].

From 6 to 7 o'clock is a busy time; breakfast is to be eaten, the tents struck, the wagons loaded and the teams yoked and brought up in readiness to be attached to their respective wagons. All know when, at 7 o'clock, the signal to march sounds, that those not ready to take their proper places in the line of march must fall into the dusty rear for the day.

There are sixty wagons. They have been divided into fifteen divisions or platoons of four wagons each, and each platoon is entitled to lead in its turn. The leading platoon today will be the rear one tomorrow . . . It is within ten minutes of seven; the corral . . . is everywhere broken, the teams [are] attached to the wagons. The women and children have taken their places in them. The pilot (a borderer [frontiersman] who has passed his life on the verge of civilization and has been chosen to the post of leader from his knowledge of the savage and his experience in travel through roadless wastes), stands ready . . . to mount and lead the way. Ten or fifteen young men, not today on duty, form another cluster. They are ready to start on a buffalo hunt, are well mounted and well armed, as they need be, for the unfriendly Sioux have driven the buffalo out of the Platte, and the hunters must ride fifteen or twenty miles to reach them. . . .

It is on the stroke of seven . . . Fortunately every one has been found and every teamster is at his post. The clear notes of a trumpet sound in the front; the pilot and his guards mount their horses; the leading divisions of the wagons move out of the encampment, and take up the line of march; the rest fall into their places with the precision of clock work, until the spot so lately full of life sinks back into that solitude that seems to reign over the broad plain and rushing river . . .

It is not yet 8 o'clock when the first watch is to be set; the evening meal is just over, and the corral now free from the intrusion of cattle or horses, groups of children are scattered over it. The larger are taking a game of romps ... Before a tent near the river a violin makes lively music ... It has been a prosperous day; more than twenty miles have been accomplished of the great journey. . . .

1. Would you have liked to be a part of this group? Why or why not?

2. What seem to be the reasons for leading this kind of life?

3. What is the role of the individual in this account?

8. Getting a Start in Ohio, 1840

William Cooper Howells, an editor in Ohio, described life in that state.

Particularly remarkable was the general equality and the general dependence of all upon the neighborly kindness and good offices of others. Their houses and barns were built of logs, and were raised by the collection of many neighbors together on one day, whose united strength was necessary to the handling of the logs. As every man was ready with the ax and understood this work, all came together within the circle where the raising was to be done, and all worked together with about equal skill. The best axmen were given charge of the placing of the logs on the wall, and some one of experience took the general direction. The logs of the width and length of the house were usually of different lengths. Those intended for the two sides were placed in a convenient place, some distance from the foundation; those for the ends, in another place. The first two side logs were put in place at the back and front; then the end logs were notched down in their places; then two side logs would be rolled up on skids, and notched in their places. At the corners the top of the log, as soon as it was put in place, would be dressed up [notched] by the cornerman; and when the next logs were rolled up they would be notched, which notch would be turned downwards upon the saddle made to receive it, when the cornerman would saddle that log ready for the next. This kept the logs in their places like a dovetail and brought them together so as to form a closer wall. The ends of the skids would be raised on each new log as it was laid down to make a way for the next. The logs on these skids would be rolled as long as the men could handle them from the ground, but when the wall got too high, then they would use forks, made by cutting a young notched tree, with which the logs

The Heritage of America, edited by Henry Steele Commager and Allan Nevins (Boston: Little, Brown and Company, 1949), pp. 275-276. Copyright 1939, 1949 by Henry Steele Commager and Allan Nevins. Reprinted by permission of the publisher. Slightly adapted.

"Skids," here, are planks up which logs are rolled to their places in the wall.

A "dovetail" is a V-shaped joint between two pieces.

would be pushed up. By using a fork at each end of the log, it could be pushed up with ease and safety. The men understood handling timber, and accidents seldom happened, unless the logs were icy or wet or the whisky had gone round too often. I was often at these raisings, because we had raisings of the kind to do, and it was the custom always to send one of the family to help, so that you could claim like assistance in return. At the raisings I would take the position of cornerman, if the building was not too heavy, as it was a post of honor, and my head was steady when high up from the ground. In chopping on the corners we always stood up straight and it required a good balance.

This kind of mutual help of the neighbors was extended to many kinds of work, such as rolling up the logs in a clearing, grubbing out the underbrush, splitting rails, cutting logs for a house, and the like. When a gathering of men for such a purpose took place, there was commonly some sort of mutual job laid out for the women, such as quilting, sewing, or spinning up a lot of thread for some poor neighbor. This would bring together a mixed party, and it was usually arranged that after supper there should be a dance or at least plays which would occupy a good part of the night and wind up with the young fellows seeing the girls home in the short hours, or, if they went home early, sitting with them by the fire in that kind of interesting chat known as sparking.

1. Compare Howell's story with the account of traveling on the Oregon Trail. What similarities do you note?

2. How can you explain these similarities?

9. A Frenchman Observes Frontier Settlement, 1786

The Marquis de Chastellux, a French officer who served in the American Revolution, recorded, in 1786, his observations of frontier settlement. You read a selection from his writings in Unit IV.

... [A frontiersman] begins by felling all the smaller trees, and some strong branches of the large ones: these he makes use of as fences to the first field he wishes to clear; he next boldly attacks those immense oaks, or pines, which one would take for the ancient lords of the territory he is usurping [taking over]; he strips them of their bark, or lays them open all round with his axe. These trees mortally wounded, are the next spring robbed of their honors [life]; their leaves no longer spring, their branches fall, and their trunk becomes a hideous skeleton. This trunk still seems to brave the efforts of the new colonist; but where there are the

American History Told by Contemporaries, edited by Albert Bushnell Hart (New York: The Macmillan Company, 1898), Vol. II, pp. 392-393.

smallest chinks or crevices, it is surrounded by fire, and the flames consume what the iron was unable to destroy. But it is enough for the small trees to be felled, and the great ones to lose their sap. This object compleated, the ground is cleared; the air and the sun begin to operate upon that earth which is wholly formed of rotten vegetables, and teems with [is full of] the latent [undeveloped] principles of production. The grass grows rapidly; there is pasturage for the cattle the very first year; after which they are left to increase, or fresh ones are brought, and they are employed in tilling a piece of ground which yields the enormous increase of twenty or thirty fold. The next year the same course is repeated; when, at the end of two years, the planter has wherewithal to subsist [exist] and even to send some articles to market: at the end of four or five years, he completes the payment of his land, and finds himself a comfortable planter. Then his dwelling, which at first was no better than a large hut formed by a square of the trunks of trees, placed one upon another, with the intervals filled by mud, changes into a handsome wooden house, where he contrives [builds] more convenient, and certainly much cleaner apartments than those in the greatest part of our small towns. This is the work of three weeks or a month. His first habitation, that of eight and forty hours. I shall be asked, perhaps, how one man, or one family can be so quickly lodged? I answer, that in America a man is never alone, never an isolated being. The neighbours, for they are every where to be found, make it a point of hospitality to aid the new farmer. A cask of cyder [cider] drank [drunk] in common, and with gaiety, or a gallon of rum, are the only recompense [payment] for these services. Such are the means by which North America, which one hundred years ago was nothing but a vast forest, is peopled with three millions of inhabitants . . .

An "increase of thirty fold" means that the crop is thirty times greater than before.

CONCLUDING EXERCISE

1. Do the problems you listed while studying the maps and pictures match the problems you found in these contemporary accounts? Are there differences? Explain.

2. What kinds of solutions to frontier problems begin to emerge? How do you explain this?

3. Was the pioneer self-sufficient? That is, could he solve most of his problems by himself? Explain.

4. What kind of people went to the frontier? Do you think the frontier would attract such people? Would it bring out the traits they displayed? Explain.

5. Are there common experiences and traits in all frontier areas?

391

A FURTHER LOOK
AT PROBLEMS AND SOLUTIONS

10. Farm and Factory Products

You have studied some of the problems settlers encountered while they traveled west. You have also read about the problems of settlers who established their homes at the most distant outposts of the frontier. Now you will study the problems of a somewhat more developed and populated frontier area.

Between 1800 and 1830, the area between the Appalachian Mountains and the Mississippi River grew so quickly that five new states were created from it. The five states were Illinois, Indiana, Ohio, Mississippi, and Alabama. On the western bank of the Mississippi River, Missouri and Louisiana also achieved statehood. Most Americans still lived in the East, and the largest concentrations of population were in the Northeast. (See the selection and the maps on pages 299–302.) However, the growth of the region around the Ohio and Mississippi rivers drained large numbers of people from the older areas of the country.

POINTS TO CONSIDER

How the five following maps suggest possible problems for settlers in the Ohio and Mississippi rivers area.

Agricultural Production
- ⠿ WHEAT
- ⠿ CORN
- ⠿ COTTON
- ⠿ TOBACCO
- ‡ RICE, SUGAR
- ✕ CATTLE

Industrial Centers
- ◯ COAL
- ◓ COTTON SPINNING
- ● IRON AND STEEL

CENTERS OF AGRICULTURAL PRODUCTION IN THE 1830's

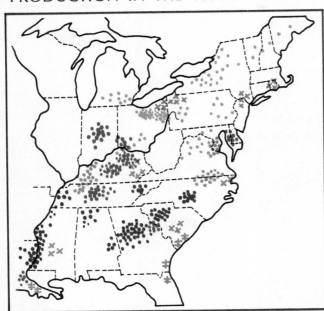

INDUSTRIAL CENTERS IN THE 1830's

1. In which parts of the country were most farm products grown? Where were most industrial products manufactured?

2. What obstacles to east-west transportation are revealed by the maps, pictures, and stories you studied earlier in this unit?

3. Consider the information on these maps, and think about what the western settler's needs might be. Would the difficulties of east-west transport be a serious problem for him? Why or why not?

4. If the transportation problem was a serious one, how could the settler solve it?

11. Land and Water Transportation

The following two pictures show the kind of transportation that was common in the early 1800's. The first drawing shows stage-coach travel to the West in 1812. The second shows a flat-bottomed barge, which was used for carrying men and goods down rivers. The map following the pictures indicates the main route used by westerners to transport their products to the East.

TRAVELING BY LAND

TRAVELING BY WATER

What difficulties would the western settler encounter as he tried to use these forms of transport?

WESTERNERS' PRINCIPAL ROUTE FOR MOVING PRODUCTS EAST

After 1814, another route that went around the southern end of the Appalachian Mountains was used.

394

1. How do the pictures of land and water transportation help to explain the use of this route?

2. Does the use of this route confirm your ideas about problems settlers might have faced? Does it suggest additional problems? Explain.

3. What further problems would accompany the use of this type of transportation if the population continued to grow?

12. Canals and Railroads

The following maps show canals and railroads built between 1800 and 1860. The canal map indicates some of the roads that provided links between canals.

POINTS TO CONSIDER

Whether these forms of transportation helped solve some of the problems of the western settler.

PRINCIPAL CANALS IN 1840

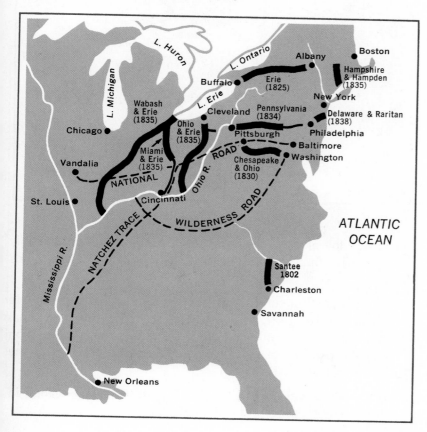

RAILROADS IN 1840 AND 1860

KEY

■■■■■ RAILROADS IN 1840

──── RAILROADS IN 1860

Most canals were built by 1840, whereas railroads developed extensively between 1840 and 1860.

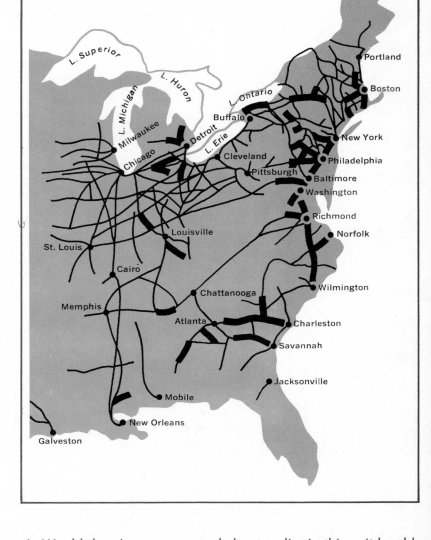

1. Would the pioneers you read about earlier in this unit be able to provide these facilities to solve their problems? Who would? Why?

2. The marginal picture shows workers building part of the Erie Canal near Lockport, New York. The total cost of the Erie Canal was around $8 million. What effect does this information and the picture have on the conclusion you reached in the previous question?

3. How would you explain the fact that there are few canals in the southern part of the United States?

13. The Story of the Six-Shooter

Definition or description of a weapon that is known and recognized the world over is hardly necessary. Briefly, the revolver is a pistol with a rotating cylinder containing ordinarily five or six chambers, each of which discharges through a single barrel. It is six pistols encompassed in one, commonly known to its familiars as a "gun," "six-gun," "shooting iron," "six-shooter," or "Colt." The Colt was the original revolver, so far as American history is concerned, and it furnished the principle upon which other models were constructed. This is the story of how the revolver originated . . .

The arms originally carried by the Texas Ranger were those of the American pioneers east of the Mississippi. The American long rifle has been designated as one of the principal factors in the conquest of America. This weapon, however, was designed for use on the ground, not on horseback. It developed in the woods for service in the forests and glades when the user had both feet planted firmly on solid earth. The "hair trigger," the "double sights," the "fine bead," are terms significant of a weapon nicely adjusted and to be carefully aimed. Moreover, in the decade 1830–1840 the cap-and-ball rifle was still in use, the loading of which was a meticulous and time-consuming task. The powder had to be measured and poured, the ball had to be rammed down the barrel with a long rod, the tube must be "primed," and the cap or flint had to be adjusted. All this took about a minute, and in a fight much can happen in a minute. That the rifle was no horseman's weapon needs no demonstration.

The sword and lance, the horseman's traditional weapons, were outworn relics of the pre-gunpowder era. The Mexicans used the lance, as did the Plains Indians, but the Texans never used either lance or sword. The sword was ineffective against the Mexican, who was an artist with a knife and a rope; it was useless against the Comanche, who refused to engage in close combat. Once when there was talk of equipping the Texas Rangers with swords, an old Texan remarked, "They would doubtless be of great service to the Rangers, especially in a snake country."

The American pioneer did take to Texas with him the pistol—the old single-shot dueling piece, or the smaller derringer-like weapon, or the large horse pistol. The horse pistol could be used on horseback, but a horseman could hardly carry more than two of them. At best it was possible for the early Texan to carry on horseback three shots, one in his rifle and one in each of the two pistols in his belt. The first was practically useless to a mounted

Walter Prescott Webb, **The Great Plains** (Waltham, Mass.: Blaisdell Publishing Company, a Division of Ginn and Company, 1931), pp. 167-169. Reprinted by permission of the publisher.

A "meticulous" task requires precision and careful attention.

A "derringer" is a short-barreled pistol.

397

man, and the two pistols were bulky and unwieldy and had the same disadvantages of loading as the rifle had.

Let us turn next to an examination of Comanche weapons. For defense the warrior carried a rawhide shield hung on his left arm; for offense a fourteen-foot spear, a plain or sinew-backed bow, and a quiver of arrows tipped with flint or steel. These he used effectively on both game and enemy.

Imagine now a battle between the Texans and the Comanches, and observe the relative advantages in weapons possessed by each. In most respects the Indian had the best of it. In the first place, the Texan carried at most three shots; the Comanche carried twoscore [forty] or more arrows. It took the Texan a minute to reload his weapon; the Indian could in that time ride three hundred yards and discharge twenty arrows. The Texan had to dismount in order to use his rifle effectively at all, and it was his most reliable weapon; the Indian remained mounted throughout the combat. Apparently the one advantage possessed by the white man was a weapon of longer range and more deadly accuracy than the Indian's bow, but the agility of the Indian and the rapidity of his movements did much to offset this advantage.

Imagine now the three probable issues [tactics] of an Indian battle. The most common form of encounter was that in which the white men stood and received the attack. Such engagements are often represented in pictures by a body of plumed warriors riding in a circle, the center of which is a group of white men and women huddled together in the open plain and protected by whatever barricades they could hastily improvise. This picture had its justification in practice upon the trans-Plains trails leading from Missouri to Oregon, California, and Santa Fe. The purpose of the Indian tactics was to exhaust the ammunition of the white men by "drawing their fire," and then rush upon them before they could reload. The white men saved themselves by conserving their ammunition, firing slowly and in rotation by the platoon system, so that some of the weapons were always primed. It was a situation which called for great economy and precaution. It gave rise to such admonitions as "Hold your fire," "Take steady aim," "Make every shot tell." The marvelous marksmanship of that early day was due to the fact that the first shot was frequently the only shot.

But let us assume as a second possible procedure in battle that the Indians retreat and the Rangers pursue. In this event the white men would discharge their rifles first, then mount, and go in pursuit. At most they had only two shots each, and these were soon spent. In the meantime the Indian could discharge his arrow from his running horse, and as soon as his adversary's guns were empty could turn upon him with arrows and spear.

As a third possibility the Texans would retreat and the Indians pursue. Here was a situation which the Rangers and all who fought Plains Indians found most dangerous, and one in which escape depended on the speed of one's horse. All the Comanche's weapons were peculiarly adapted to the situation, and he liked nothing better than to have his enemy running before him on the open plain. Arrow would follow arrow from his snapping bow, and if better mounted than his enemy he could push up and spear him from a distance of ten or twelve feet. Timber to hide in or a fast horse to ride offered the Ranger his only safety. Lacking these, he lost his scalp to the Indian, who left the mangled body to the birds and wolves.

Undoubtedly the Texans needed a new weapon, something with a reserve power and capable of "continuous" action—a weapon more rapid than the Indian's arrows, of longer reach than his spear, and, above all, one adapted to use on horseback. The man who supplied the weapon that fulfilled all these necessities was a Connecticut Yankee by the name of Samuel Colt. . . . [Another scholar states:]

Colt found the pistol a single-shooter and left it a six-shooter. Thus judged the Texan rangers, when they coined this new word "six-shooter," to describe a thing no less new among men, an engine which rendered them victorious against fearful odds, and over both Mexicans and Indians.

In 1830 Samuel Colt, at the age of sixteen, shipped as a sailor from Boston to Calcutta. On this voyage he whittled from wood his first model of a revolving pistol; in that same year trouble was brewing between the Texans and the Mexicans—two events apparently without relation. In 1835 Colt took out his first patent in England, and in that year the Texan revolt began; in 1836 he took out a patent in America, and in the same year the Texans established their independence and the Republic of Texas. By 1838 a company had been organized at Paterson, New Jersey, for the manufacture of Colt's patent firearms. It seems that this company took over Colt's patents and models with a view to manufacturing the arms in commercial quantities, and Colt was to receive a royalty, improve the invention, and further the introduction of the new arms, particularly by interesting the United States government in his weapon. Among the patents which he gave up was a model of a six-chambered revolver of .34 caliber, which the company began to manufacture about 1838. It was described as "the first revolver which came at all into general use" and as the one "which won its fame and fortune."

There are several things about this revolver to interest us. It could not be sold to the government or in quantity to private citizens of the United States; but for some reason orders began to come in from the far-off Republic of Texas, and . . . it was used to some extent on the Santa Fe Trail. Just how the revolvers found their way to Texas is unknown; but the fact remains that the six-shooter or the five-shooter did find its way into the hands of the Texas Rangers—those hard-pressed men who were most in need of it.

The close relationship of Texas and the Rangers to the evolution of this distinctive American weapon is exemplified in the very names given to these early revolvers. The first model, "which won its fame and fortune," was called the "Texas." A second model, with certain improvements over the old, was brought out probably about 1842. It was a Texas Ranger who suggested the improvements, and it was for him that the improved weapon was named. This man, Samuel H. Walker, captain of the Rangers, had been sent to New York to purchase a supply of the latest firearms, and while there he arranged to meet the inventor of the Texas. [This meeting is discussed in the records of the Colt Company.]

The result of several days of very friendly conference between Walker and Colt was a new type of pistol—the first military revolver. Walker suggested that, while the Texas was a wonderful weapon, it was too light; that, as it was in three pieces while being loaded, a mounted man was very liable to lose a part; that a trigger guard was necessary; that the strength and weight of the pistol should be such as to render it serviceable as a club when empty. The pistol which Colt produced to meet these requirements he named the "Walker Pistol."

The Texas, the Walker, and the term "six-shooter," coined by the Rangers—all these names bear evidence that the "Lone Star Republic" had much to do with the development of the new weapon.

The exact date at which the revolvers were brought to Texas remains uncertain. The early Texas Rangers, better fighters than scribes, have left but scant record of their border doings. Still there is something—a copy of a signed statement by two Rangers that the revolvers appeared in Texas in 1839. It was in the following year that John C. Hays and his men were stationed in San Antonio, and it was Hays and his men, Walker among them, who proved conclusively the value of the revolvers. Thus we are able to fix the date of introduction before 1840.

400

The battle of the Pedernales has good claims to being the first battle in which the six-shooter was used on mounted Indians. Hays and fourteen of his men had gone out from San Antonio to look for Indians, and on their return discovered that they were being followed by about seventy Comanches. A desperate battle ensued in which the Rangers "shot them down with their pistols." Some of the Rangers and more than thirty Indians were killed. Here are two accounts of the results of this engagement. Major Caperton says of the battle:

That was considered the best-contested fight that ever took place in Texas, and it showed that they [the Rangers] could whip the Indians on horseback, . . . the pistols gave them the advantage. That was the first time pistols were used in a fight with Indians.

Mrs. Mary A. Maverick, a remarkable Texas woman who as a girl lived in San Antonio and kept a charming and illuminating diary, says that Hays came to her home twelve days after the battle and gave her the account, which she wrote down at the time. The date was June 8, 1844. She mentions the tremendous odds against the Rangers, and concludes with this statement: "Hays modestly gave the credit of the victory to the wonderful marksmanship of every Ranger, and the total surprise of the Indians, caused by the new six-shooters, which they had never seen or heard of before."

Soon after this battle Hays found further opportunity to test the value of the revolver in a fight in the Nueces cañon [canyon]. Here the Indians in superior numbers made the attack, sweeping round the Rangers on both sides and discharging their arrows as they passed. Hays and his men first emptied their rifles and then sprang into their saddles for pursuit. "Never," said an old Indian fighter, "was a band of Indians more surprised than at this charge. They expected the Rangers to remain on the defensive, and to finally wear them out and exhaust their ammunition. . . . In vain the Comanches tried to turn their horses and make a stand, but such was the wild confusion of running horses, popping pistols, and yelling Rangers that they abandoned the idea of a rally and sought safety in flight." In the pursuit, which covered three miles, the Rangers literally carried out their leader's orders to "powder-burn" them, causing the Indians to drop bows, shields, and lances all along the route. Years later a Comanche chief who was in this fight said that he never wanted to fight Jack Hays and his Rangers again, that they had a shot for every finger on the hand, and that he lost half his warriors, who died for a hundred miles along the trail toward Devil's River.

In 1850 Major George T. Howard of the old Texas army and Captain I. S. Sutton of the Rangers wrote the following testimonial

401

to the effectiveness of the revolvers: "They are the only weapon which enabled the experienced frontiersmen to defeat the *mounted* Indian in his own peculiar mode of warfare. . . . We state, and with entire assurance of the fact, that your six-shooter is the arm which has rendered the name of Texas Ranger a check and terror to the bands of our frontier Indians."

1. How did the six-shooter solve a major frontier problem?

2. Why were the guns carried by earlier pioneers inadequate?

14. Inventions, 1800–1862

The six-shooter was only one of many important inventions that emerged in the first part of the nineteenth century. The following chart lists some of the others.

DATE	INVENTION	INVENTOR	INFORMATION ABOUT INVENTOR
1807	STEAMBOAT	ROBERT FULTON	PAINTER, ENGINEER, AND INVENTOR FROM PHILADELPHIA. WITH THE AID OF A FORMER UNITED STATES MINISTER TO FRANCE, HE DESIGNED THE *CLERMONT*, THE FIRST STEAMBOAT.
1812	MOWING MACHINE	PETER GAILLIARD	FROM LANCASTER, PENNSYLVANIA.
1816	PERCUSSION CAPS FOR EXPLOSIVES	JOSHUA SHAW	SEA CAPTAIN AND INVENTOR.
1819	CAST IRON PLOW	JETHROW WOOD	FROM CAYUGA COUNTY, NEW YORK.
1830	STEAM LOCOMOTIVE	PETER COOPER	FROM NEW YORK.
1830	T RAIL (A metal rail attached to a wooden tie. It was longer lasting and easier to produce than earlier rails.)	ROBERT L. STEVENS	MECHANICAL ENGINEER, NAVAL ARCHITECT, AND INVENTOR FROM NEW JERSEY.
1832	REAPER	CYRUS McCORMICK	BORN IN VIRGINIA, HE CREATED A NATION-WIDE BUSINESS MANUFACTURING HIS INVENTION.
1832	TELEGRAPH	SAMUEL MORSE	AN ARTIST AND INVENTOR, HE LIVED IN NEW YORK AND EUROPE. HE ALSO DEVELOPED THE MORSE CODE, A SYSTEM OF SYMBOLS FOR TRANSMITTING MESSAGES.
1837	STEEL PLOW	JOHN DEERE	ILLINOIS BLACKSMITH.
1860	REPEATING RIFLE	OLIVER WINCHESTER	MANUFACTURER AND INVENTOR FROM NEW ENGLAND.
1862	REVOLVING MACHINE GUN	RICHARD GATLING	BORN IN NORTH CAROLINA, HE ALSO INVENTED VARIOUS AGRICULTURAL IMPLEMENTS.

1. How would each of these inventions help solve the problems of pioneers? Could some of the settlers' problems be solved *only* with such inventions? For example, what difficulty would a settler face when he tried to set up a farm on the kind of soil found between the Mississippi River and the Rocky Mountains? How could he meet this difficulty?

2. What role did the pioneer play in creating the six-shooter and the inventions shown on this chart?

3. How might you explain the following statement: "The growth of industry in the first half of the nineteenth century made an important contribution to the conquest of the West."

INDIVIDUALISM AND THE FRONTIER

1. What is an individual? What does it mean when you call someone individualistic? What examples can you cite of individualism?

2. What is the role of an individual in society today? Are there limits to what an individual can accomplish today? What effect does this have on individuals?

3. Would you describe the frontiersmen you read about as individualistic? How do you explain this? What effect did this trait have on the frontiersman as he faced the problems you observed?

4. What did the frontiersman do when he faced problems beyond his own limitations? What did this situation do to his individualism?

THROUGH AMERICAN EYES

15. Benjamin Franklin Writes About America, 1784

In the first part of this unit you observed what one group of Americans—the pioneers—were like. Now you will continue your study of the social aspects of American life by reading observations made by Americans and by foreign visitors.

Benjamin Franklin was one of the most outstanding and widely known citizens of eighteenth-century America. During his lifetime (1706–1790) he was a printer, inventor, statesman, diplomat, and scientist. He was also a prolific, or productive, writer. (See pages 75–78 and 121–123 for some of his other writings.) In 1784,

II. The American People: 1800-1860

Franklin recorded the ideas about Americans that appear in the following account. As you read the remarks of Franklin and other observers, think about the following points.

POINTS TO CONSIDER

What Americans feel is important and what they enjoy.

What similarities and differences there are between Americans in different areas of the country.

... Strangers are welcome because there is room enough for them all, and therefore the old inhabitants are not jealous of them; the laws protect them sufficiently, so that they have no need of the patronage [protection] of great men; and every one will enjoy securely the profits of his industry. But if he does not bring a fortune with him, he must work and be industrious to live. One or two years residence give him all the rights of a Citizen; but the Government does not at present, whatever it may have done in former times, hire people to become settlers, by paying their passages, giving land, negroes, utensils, stock, or any other kind of emolument [salary] whatsoever. In short, America is the land of labour, and by no means what the English call *Lubberland,* and the French *Pays de Cocagne,* where the streets are said to be paved with half-peck loaves, the houses tiled with pancakes, and where the fowls fly about ready roasted, crying, *Come eat me!* ...

Land being cheap in that country, from the vast forests still void of inhabitants, and not likely to be occupied in an age to come, insomuch that ... an hundred acres of fertile soil full of wood may be obtained near the frontiers in many places, for eight or ten guineas, hearty young labouring men, who understand the husbandry [farming] of corn and cattle, which is nearly the same in that country as in Europe, may easily establish themselves there. A little money saved of the good wages they receive there while they work for others, enables them to buy the land and begin their plantation, in which they are assisted by the good will of their neighbours, and some credit. Multitudes of poor people from England, Ireland, Scotland, and Germany, have by this means in a few years become wealthy farmers, who in their own countries, where all the lands are fully occupied, and the wages of labour low, could never have emerged from the mean [poor] condition wherein they were born.

1. According to Franklin, what benefits did people who came to America receive?

2. What quality or trait does Franklin think people must have in order to obtain these benefits?

American History Told by Contemporaries, edited by Albert Bushnell Hart (New York: The Macmillan Company, 1900), Vol. III, pp. 23-24.

A "lubber" is someone who leads a life of ease. The "pays de cocagne" is the land of plenty.

A "guinea" is a unit of English money. Today it is equivalent to $2.94 in American money, but in 1784 it was worth a great deal more.

16. Mrs. Smith Describes Thomas Jefferson, 1801

Mrs. Samuel Harrison Smith was a recognized leader of Washington society in the first forty years of the capital's history (1800–1840). Her husband served as an adviser to Thomas Jefferson on political affairs.

Mrs. Smith wrote several books and articles. However, her personal letters are her most valuable contribution to an understanding of the social history of Washington in the early 1800's. In the following account, she describes how Thomas Jefferson lived in the White House.

... The apartment in which he took most interest was his cabinet; this he had arranged according to his own taste and convenience. It was a spacious room. In the centre was a long table, with drawers on each side, in which were deposited not only articles appropriate to the place, but a set of carpenter's tools in one and small garden implements in another from the use of which he derived much amusement. Around the walls were maps, globes, charts, books, etc. In the window recesses were stands for the flowers and plants which it was his delight to attend and among his roses and geraniums was suspended the cage of his favorite mocking-bird, which he cherished with peculiar fondness, not only for its melodious powers, but for its uncommon intelligence and affectionate disposition, of which qualities he gave surprising instances. It was the constant companion of his solitary and studious hours. Whenever he was alone, he opened the cage and let the bird fly about the room. After flitting for a while from one object to another, it would alight on his table and regale him with its sweetest notes, or perch on his [shoulder] and take its food from his lips. Often when he retired to his chamber it would hop up the stairs after him and while he took his siesta, would sit on his couch and pour forth its melodious strains. How he loved this bird! How he loved his flowers! He could not live without something to love, and in the absence of his darling grandchildren, his bird and his flowers became objects of tender care. In a man of such dispositions, such tastes, who would recognize the rude, unpolished Democrat, which foreigners and political enemies described him to be.... If his dress was plain, unstudied and sometimes old-fashioned in its form, it was always of the finest materials; in his personal habits he was fastidiously [exceedingly] neat; and if in his manners he was simple, affable [friendly] and unceremonious, it was not because he was ignorant of, but because he despised the conventional and artificial usages of courts and fashionable life. His simplicity never degenerated

Mrs. Samuel Harrison Smith, **The First Forty Years of Washington Society,** edited by Gaillard Hunt (New York: Charles Scribner's Sons, 1906), pp. 384-388.

into vulgarity, nor his affability into familiarity. On the contrary, there was a natural and quiet dignity in his demeanour that often produced a degree of restraint in those who conversed with him, unfavorable to that free interchange of thoughts and feelings which constitute the greatest charm of social life. His residence in foreign courts never imparted that polish to his manners, which courts require, and though possessed of ease, they were deficient in grace. His external appearance had no pretensions to elegance, but it was neither coarse nor awkward, and it must be owned [admitted] his greatest personal attraction was a countenance beaming with benevolence and intelligence.

A "national man," here, means that Jefferson had the characteristics typical of an American.

He was called even by his friends, a national man, full of odd fancies in little things and it must be confessed that his local and domestic arrangements were full of contrivances [devices], or *conveniences* as he called them, peculiarly his own and never met with in other houses. Too often the practical was sacrificed to the fanciful, as was evident to the most superficial observer, in the location and structure of his house at Monticello. . . .

The same fanciful disposition characterized all his architectural plans and domestic arrangements; and even in the President's House, were introduced some of these favorite contrivances, many of them really useful and convenient. Among these, there was in his dining room an invention for introducing and removing the dinner without the opening and shutting of doors. A set of circular shelves were so contrived in the wall, that on touching a spring they turned into the room loaded with the dishes placed on them by the servants without [on the other side of] the wall, and by the same process the removed dishes were conveyed out of the room. When he had any persons dining with him, with whom he wished to enjoy a free and unrestricted flow of conversation, the number of persons at table never [exceeded] four, and by each individual was placed a *dumb-waiter,* containing everything necessary for the progress of the dinner from beginning to end, so as to make the attendance of servants entirely unnecessary, believing as he did, that much of the domestic and even public discord was produced by the mutilated and misconstructed repetition of free conversation at dinner tables, by these mute but not inattentive listeners. . . .

Both Jefferson and Mrs. Smith were from the highest levels of society. Judging from this account, what do you think people of that social class considered important?

17. Timothy Dwight Portrays New Englanders, 1821–1822

Timothy Dwight was a Congregational minister, author of several books and poems, and president of Yale from 1795 to 1817. He was widely known for his attempt to correct European misconceptions about life in America. It was for this purpose that he wrote *Travels in New England and New York,* from which the following selection is taken. The book was first published in 1821–1822.

The means of comfortable living, are in New-England so abundant, and so easily obtained, as to be within the reach of every man who has health, industry, common honesty, and common sense. Labour commands such a price, that every labourer of this character may earn from one hundred and twenty-five to two hundred and fifty dollars a year. Hence every one may within a moderate period purchase himself a farm of considerable extent in the recent settlements, and a small one in those which are older. Even those, who are somewhat below the common level in these attributes, may, and do, acquire small houses, and gardens, where they usually live comfortably.

The food of the inhabitants at large, even of the poor, is principally flesh, and fish; one or other of which is eaten by a greater part of the inhabitants twice and three times a day. A breakfast, in the large towns, is chiefly bread and butter; the bread in the cool season generally toasted. In the country almost universally this is accompanied with smoke-dried beef, cheese, or some species of fish or flesh broiled, or otherwise fitted to the taste of the family. So universal is this custom, that a breakfast without such an addition is considered as scarcely worth eating. At dinner, the vegetables, which I formerly mentioned, continually succeed each other in their varieties. Fruits also, which you will remember are here very numerous and various, as well as very rich and luscious, are brought upon the dinner-table, or are eaten in other parts of the day, throughout most of the year. Supper, in most parts of the country, is like the breakfast; except that it is made up partially of preserved fruits, different kinds of cake, pies, tarts, etc. The meats, used at breakfast and supper, are generally intended to be dainties.

Puddings, formed of rice, flour, maize [corn], and sometimes of buckwheat, very frequently constitute a part of the dinner.

Pork, except the hams, shoulders, and cheeks, is never converted into bacon. I do not know, that I ever saw a flitch [side] of bacon, cured in New-England, in my life. The sides of the hog are here

Timothy Dwight, **Travels in New England and New York** (New Haven, Connecticut: S. Converse, Printer, 1822), Vol. IV, pp. 352-355.

always pickled; and by the New-England people are esteemed much superiour to bacon. The pork of New-England is fatted upon maize; a sweeter and richer food for cattle of all kinds, than any other; is more skilfully cured; and is, therefore, better than that of any other country. It is also a favourite food with most of the inhabitants.

Tea and coffee constitute a part of the breakfast, and supper, of every class; and of almost every individual. The principal drink of the inhabitants is cider. Wine, which is here very cheap, is extensively used: so in the mild season is punch. Porter, also, is drunk by fashionable people; and in small quantities, ale. In the large towns, particularly in Boston, dinners are given without number; but much more unfrequently in the smaller ones. The favourite entertainment in them is the supper. For this there are two potent [strong] reasons. One is, every body is here employed in business through the day. The evening, being the only season of leisure, furnishes the best opportunity for that agreeable inter-course [communication], which is the primary object of all enter-tainments. The other is, the want of a sufficient number of servants to take the burden of superintending the preparation of dinners from the mistress of the family. I have been present at a very great multitude of entertainments of both kinds; and am com-pelled to say, that those of the evening are much the most pleasant, and rational. There is less excess, and more leisure; the mind is more cheerful; and the conversation almost of course more sprightly, interesting, and useful.

The hours of breakfast vary in the country from six to eight in the summer, and from seven to nine in the winter: those of dinner from twelve to two: those of supper from five to eight. In the large towns all these hours vary still more. The most fashionable people breakfast late; and dine from three to four. The food of such people is principally taken at a single meal. In the summer many of the labouring people make their principal meal at supper.

The proportion of animal food, eaten in this country, is, I think, excessive.

At entertainments, the dining-table is loaded with a much greater variety of dishes than good sense will justify. A fashion, which it is difficult to resist, prevails, in this respect, over every rational consideration.

The quantity of ardent spirits, consumed chiefly by the middle and lower classes of people, is scandalous to its character, although much less in its amount than that drunk by the same number of people in Great-Britain.

"Porter," a British drink, is similar to beer and ale.

The dress of the inhabitants is chiefly formed of the manufactures, and made up in the fashions, of Europe; particularly of Great-Britain.

The principal amusements of the inhabitants are visiting, dancing, music, conversation, walking, riding, sailing, shooting at a mark, draughts [checkers], chess, and unhappily in some of the larger towns, cards, and dramatic exhibitions [plays]. A considerable amusement is also furnished in many places by the examination, and exhibitions, of the superiour schools; and a more considerable one, by the public exhibitions of Colleges.

Our countrymen also fish, and hunt.

Journeys, taken for pleasure, are very numerous; and are a very favourite object.

Boys, and young men, play at foot-ball [rugby], cricket, quoits, and at many other sports of an athletic cast; and in the winter are peculiarly fond of skating. Riding in a sleigh, or sledge, is also a favourite diversion in New-England.

Rugby, cricket, and quoits are sports played in Great Britain.

People of wealth, and many in moderate circumstances, have their children taught music; particularly on the piano-forte; and many of the young men play on the German flute; violin, clarionet, etc. Serenading is not unfrequent.

Visiting, on the plan of sociality and friendship, is here among all classes of people, especially among those who are intelligent, and refined, a very agreeable, and very rational, source of enjoyment; and is usually free from the crowds and confusion, the ceremony and frivolity, which so often render scenes of this nature wearisome in great cities, and force the hours, devoted to them, to drag heavily: while

"The heart, distrusting, asks if this be joy."

Visits are here formed for the purposes of interchanging thought, affection, hospitality, and pleasure. With far less parade, less inconvenience to the family visited, and less trouble to the visitors, they are fraught with [possess] more cordiality, more good sense, more sprightliness, and incomparably more pleasure. The themes of conversation are of a superior class; the affections, and sentiments, are set upon a higher key; and the company part, not with eagerness, but with regret.

Reading also is a favourite employment with persons in almost all conditions of life. A considerable collection of books throughout a great part of this country, is furnished to the inhabitants by the social libraries . . . Private libraries are undoubtedly much

409

more limited than in Great-Britain. Many of them are, however, sufficient collections to extend much useful information, and to supply not a small fund of pleasure to their proprietors [owners] and others. By these means a great number of persons are enabled to read as extensively as their other avocations [activities] will permit; and all, who love reading, will find, or make, opportunities for pursuing it, which in the aggregate [all told], will constitute a considerable, as well as valuable and delightful, part of their lives. Accordingly this employment is pursued by men, and women, in almost every sphere of life.

1. According to Dwight, what were the interests of New Englanders, and what did they like to do?

2. Judging from these tastes, what would you say New Englanders were like? Which seem more important, the similarities or the differences between working people and wealthier classes?

3. Dwight was a New Englander. Does he reveal his personal tastes? How does he differ from some New Englanders he describes? How does he resemble them?

4. Did New England possess any of the qualities Franklin described? Did the tastes of New Englanders resemble those of Jefferson and Mrs. Smith?

18. Thomas Low Nichols on the Shakers

Thomas Low Nichols, a nineteenth-century author, desired to lead America to social and sanitary reforms. His book, *Forty Years of American Life, 1821–1861*, is a vivid picture of America. In it, he describes a Shaker community in Ohio. The Shakers were a religious group founded in New York around 1776. By 1826, Shaker communities had been established as far west as Indiana. In these communities, all property was held in common.

Thomas Low Nichols, **Forty Years of American Life, 1821-61** (London, England: Longmans Green & Co., Ltd., 1874), pp. 253-254.

In the Shaker village are no taverns or shops, but large, plainly-built dwelling-houses, barns, workshops, and an edifice for meetings and religious exercises. Simple utility is the only rule of architecture. There is not, in the whole village, one line of ornament. The brown paint is used only to protect the woodwork of the buildings. I did not see so much as an ornamental shrub or flower in the whole domain.

One house is set apart for the entertainment of strangers, who receive attention, food, and lodging as long as they choose to remain. The brethren and sisters who are appointed to fulfil the duties of hospitality, neither demand nor refuse payment.

The women, old and young, ugly and pretty, dress in the same neat but unfashionable attire. There are no bright colours; no ruffles or flounces or frills; no embroidery or laces; no ribbons or ornaments of any kind. The hair is combed smoothly back under a plain cap; a three-cornered kerchief of sober brown covers the bosom, and the narrow gored skirt had no room for crinoline.

The rooms and furniture are as plain and homely as the external architecture. There is not a moulding nor any coloured paper; not a picture nor print adorns the walls, nor is there a vase or statue. The only books are a few of their own religious treatises, collections of hymns, and works of education, science, and utility.

But there is everywhere the perfection of order and neatness. The floors shine like mirrors. Every visible thing is bright and clean. There is a place for everything, and everything is in its place. This order and neatness is carried out in the workshops, the farmyards, everywhere.

A community of two or three hundred industrious persons, all engaged in agriculture and useful manufactures, paying no rents, having no costly vices, producing for themselves all the necessaries of life, and selling their surplus produce, cannot fail to grow rich. I found this community living in comfort and abundance, surrounded with a great wealth of houses and lands, flocks and herds, and, as I was told, with large sums invested in the best securities. Men, women, and children all work, there are no idlers, and no time is lost. As the honesty of the Shakers is proverbial, they have the command of the best markets for their wooden wares, agricultural implements, brooms, garden seeds, preserved fruits and vegetables, and the surplus of their cloth, leather, etc. There is nothing, therefore, to hinder them from accumulating property to an immense extent; as can easily be done by any honest community in any country.

1. What do Shakers seem to consider important in life?

2. Have you seen any examples of similar ideas in the other readings in this section?

19. Mountain Men: Washington Irving, 1837

Washington Irving (1783–1859), one of America's foremost authors, published works on history, tales such as "Rip Van Winkle," and descriptions of his travels to the West. Among his many widely read accounts of life in the Rocky Mountain area is his book, *The Adventures of Captain Bonneville, U.S.A.* The following description of a rendezvous of mountain men is taken from this book. Mountain men were the men who trapped furs in the Rocky Mountains. From 1820 to 1845, the activities of these hardy, daring men were at their height.

Washington Irving, **The Adventures of Captain Bonneville, U.S.A.** (Philadelphia: J. B. Lippincott Company, 1870), pp. 180-181.

The Green River valley was at this time the scene of one of those general gatherings of traders, trappers, and Indians, that we have already mentioned. The three rival companies, which, for a year past had been endeavoring to out-trade, out-trap, and out-wit each other, were here encamped in close proximity, awaiting their annual supplies. About four miles from the rendezvous of Captain Bonneville was that of the American Fur Company, hard by [near] which, was that also of the Rocky Mountain Fur Company.

After the eager rivalry and almost hostility displayed by these companies in their late campaigns, it might be expected that, when thus brought in juxtaposition, they would hold themselves warily and sternly aloof from each other, and, should they happen to come in contact, brawl and bloodshed would ensue.

"In juxtaposition," here, means near each other.

No such thing! Never did rival lawyers, after a wrangle at the bar, meet with more social good humor at a circuit dinner. The hunting season over, all past tricks and manoeuvres are forgotten, all feuds and bickerings buried in oblivion. From the middle of June to the middle of September, all trapping is suspended; for the beavers are then shedding their furs, and their skins are of little value. This, then, is the trapper's holiday, when he is all for fun and frolic, and ready for a saturnalia [festival] among the mountains.

At the present season, too, all parties were in good humor. The year had been productive. Competition, by threatening to lessen their profits, had quickened their wits, roused their energies, and made them turn every favorable chance to the best advantage; so that, on assembling at their respective places of rendezvous, each company found itself in possession of a rich stock of peltries [pelts].

The leaders of the different companies, therefore, mingled on terms of perfect good fellowship; interchanging visits, and regaling [entertaining] each other in the best style their respective camps afforded. But the rich treat for the worthy captain was to see the "chivalry" of the various encampments, engaged in contests of skill at running, jumping, wrestling, shooting with the rifle, and running horses. And then their rough hunters' feastings and carousals. They drank together, they sang, they laughed, they whooped; they tried to outbrag and outlie each other in stories of their adventures and achievements. Here the free trappers were in all their glory. . . .

1. Are there any similarities between these Americans and the ones described by Franklin and Dwight?

2. Do these Americans have anything they seem to consider especially important? Why do you think they have such values?

20. Louisiana Planters: Timothy Flint, 1816–1826

You read a selection from Flint's writings on the Mississippi Valley earlier in this unit (see pages 386–387). In the following excerpt, he describes the planters of Louisiana.

The opulent [rich] planters of this state have many amiable traits of character. They are high-minded and hospitable in an eminent degree. I have sojourned [stayed] much among them and have never experienced a more frank, dignified, and easy hospitality. It is taken for granted that the guest is a gentleman and that he will not make an improper use of the great latitude [freedom] that is allowed him. If he [does] not pass over the limits which just observance prescribes, the more liberties he takes and the more ease he feels within those limits, the more satisfaction he will give to his host. You enter without ceremony, call for what you wish, and intimate [announce] your wishes to the servants. In short, you are made to feel yourself at home. This simple and noble hospitality seems to be a general trait among these planters, for I have not yet called at a single house where it has not been exercised toward me. Suppose the traveler to be a gentleman, to speak French, and to have letters to one respectable planter, it becomes an introduction to the settlement, and he will have no occasion [need] for a tavern.

It results in some way from their condition, from their ample income, or perhaps, as they would say, from the influence of slavery, that they are liberal in their feelings, as it respects expenditure, and are more reckless of [unconcerned about] the value of money than any people that I have seen. The ladies no doubt have their tea-table or rather their coffee-table scandal [gossip]. But I confess that I have seen less of that prying curiosity to look into the affairs of neighbors and have heard less scandal here than in other parts of the United States.

The luxury of the table is carried to a great extent among them. They are ample in their supply of wines, though claret is generally drunk. Every family is provided with claret, as we at the North

Timothy Flint, **Recollections of the Last Ten Years ... in the Valley of the Mississippi** (Boston: Cummings, Hilliard, and Company, 1826), pp. 447-449.

"Letters," here, are letters of introduction.

413

are with cider. I have scarcely seen an instance of intoxication among the respectable planters. In drinking, the guests universally raise their glasses and touch them together instead of [making a toast to someone's] health. In the morning, before you rise, a cup of strong coffee is offered you. After the dessert at dinner you are offered another. It is but very recently that the ladies have begun to drink tea. During the warm months, before you retire, it is the custom in many places for a black girl to take off your stockings and perform the ancient ceremonial of washing the feet.

They are easy and amiable in their intercourse with one another and excessively attached to balls and parties. They certainly live more in sensation than in reflection. The past and the future are seasons with which they seem little concerned. The present is their day, and "a short life and a merry one" their motto. Their feelings are easily excited. Tears flow. The excitement passes away, and another train of sensations is started. In the pulpit they expect an ardor [fiery passion], an appeal to the feelings, which the calmer and more reflecting manner of the North would hardly tolerate.

An intelligent and instructed planter's family is certainly a delightful family in which to make a short sojourn, and they have many of the lesser virtues, exercised in a way so peculiar and appropriate in their modes [ways] of existence as to impress you with all the freshness of novelty. Unhappily, as appertains to [is true of] all earthly things, there is a dark ground to the picture. The men are "sudden and quick in quarrel." The dirk [dagger] or the pistol is always at hand. Fatal duels frequently occur. They are profane and excessively addicted to gambling. This horrible vice, so intimately associated with so many others, prevails like an epidemic. Money got easily and without labor is easily lost. Betting and horse racing are amusements eagerly pursued, and oftentimes to the ruin of the parties. A Louisianian will forego any pleasure to witness and bet at a horse race. Even the ladies visit these amusements and bet with the gentlemen.

It is true that there are opulent French planters, reared in the simplicity of the early periods of Louisiana, who can neither read nor write. I have visited more than one such. But it is also true that the improving spirit of the age, the rapid communication by steamboats, which brings all the luxuries, comforts, and instructions of society immediately to their doors, is diffusing among the planters a thirst for information, an earnest desire that their children should have all the advantages of the improved modes of present instruction. They have, in many instances, fine collections

414

of books. A piano is seen in every good house. Their ear, taste, and voice and their excitability of character fit the ladies for excellence in music. In common with those in other parts of the Union, great and too much stress is laid upon accomplishments merely external, and there is not attached sufficient importance to that part of education which fits for rational conversation and usefulness. It is asserted here, even to a proverb, and so far as my observation extends, with great truth, that the Creole ladies are, after marriage, extremely domestic, quiet, affectionate, and exemplary wives and mothers.

"Creole," here, refers to the descendants of French settlers in Louisiana.

1. Are the values of Louisiana planters similar to the values of any other group you have read about? Are they different?

2. How does Flint express his own values in describing planters of the South?

3. Do you think that the differences between the way wealthy people lived and the way other groups lived would be greater in New England or in Louisiana? Why?

4. According to Franklin, what does America make possible? Would this be true for all groups in Louisiana? Explain.

21. Boston Society in the 1820's and 1830's: Edward Everett Hale

In the following selection, Edward Everett Hale describes his boyhood days in Boston. Hale was born in Boston in 1822. Graduated from Harvard College in 1839, he served as a Unitarian minister in Worcester, Massachusetts, and in Boston. He did not record his memories of Boston until 1893.

... [So] far as I remember the houses themselves and the life in them, everything was quite as elegant and finished as it is now. Furniture was stately, solid, and expensive. I use chairs, tables, and a sideboard in my house to-day, which are exactly as good now as they were then. Carpets, then of English make, covered the whole floor, and were of what we should now call perfect quality. In summer, by the way, in all houses of which I knew anything, these carpets were always taken up, and India mattings substituted in the "living-rooms." Observe that very few houses were closed in summer. Dress was certainly as elegant and costly as it is now; so were porcelain, glass, table linen, and all table furniture. In the earlier days of which I write, a decanter of wine would invariably have stood on a sideboard in every parlor, so that a glass of wine could readily be offered at any moment to any guest. All

Edward Everett Hale, **A New England Boyhood and Other Bits of Autobiography** (Boston: Little, Brown and Company, 1927), pp. 4-6, 132-133.

through my boyhood it would have been matter of remark if, when a visitor made an evening call, something to eat or drink was not produced at nine o'clock. It might be crackers and cheese, it might be mince pie, it might be oysters or cold chicken. But something would appear as certainly as there would be a fire on the hearth in winter. Every house, by the way, was warmed by open fires; and in every kitchen cooking was done by an open fire. I doubt if I ever saw a stove in my boyhood except in a school or an office. Anthracite coal was first tried in Boston in 1824. Gas appeared about the same time. I was taken, as a little boy, to see it burning in the shops in Washington Street, and to wonder at an elephant, a tortoise, and a cow, which spouted burning gas in one window. Gas was not introduced into dwelling-houses until Pemberton Square was built by the Lowells, Jacksons, and their friends, in the years 1835, 1836, and later. . . .

A handsome parlor then, differed from a handsome parlor now, mostly in the minor matters of decoration. The pictures on the walls were few, and were mostly portraits. For the rest, mirrors were large and handsome. You would see some copies from well-known paintings in European galleries, and any one who had an Allston would be glad to show it. But I mean that most walls were bare. In good houses, if modern, the walls of parlors would invariably be painted of one neutral tint; but in older houses there would be paper hangings, perhaps of landscape patterns. The furniture of a parlor would generally be twelve decorous heavy chairs, probably hair-seated, with their backs against the walls; a sofa which matched them, also with its back against the wall; and a heavy, perhaps marble-topped centre table. There might be a rocking-chair in the room also; but so far as I remember, other easy-chairs . . . were unknown. . . .

. . . Boston was still a wooden town, and the danger of fire was, as it is in all American cities, constantly present. There hung in our front entry two leather buckets; in each of them was certain apparatus which a person might need if he were in a burning house. Strange to say, there was a bed-key, that he might take down a bedstead if it were necessary. These were relics of a time when my father had been a member of one of the private fire companies. In those associations each man was bound to attend at any fire where the property of other members of the association was in danger; and there were traditions [stories] of father's having been present at the great Court Street fire, for instance. But these fire clubs either died out or became social institutions, as the Fire Club in Worcester exists to this day; and nothing was left but the bucket as a sort of memorial of a former existence.

Washington Allston was a well-known American artist of the early nineteenth century.

416

Before our day the volunteer fire department system of Boston had been created, and there were similar systems in all large cities. Of course we boys supposed that ours was the best in the world; each boy in Boston supposed that the engine nearest his house was the best engine in the world, and that, on occasion, it could throw water higher than any other engine. . . .

1. What do the Bostonians in Hale's account seem to enjoy?

2. What do they consider important?

3. Are their tastes closer to those of wealthy people in Washington or in Louisiana? Do the Bostonians resemble any of the ordinary citizens you have studied? Explain.

CONCLUDING EXERCISE

1. Why did Franklin think Americans would be able to enjoy equality in social and political matters? Did he predict accurately?

2. What tentative conclusions can you form about the characteristics of Americans from the accounts you have read?

3. How do these characteristics compare with those of the pioneers you studied earlier in the unit?

4. How can you explain these characteristics? Is there anything about America that may have shaped the American personality?

EVENTS THAT STIRRED THE NATION

22. A Whaling Expedition: Herman Melville

Another aspect of the study of social life and conditions is the excitement generated by certain events. During the first half of the nineteenth century, whaling, steamboats, and the Pony Express captured the imaginations of many Americans and dominated their conversations. The readings in this section deal with these events.

The first account is about whaling, which was at its height of activity from 1840 to 1860. New England was the center of the whaling industry. Whaling dominated the way of life of many seacoast towns in the Northeast. Hundreds of vessels put out to sea from ports such as New Bedford, Massachusetts, to search for whales. Herman Melville describes the excitement of searching for whales—an excitement told over and over in tales of the sea. The following selection is from his novel, *Moby Dick,* written in 1851.

417

POINTS TO CONSIDER

What qualities the participants in these events had.

What the events had in common.

What public excitement over these events shows about the interests and values of the American people.

Herman Melville, **Moby Dick, or The Whale,** edited by Willard Thorp (New York: Oxford University Press, 1947), pp. 209-211.

"Leeward" means the direction in which the wind is blowing.

To a landsman, no whale, nor any sign of a herring, would have been visible at that moment; nothing but a troubled bit of greenish white water, and thin scattered puffs of vapor hovering over it, and suffusingly blowing off to leeward, like the confused scud [foam] from white rolling billows. The air around suddenly vibrated and tingled, as it were, like the air over intensely heated plates of iron. Beneath this atmospheric waving and curling, and partially beneath a thin layer of water, also, the whales were swimming. Seen in advance of all the other indications, the puffs of vapor they spouted, seemed their forerunning couriers and detached flying outriders.

All four boats were now in keen pursuit of that one spot of troubled water and air. But it bade fair [promised] to outstrip them; it flew on and on, as a mass of interblending bubbles borne down a rapid stream from the hills.

"Pull, pull, my good boys," said Starbuck, in the lowest possible but intensest concentrated whisper to his men; while the sharp fixed glance from his eyes darted straight ahead of the bow, almost seemed as two visible needles in two unerring binnacle compasses. He did not say much to his crew, though, nor did his crew say anything to him. Only the silence of the boat was at intervals startlingly pierced by one of his peculiar whispers, now harsh with command, now soft with entreaty [begging].

A "binnacle compass" is a compass fixed in a stand (binnacle), usually in front of a ship's steering equipment.

How different the loud little King-Post. "Sing out and say something, my hearties. Roar and pull, my thunderbolts! Beach me, beach me on their black backs, boys; only do that for me, and I'll sign over to you my Martha's Vineyard plantation, boys; including wife and children, boys. Lay me on—lay me on! O Lord, Lord! but I shall go stark, staring mad! See! see that white water!" And so shouting, he pulled his hat from his head, and stamped up and down on it; then picking it up, flirted [flung] it far off upon the sea; and finally fell to rearing and plunging in the boat's stern [rear] like a crazed colt from the prairie. . . .

To "tantalize" is to tempt and threaten at the same time.

Meanwhile, all the boats tore on. The repeated specific allusions of Flask to "that whale," as he called the fictitious monster which he declared to be incessantly tantalizing his boat's bow [front] with its tail—these allusions of his were at times so vivid and life-like, that they would cause some one or two of his men to snatch a fearful look over his shoulder. But this was against all rule; for the oarsmen must put out their eyes, and ram a skewer through their necks; usage [custom] pronouncing that they must have no organs but ears, and no limbs but arms, in these critical moments.

It was a sight full of quick wonder and awe! The vast swells of the omnipotent [all-powerful] sea; the surging, hollow roar they made, as they rolled along the eight gunwales, like gigantic bowls in a boundless bowling-green; the brief suspended agony of the boat, as it would tip for an instant on the knife-like edge of the sharper waves, that almost seemed threatening to cut it in two; the sudden profound dip into the watery glens and hollows; the keen spurrings and goadings to gain the top of the opposite hill; the headlong, sled-like slide down its other side;—all these, with the cries of the headsmen and harpooners, and the shuddering gasps of the oarsmen, with the wondrous sight of the ivory Pequod bearing down upon her boats with outstretched sails, like a wild hen after her screaming brood;—all this was thrilling. Not the raw recruit, marching from the bosom of his wife into the fever heat of his first battle; not the dead man's ghost encountering the first unknown phantom in the other world;—neither of these can feel stranger and stronger emotions than that man does, who for the first time finds himself pulling into the charmed, churned circle of the hunted sperm whale.

The "Pequod" is the whaling ship from which the boats were launched.

23. Launching a Steamboat: J. H. B. Latrobe

Robert Fulton attracted widespread attention with the success of his Hudson River steamboat in 1807. He and his associates realized the advantages of the steamboat for use on the rivers of the western areas. Fulton and Robert R. Livingston, former minister to France and chancellor, or judge, of New York, made plans for the use of steamboats on the Mississippi River. Nicholas Roosevelt joined them to direct the building and launching of the *New Orleans*, the first steamboat to navigate a river of the interior. The following account by J. H. B. Latrobe, a nineteenth-century lawyer, historian, and author, describes the initial voyage of the *New Orleans* down the Ohio River to the Mississippi.

Prior to the introduction of steamboats on the Western waters, the means of transportation thereon consisted of keel boats, barges and flat boats. Keel boats and barges ascended, as well as descended, the stream. The flat boat was an unwieldy box, and was broken up, for the lumber it contained, on its arrival at the place of destination. The keel boat was long and slender, sharp

John Hazlehurst Boneval Latrobe, **The First Steamboat Voyage on the Western Waters** (Baltimore, Md.: The Maryland Historical Society, 1871), pp. 5-6, 12, 14, 20-21.

419

fore and aft, with a narrow gangway [walk] just within the gunwale, for the boatmen as they poled or warped up the stream when not aided by the eddies that made their oars available [useful]. When the keel boat was covered with a low house, lengthwise, between the gangways, it was dignified with the name of "barge." The only claim of the flat boat, or "broad horn," to rank as a vessel was due to the fact that it floated upon water and was used as a vehicle for transportation. Keel boats, barges, and flat boats had prodigious [big] steering oars, and oars of the same dimensions were hung on fixed pivots on the sides of the last named, by which the shapeless and cumbrous [clumsy] contrivance was, in some sort, managed. Ignorant of anything better, the people of the West were satisfied with these appliances of trade in 1810.

Whether steam could be employed on the Western rivers was a question, that its success between New York and Albany was not regarded as having entirely solved: and after the idea had been suggested of building a boat at Pittsburg, to ply [sail] between Natchez and New Orleans, it was considered necessary that investigations should be made, as to the currents of the rivers to be navigated, in regard to the new system. These investigations, Mr. Roosevelt undertook, with the understanding, that if his report were favorable, Chancellor Livingston, Mr. Fulton and himself, were to be equally interested in the undertaking. The Chancellor and Fulton were to supply the capital, and Roosevelt was to superintend the building of the boat and engine. . . .

. . . At length, however, all difficulties were overcome by steady perseverance, and the boat was launched—and called, from the place of her ultimate destination, the New Orleans. It cost in the neighborhood of $38,000. . . .

The people of Pittsburg turned out in mass and lined the banks of the Monongahela to witness the departure of the Steamboat; and shout after shout rent the air, and handkerchiefs were waived, and hats thrown up by way of "God speed" to the voyagers, as the anchor was raised, and heading up stream for a short distance, a wide circuit brought the New Orleans on her proper course, and, steam and current aiding, she disappeared behind the first headlands on the right bank of the Ohio.

. . . Morning after morning, the rise in the [Ohio] river during the night was reported; and finally, in the last week in November, it was ascertained that the depth of water in the shallowest portion of the Falls, exceeded by five inches the draught of the boat. It was a narrow margin. . . . To get into the Indiana channel, which was the best, a wide circuit had to be made bringing her head down stream, completing which, the New Orleans began the descent. Steerage way depended upon her speed exceeding that of the current. The faster she could be made to go, the easier would it be to guide her. All the steam the boiler would bear was put upon her. The safety valve shrieked: The wheels revolved faster than they had ever done before; and the vessel, speaking figuratively, fairly flew away from the crowds collected to witness her departure from Louisville [Kentucky]. Instinctively, each one on board now grasped the nearest object, and with bated breath awaited the result. Black ledges of rock appeared only to disappear as the New Orleans flashed by them. The waters whirled and eddied, and threw their spray upon the deck, as a more rapid descent caused the vessel to pitch forward to what at times seemed inevitable destruction. Not a word was spoken. The pilots directed the men at the helm by motions of their hands. Even the great Newfoundland dog seemed affected by the apprehension of danger, and came and crouched at Mrs. Roosevelt's feet. The tension on the nervous system was too great to be long sustained. Fortunately, the passage was soon made; and, with feelings of profound gratitude to the Almighty, at the successful issue [outcome] of the adventure, on the part of both Mr. Roosevelt and his wife, the New Orleans rounded to in safety below the Falls. . . .

To "round to," here, means to bring a boat around so that its bow, or front, is pointing upstream.

1. After reading this account of the early steamboat experiment, what qualities would you say Americans possess?

2. Does anything similar happen today in America?

24. Glimpsing the Pony Express: Mark Twain

The Pony Express, the most famous mail route in American history, was planned by William M. Gwin, a senator from California. In 1854, Gwin tried to persuade Congress to provide for a line of fast mail riders across the plains to California. Congress rejected the plan, but the firm of Russell, Majors, and Waddell decided to undertake the venture. The first runs were made between St. Joseph, Missouri, and Sacramento, California, in April 1860. At the height of its fame, the Pony Express used 420 horses, 400 station men and helpers, and 125 riders. Each rider covered from 75 to 125 miles. He changed horses at relay stations 10 or 15 miles apart.

Mark Twain, who traveled to the West in 1861, studied the Pony Express with keen interest. The following account is from Twain's famous book, *Roughing It.*

421

Mark Twain, **Roughing It** (Hartford, Connecticut: American Publishing Co., 1872), pp. 70-72.

A "roundabout" is a short, close-fitting jacket.

In a little while all interest was taken up in stretching our necks and watching for the "pony-rider"—the fleet messenger who sped across the continent from St. Joe to Sacramento, carrying letters nineteen hundred miles in eight days! Think of that for perishable horse and human flesh and blood to do! The pony-rider was usually a little bit of a man, brimful of spirit and endurance. No matter what time of the day or night his watch came on, and no matter whether it was winter or summer, raining, snowing, hailing, or sleeting, or whether his "beat" was a level straight road or a crazy trail over mountain crags and precipices, or whether it led through peaceful regions or regions that swarmed with hostile Indians, he must be always ready to leap into the saddle and be off like the wind! There was no idling-time for a pony-rider on duty. He rode fifty miles without stopping, by daylight, moonlight, starlight, or through the blackness of darkness—just as it happened. He rode a splendid horse that was born for a racer and fed and lodged like a gentleman; kept him at his utmost speed for ten miles, and then, as he came crashing up to the station where stood two men holding fast a fresh, impatient steed, the transfer of rider and mail-bag was made in the twinkling of an eye, and away flew the eager pair and were out of sight before the spectator could get hardly the ghost of a look. Both rider and horse went "flying light." The rider's dress was thin, and fitted close; he wore a "roundabout," and a skull-cap, and tucked his pantaloons into his boot-tops like a race-rider. He carried no arms—he carried nothing that was not absolutely necessary, for even the postage on his literary freight was worth *five dollars a letter*. He got but little frivolous correspondence to carry—his bag had business letters in it, mostly. His horse was stripped of all unnecessary weight, too. He wore a little wafer of a racing-saddle, and no visible blanket. He wore light shoes, or none at all. The little flat mail-pockets strapped under the rider's thighs would each hold about the bulk of a child's primer. They held many and many an important business chapter and newspaper letter, but these were written on paper as airy and thin as gold-leaf, nearly, and thus bulk and weight were economized. The stage-coach traveled about a hundred to a hundred and twenty-five miles a day (twenty-four hours), the pony-rider about two hundred and fifty. There were about eighty pony-riders in the saddle all the time, night and day, stretching in a long, scattering procession from Missouri to California, forty flying eastward, and forty toward the west, and among them making four hundred gallant horses earn a stirring livelihood and see a deal of scenery every single day in the year.

We had had a consuming desire, from the beginning, to see a pony-rider, but somehow or other all that passed us and all that met us managed to streak by in the night, and so we heard only a whiz and a hail [call], and the swift phantom of the desert was gone before we could get our heads out of the windows. But now we were expecting one [any] moment, and would see him in broad daylight. Presently the driver exclaims: "Here he comes!"

Every neck is stretched further, and every eye strained wider. Away across the endless dead level of the prairie a black speck appears against the sky, and it is plain that it moves. Well, I should think so! In a second or two it becomes a horse and rider, rising and falling, rising and falling—sweeping toward us nearer and nearer—growing more and more distinct, more and more sharply defined—nearer and still nearer, and the flutter of the hoofs comes faintly to the ear—another instant a whoop and a hurrah from our upper deck, a wave of the rider's hand, but no reply, and man and horse burst past our excited faces, and go winging away like a belated fragment of a storm!

So sudden is it all, and so like a flash of unreal fancy, that but for the flake of white foam left quivering and perishing on a mail-sack after the vision had flashed by and disappeared, we might have doubted whether we had seen any actual horse and man at all, maybe. . . .

1. What does the creation of the Pony Express tell you about the traits of the American people?

2. What kind of details does Mark Twain notice about the Pony Express rider?

3. Why do you think Twain was so interested in such details? Do Americans today like to hear about such details? Why?

4. Aside from these details, how does Twain describe the Pony Express rider? Why does Twain react this way?

5. What was there about a mail route that could excite the imagination of Americans?

WHAT EVENTS SHOW ABOUT PEOPLE

1. What do the three events described here have in common? For example, what kind of activities are they? How could you characterize their purposes?

2. How do Herman Melville and Mark Twain, in particular, describe these events? Why do activities like hunting whales and carrying mail inspire them to react this way?

3. What does American interest in this kind of activity show about Americans? Have you noticed similar traits elsewhere in this unit?

4. Melville and Twain provide good examples of the *way* Americans reacted to these events. What does this show about American characteristics?

5. What characteristics did people need to initiate such activities or to participate in them? Have you noticed traits like these elsewhere in the unit?

6. From your study of these events, do you think that the American people have been influenced by the kind of land they live in? Explain.

7. Do you think the American people today react in the same way to the same kind of events you read about here? Give examples to back up your answer.

THROUGH THE EYES OF OTHERS

25. America Is Different: St. John Crèvecoeur

The following selections are comments of foreign visitors to America. The first one is by J. Hector St. John Crèvecoeur, a Frenchman who migrated to America prior to the American Revolution. In 1782, Crèvecoeur sought an answer to the question, "What is an American?"

POINTS TO CONSIDER

Whether these foreign observers notice any of the same traits.

Whether foreign and American observers agree about what Americans are like.

J. Hector St. John Crèvecour, **Letters from an American Farmer** (New York: Fox, Duffield & Company, 1904), pp. 49-55.

"Ecclesiastical dominion" refers to the important and influential role religion played in many European governments at this time.

[America] is not composed, as in Europe, of great lords who possess everything, and of a herd of people who have nothing. Here are no aristocratical families, no courts, no kings, no bishops, no ecclesiastical domination, no invisible power giving to a few a very visible one [power]; no great [industrial] manufacturers employing thousands, no great refinements of luxury. The rich and the poor are not so far removed from each other as they are in Europe. Some few towns excepted, we are all tillers of the earth, from Nova Scotia to West Florida. We are a people of cultivators, scattered over an immense territory, communicating with each other by means of good roads and navigable rivers, united by the silken bands of mild government, all respecting the laws, without dreading their power, because they are equitable [fair]. We are all animated with the spirit of an industry which is unfettered and unrestrained, because each person works for himself. If [a European] travels through our rural districts he views not the hostile castle, and the haughty mansion, contrasted with the clay-built hut and the miserable cabin, where cattle and men help to keep each other warm, and dwell in meanness [poverty], smoke, and indigence [unemployment]. A pleasing uniformity of decent competence appears throughout our habitation. Lawyer or merchant are the fairest titles our towns afford; that of a farmer is the only appellation [social title] of the rural inhabitants of our country. It must take some time ere he can reconcile himself to our dictionary, which is but short in words of dignity, and names of honor. There, on a Sunday, he sees a congregation of respectable farmers and their wives, all clad in neat homespun, well mounted or riding in their own humble wagons. There is not among them an esquire, saving the unlettered magistrate [judge]. There he sees a parson as simple as his flock, a farmer who does not riot on the labor of others. We have no princes, for whom we toil, starve, and bleed ... Here man is free as he ought to be; nor is this pleasing equality so transitory [short-lived] as many others are. Many ages will not see ... the unknown bounds of North America entirely peopled. Who can tell how far it extends? Who can tell the millions of men whom it will feed and contain? for no European foot has as yet traveled half the extent of this mighty continent!

The next wish of this traveler will be to know whence came all these people? They are a mixture of English, Scotch, Irish, French, Dutch, Germans, and Swedes. From this promiscuous [mixed] breed, that race now called Americans have risen. . . .

In this great American asylum [refuge], the poor of Europe have by some means met together, and in consequence of various causes; to what purpose should they ask one another what countrymen they are? Alas, two thirds of them had no country. . . . [Urged] by a variety of motives, here they came. Every thing has tended to regenerate [restore] them; new laws, a new mode of living, a new social system; here they are become men: in Europe they were as so many useless plants, wanting vegetative mould [fertile soil], and refreshing showers; they withered, and were mowed down by want, hunger, and war; but now by the power of transplantation, like all other plants they have taken root and flourished! Formerly they were not numbered in any civil lists of their country, except in those of the poor; here they rank as citizens. . . .

"Competence," here, is the food, shelter, etc., necessary to live properly.

"Esquire" is an English term of respect formerly used to distinguish property owners from unpropertied tradesmen and laborers.

A farmer who "riots" on others' labor enjoys life while others work his land for him, either as renters or as hired laborers.

"What countrymen they are" means what country they or their forefathers came from.

425

What attachment can a poor European emigrant have for a country where he had nothing? The knowledge of the language, the love of a few kindred as poor as himself, were the only cords that tied him: his country is now that which gives him land, bread, protection, and consequence [importance] . . . What then is the American, this new man? He is [neither a] European nor the descendant of [a] European, hence that strange mixture of blood . . . which you will find in no other country. He becomes an American by being received in the broad lap of our great *Alma Mater* [sustaining mother]. Here individuals of all nations are melted into a new race of men, whose labors and posterity [future generations] will one day cause great changes in the world. Americans are the western pilgrims, who are carrying along with them that great mass of arts, sciences, vigor, and industry which began long since in the east [Europe]; they will finish the great circle. The Americans were once scattered all over Europe; here they are incorporated into one of the finest systems of population which has ever appeared, and which will hereafter become distinct by the power of the different climates they inhabit. The American ought therefore to love this country much better than that [in which] either he or his forefathers were born. Here the rewards of his industry follow with equal steps the progress of his labor . . .

1. What, for Crèvecoeur, is America's important quality?

2. How do his observations compare with Franklin's ideas on America? What does this do to any conclusions you drew from reading Franklin's account?

3. What does Crèvecoeur say an American is? What is the basis for his conclusion?

26. What White Men Are Like: The Delaware Indians, 1817

The first Americans were the Indians. Prior to 1492, Indian society had little contact with other societies. Then, a new way of life was established by the settlers who came to America. In 1817, this way of life was still foreign to most Indians. The following account presents the opinion of American society which many Indians held. It was written by the Reverend John Heckewelder, an English missionary who lived among the Delaware Indians.

. . . "We and our kindred tribes," say they, "lived in peace and harmony with each other, before the white people came into this country; our council house extended far to the north and

American History Told by Contemporaries, edited by Albert Bushnell Hart (New York: The Macmillan Company, 1900), Vol. III, pp. 469-470.

far to the south. In the middle of it we would meet from all parts to smoke the pipe of peace together. When the white men arrived in the south, we received them as friends; we did the same when they arrived in the east. It was we, it was our fore-fathers, who made them welcome, and let them sit down by our side. The land they settled on was ours. We knew not but the Great Spirit had sent them to us for some good purpose, and therefore we thought they must be a good people. We were mistaken; for no sooner had they obtained a footing on our lands, than they began to pull our council house down first at one end and then at the other, and at last meeting each other at the centre, where the council fire was yet burning bright, they put it out, and extinguished it with our own blood! with the blood of those who with us had received them! who had welcomed them in our land! Their blood ran in streams into our fire, and extinguished it so entirely, that not one spark was left us whereby to kindle a new fire; we were compelled to withdraw ourselves beyond the great swamp, and to fly to our good uncle the *Delamattenos* [an Indian tribe], who kindly gave us a tract of land to live on. How long we shall be permitted to remain in this asylum, the Great Spirit only knows. The whites will not rest contented until they shall have destroyed the last of us, and made us disappear entirely from the face of the earth."

... [One Delaware Indian chief said:] "I admit there are good white men, but they bear no proportion to the bad; the bad must be the strongest, for they rule. They do what they please. They enslave those who are not of their colour, although created by the same Great Spirit who created us. They would make slaves of us if they could, but as they cannot do it, they kill us! There is no faith to be placed in their words. They are not like the Indians, who are only enemies, while at war, and are friends in peace. They will say to an Indian, 'my friend! my brother!' They will take him by the hand, and at the same moment destroy him. And so you (addressing himself to the Christian Indians) will also be treated by them before long. Remember! that this day I have warned you to beware of such friends as these. I know the *long knives;* they are not to be trusted."

1. How does this view of Americans compare with those you read earlier in this unit? How do you account for this?

2. Can you think of any other inhabitants of the United States who might have described Americans in a similar way?

3. What does this kind of account do to your own conclusions about Americans? Why?

"Council house" means the territory held by the Indians.

427

27. Mrs. Trollope Comments on Cincinnati, 1828

Mrs. Frances Trollope, an English novelist, came to America in 1827 to earn a living in business. When she failed, she turned to writing about her travels. The following remarks about Cincinnati were written in 1828.

Frances Trollope, **Domestic Manners of the Americans** (London, England: Whittaker, Treacher & Co., 1832), pp. 50-51, 55-56, 66, 116-117.

We were soon settled in our new dwelling, which looked neat and comfortable enough, but we speedily found that it was devoid [empty] of nearly all the accommodations that Europeans conceive necessary to decency and comfort. No pump, no cistern, no drain of any kind, no dustman's cart, or any other visible means of getting rid of the rubbish, which vanishes with such celerity [rapidity] in London, that one has no time to think of its existence; but which accumulated so rapidly at Cincinnati, that I sent for my landlord to know in what manner refuse of all kinds was to be disposed of.

"Your help will just have to fix them all into the middle of the street, but you must mind, old woman, that it is the middle. I expect you don't know as we have got a law what forbids throwing such things at the sides of the streets; they must just all be cast right into the middle, and the pigs soon takes them off."

In truth, the pigs are constantly seen doing Herculean [heroic] service in this way through every quarter of the city; and though it is not very agreeable to live surrounded by herds of these unsavoury animals, it is well they are so numerous, and so active in their capacity of scavengers, for without them the streets would soon be choked up with all sorts of substances in every stage of decomposition. . . .

The "simple" manner of living in Western America was more distasteful to me from its levelling effects on the manners of the people, than from the personal privations [wants] that it rendered necessary; and yet, till I was without them, I was in no degree aware of the many pleasurable sensations enjoyed by the middle classes in Europe. . . .

. . . The gentlemen spit, talk of elections and the price of produce, and spit again. The ladies look at each other's dresses till they know every pin by heart; talk of parson somebody's last sermon on the day of judgment, on Dr. t'otherbody's new pills for dyspepsia [indigestion], till the "tea" is announced, when they all console themselves together for whatever they may have suffered in keeping awake, by taking more tea, coffee, hot cake and custard, hoe cake, johnny cake, waffle cake, and dodger cake, pickled peaches, and preserved cucumbers, ham, turkey, hung beef, apple sauce, and pickled oysters than ever were prepared in any other country of the known world. After this massive meal is over, they return to the drawingroom, and it always appeared to me that they remained together as long as they could bear it, and then they rise *en masse*, cloak, bonnet, shawl, and exit. . . .

"En masse" is French for "as a crowd."

The theatre was really not a bad one, though the very poor receipts rendered it impossible to keep it in high order; but an annoyance infinitely greater than decorations indifferently clean, was the style and manner of the audience. Men came into the lower tier [row] of boxes without their coats; and I have seen shirt-sleeves tucked up to the shoulder; the spitting was incessant, and the mixed smell of onions and whiskey was enough to make one feel even the Drakes' acting dearly bought by the obligation of enduring its accompaniments. The bearing and attitudes of the men are perfectly indescribable; the heels thrown higher than the head, the entire rear of the person presented to the audience, the whole length supported on the benches, are among the varieties that these exquisite posture-masters exhibit. The noises, too, were perpetual, and of the most unpleasant kind; the applause is expressed by cries and thumping with the feet, instead of clapping; and when a patriotic fit seized them, and "Yankee Doodle" was called for, every man seemed to think his reputation as a citizen depended on the noise he made.

"Receipts," here, means the money collected on tickets.

1. How do Mrs. Trollope's views of social life in America compare with those of Mrs. Smith or Edward Everett Hale (see pages 405–406 and 415–417)? How do they compare with the remarks of Timothy Dwight or Timothy Flint (see pages 407–410 and 413–415)?

2. How does this affect your conclusions about these matters? Explain.

28. Patrick Shirreff Describes Chicago, 1833

Patrick Shirreff, a Scotch farmer, was a pioneer in the development of better grains and cereals. After coming to America in 1833 to study agriculture, he recorded his observations of American life.

Chicago consists of about 150 wood houses, placed irregularly on both sides of the river, over which there is a bridge. This is already a place of considerable trade, supplying salt, tea, coffee, sugar, and clothing to a large tract of country to the south and

American History Told by Contemporaries, edited by Albert Bushnell Hart (New York: The Macmillan Company, 1900), Vol. III, pp. 475-478.

west; and when connected with the navigable point of the river Illinois, by a canal or railway, cannot fail of rising to importance. Almost every person I met regarded Chicago as the germ of an immense city, and speculators have already bought up, at high prices, all the building-ground in the neighborhood. Chicago will, in all probability, attain considerable size . . .

Besides the assemblage of Indians, there seemed to be a general fair at Chicago. Large wagons drawn by six or eight oxen, and heavily laden with merchandise, were arriving from, and departing to, distant parts of the country. There was also a kind of horse-market, and I had much conversation with a dealer from the State of New York, having serious intentions of purchasing a horse to carry me to the banks of the Mississippi, if one could have been got suitable for the journey. The dealers attempted to palm colts on me for aged horses, and seemed versed [skilled] in all the trickery which is practised by their profession in Britain.

A person showed me a model of a thrashing-machine and a churn, for which he was taking orders, and said he furnished the former at $30 . . . There were a number of French descendants, who are engaged in the fur-trade, met in Chicago, for the purpose of settling accounts with the Indians. They were dressed in broadcloths and boots, and boarded in the hotels. They are a swarthy [dark-complexioned] scowling race, evidently tinged with Indian blood, speaking the French and English languages fluently, and much addicted to swearing and whiskey. . . .

Undressing for the night had become a simple proceeding, and consisted in throwing off shoes, neck-cloth, coat, and vest, the two latter being invariably used to aid the pillow, and I had long dispensed with a nightcap. I was [awakened] from a sound sleep towards morning, by an angry voice uttering horrid imprecations [curses], accompanied by a demand for the bed I occupied. A lighted candle, which the individual held in his hand, showed him to be a French trader, accompanied by a friend, and as I looked on them for some time in silence, their audacity [boldness] and brutality of speech increased. At length I lifted my head from the pillow, leant on my elbow, and with a steady gaze, and the calmest tone of voice, said . . . "If you will ask the favour in a proper manner, I shall give you an answer." He was now either ashamed of himself, or felt his pride hurt, and both left the room without uttering a word. Next morning, the individuals who slept in the apartment with me, discovered [revealed] that the intruders had acted most improperly towards them, and the most noisy of the two entered familiarly into conversation with me during breakfast . . .

1. What characteristics does Shirreff attribute to the Americans he observes?

2. Have the characteristics seen here been observed by others?

3. Do you think Washington Irving would describe the same people differently? Why?

4. What conclusions can you draw about the characteristics Shirreff describes? Why?

29. A Steamboat Trip in the South: Charles Dickens, 1842

Charles Dickens, the famous English writer, toured parts of America in 1842. In the following account, he describes his experiences on a steamboat in the South.

We were to proceed in the first instance by steamboat; and as it is usual to sleep on board, in consequence of the starting-hour being four o'clock in the morning, we went down to where she lay, at that very uncomfortable time . . . when . . . a familiar bed . . . looks uncommonly pleasant. . . .

I go on board . . . open the door of the gentlemen's cabin; and walk in. Somehow or other—from its being so quiet, I suppose —I have taken it into my head that there is nobody there. To my horror and amazement it is full of sleepers in every stage, shape, attitude, and variety of slumber: in the berths, on the chairs, on the floors, on the tables, and particularly round the stove . . . I take another step forward, and slip on the shining face of a black steward, who lies rolled in a blanket on the floor. He jumps up, grins, half in pain and half in hospitality; whispers my own name in my ear; and groping among the sleepers, leads me to my berth. Standing beside it, I count these slumbering passengers, and get past forty. There is no use in going further, so I begin to undress. As the chairs are all occupied, and there is nothing else to put my clothes on, I deposit them upon the ground: not without soiling my hands, for it is in the same condition as the carpets in the Capitol, and from the same cause. Having but partially undressed, I clamber on my shelf, and hold the curtain open for a few minutes while I look round on all my fellow travellers again. That done, I let it fall on them, and on the world: turn round: and go to sleep.

I wake, of course, when we get under weigh, for there is a good deal of noise. The day is then just breaking. Everybody wakes at the same time. Some are self-possessed directly, and some are

Charles Dickens, **American Notes and Pictures from Italy** (London, England: Oxford University Press, 1957), pp. 128-130. Reprinted by permission of the publisher.

To "weigh" anchor means to set sail.

much perplexed [troubled] to make out where they are until they have rubbed their eyes, and leaning on one elbow, looked about them. Some yawn, some groan, nearly all spit, and a few get up. I am among the risers: for it is easy to feel, without going into the fresh air, that the atmosphere of the cabin is vile in the last degree. I huddle on my clothes, go down into the fore-cabin, get shaved by the barber, and wash myself. The washing and dressing apparatus for the passengers generally, consists of two jack-towels, three small wooden basins, a keg of water and a ladle to serve it out with, six square inches of looking-glass, two ditto ditto [square inches] of yellow soap, a comb and brush for the head, and nothing for the teeth. Everybody uses the comb and brush, except myself. Everybody stares to see me using my own . . .

A "jack-towel" is a coarse towel on a roller.

1. How does Dickens' account of American customs compare with Mrs. Trollope's description?
2. How do you think Dickens would have described the rendezvous of the mountain men (see pages 411–413)? Does this have any effect on the way you use these accounts to form your own conclusions about Americans?

30. Americans and Money: Friedrich von Raumer, 1844

Professor Friedrich von Raumer, a German historian, visited the United States twice. However, his account of America probably draws more heavily on what he read about America than on what he observed.

American History Told by Contemporaries, edited by Albert Bushnell Hart (New York: The Macmillan Company, 1900), Vol. III, p. 530.

. . . The American looks on money essentially as the means of further activity; he does not lock it up in coffers, or accumulate for the mere purpose of leaving it to a few lazy heirs; he is no miser that never makes use of his wealth, nor is he a spendthrift that squanders it away; but his endeavor is, to employ it in the truest advantage. Mistakes in this respect are only the exceptions, and do not form the rule, as with prodigals [wasters] and misers. The Americans are reasonably disinclined to all useless expenses, which in Europe so often impoverish both individuals and states . . .

1. According to Von Raumer, what is the American attitude toward wealth?
2. Is Von Raumer's view supported by any other accounts you have read? Explain.

31. Work and Progress in America: Alexis de Tocqueville, 1835

The French government sent Alexis de Tocqueville to America in 1831 to observe the American prison system. De Tocqueville, however, did not confine his attention to prisons. In 1835, he described his impressions of America in *Democracy in America*. This book is used widely in the study of American democracy.

Amongst a democratic people, where there is no hereditary wealth, every man works to earn a living, or has worked, or is born of parents who have worked. The notion of labour is therefore presented to the mind on every side as the necessary, natural, and honest condition of human existence. Not only is labour not dishonourable amongst such a people, but it is held in honour: the prejudice is not against it, but in its favour. In the United States a wealthy man thinks that he owes it to public opinion to devote his leisure to some kind of industrial or commercial pursuit, or to public business. He would think himself in bad repute if he employed his life solely in living. It is for the purpose of escaping this obligation to work, that so many rich Americans come to Europe, where they find some scattered remains of aristocratic society, amongst which idleness is still held in honour.

Alexis de Tocqueville, **Democracy in America**, translated by Henry Reeve (London, England: Saunders & Otley, 1840), Vol. III, pp. 312-313, 315, 322-324.

. . . In America no one is degraded because he works, for every one about him works also; nor is any one humiliated by the notion of receiving pay, for the President of the United States also works for pay. He is paid for commanding,—other men for obeying orders. In the United States professions are more or less laborious, more or less profitable; but they are never either high or low: every honest calling is honourable. . . .

The United States of America have only been emancipated [freed] for half a century from the state of colonial dependence in which they stood to Great Britain: the number of large fortunes there is small, and capital is still scarce. Yet no people in the world has made such rapid progress in trade and manufacturing as the Americans: they constitute at the present day the second maritime nation in the world; and although their manufactures have to struggle with almost insurmountable natural impediments, they are not prevented from making great and daily advances.

In the United States the greatest undertakings and speculations are executed without difficulty, because the whole population is engaged in productive industry, and because the poorest as well as the most opulent [wealthy] members of the commonwealth are ready to combine their efforts for these purposes. The consequence is, that a stranger is constantly amazed by the immense

433

public works executed by a nation which contains, so to speak, no rich men. The Americans arrived but as yesterday on the territory which they inhabit, and they have already changed the whole order of nature for their own advantage. They have joined the Hudson to the Mississippi, and made the Atlantic Ocean communicate with the Gulf of Mexico, across a continent of more than five hundred leagues in extent which separates the two seas. The longest railroads which have been constructed up to the present time are in America.

But what most astonishes me in the United States, is not so much the marvellous grandeur of some undertakings, as the innumerable multitude of small ones. Almost all the farmers of the United States combine some trade with agriculture; most of them make agriculture itself a trade. It seldom happens that an American farmer settles for good upon the land he occupies: especially in the districts of the far west he brings land into tillage in order to sell it again, and not to farm it: he builds a farmhouse on the speculation, that, as the state of the country will soon be changed by the increase of population, a good price will be gotten for it.

Every year a swarm of the inhabitants of the North arrive in the Southern states, and settle in the parts where the cotton-plant and the sugar-cane grow. These men cultivate the soil in order to make it produce in a few years enough to enrich them; and they already look forward to the time when they may return home to enjoy the competency [livelihood] thus acquired. Thus the Americans carry their business-like qualities into agriculture; and their trading passions are displayed in that, as in their other pursuits.

1. What does De Tocqueville say about the American attitude toward work? What other observers, foreign or American, mentioned this attitude? How do their observations and explanations compare with De Tocqueville's?

2. For what reason was De Tocqueville impressed with "public works" in America? Were Americans themselves ever impressed by the same things? Explain.

3. What traits did pioneers display in the way they solved their problems? How does this compare with De Tocqueville's observations about Americans?

4. According to Von Raumer, what was the American attitude toward wealth? How does De Tocqueville help to explain reasons for this?

5. What other traits does De Tocqueville point out? How do his comments compare with other accounts?

6. How do you think De Tocqueville would describe the scenes in Chicago portrayed by Shirreff? Explain.

EVALUATING AMERICANS, 1800–1860

1. What are the general characteristics Americans saw in themselves? What did the American think he valued and enjoyed? Did all the American observers you read agree on these points? What were the differences?

2. Did the foreign observations agree with any of the conclusions made by Americans? Explain. What were the differences? How do you explain this?

3. What did American reactions to the events you studied show about the American people?

4. How does the information on the characteristics of the frontiersmen in Section I of this unit compare with what you have read about Americans in Section II? How do the accounts agree or disagree? Do they aid you in drawing your own conclusions?

5. Now that you have made a study of America in the period 1800–1860, what is your answer to Crèvecoeur's question, "What is an American?"

III. Folklore of the Frontier

32. Davy Crockett

Part of the heritage of America is its folklore, or the traditional sayings, tales, and songs about the country and its people. Although folklore is usually passed orally from one generation to another, much of it has been preserved in recordings and on paper. The selections you are about to read are folk songs and stories of the frontier life you studied earlier in this unit.

Davy Crockett, born in Tennessee, was the typical unschooled frontiersman, hunter, and adventurer. He fought with Andrew Jackson against the Creek Indians in 1813. He served in the House of Representatives from 1827 to 1831, and from 1833 to 1835. Crockett was killed in 1836 in Texas while defending the Alamo from a Mexican attack. Numerous almanacs that appeared in his time related his many legendary doings. The first selection depicts Crockett's attitude toward himself. The second shows how Crockett was portrayed in a cartoon that appeared in an almanac in the 1830's.

Sketches and Eccentricities of Col. David Crockett, of West Tennessee (New York: J. J. Harper, 1833), p. 164.

CROCKETT'S BRAG

I'm that same David Crockett, fresh from the backwoods, half-horse, half-alligator, a little touched with the snapping-turtle; can wade the Mississippi, leap the Ohio, ride upon a streak of lightning, and slip without a scratch down a honey locust; can whip my weight in wild cats,—and if any gentleman pleases, for a ten dollar bill, he may throw in a panther,—hug a bear too close for comfort, and eat any man opposed to Jackson.

A CARTOON FROM AN ALMANAC

COURTESY, AMERICAN ANTIQUARIAN SOCIETY

Do the cartoon and the brag suggest any characteristics of Americans that you have already observed?

33. Mike Fink

Probably the most famous keelboatman of the Mississippi River was Mike Fink. He embodied the spirit of the rivermen who opened up the vast network of river transportation in the West. In 1822, Fink embarked on an expedition up the Missouri River. During the trip, he became involved in a quarrel. After killing one man, Fink was killed by another member of the expedition. The following are selections from "Fink's Brag."

436

. . . Hurray for me, you scapegoats! . . . I can lick five times my own weight in wildcats. I can use up Injens by the cord. . . .

I'm a Salt River roarer! I'm a ring-tailed squealer! I'm a reg'lar screamer from the ol' Massassip'! WHOOP! I'm the very infant that refused his milk before its eyes were open, and called out for a bottle of old Rye! I love the women an' I'm chockful o' fight! I'm half wild horse and half cock-eyed alligator and the rest o' me is crooked snags an' red-hot snappin' turkle. I can hit like fourth-proof lightnin' an' every lick I make in the woods lets in an acre o' sunshine. I can out-run, out-jump, out-shoot, out-brag, out-drink, an' out-fight, rough-an'-tumble, no holts [holds] barred, ary [any] man on both sides [of] the river from Pittsburgh to New Orleans an' back ag'in to St. Louiee. Come on, you flat-ters, you bargers, you milk-white mechanics, an' see how tough I am to chaw! I ain't had a fight for two days an' I'm spilein' for exercise. Cock-a-doodle-do!

A "lick" is a swing of the axe.

"Spilein' (spoiling) for" means looking for.

1. What similarities do you see between Fink and Crockett? What do these brags reveal about the characteristics of such frontiersmen?

2. What relationship do you see between the characteristics of Fink and Crockett and the frontier life you studied about in Section I?

3. Would you apply the term "individualistic" to Fink or Crockett? Explain.

34. Jim Bridger

Jim Bridger was one of the most famous trailblazers of the Rocky Mountains. He hunted, trapped, traveled, and guided others through the rocky ranges. He is credited with being the first frontiersman to see the Great Salt Lake. This was in 1824. Bridger was a well-known storyteller. Here are some of his tall tales.

. . . Jim was pretty generally known as Old Gabe. He'd been a hunter, trapper, fur-trader and guide so many years that he was the best known old-timer in any of those lines in the West. He'd also discovered a mess of places scattered all over the West—Salt Lake, South Pass, parts of Yellowstone Park, and so forth. Even more—he'd figured out what to *do* about some of the strangest of these places, and he'd been most generous and open-handed in telling people.

Letting people know was his favorite pastime. Let Old Gabe corner somebody in a tavern or a trading post or by a campfire, and he'd just pour out wisdom by the gallon.

One night in a camp in the Teton Mountains [in Wyoming], for instance, he got started in a talk about using nature in a scientific way. There was a bunch of men there, sitting around in the shadows, with the firelight showing their faces in the darkness now and then. There were only three men, it happened, though, that did much talking that night—Old Gabe, another old-timer named Jack Something-or-other, and the tenderfoot.

"Trouble is," Old Gabe said, "that though we've got more wonders of Nature out in this country here than there are in any other part of the world, very few folks make much use of them. Take the way people fail to reckon time. They do it with trees, sure, counting the tree rings. But why don't they do it other ways that don't put a body to the work of chopping down a tree?"

This uppity young tenderfoot that had got himself educated at Yale said, "What, precisely, do you have in mind, Mr. Bridger?"

"I'll tell you," says Gabe. "You see that hill over there, that one that's shaped something like a Ute Indian's nose? Well, that used to be a hole in the ground. But in this salubrious and healthy climate, the thing went and grew into a hill."

"Salubrious" is another word for healthy.

"Indeed?" the tenderfoot said. "And how, pray, did you know that?"

"Saw it with my own eyes, back in 1820, when it was a hole. Jack here did the same. Didn't you, Jack?"

The other old-timer shook his head. "No," he said, "I didn't come along and get my first squint at it until in 1825, when it was more in the nature of a mound. But it's sure growed since then, the way you say."

"Course it has," Old Gabe said. "Point I want to make is, if you knew about the rate of growth in a thing like that, you could measure time. Or take that stone I heaved across the Sweetwater a good while back. Go and look at it now, and you'll see it's grown up and got to be Independence Rock. We've got a lot to learn about how holes and rocks grow, but when we learn it, it'll be right helpful. And another thing we haven't learned to use properly out here is the handy arrangements of the scenery."

"Perhaps," the uppity tenderfoot said, slapping at a mosquito, "you will provide me with a specific example or two."

438

"Of course," Old Gabe said, "and I'll show you how I worked it once or twice too. Don't suppose anybody here—" (he looked at the men around the fire) "—anybody outside of Jack, at least, remembers the Year of the Big Snow. The way you could tell it from other winters is this, that for seventy days a foot of snow fell every single day. Let's see, that added up to a good deal of snow, as you'd find out for yourself if you multiplied and so forth. Let's say, roughly, that it came to about seventy feet of snow— that's the depth I found by measuring some places, anyhow. Well, I was scouting around Salt Lake the next spring, and I saw all these white statues that looked like animals—buffalo mostly, but here and there a bear or a deer. What they really were, you see, was real animals that had friz. So I toted them over to Salt Lake, and heaved the varmints in. The lake then pickled and cured them —and I had vittles on hand for me and the Ute Indians to last for years."

"Mr. Bridger," the tenderfoot said, "that sounds dubious [doubt-ful]. Can you establish the veracity [truth] of your allegations [statements]?"

Bridger had been throwing some wood on the fire. Now he dusted his hands off, sat down, and answered the tenderfoot back. "Of course I can, and I can prove what I said was true, too —or you can do it, if you're a mind to. Just hunt all over the Wasatch and Humboldt Mountains, young man, and if you find a single buffalo, or a married one, I'll eat the critter, horns and all. There's not a buffalo in the whole district. Ain't that true, Jack?"

"True as gospel," Jack said. "I can tell, too, of another time Old Gabe took advantage of the way things had got laid out—over in Yellowstone. I only had a chance to eat that salted buffalo, and had to take his word for how he'd saved it. But this time I was along, to see with my own two eyes. In this camp we had, just before we turned in for the night, he'd holler out, 'Time to git up!' Six hours later—"

"Six hours and seven minutes," Jim Bridger cut in.

"Six hours and seven minutes later, the echo would come back and wake us for breakfast," Jack said. "Gabe knew, by testing it out, about acoustics and such—knew how long it took a medium-sized echo to travel. After we'd been woke that way, we'd catch our breakfast in Fire Hole River—just pulled our trouts out, took them off the hooks, and ate them, then and there."

"Ate them?" says the tenderfoot, looking sickish. "Raw?"

"Course not," Jack told him. "Fire Hole River's a body of water Jim went and discovered. It's cold on the bottom, so trouts live there, but it biles [boils] on top. These trouts would be cooked beautiful by the time they'd been landed—all except the seasoning, which we'd take along with us when we fished."

1. Compare Bridger with Fink and Crockett. Do they have any traits in common?
2. If so, why do you think they developed these traits?

35. Pioneers Comment on the Weather

Some indication of the temperament of the pioneers is found in their humorous expressions about the conditions they encountered. Here are sample comments from the early settlers in the arid regions of the West.

Russell Lord, **Behold Our Land** (Boston: Houghton Mifflin Company, 1938), pp. 2, 211. Reprinted by permission of the publisher.

... Of course it gets dry out there, they say, so dry sometimes that the cattle starve down and climb through the holes in the chicken wire, and hide among the chickens, and that's annoying ...

A drop of water hit a man, and they had to throw two buckets of dirt in his face to bring him to. ... We keep track of the wind by hanging a log chain on a post. If it stands out straight, that's a breeze, but when it gets to whipping around, and links snap off, look out; it's likely to be windy by sundown.

1. How do the claims made about the climate and conditions in this area compare with what you observed from the maps in Section I?
2. How do these tales resemble Bridger's stories? Why do you think frontiersmen told such stories?

36. Big-Foot Wallace

Born in Virginia, William Wallace went to Texas after it won its independence from Mexico. He protected settlers and the mail runs from Indian attacks and served in the army during the Mexican War (1846–1848). After the war, he and a partner bought some land and became ranchers. The following story about Wallace is told by one of his friends, Jack Dobell. It begins when Dobell comes upon Wallace unexpectedly near San Antonio, Texas.

Some years ago, while on my way to the city of San Antonio, I lost my road, and after wandering about the prairies till nearly sunset, I concluded to strike camp, and make a fresh start in the morning. But just as I made up my mind to pass the night at "Sprawls," and put up as well as I could with such accommodations as are usually furnished by that extensive establishment, I thought I saw some faint symptoms of a "settlement" ahead of me. Spurring on my jaded [tired] horse, I at length came to a sort of hybrid [cross] between a log cabin and a half-faced camp, in front of which a man was seated on a fallen tree, busily engaged in rubbing up his rifle.

"Can you give me such directions, my friend," said I, "as will enable me to find my way back to the main road to San Antonio?"

The man looked up . . . and to my astonishment I recognized my old friend and messmate, Big-Foot Wallace.

"Why, hello, Foot," said I, "have you forgotten your old 'compadre,' Jack Dobell?"

Big-Foot looked at me dubiously for a minute, then, springing up from the log, he seized me by the hand and gave it such a grip that my fingers stuck together for five minutes afterward.

"Get down, Dobell," said he, "and rest your face and hands. You must stay with me all night, and in the morning I'll pilot you out to the road myself. It's a fact, though," continued Big-Foot, looking ruefully [sorrowfully] around upon the apparently scant accommodations afforded by his "ranch," "it's a fact, though, I haven't got much to offer you. Crops have failed entirely, but there's pretty smart [a good amount] of good grass in that hollow yonder for your nag; and my partner, Jackson, was lucky enough to kill a fat buck to-day. So get down at once, for I have a heap to tell you about what has happened to me since we last met. . . ."

"You needn't be afraid to stake [your horse] so far from camp— there's no Indians about here now," said Big-Foot, with a melancholy expression of countenance, as if he was heartily sick of "these piping times of peace," and longed to see once more the stirring scenes of [bygone] days. "I do believe there hasn't been an Indian in ten miles of this place for the last twelve months."

"Why, you don't tell me, Big-Foot," said I, "that you have been all that time without a single 'scrimmage' with the Mexicans or Indians?"

"Yes," said he, "with the exception of a little 'tussle' I had with the 'Tonks' [Tonkawa Indians of Texas] about six months ago, on the Llaño [River], I haven't had a row of any sort since I 'drove my megs down' in this settlement. And no wonder, neither, for

John C. Duval, **The Adventures of Big Foot Wallace, The Texas Ranger and Hunter** (Macon, Ga.: 1870); reprinted from **A Treasury of American Folklore**, edited by B. A. Botkin (New York: Crown Publishers, Inc., 1944), pp. 169-171.

441

A "corn crib" is a place where corn is stored.

the people are 'piling in' here as thick as pig-tracks around a corn-crib door; and they have fenced up the prairies in such a way that the Indians won't venture in, for fear of being 'hemmed up.' If I only knew where all these people come from, I'd go there right off, for there can't be any one left behind, and a fellow wouldn't be 'scrouged' [squeezed] to death, as he is here now. Of all things in the world, I hate being 'fenced up'; I want plenty of elbow-room and plenty of 'outlet,' but here you can't travel half a dozen miles in any direction, without being headed off by somebody's fence."

On our return to the "ranch," we took a seat on the log which answered Big-Foot in place of a sofa, and he said to me, "Well, in the first place, I suppose you would like to know how I came to settle here, and take up with the business of farming.

"You see, after the Mexican war had ended, and that chap with the gold epaulets on his shoulders and the 'chicken fixings' on his coat-sleeves had mustered us out of the service and paid us off, Jackson and I concluded, as we had saved up a smart pile of money between us, that we would try our hands at 'ranching.' Neither of us knew anything about it, but we thought it would be plain sailing enough, as things appeared to grow in this country pretty much of their own accord anyhow, without requiring a great deal of hard work, of which neither of us were 'overly' fond. So we bought two hundred acres of land here, from Uncle Josh (and by the same token, he made us pay a 'swingeing' [whopping] price for it—twenty-five cents an acre, half cash down).

". . . [After] Jackson and I had bought this piece of land from 'Uncle Josh,' the first thing we did was to build this shanty, and fence in that 'truck-patch' [vegetable garden] you see yonder; and long before we got through with the job, I tell you I had taken a perfect disgust for farming. To sit here comfortably on this log, and look at that little shanty and the truck-patch alongside of it, you would think them a mere circumstance; and, in fact, they don't make a very imposing show in the way of improvements; but just you try your hand at riving [splitting] a few hundred boards out of these knotty post-oaks, that split just as well crossways as lengthways, and if you don't lather [angrily destroy] 'a few,' and cuss a few more, then I'm mistaken. And if that don't satisfy you, just pitch into that chaparral out yonder, where the thorns are as sharp and as crooked as cats' claws, and perhaps, by the time you are tattooed all over like a New-Zealander, and there's nothing left of your pants but the waistbands, and only the collar of your shirt, you will come to the

"Chaparral" is a thicket of shrub-like oak trees.

same conclusion that I did, that farming ain't quite so pleasant a business as following an Indian trail on an easy-going horse. . . ."

1. How would you describe Big-Foot Wallace?

2. Do you see here any new attitude of the frontiersman that you have not previously observed?

37. "Texian Boys"

The remaining readings in this section are folk songs and ballads that tell about frontier life. The following folk song describes the settlers of Texas.

Lou'siana gals, come and listen to my noise,
Don't go marry those Texian boys,
For, if you do, your fortune will be
Johnnycake and venison and sassafras tea,
Johnnycake and venison and sassafras tea.

Folk Song, U.S.A., edited by John A. and Alan Lomax (New York: Duell, Sloan and Pearce, 1947), p. 45.

"Johnnycake" is a flat cornmeal cake. "Venison" is deer meat. "Sassafras" is a root used for flavoring.

When they go to preachin', let me tell you what they wear,—
An old leather coat all picked and bare,
An old straw hat more brim than crown,
And a pair of dirty socks they've worn the winter round,
A pair of dirty socks they've worn the winter round.

When they go a-courtin', I'll tell you what they ride,—
An old pack-saddle all covered with hide,
An old hair girth made out of a rope,
A-straddle of a horse that can't fetch a lope,
A-straddle of a horse that can't fetch a lope.

A "girth" is a strap that holds a saddle to a horse. A "lope" is a slow gallop.

For your wedding supper there's beef and cornbread,
There it is to eat when the ceremony's said;
And when you go to milk, you'll milk in a gourd,
Set it in a corner and cover it with a board,
Set it in a corner and cover it with a board.

They live in a hut with a hewed log wall,
But it ain't got any windows at all;
With a clapboard roof and a puncheon floor,
And that's the way all Texas o'er,
And that's the way all Texas o'er.

"Clapboards" are overlapping boards. "Puncheon" is split lumber with only one smooth side.

They will take you out on a live-oak hill,
And there they'll leave you against your will.
They'll leave you on the prairie and starve you on the plains,
For that is the way with the Tex-i-ans,
For that is the way with the Tex-i-ans.

Brandy is brandy any way you mix it,
A Texian's a Texian any way you fix him,
When other good folk are all gone to bed,
The devil is a-workin' in a Texian's head,
The devil is a-workin' in a Texian's head.

1. Does this song reflect any ideas you already have about pioneer life? How does pioneer life in Texas compare with life in New England or the South?

2. What does the writer of the song think Texas pioneers are like? Does he approve or disapprove of them? In his attitude toward the Texas pioneers, which of the observers of American life does this writer resemble most?

3. What are this song-writer's values? How do they compare with the values of pioneers like Davy Crockett and Mike Fink? Big-Foot Wallace? of other Americans you have studied?

38. "Sweet Betsy from Pike"

Pioneers rushed to California after gold was discovered there in 1849. The following ballad tells the story of one of these pioneers, "Sweet Betsy from Pike." Whether Betsy really came from Pike County in northeastern Missouri is uncertain since the Californians called all migrants "Pikes."

Did you ever hear tell of Betsy from Pike,
Who crossed the wide mountains with her lover Ike.
With two yoke of cattle and one spotted hog,
A tall Shanghai rooster and an old yellow dog.

They swam the wide rivers and crossed the tall peaks,
And camped on the prairie for weeks upon weeks.
Starvation and cholera and hard work and slaughter,
They reached California spite of hell and high water.

The Injuns came down in a wild yelling horde,
And Betsy was skeered they would scalp her adored;
Behind the front wagon-wheel Betsy did crawl,
And fought off the Injuns with musket and ball.

They soon reached the desert, where Betsy gave out,
And down in the sand she lay rolling about;
While Ike in great terror looked on in surprise,
Saying, "Get up now, Betsy, you'll get sand in your eyes."

The Shanghai ran off and the cattle all died,
The last piece of bacon that morning was fried;
Poor Ike got discouraged, and Betsy got mad,
The dog wagged his tail and looked wonderfully sad.

Folk Song, U.S.A., edited by John A. and Alan Lomax (New York: Duell, Sloan and Pearce, 1947), p. 179.

"Cholera" is an intestinal disease.

444

Long Ike and sweet Betsy attended a dance,
Where Ike wore a pair of his Pike County pants;
Sweet Betsy was covered with ribbons and rings.
Said Ike, "You're an angel, but where are your wings?"

A miner said, "Betsy, will you dance with me?"
"I will that, old hoss, if you don't make too free;
But don't dance me hard. Do you want to know why?
Doggone you, I'm chock-full of strong alkali."

Long Ike, and sweet Betsy got married of course,
But Ike, getting jealous, obtained a divorce;
And Betsy, well satisfied, said with a shout,
"Good-bye, you big lummux, I'm glad you backed out."

1. What was "sweet Betsy" like?

2. As a pioneer woman, what contributions did Betsy make to the success of this particular migration?

3. How does the trip described here compare with those you read about earlier in this unit?

4. How would someone like Mrs. Trollope describe Betsy? Why?

39. "Root, Hog, or Die"

The first vehicle to overcome the problems of crossing the plains was the prairie schooner, an ox-drawn covered wagon. The driver of the oxen was called a bull-whacker because of the twenty-foot blacksnake whip he used. He was largely responsible for the group's safety. This ballad is about such a driver. The title is a pioneer saying that means do the job or suffer the consequences.

I'm a lonely bull-whacker
On the Red Cloud Line,
I can lick any son-of-a-gun
Can yoke an ox of mine.
If I can catch him
You bet I will or try,
I'll lick with him an ox-bow,
Root, hog, or die.

Well, it's out upon the road
With a very heavy load,
With a very awkward team
And a very muddy road,
You may whip and you may holler,
If you cuss it's on the sly,
Then it's whack the cattle on, boys,
Root, hog, or die.

By this time the couple had arrived in California.

"Alkali," here, means alkali water, which is poisonous.

The Folk Songs of North America, edited by Alan Lomax (Garden City, N.Y.: Doubleday and Company, 1960), pp. 333-334. New words and new music adaptation by Alan Lomax. © copyright 1960, Ludlow Music, Inc. Reprinted by permission of Ludlow Music, Inc.

An "oxbow" is part of the yoke (harness) of an ox team. It is U-shaped, to fit under the neck of an ox.

Now perhaps you'd like to know, boys,
What we have to eat,
A little piece of bread
And a little dirty meat,
A little black coffee
And whisky on the sly,
It's whack the cattle on, boys,
Root, hog, or die.

There's hard times on Bitter Creek
Never can be beat,
It was root, hog, or die
Under every wagon sheet;
We cleaned up all the Injuns,
Drank all the alkali,
And it's whack the cattle on, boys,
Root, hog, or die.

O I'm a-goin' home
Bull-whackin' for to spurn,
I ain't got a nickel,
And I don't give a durn.
'Tis when I meet a purdy gal
You bet I will or try,
I'll whack her with my ox-bow,
Root, hog, or die.

Does this song reflect any of the problems or characteristics of the frontiersmen you read about in this section? Explain.

USING FOLKLORE IN HISTORY

1. Has your study of frontier folklore confirmed any ideas you had about the traits of pioneers? Has it given you new ideas about what pioneers were like? Has it helped to show reasons why pioneers had such traits? Explain.

2. What connections do you now see between the traits of pioneers and of other Americans in the period 1800–1860? To what extent does the frontier seem to have shaped American character?

3. In Section I you studied the conditions and problems of frontier life. What is the relationship between folklore and this part of history?

4. Do we have folklore today? Explain. What is its role? How do you use folklore in writing the history of a people?

THE AMERICAN PEOPLE, PAST AND PRESENT

1. What were the principal traits of Americans in the period 1800–1860?

2. Can you think of any explanations for these traits?

3. Are early nineteenth-century Americans in any way like the colonial Americans you studied in Unit I? If so, how?

4. Are Americans today like Americans in the first part of the nineteenth century? Which traits have lasted? Which ones are no longer important?

5. Can you think of any explanations for your answers to the last two questions?

TIME LINE

1803 LOUISIANA PURCHASED FROM FRANCE.

1804 LEWIS AND CLARK EXPEDITION.

1807 ROBERT FULTON SUCCESSFULLY DEMONSTRATES THE USE OF A STEAMBOAT ON THE HUDSON RIVER.

1808 AMERICAN FUR COMPANY ORGANIZED IN THE NORTHWEST.

1812 WAR OF 1812 BEGINS.

1812 MOWING MACHINE INVENTED.

1815 WAR OF 1812 ENDS.

1819 FLORIDA PURCHASED FROM SPAIN.

1819 CAST IRON PLOW INVENTED.

1821 AMERICANS SETTLE IN TEXAS.

1821 MEXICO GAINS HER INDEPENDENCE FROM SPAIN.

1822 ROCKY MOUNTAIN FUR COMPANY ORGANIZED IN THE NORTHWEST.

1825 ERIE CANAL OPENED.

1827 MRS. TROLLOPE VISITS THE U.S.

1828 FIRST PASSENGER RAILROAD IN THE U.S., THE BALTIMORE & OHIO.

1830 STEAM LOCOMOTIVE INVENTED.

1831 ALEXIS DE TCCQUEVILLE VISITS THE U.S.

1832 REAPER INVENTED.

1832 TELEGRAPH INVENTED.

1833 PATRICK SHIRREFF VISITS THE U.S.

1835 SIX-SHOOTER INVENTED BY COLT.

1836 TEXAS DECLARES ITS INDEPENDENCE FROM MEXICO.

1837 WASHINGTON IRVING WRITES *THE ADVENTURES OF CAPTAIN BONNEVILLE.*

1837 STEEL PLOW INVENTED.

1842 CHARLES DICKENS VISITS THE U.S.

1845 TEXAS ANNEXED TO THE U.S.

1846 WAR WITH MEXICO BEGINS.

1848 U.S. GAINS CONTROL OF THE OREGON TERRITORY SOUTH OF THE 49TH PARALLEL.

1848 MEXICAN WAR ENDS. MEXICO CEDES THE TERRITORY THAT BECOMES CALIFORNIA, NEW MEXICO, ARIZONA, UTAH, AND NEVADA TO THE U.S.

1848 GOLD DISCOVERED IN CALIFORNIA.

1851 HERMAN MELVILLE'S BOOK, *MOBY DICK,* PUBLISHED.

1856 FIRST RAILROAD CROSSES THE MISSISSIPPI RIVER.

1858 FIRST TRANSATLANTIC CABLE LAID.

1859 FIRST OIL WELL DRILLED AT TITUSVILLE, PA.

1859 SILVER DISCOVERED IN NEVADA.
1860 PONY EXPRESS MAIL ROUTE OPENED FROM MISSOURI TO CALIFORNIA.
1860 REPEATING RIFLE INVENTED.

BIBLIOGRAPHY

COATSWORTH, ELIZABETH. HERE I STAY. New York: Coward-McCann, 1938.
Early nineteenth century Maine is the scene of this novel. A young lady chooses to remain on the land she has grown to love rather than follow the many other young people leaving for new lands in Ohio.

*DANIELS, JONATHAN. THE DEVIL'S BACKBONE. New York: McGraw-Hill Book Co., Inc., 1962.
This story of the men who traveled the wilderness trail between Nashville, Tennessee, and Natchez, Mississippi, is richly varied in mystery, tragedy, and romance.

THE ERIE CANAL. New York: American Heritage Publishing Co., Inc., 1964.
The illustrations and text combine to present a vivid picture of the reasons for building the Erie Canal and the problems encountered during its construction.

GARST, SHANNON. JIM BRIDGER. Boston: Houghton Mifflin Company, 1952.
This action-filled biography tells the story of one of the men who helped to blaze the trails to the Far West.

*LAVENDER, DAVID. WESTWARD VISION. New York: McGraw-Hill Book Co., Inc., 1963.
While telling the exciting story of the Oregon Trail, the author probes into the motives that caused men to look westward.

THE LIFE TREASURY OF AMERICAN FOLKLORE. New York: Time Inc., 1961.
Colorfully illustrated, this collection of familiar American folktales covers a wide span of history, from the period of exploration to the present.

LOMAX, JOHN A. and ALAN. FOLK SONG: U.S.A. New York: Duell, Sloan and Pearce, 1960. †New York: New American Library of World Literature, Inc., 1966.
Two of the foremost authorities on folk songs have compiled various songs about the frontier, miners, Negroes, cowboys, and lumbermen.

PARKMAN, FRANCIS. THE OREGON TRAIL. New York: Holt, Rinehart and Winston, Inc., 1931. †New York: New American Library of World Literature, Inc., 1961.
This book is the record of the adventures of Parkman and his four companions, who joined the great westward movement in 1846.

TWAIN, MARK (CLEMENS, SAMUEL). ADVENTURES OF TOM SAWYER. New York: Harcourt, Brace & World, Inc., 1963. †New York: Dell Publishing Co., Inc., 1963.
A classic novel, based on the author's boyhood experiences, presents a picture of life along the Mississippi River in the mid-nineteenth century.

WELLS, HELEN. ADAM GIMBEL, PIONEER TRADER. New York: David McKay Co., Inc., 1955.
Adam Gimbel supplied many necessary wares to settlers on the frontier. His rise from frontier peddler to store owner is told in this biographical novel.

* Denotes more advanced reading.
† Denotes paperback edition.

unit VI
THE CIVIL WAR
AND ITS
AFTERMATH 1860-1877

Long, too long America,
Traveling roads all even and peaceful you learn'd from joys and
*   prosperity only,*
But now, ah now, to learn from crises of anguish . . .   WALT WHITMAN
                                              "LONG, TOO LONG AMERICA," 1865

INTRODUCTION

We're tenting tonight on the old Camp Ground
   Give us a song to cheer
Our weary hearts, a song of home
   And friends we love so dear.

Many are the hearts that are weary tonight,
   Wishing for the war to cease;
Many are the hearts looking for the right
   To see the dawn of peace.
Tenting tonight, Tenting tonight,
   Tenting on the old Camp Ground.

We are tired of war on the old Camp Ground
   Many are dead and gone
Of the brave and true who've left their homes
   Others been wounded long.

Many are the hearts that are weary tonight,
   Wishing for the war to cease;
Many are the hearts looking for the right,
   To see the dawn of peace.
Dying tonight, Dying tonight,
   Dying on the old Camp Ground.

Although a Union song, "Tenting on the Old Camp Ground" describes the feelings and sufferings of both sides in the final stages of the Civil War. The war was fought between the eleven southern states of the Confederacy and the twenty-three northern states of the Union. It began on April 12, 1861, when General Pierre Beauregard's southern forces bombarded Fort Sumter and ended when General Robert E. Lee surrendered to Union General Ulysses S. Grant at Appomattox Courthouse on April 9, 1865.

From the earliest days of colonization, the areas that were to become the United States developed in different ways. Social life, political ideas, and economic pursuits varied from place to place. These differences were not sufficient to prevent a union of states in 1787. But they remained present, and sometimes rose to the surface.

In 1796, for example, conflict erupted over the Alien and Sedition

450

Acts. (See Unit III, pages 259-261.) The Sedition Act imposed penalties for false or malicious criticism of the government. The Alien Act required foreigners to register with the federal government and allowed the President to deport without a trial those he considered dangerous to the United States. There was also a new Naturalization Act, which lengthened the residence requirements for citizenship. The Acts were directed primarily at French immigrants.

Many of these immigrants had been severely criticizing the government at a time when the country was engaged in an undeclared naval war with France. But there was another aspect to the problem. The Acts were passed by a Federalist Congress, and the French immigrants were mostly Republicans. (Furthermore, the Federalists in general tended to draw their strength from eastern cities, while the Republicans were popular in rural areas and in the West.) The situation prompted the Republican legislatures of Kentucky and Virginia to pass resolutions declaring the Alien and Sedition Acts null and void in their states. The Acts were never strictly enforced however, so there was never an outright clash between Kentucky and Virginia and the federal government.

The War of 1812 brought another crisis that endangered the unity of the country. The New England states, which depended heavily on trade, opposed the war all along. Two years after it began, their fears were realized. Trade was at a standstill. In response, delegates from the New England states met at Hartford, Connecticut. They demanded seven amendments to the Constitution to increase the power of New England. They seemed to threaten that New England would secede from the Union if its demands were not met. One of their demands was that southern states no longer be permitted to count part of their slaves in determining representation to Congress. Nothing was ever done about the demands of the Hartford Convention, because the war ended soon after it met.

Still another crisis arose in the late 1820's and early 1830's. Southerners, for reasons you will consider in this unit, opposed high tariffs, or taxes on goods entering the country. In 1828, Congress enacted a new group of high tariffs. The law was so fiercely opposed in some quarters that it was called the "Tariff of Abominations." South Carolina, in particular, opposed the tariff. Its response was the "South Carolina Exposition," which declared that states had the right to decide whether a federal law was constitutional. According to this theory, states could declare laws they considered unconstitutional null and void within their borders. This *nullification* theory was the occasion of many heated debates in Congress. President Jackson, who felt that nullification threatened the union, surprised his southern friends by opposing the idea. (See Unit IV, pages 360-365.)

Then, in 1832, Congress passed another tariff law. Again the rates were high. This time South Carolina declared the tariff null and void within the state. Jackson warned that he would enforce the law. At his request, Congress passed a bill in 1833 giving him the power to suppress opposition in South Carolina by force. A clash was avoided by passage of a compromise tariff bill on the same day.

In each of these three situations, the crisis passed without serious incident. The threat to the Union was averted. But in 1861, a crisis arose which erupted into war. The war was fought between two distinctly different sections of the country, the North and the South. In this unit you will make a detailed study of the differences between the two sections, events of the period prior to the war, and opinions of both northerners and southerners about the issues that arose to divide the sections. You will be asked to form your own conclusions about the nature and extent of the differences between North and South. You will also be asked to think about whether war was the only answer to the conflicts of interest that developed. You will be able to decide for yourself at what point and by what means war might have been avoided, if it could have been avoided at all. All of these considerations will help you to form an opinion about what caused the Civil War.

In the second part of the unit, you will take a brief look at the period of the war itself. Here you will judge the extent to which the aims of the government during the war matched the causes of the war. You will also be able to decide which conflicts seemed to have been decided by the military events. Finally, you will be asked to consider what other results the war might have had.

The last part of the unit deals with the years 1865-1877, the period generally known as Reconstruction. Here you will be able to see what some of the results of the war were. You will be able to make a better judgment about whether the war solved the problems that caused it.

VIEWS OF SLAVERY, 1800–1830

I. The North and the South

1. Southern Views of Slavery

What were the North and South like in the period preceding the Civil War? Were they very different from each other? In Unit V, you compared the characteristics and social life of northerners and southerners. Now you will compare their economies, population patterns, and attitudes toward slavery.

The following two selections present southern views of slavery in the period 1800–1830. In the first account Elias Horry, a South Carolina plantation owner, tells how his slaves lived. Some slaves did not fare as well as those on Horry's plantation. However, Horry's attitude toward his slaves is typical of what very many slaveowners thought.

James Madison, President from 1809 to 1817, presents the views of some of the more aristocratic slaveowners. Many of those who shared his views were fellow Virginians, such as Thomas Jefferson and James Monroe.

ELIAS HORRY, 1826

With regard to the accommodation [housing] and general comfort of the slaves in this country, there is no question but that they enjoy a greater share of the blessings of life than falls to the lot of the laboring poor of most countries. Their dwellings, on my plantation, are built in such a manner as to afford them every protection and comfort, and are generally about forty feet in length and twenty feet wide, with a double brick chimney in the centre that forms two tenements [dwellings]; each tenement has two rooms and a hall.

Their food consists of hominy, potatoes, peas, and small-rice, and is regularly given out to them every week. The waters of the Santee, upon which I live, abound with the finest fish, and all the grown Negroes, and many of the children, are supplied with fishhooks and lines by which they are enabled to get a regular supply of fish from the river. In the summer season salted fish is occasionally given to them. Each grown Negro is allowed a small field, say from a quarter to a half acre of land, or more if he desires it, which he plants, and the profits of which he appropriates [keeps] exclusively to his own use. They are permitted to raise poultry of every description which they either sell to their master or send to market. In cases of sickness they have every medical attention necessary. . . . In addition to which, in cases of severe illness, one or more of the family to which the invalids may belong are permitted to wait upon them. . . .

Edward Brown, **Notes on the Origin and Necessity of Slavery** (Charleston, South Carolina: A. E. Miller, 1826), pp. 56-57.

453

"Plains" are simple clothes.

Their clothing consists of white plains, and they are also furnished with London duffil blankets of the best quality, a pair of shoes, and a Scotch cap. The blankets are given out once every three years; and it often occurs from the nature of his work, that a laborer may require another pair of shoes, which is given to him. Every woman has an additional blanket at the birth of every child, as well as clothes for her infant.

Their labor is, comparatively, *light and easy,* so that an industrious negro can very easily accomplish his task early in the afternoon, and the rest of the time is at his own disposal. . . . [If those] of my negroes who are mechanics . . . are called upon to do any extra work, in their *own time,* they are regularly paid for it. In one instance I paid in one year to a carpenter belonging to me, $150, for the *extra* services of himself and two sons, in rearing [building] the frames of five negro houses. . . . The head of every family has a small garden allowed him, contiguous to [next to] his dwelling, independent of the little field I have mentioned, from which he gathers as many vegetables as supply his wants. They appear happy and contented, and the discipline used to keep them in proper order is by no means severe, but is always consistent with the feelings of justice and of humanity.

1. According to this account by Horry, what was life like for slaves on his plantation?

2. How would you describe Horry's attitude toward slaves?

3. Does Horry seem to think slavery is right or wrong? Why?

JAMES MADISON, 1819–1829

Letters and Other Writings of James Madison, (Philadelphia: J. B. Lippincott & Company, 1865), Vol. III, pp. 239, 133-134.

The negro slavery is . . . a sad blot on our free country . . . No satisfactory plan has yet been devised for taking out the stain . . . .

[If emancipation is to be just] . . . the consent of both the master and the slave should be obtained . . . .

To be consistent with existing and probably unalterable [unchangable] prejudices in the United States, the freed blacks ought to be permanently removed beyond the region occupied by, or allotted to, a white population . . . .

Letters and Other Writings of James Madison, Vol. IV, p. 53.

. . . It is due to justice; due to humanity; due to truth; to the sympathies of our nature; in fine, to our character as a people, both abroad and at home, that [the slaves] should be considered, as much as possible, in the light of human beings, and not as mere property . . . . They may be considered as making a part, though a degraded part, of the families to which they belong . . . .

... [The] mere circumstance of complexion cannot deprive them of the character of men ....

[Regarding the] condition of slaves in Virginia it may be ... stated, as better beyond comparison, than it was before the Revolution. ... [Their] food ... includes a much greater proportion of [meat], than is attainable by the free labourers even in [Europe]. ...

The Writings of James Madison, edited by Gaillard Hunt (New York: G. P. Putnam's Sons, 1908), Vol. VIII, pp. 426-427.

1. Does Madison have any of the same views as Horry?

2. How does his attitude toward slavery differ from Horry's?

2. Northern Views of Slavery

James Fenimore Cooper was a famous novelist from New York. John Quincy Adams, who became President in 1825, was from Massachusetts. Most northerners felt the way either Cooper or Adams did about slavery. Cooper's views are probably more typical of northern attitudes.

JAMES FENIMORE COOPER, 1828

There is scarcely a nation in Europe ... that has not a proportion of its population ... which, as a whole, endure much more physical suffering than the negroes of America.

James Fenimore Cooper, **Notions of the Americans** (New York: Frederick Ungar Publishing Company, 1963), Vol. II, pp. 260, 276, 261. Reprinted by permission of the publisher.

The condition of the American slave varies, of course, with circumstances. In some few portions of the country, he is ill dealt by. In most districts his labour is sufficiently light, his clothing is adapted to the climate, and his food is, I believe, everywhere abundant. The strongest evidence, after all, which can be given, that the amount of animal suffering among the American slaves is not great, (there are exceptions, of course,) is the fact that they are a lighthearted and a laughing race. I am very ready to grant that ... some of the most degraded and least intellectual people of the earth, are among the gayest; but I believe that it is a rule in nature, that where there is much animal suffering there is an animal exhibition [display] of its existence. ...

But physical suffering, especially in a country like this, is not the prominent grievance [main wrong] of slavery. ... God has planted in all our spirits secret but lasting aspirations [ambitions] after a state of existence higher than that which we enjoy, and no one has a right to say that such are the limits beyond which [one] shall not pass.

... [Public] opinion is making a steady advance to the general improvement, and I think, to the final liberation of the race. Although these changes are not as rapid as they might be ... and far less rapid than most good men could wish, it is a course that is more likely to be attended with less positive injury to the [slaves than sudden emancipation.]

JOHN QUINCY ADAMS, 1820

... [What] can be more false and heartless than this doctrine which makes the first and holiest rights of humanity to depend upon the color of the skin? ... [Slavery] reduces men endowed with logical powers to maintain that [it] is sanctioned [approved of] by the Christian religion, that slaves are happy and contented in their condition, [and] that between master and slave there are ties of mutual attachment and affection ... while at the same time they ... burn at the stake negroes convicted of crimes for the terror of the example, and writhe in ... fear at the very mention of human rights as applicable to men of color. ...

1. How would you summarize Cooper's attitude toward slavery? What is the difference between Cooper's and Adams' opinions?

2. To what extent did northern and southern attitudes toward slavery differ?

3. Would differences like these be likely to cause a war? Explain.

POPULATION AND ECONOMY, 1790–1860

3. Population Growth

The next six readings sketch the populations and economies of the North and South in the era preceding the Civil War.

POINTS TO CONSIDER

What differences there are between North and South.

How people would feel about these differences.

POPULATION GROWTH IN THE UNITED STATES, 1790–1860

YEAR	NORTHEAST*	NORTH CENTRAL*	SOUTH*
1790	1,968,040	---	1,961,174
1800	2,635,576	51,006	2,621,901
1810	3,486,675	292,107	3,461,099
1820	4,359,916	859,305	4,419,232
1830	5,542,381	1,610,473	5,707,848
1840	6,761,082	3,351,542	6,950,729
1850	8,626,951	5,403,595	8,982,612
1860	10,594,268	9,096,716	11,133,361

*The Northeast includes the New England states, New York, New Jersey, and Pennsylvania. North Central includes Ohio, Indiana, Illinois, Michigan, Wisconsin, Iowa, Missouri, Minnesota, and the territories of Kansas and Nebraska. The South includes Delaware, Maryland, Virginia, North and South Carolina, Georgia, Florida, Kentucky, Tennessee, Alabama, Mississippi, Arkansas, Texas, Louisiana, and the Oklahoma Territory. Population west of the areas listed above was 178,818 in 1850, and 618,976 in 1860.

1. How does the population of the Northeast compare with that of the South? How does the total population of the northern areas compare with that of the South? Which area was growing the fastest?

2. Do you think northerners or southerners would have any reaction to these facts? If so, what?

4. The Slave Population

SLAVE POPULATION OF THE UNITED STATES, 1790–1860*

YEAR	NORTHEAST	NORTH CENTRAL	SOUTH
1790	40,354	—	657,327
1800	36,370	135	857,097
1810	27,081	3,304	1,160,977
1820	18,001	11,329	1,508,692
1830	2,780	25,879	1,980,384
1840	765	58,604	2,427,986
1850	236	87,422	3,116,629
1860	18	114,948	3,838,765

*The areas on this chart are the same as those in the chart on the opposite page.

1. What does the chart show about the slave population of the United States?

2. How can you explain the differences in distribution of slaves between the North and the South?

SLAVERY, 1840–1860

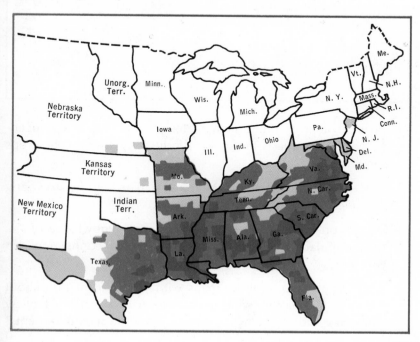

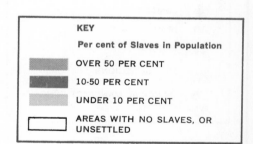

KEY

Per cent of Slaves in Population

OVER 50 PER CENT

10-50 PER CENT

UNDER 10 PER CENT

AREAS WITH NO SLAVES, OR UNSETTLED

457

1. What does the map show you about slave population that was not revealed by the chart?

2. How do you think the people in each section would react to the situation shown on this map?

5. Industry and Agriculture

AMERICAN INDUSTRY, 1860

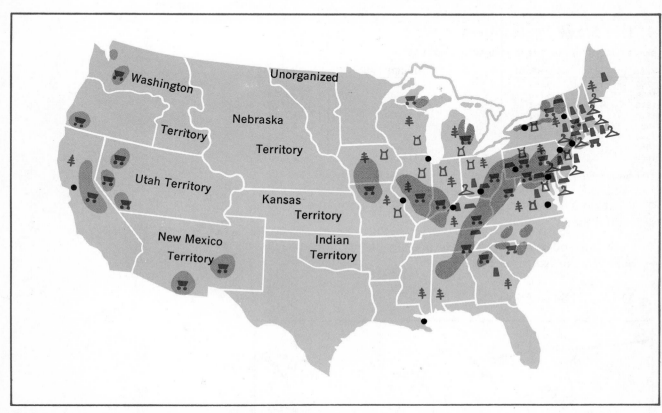

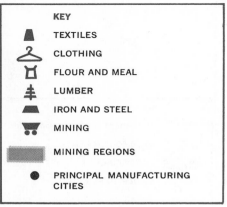

KEY

🔺 TEXTILES

👕 CLOTHING

🏺 FLOUR AND MEAL

🌲 LUMBER

🔻 IRON AND STEEL

🛒 MINING

▬ MINING REGIONS

● PRINCIPAL MANUFACTURING CITIES

1. In what area of the United States is most industry concentrated? What area is the major producer of each of the crops shown?

2. What might explain these differences? (For help in answering this question, see Unit I, pages 50–54.)

3. When you compare these maps with your knowledge of the total population of the United States, what connections do you see?

4. When you compare these maps with your information about the slave population, what hypotheses can you make? Review what was said about hypotheses in "A Note to the Student."

5. What products do you think are the greatest sources of revenue for the North? For the South?

6. Would these differences affect northern and southern attitudes toward slaves? Explain.

AGRICULTURAL PRODUCTS, 1860

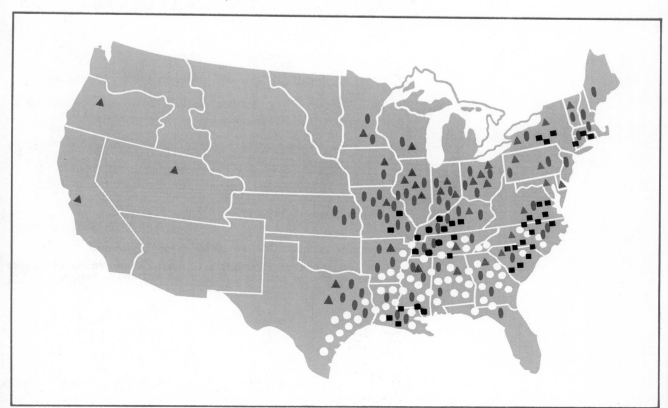

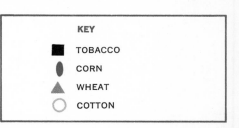

KEY

■ TOBACCO

● CORN

▲ WHEAT

○ COTTON

6. Economic Growth: Production of Goods

The next selection deals with economic growth in the North and South. There are two ways in which a country or section can become more wealthy, or achieve economic growth. One way is to produce more goods. The other is to sell more goods, usually by finding new buyers.

POINTS TO CONSIDER

Which section was growing faster.

Which section was likely to grow fastest in the future.

How northerners and southerners would react to these trends.

COTTON AND MANUFACTURED GOODS, 1800–1860

YEAR	VALUE OF COTTON IN MILLIONS OF DOLLARS	VALUE OF MANUFACTURED GOODS IN MILLIONS OF DOLLARS*
1800	10	—
1810	19	199
1820	29	—
1830	36	—
1840	75	—
1850	117	1,019
1860	207	1,900

*Fewer than one out of five people were employed by industry in 1860. No figures are available for manufactured goods in 1800, 1820, 1830, and 1840.

1. What is happening to the value of cotton? What is happening to the value of manufactured goods?

2. What contrasts can you see between the two columns?

3. Which section do you think would have a better chance of increasing its wealth quickly in the future? Why?

4. What would the southern planter need if he wanted to grow more cotton?

7. Economic Growth: Selling Goods

THE ROLE OF COTTON IN UNITED STATES EXPORTS, 1800–1860

YEAR	VALUE OF COTTON EXPORTS IN MILLIONS OF DOLLARS	VALUE OF UNITED STATES EXPORTS IN MILLIONS OF DOLLARS
1800	—	71
1810	15	67
1820	22	70
1830	30	74
1840	64	132
1850	72	152
1860	192	400

1. What has been happening to the South's percentage of total exports?

2. Compare the value of cotton exports with the value of cotton produced. (See the chart at the top of the page.) Is most of the cotton sold in the United States or abroad?

3. Would you say most manufactured goods were sold in the United States or abroad? How did you find out?

4. What, then, was the biggest market for the North? For the South?

COST OF EUROPEAN AND AMERICAN PRODUCTS

European manufactured products usually cost less than American ones. In 1828, for example, British woolen cloth cost about $1.00 per yard, while American wool cost $1.65 per yard. The same year, British calico (a type of cotton cloth) cost about 13¢ per yard, while American calico cost 30¢.

1. What attitude do you think the North would have toward the difference between European and American prices on manufactured goods? What attitude would the South have? Why?

2. A *tariff* is a tax on goods coming into a country. The effect of a tariff is to raise the price of the foreign goods. How would the North and South feel about tariffs? Why?

8. Canals and Railroads

CANALS, 1860

RAILROADS, 1860

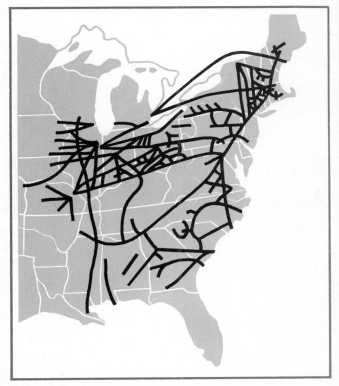

For more details see the maps on pages 395-396.

FINANCING CANALS AND RAILROADS
The federal government helped state and local governments and private companies pay the costs of building canals and railroads. By 1860, it had purchased over $3 million worth of canal stock. It also granted 4 million acres of public lands for canal construction. By 1857, the federal government had granted the railroads 18 million acres of land. It also helped the railroads by

To purchase stock is to buy a share of a business. The money a company gets from selling its stock can be used to help pay the company's expenses.

461

conducting land surveys and by reducing the tariff on iron between 1830 and 1843. This saved the railroads $6 million.

1. How does the distribution of railroads and canals differ in the North and in the South?

2. What information in this section might explain the difference?

3. How do you think the North would feel about the role of the federal government in financing railroads and canals? How would the South feel?

THE DIFFERENCES BETWEEN THE SECTIONS

1. Summarize the sectional differences you have noticed.

2. The first four readings in this section presented some typical northern and southern views of slavery. Has your study of charts and maps helped to explain these views? Has it suggested new ideas about the attitudes North and South might have toward slavery? Explain.

3. Do you think that the differences between North and South that you have noticed could lead to war? Do you think that these differences make war inevitable? Explain.

II. The Approaching Storm

THE NEW LANDS

9. The Northwest Ordinance of 1787

In this section you will scan the major events and movements that are considered to have caused the Civil War. The first topic is the events initiated by United States land acquisitions between 1787 and 1848. You have already studied the acquisitions in Unit IV. Now you will see some of their results.

The first landmark on the road to Civil War is the Northwest Ordinance of 1787. The Ordinance was a response to the acquisition of the Northwest Territory after the Revolutionary War. The Ordinance established a government for the territory and procedures by which districts of the territory could become states. (See pages 277–278). Article VI, which follows, dealt with slavery.

POINTS TO CONSIDER
How northerners and southerners would feel about the events described in this section. Consider the interests and attitudes you observed in Section I.

How these events could contribute to a clash between North and South.

Whether these events made the Civil War inevitable.

There shall be neither slavery nor involuntary servitude in the said territory, otherwise than in the punishment of crimes whereof the party shall have been duly convicted: *Provided, always,* That any person escaping into the same, from whom labor or service is lawfully claimed in any one of the original States, such fugitive may be lawfully reclaimed and conveyed to the person claiming his or her labor or service . . .

1. In 1787, which Americans would have wanted to forbid slavery in the Northwest Territory? Why?

2. Which Americans would have insisted on the clause concerning the return of fugitive, or runaway, slaves? Why?

10. The Missouri Compromise, 1820

In 1819, Missouri requested admission to the Union as a slave state. Many northerners objected to Missouri's entry. Maine also desired admission to the Union, but as a free state. The South objected to this. Congress admitted Missouri and Maine, but prohibited slavery in the remaining area of the Louisiana Purchase north of 36°30′.

Documents of American History, edited by Henry Steele Commager (Seventh edition; New York: Appleton-Century-Crofts, 1963), p. 132. Reprinted by permission of the publisher.

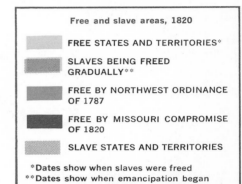

Free and slave areas, 1820

FREE STATES AND TERRITORIES*

SLAVES BEING FREED GRADUALLY**

FREE BY NORTHWEST ORDINANCE OF 1787

FREE BY MISSOURI COMPROMISE OF 1820

SLAVE STATES AND TERRITORIES

*Dates show when slaves were freed
**Dates show when emancipation began

THE MISSOURI COMPROMISE AND SLAVERY

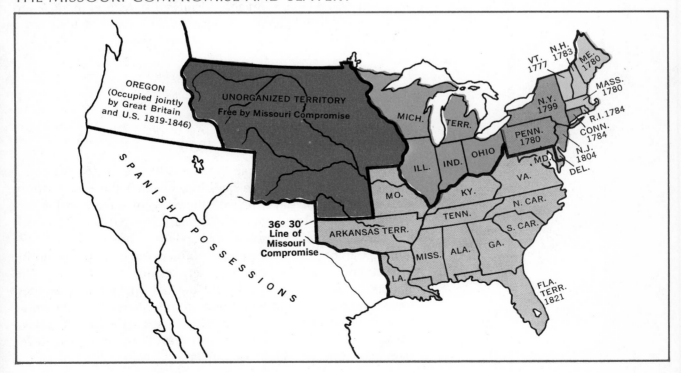

1. What did the South gain from the Missouri Compromise? How does this compare with the South's gains from the Northwest Ordinance?

2. What changes had occurred in the southern economy between 1787 and 1820? How could this affect the South's demands?

3. Review the northern and southern interests you observed in Section I. How could the admission of Maine or Missouri into the Union affect interests other than slavery?

4. Did the North or South have more people in 1820? Which section had a higher rate of population growth? How could this affect northern and southern interests? How would it affect northern and southern attitudes toward the Maine-Missouri issue?

5. When the Maine-Missouri issue arose, the aging Jefferson said, "This momentous question, like a fireball in the night, awakened and filled me with terror." What do you imagine his fears were? Why?

11. States Entering the Union, 1822–1850

Following the admission of Missouri to the Union in 1821, no states were created until 1836. From 1836 to 1850, six states were admitted to the Union. Arkansas achieved statehood in 1836 and Michigan in 1837. Florida and Texas became states in 1845; Iowa was admitted in 1846 and Wisconsin in 1848.

1. What pattern do you see in these events?

2. How can you explain it?

12. The Compromise of 1850

With the end of the Mexican War in 1848, the United States acquired vast new lands. The question, whether the new territory was to be free or slave, revived the issue of slavery in the territories. Debate flared when California requested admission as a free state and the South objected. Congress compromised by admitting California as a free state and by organizing the territories of Utah and New Mexico without any restrictions on slavery. The settlers of these territories would decide whether they wanted slavery or not. Leaving the choice to the citizens was known as "popular sovereignty." Congress also passed a rigid fugitive slave act to insure the return of runaway slaves and abolished slave-trading in the District of Columbia.

FREE AND SLAVE AREAS, 1850

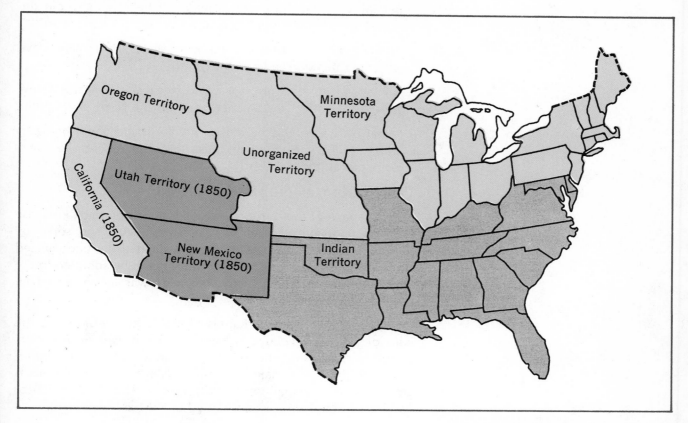

Oregon Territory

Minnesota Territory

Unorganized Territory

California (1850)

Utah Territory (1850)

New Mexico Territory (1850)

Indian Territory

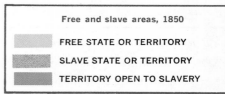

Free and slave areas, 1850

FREE STATE OR TERRITORY

SLAVE STATE OR TERRITORY

TERRITORY OPEN TO SLAVERY

1. John C. Calhoun of South Carolina was one of the foremost champions of southern interests in the Senate. In the debate over the Compromise of 1850, he declared, "[The South] has no concession or surrender to make. She has already surrendered so much that she has little left to surrender." Do the settlements of 1787 and 1820 provide any basis for his statement? Explain.

2. In terms of new territory or states, what did the South gain from the Compromise of 1850? What did the North gain? Do you think the settlement gave equal advantages to both sides? Explain.

3. Senator Daniel Webster of Massachusetts feared that a ban on slavery in the new territories would anger the South and destroy the Union. In a speech to the Senate, he pleaded with the North not to ban slavery in the lands acquired from Mexico. Webster argued that slavery was "excluded from . . .

465

those territories by ... the law of nature—of physical geography." What did Webster mean? If he was right, did the Compromise of 1850 give equal advantages to both sides?

4. In 1850, how many free states were there? How many slave states? Which side had a majority?

5. Which territories were not yet organized into states? How would they affect the balance between the North and South?

6. What changes had occurred in the North and South between 1820 and 1850? How would these changes affect northern and southern attitudes toward new territory in 1850?

13. The Kansas-Nebraska Act, 1854

In 1854, much of the territory included in the Louisiana Purchase was still unorganized. The Kansas-Nebraska Act, sponsored by Senator Stephen A. Douglas of Illinois, divided the unorganized lands into two territories. The territories could be admitted to the Union with or without slavery; the issue was to be settled by popular sovereignty.

Douglas believed that the Kansas-Nebraska Act would settle the issue of slavery peacefully. Instead, civil war broke out in Kansas. Northerners and southerners raced to Kansas to build up an antislavery or proslavery majority. Both sides organized governments and demanded recognition from Congress. After heated debate and bloodshed, Kansas was admitted in 1861 as a free state.

AREAS OPEN TO SLAVERY, 1854

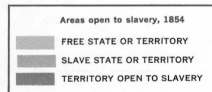

Areas open to slavery, 1854

FREE STATE OR TERRITORY

SLAVE STATE OR TERRITORY

TERRITORY OPEN TO SLAVERY

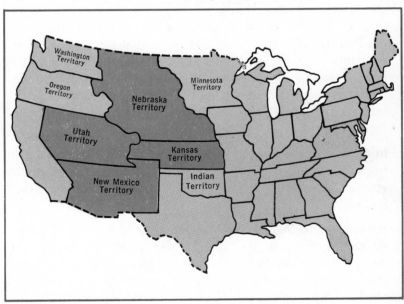

466

1. What earlier agreement dealt with slavery in the area of Kansas and Nebraska? Which section would have supported the Kansas-Nebraska Act? How would the other section react?

2. The Kansas-Nebraska Act was the last of a series of settlements concerning new territory that began in 1787. Previously the North and South had obeyed the settlements peacefully. Why do you think both sides resorted to violence in Kansas?

3. How do you think northerners and southerners would react to reports of violence against free and slave communities? How might this affect later attempts to reach peaceful agreements?

14. The Dred Scott Decision, 1857

In 1834, a slave named Dred Scott was taken by his owner from Missouri to Illinois, a free state. He remained on free soil for most of the period from 1834 to 1838. A few years after his return to Missouri, Scott sued for his freedom. He claimed that because he had lived on free soil he was a free man. The case was appealed to the Supreme Court, which ruled against Scott in 1857. The Court declared, in part, that Scott's residence on free soil did not make him a free man and that the Missouri Compromise was unconstitutional because Congress did not have the power to exclude slavery from the territories.

1. Look at the map on page 466. How would the Dred Scott decision affect Washington, Oregon, and Minnesota?

2. If you were a northerner in 1857, what trend would you see in the Kansas-Nebraska Act and the Dred Scott decision?

3. Many northerners who remained indifferent to the moral issue of slavery were angered by the Dred Scott decision. How can you explain this?

THE NEW TERRITORIES

1. In 1833, 1846, and 1857, Congress voted for lower tariffs. In 1833 and 1846, a large majority of southern congressmen supported the lower rates. In 1857, the southern vote for lower rates was unanimous. How could this voting pattern affect northern reactions to events you studied in this section?

2. In Section I, you noticed some of the differences between the North and South and the special interests of each side. Did you think that these differences, by themselves, would lead to a clash between the sections? Why?

3. Do you think the events you have just studied would lead to a clash? Why?

467

THE SLAVES: FLIGHT AND REBELLION

15. The Fugitive Slave Law of 1793

In 1793, Congress passed a law which provided that a slave-owner could recover a fugitive slave *anywhere in the country* by declaring before a judge that the slave belonged to him. The law also stated that anyone who interfered with the recapture of runaway slaves was subject to a fine of five hundred dollars.

If you were a northerner who disapproved of slavery, how would you feel about this law?

16. The Underground Railroad

Negroes and many white people who opposed slavery established a system of secret escape routes known as the Underground Railroad. Slaves from the South were guided north by Underground Railroad agents called "conductors." The "conductors" put the slaves in contact with other agents who arranged their escape to Canada. Slaves were hidden during the day in attics, cellars, and haylofts. At night, they were taken to the next "station," or home of a member of the underground. Runaway slaves often made the hazardous journey concealed in farm wagons.

UNDERGROUND RAILROAD ROUTES, 1840–1860

KEY

MAIN ROUTES OF THE
UNDERGROUND RAILROAD

● PRINCIPAL STATIONS

In addition to the routes shown here, there was a sea route from Charleston, South Carolina, to Philadelphia via the Delaware River. Other routes went from Cleveland and Sandusky to Canada.

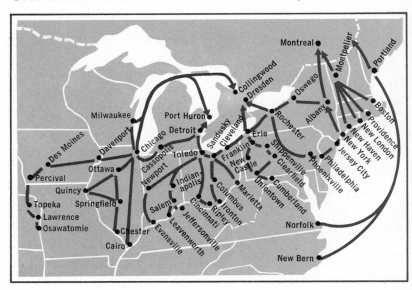

1. What would you expect southern slaveholders to think of this activity, which was mainly conducted by northerners? How would it affect southern interests?

2. How would people like John Quincy Adams be likely to regard the Underground Railroad? Do you see any problem developing? Explain.

3. Look at the map of the Underground Railroad. Did the Compromise of 1850 succeed? How can you explain this?

17. Personal Liberty Laws

Southerners sometimes employed professional slave-catchers to retrieve escaped slaves. The slave-catchers often kidnaped free northern Negroes and took them south to become slaves. Nine northern states passed personal liberty laws to meet this problem. The following is from the Massachusetts law, passed in 1855.

Any sheriff, deputy sheriff, jailer, coroner, constable or other officer of this Commonwealth, or the police of any city or town, or any district, county, city or town officer, or any officer or other member of the volunteer militia of this Commonwealth, who shall hereafter arrest, imprison, detain or return, or aid in arresting, imprisoning, detaining or returning, any person for the reason that [the said person] is claimed or adjudged to be a fugitive from service or labor, shall be punished by fine . . . and by imprisonment. . . .

The volunteer militia of the Commonwealth shall not act in any manner in the seizure, detention or rendition [return] of any person for the reason that he is claimed or adjudged to be a fugitive from service or labor. Any member of the same who shall offend against the provisions of this section shall be punished by fine . . . and by imprisonment. . . .

Acts and Resolves of the General Court of the Commonwealth of Massachusetts for the Year 1855, Chapter 489.

1. What reaction would southerners have to these laws? Would their attitude be justified? Explain.

2. Why might northern states want to pass such laws, other than to block professional slave-catchers? Would such motives be justified? Explain.

18. Slave Revolts

Many slaves did not give in quietly to their fate. There were several forms of resistance. Some threw themselves overboard from the decks of slave ships before they reached American shores. Others did as little work as possible, secretly damaged their owners' property, or escaped to the North.

The most extreme form of protest was the slave revolt. Between 1700 and 1860, there were at least one hundred revolts, most of them between 1800 and 1860. A major revolt took place in Charleston, South Carolina, in 1822. It was led by Denmark Vesey, a free Negro who organized slaves to capture the city. The revolt was betrayed by one of the participants, and thirty-seven Negroes were executed for their role in it.

The most famous revolt of all was the one that occurred in Virginia, in 1831. The leader was Nat Turner, a slave preacher who had been considered a model, obedient slave. He and his followers killed the family who owned Turner, and then, marched through the countryside encouraging others to join the revolt. The rebellion cost the lives of fifty-seven white people and about one hundred Negroes before it was put down. Many of the Negroes who lost their lives were not involved in the uprising, but were killed in the manhunt for Turner and his followers. Turner and about twenty Negroes were executed after being brought to trial.

How would southerners react to slave revolts? Why? Use the information in Section I in order to give as complete an answer as possible.

ABOLITIONISTS

19. *Uncle Tom's Cabin:* Harriet Beecher Stowe

In 1831, William Lloyd Garrison published the first issue of a newspaper called the *Liberator*. In 1833, Garrison and some sixty others met in Philadelphia to organize the National Anti-Slavery Society. There had been local antislavery societies in the United States before the 1830's, but now their number increased. Members of these societies were known as abolitionists because they wanted to abolish, or do away with, slavery. Abolitionists published newspapers and books, lectured, and participated in the activities of the Underground Railroad. They aroused opposition in the North as well as the South. Garrison was almost killed when an angry mob dragged him through the streets of Boston.

Abolitionist activity in the United States was part of a worldwide movement to end slavery. Between 1833 and 1854, slavery was abolished in the British and French colonies and in most Latin American republics. In the United States, all the northern states had ended slavery by 1804.

470

One of the most famous, influential writings about slavery is *Uncle Tom's Cabin, or Life Among the Lowly*. The author, Harriet Beecher Stowe, was the daughter of a Connecticut abolitionist minister. She based the book partly on what she had seen during a visit to a Kentucky plantation. Published in 1852, *Uncle Tom's Cabin* became a best-seller. It also became a popular play. The following selection from the book is about the death of the slave, Uncle Tom.

[Simon] Legree drew in a long breath; and, suppressing his rage, took Tom by the arm, and, approaching his face almost to his, said, in a terrible voice, "Hark'e, Tom!—ye think, 'cause I've let you off before, I don't mean what I say; but, this time, I've *made up my mind,* and counted the cost. You've always stood it out agin me: now, I'll *conquer ye or kill ye!*—one or t'other. I'll count every drop of blood there is in you, and take 'em, one by one, till ye give up!"

Tom looked up to his master, and answered, "Mas'r, if you was sick, or in trouble, or dying, and I could save ye, I'd *give ye* my heart's blood . . .

Like a strange snatch of heavenly music, heard in the lull of a tempest [storm], this burst of feeling made a moment's blank pause. Legree stood aghast, and looked at Tom; and there was such a silence that the tick of the old clock could be heard, measuring, with silent touch, the last moments of mercy . . .

It was but a moment. There was one hesitating pause . . . and the spirit of evil came back [to Simon Legree], with sevenfold vehemence; and Legree, foaming with rage, smote [struck] his victim [Tom] to the ground.

Harriet Beecher Stowe, **Uncle Tom's Cabin** (Boston: Houghton Mifflin Company, 1896), pp. 489-490.

1. How does this account of slave treatment compare with the one by Elias Horry?

2. Which account do you suppose is more reliable? Why?

3. What effect do you think Mrs. Stowe's account would have on its readers in the North? How would southerners react? Why?

20. The Slave Trade: Frederick Douglass

Before the Civil War, slaves were bought and sold in the market places of the South. Frederick Douglass was born a slave in Maryland in 1817. As a house servant, he was taught to read and write. In 1838, he escaped to the North and became an outspoken critic of slavery. He published his own newspaper and lectured as a representative of the Massachusetts Anti-Slavery

Society. The following excerpt is from a speech Douglass delivered on July 4, 1852, in Rochester, New York.

Life and Writings of Frederick Douglass, edited by Philip S. Foner (New York: International Publishers Co., Inc., 1950), Vol. II, pp. 194-195. Copyright 1950. Reprinted by permission of the publishers.

... To me the American slave trade is a terrible reality. When a child, my soul was often pierced with a sense of its horrors. I lived on Philpot Street, Fell's Point, Baltimore, and have watched from the wharves the slave ships in the Basin, anchored from the shore, with their cargoes of human flesh, waiting for favorable winds to waft them down the Chesapeake. There was, at that time, a grand slave mart kept at the head of Pratt Street, by Austin Woldfolle. His agents were sent into every town and county in Maryland, announcing their arrival, through the papers, and on flaming "*hand-bills,*" headed cash for Negroes. These men were generally well dressed men, and very captivating in their manners; ever ready to drink, to treat, and to gamble. The fate of many a slave has depended upon the turn of a single card and many a child has been snatched from the arms of its mother by bargains arranged in a state of brutal drunkenness.

The flesh-mongers gather up their victims by dozens, and drive them chained, to the general depot at Baltimore. When a sufficient number has been collected here, a ship is chartered for the purpose of conveying the forlorn crew to Mobile, or to New Orleans. . . .

In the deep, still darkness of midnight, I have been often aroused by the dead, heavy footsteps, and the piteous cries of the chained gangs that passed our door. . . .

Fellow-citizens, this murderous traffic is, to-day, in active operation in this boasted republic. In the solitude of my spirit . . . I see the bleeding footsteps; I hear the doleful [mournful] wail of fettered [chained] humanity on the way to the slave-markets, where the victims are to be sold like *horses, sheep,* and *swine,* knocked off to the highest bidder. There I see the tenderest ties ruthlessly broken, to gratify the . . . [whims and greed] of the buyers and sellers of men. My soul sickens at the sight.

1. What impression would a northern audience have about southerners after hearing Douglass' speech?

2. How does this compare with the impression of southerners created by the excerpt from *Uncle Tom's Cabin?*

3. How reliable do you think Douglass' report was? Why?

4. How would a southerner regard speeches like this?

21. John Brown's Raid, 1859

John Brown, son of an abolitionist, envisioned a plan to invade the South and free the slaves. In 1859, with financial support from abolitionists, Brown made plans to start a slave rebellion in Virginia, to establish a free state in the Appalachian Mountains, and to spread the rebellion through the South. On October 16, 1859, Brown and eighteen of his men captured the federal arsenal at Harper's Ferry, in the present state of West Virginia. Brown planned to distribute the weapons in the arsenal to slaves who joined the rebellion. However, no slaves came to Brown's aid. He and his men were captured by a force of marines. Brown was brought to trial and convicted of treason against Virginia, murder, and criminal conspiracy. He was hanged on December 2, 1859.

Do you think this attack would have a serious effect on relations between North and South? Why or why not?

CONCLUDING EXERCISE

1. In thinking about how Americans would respond to abolitionist activities, did you consider the northern and southern attitudes toward slavery that you studied in Section I? How could these attitudes influence reactions to the abolitionists?

2. Do you think the actions of the abolitionists would change the attitudes you observed in Section I? Explain.

3. Review the events in Section II. Compare the dates of these events with the dates of abolitionist activities, starting with Garrison's newspaper in 1831. How could the events have influenced reactions to the abolitionists?

THE MOOD OF THE SOUTH, 1820–1860

22. Slave Codes

All of the southern states instituted laws to govern slave life. These laws, known as slave codes, were basically the same throughout the South. Some of the laws forbade slave owners to abuse or neglect their slaves. Most of the laws, however, were for controlling and punishing slaves. A slave could not leave his owner's property without a written pass unless he was accompanied by a white person. Slaves, generally, were not allowed to work for pay, grow food and raise cattle for themselves, or buy and sell goods. They could not blow horns, beat drums, own guns, buy liquor, or meet in groups unless a white person was present.

Those who violated the law were punished severely. Whipping, branding, loss of an ear, and death were some of the penalties for running away or stealing. A slave could be executed for attempted murder, rebellion, arson, or striking a white person.

Since colonial times, slave codes had been slowly strengthened. The following chart gives examples of provisions added to the codes of six states between 1818 and 1848.

SAMPLE ADDITIONS TO SLAVE CODES, 1818–1848

LAW	STATE	YEAR
FREE NEGROES MAY NOT ENTER THE STATE.	GEORGIA	1818
	SOUTH CAROLINA	1820
	MISSISSIPPI	1822
	NORTH CAROLINA	1826
	TENNESSEE	1831
	VIRGINIA	1834
*FREE NEGROES LEAVING THE STATE MAY NOT RETURN.	SOUTH CAROLINA	1822
NEGRO SEAMEN MUST BE IMPRISONED WHILE THEIR SHIPS ARE IN PORT.	SOUTH CAROLINA	1822
SLAVES MAY NOT PREACH.	NORTH CAROLINA	1831
	VIRGINIA	1832
	GEORGIA	1833
SLAVES MAY NOT LEARN TO READ OR WRITE.	NORTH CAROLINA	1830
	VIRGINIA	1831
	SOUTH CAROLINA	1834
CIRCULATION OF ANTISLAVERY LITERATURE PROHIBITED.	NORTH CAROLINA	1830
	MISSISSIPPI	1830
	VIRGINIA	1836
DEATH PENALTY FOR ASSISTING AN ESCAPED SLAVE.	NORTH CAROLINA	1832
DEATH PENALTY FOR PUBLISHING MATERIAL THAT MAY INCITE A SLAVE REVOLT.	GEORGIA	1829
	VIRGINIA	1847–48
DEATH PENALTY FOR INCITING SLAVE REBELLION.	SOUTH CAROLINA	1822
	GEORGIA	1829
	TENNESSEE	1835
	VIRGINIA	1847

*By 1860, ten states had constitutional provisions preventing the emancipation of slaves.

1. Why do you think southern states added these laws to their slaves codes?

2. How could you check your hypothesis? Can any of the information in this unit be used as a check? If so, how?

23. The "Morality" of Slavery

The following passages are excerpts from a book written by George Fitzhugh in 1854. Fitzhugh was a lawyer and sociologist from Virginia. The opinions expressed by Fitzhugh are typical of views that first became popular in the South during the 1830's. By 1850, they had become far more prominent.

We find slavery repeatedly instituted by God, or by men acting under his immediate care and direction, as in the instances of

Arthur J. Link and Richard Leopold, **Problems in American History** (Second edition; Englewood Cliffs, N. J.: Prentice-Hall, Inc., 1957), pp. 322-323. © 1957. Reprinted by permission of Prentice-Hall, Inc.

Moses and Joshua. Nowhere in the Old or New Testament do we find the institution condemned, but frequently recognized and enforced. . . . It is probably no cause of regret that men are so constituted as to require that many should be slaves. Slavery opens many sources of happiness and . . . encourages the exercise of many virtues and affections which would be unknown without it. It begets friendly, kind and affectionate relations, just as equality engenders [causes] antagonism and hostility on all sides. . . .

An essay on the subject of slavery would be very imperfect, if it passed over without noticing . . . [the Declaration of Independence and the Virginia Bill of Rights]. The abstract principles which they enunciate [put into words], we candidly [frankly] admit, are wholly at war with slavery; we shall attempt to show that they are equally at war with all government, all subordination, all order. . . .

"Subordination," here, means obedience.

It is, we believe, conceded on all hands, that men are not born physically, morally or intellectually equal. . . . Their natural inequalities beget inequalities of rights. The weak in mind or body require guidance, support and protection; they must obey and work for those who protect and guide them. . . . Nature has made them slaves; all that law and government can do, is to regulate, modify and mitigate [soften] their slavery. In the absence of legally instituted slavery, their condition would be worse under that natural slavery of the weak to the strong, the foolish to the wise and cunning. The wise and virtuous, the brave, the strong in mind and body, are by nature born to command and protect, and law but follows nature in making them rulers, legislators, judges, captains, husbands, guardians . . . and masters. . . .

Men are not "born entitled to equal rights!" It would be far nearer the truth to say, "that some were born with saddles on their backs, and others booted and spurred to ride them,"—and the riding does them good. They need the reins, the bit and the spur. . . .

1. How does this view of slavery compare with the views expressed by James Madison and Elias Horry in the 1820's?

2. How can you explain the changes in southern opinion since the 1820's?

24. The Undebatable Issue

After the Nat Turner rebellion in 1831, the Virginia legislature moved to abolish slavery throughout the state. The proposal was

475

defeated. However, there was some feeling in favor of abolition. Out of 131 representatives, 58 wanted to end slavery.

Later on, it became much more difficult to express such opinions in the South. As you learned, views like George Fitzhugh's became widespread during the 1830's. By 1850, proslavery views were the only acceptable views a southerner could voice safely in public.

At the same time, southerners tried to prevent criticism of slavery in Congress. The issue arose when abolitionists sent petitions to Congress calling for the end of slavery and the slave trade in the District of Columbia. The flood of petitions reached a peak in 1836. The southerners reacted by passing, with the aid of northern Democrats, a "gag rule" which prevented the consideration of antislavery petitions in the House of Representatives. John Quincy Adams, as a representative from Massachusetts, led the fight to have the "gag rule" repealed. He succeeded in 1844.

1. How do you think northerners would feel about southerners suppressing criticism of slavery within the South?

2. How would northerners react to the "gag rule"? Would this issue disturb people other than abolitionists? Why or why not?

CONCLUDING EXERCISE

1. How would southern slave codes, arguments about slavery, and suppression of criticism of slavery be likely to affect northern opinions about southerners?

2. Do you think these developments would affect the reactions of northerners to abolitionist views? Explain.

3. Which of these three developments do you think the North would find most disturbing? Why?

4. During the 1840's southern congressmen pressed for the admission of Texas into the Union. They also favored war with Mexico to obtain the area from Texas to the Pacific Ocean. How might these efforts appear to northerners who had followed the developments sketched in the last three readings?

5. How could the developments described in the last three readings influence northern interpretations of other events?

THE ELECTION OF 1860

25. Abraham Lincoln: "A House Divided," 1858

Dissatisfaction with the Kansas-Nebraska Act led antislavery forces to form a new political party. The Republican party was founded

476

in 1854 and was soon running candidates for office. Abraham Lincoln ran on the Republican ticket in Illinois in the senatorial race of 1858. He opposed Stephen A. Douglas who was running for re-election. Douglas was victorious, but Lincoln emerged from the campaign a national figure. He opposed Douglas again in the Presidential election of 1860.

The following selection presents some of the views Lincoln expressed in a speech before the Republican state convention that nominated him to run for senator. During the campaign, Lincoln stressed that he opposed the extension of slavery into the territories, but that he was not an abolitionist.

The Collected Works of Abraham Lincoln, edited by Ray P. Basler (New Brunswick, N. J.: Rutgers University Press, 1953), Vol. II, pp. 461-462.

We are now far into the *fifth* year, since a policy [the Kansas-Nebraska Act] was initiated, with the *avowed* object, and *confident* promise, of putting an end to slavery agitation.

Under the operation of that policy, that agitation has not only, *not ceased,* but has *constantly augmented* [increased].

In *my* opinion, it *will* not cease, until a *crisis* shall have been reached, and passed.

"A house divided against itself cannot stand."

I believe this government cannot endure, permanently half *slave* and half *free.*

I do not expect the Union to be *dissolved*—I do not expect the house to *fall*—but I *do* expect it will cease to be divided.

It will become *all* one thing, or *all* the other.

Either the *opponents* of slavery, will arrest the further spread of it, and place it where the public mind shall rest in the belief that it is in course of ultimate extinction; or its *advocates* will push it forward, till it shall become alike lawful in *all* the States, *old* as well as *new*—*North* as well as *South.*

1. What is Lincoln's position regarding the problems you have seen developing over slavery?

2. What would be the attitude of each section toward his ideas?

26. The Election Returns, 1860

In the Presidential election of 1860, the Democratic party was split. One group of Democrats, mostly southerners, nominated John C. Breckinridge of Kentucky. They called for support of slavery in the territories. The northern Democrats nominated Stephen A. Douglas. They emphasized that the issue of slavery in the territories should be decided by popular sovereignty.

The Republicans were united behind Abraham Lincoln. They opposed slavery in the territories, but did not call for interference with slavery in the states. They also supported a protective tariff.

A new political party, the Constitutional Union party, also entered the race in 1860. They nominated John Bell of Tennessee and called for support of the Constitution. Their platform did not mention slavery.

The following map shows the results of the election of 1860. The numbers on the map indicate electoral votes. In the popular vote, Douglas had about 500,000 votes less than Lincoln.

RESULTS OF THE ELECTION OF 1860

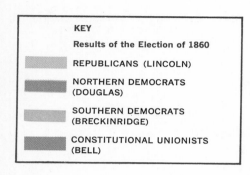

KEY

Results of the Election of 1860

REPUBLICANS (LINCOLN)

NORTHERN DEMOCRATS (DOUGLAS)

SOUTHERN DEMOCRATS (BRECKINRIDGE)

CONSTITUTIONAL UNIONISTS (BELL)

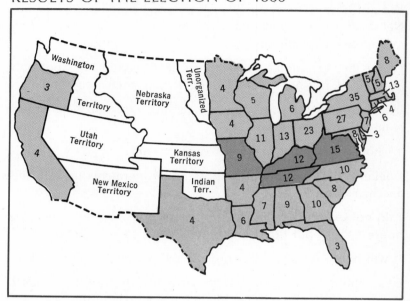

1. What does the election show about the mood of each section?

2. How could you explain the results of this election in terms of events you studied in this section?

3. What effects would you expect this election to have? Why?

AN UNAVOIDABLE CONFLICT?

1. In 1861, the Civil War began. What do you think caused it?

2. Did you think that the differences between North and South outlined in Section I made war inevitable? Why or why not?

3. Do you think that any of the events described in this section made war inevitable? Explain.

4. What relationship, if any, do you see between the different sectional interests suggested in Section I and the events described in Section II?

478

THE SOUTH STATES ITS CASE

27. "We All Support Slavery"

In this section, you will examine first the views of southerners, and then the views of northerners about the issues you have studied so far. The following selection is from a speech by Albert Gallatin Brown, a Democratic senator from Mississippi. Brown was a prominent spokesman for the southern position. In 1856, he replied to a speech by Senator William H. Seward of New York. Seward had suggested that the non-slaveholders of the South might turn against a system which was advantageous only to the wealthy and aristocratic.

POINTS TO CONSIDER
What interests southerners wished to safeguard.
Why southerners felt these interests could not be preserved within the Union.
How widespread such feelings were in the South.
How the events of 1800–1860 could have contributed to such feelings.

There are three hundred and fifty thousand slaveholding aristocrats in the South, says the senator—men at war with liberty, and dangerous to the republic. They are only one in one hundred of the entire population; or if you add, he says, "the children, relatives, and dependants, they are one in fifteen;" consequently fourteen parts out of every fifteen of the entire population have no interest in slavery. They are, as he seems to conclude, mere hewers [cutters] of wood and drawers of water to the slaveholding aristocrats.

...If he [Seward] expects, by appeals like these, to turn the hearts of the non-slaveholders of the South against slavery, he will miss his aim. They may have no pecuniary interest in slavery, but they have a social interest at stake that is worth more to them than all the wealth of all the Indies. Suppose the senator shall succeed in his ideas of universal abolition—what is to be the social condition of the races in the South? Can they live together in peace? No one pretends to think they can. Will the white man be allowed to maintain his superiority there? Let us examine this proposition. There are in my state about three hundred and fifty thousand whites, and about an equal number of blacks. Suppose the negroes were all set free. What would be the immediate and necessary consequence? A struggle for the supremacy would instantly ensue [follow]. White immigration to the state would cease of course. The whites already there would have but little motive to struggle in the maintenance of the unequal contest

III. The Views on Both Sides

David M. Potter and Thomas G. Manning, **Nationalism and Sectionalism in America, 1775-1877** (New York: Holt, Rinehart and Winston, Inc., 1961), p. 177. Copyright 1949 by Holt, Rinehart and Winston, Inc. Reprinted by permission of the publisher.

A "pecuniary interest" involves money.

between the blacks and their millions of sympathizing friends in the free states. The consequence would be that the men of fortune would gather up their transferable property, and seek a home in some other country. The poor men—those of little means—the very men on whom the senator relies to aid him in carrying out his great scheme of emancipation, would alone be compelled to remain: their poverty, and not their will, would compel them to remain. In the course of a few years, with no one going to the state, and thousands on thousands leaving it in one constant stream, the present equilibrium [balance] between the races would be lost. In a few years, the disparity [inequality] would probably be some three, four, or five to one in favor of the blacks. In this state of things, it is not difficult to see what would be the white man's condition. If he should be allowed to maintain his equality he might think himself fortunate; superiority would be a thing not to be dreamed of. The negroes being vastly in the majority, would probably claim the ascendency [superior position] in the social, and in all other circles. If the white man, reduced to such a condition, were allowed to marry his sons to negro wives, or his daughters to negro husbands, he might bless his stars. If the senator from New York expects the aid of non-slaveholders in the South in bringing about this state of social relations, let me tell him he is greatly mistaken.

1. According to Brown, what would a non-slaveholder have to fear from abolition?

2. Considering the information on population that you studied in Section I (pages 456–457), how valid do you think Brown's population figures are?

3. Brown professes to speak for most of the people of the South. Do you think he probably *did* speak for them? Why or why not? How would you go about finding out whether he has represented their views accurately?

28. The Threat from Northern Politicians

By the 1850's, various political groups had formed in the North to challenge the expansion of slavery. The Free-Soil party, organized in 1848, was one such group. Jefferson Davis stated the southern position in an attack on the Free-Soil party. Davis, a planter and political leader from Mississippi, became president of the Confederate States of America, the government formed by the states that withdrew from the Union.

What do you propose, gentlemen of the Free-Soil Party? Do you propose to better the condition of the slave? Not at all. What

Charles A. and Mary R. Beard, **The Rise of the Industrial Era** (New York: The Macmillan Company, 1933), Vol. II, pp. 5-6. Copyright 1933 by The Macmillan Company, copyright renewed 1961 by William Beard and Miriam Beard Vagts. Reprinted by permission of the publisher.

then do you propose? You may say you are opposed to the expansion of slavery . . . Is the slave to be benefited by it? Not at all. It is not humanity that influences you in the position which you now occupy before the country . . . It is that you may have an opportunity of cheating us that you may have a majority in the Congress of the United States and convert the Government into an engine of northern aggrandizement. It is that your section may grow in power and prosperity upon treasures unjustly taken from the South, like the vampire bloated and gorged [stuffed] with the blood which it has secretly sucked from its victims . . . You desire to weaken the political power of the southern states; and why? Because you want, by an unjust system of legislation, to promote the industry of the New England states, at the expense of the people of the South and their industry.

"Aggrandizement" is the acquisition of great power, wealth, etc.

1. What does Davis claim is the real reason for northern opposition to the expansion of slavery?

2. What southern interest, in particular, does Davis feel that the Free-Soil party threatens?

3. Are there any facts about the North and South in the 1850's that could have fed Davis' suspicions? Explain.

29. The Trouble with Union

Some southern congressmen continued to attend meetings of Congress after their states had seceded, or withdrawn, from the Union. Senator Louis T. Wigfall from Texas made the following speech in the Senate in March 1861. Although this speech was made after most of the South had seceded, it represents ideas frequently expressed before secession.

This Federal Government is dead. The only question is whether we will give it a decent, peaceable . . . burial . . .

American History Told by Contemporaries, edited by Albert Bushnell Hart (New York: The Macmillan Company, 1901), Vol. IV, pp. 172, 174-175.

I owe my allegiance—and Senators are not mistaken about that, for I have said it frequently—to the State which I here represent. I do not owe my allegiance to this Government. . . . Your President elect [Lincoln], a short time ago, in a speech, asked the question gravely, what is the difference between a State and a county? And he seemed to be really in quest of information. Now, I was not astonished at that, for I did not expect anything better of him. From a man who is taken up because he is an ex-rail splitter, an ex-grocery keeper, an ex-flatboat captain, and an ex-Abolition lecturer, and is run upon that question, I would not expect any great information as to the Government which he was to administer. . . .

Senator Wigfall was a "fire eater." This name was given to the southern politicians who were most extreme in their hostility toward the North and toward antislavery agitation.

"Sovereignty" means independent power.

A "husting" is a place where political speeches are made.

[A] party has come into power that represents the antagonism to my own section of the country. It represents two million men who hate us, and who, by their votes for such a man as they have elected, have committed an overt act of hostility.... Our objection to living in this Union, and therefore the difficulty of reconstructing it, is not your personal liberty bill, not the territorial question, but that you utterly and wholly misapprehend [misunderstand] the form of government. You deny the sovereignty of the States; you deny the right of self-government in the people; you insist upon negro equality; your people interfere impertinently with our institutions and attempt to subvert them; you publish newspapers; you deliver lectures; you print pamphlets, and you send them among us, first, to excite our slaves to insurrection against their masters, and next, to array [organize] one class of citizens against the other; and I say to you that we cannot live in peace, either in the Union or out of it, until you have abolished your Abolition societies; not, as I have been misquoted, abolish or destroy your schoolhouses; but until you have ceased in your schoolhouses teaching your children to hate us; until you have ceased to convert your pulpits into hustings; until you content yourselves with preaching Christ, and Him crucified, and not delivering political harangues [speeches] on the Sabbath; until you have ceased inciting your own citizens to make raids and commit robberies; until you have done these things we cannot live in the same Union with you. Until you do these things, we cannot live out of the Union at peace....

1. Wigfall presents a long list of objections to living in the Union. How could you summarize this list? What does Wigfall think is at stake?

2. How does Wigfall's view of northern intentions toward the South compare with the views of Brown and Davis?

3. How could specific events in the period 1800–1860 have led Wigfall to these opinions?

30. A Loss of Faith

Despair gripped many southerners when Abraham Lincoln won the Presidential election of 1860. Many turned to secession as the only course open to them. The first of the following selections is from an address issued by a group of southern congressmen to their constituents on December 13, 1860. The second is a statement by David F. Jamison, president of the special convention called by the South Carolina legislature to consider secession. South Carolina seceded on December 20, 1860. It was the first state to withdraw from the Union.

SOUTHERN CONGRESSMEN ADDRESS THEIR PEOPLE

The argument is exhausted. All hope of relief in the Union, through the agency of committees, Congressional legislation, or constitutional amendments, is extinguished, and we trust the South will not be deceived by appearances or the pretence of new guarantees. The Republicans are resolute in the purpose to grant nothing that will or ought to satisfy the South. We are satisfied the honor, safety, and independence of the Southern people are to be found only in a Southern Confederacy—a result to be obtained only by separate State secession—and that the sole and primary aim of each slaveholding State ought to be its speedy and absolute separation from an unnatural and hostile Union.

J. G. Randall and David Donald, **The Civil War and Reconstruction** (Second edition; Boston: D. C. Heath and Company, 1961), p. 148.

Several congressional committees were trying to head off secession by finding ways to compromise. But many Republicans and southerners opposed compromise.

A SPOKESMAN FOR SOUTH CAROLINA

Written Constitutions are worthless unless they are written at the same time in the hearts, and founded on the interests of a people; and there is no common bond of sympathy between the North and the South. All efforts to preserve this Union will not only be fruitless, but fatal to the less numerous section. . . .

Rollin Gustav Osterweis, **Romanticism and Nationalism in the Old South** (New Haven: Yale University Press, 1949), p. 150.

1. Why did these southerners feel they could no longer preserve their interests within the Union?

2. Which events might have led them to this belief?

31. The South Decides

By February 1, 1861, six states of the lower South had followed South Carolina in seceding from the Union. These states, in order of secession, were: Mississippi, Florida, Alabama, Georgia, Louisiana, and Texas.

As the states seceded from the Union, their troops occupied federal forts and navy yards located within their borders. However, the federal government retained control of Fort Sumter, at Charleston, South Carolina. Southern troops surrounded the fort, but did not attack it. In April 1861, Lincoln notified South Carolina that an expedition was on its way with provisions for the soldiers of the fort. The Confederate forces feared that Lincoln was also sending reinforcements. They demanded the surrender of the fort. When the fort was not surrendered, the Confederate troops opened fire. The northern forces returned the fire. The Civil War was under way. Fort Sumter was taken by the Confederate forces on April 13, 1861.

Virginia, the first of the four states of the upper South to secede, withdrew from the Union on April 17, 1861. As recently as April 4, secession had been voted down in Virginia. By May 20, 1861,

Arkansas, Tennessee, and North Carolina had also seceded. Tennessee, like Virginia, had previously rejected secession.

The following map shows the results of the final vote on secession in the eleven southern states. The selection that follows the map is an editorial from the Charlottesville, Virginia, *Review*, of January 4, 1861. The views in this article are representative of those expressed in the four states of the upper South.

THE VOTE ON SECESSION

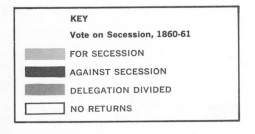

KEY

Vote on Secession, 1860-61

- FOR SECESSION
- AGAINST SECESSION
- DELEGATION DIVIDED
- NO RETURNS

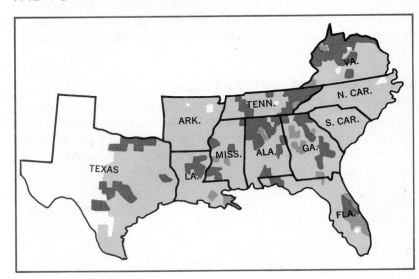

1. Was secession a unanimous decision? How can you explain this? What information from other sections of this unit might help you to answer this question?

2. How could you use this map to test the accuracy of the statement by Brown? (See pages 479–480.)

AN EDITORIAL FROM A STATE OF THE UPPER SOUTH

So important do we regard the Union, so much do we cherish it, that the pulling down of its splendid columns is to us like the fall of the paternal walls and roof, and the demolition [destruction] of all the most endearing emblems of home. We know that we shall never find any other such country. We know that we shall never see any other such flag. We know we shall never stand up as proudly and as exultant [joyously] under any other nationality.

Therefore . . . we entertain towards South Carolina the most bitter resentment. We feel that she has not only precipitately [reck-

Editorial from Charlottesville **Review**, reprinted in **Southern Editorials on Secession**, edited by Dwight L. Dumond (Washington, D. C.: American Historical Association, 1931), pp. 388-389. Copyright 1931 by the American Historical Association, copyright renewed 1959 by Dwight L. Dumond. Reprinted by permission of the publisher.

lessly] thrown down the bulwarks of the Union ... but she has done so with the full knowledge—aye, the intention—to hold Virginia and the border States between her and the Storm ...

But—however it has been done—an issue has been made. The subjection [conquest] of South Carolina or any seceding State ... is a blow at the entire South—subjection to all. We are, thenceforth, humiliated. We are conquered. We could not hold up our heads in that Union any more ...

Our fellow-countrymen at the North can undertake to preserve this Union with the sword, if they shall deem it wise. ... The naked fact is, that ... upon any display of force ... every [southern] sword will leap from its scabbard from the mouth of the Susquehanna to ... the Mississippi.

1. How does this writer feel about the Union?

2. Would he have the same reasons for separation from the Union as the spokesmen for the South you encountered in Reading 30? Explain.

3. How would you evaluate Brown's statement after looking at the map and editorial? Is it likely that his statement is all true? Completely inaccurate? Explain.

32. "The Bonnie Blue Flag"

Many songs came out of the Civil War. The following selection is one that southern soldiers often sang as they marched to battle. Some of the verses, praising each state that had joined the Confederacy, have not been included.

We are a band of brothers, and native to our soil,
Fighting for our liberty, with treasure blood and toil;
And when our rights were threatened, the cry rose near and far:
Hurrah for the Bonnie Blue Flag that bears a single star!

(Chorus) Hurrah! Hurrah! For Southern rights, hurrah!
Hurrah for the Bonnie Blue Flag that bears a single star.

Then here's to our Confederacy, strong we are and brave,
Like patriots of old we'll fight, our heritage to save;
And rather than submit to shame, to die we would prefer,
So cheer for the Bonnie Blue Flag that bears a single star.

1. How does this song reflect the southern position?

2. Does this song add anything to your views about popular support for war in the South? Explain.

Songs of the Civil War, edited by Irwin Sibler (New York: Columbia University Press, 1960), pp. 65-67. Slightly adapted. Reprinted by permission of the publisher.

WHY STUDY VIEWS?

1. Has anything in this section changed your ideas about the causes of the Civil War? Explain.

2. Is it necessary to examine materials like the ones in this section in order to understand why a war takes place? Or is it enough to study differences between the two sides, as you did in Section I, and events leading to the war, as you did in Section II? Give reasons for your answers.

THE NORTH'S POSITION

33. "We Are All Abolitionists"

How did northerners view southern interests and attitudes? Over which issues were northerners willing to fight? The rest of this section deals with the issues dividing the North and South, as seen from northern points of view.

The following reading is taken from a speech made in New York by William Lloyd Garrison. Garrison was considered the foremost leader of the abolitionist cause in America. (See page 470.) In his speech, Garrison presents an interpretation of northern feelings about slavery. The views on which Garrison comments were substantially the same before the war as they were in 1862, when he gave the speech.

The Patriotic Speaker, edited by Robert R. Raymond (New York: A. S. Barnes & Burr, 1864), pp. 209-210.

I know that to be an abolitionist is not to be with the multitude —on the side of the majority—in a popular and respectable position; and yet I think I have a right to ask of you . . . why it is . . . that, while you profess to be opposed to slavery, you nevertheless desire the whole world to understand that you are not radical abolitionists? . . . Why are you not all abolitionists? Your principles are mine. What you have taught me, I adopt. What you have taken a solemn oath to support, as essential to a free government, I recognize as right and just. The people of this State profess to believe in the Declaration of Independence. That is my abolitionism. Every man, therefore, who disclaims abolitionism, repudiates the Declaration of Independence. Does he not? "All men are created equal, and endowed by their Creator with an inalienable right to liberty." Gentlemen, that is my fanaticism—that is all my fanaticism. All I ask is, that this declaration may be carried out everywhere in our country and throughout the world. It belongs to mankind. Your Constitution is an abolition Constitution. Your laws are abolition laws. Your institutions are abolition institutions. Your free schools are abolition schools. I believe in them all; and all that I ask is, that institutions so good, so free, so noble, may be everywhere propagated [spread], everywhere accepted. And thus it is that I desire, not to curse the South, or any portion of her people, but to bless her abundantly, by abolishing her infamous and demoralizing slave institution, and erecting the temple of liberty on the ruins thereof. . . .

We profess to be Christians. Christianity—its object is to redeem, not to enslave men! Christ is our Redeemer. I believe in Him. He leads the anti-slavery cause, and always has led it. The Gospel is the Gospel of freedom; and any man claiming to be a Christian, and to have within him the same mind that was in Christ Jesus, and yet dares to hold his fellow-man in bondage, as a mere piece of perishable property, is recreant [unfaithful] to all the principles and obligations of Christianity. . . .

1. What does Garrison reveal about the actual attitude of most northerners toward the abolitionist cause?

2. Why does Garrison say to his audience, "Your principles are mine"? Do you suppose he was right? Do you think that speeches like this would change the attitude of northerners toward abolition? Explain.

3. Review the speeches by senators Brown and Wigfall at the beginning of this section. How do you evaluate them now?

4. Suppose that Senator Brown was correct in evaluating southern opinion, and that Garrison was correct about the basic feelings of most northerners. How would this affect the ability of the sections to avoid war?

34. The Threat from Slaveholders

William H. Seward of New York, a senator from 1849 to 1861, was one of the principal antislavery spokesmen in Congress. When the Republican party was organized in 1854, he soon became one of its leaders. He made the following speech in Michigan in 1856. At this time, 15 out of 62 senators were Republicans. In the House of Representatives, Republicans controlled 108 seats out of 234.

. . . [The] slaveholding class of the American people is systematically and successfully perverting [misusing] the administration of the government, especially in regard to the territories, so as to change the constitution and endanger the stability, welfare and liberty of the Union. . . .

. . . This class spreads . . . from the banks of the Delaware to those of the Rio Grande. . . . [It] has become the governing power in each of the slaveholding states, and it practically chooses thirty of the sixty-two members of the senate, ninety of the two hundred

The Works of William H. Seward, edited by George E. Baker (Boston: Houghton Mifflin Company, 1884), Vol. IV, pp. 253, 257-258, 265, 272.

and thirty-three members of the house of representatives, and one hundred and five of the two hundred and ninety-five electors of president and vice-president of the United States. . . .

. . . The [supreme] court consists of a chief justice and eight associate justices. Of these, five were called from slave states, and four from free states. . . .

Perhaps you expect the slaveholding class will abate [reduce] its [ambition] . . . How long, and with what success, have you waited already for that reformation? Did any property class ever so reform itself? . . . Does the slaveholding class even seek to beguile [tempt] you with such a hope? Has it not become [greedy], arrogant, defiant? . . .

1. Why does Seward talk about matters like the number of southerners in Congress? What point is he trying to make?

2. What did Seward mean by saying that a "reformation" of the slaveholding class would never occur?

3. How could you summarize his views of the slaveholders' aims?

4. What events might have led Seward to these opinions?

5. How does Seward's view of southern intentions compare with Davis' and Wigfall's views of northern intentions?

35. The Need for Union

When Lincoln became President, he appointed Seward Secretary of State. Seward made the following speech in 1861 after several states had seceded from the Union. His ideas are representative of those expressed by most Republicans.

The Patriotic Speaker, edited by Robert R. Raymond (A. S. Barnes & Burr, 1864), pp. 104-105.

A "confederacy" is a league or union of states. It implies a looser union than that formed under a federal government.

Dissolution would not only arrest, but extinguish the greatness of our country. Even if separate confederacies could exist and endure, they could severally [separately] preserve no share of the common *prestige* of the Union. . . . Nor will great achievements be possible for the new confederacies. . . . No petty confederacy that shall follow the United States can prolong, or even renew, the majestic drama of national progress. . . .

The public prosperity! how could it survive the storm? Its elements are industry in the culture of every fruit; mining of all the metals; commerce at home and on every sea; material improvement that knows no obstacle and has no end; invention that ranges throughout the domain of nature; increase of knowledge as broad as the human mind can explore; perfection of art as high as human genius can reach; and social refinement working for the renovation [renewal] of the world. How could our successors prosecute these noble objects in the midst of brutalizing civil conflict? . . . What leisure will the citizen find for study or invention, or art, under the reign of conscription; nay, what interest in them will society feel when fear and hate shall have taken possession of the national mind? Let the miner in California take heed; for its golden wealth will become the prize of the nation that can command the most iron. Let the borderer [frontiersman] take care; for the Indian will again lurk around his dwelling. Let the pioneer come back into our denser settlements; for the railroad, the post-road, and the telegraph, advance not one furlong farther into the wilderness. With standing armies consuming the substance of our people on the land, and our navy and our postal steamers withdrawn from the ocean, who will protect or respect, or who will even know by name our petty confederacies? The American man-of-war is a noble spectacle. I have seen it enter an ancient port in the Mediterranean. All the world wondered at it, and talked of it. Salvos [volleys] of artillery, from forts and shipping in the harbor, saluted its flag. Princes and princesses and merchants paid it homage, and all the people blessed it as a harbinger [messenger] of hope for their own ultimate freedom. I imagine now the same noble vessel again entering the same haven. The flag of thirty-three stars and thirteen stripes has been hauled down, and in its place a signal is run up, which flaunts [shows] the device of a lone star or a palmetto tree. Men ask, "Who is the stranger that thus steals into our waters?" The answer contemptuously given is, "She comes from one of the obscure republics of North America. Let her pass on."

To "prosecute an object," here, means to work toward a goal.

"Conscription" is another term for "draft," a law requiring men to perform military service.

A "furlong" is a measure of distance equal to 1/8 of a mile.

The "palmetto," a kind of palm tree, is the state emblem of South Carolina.

1. What is Seward's main idea here?

2. Judging from this speech, do you think Seward would be willing to compromise with the southern states? Explain. How does Seward's attitude here compare with his former attitude?

3. Does this comparison have any effect on your view of the causes of the Civil War?

4. How does Seward's attitude toward union compare with the attitudes of some of the southern congressmen you studied?

36. Grounds for Faith

As you learned earlier, many southerners lost faith in the Union when the Republicans were victorious in the Presidential election of 1860. In response, a concerned North tried to restore southern confidence. Two attempts to reassure the South are presented in this reading. The first attempt was a constitutional amendment considered by Congress in December 1860, the month following the election. At the time, South Carolina had already seceded. By March 2, 1861, the amendment had passed both houses of Congress with the two-thirds vote required for its adoption. If ratified by three-fourths of the states, it would have become part of the Constitution. The second attempt at reassurance was a passage in Lincoln's first inaugural address, delivered on March 4, 1861. By then, seven southern states had seceded and formed the beginnings of the Confederate States of America.

A PROPOSED CONSTITUTIONAL AMENDMENT

No Amendment shall be made to the Constitution which will authorize or give the Congress the power to abolish or interfere, within any State, with the domestic institutions thereof, including that of persons held to labor or service by the laws of said State.

What did this proposed amendment prohibit?

LINCOLN'S FIRST INAUGURAL ADDRESS

That there are persons in one section, or another who seek to destroy the Union at all events, and are glad of any pretext [excuse] to do it, I will neither affirm or deny; but if there be such, I need address no word to them. To those, however, who really love the Union, may I not speak? . . .

Physically speaking, we cannot separate. We cannot remove our respective sections from each other, nor build an impassable wall between them. A husband and wife may be divorced, and go out of the presence, and beyond the reach of each other; but the different parts of our country cannot do this. They cannot but remain face to face; and intercourse [association], either amicable [friendly] or hostile, must continue between them. Is it possible then to make that intercourse more advantageous, or more satisfactory, *after* separation than *before*? Can aliens make treaties easier than friends can make laws? Can treaties be more faithfully enforced between aliens, than laws can among friends? Suppose you go to war, you cannot fight always; and when, after much loss on both sides, and no gain on either, you cease fighting, the identical old questions, as to terms of intercourse, are again upon you.

This country, with its institutions, belongs to the people who inhabit. it. Whenever they shall grow weary of the existing government, they can exercise their *constitutional* right of amending it, or their *revolutionary* right to dismember, or overthrow it. . . .

By the frame of the government under which we live, this same

The Collected Works of Abraham Lincoln, edited by Ray P. Basler (New Brunswick, N. J.: Rutgers University Press, 1953), Vol. IV, pp. 266, 269-271.

people have wisely given their public servants but little power for mischief; and have, with equal wisdom, provided for the return of that little [power] to their own hands at very short intervals.

While the people retain their virtue, and vigilance, no administration, by any extreme of wickedness or folly, can very seriously injure the government, in the short space of four years. . . .

In *your* hands, my dissatisfied fellow countrymen, and not in *mine,* is the momentous issue of civil war. The government will not assail [attack] *you.* You can have no conflict, without being yourselves the aggressors. *You* have no oath registered in Heaven to destroy the government, while *I* shall have the most solemn one to "preserve, protect and defend" it.

I am loth [reluctant] to close [end this speech]. We are not enemies, but friends. We must not be enemies. Though passion may have strained, it must not break our bonds of affection. The mystic chords of memory, stretching from every battle-field, and patriot grave, to every living heart and hearthstone, all over this broad land, will yet swell the chorus of the Union, when again touched, as surely they will be, by the better angels of our nature.

1. Judging from these two documents, what was the official attitude of the United States government toward the existence of slavery?

2. What different reasons does Lincoln give the South for staying in the Union?

3. Review the southern objections to the Union on pages 481–483. Do you think the actions of Lincoln and Congress adequately meet these objections?

4. On March 11, 1861, seven days after Lincoln's speech, the Confederate States of America adopted a permanent constitution. How can you explain the failure of Lincoln and Congress to preserve the Union?

37. Some Grass Roots Opinions

The next two selections are examples of public opinion in the North. The first is an excerpt from a letter written in 1835 by John Jones, a resident of Glasgow, Kentucky. Although Kentucky was a slave state, it sided with the North in the Civil War. Jones wrote to James G. Birney, an abolitionist who ran for President in 1840 and again in 1844 on an antislavery platform. Birney had been a slaveholder, but had freed his slaves in the 1830's. The second selection is an editorial from the Concord, New Hampshire, *Patriot and State Gazette,* published on May 8, 1861.

Letter by John Jones to James G. Birney, July 25, 1935, reprinted in **Letters of James Gillespie Birney,** edited by Dwight L. Dumond (Washington, D. C.: American Historical Association, 1938), Vol. I, pp. 183-184, 223-224. Copyright 1938 by the American Historical Association. Reprinted by permission of the publisher.

The American Colonization Society was founded in 1817 to return free Negroes to Africa. Comparatively few Negroes were deported.

Editorial from **New Hampshire Patriot and State Gazette,** reprinted in **Northern Editorials on Secession,** edited by Howard C. Perkins (Washington, D. C.: American Historical Association, 1942), Vol. II, p. 830. Copyright 1942 by the American Historical Association. Reprinted by permission of the publisher.

FREEDOM NOW?: OPINION IN KENTUCKY, 1835

The principle of immediate emancipation is very unpopular: the great Bugbear. Ask the questions: Is not slavery wrong? "Granted." Is it not a very great sin against God, and contrary to every precept of the Gospel of Christ? "Admitted." Is it not at variance with the genius of our Civil Institutions, and a reproach to our nation? "Certainly." Is it not an evil of a destructive character, and is it not growing upon us? "We think so." Ought we not to get rid of this evil? "Certainly." As it has become evident that delay is dangerous ought we not to act efficiently, and immediately emancipate the slaves? "No we cannot agree to that. If some way could be contrived [devised] for sending them all out of our country, we would be glad to see them free; not otherwise." Would not that be cruel? . . . "It would seem [so; but] set them free, and there would immediately commence such scenes of house burning, housebreaking, stealing, robbing, throatcutting, headbreaking, stonethrowing, brickbatting, etc. etc. as was never heard of before. . . . [Sir], we must confess this [idea of freeing the slaves] looks reasonable; but we have an unconquerable aversion [dislike] to having the negroes free among us."

A REASON FOR WAR: OPINION IN NEW HAMPSHIRE, 1861

The course of a portion of the republican papers and their pulpit orators has raised a vitally important question as to the object and purpose of the war. . . . That question is this: Is this a war in support of the Government, the Constitution, the Union, and the dearly-purchased rights of a free people, or a negro crusade for the abolition of slavery? . . . [There] is no question that the great mass of [the people] have responded to the summons to war with the distinct understanding that they were called upon to *preserve* national institutions and constitutional privileges, and not to *destroy* them—to sustain and perpetuate the Constitution and the Union, to uphold the Government, and to put down armed rebellion seeking their overthrow.

If such is the real . . . purpose of the war, it must and will be cordially supported . . . by the united people of the North; but if it is an abolition crusade, designed to destroy the rights and institutions of the South recognized by the Constitution, then it is a wicked and treasonable war and will not be participated in by any man who loves the old Union, reveres the Constitution and has a patriot's devotion to the Government and flag of our country.

We do not doubt that the President and his constitutional advisers entered upon this great contest with a single view to [maintaining] the integrity of the Union, the authority of the Government, the

492

perpetuity [continuation] of the Constitution, the honor, rights, welfare and glory of the country, its flag and its people; and those who now seek to give it a different direction and purpose, have no countenance [support] from those in authority.

1. What do these samples of popular feeling in the North show about some northerners' attitudes toward slavery? Was Garrison right when he said that northerners' principles were the same as his?

2. On the basis of these two statements, what hypothesis could you form about northerners' reasons for supporting the Civil War? What specific information would help you to form a more definite conclusion?

3. How does the New Hampshire editorial compare with the Charlottesville, Virginia, editorial? (See pages 484–485.) Does this influence your view of the causes of the war? Explain.

38. "Rally Around the Cause, Boys"

The following selection is an example of the songs that northern troops sang during the Civil War.

We will rally around the cause, boys, we'll rally in our might
Singing the holy cause of freemen.
We will battle for our Union the sacred cause of right
Singing the holy cause of freemen.

(Chorus) For Lincoln and Johnson huzza, boys, huzza.
Down with rebellion and on with the war.
While we rally round the cause, boys, we'll rally in our might
Singing the holy cause of freemen.

To reunite the states we have got a General Grant
Singing the holy cause of freemen.
We are sick of cries for peace and other rebel cant,
Singing the holy cause of freemen. . . .

The Union Sundered [Record no. 5; supplement to "Life History of the United States" (New York: Time, Inc., 1964)].

Andrew Johnson was Lincoln's Vice-President.

"Cant" is whining speech.

How does this song affect your view of the reasons the North had for supporting the Civil War?

FACTS AND OPINIONS

1. Define the terms "fact" and "opinion."

2. What examples can you give of facts? Why are they facts?

3. Do you have any opinions? What are they? Why are they opinions?

493

4. Is there any reason to distinguish between fact and opinion? Why?

5. What parts of the statements by southerners and northerners that you have just studied are fact and what parts are opinion? What effect does this have on the way you use them in forming your own hypothesis?

6. Could opinion have anything to do with causing a war? Explain.

THE CAUSES OF THE WAR

1. For what cause were most northerners willing to go to war?

2. At what point in the period leading to war did this issue become important?

3. Would you say that the South's threat to this concern was the major reason for the war? Why or why not?

AN UNAVOIDABLE CONFLICT?: REVIEWING THE QUESTION

1. Did you think that war between the North and South was inevitable because of the differences between the two sections? Did you think that the events of the period 1800–1860 made war inevitable? Have you changed your mind? Why or why not?

2. Do you think that the Civil War could have been prevented at any point? If so, how? If not, why not?

IV. The War

39. Events of the War

Up to this point you have been concentrating on causes of the Civil War. Now you will examine some events of the war. Follow the events on the map showing the sites of major battles.

MAJOR EVENTS OF THE CIVIL WAR	
1861	
FEBRUARY 4	MISSISSIPPI, FLORIDA, ALABAMA, GEORGIA, LOUISIANA, AND TEXAS JOIN SOUTH CAROLINA TO FORM THE CONFEDERATE STATES OF AMERICA (CSA).
MARCH 4	ABRAHAM LINCOLN INAUGURATED PRESIDENT.
APRIL 4	LINCOLN DECIDES TO HOLD FORT SUMTER IN SOUTH CAROLINA. CONFEDERATE TROOPS HAVE ALREADY SEIZED MOST OF THE FEDERAL PROPERTY IN SOUTHERN STATES.
APRIL 12	GENERAL PIERRE BEAUREGARD (CSA) ORDERS FORT SUMTER TO SURRENDER AND, UPON ITS REFUSAL, OPENS FIRE.

APRIL 13	FORT SUMTER IS SURRENDERED.
APRIL 15	LINCOLN CALLS FOR 75,000 VOLUNTEERS.
APRIL 17	VIRGINIA SECEDES, BUT WESTERN COUNTIES REMAIN LOYAL TO THE UNION.
APRIL 19	LINCOLN ORDERS ALL SOUTHERN PORTS BLOCKADED.
MAY	ARKANSAS, TENNESSEE, AND NORTH CAROLINA SECEDE. RICHMOND, VIRGINIA, BECOMES THE CAPITAL OF THE CONFEDERACY.
JULY 21	NORTHERN TROOPS DEFEATED AT MANASSAS JUNCTION NEAR BULL RUN CREEK. THEY RETREAT IN CHAOS TO WASHINGTON, D. C.
AUGUST– DECEMBER	THE UNION FORCES CONCENTRATE ON TRAINING.
1862 FEBRUARY 16	GENERAL ULYSSES GRANT (USA) CAPTURES FORT DONELSON ON THE CUMBERLAND RIVER. HE DEMANDS, "NO TERMS BUT UNCONDITIONAL AND IMMEDIATE SURRENDER."
MARCH 9	THE FIRST BATTLE BETWEEN IRONCLAD SHIPS, THE U.S. MONITOR AND THE CONFEDERATE VIRGINIA (MERRIMAC), ENDS IN A DRAW.
APRIL 6–7	GRANT DEFEATS THE CONFEDERATE FORCES UNDER GENERAL ALBERT JOHNSTON (CSA) AT SHILOH, ON THE TENNESSEE RIVER.
APRIL 16	THE CONFEDERACY MAKES WHITE MEN 18–35 YEARS OLD LIABLE FOR MILITARY SERVICE; ALTHOUGH MEN IN CERTAIN OCCUPATIONS ARE EXEMPT, AND DRAFTED MEN CAN HIRE SUBSTITUTES.
APRIL 25	ADMIRAL DAVID FARRAGUT (USA) CAPTURES THE SOUTH'S LARGEST CITY, NEW ORLEANS.
JUNE 25	CONFEDERATE TROOPS ENGAGE GENERAL McCLELLAN (USA), WHO IS IN POSITION TO ATTACK RICHMOND, IN A SERIES OF COUNTERATTACKS KNOWN AS THE SEVEN DAYS' BATTLES. McCLELLAN IS FORCED TO RETREAT.
AUGUST 29–30	GENERAL JOHN POPE (USA) IS DEFEATED AT THE SECOND BATTLE OF BULL RUN IN AN ATTEMPT TO MOVE ON RICHMOND. McCLELLAN IS RESTORED TO COMMAND.
SEPTEMBER 4–17	GENERAL ROBERT E. LEE (CSA) CROSSES THE POTOMAC INTO THE NORTH. McCLELLAN ATTACKS LEE AT SHARPSBURG, NEAR ANTIETAM CREEK. THE BATTLE IS A DRAW, BUT LEE WITHDRAWS TO VIRGINIA.
SEPTEMBER 22	LINCOLN ISSUES THE EMANCIPATION PROCLAMATION WHICH PROVIDES THAT ALL SLAVES IN THE CONFEDERACY WILL BE FREE AS OF JANUARY 1, 1863.
DECEMBER 13	GENERAL AMBROSE BURNSIDE (USA), WHO HAS REPLACED McCLELLAN, ATTACKS LEE'S CAMP AT FREDERICKSBURG, VIRGINIA. BURNSIDE IS FORCED TO RETREAT AND IS REPLACED BY GENERAL JOSEPH HOOKER.
1863 MARCH 3	CONGRESS PASSES THE FIRST DRAFT LAW MAKING ALL MEN 20–45 LIABLE FOR MILITARY SERVICE. HOWEVER, SERVICE CAN BE AVOIDED BY PAYMENT OF $300 OR BY FINDING A SUBSTITUTE.
MAY 2–4	LEE AND GENERAL "STONEWALL" JACKSON (CSA) DEFEAT GENERAL HOOKER (USA) AT CHANCELLORSVILLE, VIRGINIA.
MAY 22–JULY 4	AFTER A SIX WEEK SEIGE BY GRANT, VICKSBURG SURRENDERS. THE UNION NOW CONTROLS THE MISSISSIPPI RIVER. THE CONFEDERACY IS SPLIT IN TWO.
JULY 1–3	GENERAL GEORGE MEADE (USA), WHO HAS REPLACED HOOKER, MEETS LEE AT GETTYSBURG, PENNSYLVANIA. LEE LOSES ABOUT ONE-THIRD OF HIS ARMY, AND IS FORCED TO RETREAT INTO VIRGINIA.
JULY 13–16	RIOTS AGAINST THE DRAFT OCCUR IN NEW YORK CITY. UNION FORCES ARE CALLED IN TO PUT DOWN THE RIOTS.
NOVEMBER 23–25	GRANT DEFEATS THE CONFEDERATE TROOPS NEAR CHATTANOOGA, TENNESSEE.
1864 MARCH 9	GRANT BECOMES SUPREME COMMANDER OF THE UNION FORCES.

	MAY 5–JUNE 3	AS GRANT ADVANCES TOWARD RICHMOND, HE IS MET BY LEE. DESPITE HEAVY LOSSES, GRANT MOVES CLOSER TO RICHMOND.
	MAY 7–DECEMBER 22	GENERAL WILLIAM SHERMAN (USA) SETS OUT FROM CHATTANOOGA TO INVADE GEORGIA. ON SEPTEMBER 2, HE OCCUPIES ATLANTA. ON NOVEMBER 14, HE STARTS ACROSS GEORGIA, DESTROYING MUCH IN HIS PATH. HE ENTERS SAVANNAH ON DECEMBER 22.
	OCTOBER	GENERAL PHILIP SHERIDAN (USA) MOVES THROUGH THE SHENANDOAH VALLEY, IN VIRGINIA, DESTROYING CONFEDERATE GRAIN AND FOOD SUPPLIES.
	1865 JANUARY 16–MARCH 21	SHERMAN MOVES THROUGH SOUTH AND NORTH CAROLINA LEAVING A PATH OF DESTRUCTION.
	APRIL 2	LEE ABANDONS RICHMOND AND RETREATS TO THE WEST.
	APRIL 9	LEE SURRENDERS TO GRANT AT APPOMATTOX COURTHOUSE.

	COST	MEN IN ARMED FORCES	BATTLE DEATHS	*OTHER DEATHS
NORTH	$6,190,000,000	2,213,363	140,414	224,097
SOUTH	$3,000,000,000	1,000,000	94,000	164,000

*Other deaths include deaths from disease, accidents, and other causes not directly connected with the actual fighting.

MAJOR BATTLES, 1861–1865

KEY

UNITED STATES

CONFEDERATE STATES

X IMPORTANT BATTLE

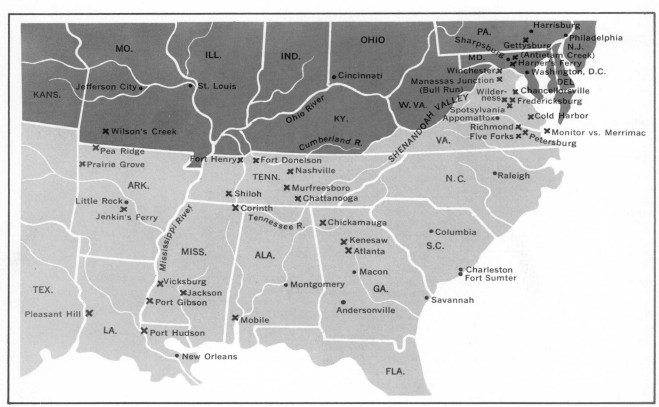

1. What advantages or disadvantages did each side have in fighting the war? Do you see any reasons for the Union's victory?

2. Do you think the war would be likely to affect any of the differences between the North and South that you noticed in Section 1? If so, how?

3. What problems do you think the United States might have as a result of the war?

4. Does the information you have examined on the war raise any questions in your mind? Explain. How would you find answers to your questions? Use the instructions for library research in Unit II as a guide for your investigation. (See pages 190–192.)

40. The Emancipation Proclamation

On September 22, 1862, President Lincoln issued a proclamation concerning slavery in the Confederate states. A portion of the proclamation appears below.

[On] the first day of January, in the year of our Lord one thousand eight hundred and sixty-three, all persons held as slaves within any State, or designated part of a State, the people whereof shall then be in rebellion against the United States, shall be then, thenceforward, and forever free; and the Executive Government of the United States, including the military and naval authority thereof, will recognize and maintain the freedom of such persons, and will do no act or acts to repress such persons, or any of them, in any efforts they may make for their actual freedom.

[The] Executive will, on the first day of January . . . designate the States and parts of States . . . in which the people thereof . . . shall then be in rebellion against the United States; and the fact that any State, or the people thereof, shall on that day be in good faith represented in the Congress of the United States . . . shall . . . be deemed conclusive [final] evidence that such State and the people thereof are not then in rebellion against the United States. . . .

Abraham Lincoln, Complete Works, edited by John G. Nicolay and John Hay (New York: Appleton-Century-Crofts, 1894), Vol. II, p. 287.

1. What does Lincoln promise in this proclamation?

2. What was the Union's position in the war when Lincoln issued the proclamation? Does this suggest any reasons for his action? Does it suggest any problems Lincoln might have in fulfilling his promise?

3. What effect do you think the proclamation would have on southern states, northern states, and other nations? Do your answers suggest any reasons for issuing the proclamation?

4. How does the proclamation relate to your view of the causes of the war? How can you explain the time that passed between the beginning of the war and the issuing of the proclamation?

41. The Gettysburg Address

Abraham Lincoln, Complete Works, edited by John G. Nicolay and John Hay (New York: Appleton-Century-Crofts, 1894), Vol. II, p. 493.

The Union lost 23,000 men in the battle of Gettysburg. Lincoln made one of his most notable speeches on November 19, 1863, during the dedication of a national cemetery at the battlefield.

Fourscore and seven years ago our fathers brought forth on this continent a new nation, conceived in liberty, and dedicated to the proposition that all men are created equal.

Now we are engaged in a great civil war, testing whether that nation, or any nation so conceived and so dedicated, can long endure. We are met [meeting] on a great battle-field of that war. We have come to dedicate a portion of that field as a final resting place for those who here gave their lives that that nation might live. It is altogether [completely] fitting and proper that we should do this.

"Consecrate" and "hallow" mean to make holy, to sanctify.

But, in a larger sense, we cannot dedicate—we cannot consecrate—we cannot hallow—this ground. The brave men, living and dead, who struggled here, have consecrated it far above our poor power to add or detract [lessen]. The world will little note nor long remember what we say here, but it can never forget what they did here. It is for us, the living, rather, to be dedicated here to the unfinished work which they who fought here have thus far so nobly advanced. It is rather for us to be here dedicated to the great task remaining before us—that from these honored dead we take increased devotion to that cause for which they gave the last full measure of devotion; that we here highly resolve that these dead shall not have died in vain; that this nation, under God, shall have a new birth of freedom; and that government of the people, by the people, for the people, shall not perish from the earth.

1. What do you think Lincoln's main idea is? How does this relate to what you know of the Civil War and its causes?

2. What qualities does the speech have that may have contributed to its greatness in the years since it was delivered? What is the basis for your decision? Have you heard other speeches that possess such characteristics? Explain.

1. What did Lincoln emphasize as the major goal of the North?

2. Did this goal grow out of the most important issues that led to war? Explain.

3. In 1865, when the war ended, what did the North achieve with its victory? Which of the issues that brought on the war were decided in the North's favor?

V. Rebuilding the Nation

42. The South and the War

The next two selections describe what southerners felt and experienced during the war. The first is an editorial from a Louisiana newspaper. The second is a description by a New England newspaperman of Charleston, South Carolina, after the war.

A LOUISIANA EDITORIAL, 1861

The more moderate of the Northern papers still [insist] that the people of that section have taken up arms simply to preserve the Union. . . . We say it is not true . . . Unless he [Lincoln] is a born idiot, which we do not believe, he must be aware that to send armies to occupy the South, and fleets to blockade her ports; to seize on all provisions and other articles destined for the South; to maltreat all who sympathize with us, and to display . . . hostility to us [in] every possible [way], is not exactly calculated to increase the [ties] between the South and North. LINCOLN, instead of [strengthening the ties], is driving in the wedge of separation with all his force. He has acted as if his real design had been to place an eternal and impassable barrier between the two sections. This has been the effect, let his views have been what they may.

Editorial from New Orleans **Bee,** reprinted in **Southern Editorials on Secession,** edited by Dwight L. Dumond (Washington, D. C.: American Historical Association, 1931), pp. 511-512. Copyright 1931 American Historical Association, copyright renewed 1959 by Dwight L. Dumond. Reprinted by permission of the publisher.

1. How does this editorial compare with the one on page 484?

2. Does this editorial change your opinion about what the war accomplished? Why or why not?

3. What post-war problems do you see here for Lincoln?

CHARLESTON: SEPTEMBER 1865

A city of ruins, of desolation, of vacant houses, of widowed women, of rotting wharves, of deserted warehouses, of weed-wild gardens, of miles of grass-grown streets, of acres of pitiful and voiceful barrenness—that is Charleston, wherein Rebellion loftily reared its head . . . on whose beautiful promenade the fairest of cultured women gathered with passionate hearts to applaud the assault of ten thousand upon the little garrison of Fort Sumter!

The Heritage of America, edited by Henry Steele Commager and Allan Nevins (Boston: Little, Brown and Company, 1949), pp. 800, 802-803. Copyright 1939, 1949 by Henry Steele Commager and Allan Nevins.

It would seem that it is not clearly understood how thoroughly Sherman's army destroyed everything in its line of march—destroyed it without questioning who suffered by the action. That this wholesale destruction was often without orders and often against most positive orders does not change the fact of destruction. The rebel leaders were, too, in their way, even more wanton [unrestrained] and just as thorough as our army in destroying property. They did not burn houses and barns and fences as we did, but during the last three months of the war they burned immense quantities of cotton and rosin.

"Rosin" is hardened pine pitch used to make varnish, soap, etc.

The action of the two armies put it out of the power of men to pay their debts. . . . Thousands of men who were honest in purpose have lost everything but honor. The cotton with which they meant to pay their debts has been burned, and they are without other means. What is the part of wisdom in respect to such men? It certainly cannot be to strip them of the last remnant. Many of them will pay in whole or in part if proper consideration be shown them. It is no question of favor to any one as a favor, but a pure question of business—how shall the commercial relations of the two sections be re-established? In determining it, the actual and exceptional condition of the state with respect to property should be constantly borne in mind.

1. What solution is suggested to the problem that is described here?

2. Do you see any possible difficulties with this solution?

43. The Attitude of Lincoln

Lincoln began his second term as President on March 4, 1865. His second inaugural address and his plan for reuniting the southern states and the national government reflect his attitude toward the South. On April 14, a few days after the northern victory, Lincoln was assassinated. By that time, his plan for restoring the Union had been accepted by Virginia, Tennessee, Arkansas, and Louisiana.

SECOND INAUGURAL ADDRESS

The Collected Works of Abraham Lincoln, edited by Ray B. Basler (New Brunswick, N. J.: Rutgers University Press, 1953), Vol. VIII, p. 333.

. . . With malice toward none; with charity for all; with firmness in the right, as God gives us to see the right, let us strive on to finish the work we are in; to bind up the nation's wounds; to care for him who shall have borne the battle, and for his widow, and his orphan—to do all which may achieve and cherish a just, and a lasting peace, among ourselves, and with all nations.

PLAN FOR REBUILDING THE UNION

Those who rebelled against the Union would be pardoned and granted full citizenship if they took an oath to support the Constitution and all United States laws and proclamations made during the war. Pardon was not extended to officers of the Confederate government or army or to men who had left posts in the United States government or army to serve the Confederacy.

The United States would recognize any constitutional state government established by at least one-tenth of the voters of a former Confederate state. Only those who took the above oath could vote.

1. How could southern states qualify to rejoin the Union under Lincoln's plan?

2. Does this plan reflect the attitude toward the South that Lincoln expressed in his second inaugural address? Explain.

3. Would you expect all northerners to accept Lincoln's plan? Why or why not?

44. The Thirteenth Amendment, 1865

Congress accepted the Thirteenth Amendment to the Constitution early in 1865. By December, it was part of the Constitution.

Section 1. Neither slavery nor involuntary servitude, except as a punishment for crime whereof the party shall have been duly convicted, shall exist within the United States, or any place subject to their jurisdiction.

Section 2. Congress shall have power to enforce this article by appropriate legislation.

1. Why do you think this amendment was necessary? Wasn't the Emancipation Proclamation sufficient? Why?

2. What relationship does this amendment have to the causes of the Civil War? Explain.

45. Black Codes

Andrew Johnson, who became President after Lincoln's assassination, carried out a plan similar to Lincoln's for restoring the Union. One new requirement in Johnson's plan was that the southern states ratify the Thirteenth Amendment. The states not restored under Lincoln's plan complied with Johnson's plan. Then most of them passed state laws known as "black codes" for the newly

This plan was declared official policy on December 8, 1863.

501

freed slaves. The following laws from Mississippi and Florida are examples of these "black codes."

A MISSISSIPPI LAW, NOVEMBER 1865

American History Told by Contemporaries, edited by Albert Bushnell Hart (New York: The Macmillan Company, 1901), Vol. IV, p. 479.

[All] freedmen, free negroes, and mulattoes in this State, over the age of eighteen years, found on the second Monday in January, 1866, or thereafter, with no lawful employment or business, or found unlawfully assembling themselves together, either in the day or night time . . . shall be deemed vagrants [tramps], and on conviction thereof shall be fined [a] sum . . . not exceeding . . . fifty dollars . . . and imprisoned, at the discretion [judgment] of the court . . . not exceeding ten days.

A FLORIDA LAW, JANUARY 1866

American History Told by Contemporaries, edited by Albert Bushnell Hart, Vol. IV, pp. 480-481.

. . . [It] is provided that when any person of color shall enter into a contract . . . to serve as a laborer for a year, or any other specified term, on any farm or plantation in this State, if he shall refuse or neglect to perform the stipulations [conditions] of his contract by wilful disobedience of orders, wanton [rebellious] impudence or disrespect to his employer, or his authorized agent, failure or refusal to perform the work assigned to him, idleness, or abandonment of the premises or the employment of the party with whom the contract was made, he or she shall be liable, upon the complaint of his employer or his agent, made under oath before any justice of the peace of the county, to be arrested and tried before the criminal court of the county, and upon conviction shall be subject to all the pains and penalties prescribed for the punishment of vagrancy . . .

The employer could decide whether the laborer should be punished or placed in his custody. The employer's complaint could be dismissed if false, and the laborer could then sue for damages.

[If] any negro, mulatto, or other person of color, shall intrude himself into any religious or other public assembly of white persons, or into any railroad car or other public vehicle set apart for exclusive accommodation of white people, he shall be deemed to be guilty of a misdemeanor [minor crime], and upon conviction shall be sentenced to stand in the pillory for one hour, or be whipped, not exceeding thirty-nine stripes [lashes], or both, at the discretion of the jury; nor shall it be lawful for any white person to intrude himself into any religious or other public assembly of colored persons, or into any railroad car or other public vehicle, set apart for the exclusive accommodation of persons of color, under the same penalties.

A "pillory" is a wooden frame with openings in which the head and hands are locked. Pillories were set in public places to disgrace the people being punished.

1. What do the southern legislators appear to be doing? Why?

2. Would these laws have any effect on northern attitudes toward Lincoln's and Johnson's plans to restore the Union? Why?

3. Is there any relationship between these laws and the issues that you considered causes of the Civil War? Explain.

46. Congress Takes Over

Many Republican leaders disapproved of Lincoln's and Johnson's plans for readmitting the southern states to the Union. The Thirty-Ninth Congress, which met in December 1865, had a majority of Republican members. In June 1866, a congressional committee reported that the new southern state governments were unsatisfactory, and did not deserve to have representatives in Congress. Congress set up new requirements for the southern states. It made them accept the Fourteenth Amendment, the First Reconstruction Act, and the Fifteenth Amendment. Johnson vetoed the bills passed by Congress, but Congress often passed the laws over his veto. In 1868, Congress impeached Johnson, trying him for bad conduct. This attempt to remove him from office failed by one vote. But Congress had taken over the rebuilding of the Union.

POINTS TO CONSIDER
Why Congress established new requirements for the southern states.

THE FOURTEENTH AMENDMENT, JULY 1868

Section 1. All persons born or naturalized in the United States, and subject to the jurisdiction thereof, are citizens of the United States and of the State wherein they reside. No State shall make or enforce any law which shall abridge the privileges or immunities of citizens of the United States; nor shall any State deprive any person of life, liberty, or property, without due process of law; nor deny to any person within its jurisdiction the equal protection of the laws.

Section 2. [Representation in Congress shall be based on the total number of persons in each state. Whenever a state denies the right of voting to any of its male inhabitants who have reached the age of twenty-one and are citizens of the United States, the representation of that state in Congress shall be reduced.]

Section 3. No person shall . . . hold any office, civil or military, under the United States, or under any State, who, having previously taken an oath, as [an official], to support the Constitution of the United States, shall have engaged in insurrection or rebellion against the same, or given aid or comfort to the enemies thereof. But Congress may by a vote of two thirds of each house, remove such disability.

The Fourteenth Amendment was submitted to the states for ratification in June 1866.

503

The Confederacy had borrowed $2 billion, most of it from citizens and institutions of the South.

Section 4. [All United States public debt incurred for the purpose of suppressing the rebellion shall be valid. Any claim for repayment of money loaned to aid the rebellion or any claim for the loss of slaves shall be illegal and void.]

Section 5. The Congress shall have power to enforce by appropriate legislation the provisions of this article.

All of the southern states except Tennessee rejected the Fourteenth Amendment. How can you explain this?

THE FIRST RECONSTRUCTION ACT, MARCH 1867
The ten southern states that rejected the Fourteenth Amendment were organized into five military districts. Each district was placed under the command of a high-ranking military officer who was authorized to use federal troops to maintain law and order.

These states were required to call conventions to draft constitutions guaranteeing Negro suffrage. Delegates to the conventions were to be elected by all adult males except former Confederate leaders, who were deprived of the right to vote. The new constitutions had to be approved by a majority of the voters.

Each state then had to ratify the Fourteenth Amendment. When all of these steps had been taken and when the amendment had become part of the federal Constitution, Congress would consider readmitting the states to the Union.

What seem to be the major goals of this act?

THE FIFTEENTH AMENDMENT, MARCH 1870
Section 1. The right of citizens of the United States to vote shall not be denied or abridged by the United States or any State on account of race, color, or previous condition of servitude.

Section 2. The Congress shall have power to enforce this article by appropriate legislation.

1. Why would Congress feel it necessary to propose the Fifteenth Amendment?

2. How does Congress' program for readmitting southern states to the Union differ from Lincoln's and Johnson's plans?

3. Why do you think Congress insisted on this program?

4. Is there any connection between Congress' program and the issues that led to the Civil War? Explain.

504

47. New Legislatures in the South

By the summer of 1868, seven of the ten southern states had been readmitted to the Union under the congressional plan. The newly elected state legislatures had begun their sessions. James S. Pike, a northern observer, recorded his impressions of one such legislature, the South Carolina House of Representatives. Before the war, Pike had been a reporter for the *New York Tribune*. He had shared the views of abolitionists and of Republicans like Seward.

They were such a . . . body of men as might pour out of a market-house or a court-house at random in any Southern State. Every negro type . . . was here to be seen, from the genteel serving-man to the rough-hewn customer from the rice or cotton field. Their dress was as varied as their countenances [faces]. There was the second-hand black frock-coat of infirm gentility, glossy and threadbare. There was the stove-pipe hat of many ironings and departed styles. There was also to be seen a total disregard of the proprieties [proper standards] of costume in the coarse and dirty garments of the field; the stub-jackets and slouch hats of soiling labor. In some instances, rough woolen comforters [scarves] embraced the neck and hid the absence of linen. Heavy brogans [work shoes], and short, torn trousers, it was impossible to hide. . . . These were the legislators of South Carolina. . . .

[The] blacks outnumber the whole body of whites in the House more than three to one. On the mere basis of numbers [of people] in the State the injustice of this . . . is manifest [clear], since the black population is relatively four to three of the whites. A just [correction] of the disproportion, on the basis of population merely, would give fifty-four whites to seventy black members. . . .

One of the things that first strike a casual observer in this negro assembly is the fluency [easy flow] of debate. . . . The leading topics of discussion are all well understood by the members . . . When an appropriation bill is up to raise money to catch and punish the Ku-klux, they know exactly what it means. . . . So, too, with educational measures. The free school comes right home to them; then the business of arming and drilling the black militia. . . . The intellectual level is [low] . . . [The Negro legislator] will speak half a dozen times on one question, and every time say the same things without knowing it. He answers completely to the description of a stupid speaker in Parliament. . . It was said of him that he did not know what he was going to say when he got up; he did not know what he was saying while he was speaking, and he did not know what he had said when he sat down. . . .

James S. Pike, **The Prostrate State** (New York: Appleton-Century-Crofts, 1874), pp. 10, 14-15, 17-21.

"Gentility" means members of the upper class. "Infirm" refers to those who were not secure or firm in their positions.

The "Ku Klux Klan," a secret society, was organized to frighten Negroes and keep them powerless.

...No one is allowed to talk five minutes without interruption, and one interruption is the signal for another and another, until the original speaker is smothered under an avalanche of them. ...Every one esteems himself as good as his neighbor, and puts in his oar, apparently as often for love of riot and confusion as for any thing else....

But underneath all this shocking burlesque [mockery] upon legislative proceedings, we must not forget that there is something very real to this uncouth and untutored multitude....Seven years ago these men were raising corn and cotton under the whip of the overseer. To-day they are raising points of order and questions of privilege. They find they can raise one as well as the other. They prefer the latter....It means liberty....

"Uncouth" means rough and unpolished in manners or appearance. Someone who is "untutored" has not been taught.

1. How do you think former southern leaders would react to these new legislatures?

2. What would you expect them to do about it? Why?

48. The Election of 1868

In 1868, the Republicans nominated the hero of the war, Ulysses S. Grant, for President. The Democrats nominated the little known war-time governor of New York, Horatio Seymour. The following maps show the results of the election. As you look at them, remember that in 1865 southern white people generally favored the Democrats over the Republicans.

ELECTORAL VOTE BY STATES

ELECTORAL VOTE—317

GRANT, REPUBLICAN—214

SEYMOUR, DEMOCRAT—80

NOT PARTICIPATING—23

Unreconstructed States—States that had not accepted Congress's Reconstruction plan could not vote.

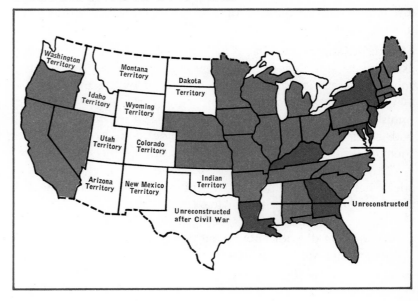

POPULAR VOTE BY COUNTIES

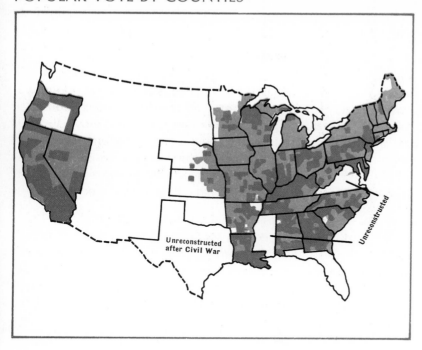

Popular vote 5,724,701

GRANT, REPUBLICAN—3,015,068

SEYMOUR, DEMOCRAT—2,709,633

No breakdown of the popular vote was available for Florida.

1. What effect, if any, do you think the congressional plan for restoring the Union had upon these election results?

2. How does the outcome of this election relate to the issues that led to war?

49. The Ku Klux Klan

Many northerners went south to participate in the new southern state governments. Some of them genuinely wished to help the freed Negroes. Others wanted to take advantage of the uneducated Negroes' igorance to get profitable jobs. These northerners were called "carpetbaggers" because their traveling bags were made of carpet material. Southerners who cooperated with these northerners were called "scalawags."

In 1872, the former southern white leaders were pardoned. Meanwhile, military rule was gradually ending in the South. The old governing group returned to power.

One of the most famous "carpetbaggers," Albion W. Tourgée, wrote a novel describing the reaction of southern whites to Negro rule. The following passage is about the Ku Klux Klan, a secret group that was organized to frighten Negroes and keep them from voting.

Albion W. Tourgée, **A Fool's Errand** (New York: Fords, Howard and Hulbert, 1880), pp. 225-228.

It was a chill, dreary night. A dry, harsh wind blew from the north. The moon was at the full, and shone clear and cold in the blue vault.

There was one shrill whistle, some noise of quietly-moving horses; and those who looked from their windows saw a black-gowned and grimly-masked horseman sitting upon a draped horse at every corner of the streets, and before each house,— grim, silent, threatening. Those who saw dared not move, or give any alarm. Instinctively they knew that the enemy they had feared had come, had them in his clutches, and would work his will of them, whether they resisted or not. So, with the instinct of self-preservation, all were silent—all simulated sleep.

Five, ten, fifteen minutes the silent watch continued. A half-hour passed, and there had been no sound. Each masked sentry sat his horse as if horse and rider were only some magic statuary with which the bleak night cheated the affrighted eye. Then a whistle sounded on the road toward Verdenton. The masked horsemen turned their horses' heads in that direction, and slowly and silently moved away. Gathering in twos, they fell into ranks with the regularity and ease of a practiced soldiery, and, as they filed on towards Verdenton, showed a cavalcade of several hundred strong; and upon one of the foremost horses rode one with a strange figure lashed securely to him.

When the few who were awake in the little village found courage to inquire as to what the silent enemy had done, they rushed from house to house with chattering teeth and trembling limbs, only to find that all were safe within, until they came to the house where old Uncle Jerry Hunt had been dwelling alone since the death of his wife six months before. The door was open.

The house was empty. The straw mattress had been thrown from the bed, and the . . . cord on which it rested had been removed.

. . . Upon the limb of a low-branching oak not more than forty steps from the Temple of Justice, hung the lifeless body of old Jerry. The wind turned it slowly to and fro. The snowy hair and beard contrasted strangely with the dusky pallor of the peaceful face . . .

The Fool asked of some trusty friends the story of the night before. With trembling lips one told it to him,

"I heard the noise of horses—quiet and orderly, but many. Looking from the window in the clear moonlight, I saw horsemen passing down the street, taking their stations here and there, like

The fool is Tourgée, the author.

guards who have been told off for duty, at specific points. Two stopped before my house, two opposite Mr. Haskin's, and two or three upon the corner below. They seemed to have been sent on before as a sort of picket-guard for the main body, which soon came in. I should say there were from a hundred to a hundred and fifty still in line. They were all masked, and wore black robes. The horses were disguised, too, by drapings. There were only a few mules in the whole company. They were good horses, though: one could tell that by their movements. Oh, it was a respectable crowd! No doubt about that, sir. Beggars don't ride in this country. I don't know when I have seen so many good horses together since the Yankee cavalry left here after the surrender. They were well drilled too. Plenty of old soldiers in that crowd. Why, every thing went just like clock-work. Not a word was said —just a few whistles given. They came like a dream, and went away like a mist. I thought we should have to fight for our lives; but they did not disturb any one here. They gathered down by the court-house. I could not see precisely what they were at, but, from my back upper window, saw them down about the tree. After a while a signal was given, and just at that time a match was struck, and I saw a dark body swing down under the limb. I knew then they had hung somebody, but had no idea who it was. To tell the truth, I had a notion it was you, Colonel. I saw several citizens go out and speak to these men on the horses. There were lights in some of the offices about the court-house, and in several of the houses about town. Every thing was as still as the grave,—no shouting or loud talking, and no excitement or stir about town. It was evident that a great many of the citizens expected the movement, and were prepared to co-operate with it by manifesting no curiosity, or otherwise endangering its success. I am inclined to think a good many from this town were in it. I never felt so powerless in my life. Here the town was in the hands of two or three hundred armed and disciplined men, hidden from the eye of the law, and having friends and co-workers in almost every house. I knew that resistance was useless."

"But why," asked the Fool, "has not the body been removed?"

"We have been thinking about it," was the reply; "but the truth is, it don't seem like a very safe business. And, after what we saw last night, no one feels like being the first to do what may be held an affront by those men. I tell you, Colonel, I went through the war, and saw as much danger as most men in it; but I would rather charge up the Heights of Gettysburg again than be the object of a raid by that crowd."

An "inquest" is an official inquiry or examination, often held before a jury.

After some parley, however, some colored men were found, and a little party made up, who went out and saw the body of Uncle Jerry cut down, and laid upon a box to await the coming of the coroner, who had already been notified. The inquest developed only these facts, and the sworn jurors solemnly and honestly found the cause of death unknown....

1. How do the actions described here relate to the causes of the Civil War? What conclusion can you draw from this?

2. What problems do you see here for the United States? What solutions can you suggest?

RECONSTRUCTION

The term "Reconstruction" is generally used to describe the period following the Civil War, from 1865 to 1877. What is the meaning of this term? Would you use it to describe this period? Why? What other term might be used to describe this period? What is the value of using terms to describe periods of history?

WAR AND CHANGE

You have formed your own hypothesis about the causes of the Civil War and have studied the period following the war. What conclusions can you form about the relationship between the causes of war and the situation following it?

1. Were any of the conflicts that brought on the war decided by the war? Explain.

2. Were there problems that were not solved by the war?

3. Did the material in this section on the post-war period relate to *all* the conflicts that led to war? If not, which conflicts were not touched upon? What information would you need in order to know how the war affected these issues? Explain.

4. Is there a difference between the kind of questions the war settled and the kind it did not settle? Be specific.

5. What does your answer tell you about war as a technique for solving a nation's problems?

THE CIVIL WAR PERIOD AND THE NEGRO

Earlier in this unit you considered the question, "Was the Civil War inevitable?" Whether or not it was inevitable, a further question can be asked: "Is it good that the war was

510

fought?" One of the most important problems to consider before answering this question is how the Civil War affected the Negro. The abolition of slavery *by force* was one result of the Civil War. Was this the only solution to the problem of slavery? Was it the best one?

1. Many southern slaveowners felt that the cost of maintaining slaves from infancy through old age was greater than the value of the slaves' labor. If slavery *was* unprofitable, do you think it would have disappeared by itself? Why or why not?

2. Was it necessary to have a group like the abolitionists in order to bring about the end of slavery? Do you need additional information to answer this question? If so, what? If not, why not?

3. Did the abolitionists, the Emancipation Proclamation, the experience of the war, and the new amendments to the Constitution have any *bad* results for the Negro? Explain.

4. Is it better *not* to force changes like the abolition of slavery, if it seems that change might occur peacefully? Assume that there *was* reason to hope that slavery would eventually die out by itself. Should opponents of slavery simply have waited for it to end? Should they have refrained from trying to force the end of slavery? Why or why not?

5. Assume that slavery was allowed to die by itself. Suppose this meant that three or four additional generations had to live as slaves. Does this change your judgment about the best way to end slavery? Explain.

BIBLIOGRAPHY

THE AMERICAN HERITAGE PICTURE HISTORY OF THE CIVIL WAR. New York: American Heritage Publishing Co., 1960.
    One of the finest collections of Civil War photographs and illustrations. The narrative describes the events of the period concisely and colorfully.
BUCKMASTER, HENRIETTA. FLIGHT TO FREEDOM: THE STORY OF THE UNDERGROUND RAILROAD. New York: Thomas Y. Crowell Company, 1958.
    The story of the Underground Railroad, viewed through the lives of people who participated in it.
CASE, ELINOR. YANKEE TRAITOR, REBEL SPY. Philadelphia: The Westminster Press, 1956.
    An exciting novel about the Civil War soldiers who had to fight cousins on the enemy side and traitors in their own ranks.
CATTON, BRUCE. THIS HALLOWED GROUND. New York: Doubleday & Company, Inc., 1962. †New York: Pocket Books, 1961.
    This special edition for teen-agers is from Catton's Pulitzer Prize winning history of the Civil War.

CRANE, STEPHEN. THE RED BADGE OF COURAGE. New York: The Macmillan Company, 1962. †New York: Holt, Rinehart and Winston, Inc., 1956.

This popular and exciting novel portrays the fears and doubts of a young man entering combat for the first time.

FREEMAN, DOUGLAS SOUTHALL. LEE OF VIRGINIA. New York: Charles Scribner's Sons, 1958.

The leading authority on the life of Robert E. Lee presents a stirring picture of the commander of the Confederate forces. Especially written for young readers.

NOLAN, JEANETTE C. ABRAHAM LINCOLN. New York: Julian Messner, Inc., 1953. Covering the period from Lincoln's boyhood through the stormy years of his Presidency, this biography shows the greatness of Lincoln as he dealt with the problems of his era.

†Denotes paperback edition.

TIME LINE

1816	PROTECTIVE TARIFF ADOPTED BY CONGRESS.
1820	MISSOURI COMPROMISE.
1825	ERIE CANAL COMPLETED.
1828	TARIFF RATES RAISED.
1831	*THE LIBERATOR*, AN ABOLITIONIST NEWSPAPER, BEGINS PUBLICATION.
1832	NEW TARIFF ACT PASSED.
1832	SOUTH CAROLINA NULLIFIES THE TARIFFS OF 1828 AND 1832.
1833	COMPROMISE TARIFF BILL PASSED.
1833	NATIONAL ANTI-SLAVERY SOCIETY FOUNDED.
1848	FREE SOIL PARTY ORGANIZED.
1850	COMPROMISE OF 1850.
1852	*UNCLE TOM'S CABIN* PUBLISHED.
1854	REPUBLICAN PARTY FOUNDED.
1854	KANSAS-NEBRASKA ACT.
1856	VIOLENCE ERUPTS IN KANSAS.
1857	DRED SCOTT DECISION HANDED DOWN BY THE SUPREME COURT.
1859	JOHN BROWN'S RAID ON HARPER'S FERRY.
1860	LINCOLN ELECTED PRESIDENT.
1860	SOUTH CAROLINA SECEDES.
1861	CONFEDERACY FORMED.
1861	FORT SUMTER SURRENDERS TO SOUTHERN TROOPS.
1863	THE UNION IS IN CONTROL OF THE MISSISSIPPI RIVER AFTER CAPTURING VICKSBURG.
1863	EMANCIPATION PROCLAMATION ISSUED.
1863	BATTLE OF GETTYSBURG.
1864	SHERMAN'S MARCH THROUGH GEORGIA.
1864	GRANT DRIVES TOWARD RICHMOND.
1864	LINCOLN RE-ELECTED PRESIDENT.
1865	LEE SURRENDERS AT APPOMATTOX.
1865	LINCOLN ASSASSINATED.
1865	THIRTEENTH AMENDMENT RATIFIED.
1865	SOUTHERN STATES ENACT "BLACK CODES."
1867	FIRST RECONSTRUCTION ACT PASSED.
1868	PRESIDENT JOHNSON IMPEACHED.
1868	FOURTEENTH AMENDMENT RATIFIED.
1868	ULYSSES S. GRANT ELECTED PRESIDENT.
1870	FIFTEENTH AMENDMENT RATIFIED.
1871	ACT AGAINST THE KU KLUX KLAN PASSED.
1872	CONFEDERATE LEADERS ARE PARDONED.
1872	GRANT RE-ELECTED PRESIDENT.
1877	LAST FEDERAL TROOPS REMOVED FROM THE SOUTH.

unit VII
THE LAST WEST
AND
INDUSTRIALISM 1860-1920

Our thought has been "Let every man look out for himself, let every generation look out for itself," while we reared giant machinery which made it impossible that any but those who stood at the levers of control should have a chance to look out for themselves. We had not forgotten our morals. . . . But we were very heedless and in a hurry to be great.

WOODROW WILSON
INAUGURAL ADDRESS OF 1913

INTRODUCTION

During and after the Civil War, two different developments were proceeding side by side in American life. One was the settlement of our last frontier, the "Last West." This occurred mainly between about 1860 and 1890. The other development was the growth of industries and cities between 1870 and 1920.

The "Last West" was the area of the Great Plains and the Rocky Mountains. It had a flavor all its own. There were the famous bad men such as Jesse James and William Bonney, alias Billy the Kid. There were events like the massacre of General George Custer's troops by Sitting Bull and his Sioux Indians. There was the excitement generated by completion of the nation's first transcontinental railroad, when the Central Pacific and the Union Pacific met at Promontory Summit, Utah, in 1869. Finally, there was the last major rush for free land in Oklahoma in 1889.

	THE LAST WEST

Personalities and events like these helped to form the ideas most Americans held about the West. This unit begins with a comparison of popular ideas about the West and pictures and accounts of the West as it really was. You will see, first, how the West was represented in popular novels and movies around the turn of the

514

century. Then you will examine photographs, paintings, and personal recollections about life on the Great Plains in the late decades of the 1800's. As you decide which popular ideas about the West were factual and which were fiction, you might consider the reasons for the ideas we have today about the Last West.

The second section focuses on the importance of the Last West to the United States. The Last West was really the last part of the frontier. Thus the problem here is what the frontier meant for American history. In Unit IV you examined Frederick Jackson Turner's ideas about the relationship between the frontier and the growth of democracy. In Unit V you studied the kind of personal characteristics that frontier life encouraged. In particular, you formed opinions about how much individualism, in the sense of self-reliance, was possible on the frontier. Now you will conclude your study of the impact of the frontier. You will read statements by a congressman from Ohio, Frederick Jackson Turner, and an American novelist on what the frontier meant for the American economy and character. You will compare the ideas of these men with two interpretations of settlement, farming, and ranching in the Great Plains. In part, you will be reviewing the idea of individualism to see how it applied to life in the Last West.

From the rural setting and relatively simple life of the Last West, the unit moves to the city environment that grew up around the new factories. The central issues in this part of the unit are like the ones you considered when studying the last frontier. What did the growth of industry and big business mean for the American economy? How did the new problems of industrial and urban life affect traditional American values like individualism?

Industrial America is presented from two different viewpoints. In the third section, you will learn about the growth of wealth which was one result of the growth of industry. You will study the forms of business organization which arose as businesses became larger, and you will read the success stories of millionaires like Andrew Carnegie and John D. Rockefeller. Then you will glimpse the kind of life that was led by the newly wealthy, the life of the "Gilded Age." The rest of the third section is devoted to the ideas of those who felt that big business was beneficial to the country. In particular, you will study what these people considered to be the secret of success, and how they viewed the role of the big businessman in society. You will also study their ideas about business competition and about the proper relationship between government and business.

The fourth section presents the ideas of the critics of big business.

515

These were people who pointed out the problems of the new industrial age, and who felt that large corporations bore much of the responsibility for the problems. This section concludes with an account of the laws passed by Congress to solve the problems. As you study the ideas of the champions and critics of big business, and the solutions to the problems of this new era, you will be asked to think about whether industrialism changed American values.

The last section of the unit focuses on immigrants, especially those who came to the United States in large numbers during the late nineteenth and early twentieth centuries. First you will read the stories of several immigrants about their reasons for coming to this country. You will be able to compare their motives with the motives of earlier immigrants, such as those who came during the colonial period. This comparison will give you some insight into the values of the new immigrants. You will be able to judge whether their values resembled the values of other Americans. You will also learn about the experiences of immigrants when they arrived in the United States. Here you can again examine the American value of individualism. Did the immigrants work hard and try to achieve success through their own efforts? If so, was individual effort sufficient to bring them success?

As you study this period in American history, you might consider some of the larger problems it suggests. For example, after you decide which parts of the popular image about the Last West were fictional, you might think about why Americans had such an image of the West. In particular, why did they form such an image during the late 1800's and early 1900's? Was there anything about that period which made the image they had especially appealing? You might also consider what ideas Americans have today about business and success, and why we have these ideas.

The Last West

WHAT WAS THE WEST LIKE?

The "Last West," as you learned in the introduction, was the area of the Great Plains and Rocky Mountains, from what is now North Dakota, Montana, and Idaho in the north, to Arizona and New Mexico in the south. Texas, which lies at the southeastern base of the plains, was the first part of this area to be settled. Settlement of Texas began before the Civil War.

Most of us have some mental picture of what this American West was like. Before you begin your study of the West, write down your ideas about it. Compare them with those of your classmates.

THE WEST IN NOVELS AND MOVIES

1. Novels: Buck Taylor and *The Virginian*

Around 1860, short paperback books called dime novels appeared on the American scene. At the turn of the century, the first motion pictures were shown. These novels and movies were often about the West. They provided many Americans with their major impressions of western life. In the following pages, you will find examples of the way the West was represented to earlier Americans in novels and on the screen.

Two typical heroes of western novels were Buck Taylor and the Virginian. Buck Taylor was created by Prentiss Ingraham. Ingraham was a soldier, a press agent for Buffalo Bill's Wild West Show, and the author of many popular dime novels. The first two passages are from Ingraham's writings about Buck Taylor. The third account is taken from Owen Wister's *The Virginian, A Horseman of the Plains*. This book was a hard-cover novel about cowboy life in Wyoming in the 1870's and 1880's. Since publication of the book in 1902, over 3 million copies have been sold. The story was also made into a Broadway play, a movie, and a television series.

POINTS TO CONSIDER

What is meant by "image."

The image of the Last West which emerged from 1860 to 1920.

A PORTRAIT OF BUCK TAYLOR

He was dressed in somewhat gaudy attire, wore a watch and chain, diamond pin in his black scarf, representing a miniature

Henry Nash Smith, **Virgin Land, The American West as Symbol and Myth** (Cambridge, Mass.: Harvard University Press, 1950), pp. 110-111. Copyright 1950 by the President and Fellows of Harvard College.

spur, and upon the small finger of his right hand there was a ring, the design being a horseshoe of rubies.

About his broad-brimmed, dove-colored sombrero was coiled a miniature [lariat], so that the spur, horseshoe and lasso designated his calling.

A "sombrero" is a wide-brimmed Mexican hat.

BUCK TAYLOR DESCRIBES HIS LIFE

... We lead a wild life, get hard knocks, rough usage and our lives are in constant peril, and the settling of a difficulty is an appeal to revolver or knife; but after all we are not as black as we are painted.

Owen Wister, **The Virginian, A Horseman of the Plains** (New York: Grosset & Dunlap, Inc., Publishers, 1902), pp. 2-4, 28-30.

THE VIRGINIAN

... I noticed a man who sat on the high gate of the corral, looking on. For he now climbed down with the undulations [waving motions] of a tiger, smooth and easy, as if his muscles flowed beneath his skin. The others had all visibly whirled the rope, some of them even shoulder high. I did not see his arm lift or move. He appeared to hold the rope down low, by his leg. But like a sudden snake I saw the noose go out its length and fall true... As the captured pony walked in with a sweet, church-door expression, our train moved slowly on to the station, and a passenger remarked, "That man knows his business. . . ."

[Another view of the same man . . .] Lounging there at ease against the wall was a slim young giant, more beautiful than pictures. His broad, soft hat was pushed back; a loose-knotted, dull-scarlet handkerchief sagged from his throat; and one casual thumb was hooked in the cartridge-belt that slanted across his hips. . . .

[During a card game, Trampas, the villain of the novel, insults the Virginian.]

The Virginian's pistol came out, and his hand lay on the table, holding it unaimed. And with a voice as gentle as ever, the voice that sounded almost like a caress, but drawling a very little more than usual, so that there was almost a space between each word, he issued his orders to the man Trampas:—

"When you call me that, *smile!*" And he looked at Trampas across the table. . . .

. . . [Silence], like a stroke, fell on the large room. All men present, as if by some magnetic current, had become aware of this crisis. . . . I stood stock-still, and noticed various people crouching, or shifting their positions.

"Sit quiet," said the dealer, scornfully to the man near me. "Can't you see he don't want to push trouble? He has handed Trampas the choice to back down or draw his steel [pistol]."

Then, with equal suddenness and ease, the room came out of its strangeness. Voices and cards, the click of chips, the puff of tobacco, glasses lifted to drink,—this level of smooth relaxation hinted no more plainly of what lay beneath than does the surface tell the depth of the sea.

For Trampas had made his choice. And that choice was not to "draw his steel. . . ."

1. What are Buck Taylor and the Virginian like?

2. How do they compare with your image of the West?

2. Dime Novel Covers

Some dime novels sold as many as 500,000 copies. The next two selections are covers of late nineteenth-century dime novels. Kit Carson, who appears on the second cover, was a scout and a cowboy.

A DIME NOVEL COVER: LONE STAR

1. How do Lone Star and Kit Carson differ from Buck Taylor and the Virginian?

2. How do figures like Lone Star and Carson compare with your image of the West?

3. The Early Movies: William S. Hart

One of the most popular of the early silent movies was *The Gun Fighter*. Made in 1916, it starred William S. Hart. Hart was one of the first film actors to become famous for his portrayals of western heroes. In the following scene from *The Gun Fighter*, Hart is in the center. The second illustration is from a later movie in which Hart appeared. In both movies, he played an outlaw.

520

A SCENE FROM *THE GUN FIGHTER*

THE MUSEUM OF MODERN ART/FILM STILLS ARCHIVE

A SCENE FROM A LATER WESTERN

THE MUSEUM OF MODERN ART/FILM STILLS ARCHIVE

1. How would you describe the westerners that William S. Hart portrayed?

2. How do these movie figures compare with the westerners in the novels discussed in this section?

521

1. What image of the Last West emerges from the western novels and the early movies?

2. How does this image compare with your own impressions of the West? What is the basis for your impressions?

RANCH LIFE

4. Photographs of Ranch Life

The cattle kingdom originated on the Spanish, later Mexican, ranches of southeast Texas. By 1860, there were over 5 million head of cattle grazing on Texas plains. Cattlemen were slow to extend their grazing lands into the Great Plains area, which includes parts of the present states of Montana, North and South Dakota, Wyoming, Nebraska, Colorado, Kansas, and New Mexico. Early explorers had established the idea that this area was desert. It was labeled the Great American Desert on maps. Within ten years after the Civil War, however, the cattle industry had spread to all states in the Great Plains.

The next group of selections deals with ranch life and the cattle kingdom in the Last West. The following pictures show different aspects of a cowboy's life.

POINTS TO CONSIDER

How the popular image of the Last West compares with actual ranch life.

How factual the popular image was.

COWBOYS PREPARE FOR A HUNT

ERWIN E. SMITH PHOTOGRAPH. COURTESY, LIBRARY OF CONGRESS AND MRS. L. M. PETTIS

522

COWBOYS RELAX ON THE RANGE

COWBOYS IN TOWN

5. The S. M. S. Ranch

Frank S. Hastings managed the S. M. S. Ranch, one of the largest in Texas, for many years. The following selection is from his book, *The Story of the S. M. S. Ranch,* which was published in 1919.

A Ranch in its entirety is known as an "Outfit," and yet in a general way the word "Outfit" suggests the wagon outfit which does the cow-work and lives in the open from April 15th, when work begins, to December 1st, when it ends.

The wagon outfit consists of the "Chuck Wagon" which carries the food, bedding and tents, and from the back of which the food is prepared over an open fire. The "Hoodlum Wagon," which carries the water barrel, wood and branding irons, furnishes the Chuck Wagon with water and wood, the branding crew with wood, and attends all round-ups or branding pens with supply of drinking water.

The Remuda (cow ponies) and Horse Wrangler always travel with the "Wagon." Remuda is the Spanish word for Saddle Horses.

The wagon crew consists of the Wagon Boss, usually foreman of the ranch, Cook, Hoodlum Driver, Horse Wrangler, Straw Boss, next in authority to Wagon Boss, and eight to twelve men as the work may demand. In winter the outfit is reduced to the regular year-around men who are scattered over the different ranch camps.

In almost everything industrial the problem is reduced to "Men," but in the Ranch it is reduced to "Men and horses." One might almost say to horses; since the love of a horse explains why there are cowboys—not rough riders, or the gun-decorated hero of the moving picture, but earnest, everyday, hardworking boys who will sit twenty-four hours in a saddle and never whimper, but who "Hate your guts" if you ask them to plow an acre of land or do anything else "afoot."

Every cowboy has a mount of from eight to fourteen horses regulated by his work, and the class of horses. A line rider can get along with fewer horses than a "wagon" man, and a man with a good many young horses needs more than the man with an older or steadier mount. Every one of these men will claim they are "afoot" and that "There ain't no more good cow ponies," but woe to the "outfit" that tries to take one of the no-accounts away, or, as the saying is, "Monkey with a man's mount."

Frank S. Hastings, **The Story of the S.M.S. Ranch,** reprinted in Walter Prescott Webb, **The Great Plains** (New York: Grosset & Dunlap, Inc., Publishers, 1931), pp. 251-255. Reprinted by permission of the SMS Ranch, Stamford, Texas.

A "mount" is the group of horses a cowboy uses for his work. A "line rider" patrols boundaries, turns back stray cattle, repairs fences, and checks grazing and water conditions.

Young horses apparently tire more easily than experienced ones.

Horses are assigned, and then to all intents and purposes they become the property of the man. Some foremen do not let their men trade horses among themselves, but it is quite generally permitted under supervision that avoids "sharking."

"Sharking" probably refers to gambling for horses.

Every horse has a name and every man on the ranch knows every horse by name, and in a general way over all the S. M. S. Ranches with over 500 cow ponies in service the men know all the horses by name, and what horses are in each man's mount. A man who does not love his mount does not last long in the cow business. Very few men are cruel to their horses, and a man who does not treat his mount well is only a "bird of passage" on most ranches, and always on the S. M. S. Ranch. There is an old ranch saying that between the shoulder and the hip [the horse] belongs to the rider, and the rest to the company. Beating over the head or spurring in the shoulder means "time check." Cowboys' principal topic is their horses or . . . men who ride, and every night about the camp fire they trade horses, run imaginary horse races, or romance about their pet ponies.

"Time check" means to be fired from the job.

I shall speak of horses in the main as with the wagon. All the saddle horses of an outfit thrown together are called the Remuda —pronounced in Texas "Remoother"—slurring the "ther." The Remuda is in charge [in the care] of a man, usually a half-grown boy known as the "Horse Wrangler," whose duty it is to have them in a band when wanted to change mounts, and to see that they are watered and grazed and kept from straying. They are always assembled early morning, at noon and at night, and at such other times as the work may demand a change, as, for instance, in making a round the boys use their wildest and swiftest horses —usually their youngest—to tame them down. When the round-up is together they use their "cutting" horses, which are as a rule their oldest and best horses. . . .

"Making a round" is gathering the cattle into a single, compact group.

"Cutting" is going into the herd to bring out those that need to be branded.

An "Outlaw" is a horse which no amount of riding or handling will subdue. He is "turned in" and sold in the "Scalawag" bunch which goes out every year, and includes the horses no longer fit for cow use. They are bought by traders who take them into some of the older Southern States and sell them to the negro tenants for cotton horses.

A "Sunday Hoss" is one with an easy saddle gait—usually a single footer with some style. The boys go "Gallin" Sundays, and in every mount of the younger men there is apt to be such a horse, but not in any sense saved from the regular work for Sunday.

A "single footer" is a horse that picks up one foot at a time, while moving at the speed of a trot.

525

"An Individual" is the private property of a cowboy and not very much encouraged, as it is only natural that he does not get much work, and is an encouragement to go "Gallin" when the foreman holds the boys down on ranch horses more on the boys' account because it is often a long night ride and impairs the boys' capacity for a hard day's work in busy times. . . . The owner of an "Individual" may be the embodiment of general honesty, but seems to feel that oats sneaked out for "his hoss" is at worst a very small venial sin.

A cow horse is trained so that he is tied when the reins are [hanging] down. He can, of course, drift off and when frightened run, but stepping on the reins seems to intimidate him into standing still as a rule. There are two reasons for this: first, the cowboy frequently has work where it is vital to leap from his horse and do something quick; second, that there is rarely anything to tie him to; though even when tying a horse a fairly even pull will loosen the reins. Cow horses are easily startled and apt to pull back and break the reins.

The regular cowboy gait for pasture riding or line work or ordinary cross-country riding is a "Jiggle"—a sort of fox trot that will make five miles per hour. For the round-up hard running is necessary part of the time and usually a stiff gallop the balance.

Cowboy life is very different from the ideas given by a Wild West Show or the "Movies." It is against Texas law to carry a pistol, and the sale is unlawful. This, however, is evaded by leasing [renting a pistol for] 99 years. Occasionally a rider will carry a Winchester on his saddle for coyotes or Lobo wolves, but in the seventeen years the writer has been intimate with range life he has never seen a cowboy carry a pistol hung about him, and very few instances where one was carried concealed. There is always a gun of some sort with the outfit carried in the wagon.

Every cowboy furnishes his own saddle, bridle, saddle blanket, and spurs; also his bedding, known as "Hot Roll," a 16 to 20 oz. canvas "Tarp" [tarpaulin] about 18 feet long doubled and bedding in between, usually composed of several quilts known as "suggans" and blankets—rarely a mattress, the extra quilts serving for mattress. The top "Tarp" serves as extra covering and protects against rain.

Working outfits are composed as far as possible of unmarried men, with the exception of the Wagon Boss, who is usually the Ranch foreman. They rarely leave the wagon at night, and as the result of close association an interchange of wit, or "josh," as it is called, has sprung up. There is nothing like the chuck-wagon josh in any other phase of life, and it is almost impossible to describe, because so much of it revolves about or applies to the technical part of ranching. It is very funny, very keen, and very direct, and while the most of it is understood by an outsider, he cannot carry it away with him.

At headquarters a bunk house is always provided which is usually known as "the Dog House" or "the Dive." No gambling is permitted on the ranches, but the cowboys' great game, "Auction Pitch," or dominoes or stag dances or music fill the hours of recreation, divided with the great cowboy occupation of "Quirt" [whip] making, in which they are masters. The use of liquor is not permitted on the S. M. S. Ranches or by the men when on duty away from the ranches.

1. What was life like for a cowboy on a ranch?

2. After reading this account, what kind of people do you think cowboys were? What parts of this description give you that impression?

6. The Cattle Drive

As the railroads moved westward in the 1860's, ranchers herded their cattle to towns located along the railroads for shipment to markets in the East. Texans were among the first cattlemen to use the cattle drive as a means of transportation. Cattle drives continued on a large scale until 1890. The next two accounts relate the experiences of two cowboys, Charles Goodnight and Andy Adams, on cattle drives. One of the trails shown on the map in the margin is named after Goodnight.

CHARLES GOODNIGHT DESCRIBES A CATTLE DRIVE

Sometimes the demands were so urgent that a man's boots would not be taken off his feet for an entire week. The nerves of the men usually became wrought up to such a tension that no man was to be touched by another when he was asleep until after he had been spoken to. The man who suddenly aroused a sleeper was liable to be shot, as all were thoroughly armed and understood the instant use of the revolver or the rifle. . . .

[In a stampede, the] task of the men was to gain control of the herd and gradually turn the cattle until they were moving in a circle. Then, although they might break each other's horns off and crush one another badly, the great danger was past. A well-trained night-horse needed but little guidance, and knew that if

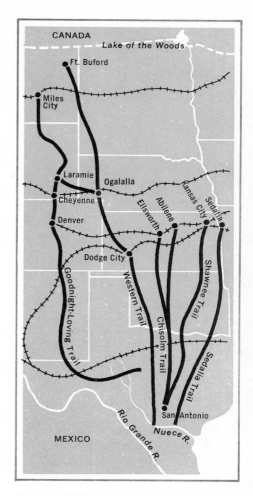

FIVE MAIN TRAILS OF THE CATTLE DRIVE

Walter Prescott Webb, **The Great Plains** (New York: Grosset & Dunlap, Inc., Publishers, 1931), pp. 264-265.

527

the herd came his way, all that he had to do was to lead. The speed of the herd was terrific, but the position at the head of the stampede was what the trail man desired, for there he was in position to start the herd turning. . . .

In the excitement of a stampede a man was not himself, and his horse was not the horse of yesterday. Man and horse were one, and the combination accomplished feats that would be utterly impossible under ordinary circumstances. Trained men generally would be found near the "point" at both sides of the herd. When the man on one side saw the herd bending [turning] his way he would fall back, and if the work were well done on the other side of the herd the stampede then gradually came to an end; the strain was removed, the cowboys were the happiest men on earth, and their shouts and laughter could be heard for miles over the prairie.

ANDY ADAMS TELLS OF HIS EXPERIENCES

Holding the herd this third night required all hands. Only a few men at a time were allowed to go into camp and eat, for the herd refused even to lie down. What few cattle attempted to rest were prevented by the more restless ones. By spells they would mill [move aimlessly], until riders were sent through the herd at break-neck pace to break up the groups. . . . As the horses were loose for the night, we could not start them on the trail until daybreak gave us a change of mounts, so we lost the early start of the morning before.

Good cloudy weather would have saved us, but in its stead was a sultry morning without a breath of air, which bespoke another day of sizzling heat. We had not been on the trail over two hours before the heat became almost unbearable to man and beast. Had it not been for the condition of the herd, all might yet have gone well; but over three days had now elapsed without water for the cattle, and they became feverish and ungovernable. The lead cattle turned back several times, wandering aimlessly in any direction, and it was with considerable difficulty that the herd could be held on the trail. The rear overtook the lead, and the cattle lost all semblance of a trail herd. Our horses were fresh, however, and after about two hours' work, we once more got the herd strung out in trailing fashion; but before a mile had been covered, the leaders again turned, and the cattle congregated into a mass of unmanageable animals, milling and lowing [mooing] in their fever and thirst. . . . No sooner was the milling stopped than they would surge hither and yon, sometimes half a mile, as ungovernable as the waves of an ocean. After wasting several hours in this

The "point" is the front of a group of cattle. Fewer cattle are placed in the front so that the herd cannot easily go astray.

Andy Adams, **Log of a Cowboy**, reprinted in Walter Prescott Webb, **The Great Plains**, pp. 266-267. Copyright 1955 by Houghton Mifflin Company. Reprinted by permission of Houghton Mifflin Company.

manner, they finally turned back over the trail, and the utmost efforts of every man in the outfit failed to check them. We threw our ropes in their faces, and when this failed, we resorted to shooting; but in defiance of the fusillade and the smoke they walked sullenly through the line of horsemen across their front. Six-shooters were discharged so close to the leaders' faces as to singe their hair, yet, under a noonday sun, they disregarded this and every other device to turn them, and passed wholly out of our control. In a number of instances wild steers deliberately walked against our horses, and then for the first time a fact dawned on us that chilled the marrow in our bones—*the herd was going blind.*

A "fusillade" is the firing of shots in rapid succession.

1. What problems did cowboys encounter on the trail?

2. What are "traits"? Cite some examples of traits. What traits did the cowboys have to possess in order to overcome their problems?

3. How do the life, problems, and traits of real cowboys compare with the popular image of the West?

CONCLUDING EXERCISE

1. How do the actual reports and pictures of ranch life compare with the image of the West offered in the western novels and early movies?

2. To what extent does the popular image seem to have been based on fact?

THE SOD HOUSE FRONTIER

7. A Photograph of Early Nebraska

You learned earlier that pioneers were reluctant to settle on the Great Plains because they believed it to be the Great American Desert. There was some settlement of this area in the 1850's, but it was not until after the Civil War that large-scale settlement took place.

One of the problems that confronted settlers of the Great Plains was the lack of building materials. Many pioneers built their homes out of sod, the grass-covered surface of the soil. They cut the sod into bricklike chunks. The following picture shows a typical sod house of the Great Plains area.

A NEBRASKA FAMILY AROUND 1880

How did immigrants on the sod house frontier live?

8. Settling the Sod House Frontier

The Homestead Act of 1862 stimulated settlement of the western lands. Under this act, a person was granted 160 acres of unoccupied public land upon the payment of a small fee. After five years of residence, he became the owner of his farm or homestead. The next selection describes conditions that homesteaders faced on the Great Plains.

Leroy R. Hafen and Carl Coke Rister, **Western America** (Second edition; Englewood Cliffs, N. J.: Prentice-Hall, Inc., 1950), pp. 391-394. © 1950. Reprinted by permission of Prentice-Hall, Inc.

A "perennial" stream is one that flows all year round.

Henry Howe was a nineteenth-century American historian.

. . . [Settlers] employed new techniques in adapting themselves to the country. Homesteaders found the wood and water problem ever present. Cottonwood, elm, willow, hackberry, and ash grew sparsely along the streams, and occasionally copses [groves] of cedar about escarpments [steep slopes] and eroded terrain; but seldom was timber of sufficient size and quantity to supply building needs. In certain areas not even firewood was to be had . . . Moreover, the land was semi-arid, and there were few springs or perennial streams. On the high plains the larger streams were sand-filled, and their waters were bitter or salty. So the homesteader's usual quest for wood and water was unsatisfied here. In 1873 Henry Howe noticed the scarcity of timber in western Kansas, but he said that there was enough rock for building purposes. This was untrue. In much of the prairie country no stone could be found. Indeed, Howe must have seen this; for as he moved westward over the Kansas Pacific Railroad, he noticed along his line of travel "subterranean houses" (dugouts) and adobes in eastern Colorado. The dugout, he said, was an excavation, some 10 feet wide, 20 long, and 6 or 8 deep. Over this were timbers, put up like rafters, and the whole was covered with prairie and sod.

The first Kansas and Nebraska settlers generally built sod houses and dugouts, either because they were too poor to provide a frame or brick structure or because of the inconvenience of hauling lumber from a distant town over the roadless prairie. Since they knew little about sod building, the first sod houses erected leaked badly during occasional periods of rainy weather. But later they were improved. . . . W. E. Webb, who visited the Kansas-Nebraska border in 1872, watched a sod house turn to mud during a heavy rain.

Community structures (schoolhouses and churches) were also made of sod. . . . A community sod-house building day was as much of an occasion for Great Plains people as was that of an Eastern log-raising. "The site being decided upon," writes [an observer of conditions in Kansas], "the neighborhood gathered with horses, plows, and wagons. A piece of virgin sod would be selected, the sod-breaking plow would be started; the sharp share would cut the grass roots and slice out a long piece of the sod from two to four inches in thickness, by twelve to fourteen inches in width." From these slices were cut bricklike segments to build the walls. Window and door frames were made of poles, and openings were covered with buffalo or cow hide. Brush was laid over pole rafters, and the whole, covered with sod and sand, packed down. But in parts of the country, dugouts were used for churches and schoolhouses, particularly where but few settlers lived within a community, or where the prairie sod was not sufficiently matted. Both types were comfortable in winter and saved the lives of many Kansas and Nebraska homesteaders during blizzard visitations of the seventies and eighties, a fact which was proved by the greater proportion of deaths among those who sought shelter in flimsily constructed frame and log houses.

"Adobes" are buildings made of sun-dried brick of earth and straw.

"Matted," here, means held together by grass roots.

CONCLUDING EXERCISE

1. Judging from this description and the picture of Nebraska, what was life like on the sod house frontier?

2. What do you think the settlers of this frontier were like? What are the reasons for your opinion?

3. How does your idea compare with the West as portrayed in the novels and early movies you studied?

4. Why do you suppose settlers moved westward?

LIFE ON THE PRAIRIE

9. Paintings of the Old Dakota Territory

Settlement of North and South Dakota did not take place until the late 1870's and early 1880's. Harvey Dunn, who was born in a homestead shack, painted his impressions of life in the Dakota Territory. The next three selections are pictures of the Dakota Territory painted in the late 1800's and early 1900's.

THE PRAIRIE IS MY GARDEN

COURTESY, SOUTH DAKOTA STATE UNIVERSITY

OLD SETTLERS

COURTESY, SOUTH DAKOTA STATE UNIVERSITY

BUFFALO BONES ARE PLOWED UNDER

COURTESY, SOUTH DAKOTA STATE UNIVERSITY

1. What was life like in the Dakota Territory?

2. Judging from the illustrations, what were some of the advantages and disadvantages of living in this area?

3. How would you describe the people in the paintings?

10. *A Son of the Middle Border:* Hamlin Garland

Hamlin Garland is well-known for his writings about life in the Midwest in the late nineteenth century and early twentieth century. He spent his early years on a farm in Iowa. The following passage from his novel, *A Son of the Middle Border,* tells about Garland's life in Iowa. Since Iowa was settled earlier than the areas of the Great Plains you have been reading about, farming was more advanced there than it was in areas farther west. However, Garland's description can apply to many Great Plains farms of the late nineteenth century.

Hamlin Garland, **A Son of the Middle Border** (New York: The Macmillan Company, 1917), pp. 147-153. Copyright 1917 by Hamlin Garland, renewed 1945 by Mary I. Lord and Constance G. Williams. Reprinted by permission of The Macmillan Company.

As I look back over my life on that Iowa farm the song of the reaper fills a large place in my mind. We were all worshippers of wheat in those days. The men thought and talked of little else between seeding and harvest, and you will not wonder at this if you have known and bowed down before such abundance as we then enjoyed.

Deep as the breast of a man, wide as the sea, heavy-headed . . . many-voiced . . . a meeting place of winds and of sunlight—our fields ran to the world's end. . . .

"Haying" is harvesting hay.

Haying was over, and day by day we boys watched with deepening interest while the hot sun transformed the juices of the soil into those stately stalks. I loved to go out into the fairy forest of it, and lying there, silent in its swaying deeps, hear the wild chickens peep and the wind sing its subtle [gentle] song over our heads. Day by day I studied the barley as it turned yellow, first at the root and then at the neck (while the middle joints, rank [thick] and sappy, retained their blue-green sheen), until at last the lower leaves began to wither and the stems to stiffen in order to uphold the daily increasing weight of the milky berries, and then almost in an hour—lo! the edge of the field became a banded ribbon of green and yellow, languidly [slowly] waving in and out with every rush of the breeze.

A "reaper" is a machine which harvests grain.

Now we got out the reaper, put the sickles [blades] in order, and father laid in a store of provisions. . . .

Reaping generally came about the 20th of July, the hottest and driest part of the summer, and was the most pressing [urgent] work of the year. It demanded early rising for the men, and meant an all day broiling over the kitchen stove for the women. Stern, incessant toil went on inside and out from dawn till sunset, no matter how the thermometer sizzled. On many days the mercury mounted to ninety-five in the shade, but with wide fields all yellowing at the same moment, no one thought of laying off.

A storm might sweep it flat, or if neglected too long, it might "crinkle" [dry up]. . . .

No task save that of "cradling" surpassed in severity "binding on a station." It was a full-grown man's job, but every boy was ambitious to try his hand, and when at fourteen years of age I was promoted from "bundle boy" to be one of the five hands to bind after the reaper, I went to my corner with joy and confidence. For two years I had been serving as binder on the corners, (to keep the grain out of the way of the horses) and I knew my job.

"Cradling" is mowing grain by hand with a scythe. "Binding on a station" is tying the grain stalks into sheaves, or bundles, as they fall from the reaper.

I was short and broad-shouldered with large strong hands admirably adapted for this work, and for the first two hours, easily held my own with the rest of the crew, but as the morning wore on and the sun grew hotter, my enthusiasm waned. A painful void developed in my chest. My breakfast had been ample, but no mere stomachful of food could carry a growing boy through five hours of desperate toil. Along about a quarter to ten, I began to scan the field with anxious eye, longing to see Harriet and the promised luncheon basket.

Just when it seemed that I could endure the strain no longer she came bearing a jug of cool milk, some cheese and some deliciously fresh fried-cakes. With keen joy I set a couple of tall sheaves together like a tent and flung myself down flat on my back in their shadow to devour my lunch.

Tired as I was, my dim eyes apprehended something of the splendor of the shining clouds which rolled like storms of snow through the deep-blue spaces of sky and so, resting silently as a clod I could hear the chirp of the crickets, the buzzing wings of flies and the faint, fairy-like tread of smaller unseen insects hurrying their way just beneath my ear in the stubble. Strange green worms, grasshoppers and shining beetles crept over me as I dozed.

"Stubble" is the short stubs of stalks which remain after the grain has been mowed.

This delicious, dreamlike respite was broken by the far-off approaching purr of the sickle, flicked by the faint snap of the driver's whip, and out of the low rustle of the everstirring [miniature] forest came the wailing cry of a baby wild chicken lost from its mother—a falling, thrilling, piteous little pipe. . . .

At noon we hurried to the house, surrounded the kitchen table and fell upon our boiled beef and potatoes with such ferocity that in fifteen minutes our meal was over. There was no ceremony and very little talking till the [hidden] wolf was appeased. Then came a heavenly half-hour of rest on the cool grass in the shade of the trees, a siesta as luxurious as that of a Spanish monarch—but alas!—this "nooning," as we called it, was always cut short by father's word of sharp command, "Roll out, boys!" and again the big white jugs were filled at the well, the horses, lazy with food, led the way back to the field, and the stern contest began again.

All nature at this hour seemed to invite to repose rather than to labor, and as the heat increased I longed with wordless fervor for the green woods of the Cedar River. At times the gentle wind hardly moved the bended heads of the barley, and the hawks hung in the air like trout sleeping in deep pools. The sunlight was a golden, silent, scorching cataract [waterfall]—yet each of us must strain his tired muscles and bend his aching back to the harvest.

Supper came at five, another delicious interval—and then at six we all went out again for another hour or two in the cool of the sunset.—However, the pace was more leisurely now for the end of the day was near. I always enjoyed this period, for the shadows lengthening across the stubble, and the fiery sun, veiled by the gray clouds of the west, had wondrous charm. The air began to moisten and grow cool. The voices of the men pulsed powerfully and cheerfully across the narrowing field of unreaped grain, the prairie hens led forth their broods to feed, and at last, father's long-drawn, and musical cry, "Turn out! All hands turn out!" rang with restful significance through the dusk. Then, slowly, with low-hung heads the freed horses moved toward the barn, walking with lagging steps like weary warriors going into camp. . . .

1. How would you describe life in Iowa in the 1870's?

2. How does this compare with Dunn's paintings?

3. What appears to be the appeal of this kind of life?

THE LAST WEST: FACT OR FICTION?

1. What general conclusions can you form about the Last West?

2. How does this differ from the idea of the West presented in the dime novels and early movies? From your own ideas about the early West?

3. Why do you think popular ideas about the West arose? Do they have any basis in fact?

4. Do you like "westerns"? Would you be just as interested in the exploits of adventurous French knights during the Crusades, or in the exploits of Japanese warriors? Why?

---

11. Oklahoma: The Last Chance

Prior to 1889, most of Oklahoma had been a large Indian reservation. In April 1889, the federal government opened the territory for settlement. The following selection from the *St. Louis Globe Democrat* describes what happened.

Arkansas City, [Kansas], April 22, 1889.—Few of the thousands of seekers of something for nothing, who have used this city as their last halting place prior to making the rush into Oklahoma, went to bed last night. They spent the night on the street, at the depot, and in and out of hotel lobbies. Yesterday's influx [flood] of visitors was enormous. The regular trains have had to run in sections. And this extra accommodation has not sufficed. The aisles have been crowded to excess, and the suffering of the cooped-up speculators and boomers must have been great. Fortunately there were very few women in the crowds.

The depot was crowded all night, and the sale of tickets kept steadily on, nine-tenths of those issued being to Guthrie and most of the balance to Arthur. This latter is just five miles over the line, and as all trains will stop before leaving the Cherokee strip, the holders of tickets to Arthur propose to jump off at the line. Every one seemed to be talking, and there was a perfect babel, but the grand rush commenced about six, when the people who had slept uptown joined their less fortunate brethren. Some carried absolutely nothing in their hands, evidently thinking they could do the rushing better for not being handicapped. But a marked characteristic of the crowd was the great number of spades and axes carried. The [railroad] company's arrangements to prevent a great rush to one train was to so arrange matters that no one could know which train could pass first, and the secret has been admirably kept.

The trip south commenced amid shouting and cheering. There could not have been less than five thousand men who failed to secure seats, although a score of flatcars had been fitted up with plank seats, which were crowded with eager boomers.

II. The Last West: The End of a Dream

The Heritage of America, edited by Henry Steele Commager and Allan Nevins (Revised and enlarged edition; Boston: Little, Brown and Company, 1949), pp. 872-875. Copyright 1939, 1949, by Henry Steele Commager and Allan Nevins. Reprinted by permission of Little, Brown and Company.

A "speculator" is one willing to assume a business risk in hope of some gain. Here, a speculator is one who buys land in hopes of selling it at a higher price. "Boomers" were people who took advantage of the land boom to settle in Oklahoma. The land boom was the sudden increase in available free land.

The "Cherokee strip" was not opened for settlement until 1893.

Two men got on the cowcatcher of a locomotive but had to be removed. On a later train, however, a man rode the whole journey of eighty-nine miles on the cowcatcher. There were only two ladies on the train. Each . . . expressed confidence in the gallantry of the men to enable them to locate claims. The conductor collected ten hundred and twenty-four tickets on this train.

At twelve-fifteen precisely there was a loud whistle from the engine, answered by a shout from the train, and we were in Oklahoma at last. Before the train had crossed the line fifty yards a man sprang off, regardless of the danger. He fell pretty heavily but was on his feet in a few seconds, collected his baggage, which he had thrown out ahead, and was turning sods [digging into the soil] before the train was out of sight. A little farther south a man had evidently just alighted from the mule which was standing by him and whose pack he was unloading. So far it was just possible that every boomer seen had waited till twelve o'clock before he crossed the line, but squatters pure and simple now came in view. They sprang out of the woods on every side, and it was evident from the appearance of some of them that they had been in hiding for weeks. . . .

When the word was given to advance at the north line, the boomers started forward at various rates of speed. All who desired to locate anywhere near the track in the north end of the Territory found themselves forestalled. Some turned back in disgust, and others pushed farther on into the interior. But for absolute contempt of the President's reminder of the danger of premature occupation, Guthrie takes the lead. It could not legally be reached by road in advance of the train; yet when the town site came in view, it was literally covered with lot claimants. The location is well suited for a town. The railroad runs along a valley on the west of which is a creek which forms a picturesque background to the depot. The town, or town site, is on the other side of the track; and the ground slopes gradually up to the summit of a little ridge. At the summit is the land office.

What happened when the train began to slacken [slow down] beggars all description. Boys, middle-aged men, and old fellows threw themselves off the platform and commenced a wild rush. They fell upon each other, scrambled to their feet, and made off, some carrying their grips and others dropping everything in the eagerness of the chase. As the train went on toward the depot the passengers kept jumping off. The town-lot craze seemed to lend speed even to cripples. A man with a wooden leg was among the first to make the dangerous jump, and he held his

538

own in the race. Not a passenger by this first train went past Guthrie, so that the population of the new city was increased by this rush to the extent of nearly a thousand. All roads seemed to lead to the land office at which a line over one hundred yards long was already formed. For a second the runners paused.

Then they commenced a wild tear [race] out east, and each man, as he found an unclaimed lot, proceeded to stake it out and hold it down. The process of securing the lots, as in general adoption, is simple in the extreme. First of all a stake is driven in the ground, with or without a placer attached, setting forth the name of the claimant. Then the new owner paces off the ground he proposes to occupy for a residence or business house. There is at least a charm of variety about the laying out of Guthrie. Some people contented themselves with twenty-five feet frontage, others took forty feet, and others fifty; but most of the claimants had a fair idea of where the streets ought to be and left the necessary space for them. By the time the men on Train No. 1 had each selected his lot the town site had extended away beyond the half section reserved, and long before the majority had quit running, Train No. 2 pulled in, quite as heavily loaded as its predecessor. The same process was carried out to the letter.

Among those hurrying up the hill were two ladies who succeeded in securing a claim each and will hold it. These ladies are from California. They are going into business at once.

There was a considerable interval before another train arrived, but the third and fourth came in close together, each discharging its cargo of passengers to add to the astounding crush. The limits of the city kept on increasing, and by the time the fifth and sixth trains had unloaded, the city extended far away to the distance. Altogether ten trains got in before three o'clock, and making allowance for those who went on to Oklahoma City, there must have been at least six thousand people in Guthrie three hours after the Territory was legally opened for settlement. It was wonderful, the manner in which disputes among the newcomers were settled in this early part of the proceedings. Sometimes half a dozen men would pounce on a lot simultaneously or nearly so. Each would commence to stake out, but after a little while a general agreement would be come to, and every applicant but one would rush off and secure an undisputed lot. There has been so far no unpleasantness of any kind.

1. How would you describe the behavior of these people?

2. What seems to be the reason for this behavior?

12. The Meaning of the West: Brinkerhoff and Turner

Between 1865 and 1900, nine states, all located west of the Mississippi River, entered the Union. By 1900, the nation consisted of forty-five states. By 1912, Oklahoma, New Mexico, and Arizona had been admitted to bring the total to forty-eight.

The next two selections are concerned with what the western lands meant to the people of the United States. The first account is from a speech by Jacob Brinkerhoff, a Democratic congressman from Ohio. Brinkerhoff made the speech in 1845 during the congressional debate on the annexation of Texas. The second selection is from a paper delivered by Frederick Jackson Turner in 1893 before the American Historical Association. It was entitled "The Significance of the Frontier in American History."

JACOB BRINKERHOFF, 1845

Congressional Globe, 28th Cong., 2d Sess., Appendix, 121.

. . . There were few gentlemen here but knew the advantage of having a great West to go to; where, away from the spirit of monopoly, the effects of family influence, the power of associated wealth, and the thousand other adverse influences which met a young man in the eastern portion of the Union, and kept down his efforts at achieving an independence, or treading with success the pathway of an honorable ambition; where none of these hindrances [obstacles] were in his way, but where there was "ample room and verge enough," and where the race was to the swift, and the battle was to the strong.

"Verge," here, means a border area. It refers to the frontier that bordered the settled regions.

FREDERICK JACKSON TURNER, 1893

Frederick Jackson Turner, **The Frontier in American History** (New York: Holt, Rinehart and Winston, Inc., 1962), pp. 1, 37-38.

In a recent bulletin of the Superintendent of the Census for 1890 appear these significant words: "Up to and including 1880 the country had a frontier of settlement, but at present the unsettled area has been so broken into by isolated bodies of settlement that there can hardly be said to be a frontier line. In the discussion of its extent, its westward movement, etc., it cannot, therefore, any longer have a place in the census reports." This brief official statement marks the closing of a great historical movement. Up to our own day American history has been in a large degree the history of the colonization of the Great West. The existence of an area of free land, its continuous recession, and the advance of American settlement westward, explain American development.

. . . Since the days when the fleet of Columbus sailed into the waters of the New World, America has been another name for opportunity . . . He would be a rash prophet who should assert that the expansive character of American life has now entirely ceased. Movement has been its dominant fact, and, unless this training has no effect upon a people, the American energy will continually demand a wider field for its exercise. But never again will such gifts of free land offer themselves. . . . [Each] frontier did indeed furnish a new field of opportunity, a gate of escape from the bondage of the past; and freshness, and confidence, and scorn of older society, impatience of its restraints and its ideas, and indifference to its lessons, have accompanied the frontier. . . .

1. What was the appeal of the West according to Brinkerhoff and Turner?

2. What did Turner feel that the end of the frontier meant for America?

3. According to Brinkerhoff, what was necessary for success on the frontier? Why?

4. According to Turner, what characteristics or traits did the frontier encourage?

5. Did Brinkerhoff seem to approve of the motives for going west and the traits necessary for success there? Did Turner appear to admire the traits encouraged by the frontier?

6. What is a value? What values of Brinkerhoff and Turner emerge from these selections?

7. How are the values of Brinkerhoff and Turner related to each other?

13. The Homestead Act: Two Interpretations

You read about the Homestead Act of 1862 earlier in this unit. You will recall that under this act, a person could gain possession of 160 acres of public land by paying a small fee and by occupying the land for five years. The Homestead Act also provided that land could be acquired after six months residence at $1.25 an acre.

In the next two accounts, two historians present their interpretations of the Homestead Act and other land legislation. The first selection was written by Bernard A. Weisberger, an authority on United States history of the period 1860–1900. Henry Nash Smith, the author of the second account, is well known for his writings on the American West.

Bernard A. Weisberger, **The Age of Steel and Steam** ("The Life History of the United States," Vol. VII [New York: Time, Inc., 1964]), pp. 57-58. Copyright 1964, Time, Inc. Reprinted by permission of Time-Life Books.

"Capital investment" is investment in capital goods. Capital goods are goods used to produce other goods. Examples are land, factory or farm buildings, and machines.

The 98th meridian is often used to mark the beginning of the Great Plains. The westward advance came to a temporary halt at this point in the early 1800's.

"Dummy entries" were claims filed by individuals who agreed to resell immediately to big land investors.

BERNARD A. WEISBERGER

. . . A host of . . . farm machines that arrived in the 1870s let horse power and steam power harvest bumper crops with a family-size work force.

The trouble was that the Homestead Act did not provide families with the several thousand dollars needed to buy this machinery. Moreover, the basic 160-acre farm unit was not large enough to raise sufficient crops to give a reasonable return on this heavy capital investment. And [the farm's] limited area was too small to provide enough water. Finally, neither free land nor new gadgets could save those trusting souls who, late in the '70s, edged out into western Kansas and Nebraska beyond the 98th meridian, where the average annual minimum rainfall would not sustain normal farming. Thousands of these optimistic families limped back in defeat; Kansas editor William Allen White watched a pair of wagons pass through Emporia [Kansas] one day in the '90s, driven by men who had given up "only after a ten years' hard vicious fight . . . which had left its scars on their faces, had bent their bodies, had taken the elasticity [spring] from their steps. . . . They had such high hopes when they went out there; they are so desolate now."

Irrigation might have helped, but irrigation usually required joint effort. Co-operative colonies with their pooled capital, like those founded in Anaheim, California, or Greeley, Colorado, might make a go of irrigated farming. So could the Mormons, banded together under tight church discipline in Utah. That was not yet the way of the American farmer.

[The Homestead Act did not always succeed in providing small farmers with cheap land, either. It] was widely used to secure choice land for powerful operators through "dummy" entries. Further, Congress let the act fight for existence among other, conflicting policies. A Desert Land Act of 1877 offered mile-square tracts at $1.25 an acre to anyone who would irrigate them. Cattlemen filed claims in the names of complaisant [obliging] ranch hands, made token gestures at irrigation and ended with huge parcels. The Timber and Stone Act of 1878 allowed individuals to buy 160-acre blocks of timberland at $2.50 an acre. Timber magnates [large owners] filed thousands of "dummy entries" which, bought for the price of one good log, produced thousands of feet of marketable boards and shingles.

Congress parceled out over 180 million acres to the railroads along their rights-of-way. The lines, however, could choose which sections they wanted in the reserved strips . . . through which the tracks ran. [The strips ran from 20 to as much as 120 miles in width.] Controlling this valuable land, the railroads could wait until farmers gave in and bought at railroad prices . . . Congress also gave the states princely grants under acts to aid education and other public-spirited programs. The Morrill Land Grant Act of 1862 was a forward-looking way of allowing states to endow agricultural colleges with money realized from sales of Federal land grants. Yet the 140 million acres thus donated undercut the Homestead Act's basic principle. The states passed out their shares to speculators, lumbermen, mining magnates—anyone who had the ear of the legislature, as the 160-acre farmer seldom did. In addition, there were state-owned lands that were given away. Texas, always ready to operate on a big scale, handed out three million acres in land-grant and state lands to a Chicago syndicate [business association] to create the XIT ranch. In return, the Chicagoans built Texas a state capital costing $1.5 million. The cost of the ranch worked out to 50 cents an acre in a swath [strip] that extended for 200 miles.

All told, half a billion acres of the public domain had been disposed of by 1900; only 80 million of these acres were patented [given as grants] under the Homestead Act—many of them issued to loggers or cowhands acting as "dummy" entrymen for the boss. No wonder the land giveaway of the 30 years after the Civil War was called a great barbecue, at which those strong enough to elbow their way to the tables got the choicest cuts.

Still the farmers came on. Assailed by drought, they made wry jokes about the man who, when hit with a raindrop, fainted from shock and had to be revived with two buckets of dust. Their hopes remained high. When a large portion of Oklahoma was opened to homesteading in 1889, a thousand eager souls were on hand, on horses and bicycles, in hacks, wagons, carriages and trains, to rush for homesteads at the sound of the starter's gun.

HENRY NASH SMITH

. . . [The] Homestead Act almost wholly failed to have the results that had been predicted. It did not lead to the settlement of large numbers of farmers on lands which they themselves owned and tilled. Vast land grants to railways, failure to repeal the existing laws that played into the hands of speculators by allowing purchase of government lands, and cynical evasion of the law determined the actual working of the public land system. Between the passage of the Homestead Act in 1862 and 1890, only 372,659 entries were perfected [completed]. At most, two millions

LAND GRANTS TO WESTERN RAILROADS

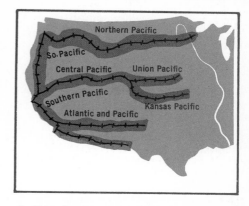

By 1900, the transcontinental railroads had received over 164,000 square miles of land. This was an area almost as big as California which covers 156,573 square miles.

Henry Nash Smith, **Virgin Land, The American West as Symbol and Myth** (Cambridge, Mass.: Harvard University Press, 1950), p. 190. Copyright 1950 by The President and Fellows of Harvard College.

of persons comprising the families of actual settlers could have benefited from the operation of the Act, during a period when the population of the nation increased by about thirty-two millions, and that of the Western states within which most of the homesteading took place, by more than ten millions. Railways alone, for example, sold more land at an average price of five dollars an acre than was conveyed [given or sold] under the Homestead Act. When the mechanical revolution introduced steam-driven tractors and threshing machines to the wheat regions of the Northwest, the pattern of small freehold subsistence farms was in danger of being wiped out. [The small farmer could not afford such machines.] The most telling index of this change is the ratio of tenancy. Eighteen per cent of the farms in Nebraska were operated by tenants in 1880, the first year for which records are available; in 1890 the figure had risen to twenty-four per cent. By 1900 more than thirty-five per cent of all American farmers had become tenants, and the ratio was increasing rapidly. Many farms technically listed as cultivated by their owners were so heavily mortgaged that the ostensible [apparent] owner was hardly his own master. . . .

1. According to Weisberger and Smith, for whom was the Last West a haven?

2. As described by Turner and the census report which he quotes, when did the frontier—cheap land for the small farmer—really end?

3. The purpose of the Homestead Act was to make the Last West the kind of frontier described by Turner. Why was that goal not achieved?

EVALUATING THE IMPACT OF THE FRONTIER

1. Do you think Turner was right about what the West meant to Americans? What were the goals of the settlers who went to the Last West? What were the goals of settlers who went to earlier frontiers? (See Units IV and V.) Could the settlers have achieved their goals without going west? What other questions could you ask to test the accuracy of Turner's idea?

2. Do you think Turner was right about the traits encouraged by the frontier? Were the pioneers you studied marked by such traits? Do Americans today display such traits?

3. Do you admire a person who has the characteristics Turner and Brinkerhoff described? Do most Americans think these

A "freehold" is land which is held for life. A "subsistence farm" produces only enough to support the people working on it.

The "ratio of tenancy" refers to the amount of farm land rented or leased as compared with the amount owned by the farmer himself.

traits are important? In other words, has admiration of such characteristics become an American *value*?

4. How would you summarize the importance of the western frontier for the history of our country?

INDIVIDUALISM IN THE LAST WEST

1. What is individualism? How did you define it when you studied individualism on the frontier in Unit V?

2. How does individualism relate to the traits Turner said the frontier encouraged?

3. According to Weisberger and Smith, was individualism sufficient for achieving success in the Last West? Why or why not? How does this compare with the way Brinkerhoff interpreted the requirements for success on the frontier?

4. Review what you learned in Unit V about the problems of settlers on earlier frontiers and how they solved these problems. Was individualism sufficient for success then? Was it more or less sufficient than in the Last West?

5. Was individualism a realistic value for a settler in the Last West? Explain.

Industrialism

III. A New Era: Industry and the Growth of Wealth

THE INDUSTRIAL BOOM

14. The Growth of Industry, 1860–1900

In 1789, Samuel Slater came to America carrying a secret. He had memorized the carefully guarded details of an English machine that made cloth. Cloth made by machine could be produced much faster than cloth made by hand. Thus, machine-made cloth could be sold much more cheaply. Making cloth by machine was a good business, because people were eager to buy less expensive goods.

Moses Brown, a Rhode Island merchant, *invested* in Samuel Slater's machine. That is, Brown gave Slater money to build his machine and provided a building, or *factory,* in which to operate the machine. In return, Brown's firm, Almy & Brown, was permitted to use the machine to manufacture cotton cloth. In 1793, Slater became a member of the firm of Almy, Brown & Slater. He formed a new company in 1798 with the name of Samuel Slater & Co.

More and more machines came into use during the nineteenth century. These machines ushered in the *industrial era.* Most of them were used to manufacture goods in factories. But machines also came to be employed in mining and processing minerals and in farming. These developments speeded industrial growth.

As industrial growth proceeded, people left their farms to work in factories. The new factories, which were located in towns and cities, also attracted people from abroad. The following statistics and charts describe industrial growth in the United States between 1860 and 1900. They also show the effect of industrial growth on population patterns. Some of the figures in these charts are rounded off.

INDUSTRIAL PRODUCTION

STEEL
Production in Tons
    1867—   19,643
    1875—   389,799
    1901—13,473,595
Production of Closest Rival, Germany
    1901— 8,000,000

RAILROADS
Number of Transcontinental Lines
    1869—1
    1881—2
    1893—5
Mileage of Track Operated
    1865— 35,085
    1900—258,784

MANUFACTURES
Value
    1860—$2 BILLION
    1890—$9 BILLION

MEAT PACKING INDUSTRY
Value
    1870— $65,000,000
    1890—$500,000,000

OIL
    1859—OIL DISCOVERED AT TITUS-VILLE, PENN.
    1885—28,000,000 TONS PRODUCED BY STANDARD OIL COMPANY, WHICH CONTROLLED 90% OF THE REFINING INDUSTRY.

TEXTILES: COTTON
Production of One Worker
    1840— 9,600 YARDS IN 14 HOURS
    1886—30,000 YARDS IN 10 HOURS

TELEPHONES
    1876—TELEPHONE INVENTED.
    1900—1,356,000 TELEPHONES IN USE.

DISCOVERIES AND INVENTIONS

1829 EXTRACTION OF COTTONSEED OIL (THIS PRODUCT IS USED FOR SALAD AND COOKING OILS, COSMETICS, MARGARINE, SOAP, CANDLES, DETERGENTS, OILCLOTH, ETC.)

1830 T-RAIL (A METAL RAIL ATTACHED TO A WOODEN TIE. IT LASTED LONGER AND WAS EASIER TO PRODUCE THAN EARLIER RAILS.)

1831 REAPER

1834 ELECTRIC MOTOR

1839 VULCANIZATION OF RUBBER (THE PROCESS OF CHEMICALLY TREATING RUBBER TO GIVE IT ELASTICITY, STRENGTH, AND STABILITY.)

1843 TYPEWRITER

1844 TELEGRAPH

1846 SEWING MACHINE

1846 ROTARY PRINTING PRESS (THIS ADVANCED THE NEWSPAPER INDUSTRY BY MAKING IT POSSIBLE TO PRINT 20,000 SHEETS PER HOUR.)

1851 BESSEMER PROCESS OF STEELMAKING (LARGE QUANTITIES OF STEEL COULD BE PRODUCED CHEAPLY BY BLASTING AIR THROUGH THE MELTED IRON TO REMOVE THE IMPURITIES.)

1852 PASSENGER ELEVATOR

1858 SHOE MACHINE (SEWS THE SOLE TO THE UPPER PART OF THE SHOE.)

1860 FIRST PETROLEUM REFINERY

1862 IRON AND STEEL SHIPS

1864 PULLMAN SLEEPING CAR

1865 COMPRESSION ICE MACHINE (MADE THE FIRST ARTIFICIAL ICE IN THE UNITED STATES.)

1868 OPEN HEARTH PROCESS OF STEELMAKNG (MELTED IRON IS BAKED WITH SCRAP METALS. SAMPLES CAN BE TAKEN TO DETERMINE THE DESIRED CARBON CONTENT OF THE STEEL. THEREFORE, LOW GRADE IRON AND SCRAPS CAN BE USED.)

1868 AIR BRAKE (THIS MADE HIGH-SPEED RAIL TRAVEL SAFE.)

1876 TELEPHONE

1879 ELECTRIC LIGHT

1879 AUTOMOBILE

1888 HAND CAMERA

1889 ELECTRIC SEWING MACHINE

1891 RADIO

1896 ELECTRIC STOVE

NUMBER OF WORKERS BY OCCUPATION

Year	Farming	All Non-farming Workers	Manufacturing and Construction
1860	6,210,000	5,320,000	1,930,000
1880	8,610,000	8,780,000	4,000,000
1900	10,710,000	18,360,000	8,000,000

TOWNS AND CITIES BY SIZE OF POPULATION

Size of population	1880	1890	1900	1910	1920
1,000,000 OR MORE	1	3	3	3	3
500,000 TO 1,000,000	3	1	3	5	9
250,000 TO 500,000	4	7	9	11	13
100,000 TO 250,000	12	17	23	31	43
50,000 TO 100,000	15	30	40	59	76
25,000 TO 50,000	42	66	82	119	143
10,000 TO 25,000	146	230	280	369	465

1. How would you summarize the preceding statistics? What took place in America between 1860 and 1900?

2. Could the term "revolution" be applied to any of these developments? Why or why not?

15. Corporations

A corporation is a form of business organization that came into wide use between 1865 and 1900. Before the Civil War, most businesses in the United States were owned by one man, or by two or more partners. Corporations are owned by many people, who are known as *stockholders*. They become part-owners of the business by purchasing *shares* of *stock,* or ownership, in the company.

547

As owners of a corporation, stockholders have the right to help make decisions about the company's business. Each share of stock permits its owner to cast one vote. The organization of a corporation looks like this:

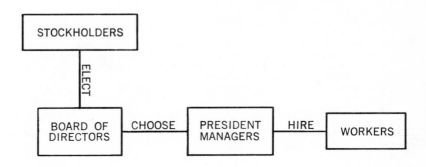

People invest in a business, or give money to support it, because they expect the business to make a good profit. They hope to share in the profit and thereby earn money through their investment. Stockholders receive part of a corporation's profits in the form of *dividends*. Stockholders can also make money by selling their stock as the corporation becomes more prosperous. If the value of their stock rises, they can sell it for more money than they paid to buy it. A *stock exchange* provides a centralized market where stocks of many companies can be easily bought and sold.

Corporations have two major advantages over partnerships and one-man businesses. First, the stockholders are not personally responsible for the company's debts. Thus, if the company goes bankrupt, the owners lose only the money they originally invested. Furthermore, stockholders can sell their stock at any time.

Secondly, by selling stock to many people, corporations can raise money more easily than partnerships or individually owned businesses. This became an important advantage after the Civil War. As businesses grew larger and more complicated, they also became more expensive to establish. Businessmen needed large amounts of money to build, equip, and operate a steel mill, an oil refinery, or a railroad.

Why did corporations first become important between 1865 and 1900?

16. Andrew Carnegie Becomes a Businessman

Andrew Carnegie, at one time a penniless immigrant from Scotland, amassed a fortune in the steel industry. The following selection is an autobiographical account of how he obtained his start in the business world.

Andrew Carnegie, "How I Served My Apprenticeship As a Business Man," **Youth's Companion,** Vol. LXX, no. 17 (1896), pp. 216-217.

. . . I am sure that I should never have selected a business career if I had been permitted to choose.

The eldest son of parents who were themselves poor, I had, fortunately, to begin to perform some useful work in the world while still very young, in order to earn an honest livelihood . . . What I could get to do, not what I desired, was the question.

When I was born my father was a well-to-do master-weaver in Dunfermline, Scotland. He owned no less than four damask looms and employed apprentices. This was before the days of steam factories for the manufacture of linen. A few large merchants took orders and employed "master-weavers," such as my father, to weave the cloth, the merchants supplying the materials.

"Damask" is a high-quality fabric.

As the factory system developed, handloom weaving naturally declined, and my father was one of the sufferers by the change. The first serious lesson of my life came to me one day when he had taken in the last of his work to the merchant and returned to our little home greatly distressed because there was no more work for him to do. I was then just about ten years of age, but the lesson burned into my heart, and I resolved then that "the wolf of poverty" would be driven from our door some day, if I could do it.

The question of selling the old looms and starting for the United States came up in the family council, and I heard it discussed from day to day. It was finally resolved to take the plunge and join relatives already in Pittsburgh. I well remember that neither father nor mother thought the change would be otherwise than a great sacrifice for them, but that "it would be better for our two boys. . . ."

Arriving in Allegheny City, four of us,—father, mother, my younger brother and myself,—father entered a cotton factory. I soon followed and served as a "bobbin boy," and this is how I began my preparation for subsequent apprenticeship as a business man. I received one dollar and twenty cents a week, and was then just about twelve years old.

A "bobbin boy" tended the spools in the spinning of thread.

I cannot tell you how proud I was when I received my first week's own earnings. One dollar and twenty cents made by myself and given to me because I had been of some use in the

world! No longer entirely dependent upon my parents, but at last admitted to the family partnership as a contributing member and able to help them! I think this makes a man out of a boy sooner than almost anything else. . . . It is everything to feel that you are useful. . . .

For a lad of twelve to rise and breakfast every morning, except the blessed Sunday morning, and go into the streets and find his way to the factory, and begin work while it was still dark outside, and not be released until after darkness came again in the evening, forty minutes' interval only being allowed at noon, was a terrible task.

But I was young . . . and something within always told me that . . . I should some day get into a better position. . . .

A change soon came, for a kind old Scotsman, who knew some of our relatives, made bobbins and took me into his factory before I was thirteen. But here for a time it was even worse than in the cotton factory, because I was set to fire a boiler in the cellar, and actually to run the small steam-engine which drove the machinery.

The firing of the boiler was all right, for fortunately we did not use coal, but the refuse wooden chips, and I always liked to work in wood. But the responsibility of keeping the water right and of running the engine, and the danger of my making a mistake and blowing the whole factory to pieces, caused too great a strain, and I often awoke and found myself sitting up in bed through the night trying the steam-gages. But I never told them at home that I was having a "hard tussle." No! no! everything must be bright to them.

This was a point of honor, for every member of the family was working hard except, of course, my little brother, who was then a child, and we were telling each other only all the bright things. Beside this no man would whine and give up—he would die first. . . .

My kind employer, John Hay, peace to his ashes! soon relieved me of the undue strain, for he needed some one to make out bills and keep his accounts, and finding that I could write a plain schoolboy hand, and could "cipher" [work with numbers], I became his only clerk. But still I had to work hard up-stairs in the factory, for the clerking took but little time. . . .

I come now to the third step in my apprenticeship, for I had already taken two, as you see, the "cotton factory" and then the "bobbin factory" . . . I obtained a situation as messenger-boy in the telegraph office of Pittsburgh when I was fourteen. Here I entered a new world.

Amid books, newspapers, pencils, pen and ink and writing pads, and a clean office, bright windows and the literary atmosphere, I was the happiest boy alive.

My only dread was that I should some day be dismissed because I did not know the city; for it is necessary that a messenger-boy should know all the firms and addresses of men who are in the habit of receiving telegrams. But I was a stranger in Pittsburgh. However, I made up my mind that I would learn to repeat successively each business house in the principal streets, and was soon able to shut my eyes and begin at one side of Wood Street, and call every firm successively to the top, then pass to the other side and call every firm to the bottom. Before long I was able to do this with the business streets generally. My mind was then at rest upon that point.

Of course, every ambitious messenger-boy wants to become an operator, and before the operators arrived in the early mornings the boys slipped up to the instruments and practised. This I did and was soon able to talk to the boys in the other offices along the line, who were also practising.

One morning I heard Philadelphia calling Pittsburgh and giving the signal, "Death Message." Great attention was then paid to "Death Messages," and I thought I ought to try to take this one. I answered and did so, and went off and delivered it before the operator came. After that the operators sometimes used to ask me to work for them.

A "death message" is a notification of someone's death.

Having a sensitive ear for sound I soon learned to take messages by the ear, which was then very uncommon—I think only two persons in the United States could then do it. Now every operator takes by ear, so easy is it to follow and do what any other boy can—if you only have to. This brought me into notice, and finally I became an operator and received the—to me—enormous recompense [salary] of twenty-five dollars per month, three hundred dollars a year!

To "take a message by ear," one must interpret the coded clicks of the telegraph and figure out the words without writing down each letter.

This was a fortune; the very sum that I had fixed when I was a factory-worker as the fortune I wished to possess, because the family could live on three hundred dollars a year and be almost, or quite, independent. Here it was at last! But I was soon to be in receipt of extra compensation for extra work.

The six newspapers of Pittsburgh received telegraphic news in common. Six copies of each despatch were made by a gentleman who received six dollars per week for the work, and he offered me a gold dollar every week if I would do it, of which I was very glad, indeed, because I always liked to work with news and scribble for newspapers. . . .

I think this last step of doing something beyond one's task is fully entitled to be considered "business." The other revenue, you see, was just salary obtained for regular work; but here was a "little business operation" upon my own account, and I was very proud indeed of my gold dollar every week.

The Pennsylvania Railroad shortly after this was completed to Pittsburgh, and that genius, Thomas A. Scott, was its superintendent. He often came to the telegraph office to talk to his chief . . . and I became known to him in this way.

When that great railway system put up a wire of its own, he asked me to be his "clerk and operator." So I left the telegraph office . . . and became connected with the railways.

The new appointment was accompanied by a, to me, tremendous increase of salary. It jumped from twenty-five to thirty-five dollars per month. Mr. Scott was then receiving one hundred and twenty-five dollars per month, and I used to wonder what on earth he could do with so much money.

I remained for thirteen years in the service of the Pennsylvania Railroad Company, and was at last superintendent of the Pittsburgh division of the road, successor to Mr. Scott, who had in the meantime risen to the office of vice-president of the company.

One day Mr. Scott, who was the kindest of men, and had taken a great fancy for me, asked if I had or could find five hundred dollars to invest.

Here the business instinct came into play. I felt that as the door was opened for a business investment with my chief, it would be wilful flying in the face of providence if I did not jump at it; so I answered promptly:

"Yes, sir, I think I can."

"Very well," he said, "get it; a man has just died who owns ten shares in the Adams Express Company, which I want you to buy. It will cost you sixty dollars per share, and I can help you with a little balance if you cannot raise it all."

Here was a queer position. The available assets of the whole family were not five hundred dollars. . . .

Indeed, had Mr. Scott known our position he would have advanced it himself, but the last thing in the world the proud Scot will do is to reveal his poverty and rely upon others. The family had managed by this time to purchase a small house, and paid for it in order to save rent. My recollection is that it was worth eight hundred dollars.

The matter was laid before the council of three that night, and the oracle spoke. "Must be done. Mortgage our house. I will take the steamer in the morning for Ohio and see uncle, and ask him to arrange it. I am sure he can." This was done. Of course her visit was successful—where did she ever fail?

The money was procured; paid over; ten shares of Adams Express Company stock was mine, but no one knew our little home had been mortgaged "to give our boy a start."

Adams Express Stock then paid monthly dividends of one per cent, and the first check for ten dollars arrived. I can see it now, and I well remember the signature of "J. C. Babcock, cashier . . ."

Here was something new to all of us, for none of us had ever received anything but from toil. A return from capital was something strange and new.

How money could make money . . . led to much speculation upon the part of the young fellows [Carnegie's friends], and I was for the first time hailed as a "capitalist. . . ."

A very important incident in my life occurred when one day in a train a nice, farmer-looking gentleman approached me, saying that the conductor had told him I was connected with the Pennsylvania Railroad, and he should like to show me something. He pulled from a small green bag the model of the first sleeping-car. This was Mr. Woodruff, the inventor.

Its value struck me like a flash. I asked him to come to Altoona the following week, and he did so.

Mr. Scott, with his usual quickness, grasped the idea. A contract was made with Mr. Woodruff to put two trial cars on the Pennsylvania Railroad. Before leaving Altoona Mr. Woodruff came and offered me an interest in the venture, which I promptly accepted. But how I was to make my payments rather troubled me, for the cars were to be paid for in monthly instalments after delivery, and my first monthly payment was to be two hundred and seventeen dollars and a half.

I had not the money, and I did not see any way of getting it. But I finally decided to visit the local banker and ask him for a loan, pledging myself to repay at the rate of fifteen dollars per month. He promptly granted it. Never shall I forget his putting his arm over my shoulder, saying, "Oh, yes, Andy, you are all right."

A "note" is a written promise to repay a debt.

I then and there signed my first note. Proud day this; and surely, now, no one will dispute that I was becoming a "business man." I had signed my first note and, more important of all,—for any fellow can sign a note,—I had found a banker willing to take it as "good."

My subsequent payments were made by the receipts [money received] from the sleeping-cars, and I really made my first considerable sum from this investment in the Woodruff Sleeping Car Company, which was afterward absorbed by Mr. Pullman—a remarkable man who is now known all over the world.

Shortly after this I was appointed superintendent of the Pittsburgh Division, and returned to my dear old home, smoky Pittsburgh. Wooden bridges were then used exclusively upon the railways, and the Pennsylvania Railroad was experimenting with a bridge built of cast-iron. I saw that wooden bridges would not do for the future, and organized a company in Pittsburgh to build iron bridges.

Here again I had recourse to the bank, because my share of the capital was twelve hundred and fifty dollars and I had not the money; but the bank lent it to me, and we began the Keystone Bridge Works, which proved a great success. This company built the first great bridge over the Ohio River, three hundred feet span, and has built many of the most important structures since.

This was my beginning in manufacturing; and from that start all our other works have grown, the profits of the one works building the other. My "apprenticeship" as a business man soon ended, for I resigned my position as an officer of the Pennsylvania Railroad Company to give exclusive attention to business.

I was no longer merely an official working for others upon a salary, but a full-fledged business man working upon my own account.

1. What is Carnegie's definition of a "businessman"? What is his definition of a "capitalist"?

554

2. According to Carnegie, what different factors contributed to his success in becoming a businessman?

3. Carnegie arrived in America in 1848. He began his job with the Pennsylvania Railroad in 1853. Do you think this had anything to do with his success? If he had come to America in 1800 or 1820, do you think he would have become a millionaire? Give reasons for your answer.

17. Big Business

You have already learned how the industrial growth of the period 1865–1900 produced a new form of business organization, the corporation. This was the first step toward the development of big business. Because the corporation could command more *capital,* or wealth, than the older forms of business organization, it made bigger enterprises possible.

Big business developed further when corporations started to combine with each other. Sometimes a corporation would combine with companies that provided goods or services it needed. Andrew Carnegie, for example, started his steel empire by building steel mills in Pittsburgh. Then he bought iron ore deposits near Lake Superior and ships to carry the ore across the Great Lakes. He also built a railroad to carry the ore from the Great Lakes to Pittsburgh. He even bought coal mines in Pennsylvania to supply his steel mills with fuel.

Another form of combination was to join with or buy companies that produced the same things. John D. Rockefeller, who founded his oil refining business in 1865, enlarged it by buying other refineries. Companies often pursued both forms of combination: Carnegie eventually bought other steel mills, and Rockefeller added oil pipe lines and railroad tank cars to his Standard Oil Company.

1. What do you suppose were the business advantages of combinations like those formed by Carnegie and Rockefeller?

2. Why do you think combinations like these became common in the period 1865–1900?

3. Do you think that such combinations would benefit the people who worked for these companies? Would such combinations benefit customers? Explain your answers.

18. The Advantages of Combination: John D. Rockefeller

John D. Rockefeller, **Random Reminiscences of Men and Events** (Garden City, N. Y.: Doubleday & Company, Inc., 1909), pp. 81-83, 86-87. Copyright 1909, Doubleday & Company, Inc., copyright renewed 1936, John D. Rockefeller. Reprinted by permission of the estate of John D. Rockefeller.

The story of the early history of the oil trade is too well known to bear repeating in detail. The cleansing of crude petroleum was a simple and easy process, and at first the profits were very large. Naturally, all sorts of people went into it; the butcher, the baker, and the candlestick maker began to refine oil, and it was only a short time before more of the finished product was put on the market than could possibly be consumed. The price went down and down until the trade was threatened with ruin. It seemed absolutely necessary to extend the market for oil by exporting to foreign countries, which required a long and most difficult development . . . [It also seemed necessary] to greatly improve the processes of refining so that oil could be made and sold cheaply, yet with a profit . . . [Finally, there was a need] to use as by-products all of the materials which in the less efficient plants were lost or thrown away.

. . . To accomplish all of these tasks of enlarging the market and improving the methods of manufacture in a large way was beyond the power or ability of any concern as then constituted [set up]. It could only be done, we reasoned, by increasing our capital and availing ourselves of the best talent and experience.

It was with this idea that we proceeded to buy the largest and best refining concerns and centralize the administration of them with a view to securing greater economy and efficiency. The business grew faster than we anticipated. . . .

I ascribe the success of the Standard Oil Company to its consistent policy of making the volume of its business large through the merit and cheapness of its products. It has spared no expense in utilizing the best and most efficient method of manufacture. It has sought for the best superintendents and workmen and paid the best wages. It has not hesitated to sacrifice old machinery and old plants for new and better ones. It has placed its manufactories [plants] at the points where they could supply markets at the least expense. It has not only sought markets for its principal products, but for all possible by-products, sparing no expense in introducing them to the public in every nook and corner of the world. It has not hesitated to invest millions of dollars in methods for cheapening the gathering and distribution of oils by pipe-lines, special cars, tank-steamers, and tank-wagons. It has erected tank-stations at railroad centers in every part of the country to cheapen the storage and delivery of oil. It has had faith in American oil and has brought together vast sums of money for the purpose of making it what it is, and for holding its market against the competition of Russia and all the countries which are producers of oil and competitors against American products.

1. Why was the oil business faced with ruin early in its history?

2. What measures did Rockefeller feel would save the oil industry? How do you think each of these steps helped the oil business?

3. Why did Rockefeller think that a large company was better equipped than a small one to carry out these steps?

4. Did Rockefeller seem to feel that his big oil company was helpful to workers? To consumers? To the American public in general? Give examples to support your answer.

19. "All Hail, King Steel..."

The following selection is an excerpt from a book written by Andrew Carnegie in 1902. In it, he expresses his feelings about the steel business.

... The influence of our steel-making capacity upon development at home must be marvellous, for the nation that makes the cheapest steel has the other nations at its feet so far as manufacturing in most of its branches is concerned. The cheapest steel means the cheapest ships, the cheapest machinery, the cheapest thousand and one articles of which steel is the base. We are on the eve of a development of the manufacturing powers of the republic such as the world has never seen.

The republic's progress and commanding position as a steel-producer are told in a few words: In 1873, only twenty-seven years ago, the United States produced 198,796 tons of steel, and Great Britain, her chief competitor, 653,500 tons, more than three times as much. Twenty-six years later, in 1899, the republic made more than twice as much as the monarchy, the figures being 10,639,857 and 5,000,000 tons respectively, an eight-fold increase for Great Britain and fifty-three-fold for the republic, and it made almost 40 per cent of all the steel made in the world, which was 27,000,000 tons. Industrial history has nothing to show comparable to this. . . . .

Andrew Carnegie, "Steel Manufacture in the United States in the 19th Century," **The Empire of Business** (Garden City, N. Y.: Doubleday & Company, Inc., 1902), pp. 231-242.

Farewell, then, Age of Iron; all hail, King Steel, and success to the republic, the future seat and centre of his empire, where he is to sit enthroned and work his wonders upon the earth.

According to this statement, how does Carnegie feel about the steel business? Does his only satisfaction seem to come from making money? Explain.

20. America's Progress: Andrew Carnegie

In 1893, Carnegie made the following statement about America's progress.

Andrew Carnegie, **Triumphant Democracy, Sixty Years' March of the Republic** (Revised edition; New York: Charles Scribner's Sons, 1893), pp. 509-510.

Here is the first century's record of the harvest of Democracy in the Republic:

The majority of the English-speaking race, in a world within itself, under one republican flag, at peace, and pledged by act of all parties to offer peaceful arbitration for the settlement of international disputes.

The nation which contains the best educated, most intelligent, most religious, and the wealthiest and healthiest body of citizens in the world; the smallest proportion of white illiterates, paupers, criminals, blind, deaf and dumb, feeble-minded and insane.

The nation which spends least on war and most upon education, and has the smallest army and navy in proportion to population and wealth of any maritime power; and which provides more generously than any other for every soldier or sailor injured in its service, and for their widows and orphans.

A "philanthropic agency" is one that grants aid to those in need. The word "philantropic" literally means loving mankind.

The people which to a greater extent than any other realize that surplus wealth is but a trust to be administered during life for the good of the community. Nowhere are there so many philanthropic agencies at work.

The nation whose Constitution is so perfect that no man suggests change, and whose fundamental laws as they stand are satisfactory to all.

The nation first in public credit and in payment of debt; the wealthiest nation; the greatest in agriculture, in manufacturing, in banking, and in commerce; the nation whose citizens are the most inventive and most enterprising, and by far the most prosperous in the world, and the nation in which labor commands the steadiest employment and receives the greatest reward.

558

The nation which is, of all English-speaking communities, most truly conservative of all that is good, and which most profoundly reverences law, and decrees its most strenuous enforcement.

The nation in which the rights of the minority, the rights of property and of freedom and validity of contract, and of free labor, are most secure.

The only truly prosperous nation in the world today; a nation in which every sober man, able and willing to perform labor, can readily find employment at wages which enable him to save a competence [income] for old age.

The only nation of all the English-speaking race whose flag, wherever it floats over land and over sea, is the symbol and guarantor of the equality of the citizen.

1. How did Carnegie view America's accomplishments?

2. Judging from this selection, how do you suppose he would view America's future?

3. In the same year that Carnegie wrote this statement, Frederick Jackson Turner made a prediction about America's future (see pages 540–541). How do the two compare? How can you account for this?

CONCLUDING EXERCISE

1. How did men like Rockefeller and Carnegie react to the industrial boom?

2. How would you characterize or describe Rockefeller's building of Standard Oil?

3. Do you think that the big business combinations which arose in the period 1865–1900 were likely to be helpful or harmful to the American people? Explain.

4. According to the statistics and other accounts you have studied in this unit, was Turner's prediction about America's future correct? Explain.

THE GILDED AGE

21. Cornelius Vanderbilt's Summer "Cottage"

"Gilded" means covered with gold. Because of the style of living that emerged among the wealthy in the late nineteenth century, the era came to be called the "Gilded Age." Examples of this style of living appear in the next two readings. The photographs and selection that follow depict The Breakers, Cornelius Vanderbilt's summer home. The Breakers was completed in 1895 at a cost of $4,000,000. The Vanderbilts made their fortune in shipping and railroads.

THE BREAKERS

Bernard A. Weisberger, **The Age of Steel and Steam** ("The Life History of the United States," Vol. VII [New York: Time, Inc., 1964]), p. 149. Copyright 1964, Time, Inc. Reprinted by permission of Time-Life Books.

A "promontory" is a high point of land or rock which juts into a lake or ocean.

A DESCRIPTION OF THE BREAKERS

Cornelius [Vanderbilt], grandson of the ferryman-to-financier Cornelius . . . converted four million dollars into a 70-room "cottage," as the elite termed all summer homes. Set on an 11-acre promontory at Newport, Rhode Island, the mansion was named The Breakers and the over-all effect, succinctly [concisely] put by one observer, was "paralyzing." Two of its largest rooms were designed and built in France, torn apart, shipped to Newport and carefully rebuilt by French workmen brought over for that purpose. In addition to the standard accouterments [fixtures], its bathrooms had hot and cold running *salt* water. . . .

22. Ward McAllister Describes a New York Party

Ward McAllister, who lived during the nineteenth century, wrote about the wealthy people of his era. He was a member of the wealthy society which he described. He coined the familiar term, "The Four Hundred," which refers to the members of the exclusive social set of a community. In 1890, McAllister recorded the following observations about how some of the rich lived.

... [A] man of wealth, who had accumulated a fortune ... resolved to give New Yorkers a sensation; to give them a banquet which should exceed in luxury and expense anything before seen in this country. As he expressed it, "... [Since] the United States Government had just refunded me $10,000, exacted from me for duties upon importations ... I resolved to appropriate it to giving a banquet that would always be remembered." Accordingly he went to Charles Delmonico, who in turn went to his *cuisine classique* [kitchen staff] to see how they could possibly spend this sum on this feast. Success crowned their efforts. The sum in such skillful hands soon melted away, and a banquet was given of such beauty and magnificence, that even New Yorkers, accustomed as they were to every species of novel expenditure, were astonished at its lavishness, its luxury. The banquet was given at Delmonico's, in Fourteenth Street. There were seventy-two guests in the large ballroom, looking on Fifth Avenue.

The table covered the whole length and breadth of the room, only leaving a passageway for the waiters to pass around it. It was a long extended oval table, and every inch of it was covered with flowers, excepting a space in the centre, left for a lake, and a border around the table for the plates. This lake ... was an oval pond, thirty feet in length, by nearly the width of the table, inclosed by a delicate golden wire network, reaching from table to ceiling, making the whole one grand cage; four superb swans, brought from Prospect Park, swam in it, surrounded by high banks of flowers of every species and variety, which prevented them from splashing the water on the table. ... Then, all around the inclosure, and in fact above the entire table, hung little golden cages, with fine songsters [birds], who filled the room with their melody. ... The surface of the whole table ... was one unbroken series of undulations [waves], rising and falling like the billows of the sea, but all clothed and carpeted with every form of blossom. ...

Ward McAllister, **Society as I Have Seen It** (New York: Cassell Publishing Company, 1890), pp. 233-234.

CONCLUDING EXERCISE

1. How would you describe the style of life illustrated by The Breakers and the New York party?

2. What do you suppose made such a life possible?

3. Do you approve of the way the Vanderbilts and Ward McAllister's society lived? Why or why not?

THE IDEAS OF THE GILDED AGE: SUCCESS AND SOCIETY

23. The Views of John D. Rockefeller

The millionaires of the Gilded Age had firm opinions about why they had been successful and what their role was in society. In the readings that follow you will find examples of the opinions held by them and their admirers. The first selection is by John D. Rockefeller.

POINTS TO CONSIDER
What the wealthy valued.

John D. Rockefeller, **Random Reminiscences of Men and Events** (Garden City, N. Y.: Doubleday & Company, Inc., 1909), pp. 133-34, 144-45. Copyright 1909, Doubleday & Company, Inc., copyright renewed 1936, John D. Rockefeller. Reprinted by permission of the estate of John D. Rockefeller.

. . . The man who starts out simply with the idea of getting rich won't succeed; you must have a larger ambition. There is no mystery in business success. The great industrial leaders have told again and again the plain and obvious fact that there can be no permanent success without fair dealing that leads to widespread confidence in the man himself, and that is the real capital we all prize and work for. . . .

If I were to give advice to a young man starting out in life, I should say to him: If you aim for a large broad-gauged success, do not begin your business career, whether you sell your labor or are an independent producer, with the idea of getting from the world by hook or crook all you can. In the choice of your profession or your business employment, let your first thought be: Where can I fit in so that I may be most effective in the work of the world? . . . Investigation will show that the great fortunes which have been made in this country, and the same is probably true of other lands, have come to men who have performed great and far-reaching economic services—men who, with great faith in the future of their country, have done most for the development of its resources. The man will be most successful who confers the greatest service on the world. . . .

Probably the greatest single obstacle to the progress and happiness of the American people lies in the willingness of so many men to invest their time and money in multiplying competitive industries instead of opening up new fields, and putting their money into lines of industry and development that are needed. It requires a better type of mind to seek out and to support or to create the new than to follow the worn paths of accepted success; but here is the great chance in our still rapidly developing country. . . .

1. What does Rockefeller say a man must do in order to succeed in business?

2. What are "personal qualities"? In order to become successful, what personal qualities would a man have to possess?

3. In Rockefeller's view, does a businessman's rise to success help or harm the country? How?

24. The Millionaire and Society

The following are views on the millionaire's role in the community. The first of the following four selections was written by Mrs. Reginald de Koven, wife of an operetta composer. The second is by Andrew Carnegie, who gave millions of dollars to schools and libraries. Charles Perkins, president of the Chicago, Burlington, and Quincy Railroad, wrote the third passage. The last selection is by James T. McCleary, secretary of the American Iron and Steel Institute.

MRS. REGINALD de KOVEN: THE MILLIONAIRE'S RECORD

With an admirable frequency the millionaires of our country become its chief benefactors. Their list of charities is almost parallel with [as long as] their enlisted stocks and bonds. Libraries, museums and endowments for the development of the arts and sciences are the transmuted [changed] products of coal and iron, and the patrons of arts are as earnest and conscientious in the distribution of their wealth as they were in its early accumulation.

Mrs. Reginald de Koven, "The Influence of Great Riches Upon the Rich Themselves," The Independent, Vol. LIV, no. 2787 (1902), p. 1064.

Race courses are far less frequent than hospitals, and fewer far than the endowed institutions of learning which spring up in the large cities and even in the smaller towns of East and West.

All these indications reveal the seriousness of the rich men of our country and define the primary results of the accumulation of wealth upon the original accumulators.

ANDREW CARNEGIE: THE GOSPEL OF WEALTH

. . . Thus is the problem of rich and poor to be solved. . . . Individualism will continue, but the millionaire will be a trustee for

"Testimony of Mr. Andrew Carnegie," Industrial Relations: Final Report and Testimony Submitted to Congress by the Commission on Industrial Relations (Washington, D.C.: United States Government Printing Office, 1916), Vol. VIII, p. 7568.

the poor; entrusted for a season with the great part of the increased wealth of the community, but administering it for the community far better than it could or would have done for itself. . . . [Soon there will be] no mode of disposing of surplus wealth creditable to thoughtful and earnest men . . . save by using it year after year for the general good. . . . The day is not far distant when . . . the public verdict will . . . be, "the man who dies . . . rich dies disgraced. . . ."

CHARLES PERKINS: THE MILLIONAIRE AND PROGRESS

Edward C. Kirkland, **Industry Comes of Age** (New York: Holt, Rinehart and Winston, Inc., 1961), p. 407.

Have not great merchants, great manufacturers, great inventors, done more for the world than preachers and philanthropists? . . . Can there be any doubt that cheapening the cost of necessaries and conveniences of life is the most powerful agent of civilization and progress? Does not the fact that well-fed, well-warmed men make better citizens, other things being equal, than those who are cold and hungry, answer the question? Poverty is the cause of most of the crime and misery in the world—cheapening the cost of the necessaries and conveniences of life is lessening poverty, and there is no other way to lessen it, absolutely none. History and experience demonstrate that as wealth has accumulated and things have cheapened, men have improved . . . in their habits of thought, their sympathy for others, their ideas of justice as well as of mercy. . . . Material progress must come first and . . . upon it is founded all other progress.

JAMES T. McCLEARY: THE ADVANTAGES OF BIG BUSINESS

James T. McCleary, "Big Business and Labor," **American Academy of Political and Social Science Annals,** Vol. XLII (July, 1912), pp. 26-27.

. . . Since 1830, when railroading began, the population of the United States has increased sevenfold. But during that period the number of our people employed in transportation has increased more than a hundredfold. In other words, in the field of transportation the coming of big business in this country has multiplied each man's chance for employment by more than twelve.

. . . When the spinning of yarn and the weaving of cloth were done by hand, few people were able to find regular money-making employment in those trades. . . . The invention of the sewing machine has largely increased, compared with the increase in population, the number of persons regularly employed in making wearing apparel. The making of garments has become big business in large part, and in that part affords to each person more opportunity for work . . . The invention of the telegraph and that of the telephone have not only increased very greatly the chance for work in transmitting messages but have practically opened an entirely new field of employment.... The improvements in papermaking, in typesetting and in printing generally have resulted in big business...and at the same time have vastly increased the number of persons employed in paper and printing industries.

1. According to Mrs. de Koven and Andrew Carnegie, what was the role of the millionaire in society?

2. Why would millionaires assume this role? Why didn't they simply use their money to live lavishly?

3. How did Charles Perkins and James McCleary view the role of the millionaire? How do their views compare with the other views? With what you have learned about the growth of industry?

25. How to Succeed in Business: Horatio Alger

Horatio Alger, one of the most popular fiction writers of the late nineteenth century, wrote over 130 novels about poor boys who became successful. The following selection from *Fame and Fortune*, one of Alger's best-known stories, was written in 1868. The main characters are Richard Hunter, an orphan and former bootblack, and Mr. Rockwell, his employer. Dick Hunter, like most of Alger's heroes, does not become a millionaire. He achieves success within a small business, owned by one man, who eventually takes him into partnership. However, many readers of Alger's books believed that the requirements for success described by Alger were the key to all successful business enterprise.

... When Micky had gone out, Mr. Rockwell said, "Well, Richard, I have lost my book-keeper."

"Yes, sir," said Dick.

"And I can't say I am sorry. I will do Mr. Gilbert the justice to say that he understood his business; but he was personally disagreeable, and I never liked him. Now I suppose I must look out for a successor."

"Yes, sir, I suppose so."

"I know a very competent book-keeper, who is intending to go into business for himself at the expiration [end] of six months. Until that time I can secure his services. Now, I have a plan in view which I think you will approve. You shall at once commence the study of book-keeping in a commercial school in the evening,

Horatio Alger, **Fame and Fortune** (Boston, Mass.: A. K. Loring, 1868), pp. 273-279.

"Confederate," means partner.

and during the day I will direct Mr. Haley to employ you as his assistant. I think in that way you will be able to suceed him at the end of his term."

Dick was completely taken by surprise. The thought that he, so recently plying the trade of a boot-black in the public streets, could rise in six months to the responsible post of a book-keeper in a large wholesale house, seemed almost incredible.

"I should like nothing better," he said, his eyes sparkling with delight, "if you really think I could discharge [perform] the duties satisfactorily."

"I think you could. I believe you have the ability, and of your fidelity [faithfulness] I feel assured."

"Thank you, sir; you are very kind to me," said Dick, gratefully.

"I have reason to be," said Mr. Rockwell, taking his hand. "...I intend Michael to undertake most of your present duties, such as going to the post-office, etc. Do you think he will answer?"

"I think so," said Dick. "He has been a rough customer, but then he has never had a chance. I believe in giving everybody a chance."

"So do I," said Mr. Rockwell. "Michael shall have his chance. Let us hope he will improve it."

There are many boys, and men too, who, like Micky Maguire, have never had a fair chance in life. Let us remember that, when we judge them, and not be too hasty to condemn. Let us consider also whether it is not in our power to give some one the chance that may redeem him.

That afternoon Micky Maguire was provided with a new suit of clothes, of which he felt very proud. The next morning, on his way to the post-office, he fell in with his old confederate, Limpy Jim, who regarded him with a glance of the most bewildering surprise.

"It ain't you, Micky,—is it?" he asked, cautiously, surveying his old comrade's neat appearance. "When did you come back from the Island?"

"Shut up about the Island, Jim," said Micky. "Do I look as if I had been there?"

"You look nobby [elegant]," said Jim. "Where's your brush?"

"I've give up the blackin' [shoeshine] business," said Micky.

"You have? What are you going to do? Sell papers?"

"No," said Micky, consequentially [importantly]. "I'm in business on Pearl Street."

"Why," said Limpy Jim, surprised, "that's where that upstart Ragged Dick works."

"He aint an upstart, an' he aint ragged," said Micky. "He's a friend of mine, an' if you insult him, I'll lam' [punch] ye."

"O my eyes!" ejaculated [exclaimed] Jim, opening the organs of vision to a very wide extent; "that's the biggest joke I ever heerd of."

"You'll hear of a bigger one pretty quick," said Micky, rolling up his sleeves, and squaring off scientifically.

Limpy Jim, who had a respect for Micky's prowess [fighting ability], . . . fled, surveying Micky from a safe distance, with a look in which surprise seemed to mingle with incredulity.

"Incredulity" means disbelief.

It may seem strange, but, from that time forth, Dick had no firmer friend than Micky Maguire, who, I am glad to say, though occasionally wayward, improved vastly, and became a useful employé of the establishment which he had entered. Of course both in ability and education, though in the last he gained considerably, he was quite inferior to Dick; but he was advanced as he grew older to the position of porter, where his strength stood him in good stead. His pay increased also, and through Dick's influence he was saved from vicious habits, and converted from a vagabond to a useful member of society. . . .

In six months, at the age of seventeen, Dick succeeded to Mr. Gilbert's place with a salary, to commence with, of one thousand dollars. To this an annual increase was made, making his income at twenty-one, fourteen hundred dollars. Just about that time he had an opportunity to sell his up-town lots, to a gentleman who had taken a great fancy to them, for five times the amount he paid, or five thousand dollars. His savings from his salary amounted to about two thousand dollars more.

Meanwhile Mr. Rockwell's partner, Mr. Cooper, from ill health felt obliged to withdraw from business, and Richard, to his unbounded astonishment and gratification, was admitted to the post of junior partner, embarking [investing] the capital he had already accumulated, and receiving a corresponding share of the profits. These profits were so large that Richard was able to increase his interest yearly by investing his additional savings . . . He was no longer Ragged Dick now, but Mr. Richard Hunter, junior partner in the large firm of Rockwell & Hunter. . . .

. . . I am glad to say that Dick has not been spoiled by prosperity. He never forgets his humble beginnings, and tries to show his sense of God's goodness by extending a helping hand to the poor and needy boys, whose trials and privations he understands well from his own past experience.

1. Why did Dick Hunter and Micky Maguire become successful?
2. Why did Dick go farther than Micky?
3. What factors did Carnegie consider responsible for his early success in business? How do they compare with the reasons for Dick Hunter's success?

26. How to Succeed in Business: Darius Ogden Mills

In the wake of business growth, there appeared a large number of publications which offered instruction about how to achieve success. One such publication was a book entitled *How They Succeeded,* by Orison Swett Marden. Marden's book consisted of interviews with prominent wealthy figures, primarily businessmen. Those who were interviewed gave their opinions on work and business. Among the men Marden approached was Darius Ogden Mills, a wealthy financier. He owned eighteen business and philanthropic corporations in New York City.

Orison Swett Marden, **How They Succeeded** (Boston: Lothrop Publishing Company, 1901), pp. 139-141.

"What, Mr. Mills, do you consider the keynote of success?"

"Work," he replied, quickly and emphatically. "Work develops all the good there is in a man; idleness all the evil. Work sharpens all his faculties and makes him thrifty; idleness makes him lazy and a spendthrift. Work surrounds a man with those whose habits are industrious and honest; in such society a weak man develops strength, and a strong man is made stronger. Idleness, on the other hand, is apt to throw a man into the company of men whose object in life is usually the pursuit of unwholesome and demoralizing diversions."

"To what formative influence do you attribute your material success, Mr. Mills?" I asked.

"I was taught very early that I would have to depend entirely upon myself; that my future lay in my own hands. I had that for a start, and it was a good one. I didn't waste any time thinking about succession to wealth, which so often acts as a drag upon young men. Many persons waste the best years of their lives waiting for dead men's shoes; and, when they get them, find them entirely too big to wear gracefully, simply because they have not developed themselves to wear them.

"As a rule, the small inheritance, which, to a boy, would seem large, has a tendency to lessen his efforts, and is a great damage to him in the way of acquiring the habits necessary to success.

"No one can acquire a fortune unless he makes a start; and the habit of thrift, which he learns in saving his first hundred dollars, is of inestimable value later on. It is not the money, but the habit which counts.

"There is no one so helpless as a man who is 'broke,' no matter how capable he may be, and there is no habit so detrimental [harmful] to his reputation among business men as that of borrowing small sums of money. This cannot be too emphatically impressed upon young men."

27. The Business World and American Life

The first two statements below are taken from Orison Marden's book on success. One is from the interview with Mills and the other from an interview with Philip Armour, owner of a huge meatpacking empire. The third passage is by William Matthews, who was a journalist, teacher, and author.

DARIUS OGDEN MILLS

". . . [The] progress of science and invention has increased the opportunities [for making money] a thousandfold, and a man can find them wherever he seeks them in the United States in particular. It has caused the field of employment of labor of all kinds to expand enormously, thus creating opportunities which never existed before. It is no longer necessary for a man to go to foreign countries or distant parts of his own country to make money. Opportunities come to him in every quarter. There is hardly a point in the country so obscure that it has not felt the revolutionizing influence of commercial enterprise. Probably railroads and electricity are the chief instruments in this respect. Other industries follow closely in their wake."

Orison Swett Marden, **How They Succeeded** (Boston: Lothrop Publishing Co., 1901), pp. 142-143.

PHILIP D. ARMOUR

". . . The world is changing every day and new fields are constantly opening. We have new ideas, new inventions, new methods of manufacture, and new ways to-day everywhere. There is

Orison Swett Marden, **How They Succeeded**, p. 80.

569

plenty of room for any man who can do anything well. The electrical field is a wonderful one. There are other things equally good, and the right man is never at a loss for an opportunity. Provided he has some ability and good sense to start with, is thrifty, honest and economical, there is no reason why any young man should not accumulate money and attain so called success in life."

WILLIAM MATTHEWS

. . . The very labor a man has to undergo, the self-denial he has to cultivate, in acquiring money, are of themselves an education. They compel him to put forth intelligence, skill, energy, vigilance, zeal, bring out his practical qualities, and gradually train his moral and intellectual powers. . . .

1. In the eyes of Mills, Armour, and Matthews what were the effects of business growth on American life?

2. How do their views compare with Brinkerhoff's view of the impact of the frontier? (See page 540.)

3. What conclusions can you draw from this comparison?

SUCCESS AND SOCIETY

1. How did the wealthy view their relation to the rest of the people in the country? How did wealthy people feel they were helpful?

2. How did they explain their success? How did Horatio Alger explain success in business?

3. Why did wealthy people and their admirers view the growth of business as fortunate for the country?

4. Do these ideas seem accurate according to what you read about the industrial boom?

THE VALUES OF THE GILDED AGE

1. What kind of character traits and behavior did wealthy people and their spokesmen seem to admire?

2. Can the term "individualistic" be applied to any of these characteristics? Why or why not?

3. What did wealthy people of the late nineteenth century value? Are these values you have observed before?

4. Do you share these values?

William Matthews, **Getting on in the World** (Chicago: Scott, Foresman and Company, 1898), p. 284.

570

IDEAS OF THE GILDED AGE: COMPETITION AND GOVERNMENT

28. Social Darwinism

Among the ideas which became popular during the Gilded Age was Social Darwinism. In developing the theory of evolution, Charles Darwin maintained that only the fittest members of a species would survive. Herbert Spencer, a nineteenth-century English philosopher, applied the biological theories of Darwin to human society.

The following statements are three expressions of Social Darwinism. The first is by William Graham Sumner, a sociologist at Yale University from 1872 to 1910, who became the chief American spokesman of the philosophy.

WILLIAM GRAHAM SUMNER

"The millionaires are a product of natural selection [of the fittest], acting on the whole body of men to pick out those who can meet the requirements of certain work to be done...."

John M. Blum, Bruce Catton, Edward S. Morgan, Arthur M. Schlesinger, Jr., Kenneth M. Stampp, C. Vann Woodward, **The National Experience: A History of the United States** (New York: Harcourt, Brace & World, Inc., 1963), p. 433.

JOHN D. ROCKEFELLER

"The growth of a large business is merely a survival of the fittest ... the working out of a law of nature and a law of God."

John M. Blum, Bruce Catton, and others, **The National Experience**, p. 433.

ANDREW CARNEGIE

"[Although the idea of natural selection] may sometimes be hard for the individual, it is best for the race, because it insures the survival of the fittest in every department."

John M. Blum, Bruce Catton, and others, **The National Experience**, p. 433.

1. According to Sumner, Rockefeller, and Carnegie, is competition good for society? How do they defend their views?

2. Suppose that you were Rockefeller or Carnegie. How could you defend this position further with arguments drawn a) from your experience in the business world? b) from your ideas about the way to achieve success? and c) from your ideas about the millionaire's contributions to society?

29. Laissez-Faire

Laissez-faire is a French expression that means to let alone, or to permit someone to do as he pleases. In the second half of the nineteenth century, this phrase became the name for the dominant philosophy about the proper relation between government and business. According to laissez-faire, business should be allowed to operate in complete freedom, with no restraints. In other words, there should be no checks on the right of an individual to pursue his economic self-interest. Competition ought to proceed unhindered. The role of government in business was to remain on the sidelines.

1. Review the ideas of the Gilded Age that you have studied so far. How could a supporter of laissez-faire defend his position with these ideas?

2. Do you share the values behind the ideas of the Gilded Age? Why or why not?

3. Do you share the feeling of the Gilded Age about the role of government in business? Explain.

30. Three Senators Oppose Prohibition of Child Labor

The Industrial Revolution caused a great increase in the population of cities. The factories which emerged in the cities called for more and more workers. Thousands of men, women, and children left farms to seek the new opportunities which factory jobs presented.

Although most states had laws prohibiting the employment of children under fourteen years of age for more than a full work week, few of these laws were enforced. By the turn of the century, many people wished to put an end to child labor. Some members of Congress introduced bills to prohibit the transportation of child-made goods in interstate commerce. The three selections which follow are by senators who opposed passage of these bills. Senators Proctor and Scott were Republicans, Senator Hardwick, a Democrat.

Congressional Record, 59th Congress, 2nd Session, Vol. XLI, Pt. 1 (Dec. 10, 1906), p. 207.

SENATOR REDFIELD PROCTOR, VERMONT

. . . These child-labor laws fifty years ago in England and in New England in the early days of manufacturing were a necessary protection; but in my somewhat long life . . . I have never known any abuse of child labor. Public sentiment would correct it. I have never known an employer but who carefully guarded [against] any violation of what was right. I suppose there is a child-labor law on the statute book of Vermont. I never knew it to be invoked. . . . Public sentiment takes care of it.

SENATOR THOMAS W. HARDWICK, GEORGIA

I want to ask [the people who want to abolish child labor] today throughout this country, in the United States and out of it, what they propose to do with a child who is the sole support of his widowed mother, when they take from him his opportunity to work; what substitute are they going to give? Are you going to let them both—mother and child—starve, or become objects of public charity? I want to ask people in the United States, and out of it, what they are going to say to the honest, self-respecting orphan boy, 12 or 13 years old, born on Georgia soil, when they say to him, "You shall not work," even if the alternative is public charity? And what is the substitute that you offer?

Senators, I tell you, some of the greatest men this Republic ever produced, in my State and in each one of yours, were boys like that. Are you going to make them inmates of charitable institutions and support them at the expense of the State?

I tell you in the name of American institutions, in the name of individualism in this Republic, it would be better to let them adopt the other plan that our fathers and theirs followed; honest, self-respecting toil is far more elevating than either public or private charity.

Congressional Record, 64th Congress, 1st Session, Vol. LIII, Pt. 12 (Aug. 4, 1916), pp. 12063-12064.

SENATOR NATHAN B. SCOTT, WEST VIRGINIA

. . . A gentleman by the name of Markham, writing a magazine article not long ago, said that he had visited the glasshouses [glass factories] and had seen children—boys and girls—with emaciated forms, with their eyes, as it were, protruding from their sockets, all due to overwork. He spoke of their little bodies being blistered by the hot furnaces, and a lot more of that kind of magazine stuff, for it is nothing but stuff.

I have been engaged in the manufacture of glass for thirty-five years and over, Mr. President, and if Mr. Markham had come to see my factory . . . [he] would not [have seen] anything like that which he described in his magazine article.

. . . The glasshouse boy of today becomes the glass manufacturer of tomorrow. There is scarcely a manufacturer of glass in the city of Pittsburgh, or in the Ohio Valley, so far as my knowledge goes—and I know the majority of them—who did not commence to learn his trade, as it were, starting from what we call "warming-in boys," "sticking-up" and "carrying-in" boys, and so forth, which are familiar phrases to the glass manufacturer. They were boys who saved their money; boys who learned their trade well, and in the course of a few years became manufacturers.

Congressional Record, 59th Congress, 2nd Session, Vol. XLI, Pt. 1 (Dec. 10, 1906), p. 199.

... [Today] two-thirds of the men engaged in the manufacture of glass have come from the factory—boys who learned their trade while they were earning good wages, boys who earned from a dollar to a dollar and a half a day....

1. What arguments do these three senators use to defend child labor?

2. What do they want to preserve?

3. What are the values of these three senators?

4. Do you accept their values? Do you accept their position in opposition to the federal regulation of child labor? Explain your answer.

WAS THE INDUSTRIAL REVOLUTION GOOD FOR AMERICA?

1. Judging from all the evidence in this section, how do you think industrial growth influenced the economic life of the American people?

2. What kinds of character traits do you think the industrial boom encouraged?

3. How would you compare the effects that industrial growth and the frontier had on American life?

4. Do you think the Industrial Revolution was good for America? Why or why not?

IV. The Critics Speak

THE WORKING MAN

31. Muckrakers Attack Child Labor

By 1906, a number of writers for popular magazines had attempted to expose the social evils created by unregulated industrialism. Theodore Roosevelt, President from 1901 to 1909, labeled those writers "muckrakers." He named them after a character in John Bunyan's *Pilgrim's Progress* who carries a rake and is primarily interested in digging in the filth and muck.

Among the most common targets of muckraker attacks were the problems of workers. Child labor, in particular, drew the fire of these writers. In this reading, you will find a photograph of some young coal miners, as well as a poem and portions of a book written by muckrakers.

574

COAL MINERS IN PENNSYLVANIA

GEORGE EASTMAN HOUSE COLLECTION

None of these coal miners, whose job was to separate bits of stone from the coal, was older than twelve.

"CHILD LABOR" BY CHARLOTTE GILMAN

No fledgling feeds the father bird!
No chicken feeds the hen!
No kitten mouses for the cat—
This glory is for men:

We are the Wisest, Strongest Race—
Loud may our praise be sung!
The only animal alive
That lives upon its young!

Charlotte Gilman, "Child Labor" reprinted in **The Cry for Justice: An Anthology of the Literature of Social Protest,** edited by Upton Sinclair (New York: Holt, Rinehart and Winston, Inc., 1915), p. 662.

AN EXCERPT FROM *THE BITTER CRY OF THE CHILDREN:* JOHN SPARGO

... In the spinning and carding [combing] rooms of cotton and woollen mills, where large numbers of children are employed, clouds of lint-dust fill the lungs and menace the health. The children have a distressing cough, caused by the irritation of the throat, and many are hoarse from the same cause. In bottle factories and other branches of glass manufacture, the atmosphere is constantly charged with microscopic particles of glass. In the wood-working industries, such as the manufacture of cheap furniture and wooden boxes, and packing cases, the air is laden with fine sawdust. Children employed in soap and soap-powder factories work, many of them, in clouds of alkaline dust

John Spargo, **The Bitter Cry of the Children** (New York: The Macmillan Company, 1906), pp. 175-178.

575

"Breaker boys" break and sort big pieces of coal.

which inflames the eyelids and nostrils. Boys employed in filling boxes of soap-powder work all day long with handkerchiefs tied over their mouths. In the coal-mines the breaker boys breathe air that is heavy and thick with particles of coal, and their lungs become black in consequence. . . .

In some occupations, such as silk-winding, flax-spinning, and various processes in the manufacture of felt hats, it is necessary, or believed to be necessary, to keep the atmosphere quite moist. The result of working in a close, heated factory, where the air is artificially moistened, in summer time, can be better imagined than described. So long as enough girls can be kept working, and only a few of them faint, the mills are kept going; but when faintings are so many and so frequent that it does not pay to keep going, the mills are closed. The children who work in the dye rooms and print-shops of textile factories, and the color rooms of factories where the materials for making artificial flowers are manufactured, are subject to contact with poisonous dyes, and the results are often terrible. Very frequently they are dyed in parts of their bodies as literally as the fabrics are dyed. . . .

Children employed as varnishers in cheap furniture factories inhale poisonous fumes all day long and suffer from a variety of intestinal troubles in consequence. The gilding of picture frames produces a stiffening of the fingers. The children who are employed in the manufacture of wall papers and poisonous paints suffer from slow poisoning. The naphtha fumes in the manufacture of rubber goods produce paralysis and premature decay. . . .

1. What impressions about child labor do you get from the picture, the poem, and the passage by Spargo?

2. How do these impressions compare with the three senators' arguments about child labor? (See pages 572–574.)

3. Do the values of Gilman and Spargo differ from the senators' values? If not, why do they disagree?

32. Child Labor and Federal Power: Senator Beveridge

Many congressmen and senators wanted a law that would end the abuses of child labor. Senator Albert J. Beveridge, a Republican from Indiana, advocated such a law. He thought that the federal government could regulate child labor as a part of its constitutional right to regulate interstate commerce. He proposed to ban the interstate transportation of goods made by children. Critics attacked this proposal as an unconstitutional extension of federal power. The following selection is from a speech Beveridge made to the Senate in 1907 in answer to this criticism.

... [If] it is good for the "interests of the Nation" to *prohibit* the transportation of *insects* from State to State; if it is good for the "interests of the Nation" to *prohibit* the importation of convict-made goods ... if we have the *power* to *prohibit* convict-made goods in interstate commerce, as we have; if we have actually *prohibited* the transportation of gold and silver merely because they had two words which inconvenienced the business of certain men in New York and New Jersey, all upon the theory that it affected the "interests of the Nation," to again use Chief Justice Marshall's famous phrase, how much more have we got the *power* to *prohibit* the transportation in interstate commerce of child-made goods which affect the "interests of the Nation," aye, and the perpetuity [endurance] of the Nation?

Congressional Record, 59th Congress, 2nd Session, Vol. XLI, Pt. 2 (Jan. 29, 1907), p. 1882.

The "two words" were "U.S. Assay." Certain manufacturers did not want these words to appear on any gold or silver goods. The words had been put on some imports which competed with the manufacturers' products.

... *Why* did we never hear before of any "danger of the extension of the Federal power" when you were enacting those statutes? Why is it then only when we attempt to stop the murder of children and the debasement of our race and the ruin of our citizens by *prohibiting* the transportation of child-made goods in interstate commerce that Senators are aroused in defense of an artificial liberty?

1. How would you summarize Beveridge's argument?

2. How would Carnegie or Rockefeller have argued to show that laissez-faire was in the public interest?

3. How would Beveridge answer these arguments?

33. *The Jungle:* Upton Sinclair

Child labor was only one of many problems dramatized by the muckrakers. One of the most famous muckraker documents was a novel called *The Jungle*. Written by Upton Sinclair in 1906, the book exposed working conditions at the turn of the century in the Chicago meat packing industry. The following passage begins with a description of the inspection of slaughtered hogs.

Before the carcass was admitted here, it had to pass a government inspector, who sat in the doorway and felt of the glands in the neck for tuberculosis. This government inspector did not

Upton Sinclair, The Jungle (New York: The Viking Press, Inc., 1906), pp. 42, 116-117. All Rights Reserved. Reprinted by permission of The Viking Press, Inc.

"Ptomaines" are poisons that develop in decaying meat and vegetables.

In the "pickle-rooms" meat was treated to make it keep.

The meat was cooked before being put into cans.

A "quarter" is one fourth of a carcass.

have the manner of a man who was worked to death; he was apparently not haunted by a fear that the hog might get by him before he had finished his testing. If you were a sociable person, he was quite willing to enter into conversation with you, and to explain to you the deadly nature of the ptomaines which are found in tubercular pork; and while he was talking with you [you] could hardly be so *ungrateful* as to notice that a dozen carcasses were passing him untouched. . . .

There were the men in the pickle-rooms . . . scarce a one of these that had not some spot of horror on his person. Let a man so much as to scrape his finger pushing a truck in the pickle-rooms, and he might have a sore that would put him out of the world; all the joints in his fingers might be eaten by the acid, one by one. Of the butchers and floorsmen, the beef-boners and trimmers, and all those who used knives, you could scarcely find a person who had the use of his thumb; time and time again the base of it had been slashed, till it was a mere lump of flesh against which the man pressed the knife to hold it. The hands of these men would be criss-crossed with cuts, until you could no longer pretend to count them or to trace them. They would have no nails,—they had worn them off pulling hides; their knuckles were swollen so that their fingers spread out like a fan. There were men who worked in the cooking-rooms, in the midst of steam and sickening odors, by artificial light; in these rooms the germs of tuberculosis might live for two years, but the supply was renewed every hour. There were the beef-luggers, who carried two-hundred-pound quarters into the refrigerator-cars; a fearful kind of work, that began at four o'clock in the morning, and that wore out the most powerful men in a few years. There were those who worked in the chilling-rooms, and whose special disease was rheumatism; the time-limit that a man could work in the chilling-rooms was said to be five years. There were the wool-pluckers, whose hands went to pieces even sooner than the hands of the pickle-men; for the pelts of the sheep had to be painted with acid to loosen the wool, and then the pluckers had to pull out this wool with their bare hands, till the acid had eaten their fingers off. There were those who made the tins for the canned-meat; and their hands, too, were a maze of cuts, and each cut represented a chance for blood-poisoning. Some worked at the stamping-machines, and it was very seldom that one could work long there at the pace that was set, and not give out and forget himself, and have a part of his hand chopped off. There were the "hoisters," as they were called, whose task it was to press the lever which lifted the dead cattle off the floor.

They ran along upon a rafter, peering down through the damp and the steam; and as old Durham's architects had not built the killing-room for the convenience of the hoisters, at every few feet they would have to stoop under a beam, say four feet above the one they ran on; which got them into the habit of stooping, so that in a few years they would be walking like chimpanzees. Worst of any, however, were the fertilizer-men, and those who served in the cooking-rooms. These people could not be shown to the visitor,—for the odor of a fertilizer-man would scare any ordinary visitor at a hundred yards, and as for the other men, who worked in tank-rooms full of steam, and in some of which there were open vats [large cooking pots] near the level of the floor, their peculiar trouble was that they fell into the vats; and when they were fished out, there was never enough of them left to be worth exhibiting,—sometimes they would be overlooked for days, till all but the bones of them had gone out to the world as Durham's Pure Leaf Lard!

34. Workers and Management: Samuel Gompers

Samuel Gompers came to America as a young boy. He worked as a cigar maker and joined the cigar maker's union. He rose through the ranks of labor to become a founder of the American Federation of Labor in 1881. He was elected president of the A.F. of L. in 1886.

The A.F. of L. was the second largest union to be founded in this country. It soon overshadowed its predecessor, the Knights of Labor, which had been founded in 1869. Unlike the Knights of Labor, which tried to unite all workers into one organization, the A.F. of L. sought only skilled workers.

Gomper's union, like that of the steel and railroad workers, called for a shorter working day and better working conditions. When management refused to meet labor's demands, strikes and open violence sometimes resulted. In the following selection, Gompers sets forth some basic positions of the A.F. of L.

The efforts of the American labor movement to secure a larger share of the income are directed against all who illegitimately [illegally] stand between the workers and the attainment of a better life. This class includes all who have not made honest investment in honest enterprise. Employers, capitalists, stockholders, bondholders—the capitalist class generally—oppose the efforts of the workers in the A.F. of L. and in other organizations to obtain a larger share of the product. Very much of the opposition

Samuel Gompers, "The American Labor Movement, Its Makeup, Achievements and Aspirations," as reprinted in Alpheus Thomas Mason, **Free Government in the Making** (New York: Oxford University Press, 1949), pp. 659-660.

"The income," here, is the total amount of money earned in the nation.

"The product" is the total value of what the workers produce, or the income from its sale.

to the efforts of the working people to secure improved conditions has come from those who obtain what may be called an unearned share in the distribution [of income]. The beneficiaries of the present system of distribution desire to retain as much as possible of their present share or to increase that proportion. But an additional reason that leads to opposition [conflict between workers and management] is that there are employers who live in the twentieth century, yet who have the mental outlook of the sixteenth century in their attitude toward the working people, and who still imagine that they are 'masters of all they survey.' These employers think that any attempt upon the part of the working people to secure improvements in their condition is a spirit of rebellion that must be frowned down. . . .

1. Which people does Gompers define as capitalists?

2. According to Gompers, what is the attitude of the capitalists toward attempts to improve working conditions?

3. How, then, would Gompers explain the conditions described by Spargo and Sinclair?

4. Do you think Gompers was right in saying that capitalists do not earn their income? Does the story of John D. Rockefeller and the oil industry bear out Gomper's interpretation? (See page 556.)

5. Why do you think Gompers held this opinion?

35. Workers and Management: Woodrow Wilson

Woodrow Wilson, President from 1913 to 1921, was not a newcomer to the political world. As a professor of history and government at Princeton University, he had been accustomed to observing and interpreting American politics. He had also been president of Princeton and governor of New Jersey. Wilson made the following remarks while campaigning for the Presidency in 1912.

Woodrow Wilson, The New Freedom: A Call for the Emancipation of The Generous Energies of a People (Garden City, N. Y.: Doubleday & Company, Inc., 1913), pp. 7-12. Reprinted by permission of the estate of Edith Bolling Wilson.

In this new age we find . . . that our laws with regard to the relations of employer and employee are in many respects wholly antiquated [out-dated] and impossible. They were framed for another age which nobody now living remembers, which is, indeed, so remote [far] from our life that it would be difficult for many of us to understand it if it were described to us. The employer is now generally a corporation or a huge company of some kind; the employee is one of hundreds or of thousands brought together, not by individual masters whom they know and with whom they have personal relations, but by agents of one sort or another. Workingmen are marshaled in great numbers for the performance of a multitude of particular tasks under a common discipline. They generally use dangerous and powerful machinery, over whose repair and renewal they have no control. New rules must be devised with regard to their obligations and their rights, their obligations to their employers and their responsibilities to one another. Rules must be devised for their protection, for their compensation when injured, for their support when disabled.

There is something very new and very big and very complex about these new relations of capital and labor. A new economic society has sprung up, and we must effect a new set of adjustments. We must not pit power against weakness. The employer is generally, in our day, as I have said, not an individual, but a powerful group; and yet the workingman when dealing with his employer is still, under our existing law, an individual. . . .

. . . Our modern corporations employ thousands, and in some instances hundreds of thousands, of men. The only persons whom you see or deal with are local superintendents or local representatives of a vast organization, which is not like anything that the workingmen of the time in which our laws were framed knew anything about. A little group of workingmen, seeing their employer every day, dealing with him in a personal way, is one thing, and the modern body of labor engaged as employees of the huge enterprises that spread all over the country, dealing with men of whom they can form no personal conception, is another thing. A very different thing. You never saw a corporation, any more than you ever saw a government. Many a workingman to-day never saw the body of men who are conducting the industry in which he is employed. And they never saw him. What they know about him is written in ledgers and books and letters, in the correspondence of the office, in the reports of the superintendents. He is a long way off from them.

So what we have to discuss is, not wrongs which individuals intentionally do,—I do not believe there are a great many of those, —but the wrongs of a system. . . . The truth is, we are all caught in a great economic system which is heartless. The modern corporation is not engaged in business as an individual. When we deal with it, we deal with an impersonal element, an immaterial piece of society. A modern corporation is a means of co-operation in the conduct of an enterprise which is so big that no one man can conduct it, and which the resources of no one man are sufficient to finance. . . . Men begin to pool their earnings, little piles, big piles. A certain number of men are elected by the stockholders to be directors, and these directors elect a president. This president is the head of the undertaking, and the directors are its managers. . . .

And do our laws take note of this curious state of things? Do they even attempt to distinguish between a man's act as a corporation director and [his act] as an individual? They do not. Our laws still deal with us on the basis of the old system. The law is still living in the dead past which we have left behind. . . .

1. How, according to Wilson, was American business organization different in 1912 from what it had been in earlier times?

2. Why does he feel the government must pass laws regarding the duties of workers and employers?

3. Does Wilson have the same view as Gompers about the causes of bad working conditions?

TRUSTS

36. The Rise of Trusts

In 1879, Rockefeller's Standard Oil Company, which controlled about 90 per cent of the oil refining business, combined with companies in other branches of the oil industry. The new combination became the Standard Oil Trust.

A *trust* is a form of business organization in which stockholders of several companies turn over their stock to *trustees*. In return, the stockholders receive trust certificates which entitle them to continue receiving shares of the profits. The *trustees,* however, receive the stockholders' voting privileges. This means that the trustees can elect, for each company, boards of directors who will follow the trustees' orders.

By organizing a large combination of companies within an industry in this way, it is possible to control prices within the industry. The Standard Oil Trust was so successful that other companies soon copied its form of organization. By 1890, there were fifteen large trusts in the United States.

Eventually the term trust came to mean any company so large that it is a *monopoly*. A monopoly is a company that has exclusive control over a service or product and is thereby able to control prices within its industry.

1. Why would the ability to control prices help to make a company successful?
2. How do you think the formation of a large trust would affect employees within the industry? Customers of the industry? The public in general? Explain your answers.

37. Popular Humor About Trusts

The late nineteenth and early twentieth centuries saw a rising tide of criticism directed against trusts. One of the most effective weapons at the disposal of the critics was humor.

The next three selections give examples of this humor. The first example is taken from a series of cartoons by Frederick Opper which were popular after 1900. The second example is a dialogue between two comics. The third is a conversation between a chicken and a rat, written by a lawyer named Bolton Hall.

EXCERPTS FROM "AN ALPHABET OF JOYOUS TRUSTS"

THE GRANGER COLLECTION

Quinine is a drug used to bring down high fevers, as in malaria.

TWO COMICS DISCUSS TRUSTS

Fields: "I got nothing. You got nothing; he got nothing. Let us form a trust."

Warfield: "Let us be thieves."

Fields: "It is the same."

How does this view of trusts compare with Gompers' view of capitalists?

W. A. Swanberg, **Citizen Hearst: A Biography of William Randolph Hearst** (New York: Charles Scribner's Sons, 1961), p. 187.

583

Bolton Hall, "The Game of Life," reprinted in **The Cry for Justice: An Anthology of the Literature of Social Protest,** edited by Upon Sinclair (New York: Holt, Rinehart and Winston, Inc., 1915), p. 710.

THE PICKED CHICKEN

"Times are hard," said the Picked Chicken.

"Why," said the Rat, "this is an era of prosperity; see how I have feathered my nest."

"But," said the Picked Chicken, "you have gotten my feathers."

"You must not think," said the Rat, "that because I get more comfort you get poorer."

"But," said the Chicken, "you produce no feathers, and I keep none—"

"If you would use your teeth"—interrupted the Rat.

"If—" said the Picked Chicken.

"You could lay—"

"I—" said the Picked Chicken.

"—up as much as I do," concluded the Rat.

"Excuse me for living," said the Picked Chicken, "but—"

"Without consumers like me," said the Rat, "there would be no demand for the feathers which you produce."

"I shall vote for a change," said the Picked Chicken.

"Only those who have feathers should have the Privilege of voting," remarked the Rat.

1. What criticism does each of these dialogues and cartoons make about trusts?

2. How do these criticisms compare with the defenses of big business you read earlier?

38. How an Oil Trust Grew: Henry Demarest Lloyd

In 1894, Henry Demarest Lloyd, the author of many books on economics, wrote a book entitled *Wealth Against Commonwealth*. The book was a fierce attack on the trusts. It was based on the methods used to set up the Standard Oil Trust. The following excerpt from Lloyd's book relates one man's fight against an oil trust. Lloyd got his evidence from records of investigations into trust practices conducted by the Ohio Legislature and the United States Congress.

Henry Demarest Lloyd, **Wealth Against Commonwealth** (New York: Harper & Row, Publishers, 1894), pp. 199-210.

. . . George Rice, coming from the Green Mountains of Vermont, entered the oil business twenty-nine years ago, when he and it were young. He was one of the first comers. Beginning as a producer in the Pithole region . . . in 1865, he prospered. Escaping the ruin which overtook those who stayed too long in that too quick sand, he was one of the first to develop the new field at Macksburg, Ohio, and to see the advantages of Marietta [Ohio], on the Ohio River, as a point for refining. . . . In 1876 he had risen to the dignity of manufacturer, and had a refinery of a capacity of 500 barrels a week, and later of 2000 barrels. Owning wells, he produced, himself, a part of the crude [oil] which he refined. His position gave him access to all the markets by river and rail. Everything promised him fortune. . . .

Several other refiners, seeing the advantages of Marietta, had settled here. . . . [Some were members of an oil trust. They] determined that Marietta must be theirs. They bought up some of the refiners. Then they stopped buying. Their representative there, afterwards a member of the trust, "told me distinctly that he had bought certain refineries in Marietta, but that he would not buy any more. . . . He had another way," he said, "of getting rid of them." Of these "other ways" the independents were now to have a full exposition. In January, 1879, freight rates on oil were suddenly and without previous notice raised by the railroads leading out of Marietta, and by their connections. Some of the rates were doubled. The increase was only on oil. It was—in Ohio— only on oil shipped from Marietta; it was exacted only from the few refiners who had not been bought, because there were "other ways of getting rid of them."

This freight-tariff attack on the independent refiners was arranged by their powerful rival and the railroad managers at a secret conference, as the latter admitted. . . .

. . . Curiously enough, the minds of the managers of a dozen roads acted simultaneously and identically, over thousands of miles of country—some, as they admitted, with suggestion, and some, as they testified, without suggestion—upon so precise a detail of their business as the rates on oil at one little point. . . .

Rice was "got rid of . . ." His successful rival had but to let its Marietta refineries lie idle, and transfer to its refineries at Wheeling [Ohio] its Marietta business—and Rice's too. . . . [The business of the combination] could be transferred from one point to another without loss. One locality or another could be subjected to ruinous conditions for the extermination of competitors, and the combination, no matter how large its works there, would prosper without check. It gets the same profit as before but the competitor by its side is ruined. . . .

The demonstration against the independent refiners of Marietta was only part of a wider web-spinning, in which those at all points—New York, Boston, Philadelphia, Pittsburgh, Oil City [Pennsylvania], Titusville, Buffalo, Rochester, and Cleveland—were to be forced to "come in" as dependents, or sell out, as most of them did.

... The independents knew nothing of the increase of freights prepared for them by the railroad managers and their great competitor until after, some time after, it had gone into effect.

The railroad company gave notice to [the combination] what the rates were to be, but withheld that information from [the independents]. That was not all. Before the new rates were given all the old rates were cancelled. "For a few days," said an independent, "we could not obtain any rates at all. We had orders from our customers, but could not obtain any rates of freight."

As to many places, the withholding of rates continued. "There's many places we can't obtain any rates to. They just say we sha'n't ship to these other places at any price...."

One peculiar thing about the action of the railroads was that it was an injury to themselves. The Baltimore and Ohio, for instance, by raising its rate, cut off its oil business with Marietta entirely. "What advantage is it, then?" the freight agent of the road over which the Baltimore and Ohio reached Marietta was asked.

"There is no advantage.... We had revenue before this increase in rates, and none since."

"What would be the inducement for her (the Baltimore and Ohio) to do it, then?"

"That is a matter I am not competent to answer...."

... [The combination] was so careless of appearances that oil ordered of its works at Parkersburg would be sent from the Marietta branch, and at the old rate of 40 cents, while the other refineries could not ship because the rate to them was 65 cents; the increase at Marietta was not enforced against it, but only against the three independents...

At one stroke the independents lost the business which it had cost them years of work to get. As the testimony of [witnesses] showed, the merchants who had been their customers in Chicago, Columbus, and other places, now had to send their orders to those for whose benefit the railroad men had raised the rates....

All the independent refiners at Marietta, except Rice, [went out of business].... Rice set himself to do two things: the first, to drag into the light of day and the public view the secrets of these "better methods"; and the second, to get new business in the place of what he had lost. . . .

. . . He went South. The little family kept the refinery at Marietta running, and the father travelled about establishing new agencies in the South, and studying freight tariffs, railroad routes, and terminal facilities for loading and unloading and storing. In 1880, through all the storm and stress of these days, he was able to double the capacity of his refinery. Again he succeeded in building up a livelihood, and again his success was treated as trespass and invasion. His bitter experience in Ohio in 1879 proved to be but an apprenticeship for a still sterner struggle. Rice was getting most of his crude oil from Pennsylvania, through a little pipe line which brought it to the Alleghany. The pipe line was taken up by the oil trust.

This compelled him to turn to the Macksburg, Ohio, field for most of his petroleum. He had one tank-car, and he ran this back and forth faster than ever. Then came the next blow. The railroad over which he ran his tank-car doubled his freight to 35 cents a barrel, from 17½. That was not all. The same railroad brought oil to the combination's Marietta refineries at 10 cents a barrel, while they charged him 35. That was not all. The railroad paid over to the combination 25 cents out of every 35 cents he paid for freight. If he had done all the oil business at Marietta, and his rival had put out all its fires and let its works stand empty, it would still have made 25 cents a barrel on the whole output. . . .

. . . [The] judge who heard all the evidence and rendered the decision, which has never been reversed or impaired, declared that [the combination] "compelled" the railroad to make the arrangement, "under a threat of building a pipe line for the conveyance of its oils and withdrawing its patronage. . . ."

This "agreement [between the railroads and the combination] for the transportation of oil" had its calculated effect. It put a stop to the transportation of oil from the Ohio field by Rice over the railroad, just as the destruction by the same hands of the pipe line to the Alleghany had cut him off from access to the Pennsylvania oil-fields. He then built his own pipe line to the Ohio field. To lay this pipe it was necessary to cross the pipe line of his great rival. Rice had the pluck [courage] to do this without asking for a consent which would never have been given. His intrepidity [fearlessness] carried its point, for, as he foresaw, they dared not cut his pipe for fear of reprisals.

Rice got the Ohio Legislature to investigate the railroad's practices.

587

In turning to the South, after his expulsion from the Ohio and Western markets, the Marietta independent did but get out of one hornet's nest to sit down in another. His opponent . . . thought it was "cheaper in the long-run to make the price cheap and be done with it, than to fritter away the time with a competitor in a little competition. [He] put the price down to the bone. . . ." The people and the dealers everywhere in the South were glad to see Rice. He found a deep discontent among consumers and merchants alike. . . .

. . . From all parts came word of the anxiety of the merchants to escape from the power that held them fast. . . . From Arkansas: "The merchants here would like to buy from some other. . . ." From Mississippi: "It has gouged the people to such an extent that we wish to break it down and introduce some other oils. . . ." As Rice went about the South selling oil the agents of the cutter "to the bone" would follow, and by threats . . . would coerce the dealers to repudiate their purchases. Telegrams would pour into the discouraged office at Marietta: "Don't ship oil ordered from your agent." We hereby countermand [nullify] orders given your agent yesterday." One telegram would often be signed by all the dealers in a town, though competitors, sometimes nearly a dozen of them, showing that they were united by some outside influence they had to obey.

. . . Rice submitted to Congress letters covering pages of the Trust Report, showing how he had been tracked through Tennessee, Missouri, Nebraska, Georgia, Kansas, Kentucky, Iowa, Mississippi, Louisiana, Texas, Arkansas, Alabama. The railroads had been got to side-track and delay his cars, and the dealers terrorized into refusing to buy his oils, although they were cheaper. If the merchants in any place persisted in buying his oil they were undersold until they surrendered. When Rice was driven out prices were put back. So close was the watch kept of the battle by the generals of "co-operation" that when one of his agents got out of oil for a day or two, prices would be run up to bleed the public during the temporary opportunity. "On the strength of my not having any oil today," wrote one of Rice's dealers, "I am told they have popped up the price 3½ cents."

The railroad officials did their best to make it true that "the poor ye have with you always." By mistake some oil meant for the combination was delivered to Rice's agent, and he discovered that it was paying only 88 cents a barrel, while he was charged $1.68, a difference of 80 cents a barrel for a distance of sixty-eight miles.

1. What methods did the oil trust employ to win business away from its independent rivals?

2. How does this evidence compare with the explanations you read earlier for the success of large combinations? For the success of individuals?

39. Robert M. La Follette and the Railroads

Robert M. La Follette served Wisconsin as congressman, senator, and governor. He became a leader of the Progressive movement, a reform movement of the early 1900's which included both Democrats and Republicans. La Follette called for numerous reforms to eliminate corruption in government. In the following selection, he relates an experience he had while serving as congressman from Wisconsin.

A voluminous [extensive] bill was before the Committee on Indian Affairs providing for the opening for settlement of 11,000,000 acres of the Sioux Indian Reservation in Dakota. As it was being read in committee, we came to a provision to ratify an agreement made by the Chicago, Milwaukee and St. Paul and Chicago and Northwestern railroads with the Indians for rights of way through the reservation. My previous study of documents on Indian Affairs here became useful. I discovered that in addition to the rights of way, one company was given the exclusive right to acquire 715 acres, and the other 828 acres of land, [apparently] for "terminal facilities," and that each road was to have at intervals of every ten miles an additional 160 acres of land, presumably for "station privileges." I stopped the reading at this point.

"This looks to me like a town site job," I said. "I cannot see why these railroads should have so much more land than is necessary to use directly in connection with their business as common carriers."

I had no sooner uttered these words than the member of the committee sitting upon my right nudged me and whispered: "Bob, you don't want to interfere with that provision. *Those are your home corporations.*"

But I did interfere and had the paragraphs laid over and we adjourned the session of the committee at twelve o'clock to attend the meeting of the House. I had not been in my seat half an hour when a page announced that Senator Sawyer wanted to see me. I found him waiting for me near the cloakroom. We sat on a settee [sofa] and talked of general matters for some time. As the Senator rose to go he said, apparently as an afterthought:

Robert M. La Follette, **La Follette's Autobiography: A Personal Narrative of Political Experiences** (Madison, Wis.: The University of Wisconsin Press, 1913), pp. 71-76. Copyright 1913 by the Robert La Follette Company, second edition; copyright © 1960 by The University of Wisconsin Press. Reprinted by permission of the publisher.

An "exclusive right" is a right that only one person, company, etc. enjoys.

589

"Oh, say, La Follette, your committee will have coming up before long the Sioux Indian bill. There is a provision in it for our folks up in Wisconsin, the Northwestern and St. Paul railroad. I wish you'd look after it."

"Senator Sawyer," I said, "we have already reached that provision in the bill, and I am preparing an amendment to it. I don't think it's right."

"Is that so," said the Senator, in apparent surprise. "Come and sit down and let's talk it over."

We argued for an hour, Sawyer presenting every point in favor of granting the railroads the prior right to acquire all the land they wanted. This was the first time Sawyer had directly and personally attempted to influence me in a matter of legislation. I was respectful to him, but could not yield to his view. I told him that I thought it right to permit the railroads to acquire the land necessary for rights of way, yards, tracks, sidings, depots, shops, roundhouses, and indeed, all they needed solely for transportation purposes, and should favor such a provision. But as framed, the provision plainly allowed them to get prior and exclusive rights to much more land for town site and other speculative uses; that besides they were not required to build their lines within any definite time, and might hold the land to the exclusion of all others indefinitely, without turning a sod or laying a rail; that it was unjust to the Indians and the public, and I could not support it. He was not ill tempered, and said he would see me again about it.

Forty-eight hours later Henry C. Payne arrived in Washington. He was Secretary of the Republican State Central Committee, political manager of the Wisconsin machine, lobbyist for the St. Paul Railroad and the Beef Trust, and had the backing of the important corporate interests of the state. Obviously he had been summoned to Washington by Sawyer.

Everybody was taught to believe that Payne had some occult [secret] and mysterious power as a political manager, and that when he said a thing would happen in politics or legislation, it always did happen. He was a perfect ideal of that union of private business and politics that carried on its face apparent devotion to the public interest. A fine head and figure, meditative, introspective eyes, a quiet, clear-cut, convincing way of stating his views, he was certainly the most accomplished railroad lobbyist I ever knew. His intimate friendship and business relation with the Chairman of the Democratic State Central Committee in Wisconsin came to be one of the best-known amenities [convenient

"Speculation," here, is the practice of acquiring land cheaply in order to resell it later at higher prices.

A political "machine" is a group or party leaders which controls the politics of the party in a certain area. A "lobbyist" is someone paid by a group to represent its interests to elected politicians. A lobbyist works for the passage of laws favorable to the group he represents.

590

features] in the politics of the day in that state. It was said that there was a well-worn pathway between the back doors of their private offices.

Well, Sawyer and Payne came to see me night after night for a week or more. Payne was rather stiff and harsh, but Sawyer was fatherly—much like a parent reasoning with a wayward child.

Nils P. Haugen, Congressman from the tenth district, occupied a seat near me. One day he said:

"I want to tell you something. I saw Payne last night at the Ebbitt House, and he went for you. He said: 'La Follette is a crank; if he thinks he can buck [resist] a railroad company with 5,000 miles of line, he'll find out his mistake. We'll take care of him when the time comes.' "

Payne was as good as his word. He fought me ever afterward.

But I got my amendment through allowing the railroad to acquire the necessary right of way, twenty acres of land for stations, and only such additional land as the Secretary of the Interior should find to be a necessary aid to transportation, prohibiting the use or sale of any of said lands for town site or other purposes, and providing that each of said roads should within three years locate, construct, and operate their lines or forfeit the lands so acquired to the government.

What connection is there between "The Picked Chicken" story on page 584 and La Follette's account about railroads and the government?

40. The Fruits of Monopoly

William Jennings Bryan was the Democratic candidate for President three times. He was defeated each time—in 1896 and 1900 by William McKinley, and in 1908 by William Howard Taft.

Bryan's political backing came primarily from the agrarian areas. There was great unrest in these areas as a result of high railroad rates, high interest rates on bank loans, falling farm prices, and crop failures. Farmers' organizations, such as the Grange and the Farmers' Alliances, were founded as outlets for the agrarian complaints. Many farmers also joined national political parties which promised to help their cause. Some gave support to the Populist party (People's party), founded in 1890.

The Democratic party adopted many Populist ideas. Therefore, in 1896, the Populists supported William Jennings Bryan. Bryan represented the debtor-agrarian-laborer sentiment, as opposed

591

William Jennings Bryan, "Menace to Government and Civilization," **The Independent,** Vol. LIV (1902), pp. 1068-1069.

to the banking-creditor-industrial interests. The following selection illustrates Bryan's attitude toward the giant trusts.

The main purpose and inevitable consequence of the present concentration of wealth is monopoly... [If a man] employs the methods of a highwayman [bandit], as a private monopoly generally does, he becomes suspicious of the people, knowing that they should protest even if they have not already done so. He fears to trust them with the use of political power and in the end will seek to deprive them of participation in the government....

1. What did Bryan fear would result from monopoly power?

2. What are the main points made by the cartoons, La Follette, and Bryan? According to each, what did the giant trusts threaten?

THE NEW FREEDOM

41. A Campaign Speech by Woodrow Wilson, 1912

The controversy between the champions and the critics of big business came to a climax in the election of 1912. Four candidates dominated the race for President. President William Howard Taft was the Republican nominee. He advocated more government regulation of trusts and a milder protective tariff. Eugene V. Debs, the Socialist party candidate, campaigned for government ownership of major industries and natural resources. Theodore Roosevelt, who ran on the ticket of the newly formed Progressive party, named his program the New Nationalism. He called for tariff revision and for public control of business through a federal trade commission. Woodrow Wilson was the Democratic nominee. His program, called the New Freedom, proposed that the federal government take steps to outlaw unfair trade practices. The Democrats also campaigned for "immediate downward revision" of the tariff.

Wilson won the election. The popular vote was: Wilson—6,286,214; Roosevelt—4,126,020; Taft—3,483,922; Debs—897,011.

The next two readings will give some insight into the motives behind Wilson's program. The first is an excerpt from a campaign speech. The second is a passage from his inaugural address.

POINTS TO CONSIDER

Why Wilson wanted to regulate unfair trade practices.

What the New Freedom was.

What the popular vote in the 1912 election shows about public opinion concerning big business.

American industry is not free, as once it was free; American enterprise is not free; the man with only a little capital is finding it harder to get into the field, more and more impossible to compete with the big fellow. Why? Because the laws of this country do not prevent the strong from crushing the weak. That is the reason, and because the strong have crushed the weak the strong dominate the industry and economic life of this country. No man can deny that the lines of endeavor have more and more narrowed and stiffened; no man who knows anything about the development of industry in this country can have failed to observe that the larger kinds [amounts] of credit are more and more difficult to obtain, unless you obtain them upon the terms of uniting your efforts with those who already control the industries of the country; and nobody can fail to observe than any man who tries to set himself up in competition with any process of manufacture which has been taken under the control of large combinations of capital will presently find himself either squeezed out or obliged to sell and allow himself to be absorbed.

There is a great deal that needs reconstruction in the United States. I should like to take a census of the business men,—I mean the rank and file of the business men,—as to whether they think that business conditions in this country, or rather whether the organization of business in this country, is satisfactory or not. I know what they would say if they dared. If they could vote secretly they would vote overwhelmingly that the present organization of business was meant for the big fellows and was not meant for the little fellows; that it was meant for those who are at the top and was meant to exclude those who are at the bottom; that it was meant to shut out beginners, to prevent new entries in the race, to prevent the building up of competitive enterprises that would interfere with the monopolies which the great trusts have built up . . .

The originative part of America, the part of America that makes new enterprises, the part into which the ambitious and gifted workingman makes his way up, the class that saves, that plans, that organizes, that presently spreads its enterprises until they have a national scope and character,—that middle class is being more and more squeezed out by the processes which we have been taught to call processes of prosperity. Its members are sharing prosperity, no doubt; but what alarms me is that they are not *originating* prosperity. No country can afford to have its prosperity originated by a small controlling class. The treasury [wealth] of America does not lie in the brains of the small body of men now in control of the great enterprises that have been concentrated

Woodrow Wilson, **The New Freedom,** as reprinted in Alpheus Thomas Mason, **Free Government in the Making** (New York: Oxford University Press, 1949), pp. 665-666. Reprinted by permission of the estate of Edith Bolling Wilson.

under the direction of a very small number of persons. The treasury of America lies in those ambitions, those energies, that cannot be restricted to a special favored class. It depends upon the inventions of unknown men, upon the originations of unknown men, upon the ambitions of unknown men. Every country is renewed out of the ranks of the unknown, not out of the ranks of those already famous and powerful and in control.

There has come over the land that un-American set of conditions which enables a small number of men who control the government to get favors from the government; by those favors to exclude their fellows from equal business opportunity; by those favors to extend a network of control that will presently dominate every industry in the country, and so make men forget the ancient time when America lay in every hamlet [town]. . . .

We used to think in the old-fashioned days when life was very simple that all that government had to do was to put on a policeman's uniform, and say, 'Now don't anybody hurt anybody else.' We used to say that the ideal of government was for every man to be left alone and not interfered with, except when he interfered with somebody else; and that the best government was the government that did as little governing as possible. That was the idea that obtained [was upheld] in Jefferson's time. But we are coming now to realize that life is so complicated that we are not dealing with the old conditions, and that the law has to step in and create new conditions under which we may live, the conditions which will make it tolerable for us to live . . . Whenever bodies of men employ bodies of men, it ceases to be a private relationship . . .

1. What kind of freedom does Wilson want to restore?

2. How does Wilson explain the loss of this freedom?

3. Where does Wilson think the country's wealth originates? Review Carnegie's tale of his early investments and Rockefeller's description of how he built the oil industry. (See pages 549–554 and 556–557.) Would Wilson regard these actions as examples of how wealth is originated?

4. Would it be possible for Wilson to feel that Rockefeller and Carnegie had originated wealth and still include them in his present criticism? Explain.

5. Review Wilson's statements about why big corporations are organized. (See page 580.) How does Wilson's opinion compare with Rockefeller's? (See page 556.)

6. What does Wilson think of the theory of laissez-faire? Why?

42. Wilson's Inaugural Address, 1913

We see that in many things [our] life is very great. It is incomparably great in its material aspects, in its body of wealth, in the diversity and sweep of its energy, in the industries which have been conceived and built up by the genius of individual men and the limitless enterprise of groups of men. It is great, also, very great, in its moral force. Nowhere else in the world have noble men and women exhibited in more striking forms the beauty and the energy of sympathy and helpfulness and counsel in their efforts to rectify [set right] wrong, alleviate [ease] suffering, and set the weak in the way of strength and hope. We have built up, moreover, a great system of government, which has stood through a long age as in many respects a model for those who seek to set liberty upon foundations that will endure against fortuitous [accidental] change, against storm and accident. Our life contains every great thing, and contains it in rich abundance.

But the evil has come with the good, and much fine gold has been corroded [spoiled]. With riches has come inexcusable waste. We have squandered [wasted] a great part of what we might have used, and have not stopped to conserve the exceeding bounty of nature, without which our genius for enterprise would have been worthless and impotent, scorning to be careful, shamefully prodigal [wasteful] as well as admirably efficient. We have been proud of our industrial achievements, but we have not hitherto stopped thoughtfully enough to count the human cost, the cost of lives snuffed out, of energies overtaxed and broken, the fearful physical and spiritual cost to the men and women and children upon whom the dead weight and burden of it all has fallen pitilessly the years through. The groans and agony of it all had not yet reached our ears, the solemn, moving undertone of our life, coming up out of the mines and factories, and out of every home where the struggle had its intimate and familiar seat. With the great Government went many deep secret things which we too long delayed to look into and scrutinize with candid, fearless eyes. The great Government we loved has too often been made use of for private and selfish purposes, and those who used it had forgotten the people.

At last a vision has been vouchsafed [given to] us of our life as a whole. We see the bad with the good, the debased [corrupt] and decadent with the sound and vital. With this vision we approach new affairs. Our duty is to cleanse, to reconsider, to restore, to correct the evil without impairing the good, to purify and humanize every process of our common life without weakening or sentimentalizing it. There has been something crude and

Inaugral Addresses of the Presidents of the United States, From George Washington 1789 to John F. Kennedy 1961 (Washington, D.C.: United States Government Printing Office, 1961), pp. 200-202.

To "sentimentalize" something is to exaggerate one's feelings about it.

595

heartless and unfeeling in our haste to succeed and be great. Our thought has been "Let every man look out for himself, let every generation look out for itself," while we reared giant machinery which made it impossible that any but those who stood at the levers of control should have a chance to look out for themselves. We had not forgotten our morals. We remembered well enough that we had set up a policy which was meant to serve the humblest as well as the most powerful, with an eye [only] to the standards of justice and fair play, and remembered it with pride. But we were very heedless [careless] and in a hurry to be great.

We have come now to the sober second thought. The scales of heedlessness have fallen from our eyes. We have made up our minds to square every process of our national life again with the standards we so proudly set up at the beginning and have always carried at our hearts. Our work is a work of restoration.

. . . We shall restore, not destroy. We shall deal with our economic system as it is and as it may be modified, not as it might be if we had a clean sheet of paper to write upon; and step by step we shall make it what it should be, in the spirit of those who question their own wisdom and seek counsel and knowledge, not shallow self-satisfaction or the excitement of excursions whither they can not tell. Justice, and only justice, shall always be our motto.

And yet it will be no cool process of mere science. The Nation has been deeply stirred, stirred by a solemn passion, stirred by the knowledge of wrong, of ideals lost, of government too often debauched [corrupted] and made an instrument of evil. The feelings with which we face this new age of right and opportunity sweep across our heartstrings like some air out of God's own presence, where justice and mercy are reconciled and the judge and the brother are one. We know our task to be no mere task of politics but a task which shall search us through and through, whether we be able to understand our time and the need of our people, whether we be indeed their spokesmen and interpreters, whether we have the pure heart to comprehend and the rectified will to choose our high course of action.

This is not a day of triumph; it is a day of dedication. Here muster [gather], not the forces of party, but the forces of humanity. Men's hearts wait upon us; men's lives hang in the balance; men's hopes call upon us to say what we will do. Who shall live up to the great trust? Who dares fail to try? I summon all honest men, all patriotic, all forward-looking men, to my side. God helping me, I will not fail them, if they will but counsel and sustain me!

596

1. What does Wilson think of Social Darwinism? Why?

2. What values does this speech reflect?

3. Are these the dominant values of nineteenth-century America or new values? Explain.

THE NEW RULES OF THE GAME

43. Labor Laws

Wilson's election was a turning point. Between 1913 and 1916, many laws concerning labor, voting procedures, and business were passed. The next three readings will summarize these developments.

POINTS TO CONSIDER

Why these laws were passed.

The relationship between these laws and nineteenth-century values.

In 1908, the United States Supreme Court declared constitutional an Oregon law which limited the working day for women to ten hours. Before this, working hours had averaged twelve to fourteen hours per day. The case is known as *Muller* v. *Oregon.* Louis D. Brandeis, who later became a member of the Supreme Court, argued in favor of the law.

In 1913, Congress created the Department of Labor and made its secretary a member of the cabinet. A year later Congress approved the Clayton Antitrust Act. This act forbid the use of *injunctions* in labor disputes unless injunctions were necessary to prevent property damage. An injunction is a judicial order telling someone to take or, more commonly, not to take a certain action. Samuel Gompers hailed the act as "labor's charter of freedom." But the act did not outlaw "yellow-dog" contracts as a condition of employment. In such contracts, an employee had to promise that he would not join a labor union.

In 1916, Congress passed the Keating-Owen Child Labor Act. It forbid the shipment in interstate commerce of any goods made by children under fourteen years old. In addition, it prohibited the shipment of goods made by children between the ages of fourteen and sixteen who worked more than eight hours a day, or more than six days a week, or after 7:00 P.M., or before 6:00 A.M. Two years later, the Supreme Court declared that the act was "unconstitutional as exceeding the commerce power of Congress and invading the powers reserved to the States."

44. Voting Laws

During the Progressive Era, Lincoln Steffens, a muckraker for *McClure's Magazine,* wrote a series of articles which later appeared as a book entitled *The Shame of the Cities.* Steffens exposed the corrupt practices of political bosses on local, county, and state levels. He showed that most citizens lacked quick remedies to protect themselves against laws they felt were unfair. By 1910, six years after *The Shame of the Cities* appeared, most states had adopted (1) the *initiative,* which allowed the people to petition for a law, (2) the *referendum,* which granted the people the right to decide if an act passed by a local or state government should be kept in force, and (3) the *primary* election, which granted people the right to decide who would run on their political party's ticket. This was also the period when most states adopted the secret ballot.

Another reform of the Progressive Era concerned the election of senators. According to the Constitution, senators were to be chosen by the state legislatures, many of which were controlled by big business. There was much support for the adoption of an amendment that would permit the people to vote directly for senators. Opponents to the direct election of senators maintained that Congress had no right to interfere in matters of state elections. The Seventeenth Amendment, adopted in 1913, provided for the direct election of senators.

45. Laws About Business

In 1887, Congress approved the Interstate Commerce Act. This act declared rebates, pools, and discriminatory rates illegal. Rebates are refunds or discounts made to important clients. Pools are business combinations in which companies get together to fix prices or share business opportunities. In addition, the Interstate Commerce Act required railroads to publish their rates and made it illegal to charge less for a long run than for a short run over the same route. The act also established an Interstate Commerce Commission. This commission had the power to investigate all complaints regarding interstate commerce, particularly those related to the railroads. However, it had no power to enforce its decisions. In 1903, Congress strengthened the Interstate Commerce Act. It gave the federal courts the power to issue injunctions against violators of the act.

As a result of the rapid growth of trusts, Congress passed the Sherman Antitrust Act in 1890. It said: "Every contract, combination in the form of trust or otherwise, or conspiracy, in restraint of trade or commerce among the several states, or with foreign nations, is hereby declared to be illegal."

The Pure Food and Drug Act was passed in 1906. It provided for federal supervision of foods and drugs sold in interstate commerce.

The year 1913 saw a number of regulatory laws passed. Congress approved the Underwood Tariff. Tariffs were reduced, and many items such as iron, steel, and raw wool were placed on the free list. Spokesmen for lower tariffs argued that the giant corporations no longer needed the special protection of a tariff. The Sixteenth Amendment gave Congress the right to levy a tax on all incomes. The Federal Reserve Act was designed to make credit more readily available and to eliminate the concentration of banking capital in New York. Many parts of the country, especially the rural districts, often suffered from a lack of credit. The act set up federal reserve banks in twelve regions of the country to mobilize the banking reserves of each region. Each had the power to regulate business conditions and to assist local banks. Before then, many banks had been forced to close when large numbers of depositors attempted to draw out their funds.

During the following year the Federal Trade Commission Act and the Clayton Antitrust Act were passed. The first act established the Federal Trade Commission, which had the power to investigate violations of the antitrust laws and to eliminate unfair systems of competition. The second was designed to strengthen and supplement the Sherman Antitrust Act. It prohibited price discriminations which would create monopolies. It also forbid corporations from acquiring stock in competing firms and made officials of corporations that violated antitrust acts personally responsible.

CONCLUDING EXERCISE
What were the reasons for each of the new laws passed between 1912 and 1916? Use your knowledge of the period between 1865 and 1912 to answer this question.

DID AMERICAN VALUES CHANGE?
1. Did the critics of big business attack the values of the millionaires and their champions? If so, tell how specifically. If not, show why the values of the critics were the same as those they attacked and explain what the critics were really attacking.

2. Was the New Freedom new? Was it a departure from the ideas of the past or an attempt to restore old American values? Explain.

3. Do the laws passed between 1912 and 1916 show that American values had changed or remained the same?

V. Immigration

46. America and the Immigrant

Oscar Handlin is one of America's foremost historians of immigration. The poem by Emma Lazarus was selected in 1886 to be inscribed on the base of the Statue of Liberty.

OSCAR HANDLIN

Once I thought to write a history of the immigrants in America. Then I discovered that the immigrants *were* American history.

EMMA LAZARUS

Give me your tired, your poor,
Your huddled masses yearning to breathe free,
The wretched refuse of your teeming shore,
Send these, the homeless, tempest-tost, to me:
I lift my lamp beside the golden door . . .

1. Define the term "immigrant."

2. What do you think of Handlin's statement?

3. Suppose you were an immigrant on your way to the United States in the year 1890. What would the poem by Lazarus mean to you? Explain.

4. How does the poem by Lazarus relate to the story of Andrew Carnegie's boyhood?

Oscar Handlin, **The Uprooted** (Boston: Little, Brown and Company, 1951), p. 3.

Emma Lazarus, "The New Colossus," Statue of Liberty, New York Harbor.

47. The Journey to a New Land

Immigration to the United States occurred in waves. The English were predominant in the first wave of immigration, in the seventeenth century, while the Scotch-Irish and Germans were predominant during the eighteenth century. In the period preceding the Civil War, the greatest number of immigrants were from Ireland and Germany. From 1890 to 1918, no one nationality was predominant among the immigrants from many different countries entering the United States. Between 1901 and 1910 alone, nearly 9 million people migrated to this country—more than the combined populations of the states of New York, Maryland, and New Hampshire in 1900.

After their arrival in America, many immigrants recorded their stories. The following selections are typical of what many immigrants experienced during this period. Edward Corsi, the author of the second selection, became Commissioner of Immigration at Ellis Island twenty-four years after his arrival in America. The third selection is by O. E. Rölvaag, whose novels about pioneer life in the Last West have become American classics.

POINTS TO CONSIDER

Why these immigrants came to America.

What problems faced the immigrant.

A CZECHOSLOVAKIAN COMES TO TEXAS, 1906

Our family came to this country in 1906 for several reasons. My father had to serve in the army in Czechoslovakia, and while he was in the army, he was injured by a cavalry horse. He killed the horse in self-defense. Since there were more men than horses in the army, he was sent to prison for a time as a punishment for killing the horse.

Printed by special permission of Mrs. Annie Foyt and Margaret Hanicak.

Father's brother (my Uncle Peter) and his family were in the United States. Uncle Peter worked in a sawmill in Deweyville, Texas. When he wrote about how good it was in the United States and how much freedom there was there, my parents began to save their money to go to Deweyville.

We left in August 1906 from Novy Hrozenkov, Czechoslovakia, taking only two small trunks of clothes with us. My little brother Jan was only 18 months old. He was sick during most of the boat trip. In fact, almost everyone was sea-sick except me. I had to bring meals to some people who were too sick to walk. The trip took 26 days, and we arrived in Galveston, Texas, on my 8th birthday.

We moved to a little town called Bessmay, Texas, not far from where my uncle worked. My father got a job at the Kirby sawmill there. We liked our new home even though it was hard at first because we couldn't speak English. The children in school made fun of me and took things away from me. Then they would tell the teacher that I had taken somebody's pencil or tablet. Since I couldn't tell the teacher any different, she would punish me. The school was very small (it had only two rooms), and it was not as good as the one I had gone to in Czechoslovakia.

A bad thing happened after we had been in America for several years. My father hurt his leg in an accident at the sawmill. The men who worked with him put a tourniquet on his leg and took him to the closest hospital which was about 30 miles away. The doctors had to take off his leg because the tourniquet had been left on too long. After that things were harder for us financially. My mother took in roomers and cooked meals for them, and we kids helped, too, by running errands for the neighbors and doing odd jobs. When he was 13, my brother Jan, the oldest boy in the family, quit school and went to work fulltime at the sawmill. We all worked very hard to save enough money to buy our own home. Finally, a few years after my father died, my mother did have her own home.

AN ITALIAN COMES TO NEW YORK CITY, 1907

... My father, in his youth, had become a disciple of the Italian patriot, Giuseppe Mazzini. The longing for freedom, not for himself alone but for his fellow men, was in my father's blood. In the newspaper which he edited he waged relentless war on the entrenched classes living at the expense of the peasant ...

Our lives had always been molded by Father's life; after he died we seemed to have no future. During the years from 1903 to 1907, when immigration to America was at its height, many Italians returned to the little towns in Italy boasting of their success in the United States. We saw strangers proudly wearing heavy gold watch chains that we knew had been bought in the New World. Stories of the ease with which money could be earned in America flew through the whole peninsula. . . .

Toward the end of the fourth year after my father died, my mother married again. . . . My new father had resigned from the army. To start life over at any work beneath his caste [class] would have been embarrassing in Italy. America was different. There he could take any sort of employment at first, and no one would think the worse of him. Two months later we were on our way. . . .

I am sure that our life on the East Side [of New York] was typical of the lives of thousands upon thousands of immigrant families. There were many times when we had nothing to eat in the house. There was one period when my stepfather was out of work for eighteen months.

When I was old enough for my first job, I went to work as a lamplighter, rising at four in the morning to put out the lamps on my route. Then I would have breakfast and get to school by nine o'clock.

Edward Corsi, **In the Shadow of Liberty**, reprinted in **We Came to America**, edited by Frances Cavanah (Philadelphia: Macrae Smith Company, 1954), pp. 146-47, 151-53. Reprinted by permission of Emme Corsi.
During the nineteenth century, Giuseppe Mazzini fought for the liberation and unification of Italy.

602

All through my boyhood I worked at various odd jobs, paying my own way through school and at the same time contributing what little I could to the limited family income. I was, in turn, lamplighter, messenger, and clerk in a telegraph office. The few hours that remained for play, and they were few indeed, I spent in the streets. I enjoyed the excitement, the crowds, and the good fellowship of the East Side. I enjoyed too the company of youngsters like myself, many of whom have risen above the handicaps of their surroundings to useful careers in the community. . . .

I remember clearly the day I led my gang into that house of mystery [a community welfare center where children could play and learn]. I was shabbily dressed and embarrassed, but I think my earnestness must have impressed the head [social] worker, for she singled me out of the group and questioned me at length. She explained in terms that we could understand what she and her co-workers were doing in the neighborhood. We were admitted on probation. We were not to be rough or break windows, as other neighborhood boys had done. We were to have a meeting room and the use of the backyard gymnasium just as long as we behaved.

My admission to the Home Garden, later Haarlem House [the community center], marked a decisive advance in my career. . . .

. . . [My] settlement contacts and experiences gave me a new understanding of American life and American ideals. It was a *new* understanding, because until then such dreams as I had had of the land of promise were well nigh shattered by the grim reality of what I had been forced to undergo. It was as if a wide door to America had been opened to me.

A "settlement" is another term for a community center.

A NORWEGIAN COMES TO SOUTH DAKOTA, 1896

. . . At last I wrote to my uncle who had emigrated to South Dakota. I asked him if he could send me a ticket to America. I said that I would pay him back after I arrived. One day the next summer the ticket came. . . .

I went to a port down the coast and took ship for the New World. . . .

[In New York the] vast harbor, the teeming city, and the alien language threw me into a terrible confusion. I couldn't speak or understand a word of English. It wasn't until I got on board the train that I discovered meals weren't furnished with my railroad ticket. By that time I was down to ten cents in American money and a copper pocket piece from Norway. I went without food for

We Came to America, edited by Frances Cavanah (Philadelphia: Macrae Smith Company, 1954), pp. 198, 201-203.

three days and three nights, all the way from New York to South Dakota.

I left the train at a little station on the Dakota prairie. Looking around, I saw nothing but level land, like the sea. My uncle was to have met me but had made a mistake in the day of my arrival. I tried to ask my way, but no one at the station spoke Norwegian. At last a Swede who worked on the railroad came along, and I was able to communicate with him. He thought he knew approximately where my uncle lived, and gave me some directions; I had a twelve-mile walk ahead of me. When he found that I hadn't eaten for three days, he gave me what remained of his dinner pail—one sandwich and some coffee. I've always blessed the big Swede in my prayers!

By this time the sun was going down. I struck out on foot, soon lost my way, and walked far into the night. It was one of those still prairie nights, breathless with heat. I've learned to love them since, but then I was worn out and discouraged. I felt as if I had been dropped down in the midst of nowhere. At last I came upon something in the darkness, a man driving a horse hitched to a wagon. This man was a Norwegian, and he took me to the farm where my uncle was employed. I stumbled into the house more dead than alive.

In that experience I learned the first lesson of the immigrant, the first and perhaps the greatest lesson: a feeling of utter helplessness, as if life had betrayed me. It comes from a sense of being lost in a vast alien land. In this case it was largely physical; but I soon met the spiritual phase of the same thing: the sense of being lost in an alien culture, the sense of being thrust somewhere outside the charmed circle of life. If you couldn't conquer that feeling, if you couldn't break through the magic hedge of thorns, you were lost indeed. Many couldn't and didn't and many were lost thereby.

48. What the Immigrant Faced: Jacob A. Riis and John F. Kennedy

The first of the next two selections was written by Jacob Riis, an immigrant from Denmark, who became a New York journalist and a personal friend of Theodore Roosevelt. The passage quoted here is from a book he published in 1890 entitled *How the Other Half Lives*. It deals with the problems many immigrants faced in urban New York. The second selection is by President John F. Kennedy, whose grandfather was an Irish immigrant.

HOW THE OTHER HALF LIVES: JACOB RIIS

New York's wage earners have no other place to live, more is the pity. They are truly poor for having no better homes; waxing [growing] poorer in purse as the exorbitant rents to which they are tied . . . keep rising. The wonder is that they are not all corrupted, and speedily, by their surroundings. If on the contrary there be a steady working up . . . the fact is a powerful argument for the optimist's belief that the world is after all, growing better, not worse, and would go far toward disarming apprehension, were it not for the steadier growth of the sediment [worst parts] of the slums and its constant menace. Such an impulse toward better things there certainly is. The German ragpicker of thirty years ago, quite as low in the scale as his Italian successor, is the thrifty tradesman or prosperous farmer of today. . . . The poorest immigrant comes here with the purpose and ambition to better himself and, given half a chance, might be reasonably expected to make the most of it. To the false plea that he prefers the squalid homes in which his half chance has too long been wanting, and for the bad result he has been unjustly blamed.

Jacob A. Riis, **How the Other Half Lives: Studies Among the Tenements of New York** (New York: Charles Scribner's Sons, 1890), pp. 23-24.

A "ragpicker" collects and sells rags and junk.

"Squalid" means neglected and dirty.

THE STRUGGLE FOR AMERICANIZATION: JOHN F. KENNEDY

The Irish were among the first to meet the hostility of an already established group of "Americans." It was not long before employment circulars included the phrase "No Irish need apply."

John F. Kennedy, **A Nation of Immigrants** (New York: Anti-Defamation League of B'nai B'rith, 1964), pp. 16, 18, 19. Copyright © 1964 by the Anti-Defamation League of B'nai B'rith. Reprinted by permission of the publisher.

It is not unusual for people to fear and distrust that which they are not familiar with. Every new group coming to America found this fear and suspicion facing them. And, in their turn, members of these groups met their successors with more of the same. . . .

Toward the end of the nineteenth century, immigration to America underwent a significant change. For the first time the major sources of settlers became southern and eastern Europe rather than northern Europe and the British Isles. Large numbers of Italians, Russians and Poles came to this country and their coming created new problems and gave rise to new tensions. . . .

. . . For the most part, these were people of the land and, for the most part, too, they were forced to settle in the cities when they reached America. . . .

The history of cities shows that when conditions become overcrowded, when people are poor, and when living conditions are bad, tensions run high and crime flourishes. This is a situation that feeds on itself—poverty and crime in one group breed fear and hostility in others and this, in turn, impedes the acceptance and progress of the first group, thus perpetuating [prolonging] its

"Sally-ports" are gates in a fortified wall through which groups of soldiers can enter or leave.

The "steerage" section of a ship contains the cheapest accommodations.

depressed condition. This was the dismal situation that faced many of the southern and eastern European immigrants just as it had faced some of the earlier waves of immigrants. Indeed, one New York newspaper had these intemperate words for the newly arrived Italians: "The floodgates are open. The bars are down. The sally-ports are unguarded. The dam is washed away. The sewer is choked . . . the scum of immigration is [thickening] upon our shores. The horde of $9.60 steerage slime is being siphoned [drained] upon us from Continental mud tanks."

As it had been with their predecessors, the struggle to establish themselves in the New World was a hard one for the newcomers from southern and eastern Europe. Indeed, for many, the struggle continues to this day. Fear, bigotry, hatred—these do not die easily and since they are not based on fact and logic, they do not yield to the evidence of fact and logic. The history of new peoples in America shows clearly, however, that given time and opportunity, virtually every group has found its way up the economic and social ladder—if not the original settlers then their children or grandchildren. There is no reason to believe that this process has ended now. . . .

THE IMMIGRANT AND THE AMERICAN PROMISE

1. What reasons did immigrants offer for coming to America?

2. How do the reasons immigrants had for coming to America in the late nineteenth and early twentieth centuries compare with the reasons people had for coming to America during the colonial period?

3. What developments in the United States would have attracted immigrants in the late nineteenth and early twentieth centuries?

4. In order to achieve their goals, was it enough for immigrants to work hard? Why or why not?

5. Do you agree with the last statement in the selection by Kennedy? Why or why not?

THE FRONTIER, INDUSTRY, IMMIGRANTS, AND US

1. Comment on the following statement: The sudden growth of industry fostered the same traits and values in Americans that the frontier had encouraged.

2. Woodrow Wilson pointed out how relations between workers and employees changed when businesses became big. You have considered the effect of this change on the ability of workers to protect themselves against poor working conditions. What other effects might there be? For example, how would it feel to work in a big factory instead of a small one that had only a few employees?

3. What do you think an individual must do to achieve economic success in this industrial age? Why? How do your ideas compare with the ideas of the nineteenth century?

4. Would you admire a person who didn't care whether or not he earned a good living? If so, why or under what conditions? If not, why not?

5. Charles Perkins declared that economic progress is the source of all other progress (see page 564). What do you think of this idea?

6. Why did your ancestors come to America? How did their values compare with the nineteenth-century American values you have been reading about?

7. Do we have any immigrants today? If so, who are they? Why do you think they come here?

8. Do you think immigrants should be allowed to come to this country today? Why or why not? Should they be allowed to come only from certain countries or from anywhere? Why? Should there be any other restrictions on immigration? Why?

9. Have we inherited any values from the nineteenth century? Explain.

10. Is it useful to know the history of your values? Why or why not?

BIBLIOGRAPHY

*ADDAMS, JANE. TWENTY YEARS AT HULL HOUSE. New York: The Macmillan Company, 1910. †New York: Signet Classics, 1961.
Jane Addams, founder of Hull House, a settlement house, describes the efforts of social workers in fighting urban slum conditions in Chicago.

BARRETT, D. R. A CROSS OF GOLD. Philadelphia: Dorrance & Company, 1939.
Barrett vividly describes frontier life in early Montana.

DOBIE, J. FRANK. UP THE TRAIL FROM TEXAS. New York: Random House, Inc., 1955.
This historical novel is one of the more outstanding works on the cattle industry.

*JOSEPHON, MATTHEW. THE ROBBER BARONS: THE GREAT AMERICAN CAPITALISTS, 1861–1901. New York: Harcourt, Brace & World, Inc., 1934. †New York: Harvest Books, 1962.
Josephon is very critical of the tactics used by many big businessmen during the era.

*LUTZ, ALMA. SUSAN B. ANTHONY: REBEL, CRUSADER, HUMANITARIAN. Boston: Beacon Press, 1959.
Lutz describes a great leader in her fight for women's suffrage.

*NEVINS, ALLAN. JOHN D. ROCKEFELLER. New York: Charles Scribner's Sons, 1959.
Nevins offers a sympathetic interpretation of Rockefeller's business ventures.

*RÖLVAAG, O. E. GIANTS IN THE EARTH: A SAGA OF THE PRAIRIE. New York: Harper & Row, Publishers, 1927. †New York: Perennial Library, 1965.
Rölvaag describes the life of Norwegian settlers in South Dakota.

† Denotes paperback edition.
* Denotes more advanced reading.

TIME LINE

1862 HOMESTEAD ACT PASSED.
1865 CIVIL WAR ENDS.
1871 KNIGHTS OF LABOR FOUNDED.
1876 RECONSTRUCTION FORMALLY ENDS.
1879 STANDARD OIL TRUST FORMED.
1886 AMERICAN FEDERATION OF LABOR FOUNDED.
1887 INTERSTATE COMMERCE COMMISSION ACT PASSED.
1889 OKLAHOMA OPENED FOR SETTLEMENT.
1890 SHERMAN ANTITRUST ACT PASSED.
1892 HOMESTEAD STEEL STRIKE.
1894 EUGENE V. DEBS LEADS THE PULLMAN STRIKE.
1901 PRESIDENT WILLIAM MCKINLEY IS ASSASSINATED. THEODORE ROOSEVELT SUCCEEDS AS PRESIDENT.
1906 PURE FOOD AND DRUG ACT PASSED.
1908 *MULLER* v. *OREGON* DECISION.
1912 WOODROW WILSON ELECTED PRESIDENT.
1913 CONGRESS PASSES THE UNDERWOOD TARIFF AND THE FEDERAL RESERVE BANKING ACT.
1913 SIXTEENTH AMENDMENT, AUTHORIZING AN INCOME TAX, IS ADOPTED.
1913 SEVENTEENTH AMENDMENT, PROVIDING FOR THE DIRECT ELECTION OF SENATORS, IS ADOPTED.
1914 FEDERAL TRADE COMMISSION AND CLAYTON ANTITRUST ACTS PASSED.
1914 WORLD WAR I BEGINS.
1916 KEATING-OWEN CHILD LABOR ACT PASSED.
1917 AMERICA ENTERS WORLD WAR I.
1917 LAW LIMITING EUROPEAN IMMIGRATION ENACTED.
1920 NINETEENTH AMENDMENT, GRANTING WOMEN THE RIGHT TO VOTE, IS ADOPTED.

unit VIII
GOVERNMENT RESPONSIBILITY:
AT HOME AND ABROAD 1898-1945

The legitimate object of government is to do for a community of people, whatever they need to have done, but cannot do, at all, or so well do, for themselves...

INTRODUCTION

In 1945, the United States government was spending almost 274 times as many dollars as it had spent in 1890. This extraordinary increase reflected more than the rise in population, the rise in national wealth, and the decrease in the value of the dollar. The increase meant above all that the United States had assumed vast new responsibilities both at home and abroad.

The military budget was the most faithful mirror of American involvement in foreign affairs. In 1890 it was about $50 million. In 1915 it had risen to $300 million. In 1945 it hit $80,000 million, about 17 times as much as in 1915. The domestic budget also rose. In 1920 the federal government spent almost $2,000 million at home. By 1940, only 20 years later, it spent almost four times as much.

In this unit, you will have an opportunity to think about why the government assumed so many new responsibilities. You will also have a chance to think about whether we should have assumed these responsibilities.

After the Civil War and before the 1890's, the United States was far more concerned with industrial expansion and domestic affairs than with foreign affairs. The problems associated with Reconstruction had to be solved. Business was booming. Immigration flowed in from all over the world. Americans were so deeply involved in building at home, that many people ridiculed Secretary of State William Seward's purchase of Alaska from Russia in 1876. Alaska became known as "Seward's Folly" and "Seward's Icebox." By the 1890's, however, the United States was becoming interested in world affairs. James G. Blaine, Secretary of State in 1881 and from 1889 to 1892, tried to increase trade with Latin America and paved the way for Pan-American cooperation. In 1895, the United States took a role in a boundary dispute between Venezuela and British Guiana. Secretary of State Richard Olney invoked the Monroe Doctrine, and declared that Great Britain had no business meddling in "American affairs." In the late 1890's the United States acquired two possessions in the Pacific Ocean: Hawaii in 1898, and Samoa in 1899.

Between 1897 and 1899, the United States moved toward full involvement as a world power. The decisive event was a crisis in Cuba in which revolutionary Cubans tried to overthrow their Spanish rulers. Then, between 1899 and 1915, the United States became increasingly active in Latin America and the Pacific area. In the first section of this unit, you will study the reasons for this activity. Before you begin, you will be asked to think about why nations get involved in the affairs of other nations at all. You will also be asked to recall the particular reasons why the United States had become involved in foreign affairs earlier in American history.

Section II focuses on World Wars I and II, the League of Nations, and the United Nations. When we entered World War I we became involved in foreign affairs on a scale that was altogether new. What prompted this country to participate in two massive world wars? What prompted our willingness or unwillingness to join world organizations? Do the developments during these crises reveal any pattern in United States attitudes toward world responsibilities?

New government responsibilities at home are the topic of the second half of this unit. In 1929 the United States was plunged into an economic crisis known as the Depression. Two presidents tried to solve the problems of the Depression: Herbert Hoover and Franklin D. Roosevelt. You will study the plans each of these men devised to attack the Depression, and the ideas they expressed about how government should react to the crisis.

In 1915, President Wilson commented on the role of the United States in world affairs. He said that "there is a distinction waiting for this nation that no nation has ever yet achieved." A quarter of a century later President Roosevelt stated that "this nation has a rendezvous with destiny." What role did these leaders envision for their nation? Did they foresee that the United States would become the world's richest and most powerful nation? Did they anticipate that our nation would become involved in almost every aspect of the life of nearly every nation on earth?

The problems presented in this unit—problems about the reasons for assuming new responsibilities and the wisdon of assuming such burdens—have great meaning for the United States today. We have inherited the expanded government built by the leaders of the period 1898-1945. Today the federal government engages in more activities and spends more money, both at home and abroad, than ever before.

Does anything in the story of American involvement in foreign affairs between 1898 and 1945 help to explain the position of the United States today in foreign affairs? Does the involvement of our nation in world problems affect you in any way? And in the domestic area, how do the responsibilities assumed by government affect you? Do they limit your freedom in any way? How do they relate to your ability to solve problems that confront you? Keep these questions in mind as you begin your study of Unit VIII.

I. The United States and Latin America

Government Responsibility Abroad

THE UNITED STATES AND FOREIGN AFFAIRS

1. Why does a nation get involved with the affairs of other nations?

2. What role did Presidents Washington, Jefferson, and Monroe think the United States should play in foreign affairs? Why?

3. Has there been any pattern to United States involvement in world affairs up to the twentieth century? Explain.

4. How is the United States involved in foreign affairs today? How does this compare with our early reasons for being involved? How do you explain this?

UNITED STATES INVOLVEMENT IN THE CARIBBEAN AREA

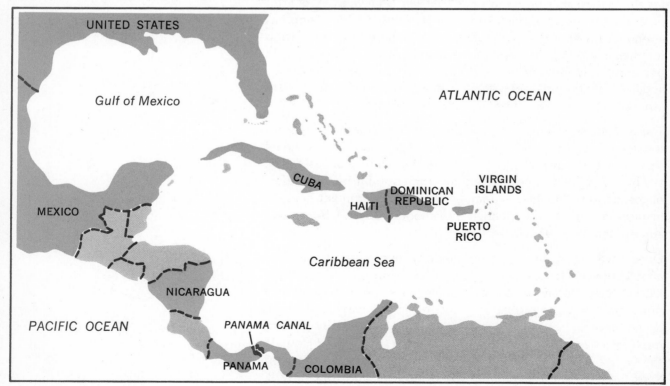

1. Cuba in the Headlines

Imagine you are a typical American in the year 1897. You know that Spain still remains in control of Cuba. You also know that since 1895 revolutionary groups on that island have attempted to oust the Spaniards. You have heard that in 1896 Spain sent to Cuba a new governor general, General Weyler. But all you really know about Cuba is what you read in the newspapers. You read one paper in particular, Joseph Pulitzer's *New York World*. Pulitzer's competitor in New York, William R. Hearst, owner of the *New York Journal,* carried similar stories and headlines. The *World,* the *Journal,* and other New York newspapers distributed their stories throughout the country by means of the wire services.

POINTS TO CONSIDER

How you would have felt about the Cuban situation in 1897-1898.

ALL CUBA AFLAME

February 20, 1897

Atrocities Are Committed Every Day Throughout the Island. . . .

200,000 PEOPLE ARE STARVING. GENERAL WEYLER TRYING "TO KILL OFF THE BREED."

April 15, 1897

. . . And he [Weyler] travels about the island not as a general at the head of his troops, but as a military despot, visiting well fortified cities that he may gloat over the misery he has wrought.

General Weyler, in an attempt to end rebel activities, placed many Cubans in barbed wire "reconcentration camps." Because the Spanish could not provide adequate food or housing, thousands died.

SHAME! SHAME! SHAME!

September 21, 1897

The *World's* Madrid correspondent cables that Gen. Woodford has informed the Spanish Government that if the pacification of Cuba is "not accomplished by the end of October, the United States must consider themselves at liberty to do whatever they shall then deem necessary to secure complete and permanent peace in Cuba."

Woodford was minister to Spain from 1897 to 1898.

"The end of October!" Why the end of October?

Why had Mr. McKinley watched murder . . . in Cuba so calmly these six months and moved to suddenly blaze out and give the Spanish Government less than five weeks' notice . . . ?

William McKinley was President from 1897 to 1901.

HORRORS OF INDIA'S PLAGUE NOW SURPASSED IN CUBA

November 7, 1897

30,000 Non-Combatants, chiefly women and children have perished within a few weeks.

You would sicken at the sight of the thousands of women and children starving to death in Cuba today. . . . Filthy skeletons dying

613

on bare, foul boards; . . . the suffering is awful. . . . The poor victims . . . die by the hundreds under the eyes of soldiers.

November 8, 1897

TRUTHS FROM CUBA THAT WILL SHOCK THE CIVILIZED WORLD

General Weyler's Policy of Killing Women and Children by Slow Starvation Under the Guns of Spain's Forts.

A multitude of sick fall dying upon garbage in the streets here, and there they lie until, after having served as . . . spectacles for nine hours, they are collected and hauled away in oxcarts used for garbage . . .

(Editorial) . . . If Spain will not put an end to murder in Cuba the United States must.

November 29, 1897: (Editorial) . . . There seems very little doubt that Mr. McKinley will be forced by Congress to accept an aggressive attitude in this matter. . . .

February 9, 1898

SPANISH MINISTER DE LOME CHARGED WITH INSULTING McKINLEY

Describes the President as "a low Politician," "Catering to the Rabble" . . .

(Editorial) . . . The Senate is growing impatient in the Cuban matter, and so are the people.

Mr. Canon, of Utah, yesterday introduced another resolution calling upon the President to insist that Spain shall "recognize the independence of the Cuban Republic" by March 4, on aim of having the United States "assert that independence within ninety days thereafter. . . ."

"Dalliance" means delay.

If the Administration continues its policy of dalliance Congress may some fine day rise up in its might as the war-making power and proclaim Cuban independence.

February 16, 1898

U.S.S. MAINE BLOWN UP IN HAVANA HARBOR

It is not known whether explosion occurred on or under the Maine.

February 17, 1898

GROWING BELIEF IT WAS NOT ACCIDENTAL

February 22, 1898

INACTIVITY OF THE ADMINISTRATION CONDEMNED

Haggling with Wreckers while the Maine Sinks Deeper in the Mud and the Nation's Dead are without a Tomb . . .

614

VULTURES PICK OUR SAILORS' BONES
PATRIOTISM WHEREVER PEOPLES GATHER

February 24, 1898

IT WAS A TORPEDO, NOT A SUBMARINE MINE THAT SUNK THE MAINE

February 26, 1898

Arms and ammunition being brought from Interior Arsenals to Navy Yard.

February 27, 1898: Brigade promised by an Oregon General . . .
Indian Volunteers are ready for an emergency . . .
Colorado Militia will join regular Army . . .
Ex-Confederates anxious to form a Regiment . . .
Danbury young men at the Recruiting Office.

CUBAN INDEPENDENCE THE INDEMNITY

"Indemnity" is payment for damage or loss.

(Editorial) . . . President McKinley's attitude, according to friends near him, is that he "will be guided by the public sentiment of the country if the Board of Inquiry shall report that the Maine was sent to the bottom through other than accidental causes."

. . . Whether Spanish treachery devised or Spanish willingness permitted this colossal crime, Spain is responsible for it.

When this fact shall be officially proclaimed, what will be the duty of the President and the Congress? . . .

On this page Senators and Representatives repudiate in scorn the suggestions that a money indemnity can be fixed and accepted.

The time and occasion have come to put an end to this. Indemnity for the families of the dead! . . .

SPAIN IS NOW ACTIVELY PREPARING FOR WAR

February 28, 1898

CABINET OFFICERS MEN OF FORTUNE

There are six millionaires in the Cabinet of President McKinley.

The richest of these is Secretary of War, Russell A. Alger.

In these times when public sentiment is aroused, when the war spirit sways people and the intimacy between Wall Street and the Government has been proven to be so intimate, it is wise to look closely into the wealth and business position of the advisors of the President . . . War would mean enormous losses to Wall Street.

$50,000,000 WAR FUND VOTED UNANIMOUSLY BY THE HOUSE

March 9, 1898

The scene in the house today cannot escape history. . . .

Mr. Cannon in introducing the bill was most impressive . . . "We stand among the first nations of the world and we must be prepared to maintain the natural honor, our dignity, justice, and the right."

Then followed the one hundred patriotic voices, who without a discordant note, voiced the sentiment of an avowed and vigilant patriotism. . . .

"We don't want war, but if it must come, let it come now. We are ready; we have got the men; we will get the ships, and we have got the money, too" . . .

March 12, 1898: (Editorial) . . . If we must have war, let it be a war for a high and noble purpose, a war right, for liberty, for humanity, for civilization. If diplomacy is to settle the matter, let the aims and exactions of our diplomacy be worthy of the great Republic and satisfying to its deep indignation.

Peace—But Free Cuba.

WAR WILL TEACH US A LESSON SAYS KIRKLAND

March 13, 1898

Admiral Kirkland, the ranking Rear Admiral of the United States Navy, says unofficially that he does not see how war with Spain can be avoided. . . .

. . . We haven't had a chance to fight against one of the big powers and this trouble with Spain will teach us a lesson. When the United States realizes the trouble she's put in being unprepared for war with a bankrupt country like Spain, it will give us some idea of what we would have to do to get into condition to fight with England or France. . . .

Mark Hanna was an industrialist and a senator from Ohio. John J. McCook was a lawyer from New York. A "trust" is a combination of business corporations, which controls a particular industry.

March 16, 1898: (Editorial) . . . The attempt of Mark Hanna, John J. McCook and the Sugar Trust syndicate to secure an early adjournment of Congress—"leaving the Spanish-Cuban question in the hands of the President"—is supported by all the peace-at-any-price elements. If these sordid plotters and anaemic protestors can only get "Congress out of the way" they are confident that they can confirm the President in his natural tendency to procrastinate [delay], and so postpone the crisis beyond the hot season. . . .

TERRIBLE PORTRAYAL OF SPAIN'S MISRULE IN CUBA

March 18, 1898

March 22, 1898: . . . "The best indication of how the people feel is the vast number of military companies being organized throughout the United States and the large number of men enlisting."

616

PRESIDENT FAVORS DIPLOMACY
CONGRESS FAVORS FORCE

March 26, 1898

March 29, 1898: . . . The majority of the House of Representatives is tonight in actual revolt against the dove-like message of President McKinley. At least a quarter of the Senate is in favor of immediate intervention in Cuba, by force if necessary. . . .

WAR SPIRIT IN CONGRESS
OVERWHELMS McKINLEY

March 30, 1898

FORTY EIGHT HOURS GIVEN
FOR SPAIN TO YIELD

March 31, 1898

SPAIN'S REPLY . . . POINTS TO WAR

April 1, 1898

She declares the United States Has No Right to Dictate Terms Between Spain and Her Colonies.

(Editorial) . . . A nation that will consent to have its ships blown up by submarine mines without demanding and enforcing instant reparation has no business with a navy. It should confine itself to growing crops, building railroads, gambling in stocks and running Sunday-Schools.

. . . We must punish Spain.

DECLARATION OF WAR!

April 16, 1898

Both Houses of Congress Have Said That Spain Must Get Off This Continent AT ONCE!

1. If you were a reader of this or similar papers, what would be your personal opinion of events concerning Cuba? Why? What would you do about it? Explain.

2. What appear to be the reasons the United States got involved in the affairs of an island ninety miles away from its shore?

3. How do these reasons compare with your prior ideas about involvement in foreign affairs?

2. Why We're in Cuba: The Atlantic Monthly, 1898

When war was finally declared on Spain over the Cuban situation, many reasons were given for United States involvement. The *Atlantic Monthly,* a literary magazine, printed one explanation in June 1898.

. . . [We] have had a Cuban question for more than ninety years. At times it has disappeared from our politics, but it has always

"The War With Spain and After," **Atlantic Monthly,** Vol. LXXXI, No. 488 (1898), pp. 722-735.

reappeared. Once we thought it wise to prevent the island from winning its independence from Spain, and thereby, perhaps, we entered into moral bonds to make sure that Spain governed it decently. Whether we definitely contracted such an obligation or not, the Cuban question has never ceased to annoy us. . . . Many of our ablest statesmen have had to deal with it . . . It has at various times been a "plank" in the platforms of all our political parties —as it was in both the party platforms of 1896,—and it has been the subject of messages of nearly all our Presidents, as it was of President Cleveland's message in December 1896, in which he distinctly expressed the opinion that the United States might feel forced to recognize "higher obligations" than neutrality to Spain. . . . [The] old trouble has . . . never been settled; nor has there recently been any strong reason for hope that it could be settled merely by diplomatic negotiation with Spain. Our diplomats have long had an experience with Spanish character and methods such as the public can better understand since war has been in progress.

The pathetic inefficiency and the continual indirection [dishonesty] of the Spanish character are now apparent to the world; they were long ago apparent to those who have had our diplomatic duties to do.

. . . More than once heretofore has there been danger of international conflict, as for instance when American sailors on the Virginius were executed in Cuba in 1873. Propositions have been made to buy the island, and plans have been formed to annex it. All the while there have been American interests in Cuba. Our citizens have owned property and made investments there, and done much to develop its fertility. They have paid tribute, unlawful as well as lawful, both to insurgents [rebels] and to Spanish officials. They have lost property, for much of which no indemnity has been paid. All the while we have had a trade with the island, important during periods of quiet, irritating during periods of unrest.

The Cuban trouble is, therefore, not a new trouble even in an acute form. It had been moving toward a crisis for a long time. Still, while our government suffered these diplomatic vexations, and our citizens these losses, and our merchants these annoyances, the mass of the American people gave little serious thought to it. The newspapers kept us reminded of an opera bouffe [musical comedy] war that was going on, and now and then there came information of delicate and troublesome diplomatic duties for our minister to Spain.

If Cuba were within a hundred miles of the coast of one of our populous states and near one of our great ports, periods of acute

The *Virginius,* a Cuban vessel illegally flying the American flag, ran guns to Cuban rebels. The Spanish navy captured it in 1873 and executed some of its crew as pirates, including one American. At the time, a number of Americans were thought to have been killed. Anti-Spanish feeling was aroused in the United States.

In 1895, before the Spanish sent Weyler to Cuba, the Cuban rebel general had forbidden any goods to be sent to towns occupied by the Spanish. He had also ordered work on the sugar plantations to cease. Many of these plantations were owned by Americans. People who gave supplies to the Spanish or continued to run their plantations had their fields burned and their houses destroyed. It was possible to bribe the rebels not to burn one's fields by paying tribute. Many chose this solution.

interest in its condition would doubtless have come earlier and oftener, and we would long ago have had to deal with a crisis by warlike measures. Or if the insurgents had commanded respect instead of mere pity, we should have paid heed to their struggle sooner; for it is almost an American maxim that a people cannot govern itself till it can win its own independence.

When it began to be known that Weyler's method of extermination was producing want in the island, and when appeals were made to American charity, we became more interested. . . .

The American public was in this mood when the battleship Maine was blown up in the harbor of Havana. The masses think in events, and not in syllogisms [logical proofs], and this was an event. This event provoked suspicions in the public mind. The thought of the whole nation was instantly directed to Cuba. The fate of the sailors on the Virginius, twenty-five years ago, was recalled. The public curiosity about everything Cuban and Spanish became intense. The Weyler method of warfare became more generally known. The story of our long diplomatic trouble with Spain was recalled. . . .

There is no need to discuss minor and accidental causes that hastened the rush of events; but such causes were not lacking either in number or in influence. . . .

But all these together could not have driven us to war if we had not been willing to be driven,—if the conviction had not become firm in the minds of the people that Spanish rule in Cuba was a blot on civilization that had now begun to bring reproach to us; and when the President, who favored peace, declared it "intolerable," the people were ready to accept his judgment.

. . . We rushed into war almost before we knew it, not because we desired war, but because we desired something to be done with the old problem that should be direct and definite and final. Let us end it once and for all. . . .

Not only is there in the United States an unmistakable popular approval of war as the only effective means of restoring civilization in Cuba, but the judgement of the English people promptly approved it,—giving evidence of an instinctive race and institutional sympathy. If Anglo-Saxon [English] institutions and methods stand for anything, the institutions and methods of Spanish rule in Cuba are an abomination and a reproach. And English sympathy is not more significant as an evidence of the necessity of the war and as a good omen for the future of free institutions than the equally instinctive sympathy with Spain that has been expressed by some of the decadent influences [decaying governments] on the Continent; indeed, the real meaning of American civilization

619

"Mediaevilism" refers to the rule of military lords over a weak peasantry.

and ideals will henceforth be somewhat more clearly understood in several quarters of the world.

American character will be still better understood when the whole world clearly perceives that the purpose of the war is only to remove from our very doors this cruel and inefficient piece of mediaevalism which is one of the two great scandals of the closing years of the century; for it is not a war of conquest.

1. How does the *Atlantic Monthly* explain our involvement in Cuban affairs?

2. Does this explanation differ in any way from the one suggested by the newspaper? Explain.

THE UNITED STATES AND THE PACIFIC AREA

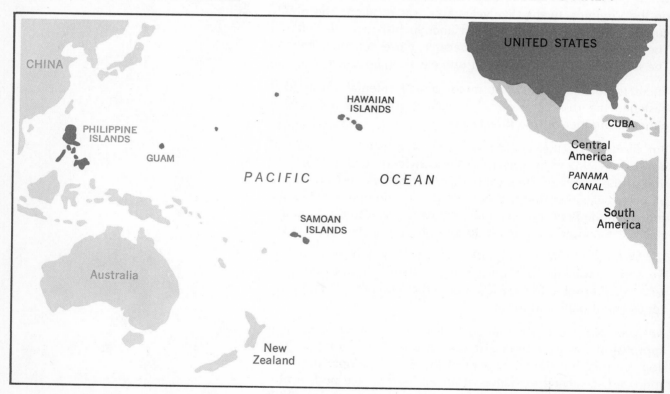

KEY

The United States and the Pacific

UNITED STATES AND POSSESSIONS

3. Aspects of the Spanish-American War

By the end of 1898, the war was over and the United States had defeated Spain. Spain gave up all claim to Cuba and gave the islands of Puerto Rico and Guam to the United States. She sold the Philippine Islands to the United States for $20 million.

The following reading tells some of the events of the Spanish-American War. It also describes world conditions prior to the war, and reactions to the war in the United States and abroad.

POINTS TO CONSIDER

How these statements relate to each other.

How these statements relate to what you have learned about the war so far.

1. In the eighteenth and nineteenth centuries, many European nations took control of areas of Asia, the Middle East, and Africa. The Europeans made these areas their *colonies*. A colony was supposed to supply the European country with new materials for its industry and to provide markets for its products.

2. The United States feared that Americans would be shut out of trade in China, where many European nations had been carving out "spheres of influence." These spheres were areas in which some nation had acquired special trading privileges.

3. The United States reasserted the Monroe Doctrine during the late nineteenth century as a warning to European countries to stay out of South America.

4. Germany became a unified nation and an industrial power in the 1870's. By that time, most of the richest areas for colonization had already been taken. Germany wanted colonies in South America.

5. In 1878, the United States agreed to protect the independence of Samoa in return for a fueling station for American ships. From 1879 on, the United States blocked German ambitions to take over Samoa.

6. In 1897, the Germans forced China to give them control of land on Kiaochow Bay, where they built a port. Americans were disturbed by this action.

7. The American business community opposed the war with Spain because they feared it would disrupt a prosperous world trade.

8. President McKinley sent his war message to Congress on April 11, 1898, two days after the Spanish had capitulated to the Cuban rebel demands.

9. The American public never learned about how Cuban rebels tried to keep food from Spanish troops, or about rebel destruction of homes and sugar plantations. The Cuban rebels had representatives in New York who managed to keep reports of such tactics out of the papers.

621

10. The *New York Journal* and the *New York World* were in fierce competition to win as many readers as possible. They tried to print stories which would arouse curiosity, horror, and indignation. They were not careful about accuracy. These practices were known as "yellow journalism."

11. Two hundred thousand Americans volunteered for the war. Fifteen thousand went to Cuba.

12. Great Britain gave moral support to the United States in its war over Cuba.

13. Germany opposed United States involvement in Cuba.

14. Great Britain feared the rivalry of Germany in world trade.

15. Theodore Roosevelt, the Assistant Secretary of the Navy, placed George Dewey in command of the American Asiatic squadron and ordered him to stand by at Manila, in the Philippines, just before the Spanish-American War began. Dewey destroyed the Spanish fleet in Manila Bay as soon as he knew war had been declared against Spain.

16. Dewey attacked the port of Manila on August 12. It fell to the Americans on August 13, 1898. Spain had already surrendered Cuba.

17. After the fall of Manila, several countries sent warships to protect their commercial interests in the Philippines. Great Britain, for example, sent two ships. Germany sent five ships. But Germany had fewer commercial interests in the Philippines than Britain. Germany also violated the blockade set up by Dewey.

18. Under great pressure from several groups in the United States, particularly businessmen and church leaders, President McKinley announced his decision to take possession of the Philippines. He made the following remarks:

    "I walked the floor of the White House night after night until midnight; and I am not ashamed to tell you, gentlemen, that I went down on my knees and prayed almighty God for light and guidance more than one night . . . And one night late it came to me this way . . . (1) that we could not give them back to Spain—that would be cowardly and dishonorable; (2) that we could not turn them over to France or Germany—our commercial rivals in the Orient—that would be bad business . . . (3) that we could not leave them to themselves—they were unfit for self-government—and they would soon have anarchy and misrule . . . and (4) that there was nothing left for us to do but to take them all, and to educate the Filipinos, and uplift and civilize and Christianize them . . ."

19. The Filipinos, on February 4, 1899, attacked the United States troops in an attempt to gain their independence. They were

supressed in a two-year war involving seventy thousand United States troops.

20. The United States granted the Philippines full independence on July 4, 1946.

21. After defeating Spain, the United States adopted the Platt Amendment. The amendment declared that the United States would withdraw its troops from Cuba providing: (1) Cuba would not make any treaty with any foreign nation which would impair its independence, (2) the United States would have the right to intervene to keep order and to protect Cuban independence, (3) the United States would be permitted to lease or buy land in Cuba for use as naval stations, and (4) Cuba could not incur debts that she would be unable to repay from her own revenues.

1. What do these statements reveal about why we entered the Spanish-American War?

2. How do these statements add to what you learned from the newspaper headlines and the magazine article?

4. Theodore Roosevelt and the Big Stick

In 1901, William McKinley was assassinated, and Theodore Roosevelt became President of the United States. In 1900, when he was Vice President, Roosevelt said that a West African proverb, "Speak softly and carry a big stick, you will go far," summed up his theory of a good policy. As President from 1901-1909, Roosevelt gave this quotation new meaning. For example, in 1903 Roosevelt used American military strength to win the right to build an American canal across Panama. Completion of a Panama Canal would remove about eight thousand miles from the sea voyage between New York and San Francisco. The people of Panama, a province of Colombia, wanted the United States to build the canal. When it was reported that Colombia had refused the United States permission to build, the Panamanians revolted against Colombia. Colombia replied by trying to send troops into Panama. Roosevelt, however, placed the United States fleet in the way of the Colombian troops. He claimed that he was carrying out the terms of a treaty Colombia had signed in 1846, which gave the United States the right to transport goods across Panama and to protect such transporting. The Panamanian revolt was successful, and Roosevelt quickly signed a treaty with Panama. One clause of the treaty gave the United States the right to take control of any land necessary for the defense of the new canal.

In 1904, Roosevelt issued a statement known as the Roosevelt Corollary to the Monroe Doctrine. At that time, the Dominican

Republic was in debt to Germany. Roosevelt feared that Germany would seize the Dominican Republic because of its failure to pay these debts. The following selection is the Roosevelt Corollary, stated in the form of an indirect warning to Germany or any other country with plans to seize power in weak Central or South American countries.

The Record of American Diplomacy, edited by Ruhl J. Bartlett (New York: Alfred A. Knopf, 1948), p. 539.

It is not true that the United States feels any land hunger or entertains any projects as regards the other nations of the Western Hemisphere save such as are for their welfare. All that this country desires is to see the neighboring countries stable, orderly, and prosperous. Any country whose people conduct themselves well can count upon our hearty friendship. If a nation shows that it knows how to act with reasonable efficiency and decency in social and political matters, if it keeps order and pays its obligations, it need fear no interference from the United States. Chronic [continual] wrongdoing . . . which results in a general loosening of the ties of civilized society, may in America, as elsewhere, ultimately require intervention by some civilized nation, and in the Western Hemisphere the adherence of the United States to the Monroe Doctrine may force the United States, however reluctantly, in flagrant [glaring] cases of such wrongdoing . . . to the exercise of an international police power. If every country washed by the Caribbean Sea would show the progress in stable and just civilization which with the aid of the Platt amendment Cuba has shown since our troops left the island, and which so many of the republics in both Americas are constantly and brilliantly showing, all question of interference by this Nation with their affairs would be at an end. . . .

1. According to President Roosevelt, what is the basis of United States involvement in the affairs of neighboring countries? How does this tie in with historic American policy as reflected in the Monroe Doctrine? What has happened to the Monroe Doctrine?

2. Roosevelt began working hard for the completion of a Panama canal when he first became President in 1901. Why do you think Roosevelt felt that the canal was important?

3. Do you think Roosevelt was concerned about the Dominican Republic for any reasons *not* stated here? Explain.

4. How does the reason for involvement that Roosevelt states here compare with the reasons for American involvement in Cuban affairs in 1898?

5. How does Roosevelt's statement compare with the reasons for recent American involvement in the affairs of other countries?

5. William Jennings Bryan: Imperialism?

William Jennings Bryan, Democratic nominee for President in 1896, 1900, and 1908, continually criticized the actions of the United States in foreign affairs. Bryan feared America was drifting toward imperialism. In accepting the nomination in 1900, he made the following remarks.

Those who would have this Nation enter upon a career of empire must consider, not only the effect of imperialism on the Filipinos, but they must also calculate its effects upon our own nation. We cannot repudiate the principle of self-government in the Philippines without weakening that principle here. . . .

William Jennings Bryan, **Speeches of William Jennings Bryan** (New York: Funk and Wagnalls Company, Inc., 1909), Vol. II, pp. 24-25.

Even now we are beginning to see the paralyzing influence of imperialism. Heretofore this Nation has been prompt to express its sympathy with those who were fighting for civil liberty. While our sphere of activity has been limited to the Western Hemisphere, our sympathies have not been bounded by the seas. We have felt it due to ourselves and to the world, as well as to those who were struggling for the right to govern themselves, to proclaim the interest which our people have, from the date of their own independence, felt in every contest between human rights and arbitrary [tyrannical] power. . . .

1. What is imperialism?

2. Do you agree with Bryan that the United States was becoming imperialistic? Why or why not?

6. President Taft's Policy

President William H. Taft (1909-1913) continued the trend of United States involvement in Latin American affairs. Taft sometimes became involved when Latin American nations failed to repay their debts to other countries or to pay the interest on their loans. The United States government then intervened, frequently by landing marines in the country, by supporting a friendly political group, or by placing the collection of customs under American supervision.

Taft's dealings with Nicaragua provide one example of his diplomacy. In 1909, a revolt in Nicaragua resulted in the establishment of a new government. The United States refused to recognize the new regime unless it agreed to borrow money from American bankers. The United States wanted Nicaragua to use this money to pay the debt it owed to Great Britain. When Nicaragua opposed this action, the United States sent a warship to Nicaragua. It remained there until the loan was made.

In the following selection, Taft expresses his ideas about relations with Latin America.

The Shaping of American Diplomacy, edited by
William Appleman Williams (Chicago: Rand McNally
& Company, 1956), p. 532.

A creditor nation is one that loans money.
A debtor nation is one that has borrowed
money and has not paid it back.

POINTS TO CONSIDER

Why Taft's policy was characterized as "substituting dollars for
bullets."

A little less than three centuries of colonial and national life have
brought the people inhabiting the United States, by a process of
evolution, natural and, with the existing forces inevitable, to a
point of distinct and radical change in their economic relations
to the rest of mankind.

During the period now past, the energy of our people, directed
by the formative power created in our early population by hered-
ity, by environment, by the struggle for existence, by individual
independence, and by free institutions, has been devoted to the
internal development of our own country. The surplus wealth produced by our labors has been applied immediately to reproduc-
tion in our own land. . . .

Since the first election of President McKinley, the people of the
United States have for the first time accumulated a surplus of
capital beyond the requirements of internal development. That
surplus is increasing with extraordinary rapidity. We have paid
our debts to Europe and have become a creditor instead of a
debtor nation; we have faced about; we have left the ranks of the
borrowing nations and have entered the ranks of the investing
nations. Our surplus energy is beginning to look beyond our own
borders, throughout the world, to find opportunity for the profitable use of our surplus capital, foreign markets for our manufacturers, foreign mines to be developed, foreign bridges and railroads and public works to be built, foreign rivers to be turned into
electric power and light. . . .

Immediately before us, at exactly the right time, just as we are
ready for it, great opportunities for peaceful commercial and industrial expansion to the south are presented. Other investing
nations are already in the field—England, France, Germany, Italy,
Spain; but the field is so vast, the new demands are so great, the
progress so rapid, that what other nations have done up to this
time is but a slight advance in the race for the grand total.

The opportunities are so large that figures fail to convey them. The
area of this newly awakened continent [South America] is 7,502,-
848 square miles—more than two and one half times as large as the
United States without Alaska, and more than double the United
States including Alaska. . . .

1. President Roosevelt's foreign policy is called "big stick diplo-

macy" by historians. What would you expect them to call Taft's foreign policy? Why?

2. Does this selection reveal any new reasons for United States involvement in world affairs?

3. Can you think of any reasons not mentioned in this reading for the United States' action in Nicaragua in 1909?

4. Are there any similarities between Taft's and Roosevelt's policies? How can you explain this?

7. President Wilson and Latin America

President Woodrow Wilson (1913-1921) was also concerned with Latin America. In 1912, the United States declared itself exempt from paying tolls in the Panama Canal. Great Britain strongly protested this action. The Hay-Pauncefote Treaty, concluded with Britain in 1901, had guaranteed equal rates to ships of all nations. In 1914, Wilson urged Congress to repeal the act exempting the United States. He argued that it was a matter of national honor that the United States carry out its treaty obligations.

Josephus Daniels, a close friend of Wilson and his Secretary of the Navy from 1913 to 1921, describes Wilson's intentions toward Latin America in the following account.

The Danish Islands of the West Indies came under the American flag during the Wilson administration. The paramount advantage to be gained by the United States from its acquisition of these islands was the large measure of safety they confer upon the Panama Canal. The strategic wisdom of gaining control of the islands lay not so much in the need of the United States of a naval base located in one of the harbors. It was the danger to the safety and amicable relations of the United States which would result from the acquirement of the islands by some other power.

Toward Puerto Rico and Hawaii and all territories separated from the continent, Wilson's attitude was expressed when he said, "We are trustees." They "are ours, indeed, but not ours to do what we please with." His whole attitude as to them and the Philippines was thus stated: "Such territories, once regarded as mere possessions, are no longer to be selfishly exploited . . . We must administer them for the people who live in them and with the same sense of responsibility to them as toward our own people in domestic affairs."

. . . Consular officers, indeed, were alert and were encouraged to advance America's good offices to promote trade in Latin-America, but no diplomacy directed to secure purely commercial

Josephus Daniels, **The Life of Woodrow Wilson 1856-1924** (New York: Holt, Rinehart and Winston, Inc., 1924), pp. 192-194. All rights reserved. Reprinted by permission of Holt, Rinehart and Winston, Inc.

The "Danish Islands" are the Virgin Islands, which the United States purchased in 1917 from Denmark.

Wilson feared that Germany would obtain the islands.

advantages to favored Americans was . . . winked at. In the presence of the diplomats from Latin-American countries, President Wilson, in his famous Mobile speech October 27, 1913, opened the way for the better understanding with those neighbor nations. He was speaking at the time of the opening of the Panama Canal, and predicted an "emancipation" of those states from "subordination to foreign enterprise." He pointed out that they had "harder bargains driven with them in the matter of loans than any other peoples in the world," and he declared, "we ought to be the first to take part in assisting in that emancipation." He then laid down this doctrine with which all his subsequent actions squared:

"We must prove ourselves their friends, and champions upon terms of equality and honor. You cannot be friends at all except upon terms of equality. We must show ourselves friends by comprehending their interest whether it squares with our interest or not. . . ."

The spirit of the Monroe Doctrine that no European country may add territory on this continent caused the President in 1914 to direct the Navy Department to bring about tranquility in the . . . island of Haiti and San [Santo] Domingo. It was necessary for this government to take action in those lands to prevent European countries landing to protect what they regarded as jeopardy of their interests by repeated revolutions. As to Haiti the aim of the United States in connection with the landing of Marines by the United States [in 1915] and the seizure of customs houses and their administration by American officials was well set forth in a statement issued by Secretary [of State] Lansing on August 25, 1915, in which he said: "We have only one purpose—that is, to help the Haitian people and prevent them from being exploited by irresponsible revolutionists. . . . The United States Government has no purpose of aggression and is entirely disinterested in promoting this protectorate." Similar purposes animated the Government in its establishment of a temporary protectorate in San Domingo.

France and Germany had sent troops to Haiti on a temporary basis. The United States feared that they might violate the Monroe Doctrine by seizing territory there.

In 1912, revolutionary forces in Santo Domingo seized two custom houses and laid seige to others which the United States government had controlled since 1907. An American official was temporarily appointed to bring things under control, but he was unable to do so. In 1916, full military occupation was established.

1. Is there anything different about Wilson's reasoning on United States involvement in the affairs of neighboring nations? Explain.

2. Does any pattern seem to be developing in United States foreign affairs?

FROM McKINLEY TO WILSON

1. For what different reasons did the United States become involved in the affairs of other nations from the time of McKinley to the time of Wilson?

2. Which reasons do you think were the main causes of our involvement? Why?

3. Do you think our involvement with other nations was justified? Was it right in some cases and wrong in others? Why?

4. Do American attitudes toward involvement in foreign affairs between 1890 and 1914 seem different from attitudes in earlier periods? How can you account for this?

5. How do the policies of the United States in the early years of the twentieth century compare with today's policies? Can you explain this?

II. World Wars and World Peace

WORLD WAR I

8. World War I: Background and Beginning

In the nineteenth century, *nationalism* became an important force in European history. A *nation* is a group of people who share a similar background, and who live in, or originally lived in, the same area. Usually a nation is also a state—a country with its own independent government. Nationalism is devotion to the interests of one's nation.

In Europe in the 1860's, people who shared the same nationality often lived in widely separated areas. They did not have their own states. Instead, they were ruled by people of other nationalities. As their feelings of nationalism developed, such groups became determined to unite and form their own national states. This often resulted in serious struggles with the ruling European powers.

The Italians are one example of a group who felt the stirrings of the new nationalism. Between 1859 and 1870, in their attempt to form an independent, united Italy, they clashed with Austria. Austria claimed areas in which a majority of the citizens were Italian. She was not willing to cede this territory to Italy.

In Austria-Hungary, the Hapsburg family ruled over many different nationalities and language groups. In addition to Italians, the Austrians ruled large groups of Germans, Hungarians, and Slavic peoples such as the Poles, Croats, and Serbs. These groups held an inferior position in matters of government. The Serbs, in particular, wanted a nation of their own. However, their people were scattered in many countries besides Austria-Hungary.

Germany became a unified country in 1871. She fought wars with both Austria and France in order to gain control of territory claimed by them. As the German national state developed, it felt the effects of the industrial revolution and the competition with

Great Britain and France for markets for trade. Great Britain and France had been the leading commercial nations since the eighteenth century. They had a vast network of colonies already established around the world.

The following map shows the nations of Europe as they had developed by 1914. After the map is a list of some of the major European events from 1870 to 1914.

POINTS TO CONSIDER

What appear to be the causes of World War I in Europe.

EUROPE IN 1914

KEY

BALKAN PENINSULA

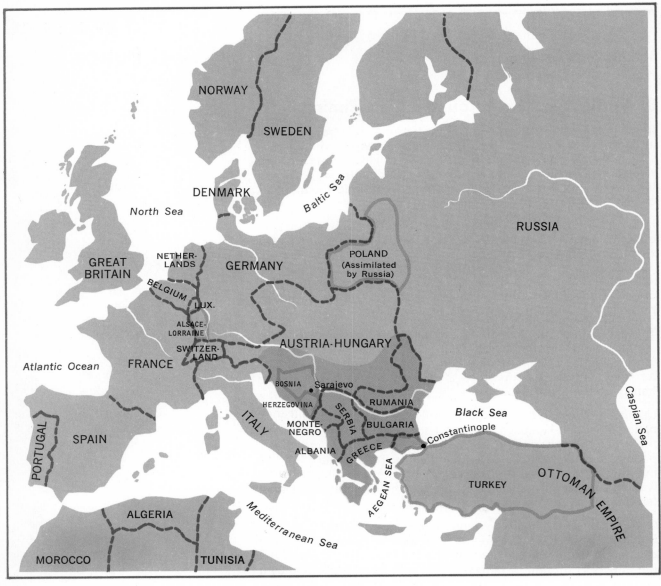

MAJOR EVENTS IN EUROPE, 1870-1914

1870-71 France and Germany were at war (Franco-Prussian War). France was defeated and required to pay a high indemnity to Germany as well as to cede Alsace and Lorraine on her eastern border.

1872 Germany made an alliance with Russia and Austria-Hungary in order to isolate her former enemy, France.

1878 Russia withdrew from the German alliance because of difficulties with Austria-Hungary.

1882 Italy joined with Germany and Austria-Hungary in a defensive alliance known as the *Triple Alliance*.

1891 France and Russia, in distrust of Germany, made a defensive alliance called the *Dual Alliance*.

1904 Great Britain, aroused by German naval moves, joined France and Russia in the *Triple Entente*.

1905 Germany interfered in French-controlled Morocco by encouraging the Sultan of Morocco to resist a French reform plan. Russia was involved in the Russo-Japanese War, so could not aid France. France submitted to the Sultan.

The czarist government of Russia suppressed a revolt.

1908 Austria-Hungary annexed Bosnia and Herzegovina. Russia protested, but took no action.

1911 Germany sent a gunboat to Morocco to aid the Moroccans against French controls. France gave Germany large areas of the Congo in Africa as a settlement.

Germany and Austria-Hungary cultivated friendship with Turkey. They helped to train a Turkish army and to plan a Berlin to Baghdad railroad to assist in furthering trade.

Russia, in need of seaports to develop her resources, wanted Constantinople, a vital link on the Berlin to Baghdad Railroad.

1912-13 A Balkan War found Serbia adding to her territory at the expense of Turkey. The Serbs failed, however, to get a port they wanted on the Adriatic Sea.

1913-14 Germany passed a new army bill that set aside $250 million for an increase in her standing army in case war should come. France, alarmed, lengthened the term of required military training from two to three years. Russia and Austria-Hungary made similar moves.

1914

June 28 The Austrian Crown Prince and Princess were killed by a young Serbian as they rode through the streets of Sarajevo, the capital of Bosnia.

July 23   Austria delivered an ultimatum to Serbia demanding that concessions be agreed to within 48 hours. England, France, and Russia tried to get an extension of the time, but they were refused. Serbia was persuaded to submit to part of the demands.

July 28   Austria-Hungary refused to accept partial compliance with her demands and declared war on Serbia. Russia warned she would not be indifferent to this action and mobilized her armies.

July 31   Germany backed Austria-Hungary and ordered Russia to cease military preparations within 12 hours. Russia made no reply.

August 1   Germany declared war on Russia. France came to Russia's aid as an ally.

August 2   Germany demanded the right to pass troops through Belgium to get to France. Belgium's neutrality was guaranteed by an 1839 treaty with Great Britain, which was pledged to defend Belgium. Belgium refused German demands.

August 4   Germany invaded Belgium. Great Britain declared war on Germany.

August 6   Austria-Hungary declared war on Russia.

1. From your study of the map and the events leading up to World War I, write several statements which reflect what you conclude to be the causes of the war. Be able to defend your ideas with the evidence that you used in coming to those conclusions.

2. Considering the causes of the war as you determined them and the situation in which Europe found itself in the years just prior to 1914, how would you think the United States might view its position toward that area of the world at that time?

9. The United States and World War I: Neutrality

Woodrow Wilson, a former college professor and governor of New Jersey, was elected President of the United States in 1912. By the summer of 1914, many events had occurred in Europe that called for a response on the part of the United States. On August 18, 1914, Wilson spoke to the nation about our position.

My Fellow Countrymen:

I suppose that every thoughtful man in America has asked himself, during these last troubled weeks, what influence the European war may exert upon the United States, and I take the liberty of address-

President Wilson's Foreign Policy: Messages, Addresses, Papers, edited by James Brown Scott (New York: Oxford University Press, 1918), pp. 66-68.

ing a few words to you in order to point out that it is entirely within our own choice what its effects upon us will be and to urge very earnestly upon you the sort of speech and conduct which will best safeguard the Nation against distress and disaster.

The effect of the war upon the United States will depend upon what American citizens say and do. Every man who really loves America will act and speak in the true spirit of neutrality, which is the spirit of impartiality and fairness and friendliness to all concerned. . . .

The people of the United States are drawn from many nations, and chiefly from the nations now at war. It is natural and inevitable that there should be the utmost . . . sympathy and desire among them with regard to the issues and circumstances of the conflict. . . .[They] may be divided in camps of hostile opinion, hot against each other, involved in the war itself in impulse and opinion if not in action.

Such divisions among us would be fatal to our peace of mind and might seriously stand in the way of the proper performance of our duty as the one great nation at peace, the one people holding itself ready to play a part of impartial mediation and speak the counsels of peace and accommodation, not as a partisan, but as a friend.

A "partisan" is one who actively takes sides.

I venture, therefore, my fellow countrymen, to speak a solemn word of warning to you against that deepest, most subtle, most essential breach of neutrality which may spring out of partisanship, out of passionately taking sides. The United States must be neutral in fact as well as in name during these days that are to try men's souls. We must be impartial in thought as well as in action, must put a curb upon our sentiments as well as upon every transaction that might be construed [viewed] as a preference of one party to the struggle before another.

1. Using this speech, describe Wilson's attitude toward European affairs at the start of World War I.

2. After examining events in Europe between 1870 and 1914, you formed an opinion about how America would react to these events. How does Wilson's policy compare with your ideas?

3. How does Wilson's attitude compare with United States attitudes toward European affairs earlier in American history?

10. The United States and World War I: Toward Involvement

In August 1914, fighting broke out in Europe. This selection presents events that affected America and Wilson's responses to them.

633

What caused the United States to enter the war.

October, 1914   The British, in their naval blockade of Germany, seized some American ships and goods headed for Germany.

October–December, 1914   The State Department of the United States protested to the British about the seizure of our ships.

DECEMBER 8, 1914: WILSON'S SECOND ANNUAL ADDRESS TO CONGRESS

President Wilson's Foreign Policy: Messages, Addresses, Papers, edited by James Brown Scott (New York: Oxford University Press, 1918), pp. 78-79.

. . . It is said in some quarters that we are not prepared for war. What is meant by being prepared? Is it meant that we are not ready upon brief notice to put a nation in the field, a nation of men trained to arms? Of course we are not ready to do that; and we shall never be in time of peace so long as we retain our present political principles and institutions. And what is it that it is suggested we should be prepared to do? To defend ourselves against attack? We have always found means to do that, and shall find them whenever it is necessary without calling our people away from their necessary tasks to render compulsory military service in times of peace.

Allow me to speak with great plainness and directness upon this matter and to avow [declare] my convictions with deep earnestness. I have tried to know what America is, what her people think, what they are, what they most cherish and hold dear. I hope that some of their finer passions are in my own heart,—some of the great conceptions and desires which gave birth to this Government and which have made the voice of this people a voice of peace and hope and liberty among the peoples of the world, and that, speaking my own thoughts, I shall, at least in part, speak theirs also, however faintly and inadequately, upon this vital matter.

We are at peace with all the world. No one who speaks counsel based on fact or drawn from a just and candid [sincere] interpretation of realities can say that there is reason to fear that from any quarter our independence or the integrity of our territory is threatened. Dread of the power of any other nation we are incapable of. We are not jealous of rivalry in the fields of commerce or of any other peaceful achievement. We mean to live our own lives as we will; but we mean also to let live. We are, indeed, a true friend to all the nations of the world, because we threaten none, covet the possessions of none, desire the overthrow of none. Our friendship can be accepted and is accepted without reservation, because it is offered in a spirit and for a purpose which no one need ever question or suspect. Therein lies our greatness. . . .

February, 1915 Germany proclaimed a "War Zone" around Great Britain, warning that she would destroy all merchant vessels found in those waters.

March, 1915 The British ship *Falaba* was sunk. One U. S. citizen was drowned.

The U. S. ship *Cushing* was attacked by Germany.

APRIL 20, 1915: WILSON SPEAKS IN NEW YORK

My interest in the neutrality of the United States is not the petty [small-minded] desire to keep out of trouble. To judge by my experience, I have never been able to keep out of trouble. I have never looked for it, but I have always found it. I do not want to walk around trouble. If any man wants a scrap that is an interesting scrap and worth while, I am his man. I warn him that he is not going to draw me into the scrap for his advertisement, but if he is looking for trouble that is the trouble of men in general and I can help a little, why, then I am in for it. But I am interested in neutrality because there is something so much greater to do than fight; there is a distinction waiting for this nation that no nation has ever yet got. That is the distinction of absolute self-control and self-mastery. Whom do you admire most among your friends? The irritable man? The man out of whom you can get a "rise" without trying? The man who will fight at the drop of the hat, whether he knows what the hat is dropped for or not? Don't you admire and don't you fear, if you have to contest with him, the self-mastered man who watches you with calm eye and comes in only when you have carried the thing so far that you must be disposed of? That is the man you respect. That is the man who, you know, has at bottom a much more fundamental and terrible courage than the irritable, fighting man. Now I covet for America this splendid courage of reserve moral force. . .

President Wilson's Foreign Policy, edited by James Brown Scott, pp. 88-89.

May, 1915 The U. S. ship *Gulflight* was sunk by the Germans. Two American lives were lost.

The British passenger ship *Lusitania* was sunk by the Germans. Eleven hundred drowned, 124 of them Americans.

MAY, 1915: WILSON SPEAKS IN PHILADELPHIA

. . . The example of America must be a special example. The example of America must be the example not merely of peace because it will not fight, but of peace because peace is the healing and elevating [uplifting] influence of the world and strife is not. There is such a thing as a man being too proud to fight. There is such a thing as a nation being so right that it does not need to convince others by force that it is right.

President Wilson's Foreign Policy, edited by James Brown Scott, p. 96.

July, 1915 It was discovered that plots against the United States were planned at the Austrian Embassy.

September, 1915 Wilson asked for the recall of the Austrian ambassador.

At Wilson's urging, the Germans pledged not to sink passenger liners without giving warning and help to the noncombatants.

DECEMBER, 1915: WILSON'S ANNUAL MESSAGE TO CONGRESS

I have spoken to you to-day, gentlemen, upon a single theme, the thorough preparation of the nation to care for its own security and to make sure of entire freedom to play the impartial role in this hemisphere and in the world which we all believe to have been providentially assigned to it. I have had in my mind no thought of any immediate or particular danger arising out of our relations with other nations. We are at peace with all the nations of the world... I am sorry to say that the gravest threats against our national peace and safety have been uttered within our own borders. There are citizens of the United States, I blush to admit, born under other flags but welcomed under our generous naturalization laws to the full freedom and opportunity of America, who have poured the poison of disloyalty into the very arteries of our national life; who have sought to bring the authority and good name of our Government into contempt, to destroy our industries wherever they thought it effective for their vindictive purposes to strike at them, and to debase our politics to the uses of foreign intrigue. Their number is not great as compared with the whole number of those sturdy hosts [large groups] by which our nation has been enriched in recent generations out of virile foreign stocks; but it is great enough to have brought deep disgrace upon us and to have made it necessary that we should promptly make use of processes of law by which we may be purged [cleansed] of their corrupt distempers [disorders]. America never witnessed anything like this before. It never dreamed it possible...

March 1916 The French liner, *Sussex,* was sunk by the Germans. Two American lives were lost. U. S. merchant ships, *City of Memphis* and *Illinois,* were sunk.

Pancho Villa of Mexico attacked a town in New Mexico and killed fifteen Americans. Brigadier General John Pershing and twelve thousand men marched into Mexico to track him down.

APRIL 18, 1916: WILSON'S MESSAGE TO GERMANY

[It is] my duty ... to say to the Imperial German Government that if it is still its purpose to prosecute relentless and indiscriminate war-

President Wilson's Foreign Policy, edited by James Brown Scott, pp. 146-147.
Wilson had asked for an increase in the nation's military forces.

"Providentially assigned" means assigned by Providence, or God. In other words, our role was destined.

"Naturalization" is the process by which a person becomes a citizen of another country.

President Wilson's Foreign Policy, edited by James Brown Scott, p. 187.

fare against vessels of commerce by the use of submarines notwithstanding the now demonstrated impossibility of [doing so] in accordance with what the Government of the United States must consider the sacred and indispensible rules of international law and the universally recognized dictates [principles] of humanity, the Government of the United States is at last forced to the conclusion that there is but one course it can pursue; and that unless the Imperial German Government should now . . . declare and effect an abandonment of its present methods of warfare [by submarines] against passenger and freight carrying vessels [the government of the United States] can have no choice but to sever diplomatic relations with the German Empire altogether.

MAY 4, 1916: GERMAN PLEDGE TO WILSON

The German Government is prepared to do its utmost to confine the operations of the war . . . to the fighting forces of the belligerents, thereby also insuring the freedom of the seas, a principle upon which the German Government believes . . . to be in agreement with the Government of the United States.

President Wilson's Foreign Policy, edited by James Brown Scott, p. 256.

"Belligerents" are countries engaged in war.

The German Government . . . notifies the Government of the United States that . . . merchant vessels . . . both within and without the area declared as naval war zone, shall not be sunk without warning and without saving human lives, unless these ships attempt to escape or offer resistance.

MAY 27, 1916: WILSON SPEAKS IN WASHINGTON, D.C.

. . . If this war has accomplished nothing else for the benefit of the world, it has at least disclosed a great moral necessity and set forward the thinking of the statesmen of the world by a whole age. . . . [The] principle of the public right must henceforth take precedence over the individual interests of particular nations, and that the nations of the world must in some way band themselves together to see that right prevails as against any sort of selfish aggression; that henceforth alliance must not be set up against alliance, understanding against understanding, but that there must be a common agreement for a common object, and that at the heart of that common object must lie the unviolable rights of peoples and of mankind. . . .

President Wilson's Foreign Policy, edited by James Brown Scott, pp. 192-193.

This is undoubtedly the thought of America. . . .

We believe these fundamental things: First, that every people has a right to choose the sovereignty under which they shall live. . . . Second, that the small states of the world have a right to enjoy the same respect for their sovereignty and for their territorial integrity that great and powerful nations expect and insist upon. And, third, that the world has a right to be free from every disturbance of its peace that has its origin in aggression and disregard of the rights of peoples and nations.

So sincerely do we believe in these things that I am sure that I speak the mind and wish of the people of America when I say that the United States is willing to become a partner in any feasible [workable] association of nations formed in order to realize these objects and make them secure against violation.

JANUARY 22, 1917: WILSON REPORTS TO THE SENATE

... We are ... nearer a definite discussion of the peace which shall end the present war. ... nearer the discussion of the international concert [accord] which must thereafter hold the world at peace. In every discussion of the peace that must end this war it is taken for granted that the peace must be followed by some definite concert of power, which will make it virtually impossible that any such catastrophe should ever overwhelm us again. ...

It is inconceivable that the people of the United States should play no part in that great enterprise. To take part ... will be the opportunity for which they have sought to prepare themselves ... since the days when they set up a new nation in the ... hope that it might in all that it was and did show mankind the way to liberty. ...

... [It] makes a great deal of difference in what way and upon what terms it [the war] is ended. The treaties and agreements ... must embody terms which will create a peace that is worth guaranteeing and preserving, a peace that will win the approval of mankind, not merely a peace that will serve the several interests and immediate aims of the nations engaged.

... [It] must be a peace without victory. ... Victory would mean peace forced upon the loser ... Only a peace between equals can last. ...

... [No] peace can last ... which does not recognize and accept the principle that governments derive their just powers from the consent of the governed ...

... [The] nations should with one accord adopt the doctrine of President Monroe as the doctrine of the world: that no nation should seek to extend its polity over any other nation or people ...

These are American principles ... And ... the principles ... of forward looking men and women everywhere ... They are the principles of mankind and must prevail!

February 3, 1917 The Germans announced that the submarine agreement of May 1916 was at an end and that the sinking of ves-

President Wilson's Foreign Policy, edited by James Brown Scott, pp. 246-247, 249-252.

Wilson gave this report to the Senate after he had sent identical messages to all the participants in the war and had received replies to his request that discussions take place to end the conflict.

"Polity" means a politically organized unit.

638

sels would resume in an unrestricted manner. The Germans were concerned over the fact that nearly $3 billion worth of United States goods was reaching Great Britain and France each year by 1917. At the start of the war, United States goods shipped to Great Britain and France were valued at only $750,000 a year. At the same time, United States trade with Germany had dropped from $345 million a year to $500,000 a year. This was due mainly to the British blockade of Europe.

FEBRUARY 3, 1917: WILSON REPORTS TO CONGRESS

... [This] Government has no alternative consistent with the dignity and honor of the United States but to take the course which, in its note of the eighteenth of April, 1916, it announced that it would take ...

President Wilson's Foreign Policy, edited by James Brown Scott, pp. 258-260.

I have, therefore, directed the Secretary of State to announce to his Excellency the German Ambassador that all diplomatic relations between the United States and the German Empire are severed ...

... I cannot bring myself to believe that they will indeed pay no regard to the ancient friendship between their people and our own ... and destroy American ships and take the lives of American citizens in the willful prosecution [carrying out] of the ruthless naval program they have announced ...

... [If] American ships and American lives should in fact be sacrificed ... I shall take the liberty of coming again before Congress, to ask that authority be given me to use any means that may be necessary for the protection of our seamen and our people ...

... We are the sincere friends of the German people and earnestly desire to remain at peace with the government that speaks for them. ...

FEBRUARY 26, 1917: WILSON'S REQUEST TO CONGRESS

... We must defend our commerce and the lives of our people ... Since it has unhappily proved impossible to safeguard our neutral rights by diplomatic means ... there may be no recourse but to *armed* neutrality, which we shall know how to maintain and for which there is abundant American precedent.

President Wilson's Foreign Policy, edited by James Brown Scott, pp. 264-266.

Since Wilson's speech of February 3, 1917, the United States had lost few ships. However, this was mainly because few ship owners had been willing to leave United States ports without adequate protection. Wilson then made this request to Congress.

It is devoutly hoped that it will not be necessary to put armed force anywhere into action. ... I am not now proposing or contemplating war or any steps that need lead to it. I merely request that you will accord me by your own vote ... the means and the authority to safeguard ... the right of a great people who are at peace ... to follow the pursuits of peace ... War can come only by the willful acts and aggressions of others.

. . . I request that you will authorize me to supply our merchant ships with defensive arms should that become necessary . . .

MARCH 1, 1917: THE ZIMMERMANN MESSAGE

The New York Times, March 1, 1917.

British code experts intercepted and decoded this message sent from Zimmermann, the German foreign secretary, to the German minister in Mexico City.

[We] intend to begin submarine warfare unrestricted. In spite of this, it is our intention to endeavor to keep neutral the United States of America.

If this attempt is not successful, we propose an alliance on the following basis with Mexico: That we shall make war together and together make peace. We shall give general financial support, and it is understood that Mexico is to reconquer the lost territory in New Mexico, Texas, and Arizona. The details are left to you for settlement.

March, 1917   The Russian Czar was overthrown.

April, 1917   By this date, 686 neutral ships had been sunk and 226 American lives lost.

APRIL 2, 1917: WILSON'S WAR MESSAGE TO CONGRESS

President Wilson's Foreign Policy, edited by James Brown Scott, pp. 274, 284, 277-279.

I have called the Congress into extraordinary session because there are serious, very serious, choices of policy to be made, and made immediately . . .

. . . [The German] Government entertains no real friendship for us and means to act against our peace and security at its convenience. That it means to stir up enemies against us at our very doors the intercepted note to the German Minister at Mexico City is eloquent evidence.

. . . The present German submarine warfare against commerce is warfare against mankind.

It is a war against all nations. American ships have been sunk, American lives taken, in ways which it has stirred us very deeply to learn of, but the ships and people of other neutral and friendly nations have been sunk and overwhelmed in the waters in the same way. There has been no discrimination. The challenge is to all mankind. Each nation must decide for itself how it will meet it. The choice we make for ourselves must be made with a moderation of counsel and a temperateness of judgment befitting our character and our motives as a nation. We must put excited feeling away. Our motive will not be revenge or the victorious assertion of the physical might of the nation, but only the vindication of right, of human right, of which we are only a single champion.

When I addressed the Congress on the twenty-sixth of February last I thought that it would suffice to assert our neutral rights with arms, our right to use the seas against unlawful interference, our right to keep our people safe against unlawful violence. But armed neutrality, it now appears, is impracticable....There is one choice we cannot make, we are incapable of making: we will not choose the path of submission and suffer the most sacred rights of our nation and our people to be ignored or violated. The wrongs against which we now array [line up] ourselves are no common wrongs; they cut to the very roots of human life.

With a profound sense of the solemn and even tragical character of the step I am taking and of the grave responsibilities which it involves, but in unhesitating obedience to what I deem my constitutional duty, I advise that the Congress declare the recent course of the Imperial German Government to be in fact nothing less than war against the government and people of the United States; that it formally accept the status of belligerent which has thus been thrust upon it; and that it take immediate steps not only to put the country in a more thorough state of defense but also to exert all its power and employ all its resources to bring the Government of the German Empire to terms and end the war.

...We are glad, now that we see the facts with no veil of false pretense about them, to fight thus for the ultimate peace of the world and for the liberation of its peoples...for the rights of nations great and small and the privilege of men everywhere to choose their way of life and of obedience. The world must be made safe for democracy....

April 6, 1917 The United States declared war on Germany.

1. Explain what caused the United States to enter the first World War despite a stated desire to remain neutral.

2. How did President Wilson picture America's role in world affairs? Why did he think this was our role?

3. How does Wilson's attitude compare with the United States' attitude in foreign affairs between 1898 and 1902?

4. Do you think Wilson was right to define America's role in world affairs as he did? Was he right to advise that we enter the war? Explain.

11. Peace Aims in the Midst of War: The Fourteen Points

By the time the United States entered the war in 1917, German plans to take France had long been thwarted. The two sides opposed each other from trenches running across Europe from Switzerland to the coast of northern France.

By July 1918, one million United States troops had joined the Allies with another million soon to follow. On January 8, 1918, in the midst of this great movement of troops, President Wilson addressed a joint session of Congress. He announced the conditions of peace that would be acceptable to the United States. These peace aims are generally referred to as the Fourteen Points.

The Messages and Papers of Woodrow Wilson (New York: George H. Doran Company, 1917), Vol. I, pp. 468-470.

...The program of the world's peace, therefore, is our program; and that program, the only possible program, as we see it, is this:

I. Open covenants [agreements] of peace, openly arrived at, after which there shall be no private international understandings of any kind but diplomacy shall proceed always frankly and in the public view.

II. Absolute freedom of navigation upon the seas ...

III. The removal, so far as possible, of all economic barriers and the establishment of ... equality of trade ... among all nations ...

IV. Adequate guarantees given and taken that national armaments will be reduced to the lowest point consistent with domestic safety.

V. A free, open-minded, and absolutely impartial adjustment of all colonial claims, based upon a strict observance of the principle that in determining all such questions of sovereignty the interests of the populations concerned must have equal weight with the ... claims of the government whose title is to be determined.

VI. The evacuation of all Russian territory and ... settlement of all questions affecting Russia as will ... assure her of a sincere welcome into the society of free nations under institutions of her own choosing. ...

VII. Belgium ... must be evacuated and restored ...

VIII. All French territory should be freed and the invaded portions restored, and the wrong done to France by Prussia in 1871 in the matter of Alsace-Lorraine ... should be righted. ...

IX. A readjustment of the frontiers of Italy should be effected along clearly recognizable lines of nationality.

"Autonomous" means to be free from outside domination.

X. The peoples of Austria-Hungary ... should be accorded the opportunity of autonomous development.

XI. Rumania, Serbia and Montenegro should be evacuated; occupied territories restored; Serbia accorded free and secure access to the sea; and the relations of the several Balkan states to one another determined by ... lines of allegiance and nationality.

XII. The Turkish portions of the present Ottoman Empire should be assured a secure sovereignty, but the other nationalities which are now under Turkish rule should be assured . . . [an] opportunity of autonomous development . . .

XIII. An independent Polish state should be erected which should include the territories inhabited by indisputably Polish populations, which should be assured a free and secure access to the sea . . .

XIV. A general association of nations must be formed under specific covenants for the purpose of affording mutual guarantees of political independence and territorial integrity to great and small states alike.

1. Have the United States' reasons for pursuing the war changed since its initial involvement?

2. From your understanding of the causes of the war in Europe, do you see any difficulty for Wilson in achieving the goals expressed in the Fourteen Points? Explain.

UNITED STATES INVOLVEMENT IN WORLD AFFAIRS

1. In summary, why did the United States get involved in World War I? How do these reasons compare with United States involvement in foreign affairs prior to this period?

2. Do you observe any pattern to United States involvement in world affairs?

THE LEAGUE OF NATIONS

12. Wilson and the League

On November 11, 1918, the Germans surrendered. In 1919, a peace conference made up of representatives of all the Allied powers was held at Versailles, just outside of Paris. Russia was absent because she had since withdrawn from the war. In November 1917, a Bolshevik, or Communist, coup had given Russia a new government which took Russia out of the war.

Four leaders gained prominence at the Versailles Peace Conference: Wilson of the United States, Prime Minister David Lloyd George of Great Britain, Premier George Clemenceau of France, and Premier Vittorio Orlando of Italy. George opposed Wilson's plan for freedom of the seas. He wanted England to retain her position of naval supremacy. Clemenceau wanted further punishment of Germany. Orlando wanted Italy to acquire parts of Austria.

The "Ottoman Empire" was founded in the late thirteenth century and lasted until the early twentieth. Its borders constantly changed, but it generally included the following countries: Turkey, Syria, Iraq, Palestine, Egypt, Barbary States, Balkan States and parts of Russia and Hungary.

The Treaty of Versailles which emerged from the conference violated many of Wilson's Fourteen Points. It allowed nations to enlarge themselves at the expense of others and to take over the colonies of the defeated nations. The Treaty also required Germany to make huge payments, or reparations, to the Allies for war damages. Wilson could not stop the Allies from making these arrangements, which had been planned in secret treaties before the United States entered the war.

However, Wilson agreed to the Treaty because he was able to have a provision for a League of Nations included in it. Wilson felt that the League provision was the most important part of the Treaty. He believed that an international society of nations could make up for the defects of the Treaty.

When Wilson returned from Europe in 1919, he poured all his energy into campaigning for American ratification of the Versailles Treaty and for entry into the League. He made thirty-seven speeches in twenty-two days. The following passages are part of a speech Wilson made in San Francisco on September 18, 1919.

The Messages and Papers of Woodrow Wilson,
edited by Albert Shaw (New York: The Review of Reviews Corporation, 1924), Vol. II, pp. 998-999.

I want to remind you how the permanency of peace is at the heart of this treaty. This is not merely a treaty of peace with Germany. . . . It is nothing less than a world settlement, and at the center of that stands this covenant for the future which we call the covenant of the League of Nations. Without it the treaty can not be worked, and without it it is a mere temporary arrangement with Germany. The covenant of the League of Nations is the instrumentality [means] for the maintenance of peace.

"Arbitration" occurs when a person or group is chosen by the parties in dispute to hear and decide upon the case in point.

How does it propose to maintain it? By the means that all forward-looking and thoughtful men have desired for generations together, by substituting arbitration and discussion for war. To hear some gentlemen talk you would think that the council of the League of Nations is to spend its time considering when to advise other people to fight. That is what comes of a constant concentration of attention upon Article X. Article X ought to have been somewhere further down in the covenant, because it is in the background; it is not in the foreground. . . . At the heart of that covenant are these tremendous arrangements: Every member of the League solemnly agrees . . . that it will never go to war without first having done one or another of two things, without either submitting the matter in dispute to arbitration, in which case it promises absolutely to abide by the verdict, or, if it does not care to submit it to arbitration, without submitting it to discussion by the council of the League of Nations, in which case it promises to lay all the documents and all the pertinent facts before that council; it consents that that council shall publish all the documents and all the pertinent facts, so that all the world shall know them; that it shall be allowed six months in which to consider the matter; and that

Under Article X, each member undertook to respect the integrity and independence of other members and to join in protecting them against aggression.

even at the end of the six months, if the decision of the council is not acceptable, it will still not go to war for three months following the rendering of the decision. So that, even allowing no time for the preliminaries, there are nine months of cooling off, nine months of discussion, nine months not of private discussion, not of discussion between those who are heated, but of discussion between those who are disinterested except in the maintenance of the peace of the world, when the purifying and rectifying influence of the public opinion of mankind is brought to bear upon the contest.

If anything approaching that had been the arrangement of the world in 1914, the war would have been impossible; and I confidently predict that there is not an aggressive people in the world who would dare bring a wrongful purpose to that jury. It is the most formidable jury in the world. . . . After all, the only overwhelming force in the world is the force of opinion.

1. What did Wilson feel the League of Nations would be able to accomplish?

2. How did he think it could achieve the result?

13. Opponents of the League: William Borah

William E. Borah, Republican Senator from Idaho, was a leader of the members of Congress who were called "isolationists." This term was used because isolationists insisted that the United States remain free of alliances that would involve the country in world affairs. As Wilson traveled around the United States to gain support for the League, many isolationists followed him to speak against the League. Borah's basic ideas are summarized in the following selection.

[This] treaty . . . imperils what I conceive to be the underlying, the very first principles of this Republic. It is in conflict with the right of our people to govern themselves free from all restraint, legal or moral, of foreign powers. . . . In opposing the treaty I do nothing more than decline to renounce and tear out of my life the sacred traditions which through fifty years have been translated into my whole intellectual and moral being. I will not, I can not, give up my belief that America must, not alone for the happiness of her own people, but for the moral guidance and greater contentment of the world, be permitted to live her own life. Next to the tie which binds a man to his God is the tie which binds a man to his country, and all schemes, all plans, however ambitious and fascinating they seem in their proposal, but which would embarrass or entangle and impede or shackle her sovereign will, which would compromise her freedom of action I unhesitatingly put behind me.

American Problems: William Borah, edited by Horace Green (New York: Duffield & Company, 1924), pp. 116-117. Reprinted by permission of Dodd, Mead and Company.

645

1. What effect does Borah think membership in the League would have on the United States?

2. Do you think that membership in the League would have had such an effect? Why or why not?

3. What information would help you to evaluate Borah's argument?

14. Opponents of the League: Henry Cabot Lodge

Henry Cabot Lodge of Massachusetts, Republican chairman of the Senate Committee on Foreign Relations, led the fight in the Senate against the League of Nations as it was proposed in the Treaty of Versailles. Lodge suggested a series of amendments to the Treaty. Most of his proposals would have reduced America's obligations to the League.

In the struggle for ratification of the Treaty, Wilson was unyielding. He refused to accept any of the amendments proposed in the Senate. When the Senate was ready to vote on the Treaty with the amendments attached to it, Wilson advised his supporters to vote against the Treaty. The Senate failed to ratify the Treaty, thereby keeping the United States out of the League of Nations.

Lodge frequently expressed his fears about the League of Nations. He made the following remarks in Boston on March 19, 1919.

League of Nations (Boston: World Peace Foundation, April, 1919), Vol. II No. 2, pp. 54-55, 62. Reprinted by permission of the publisher.

The question before us, the only question of a practical nature, is whether the League that has been drafted by the Commission of the Peace Conference and laid before it will tend to secure the peace of the world as it stands, and whether it is just and fair to the United States of America. That is the question, and I want now, very briefly, to bring it to the test.

Wars between nations come from contacts. A nation with which we have no contact is a nation with which we should never fight. But contacts, foreign relations between nations are necessary and inevitable, and the object of all diplomacy and statesmanship is to make these contacts and relations as harmonious as possible, because in these contacts is found the origin of all war.

In this scheme for a League now before us we create a number of new contracts, a number of new relations, which nations have not undertaken before to create.

The "draft" is the League charter.

. . . The draft appears to me, and I think to anyone who has examined it with care, to have been very loosely and obscurely drawn. . . .

The language of that draft is of immense importance, because it is necessary that there should be just as few differences of opinion

646

as to the meaning of the articles of that draft as human ingenuity can provide against. No man, be he president or senator, can fix what the interpretation of that draft is.

The draft itself, the articles themselves, should answer as far as possible all questions. There is no court to pass upon them. They would have to be decided by the nine powers whose representatives compose the Executive Council. The people who are for this draft of a League and those who are against it differ about the construction of nearly every article. And, not only that, but those who are for it differ among themselves, and those who are against it differ among themselves, as to its construction. There will be differences arising out of that very porous instrument. There will be differences arising before a twelvemonth has passed among the very nations that signed it. . . .

"Porous," here, means loose, or vague.

[Article X] pledges us to guarantee the political independence and the territorial integrity against external aggression of every nation a member of the League. That is, every nation of the earth. We ask no guaranties, we have no endangered frontiers; but we are asked to guarantee the territorial integrity of every nation, practically, in the world—it will be when the League is complete. As it is to-day, we guarantee the territorial integrity and political independence of every part of the far-flung British Empire.

Now mark! A guaranty is never invoked except when force is needed. If we guaranteed one country in South America alone, if we were the only guarantor, and we guaranteed but one country, we should be bound to go to the relief of that country with army and navy. We, under the clause of this treaty—it is one of the few that is perfectly clear—under that clause of the treaty we have got to take our army and our navy and go to war with any country which attempts aggression upon the territorial integrity of another member of the League.

Now, guaranties must be fulfilled. They are sacred promises—it has been said only morally binding. Why, that is all there is to a treaty between great nations. If they are not morally binding they are nothing but "scraps of paper." If the United States agrees to Art. X, we must carry it out in letter and in spirit; and if it is agreed to I should insist that we did so, because the honor and good faith of our country would be at stake.

Now, that is a tremendous promise to make. I ask those—the fathers and the mothers, the sisters and the wives and the sweethearts, whether they are ready yet to guarantee the political independence and territorial integrity of every nation on earth against external aggression, and to send the hope of their families, the hope of the nation, the best of our youth, forth into the world on that errand?

If they are, it will be done. If the American people is not ready to do it that article will have to go out of the treaty or be limited.

1. What effects does Lodge think League membership would have on the United States? On the world in general?
2. On what does Lodge base his arguments?
3. Do you think Lodge is correct in his assessment of how the League of Nations would affect the world? Why or why not?
4. How do Lodge's ideas on this subject relate to Wilson's?
5. Do you think Lodge is correct in his assessment of how the League would affect the United States? Why or why not?
6. If Lodge is right on this matter, would you favor Article X? Why or why not?
7. What does Wilson say about Article X?

15. The Post-War Mood: Thomas A. Bailey

Thomas A. Bailey, a scholar in the field of American diplomatic history, has drawn the following conclusion about President Wilson's leadership after World War I and the state of mind of the American people at that time.

Thomas A. Bailey, **A Diplomatic History of the American People** (Seventh Edition; New York: Appleton-Century-Crofts, 1964), pp. 615-616. Copyright © 1964 by Meredith Publishing Company. Reprinted by permission of Appleton-Century-Crofts.

"Inflation" exists when the price of goods goes up because there are not enough goods available to meet the demand.
The Eighteenth Amendment, ratified in 1919, provided for "prohibition." It forbid the manufacture, sale, and transportation of liquor.

Everywhere one found a strong impulse to return to old isolationist ways. Wilson's inspiring leadership had keyed the American people up to a spirit of self-sacrifice that had even resulted in the prohibition of alcoholic beverages. But all this was changing. Victory had brought an emotional letdown—"the slump in idealism." It had also brought profound disillusionment with the imperialistic and bickering Allies. The war to make the world safe for democracy had not made the world safe for democracy, nor had it ended wars. Some twenty conflicts of varying dimensions were being waged in various parts of the world. About all that America had seemingly derived from the war was debt, inflation, prohibition, influenza, and ingratitude from Allies whom she had strained herself to help— while, of course, helping defeat the common enemy.

Disgust was deepening. Hundreds of thousands of American boys were returning from Europe, irritated by the gouging [cheating] French shopkeepers and most favorably impressed by the blonde German girls. Americans everywhere were saying that Europe could jolly well "stew in its own juice." In the face of such widespread disillusionment, Wilson would have his troubles in arousing the people again . . .

1. According to Bailey, what was the mood of the country after the war? Why?

2. How would this mood be likely to affect congressional vote on whether to join the League?

3. Do you see any possible relationship between this mood and the specific arguments of Lodge? Of Borah? Explain.

MAKING JUDGMENTS

Do you think we should have joined the League of Nations? Why or why not ?

WORLD WAR II

EUROPE IN 1919

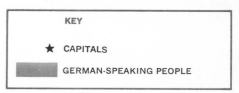

KEY

★ CAPITALS

▨ GERMAN-SPEAKING PEOPLE

16. A German Version of the Treaty of Versailles

The United States Senate rejected the Treaty of Versailles because it could not reach agreement on the League of Nations. In place of the Versailles Treaty, the United States signed a separate peace treaty with Germany in August 1921.

The rest of the Allies, however, signed the Versailles Treaty. The following selection presents Germany's complaints against the Treaty. Adolf Hitler, who became the German dictator in the early 1930's, used these complaints as an excuse for seizing territory that surrounded Germany in the late 1930's and early 1940's.

Edwin Fenton, **Thirty-Two Problems in World History** (Chicago: Scott, Foresman and Company, 1964), pp. 191-194.

The peace to be concluded with Germany was to be a peace of right, not a peace of might. . . .

The peace document shows that none of [the] repeated solemn assurances has been kept.

To begin with the territorial questions:

In the West, a purely German territory on the Saar [River] with a population of at least 650,000 inhabitants is to be separated from the German Empire [and given to France] for at least fifteen years merely for the reason that claims are asserted to the coal abounding there. . . .

Although President Wilson, in his speech of October 20th, 1916, has acknowledged that "no single fact caused the war, but that in the last analysis the whole European system is in a deeper sense responsible for the war, with its combination of alliances and understandings, a complicated texture of intrigues and espionage that unfailingly caught the whole family of nations in its meshes," "that the present war is not so simply to be explained and that its roots reach deep into the dark soil of history," Germany is to acknowledge that Germany and her allies are responsible for all damages which the enemy Governments or their subjects have incurred by her and her allies' aggression. This appears all the less tolerable as it is an indisputable historical fact that several of the hostile Powers, such as Italy and Roumania, on their part entered the war for the purpose of territorial conquests. Apart from the consideration that there is no incontestable legal foundation for the obligation for reparation imposed upon Germany, the amount of such compensation is to be determined by a commission nominated solely by Germany's enemies, Germany taking no part. . . .

Something that is "incontestable" cannot be disputed.

[It] is incompatible with the idea of national self-determination for two and one-half million Germans to be torn away from their native land against their own will. By the proposed demarcation of the boundary, unmistakably German territories are disposed of in favor of their Polish neighbors. . . . The same may be said with reference to the fact that millions of Germans in German-Austria are to be denied the union with Germany which they desire and that, further, millions of Germans dwelling along our frontiers are to be forced to remain part of the newly created Czecho-Slovakian State. . . .

The German Government agrees with the Governments of the Allied and Associated Powers in the conviction that the horrible devastation caused by this war requires the establishment of a new world order, an order which shall insure the "effective authority of the principles of international law," and "just and honorable relations between the nations." The restoration and perfection of international order in the world can only be assured if the existing authorities, in a new spirit, succeed in realizing the great idea of democracy; if, as President Wilson declared on the 4th of July, 1918, "the settlement of every question is brought about . . . upon the basis of the . . . concerned. . . ." Only the nations that enjoy freedom and independence, based upon law, may give each other the guarantee of just and honorable relations. But their fairness and honor also require that they warrant each other freedom and life as the most sacred and inalienable fundamental rights.

There is no evidence of these principles in the peace document which has been laid before us. . . . we appeal to the sense of right of men and nations, under whose token . . . the North American nation established its independence, . . . The bearers of such hallowed traditions cannot deny this right to the German people, that now for the first time has acquired in its internal politics the possibility of living in harmony with its free will based on law. A treaty such as has been proposed to Germany is incompatible with the respect for this innate [natural] right.

For what different reasons did Germany object to the Treaty of Versailles?

17. Three World Scenes

For nearly two decades following World War I, the European nations struggled to restore themselves. Other nations, like Japan, were trying to build a new prosperity. The following three scenes describe developments in Germany, Italy, and Japan that were to influence the world for many years.

POINTS TO CONSIDER
What similar patterns seem to be emerging in all three nations.

THE GERMAN SCENE IN THE 1920'S AND 1930'S

After World War I, the Germans were a discouraged, defeated, and often miserable people. The republic that had been created at the end of the war was under constant attack for not resolving Germany's problems. The Germans were not used to democracy. One group that spoke up was the German Worker's party. One of its fiery speakers was a former army corporal, Adolf Hitler. He impressed everyone with his sincerity and passion. The ideas he proposed were that the German Parliament, the Reichstag, should be abolished because it contained too many liberals and Communists. Germany should be ruled by a single master, without political parties. He pictured the German people as the "master race" who must some day rule the world.

He said that the only reason the Germans were not in their destined place was because of the Versailles Treaty, the Communists, the Socialists, and the Jews. He proposed a government that would aid the common man by controlling all business and by breaking up the large estates. His party became known as the *Nazis*.

Ideas like Hitler's are known as *fascism*. Fascism is a political philosophy that glorifies one race and one nation. Fascists favor a dictator who suppresses all opposition and who controls the economy and the society.

Hitler organized large meetings where he expounded his ideas. One group of his followers was armed and wore brown shirts. They served at Hitler's private army and often used violence against groups in opposition to their own.

In Munich, Hitler and his followers tried to overthrow the government, but they were suppressed. Hitler was convicted of treason and put in prison. While there, he wrote *Mein Kampf,* in which he told about his life and ideas. The Nazi party grew larger in the days that followed. After eight months, Hitler was out of jail.

A world depression sent the German economy into a tailspin and, in the midst of the confusion, Adolf Hitler became the nation's leader. To gain power, he abandoned his old government ideas and turned against the laborers and the unions. Businessmen flocked to his side and contributed financially to his support. In 1933, Hitler was appointed chancellor, or prime minister of Germany.

According to law, his appointment had to be approved by a vote of the Reichstag. Fearing the outcome of a vote, Hitler's followers set fire to the hall where the Reichstag met. Hitler promptly announced that the Communists had done this deed. Thousands were arrested to stop the great "conspiracy" against Germany.

A "liberal" is one who emphasizes progress and does not feel bound by traditional ways. Liberals are especially interested in promoting the freedom of individuals to exercise political and civil rights.

When elections for a new Reichstag were held, the Nazis received enough votes for Hitler to control the government. He was made dictator and was called *der Fuhrer*. Hitler dissolved the labor unions, abolished all political parties except the Nazi party, and established censorship of the radio, the press, and the movies. He thrilled the nationalistic spirit of the Germans with parades, rallies, and speeches. He glorified war and talked about the superiority of the fair-skinned race of northern Europe. He referred to the German people as the "master race" and stressed that they must not mix with inferior races, such as Jews and Slavs.

A secret police force searched out all who opposed the new regime. Many church leaders who objected to Hitler's ideas were persecuted. Jews were attacked as enemies of the people. Agents were sent to other countries to organize groups to help gain support for the new German government.

One of Hitler's first acts in 1933 was to withdraw from the League of Nations. Then, in March 1935, Hitler denounced the parts of the Versailles Treaty that limited German armed forces. Hitler rapidly built up the German Army. In 1936, he sent aid to the fascist revolutionary leader, General Francisco Franco, who was trying to overthrow the democratic government of Spain. In March 1938, after promising to recognize Austria's independence, Hitler ordered his troops into the country and took it overnight.

The English and French were alarmed, but they did nothing. Hitler's eyes moved to other lands in his drive to have an empire of world proportions under German rule—Czechoslovakia, Poland, Denmark, Norway, Finland, Belgium, the Netherlands, France. . . .

THE ITALIAN SCENE IN THE 1920'S AND 1930'S

After World War I, Italy experienced difficulty with the democratic process. Political parties were unable to accept compromise on issues affecting the nation, and there was a rapid succession of governments. Italy also felt she had not received all the territory after the war that was rightfully hers. She was especially interested in the city of Fiume in Yugoslavia. Economic problems such as inflation, rising prices, and unemployment also plagued the nation.

During this time a party called the Fascisti demanded the end of the monarchy and nobility, attacked private property and the Church, and praised the glories of Italy. They shortly abandoned these ideas and became principally anti-Communist and anti-Socialist. This group was led by Benito Mussolini who organized a private army to carry out his program. With the problems of Italy increasing rapidly, the Fascists decided to march on Rome. The king dismissed the current prime minister and called Mussolini to that position in October 1922. Parliament granted Mussolini dictatorial powers for one year in order to restore order and produce reforms. Several years later, parliamentary government had ceased to exist. Mussolini remained dictator of Italy for twenty-one years. Non-fascist cabinet members were dropped, opposition parties were disbanded, personal liberties disappeared, and the press was rigidly controlled.

To win prestige for Italy, and to gain oil, Mussolini began a war of conquest against Ethiopia in eastern Africa. The League of Nations failed to prevent his takeover of that nation. In 1936, he announced that the King of Italy was also Emperor of Ethiopia. The League of Nations had already condemned Hitler's action in 1935 when he began to rearm in defiance of the Treaty of Versailles. The League had also condemned an act of aggression by Japan in 1931. Neither condemnation had any effect. Japan had replied by withdrawing from the League. Now the League went further. It punished Italy by barring trade with her. The League Covenant provided that member nations which became aggressors could be punished in this way. However, the other members of the League did not apply the punishment strictly. In fact, they could not agree about which articles should be barred from trade with Italy. Furthermore, Germany, which had left the League, continued to trade with Italy. Failure to punish Italy showed that the League had no power to stop aggression. In 1937, Italy followed the lead of Japan and Germany and withdrew from the League.

After his success in Ethiopia, Mussolini sent his legions to aid Franco in the Spanish Civil War. In March 1939, Mussolini seized Albania.

War came to Europe in September 1939. In the spring of 1940, when Hitler seemed to be winning, Mussolini decided that Italy had better enter the war on the side of Germany.

THE JAPANESE SCENE IN THE 1920'S AND 1930'S

Japan in the 1920's was a nation of many people, but she had little of the world's goods—she was a "have not" nation. The government decided that her path to wealth and prosperity lay in expansion into the Asian mainland for resources and markets. Militarists in the government pushed a plan of aggression against China in the 1930's. The first step came in 1931, when the Japanese seized Manchuria. The United States, which favored an "open door" policy in regard to China, imposed economic restrictions on trade with Japan. The militarists under General Tojo rose in anger and called for greater war preparations. The Japanese premier attempted to reach an agreement with the United States, but under pressure from the military leaders he resigned in October 1941. He was succeeded by Tojo. The anti-American campaign was intensified. Warnings came of possible attacks on the United States, but the militarists sent envoys to Washington to help maintain the peace. Demands were made by Japan that the United States remove its boycott on trade, cease aiding China, and recognize Japan's superior position in Asia. The United States responded by demanding that Japan withdraw from China, recognize the independence of China, sign a non-aggression pact with all powers in the Pacific area, and withdraw from her association with the Axis powers of Hitler and Mussolini, which she had recently joined.

These events took place toward the end of November 1941. At the same time, some Japanese naval and air forces were moving toward Hawaii while others maneuvered in the South Pacific. Japanese forces poured into Indo-China, in southeast Asia, on December 6. President Roosevelt sent urgent appeals to Emperor Hirohito of Japan to restore order. The next afternoon, while Japanese representatives were preparing for more discussions in Washington, the armed forces of Japan attacked Pearl Harbor in Hawaii. The United States suffered greater naval losses than it had suffered in all of World War I. The dead numbered 2,343. There were 1,272 wounded and nearly 1,000 missing.

1. The events in Germany, Italy, and Japan that you have just read about led up to World War II. What do you see as the causes of the war?

2. What reaction do you imagine the United States would have to these events, if any? Would it be different from the United States' reaction to the events that led to World War I? Explain.

3. What further information about the background of World War II would help you to understand the causes better?

18. The United States' Reaction

Like President Wilson in World War I, President Roosevelt also expressed his reaction to world events. The following statements were made by Roosevelt in October 1937.

. . . The present reign of terror and international lawlessness began a few years ago.

It began through unjustified interference in the international affairs of other nations or the invasion of alien territory in violation of

Public Papers and Addresses of Franklin D. Roosevelt 1937 Vol.: The Constitution Prevails, edited by Samuel I. Rosenman (New York: The Macmillan Company, 1941), pp. 407-408, 410-411. Reprinted by permission of Samuel I. Rosenman and the estate of Franklin D. Roosevelt.

treaties; and has now reached a stage where the very foundations of civilizations are seriously threatened. The landmarks and traditions which have marked the progress of civilization toward a condition of law, order and justice are being wiped away.

Without a declaration of war and without warning or justification of any kind, civilians, including vast numbers of women and children, are being ruthlessly murdered with bombs from the air. In times of so-called peace, ships are being attacked and sunk by submarines without cause or notice. Nations are fomenting [inciting] and taking sides in civil warfare in nations that have never done them any harm. Nations claiming freedom for themselves deny it to others. . . .

Those who cherish their freedom and recognize and respect the equal rights of their neighbors to be free and live in peace, must work together for the triumph of law and moral principles in order that peace, justice and confidence may prevail in the world. . . .

It seems to be unfortunately true that the epidemic of world lawlessness is spreading.

When an epidemic of physical disease starts to spread, the community . . . joins in a quarantine of the patients in order to protect the health of the community against the spread of the disease.

It is my determination to pursue a policy of peace. It is my determination to adopt every practicable measure to avoid involvement in war. . . .

War is a contagion, whether it be declared or undeclared. It can engulf state and peoples remote from the original scene of hostilities. We are determined to keep out of war, yet we cannot insure ourselves against the disastrous effects of war and the dangers of involvement. We are adopting such measures as will minimize our risk of involvement, but we cannot have complete protection in a world of disorder in which confidence and security have broken down.

If civilization is to survive the principles of the Prince of Peace must be restored. Trust between nations must be revived.

Most important of all, the will for peace on the part of peace-loving nations must express itself to the end that nations that may be tempted to violate their agreements and the rights of others will desist from such a course. There must be positive endeavors to preserve peace.

America hates war. America hopes for peace. Therefore, America actively engages in the search for peace.

1. Review the situation in the world at this date. How does President Roosevelt's reaction compare with what you expected the United States' attitude to be?

2. How does President Roosevelt's reaction to these world events compare with Wilson's reaction to events just prior to 1914?

19. June 1940-December 1941

On June 10, 1940, Italy attacked France from the south. Germany had already begun her invasion of France through Belgium. For the next year and a half, the United States, under Roosevelt's leadership, watched the European war with alarm.

ROOSEVELT: JUNE 10, 1940

On this 10th day of June, 1940, the hand that held the dagger has struck it into the back of its neighbor. . . .

Some indeed still hold to the now somewhat obvious delusion that we of the United States can safely permit the United States to become a lone island, a lone island in a world dominated by the philosophy of force.

Such an island may be the dream of those who still talk and vote as isolationists. Such an island represents to me and to the overwhelming majority of Americans today a helpless nightmare of a people without freedom—the nightmare of a people lodged in prison, handcuffed, hungry and fed through the bars from day to day by contemptuous, unpitying masters of other continents.

It is natural also that we should ask ourselves how we can prevent the building of that prison and the placing of ourselves in the midst of it.

Let us not hesitate—all of us—to proclaim certain truths. Overwhelmingly we, as a nation—and this applies to all other American nations—are convinced that military and naval victory for the gods of force and hate would endanger the institutions of democracy in the western world, and that equally, therefore, the whole of our sympathies lies with those nations that are giving their life blood in combat against these forces.

The people and the government of the United States have seen with . . . regret and with grave disquiet the decision of the Italian Government to engage in the hostilities now raging in Europe.

ROOSEVELT: DECEMBER 29, 1940

Never before since Jamestown and Plymouth Rock has our American civilization been in such danger as now.

Public Papers and Addresses of Franklin D. Roosevelt 1940 Vol.: War—And Aid to Democracies, edited by Samuel I. Rosenman (New York: The Macmillan Company, 1941), pp. 263, 261-262. Reprinted by permission of Samuel I. Rosenman and the estate of Franklin D. Roosevelt.

Public Papers and Addresses of Franklin D. Roosevelt 1940 Vol., edited by Samuel I. Rosenman, pp. 634, 636, 640, 643.

For, on September 27, 1940, by an agreement signed in Berlin, three powerful nations, two in Europe and one in Asia, joined themselves together in the threat that if the United States of America interfered with or blocked the expansion program of these three nations—a program aimed at world control—they would unite in ultimate action against the United States. . . .

Some of us like to believe that even if Britain falls, we are still safe, because of the broad expanse of the Atlantic and of the Pacific.

But the width of those oceans is not what it was in the days of clipper ships. . . .

[We] have planes that could fly from the British Isles to New England and back again without refueling. And remember that the range of the modern bomber is ever being increased.

During the past week many people in all parts of the nation have told me what they wanted me to say tonight. Almost all of them expressed a courageous desire to hear the plain truth about the gravity of the situation. One telegram, however, expressed the attitude of the small minority who want to see no evil and hear no evil, even though they know in their hearts that evil exists. That telegram begged me not to tell again of the ease with which our American cities could be bombed by any hostile power which had gained bases in this Western Hemisphere. The gist of that telegram was, "Please, Mr. President, don't frighten us by telling us the facts."

Frankly and definitely there is danger ahead—danger against which we must prepare. But we well know that we cannot escape danger, or the fear of danger, by crawling into bed and pulling the covers over our heads.

Some nations of Europe were bound by solemn non-intervention pacts with Germany. Other nations were assured by Germany that they need never fear invasion. Non-intervention pact or not, the fact remains that they were attacked, overrun and thrown into the modern form of slavery at an hour's notice, or even without any notice at all.

The people of Europe who are defending themselves do not ask us to do their fighting. They ask us for the implements of war, the planes, the tanks, the guns, the freighters which will enable them to fight for their liberty and for our security. Emphatically we must get these weapons to them in sufficient volume and quickly enough, so that we and our children will be saved the agony and suffering of war which others have had to endure.

We must be the great arsenal of democracy. For us this is an emergency as serious as war itself. We must apply ourselves to our task

658

with the same resolution, the same sense of urgency, the same spirit of patriotism and sacrifice as we would show were we at war.

ROOSEVELT: JANUARY 6, 1941

The need of the moment is that our actions and our policy should be devoted primarily . . . to meeting [the] foreign peril. . . . First . . . we are committed to all-inclusive national defense. Second . . . we are committed to full support of all those resolute peoples, everywhere, who are resisting aggression and are thereby keeping war away from our Hemisphere. . . . Third . . . [we] know that enduring peace cannot be bought at the cost of other people's freedom. . . .

Let us say to the democracies: "We Americans are vitally concerned in your defense of freedom. We are putting forth our energies, our resources and our organizing powers to give you the strength to regain and maintain a free world. We shall send you, in ever-increasing numbers, ships, planes, tanks, guns. This is our purpose and our pledge. . . ."

I have called for personal sacrifice. I am assured of the willingness of almost all Americans to respond to that call. . . .

In the future days, which we seek to make secure, we look forward to a world founded on four essential freedoms.

The first is freedom of speech and expression—everywhere in the world.

The second is freedom of every person to worship God in his own way—everywhere in the world.

The third is freedom from want . . . everywhere in the world.

The fourth is freedom from fear—which . . . means a world-wide reduction of armaments to such a point and in such a thorough fashion that no nation will be in a position to commit an act of . . . aggression against any neighbor—anywhere in the world.

Our support goes to those who struggle to gain those rights or keep them. . . .

To that high concept there can be no end save victory.

THE ATLANTIC CHARTER: AUGUST 14, 1941

. . . [Great Britain and the United States] seek no aggrandizement [expansion] territorial or other;

. . . [They] desire no territorial changes that do not accord with the freely expressed wishes of the peoples concerned;

. . . [They] respect the right of all peoples to choose the form of government under which they live . . .

Public Papers and Addresses of Franklin D. Roosevelt 1940 Vol., edited by Samuel I. Rosenman, pp. 666-667, 669, 671-672.

Public Papers and Addresses of Franklin D. Roosevelt 1941 Vol.: The Call to Battle Stations, edited by Samuel I. Rosenman (New York: Harper & Row, Publishers, 1950), pp. 314-315. Reprinted by permission of Samuel I. Rosenman and the estate of Franklin D. Roosevelt.

On August 14, 1941, President Roosevelt and Winston Churchill met off the coast of Newfoundland to formulate a statement of common war aims. This statement became known as the Atlantic Charter.

[They will try to make available to] all states . . . access . . . to the trade and to the raw materials of the world which are needed for their economic prosperity . . .

[They desire] to bring about . . . improved labor standards, economic advancement, and social security;

. . . [After] the final destruction of the Nazi tyranny, they hope to see established a peace which will afford to all Nations the means of dwelling in safety within their own boundaries . . . in freedom from fear and want;

. . . [Such] a peace should enable all men to traverse the high seas and oceans without hindrance;

. . . [All] of the nations of the world . . . must come to the abandonment of the use of force.

THE UNITED STATES DECLARES WAR: DECEMBER 8, 1941

On December 7, 1941, the Japanese attacked the United States naval base at Pearl Harbor, Hawaii, inflicting huge losses in men and materials. President Roosevelt appeared before Congress on December 8 to request a declaration of war against Japan.

Germany and Italy, Japan's allies, then declared war on the United States. On December 11, Roosevelt asked for a declaration of war against Germany and Italy.

1. Summarize the United States' position during the years leading up to December 7, 1941, as stated by the President.

2. How does this more complete picture of United States reaction compare with your initial idea of what United States reaction would be?

3. What are the similarities and differences between the United States' actions during this period and the years between 1914 and 1918? How do you explain this?

4. How does the leadership of Roosevelt compare with that of President Wilson? Explain.

20. Plans for War and Peace

Many plans for winning the war and for maintaining peace after the war were discussed and agreed upon at a series of international meetings often attended by the three major allied leaders: Winston Churchill of Great Britain, Josef Stalin of Russia, and Franklin D. Roosevelt of the United States.

660

Casablanca Conference, February 12, 1943, (Churchill and FDR)

Unconditional surrender was demanded of all Axis powers. A statement was made that no harm was meant to the common people of those powers, but punishment was to be imposed on their "guilty and barbaric" leaders. However, the allied leaders were not yet aware of the extent of the Nazi crimes committed against Jews, Slavs, and political opponents in concentration camps. They expressed their desire to restore to all conquered peoples their sacred rights.

When Allied forces invaded Germany and Poland, they discovered that the German concentration camps were really death camps. It is estimated that the Nazis murdered some 6 million Jews. They also murdered vast numbers of Slavic people and political opponents. The exact figures are unknown.

Moscow Conference, October 1943, (Foreign ministers)

The major powers agreed to continue their joint operation and cooperation in matters relating to organizing and maintaining the peace and security of the world at the end of the war. They agreed to establish a general international organization, open to all peace-loving states, for the maintenance of international peace. They stated that democratic government must be restored to Italy and agreed upon a detailed program to bring this about. Notice was given to the Nazis that all who had been responsible for or consented to participate in massacres and executions would be tried in court for their crimes.

Cairo Conference, November 1943, (FDR, Churchill, and Chiang Kai Shek of China)

Agreement on the war against Japan was reached. Japan should be stripped of all islands and lands she had seized from others since 1914. Korea should become an independent nation.

Teheran Conference, December 1, 1943, (Stalin, FDR, and Churchill)

Plans for a drive by the United States and England to attack Germany by landing troops in Western Europe were completed. Iran was to be guaranteed independence after the war and to receive economic aid for its part in allowing goods to flow through its country to Russia. The leaders agreed to support rebel partisans in Yugoslavia and desired to get Turkey to declare war on the Axis powers.

Yalta Conference, February 1945, (FDR, Churchill, and Stalin)

It was decided to call a meeting in San Francisco to establish a world organization.

After the war, these powers would assist the European nations to re-establish democratic governments, to rebuild their economies, and to achieve the goals of the Atlantic Charter.

Germany would be disarmed, demilitarized, and dismembered by the three powers. Each would have control of an area of Germany, and France would also be given such an area to oversee.

Reparation payments would be expected of Germany. Plans were made to establish a democratic government for Poland.

It was agreed that Russia would intervene with the rest of the Allies against Japan, two or three months after Germany's defeat.

Russia would regain territory that Japan had taken from her in 1905. She would also receive some islands in the Pacific.

Connally-Fulbright Resolutions, 1943

A bipartisan group in the United States Congress asked Congress to agree in principle to the idea of membership in a world organization. The following two resolutions were passed.

Fulbright Resolution. *Resolved by the House of Representatives* . . . That the Congress hereby expresses itself as favoring the creation of appropriate international machinery with power adequate to establish and to maintain a just and lasting peace, among the nations of the world, and as favoring participation by the United States therein.

Connally Resolution. *Resolved,* That the war against all our enemies be waged until complete victory is achieved. . . .

That the United States, acting through its constitutional processes, join with free and sovereign nations in establishment and maintenance of international authority with power to prevent aggression and to preserve the peace of the world.

That the Senate recognizes the necessity of there being established at the earliest practicable date a general international organization, based on the principle of the sovereign equality of all peace-loving states, and open to membership by all such states, large and small, for the maintenance of international peace and security.

That, pursuant to the Constitution of the United States, any treaty made to effect the purposes of this resolution, on behalf of the Government of the United States with any other nation or association of nations, shall be made only by and with the advice and consent of the Senate of the United States, provided two-thirds of the Senators present concur.

1. Why do you think the leading powers made so many decisions during the war about what was to follow the end of the war? Do you think this was wise? Why?

2. Why did Congress think it necessary to pass these resolutions? Explain.

3. Do these meetings and resolutions indicate any change in the United States' attitude toward foreign affairs? Explain.

THE UNITED NATIONS

21. An Argument for the United Nations: Alben Barkley

Just before World War II ended in 1945, the United Nations was formed to replace the League of Nations. Overwhelming popular support in the United States for the United Nations was reflected in the speedy action taken by the Senate to ratify the charter in December 1945. After only six days of debate, as opposed to eight months for the League of Nations, the Senate approved United States membership by a vote of 89-2.

In the following speech, Senator Alben Barkley, Democrat of Kentucky, describes the organization of the United Nations and tells why he favors it.

The Charter creates a General Assembly in which each member may have five representatives but only one vote. The Assembly . . . is to be a sort of world-wide town meeting in which may be discussed all the problems which beset mankind and are likely to impinge upon the peace and security of the world.

The Charter provides for the creation of a Security Council as a sort of upper body, not entirely unanalogous to the United States Senate in its relations to the Congress. All nations are not represented at the Security Council. Only 11 nations at any one time may be represented. Five of them must be the five nations which are named in the Charter, to wit, China, France, Russia, England, and the United States.

. . . If the peace of the world cannot be preserved by those five nations, it cannot be preserved at all. . . .

The Charter sets up an Economic and Social Council. We know from history that in the years gone by economic conditions have contributed largely to warfare. . . .

Moreover, it sets up a Trusteeship Council to take into consideration the condition of . . . peoples who may be more backward and more helpless than other peoples, and who have not enjoyed and may not now be prepared for what we call self-government in its fullest sense. . . .

Congressional Globe 79th Congress, 1st Session (July 24, 1945), p. 7970.

"To impinge upon" means to encroach.

"Unanalogous," means different.

663

I have referred to the . . . machinery provided by the Charter for world-wide adjustment. Will [the UN] succeed? My answer is, Yes; if the peoples of the world will that it shall succeed. . . .

[Will] it fail? My answer is, Yes; it will fail if the peoples of the world permit it to be used for narrow and selfish purposes. . . .

[Are] there risks in the Charter? Of course . . . Life itself is a risk. . . .

There is no guaranty. There is no certainty. There is always risk in every venture that mankind undertakes either in his individual capacity or as a part of human society. . . .

I am for this Charter. I am for this Charter whatever risk may be involved in it. It binds all the nations that go into it to carry out the purposes and the provisions of the Charter. It provides for a military contribution on the part of all nations, for a sort of police force to put down aggression. . . .

1. Why does Barkley favor the United Nations?

2. How do his arguments compare with the arguments for and against the League of Nations?

22. An Argument Against the United Nations: Burton Wheeler

An extremely small number of critics labeled the UN a "Communist plot." More serious questions were raised by such men as Democratic Senator Burton K. Wheeler, an isolationist from Montana, who finally voted in favor of the membership. Wheeler feared the clause of the United Nations Charter which pledged members to provide armed forces to the Security Council when the Council thought it necessary to keep peace. Wheeler thought this clause would deprive the United States Senate of its right to decide whether or not to enter a war.

Congressional Record, 79th Congress, 1st Session, Vol. CI, Pt. 6 (July 24, 1945), p. 7985.

. . . I am speaking out of my deep concern for the future. The fate of my native land and the principles of democracy, of a constitutional representative republic, and all the glorious traditions and liberties with which this native land of mine has been blessed are all at stake.

. . . We in America . . . are determined that so far as lies within our power, war shall not again lay its heavy curse upon us. But, Mr. President, we must deal with the trying problems which now tax . . . the human mind . . . If . . . we should in our haste perpetuate the very policies and practices which have brought this war upon us, not even the Almighty could save us from ourselves. . . . The threat of a third world war . . . is already rooted and growing in conflict between western civilization and the Communist totalitarian tyranny in the East. . . .

If we are to participate in this proposed new world organization . . . we shall sign our own death warrant as a Nation when this charter is ratified. . . .

I believe with William Henry Chamberlin that:

An independent American policy, conceived in terms of American interest is more imperative than ever. . . .

Does any sane man in his right mind think that the terror that has been loosed upon a suffering and broken humanity has furthered the possibility of peace and security—or the guarantee of the four freedoms? . . . Are the proponents of this Charter attempting to tell the American people . . . that we may look now toward reliance upon a new reign of law and not to a reversion to trust in brute force? . . .

A "proponent" of something is one who argues in favor of it.

On July 19, 1945, Miss Dorothy Thompson wrote:

We began the war to "end war" and shall finish it with an international armaments race between the victors.

Is there any question about that, with Russia already saying that she wants a big navy, and we pleading for peacetime conscription [draft]? . . .

I predict here and now that unless the present trend in international affairs is arrested, unless the resort to the brutal and inhuman practices or power politics is killed at its roots, Dorothy Thompson's warning inevitably will be fulfilled in a third world catastrophe. . . .

1. Does Wheeler think that the world has seen the end of war in 1945? What are his reasons?

2. Is Wheeler willing to see the United States involved in further wars? Which statements of Wheeler's give you this impression?

3. What do you think Wheeler means when he says that by joining the United Nations we will become involved in "power politics"? How does his fear of such involvement compare with American foreign policy in earlier periods of our history?

4. In summary, why does Wheeler oppose United States membership in the United Nations?

5. How do Wheeler's arguments compare with arguments against the League of Nations?

THE UNITED STATES AS A WORLD POWER

1. How did the United States react in foreign affairs in 1898? In 1917? In the 1930's? In 1941?

2. Did the United States, from 1898 to 1946, become more responsible as a world power? Explain your answer.

3. What happened to the 1917 crusade designed to "make the world safe for democracy?" Was this reflected in later American action?

4. How does United States involvement in foreign affairs after World War II compare with our involvement in foreign affairs after World War I? How can you account for this?

5. "Those who cannot remember the past are condemned to repeat it." Does this phrase apply to this study of World Wars I and II? If so, how? If not, why not?

Since the Spanish-American War, the United States has become a world power. After reviewing the history of the United States from 1898 to 1946, form a hypothesis on how and why the United States became a world power. Consider:

1. The limitations of your available historical evidence.

2. The reliability of your available historical evidence.

3. Specific examples which could be used to test the validity of your hypothesis.

4. The value, if any, of forming and using hypotheses in studying history.

III. A Domestic Dilemma

Government Responsibility at Home

23. America in the Twenties: The Jazz Age

The 1920's, the decade that followed the First World War, has been called the "Jazz Age." In the selections that follow, you will observe some events and aspects of the Twenties.

POINTS TO CONSIDER

Whether the era was a "Jazz Age."

Whether the events of the Twenties seem unusual to you today.

What this tells you about life in the Twenties.
What questions would help you to learn more about the era.
How you would *interpret* the Twenties.

1920

Passage of the National Prohibition Enforcement Act, January 16. This act provided the measures necessary to enforce the Eighteenth Amendment, which had been ratified in 1919 and stated that: "After one year from the ratification of this article, the manufacture, sale, or transportation of intoxicating liquors within, the importation thereof into, or the exportation thereof from the United States and all territory subject to the jurisdiction thereof for beverage purposes is hereby prohibited."

Passage of the Nineteenth Amendment, August 26. "The right of citizens of the United States to vote shall not be denied or abridged by the United States or by any State on account of sex."

Skirts are nine inches from the ground, as compared with six inches in 1919. A writer for *The New York Times* complains that this exceeds any "modest" limit.

The first radio station, KDKA of Pittsburgh, begins broadcasting. Its first broadcast is the election returns of 1920.

Registration of passenger cars reaches 8,225,859. In 1919, less than 7,000,000 cars were registered, and in 1913 only 600,000.

Warren G. Harding becomes President. Wilson's plan for world peace is tabled. The Senate rejects the Treaty of Versailles and refuses to allow the United States to join the League of Nations.

1921

The fox-trot becomes a fashionable dance and is described by critics as "immoral."

The state of Iowa passes a law permitting adults to purchase cigarettes. Smoking of cigarettes by women becomes common, but many people consider this "shocking."

Jack Dempsey knocks out George Carpentier in four rounds.

Skirts are two inches shorter than in 1920. The first sleeveless dresses appear.

1922

Radio broadcasting occurs daily in New York.

College football games reach a new height of popularity. The Harvard-Yale game attracts 77,000 people.

There are 10,864,128 passenger cars registered.

1923

Thousands of people turn out to hear Emile Coué lecture on auto-suggestion, or self-hypnosis. He encourages his followers to repeat to themselves, "Every day in every way I am getting better and better."

Alma Cummings becomes the first "dance marathon" champion by dancing twenty-seven hours without stopping.

Hemlines are twelve to fourteen inches from the ground.

"Yes, We Have No Bananas" is the most popular song.

Registration of passenger cars reaches 13,479,608.

Warren G. Harding dies. Calvin Coolidge becomes President.

1924

Congress establishes quotas, or limits, for the number of immigrants that will be permitted to enter the country. Only 164,000 immigrants are allowed to enter every year. Each country is allowed a specific amount of this total. The English, Irish, and Germans receive the largest quotas.

Regular air mail service between New York and San Francisco begins.

Harding's Secretary of the Interior, Albert B. Fall, is sentenced to a year in jail for accepting bribes to lease government oil reserves at Teapot Dome, Wyoming, and at Elk Hills, California, to private oil operators. In 1929, one of these operators, Harry F. Sinclair, is sentenced to prison for contempt of court and of the Senate.

There are 15,450,649 passenger cars registered.

Calvin Coolidge is elected President on the Republican ticket. Despite the many scandals that occurred during the Harding administration, Coolidge receives 15,725,000 popular votes; John W. Davis, the Democratic candidate, 8,387,000; and Robert M. La Follette, the Progressive candidate, 4,823,000 votes.

1925

Labor unions strive for better working conditions.

Red Grange, star Illinois football player, is urged to run for Congress although he is under age.

Crossword puzzles become a popular fad.

The Treasury Department, responsible for enforcing prohibition, estimates that the government intercepts only about five per cent of the liquor smuggled into the country.

John T. Scopes, a biology teacher in Tennessee, violates a state law which forbids Darwin's theory of evolution to be taught in public schools. According to Darwin, man had developed, or evolved, from a lower species to his present condition. Clarence Darrow, a well-known trial lawyer, defends Scopes. William Jennings Bryan, an unsuccessful Presidential candidate in 1896, 1900, and 1908, serves as the prosecutor of the case. Scopes is convicted and fined one hundred dollars.

Florida experiences a land boom. The value of land skyrockets.

The Knights of the Ku Klux Klan, an anti-Negro, anti-Jewish, and anti-Catholic organization, reaches a membership of 5 million.

The number of registered passenger cars reaches 17,512,638.

1926
The hemlines of ladies' dresses are up to the knees.

A crowd seven blocks long lines up in New York City to view the body of the great romantic movie hero, Rudolph Valentino, which is lying in state.

Contract bridge, a new card game, is introduced.

Gene Tunney defeats Jack Dempsey for the heavyweight boxing championship before a crowd of 145,000. The gate receipts total $2,600,000 as compared with the $450,000 collected from the Dempsey championship fight in 1919.

There are 19,237,171 passenger cars registered.

1927
The unveiling of Ford's Model A attracts huge crowds in major cities.

The Jazz Singer, the first movie with sound, is a big hit.

With the coming of prohibition, bootlegging, or the illegal manufacture, sale, or transport of liquor, becomes a big business. It is estimated that the Al Capone gang controls the sale of about $60 million worth of bootleg beer and liquor. The cosmetics industry grosses about $750 million. Neither business had been important previously.

A front-page headline from *The New York Times* of May 22, 1927 declares:

LINDBERGH DOES IT! TO PARIS IN 33½ HOURS;
FLIES 1,000 MILES THROUGH SNOW AND SLEET;
CHEERING FRENCH CARRY HIM OFF FIELD
ATE ONLY ONE AND A HALF OF HIS FIVE SANDWICHES

Another headline from *The Times* proclaims:

HOME RUN RECORD FALLS AS BABE RUTH HITS 60th; PIRATES LOSE; GIANTS OUT OF RACE

1928

Stock prices rise to new levels. A person who buys "stock" in a company buys a share of the business. Therefore, by owning stock, he receives a share of the company's earnings and the right to approve or reject company policies by exercising his vote at stockholder meetings. Stock prices for some of the larger companies are: General Electric (GE), $128 per share; New York Central Railroad (NYCR), $160 per share; American Telephone and Telegraph (AT&T), $179 per share.

Herbert Hoover, the Republican Presidential candidate, defeats Al Smith, the Democratic candidate.

1929

More than 23 million automobiles are in use—over three times as many as in 1919.

On February 14, seven members of the Chicago Moran gang wait in a garage for a shipment of stolen bootleg liquor. Three men in police uniforms and two in plain clothes enter the garage, line the Moran gang against a wall, and machine-gun them to death. Then, the men in the police uniforms "arrest" the men in plain clothes and drive off. None of them are ever brought to trial.

During the past ten years, there have been about five hundred murders in Chicago.

Stock prices reach an all-time high on September 30: GE, $396 per share; NYCR, $256 per share; AT&T, $304 per share. A record 16,410,030 shares of stock are traded on October 29. By November 13, the prices have dropped drastically: GE, $168 per share; NYCR, $160 per share; AT&T, $197 per share.

Approximately 30 million Americans own shares of stock, as compared with 4 million in 1900.

24. Depression: A Scene in the Cities

On October 24, 1929, the period of prosperity that America had been enjoying came to an abrupt halt. "Black Thursday," as October 24 is called, was a day of panic on the stock market. Stock prices plunged. Many businesses failed and closed. Many workers were soon without jobs. The Great Depression, as it is called by historians, had arrived.

The Depression was felt by people from all walks of life. In the following selection, Frederick Lewis Allen, author of *Only Yesterday* and *Since Yesterday,* books concerned with the 1920's and 1930's, describes conditions in America in 1932.

POINTS TO CONSIDER
The problems city dwellers might have during a depression.
What they might do to solve their problems.

Walking through an American city, you might find few signs of the Depression visible—or at least conspicuous [obvious]—to the casual eye. You might notice that a great many shops were untenanted, with dusty plate-glass windows and signs indicating that they were ready to lease; that few factory chimneys were smoking; that the streets were not so crowded with trucks as in earlier years, that there was no uproar of riveters to assail the ear, that beggars and panhandlers were on the sidewalks in unprecedented numbers (in the Park Avenue district of New York a man might be asked for money four or five times in a ten-block walk). Traveling by railroad, you might notice that the trains were shorter, the Pullman cars fewer—and that fewer freight trains were on the line. Traveling overnight, you might find only two or three other passengers in your sleeping car. (By contrast, there were more filling stations by the motor highways than ever before, and of all the retail businesses in "Middletown" only the filling stations showed no large drop in business during the black years; for although few new automobiles were being bought, those which would still stand up were being used more than ever—to the dismay of the railroads.)

Frederick Lewis Allen, **Since Yesterday** (New York: Harper & Row, Publishers, 1940), pp. 59-65. Copyright 1939, 1940 by Harper & Row, Publishers, Incorporated. Used by permission of the publishers.

"Middletown" is a name used to indicate the average town.

Otherwise things might seem to you to be going on much as usual. The major phenomena of the Depression were mostly negative and did not assail the eye.

But if you knew where to look, some of them would begin to appear. First, the breadlines in the poorer districts. Second, those bleak settlements ironically known as "Hoovervilles" in the outskirts of the cities and on vacant lots—groups of makeshift shacks constructed out of packing boxes, scrap iron, anything that could be picked up free in a diligent combing of the city dumps: shacks in which men and sometimes whole families of evicted people were sleeping on automobile seats carried from auto-graveyards, warming themselves before fires of rubbish in grease drums. Third, the homeless people sleeping in doorways or on park benches, and going the rounds of the restaurants for leftover half-eaten biscuits, piecrusts, anything to keep the fires of life burning. Fourth, the vastly increased number of thumbers [hitchhikers] on the

"Breadlines" refers to lines that formed outside kitchens set up by charities and government agencies to feed the needy.

highways, and particularly of freight-car transients on the rail-roads: a huge army of drifters ever on the move, searching half-aimlessly for a place where there might be a job. According to [one historian], the Missouri Pacific Railroad in 1929 had "taken official cognizance" of 13,745 migrants; by 1931 the figure had already jumped to 186,028. It was estimated that by the beginning of 1933, the country over, there were a million of these transients on the move. Forty-five thousand had passed through El Paso [Texas] in the space of six months; 1,500 were passing through Kansas City [Missouri] every day. Among them were large numbers of young boys, and girls disguised as boys. According to the Children's Bureau, there were 200,000 children thus drifting about the United States. So huge was the number of freight-car hoppers in the Southwest that in a number of places the railroad police simply had to give up trying to remove them from the trains: there were far too many of them.

Among the comparatively well-to-do people of the country (those, let us say, whose pre-Depression incomes had been over $5,000 a year) the great majority were living on a reduced scale, for salary cuts had been extensive, especially since 1931, and dividends were dwindling. These people were discharging servants, or cutting servants' wages to a minimum, or in some cases "letting" a servant stay on without other compensation than board [food] and lodging. In many pretty houses, wives who had never before— in the revealing current phrase — "done their own work" were cooking and scrubbing. Husbands were wearing the old suit longer, resigning from the golf club, deciding, perhaps, that this year the family couldn't afford to go to the beach for the summer, paying seventy-five cents for lunch instead of a dollar at the restaurant or thirty-five instead of fifty at the lunch counter. When those who had flown high with the stock market in 1929 looked at the stock-market page of the newspapers nowadays their only consoling thought (if they still had any stock left) was that a judicious [wise] sale or two would result in such a capital loss that they need pay no income tax at all this year.

Alongside these men and women of the well-to-do classes whose fortunes had been merely reduced by the Depression were others who fortunes had been shattered. The crowd of men waiting for the 8:14 train at the prosperous suburb included many who had lost their jobs, and were going to town as usual not merely to look stubbornly and almost hopelessly for other work but also to keep up a bold front of activity. (In this latter effort they usually succeeded: one would never have guessed, seeing them chatting with their friends as train-time approached, how close to desperation some of them had come.) There were architects and engineers bound for offices to which no clients had come in weeks. There were doctors who thought themselves lucky when a patient paid a bill. Mrs. Jones, who went daily to her stenographic job, was now the economic mainstay of her family, for Mr. Jones was jobless and was doing the cooking and looking after the children (with singular distaste and inefficiency). Next door to the Joneses lived Mrs. Smith, the widow of a successful lawyer: she had always had a comfortable income, she prided herself on her "nice things," she was pathetically [pitifully] unfitted to earn a dollar even if jobs were to be had; her capital had been invested in South American bonds and United Founders stock and other similarly misnamed "securities," and now she was completely dependent upon hand-outs from her relatives, and didn't even have carfare in her imported pocketbook.

"Securities" are stocks and bonds.

The Browns had retreated to their "farmhouse" in the country and were trying to raise crops on its stony acres; they talked warmly about primal [primitive] simplicities but couldn't help longing sometimes for electric light and running hot water, and couldn't cope with the potato bugs. (Large numbers of city dwellers thus moved to the country, but not enough of them engaged in real farming to do more than partially check the long-term movement from the farms of America to the cities and towns.) It was being whispered about the community that the Robinson family, though they lived in a $40,000 house and had always spent money freely, were in desperate straights: Mr. Robinson had lost his job, the house could not be sold, they had realized on every asset at their command, and now they were actually going hungry—though their house still looked like the abode of affluence [wealth].

Further down in the economic scale, particularly in those industrial communities in which the factories were running at twenty per cent of capacity or had closed down altogether, conditions were infinitely worse. Frederick E. Croxton's figures, taken in Buffalo, show what was happening in such communities: out of 14,909 persons of both sexes willing and able to work, his house-to-house canvassers found in November, 1932, that 46.3 per cent were fully employed, 22.5 per cent were working part time, and as many as 31.2 per cent were unable to find jobs. In every American city, quantities of families were being evicted from their inadequate apartments; moving in with other families till ten or twelve people would be sharing three or four rooms; or shivering through the winter in heatless houses because they could afford no coal, eating meat once a week or not at all. . . . A woman clerk, offered piecework after being jobless for a year, confessed that she almost had not dared to come to the office, she had been in

A "canvasser" gathers facts and opinions.

such terror lest she wouldn't know where to hang her coat, wouldn't know how to find the washroom, wouldn't understand the boss's directions for her job.

For perhaps the worst thing about this Depression was its inexorable continuance year after year. Men who have been sturdy and self-respecting workers can take unemployment without flinching for a few weeks, a few months, even if they have to see their families suffer; but it is different after a year . . . two years . . . three years. . . . Among the miserable creatures curled up on park benches or standing in dreary lines before the soup kitchens in 1932 were men who had been jobless since the end of 1929.

Something "inexorable" cannot be changed— it is immovable.

At the very bottom of the economic scale the conditions may perhaps best be suggested by two brief quotations. The first, from Jonathan Norton Leonard's *Three Years Down,* describes the plight of Pennsylvania miners who had been put out of company villages after a blind and hopeless strike in 1931: "Reporters from the more liberal metropolitan papers found thousands of them huddled on the mountainsides, crowded three or four families together in one-room shacks, living on dandelions and wild weedroots. Half of them were sick, but no local doctor would care for the evicted strikers. All of them were hungry and many were dying of . . . diseases which enable welfare authorities to claim that no one has starved." The other quotation is from Louise V. Armstrong's *We Too Are the People,* and the scene is Chicago in the late spring of 1932:

"One vivid, gruesome moment of those dark days we shall never forget. We saw a crowd of some fifty men fighting over a barrel of garbage which had been set outside the back door of a restaurant. American citizens fighting for scraps of food like animals!"

Human behavior under unaccustomed conditions is always various. One thinks of the corporation executive to whom was delegated the job of discharging several hundred men: He insisted on seeing every one of them personally and taking an interest in each man's predicament, and at the end of a few months his hair had turned prematurely gray. . . . The Junior League girl who reported with pride a Depression economy: she had cut a piece out of an old fur coat in the attic and bound it to serve as a bathmat. . . . The banker who had been plunged deeply into debt by the collapse of his bank: he got a $30,000 job with another bank, lived on $3,000 a year, and honorably paid $27,000 a year to his creditors. . . . The wealthy family who lost most of their money but announced bravely that they had "solved their Depression problem" by discharging fifteen of their twenty servants, and showed no signs of curiosity as to what would happen to these fifteen. . . . The little

The "Junior League" is an exclusive organization of young women from socially "elite" families. The League gives voluntary service to civic and social organizations.

knot of corporation officials in a magnificent skyscraper office doctoring the books of the company to dodge bankruptcy. . . . The crowd of Chicago Negroes standing tight-packed before a tenement-house door to prevent the landlord's agents from evicting a neighbor family: as they stood there, hour by hour, they sang hymns. . . . The one-time clerk carefully cutting out pieces of cardboard to put inside his shoes before setting out on his endless job-hunting round, and telling his wife the shoes were now better than ever. . . . The man in the little apartment next door who had given up hunting for jobs, given up all interest, all activity, and sat hour by hour in staring apathy. . . .

1. What is the responsibility of government in situations like those described here? Why?

2. What is the reasoning behind your ideas? Are they based on constitutional grounds? Historical reasons? Explain.

3. Judging from this account, do you see any possible causes for the Depression? What could cause such conditions?

25. Depression: A Scene in the Country

In much of the Great Plains region, conditions during the Depression were made more severe by an extreme drought. John Steinbeck, a famous American novelist, placed the setting of one of his most popular stories in the dust bowl of Oklahoma. The following account is from his novel, *The Grapes of Wrath*.

In the water-cut gullies the earth dusted down in dry little streams. Gophers and ant lions started small avalanches. And as the sharp sun struck day after day, the leaves of the young corn became less stiff and erect; they bent in a curve at first, and then, as the central ribs of strength grew weak, each leaf tilted downward. . . .

When June was half gone, the big clouds moved up out of Texas and the Gulf, high heavy clouds, rain-heads. . . . The rain-heads dropped a little spattering and hurried on to some other country.

. . . Now the wind grew strong and hard and it worked at the rain crust in the corn fields. Little by little the sky was darkened by the mixing dust, and the wind felt over the earth, loosened the dust, and carried it away.

. . . During a night the wind raced faster over the land, dug cunningly among the rootlets of the corn, and the corn fought the wind with its weakened leaves until the roots were freed by the prying wind and then each stalk settled wearily sideways toward the earth and pointed the direction of the wind. . . .

John Steinbeck, **The Grapes of Wrath** (New York: The Viking Press, Inc., 1939), pp. 3-7, 318-320. Copyright 1939 © 1967 by John Steinbeck. Reprinted by permission of The Viking Press, Inc.

In the middle of that night the wind passed on and left the land quiet. . . . In the morning the dust hung like fog, and the sun was as red as ripe new blood. All day the dust sifted down from the sky, and the next day it sifted down. . . .

The people came out of their houses and smelled the hot stinging air and covered their noses from it. And the children came out of the houses, but they did not run or shout as they would have done after a rain. Men stood by their fences and looked at the ruined corn, drying fast now, only a little green showing through the film of dust. The men were silent and they did not move often. And the women came out of the houses to stand beside their men—to feel whether this time the men would break. The women studied the men's faces secretly, for the corn could go, as long as something else remained. The children stood near by, drawing figures in the dust with bare toes, and the children sent exploring senses out to see whether men and women would break. The children peeked at the faces of the men and women, and then drew careful lines in the dust with their toes. Horses came to the watering troughs and nuzzled the water to clear the surface dust. After a while the faces of the watching men lost their bemused perplexity and became hard and angry and resistant. Then the women knew that they were safe and that there was no break. Then they asked, What'll we do? And the men replied, I don't know. But it was all right. The women knew it was all right, and the watching children knew it was all right. Women and children knew deep in themselves that no misfortune was too great to bear if their men were whole. The women went into the houses to their work, and the children began to play, but cautiously at first. As the day went forward the sun became less red. It flared down on the dust-blanketed land. The men sat in the doorways of their houses; their hands were busy with sticks and little rocks. The men sat still — thinking — figuring. . . .

And the dispossessed, the migrants, flowed into California, two hundred and fifty thousand, and three hundred thousand. . . . And new waves were on the way, new waves of the dispossessed and the homeless, hardened, intent, and dangerous.

. . . [The] new barbarians [primitive foreigners] wanted only two things—land and food; and to them the two were one. . . . [The] wants of the Okies were beside the roads, lying there to be seen and coveted: the good fields with water to be dug for, the good green fields, earth to crumble experimentally in the hand, grass to smell, oaten stalks to chew until the sharp sweetness was in the throat. A man might look at a fallow [uncultivated] field and know, and see in his mind that his own bending back and his own

Many of the desperate farmers and their families moved to California.

An "Okie" is a migrant agricultural worker—especially one from Oklahoma.

straining arms would bring the cabbages into the light, and the golden eating corn, the turnips and carrots.

And a homeless hungry man, driving the roads with his wife beside him and his thin children in the back seat, could look at the fallow fields which might produce food but not profit, and that man could know how a fallow field is a sin and the unused land a crime against the thin children. And such a man drove along the roads and knew temptation at every field, and knew the lust to take these fields and make them grow strength for his children and a little comfort for his wife. The temptation was before him always. The fields goaded [prodded] him, and the company ditches with good water flowing were a goad to him.

And in the south he saw the golden oranges hanging on the trees, the little golden oranges on the dark green trees; and guards with shotguns patrolling the lines so a man might not pick an orange for a thin child, oranges to be dumped if the price was low.

He drove his old car into a town. He scoured the farms for work. Where can we sleep the night?

Well, there's Hooverville on the edge of the river. There's a whole raft of Okies there.

He drove his old car to Hooverville. . . .

The rag town lay close to water; and the houses were tents, and weed-thatched enclosures, paper houses, a great junk pile. The man drove his family in and became a citizen of Hooverville— always they were called Hooverville. The man put up his own tent as near to water as he could get; or if he had no tent, he went to the city dump and brought back cartons and built a house of corrugated paper. And when the rains came the house melted and washed away. He settled in Hooverville and he scoured the countryside for work, and the little money he had went for gasoline to look for work. In the evening, the men gathered and talked . . . Squatting on their hams they talked of the land they had seen.

1. Is there any action by the government in this account? How can you explain your answer?

2. Do people today face problems like the ones in these readings? What solutions are there today for such problems? Explain.

26. Steps in the Development of the Depression

During World War I American industry concentrated on producing war supplies. After the war industry converted to producing consumer goods. These goods, which had been unavailable during the war, were now much in demand. As a result of the increased demand for manufactured goods, many good jobs opened up in industry.

As people acquired well-paying jobs, their earnings rose. This meant they could purchase more goods. The demand for consumer goods rose. Business prospered, and business profits grew. These profits were often invested in stocks. As a result of business prosperity and increased demand for stocks, stock prices rose. Investment in stocks seemed to be a sure way to make money. From 1923 to 1925, the more prominent stocks in industry increased in price about seventy per cent. For example, stock worth $100 a share in 1923 sold for $170 in 1926.

As more goods were sold and more money was invested in industry through stock purchases, industry expanded by building more plants to produce more goods. It ultimately produced more than it could sell.

People who wanted to invest in the stock market were able to borrow easily. Banks made loans readily available. They wished to encourage the many people who wanted to borrow money to buy stocks or to expand their businesses. Banks profit from such borrowing, since they charge *interest* in return for lending money. By 1927, loans had increased about sixty-six per cent over previous times. Because loans were so easy to get, many people borrowed more money than they could easily pay back and used it to speculate.

In March of 1928, a group of large stockholders and wealthy businessmen began a giant buying campaign on the New York Stock Exchange, which is the main center for buying and selling stock in the United States. Large purchases at high prices gave potential investors confidence that prices would continue to rise. Thousands of people, as a result, borrowed to buy stock on credit. For example, in March a record breaking total of 3,875,000 shares of stock were sold in one day as compared with regular sales of around 2,000,000. Sales of shares increased daily. By late 1928, five to seven million shares a day were traded.

Much of the nation's wealth became concentrated in the hands of a few men. High industrial profits and a federal tax program that favored the rich aggravated uneven distribution of income. Twenty-six per cent of the national income went to five per cent of the people. This meant that the incomes of the ordinary consumers did not rise nearly as fast as the incomes of a few wealthy people. These few used their money to speculate on the stock market

"To speculate," is to take a business risk in hope of gain. Here it means to buy stocks in hopes that the stock prices will go up.

or to invest their funds in industry. As industry grew, it produced more and more goods. But consumers could not afford to buy more and more goods.

Some industries, such as coal, textiles, and construction, declined in the 1920's. Many people who had held jobs in these industries were put out of work. In other industries, new machines were installed which performed tasks previously carried out by employees. This resulted in still more unemployment. People who were unemployed could not buy the goods produced by industry.

During World War I, farmers could sell all they produced. When the demands of the war ended, the farmers were not able to sell as much. Prices of their goods fell sharply. They had difficulty making any profit. Therefore, the farmers were unable to buy as many industrial products as they had bought in the past.

International trade was out of balance. European nations, with their industries badly damaged from World War I, were forced to buy more goods from the United States than they were able to sell here. Thus they ended by owing the United States money. Europeans got most of the money to pay for American products through loans from American businessmen. The only way they could have done without the loans would have been by selling more goods to the United States. But during the 1920's, the United States adopted high tariffs. A tariff is a tax placed on an imported product. It raises the cost of the imported product above the cost of a domestic product of the same kind. A tariff encourages the consumer to buy the domestic product by making it less expensive than the imported one. Rising tariffs hurt the ability of Europeans to make payments on loans they had received from the United States. To prevent their debt to the United States from growing larger, European governments passed tariffs of their own. They wished to discourage their people from buying more American goods. This hurt the profits of American businessmen. Some businesses set up factories in Europe to avoid the tariffs.

In 1929, American businessmen stopped giving loans to Europeans. This meant Europeans could not afford to keep on buying goods from America. The Europeans had deposited gold in American banks to establish their credit, that is, to show that they could pay back money loaned to them. Since they expected to cut down on purchases, they began to withdraw their gold from the American banks. European countries also took steps to see that no more gold was sent to the United States.

Europe began to experience a depression. Many European nations had to stop payment on loans made by the United States since World War I.

In autumn of 1929, industrial production fell. The shady dealings of a famous financial speculator in London were exposed. The Boston Department of Public Utilities decided to investigate a Boston corporation and declared that its stock prices were too high as a result of speculation. These events are sometimes pictured as having shaken the confidence of a group of important investors. At any rate, several large operators on the New York Stock Exchange began to sell their stocks early in October 1929.

On October 24, 1929, many stockholders began to sell their stocks. They were frightened by the decline in stock prices that had begun in early October. When many stockholders decide to sell their stocks at once, stock prices drop. The stockholders were afraid that declining prices would eventually make their stocks worthless. They panicked and sold their stocks.

Banks had loaned much of their money for stock purchases. They were afraid that if the values of stocks dropped, people who had spent a lot of money on stocks would not be able to recover enough money to pay back bank loans. Many banks decided to call for immediate payment of loans, before it was too late. But stock values dropped very fast. Stocks became worthless. The majority of stockholders had purchased all their stocks on credit. They had no cash. They could not pay back the money they had borrowed.

Many businesses had invested a large part of their money in stocks. They lost a great deal of this money. Corporations had also invested in expansion. Often they had borrowed a part of the money to finance expansion from banks. When banks called for immediate repayment of loans, most businesses did not have the money. Furthermore, once the Depression began, people were buying fewer products. Thus, businessmen could not sell the goods they manufactured. Many businesses had to declare bankruptcy.

When a business closed, its employees did not have work. They had trouble buying food and clothing and paying rent. They could not afford to buy items such as cars or iceboxes. When people stopped buying, those who sold and made goods had to be laid off.

The farmers, who did not earn profits in the 1920's, felt the effects of the Depression more quickly than other people. Many did not own their farms. Their farms were *mortgaged*. That is, the farmer had agreed to pay for the farm in installments, or parts, over a period of time. Meanwhile, the bank owned the farm. When the Depression struck, many farmers could not meet their mortgage payments. When this happened, the bank had the right to foreclose on the mortgage, that is, to demand payment of the entire

680

remaining cost of the farm. If the farmer could not raise the money, the bank took over the farm. The bank sold the farm for whatever price it could get for it. Many farmers lost their farms in this way.

As the Depression developed, many people began to pull their savings out of banks. The banks had loaned some of this money to individuals and corporations. They were forced to call in debts. But most debtors could not meet their obligations to the banks. Consequently the banks could not meet their obligations. Many banks closed. People who had deposited money in these banks lost their savings.

By the winter of 1929-1930, total depression hit the country.

1. Do these statements relate to the scenes you previously read about the Depression? Explain.

2. According to this list of events, what were the causes of the Depression? Explain.

3. What do you think the government of the United States could do about any of these situations? Why?

TWO PROGRAMS

27. Hoover's Measures

During the Depression, Herbert Hoover and Franklin D. Roosevelt served as Presidents of the United States. Hoover, a Republican, was elected in 1928 to succeed Calvin Coolidge amid great prosperity. One year later, in 1929, the Depression arrived, and until 1932, Hoover had to deal with it. In the Presidential election of 1932, Franklin D. Roosevelt, a Democrat, defeated Hoover. Roosevelt initiated a program called the New Deal.

In the next two readings you will study the measures each of the two men took to solve the nation's economic problems. Hoover's measures appear below.

POINTS TO CONSIDER
How each measure tried to solve a cause of the Depression.
How Roosevelt's and Hoover's programs differ.
Which one was likely to be more effective and why.

1929
The Agricultural Marketing Act established a Federal Farm Board to promote agricultural cooperatives. These cooperatives were organizations set up by the farmers in order to keep production in line with demand and to market farm produce more efficiently.

IV. Hoover and Roosevelt: Two Presidents Face The Problem

681

The Federal Farm Board loaned money to the cooperatives so they could maintain prices by buying and selling on the open market.

The Hawley-Smoot Tariff established the highest tariff rates in this country's history to protect United States industry and agriculture from foreign competition.

1930
The Grain Stabilization Corporation, the Cotton Stabilization Corporation, and other such organizations were established to buy farm crops on the open market. Open market trading was expected to maintain prices. Within two years, this resulted in large government surpluses. Purchases which caused prices to fall were halted.

Hoover requested that the government spend between $100-$150 million for the construction of public works such as dams and roads.

Hoover sought the voluntary cooperation of business and labor leaders in his attempt to solve the economic problems of the nation.

1932
The Emergency Relief Organization was established to distribute the surplus wheat accumulated by the Federal Farm Board to the states for relief purposes. It also made loans to the states to support their aid programs.

The Reconstruction Finance Corporation (RFC) was created to make loans to banks, insurance companies, and other financial, industrial, and agricultural institutions. By doing this, the government hoped to stimulate business. It felt that if business became more prosperous, the prosperity would eventually "trickle down" to the people in general.

The Federal Home Loan Act established twelve Home Loan Banks to provide cheap credit for builders and homeowners.

1. How do Hoover's measures try to solve the problems that caused the Depression?

2. Do you think such a program would stop the Depression? Why or why not?

28. Roosevelt's Program: The New Deal

John Gunther, a contemporary historian and political observer, described Roosevelt's first term in office in his book *Roosevelt in*

Retrospect. The book was published in 1950, five years after Roosevelt's death. The following reading includes selections from Gunther's book and descriptions of some of the legislation passed during Roosevelt's Presidency.

JOHN GUNTHER: THE HUNDRED DAYS

The keynote of the Hundred Days [Roosevelt's early days in office] was Roosevelt's phrase, "The only thing we have to fear is fear itself." The first duty of the new President was, obviously, to restore confidence to the stricken nation, lift it to its feet. FDR had to be soothing, hortatory [encouraging], calm, decisive, and strenuously practical all at once. He blew hope into the deflated body of the country like a boy blowing up a balloon. The people listened to the inaugural address and then to the first Fireside Chat a few days later, and felt that the man in the White House was their friend, as well as leader, who would save them from further catastrophe ... Almost audibly, a sigh of relief went up through the entire land.

John Gunther, **Roosevelt in Retrospect** (New York: Harper & Row, Publishers, 1950), p. 278.

The "fireside chats" were informal radio reports to the American people. Roosevelt was the first President to effectively win public support in such a way.

FDR summoned Congress for a special session on March 9, 1933, and this remained sitting until June 16—hence the locution [expression] "Hundred Days." Seldom in any parliamentary history has so much been done so quickly.

MAJOR LEGISLATION PASSED DURING THE HUNDRED DAYS: MARCH–JUNE 1933

March 9   The Emergency Banking Relief Act closed all banks until federal examiners found them solvent.

To be "solvent" is to be able to pay one's legal debts.

March 20   The Economy Act reduced government expenditures by cutting the salaries of government employees and veterans' pensions.

March 31   The Civilian Conservation Corps (CCC) provided work in national parks, flood control projects, road construction, restoration, and prevention of soil erosion. The men hired were unmarried, 18-25 years of age, and unemployed.

April 19   The United States abandoned the gold standard. To be on the "gold standard" meant that every dollar in circulation could be exchanged for gold. The amount of gold we had, limited the amount of money in circulation. When something is available in limited amounts only, its value tends to increase. Dollars backed by gold were valuable. Thus, when we went off the gold standard the value of the dollar went down. Since the dollar was worth less, it was necessary for people who sold things to raise prices. Therefore, one result of the end of the gold standard was a rise in the prices of goods and stocks.

May 12 The Federal Emergency Relief Act made loans to states and cities for them to distribute as they pleased. The money was usually given to the unemployed in "doles," grants of money, or in handouts of food or clothing.

May 12 The Agricultural Adjustment Act (AAA) established a voluntary crop-reduction program. Farmers were to limit their production of crops and to be paid for doing this. With a limited supply of crops, prices would rise and the farmers would receive higher prices for their produce.

May 18 The Tennessee Valley Authority (TVA) was created to develop both the social and the economic well-being of the Tennessee Valley region through the control and use of the area's water resources. A program of dam construction was begun in order to aid flood control and provide electricity at reasonable rates. TVA was also to further land reclamation by planting trees and taking other measures to prevent soil erosion.

May 27 The Federal Securities Act required companies that issued securities to provide complete, accurate information to investors. There were severe penalties for failing to meet these requirements.

June 13 The Home Owners Loan Corporation was established. Through it, the government provided money for small mortgages at lower interest rates than had been charged in the past.

June 16 The Banking Act of 1933 created the Federal Bank Deposit Insurance Corporation which guaranteed bank deposits under $5,000.

June 16 The National Industrial Recovery Act (NIRA) sought a partnership between government, business, and labor. Management and labor were to draw up "codes of fair competition" which were to increase wages, reduce working hours, and increase employment. The program was under the direction of a National Recovery Administration (NRA).

June 16 The Public Works Administration (PWA) was set up under the authority of a section of the NRA act. The PWA financed projects all over the country for constructing waterworks, dams, sewers, and ships. The PWA generally hired men through private contractors.

MAJOR NEW DEAL LEGISLATION: OCTOBER 1933—JUNE 1938
October 22, 1933 Roosevelt gave the RFC authority to buy and sell gold so as to give the government "control of the gold value of our dollar."

November 8, 1933   The Civil Works Administration (CWA) gave work to jobless people in building or improving airports, roads, and schools. Some jobs involved tasks like raking leaves in parks.

January 30, 1934   The Gold Reserve Act gave the government full control over the value of the dollar.

February 2, 1934   The Export-Import Bank was established. The Bank, by a variety of measures, made it easier and safer for American farmers and businessmen to export products.

June 6, 1934   The Securities and Exchange Commission (SEC) was established. It had the power to enforce a set of new rules for the stock market. The rules were designed to stop speculation and unfair practices.

April 8, 1935   The Works Progress Administration (WPA) was established to employ jobless people. Highways, roads, and streets were built. Bridges, public buildings, parks, and airports were built or improved. WPA workers also ran community centers and surveyed government archives, or places where documents were kept. Many jobs were provided for artists, writers, actors, and musicians.

May 1, 1935   The Resettlement Administration was organized to make grants to needy farmers who were not aided by the Agricultural Adjustment Act. With these grants, they could purchase equipment and supplies. The RA was also concerned with land wastage. It purchased tracts of land where the soil was poor and planted them with trees or converted them to other uses.

May 11, 1935   The Rural Electrification Act was passed to provide government assistance in bringing electric power to rural areas.

July 5, 1935   The National Labor Relations Act granted laborers the right to organize in unions and to bargain with their employers. The National Labor Relations Board (NLRB) was established to protect the rights of laborers.

The National Labor Relations Act is generally known as the Wagner Act.

August 14, 1935   The Social Security Act provided for unemployment and old-age insurance. To obtain the necessary funds, a percentage of each person's pay was deducted and was matched by the employer.

August 29, 1935   The Farm Mortgage Moratorium Act set up a three-year moratorium, or waiting period, during which farmers could get permission to keep their farms if they could not make their mortgage payments. They were allowed to pay rent instead.

August 30, 1935   A new Revenue Act raised taxes on individual incomes over $50,000. A tax of 75% was placed on all income over

$5 million. Gift and estate taxes were also increased. Income taxes were lowered for small corporations and raised for corporations earning more than $50,000. Previously, all corporations payed income taxes at the same rate. A new tax was added on business profits where these were unusually high.

September 1, 1937 The National Housing Act was set up to direct slum clearance and construction of inexpensive housing for low-income families. The U. S. Housing Authority was established to grant loans for these purposes. It also granted rent subsidies, or money assistance, so that low rents could be charged for this housing.

June 25, 1938 The Fair Labor Standards Act established minimum wages, fixed the legal maximum of hours of work per week, and required time and a half pay for overtime. This act applied to those whose work was in or affected by interstate commerce.

1. In what different ways do you think the New Deal program was trying to fight the Depression?

2. Do you think the New Deal would halt the Depression? Why or why not?

TWO PROGRAMS: HOOVER AND ROOSEVELT

1. What similiarities and differences are there between the two programs?

2. What do you think might explain this?

3. Which program do you think meets the problems of the Depression better? Why?

THE IDEAS OF HOOVER AND ROOSEVELT

INTERPRETING FACTS
Review the programs of Roosevelt and Hoover that you have just studied. Form your own interpretation of:

1. What each man thought caused the Depression.

2. What each man thought about the role of the federal government in American society.

29. The Key to the Depression: Hoover

While studying the last two readings, you tried to judge whether Roosevelt's program or Hoover's would be more effective in combatting the Depression. Another way to judge the two programs is to weigh the ideas that inspired them. You have already made your own interpretation of these ideas. Now you will have the opportunity to compare your ideas with the ideas of the two men as recorded in their speeches. The following selection is taken from a campaign speech Hoover made in Cleveland in 1932. It gives Hoover's interpretation of the key to the Depression.

. . . Over and above and of infinitely more importance than all [the] measures I have mentioned is the problem of restoring the great mass of normal jobs in the country. Emergency jobs have helped enormously, but the normal jobs are the permanent dependence of the worker. Emergency jobs will never heal the depression.

Obviously, the normal jobs lie in the production and distribution of goods and services; in other words, the factories, the mills, the mines, the railways, the public utilities, the stores, the offices.

And every part of this mechanism is lubricated [oiled] by what we call credit. That is, the ability of the manager of a business to borrow money to buy his raw materials and to pay his labor. This credit is the very lifeblood of this whole structure. It is the lifeblood of jobs. If credit fails, the enterprise dries up; it withers or it dies. And jobs decrease or disappear.

And what is the source of credit? The savings of the people themselves. These are gathered in a myriad of tiny rivulets [streams] of their deposits in the banks, their premiums to life-insurance companies, their dues to benevolent fraternal organizations, their payments to building and loan associations, and a score of other ways. These rivulets in total volume are a mighty river. Their waters are stored in credit reservoirs. These are the banks, mortgage companies, the insurance companies, investments in the services of industry and business.

Thus credit is born of the people themselves. What the people give, the people can take away. The reservoirs of credit are built upon the confidence of the people in them. Fear is death to credit.

When the great economic earthquakes abroad struck directly at the credit structures of those foreign countries, the shocks reverberated [echoed back] to us. I have already said foreigners dumped their securities here at panic prices and demanded gold in payment. They claimed their deposits from American banks. They demanded cash for all goods they had sold to us. Our own people in fear drew out $1,500,000,000 of their savings from our own banks.

Thus credit began to dry up. The managers of business turned in vain for . . . loans to buy raw materials and to pay their labor.

Campaign Speeches of 1932, edited by Herbert Hoover and Calvin Coolidge (Garden City, N.Y.: Doubleday & Company, Inc., 1933), pp. 101-103. Reprinted by permission of the Herbert Hoover Foundation.

687

Beyond all this contraction of credit was the fear and panic through the world, spreading its destruction into the United States. It imperiled the institutions in which were the savings of every fireside —bank deposits or insurance policies or investments. In this contraction of credit lay dangers to everyone who owed money, for upon demand for immediate payment he was compelled to sell his property in a limited and vastly depreciated market and so was threatened with ruin.

1. Why does Hoover think credit is so important?

2. How does he explain the destruction of credit?

3. How does Hoover's program reflect his interpretation of the causes of the Depression?

4. Does Hoover's explanation of the Depression seem correct to you? Why?

5. What additional information would help you to judge his explanation?

30. The Key to the Depression: Roosevelt

The three selections that follow present Roosevelt's ideas about the causes of the Depression.

ROOSEVELT: A SPEECH IN WASHINGTON, 1934

. . . [The] difficult and dangerous situation into which the United States had got itself was due to the general attitude, "Every man for himself; the devil take the hindmost." Individuals were seeking quick riches at the expense of other individuals. Geographical sections were seeking economic preference for themselves to the disadvantage of other sections. Cities were recklessly offering inducements to manufacturing plants to move away from other cities. Within given industries unfair competition went on unheeded or resulted in vast consolidations whose securities were peddled to the public at dishonest prices. There was little consideration for the social point of view, and no planning whatsoever to avoid the pitfalls of overproduction or of selling methods which foisted articles on a gullible public, which the family budget could not afford.

That is a strong picture but you and I, in the bottom of our hearts, know that it is a true picture. Most of us participated in the making of that picture. . . .

. . . Through inertia [inaction] on the part of leaders and on the part of the people themselves the operations of government had

Public Papers and Addresses of Franklin D. Roosevelt, edited by Samuel I. Rosenman (New York: Random House, Inc., 1938), Vol. III, pp. 123-124. Copyright 1938 by Franklin Delano Roosevelt and renewed 1965 by Elliott Roosevelt, Hon. James Roosevelt, and Franklin Delano Roosevelt, Jr. Reprinted by permission of Random House, Inc.

fallen into the hands of special groups, some of them . . . led by people who undertook to obtain special advantages for special classes and others led by a handful of individuals who believed in their superhuman ability to retain in their own hands the entire business and financial control over the economic and social structure of the Nation.

ROOSEVELT: CAMPAIGN SPEECH IN SAN FRANCISCO, 1932

A glance at the situation today only too clearly indicates that equality of opportunity as we have known it no longer exists. Our industrial plant is built; the problem just now is whether under existing conditions it is not overbuilt. Our last frontier has long since been reached, and there is practically no more free land. More than half of our people do not live on the farms or on lands and cannot derive a living by cultivating their own property. There is no safety valve in the form of a Western prairie to which those thrown out of work by the Eastern economic machines can go for a new start. We are not able to invite the immigration from Europe to share our endless plenty. We are now providing a drab living for our own people.

Franklin D. Roosevelt: Selected Speeches, Messages, Press Conferences, and Letters, edited by Basil Rauch (New York: Holt, Rinehart and Winston, Inc., 1957), pp. 81-83.

Our system of constantly rising tariffs has at last reacted against us to the point of closing our Canadian frontier on the north, our European markets on the east, many of our Latin American markets to the south, and a goodly proportion of our Pacific markets on the west, through the retaliatory tariffs of those countries. It has forced many of our great industrial institutions who exported their surplus production to such countries, to establish plans in such countries, within the tariff walls. This has resulted in the reduction of the operation of their American plants, and opportunity for employment.

Within two years after passage of the Hawley-Smoot Tariff, twenty-five countries raised their tariffs.

Just as freedom to farm has ceased, so also the opportunity in business has narrowed. It still is true that men can start small enterprises, trusting to native shrewdness and ability to keep abreast of competitors; but area after area has been preempted [taken over] altogether by the great corporations, and even in the fields which still have no great concerns, the small man starts under a handicap. . . . Recently a careful study was made of the concentration of business in the United States. It showed that our economic life was dominated by some six hundred odd corporations who controlled two-thirds of American industry. Ten million small business men divided the other third. More striking still, it appeared that if the process of concentration goes on at the same rate, at the end of another century we shall have all American industry controlled by a dozen corporations, and run by perhaps a hundred men. . . .

Clearly, all this calls for a re-appraisal of values. A mere builder of more industrial plants, a creator of more railroad systems, an organizer of more corporations, is as likely to be a danger as a help. The day of the great promoter or the financial Titan, to whom we granted anything if only he would build, or develop, is over. Our task now is not discovery or exploitation of natural resources, or necessarily producing more goods. It is the soberer, less dramatic business . . . of adapting existing economic organizations to the service of the people. . . .

ROOSEVELT: THE "FORGOTTEN MAN" RADIO SPEECH, ALBANY, 1932

Public Papers and Addresses of Franklin D. Roosevelt, edited by Samuel I. Rosenman (New York: Random House, Inc., 1938), Vol. I, pp. 625-627. Copyright 1938 by Franklin Delano Roosevelt and renewed 1965 by Elliott Roosevelt, Hon. James Roosevelt, and Franklin Delano Roosevelt, Jr. Reprinted by permission of Random House, Inc.

These unhappy times call for the building of plans that rest upon the forgotten, the unorganized but the indispensable units of economic power, for plans . . . that build from the bottom up and not from the top down, that put their faith once more in the forgotten man at the bottom of the economic pyramid.

. . . A real economic cure must go to the killing of the bacteria in the system rather than to the treatment of external symptoms.

How much do the shallow thinkers realize, for example, that approximately one-half of our whole population, fifty or sixty million people, earn their living by farming or in small towns whose existence immediately depends on farms. They have today lost their purchasing power. Why? They are receiving for farm products less than the cost to them of growing these farm products. The result of this loss of purchasing power is that many other millions of people engaged in industry in the cities cannot sell industrial products to the farming half of the Nation. This brings home to every city worker that his own employment is directly tied up with farmer's dollar. No Nation can long endure half bankrupt. Main Street, Broadway, the mills, the mines will close if half the buyers are broke.

I cannot escape the conclusion that one of the essential parts of a national program of restoration must be to restore purchasing power to the farming half of the country. Without this the wheels of railroads and of factories will not turn.

Closely associated with this first objective is the problem of keeping the home-owner and the farm-owner where he is, without being dispossessed through the foreclosure of his mortgage. His relationship to the great banks of Chicago and New York is pretty remote. The two billion dollar fund which President Hoover and the Congress have put at the disposal of the big banks, the railroads and the corporations of the Nation is not for him.

690

His is a relationship to his little local bank or local loan company. It is a sad fact that even though the local lender in many cases does not want to evict the farmer or home-owner by foreclosure proceedings, he is forced to do so in order to keep his bank or company solvent. Here should be an objective of Government itself, to provide at least as much assistance to the little fellow as it is now giving to the large banks and corporations. That is another example of building from the bottom up.

One other objective closely related to the problem of selling American products is to provide a tariff policy based upon economic common sense rather than upon politics, hot-air, and pull. This country during the past few years, culminating with the Hawley-Smoot Tariff in 1929, has compelled the world to build tariff fences so high that world trade is decreasing to the vanishing point. The value of goods internationally exchanged is today less than half of what it was three or four years ago.

Every man and woman who gives any thought to the subject knows that if our factories run even 80 percent of capacity, they will turn out more products than we as a Nation can possibly use ourselves. The answer is that if they run on 80 percent of capacity, we must sell some goods abroad. How can we do that if the outside Nations cannot pay us in cash? And we know by sad experience that they cannot do that. The only way they can pay us is in their own goods or raw materials, but this foolish tariff of ours makes that impossible.

What we must do is this: revise our tariff on the basis of a reciprocal exchange of goods, allowing other Nations to buy and to pay for our goods, by sending us such of their goods as will not seriously throw any of our industries out of balance, and incidentally making impossible in this country the continuance of pure monopolies which cause us to pay excessive prices for many of the necessities of life.

Such objectives as these three, restoring farmers' buying power, relief to the small banks and home-owners and a reconstructed tariff policy, are only a part of ten or a dozen vital factors. But they seem to be beyond the concern of a national administration which can think in terms only of the top of the social and economic structure. It has sought temporary relief from the top down rather than permanent relief from the bottom up. It has totally failed to plan ahead in a comprehensive way. It has waited until something has cracked and then at the last moment has sought to prevent total collapse.

It is high time to get back to fundamentals. It is high time to admit with courage that we are in the midst of an emergency at least equal to that of war. Let us mobilize to meet it.

1. How does Roosevelt interpret the reasons for the Depression?

2. How do Roosevelt's and Hoover's ideas on the role of corporations in American economic life differ?

3. How does Roosevelt's program reflect his interpretation of the Depression?

4. Which interpretation of the Depression seems more convincing to you? Why?

31. The Role of the Federal Government: Hoover

The following selections focus on Hoover's and Roosevelt's ideas about the role the federal government should play in combatting the Depression.

POINTS TO CONSIDER

What each man emphasizes as the primary task of the federal government.

How each feels about making changes in the system.

A CAMPAIGN SPEECH IN WASHINGTON, 1932

. . . The spirit and devising of this Government by the people was to sustain a dual purpose—on the one hand to protect our people . . . by great national power, and on the other to preserve individual liberty and freedom through local government.

The function of the Federal Government in these times is to use its reserve powers and its strength for the protection of citizens and local governments by supporting our institutions against forces beyond their control. It is not the function of the Government to relieve individuals of their responsibilities to their neighbors, or to relieve private institutions of their responsibilites to the public, or of local government to the States, or of State governments to the Federal Government. In giving that protection and that aid the Federal Government must insist that all of them exert their responsibilities in full. It is vital that the programs of the Government shall not compete with or replace any of them but shall add to their initiative and their strength. . . .

And in all these emergencies and crises, and in all our future policies, we must also preserve the fundamental principles of our social and economic system. That system is founded upon a conception of ordered freedom. The test of that freedom is that there should be maintained equality of opportunity to every individual

Campaign Speeches of 1932, edited by Herbert Hoover and Calvin Coolidge (Garden City, N.Y.: Doubleday & Company, Inc., 1933), pp. 7-9. Reprinted by permission of the Herbert Hoover Foundation.

so that he may achieve for himself the best to which his character, ability, and ambition entitle him. . . .

. . . It does not follow, because our difficulties are stupendous [enormous], because there are some souls timorous [timid] enough to doubt the validity [soundness] and effectiveness of our ideals and our system, that we must turn to a State-controlled or State-directed social or economic system in order to cure our troubles. That . . . is tyranny. It is the regimentation [rigid control] of men under autocratic bureaucracy with all its extinction of liberty, of hope, and of opportunity. Of course, no man of understanding says that our system works perfectly. It does not. The human race is not perfect. Nevertheless, the movement of a true civilization is toward freedom rather than regimentation. This is our ideal. . . .

"Autocratic" refers to a government with absolute power and authority. A "bureaucracy" is a government that has a complicated network of departments and many officials.

Thus we have held that the Federal Government should in the presence of great national danger use its powers to give leadership to the initiative, the courage, and the fortitude [strength] of the people themselves . . .

A CAMPAIGN SPEECH IN NEW YORK, 1932

We are told by the opposition that we must have a change, that we must have a new deal. It is not the change that comes from normal development of national life to which I object, but the proposal to alter the whole foundations of our national life which have been builded through generations of testing and struggle, and of the principles upon which we have builded the nation. . . .

Campaign Speeches of 1932, edited by Herbert Hoover and Calvin Coolidge, pp. 167, 169-172.

Let us pause for a moment and examine the American system of government, of social and economic life, which it is now proposed that we should alter. Our system is the product of our race and of our experience in building a nation to heights unparalled in the whole history of the world. It is a system peculiar to the American people. It differs essentially from all others in the world. It is an American system.

It is founded on the conception that only through ordered liberty, through freedom to the individual, and equal opportunity to the individual will his initiative and enterprise be summoned to spur the march of progress.

It is by the maintenance of equality of opportunity and therefore of a society absolutely fluid in freedom of the movement of its human particles that our individualism departs from the individualism of Europe. . . .

The primary conception of this whole American system is not the regimentation of men but the cooperation of free men. It is founded upon the conception of responsibility of the individual

693

to the community, of the responsibility of local government to the State, of the State to the national Government. . . .

The implacable [unalterable] march of scientific discovery with its train of new inventions presents every year new problems to government and new problems to the social order. Questions often arise whether, in the face of the growth of these new and gigantic tools, democracy can remain master in its own house, can preserve the fundamentals of our American system. I contend that it can; and I contend that this American system of ours has demonstrated its validity and superiority over any system yet invented.

I therefore contend that the problem of today is to continue these measures and policies to restore this American system to its normal functioning, to repair the wounds it has received, to correct the weaknesses and evils which would defeat that system. To enter upon a series of deep changes to embark upon this inchoate [recently begun] new deal which has been propounded in this campaign would be to undermine and destroy our American system.

Before we enter upon such courses, I would like you to consider what the results of this American system have been during the last thirty years—that is, one single generation. For if it can be demonstrated that by means of this, our unequaled political, social, and economic system, we have secured a lift in the standards of living and a diffusion of comfort and hope to men and women, the growth of equal opportunity, the widening of all opportunity, such as had never been seen in the history of the world, then we should not tamper with it or destroy it; but on the contrary we should restore it and, by its gradual improvement and perfection, foster it into new performance for our country and for our children.

1. What does Hoover regard as the most important task of the federal government?

2. What does Hoover want the federal government to *avoid?* Why?

3. What does Hoover fear about Roosevelt's program?

4. Are Hoover's ideas about government reflected in his program? Explain.

32. The Role of the Federal Government: Franklin D. Roosevelt

A SPEECH TO THE NEW YORK LEGISLATURE, 1931

. . . Our Government is not the master but the creature of the people. The duty of the State toward the citizens is the duty of the

Franklin D. Roosevelt: Selected Speeches, Messages, Press Conferences, and Letters, edited by Basil Rauch (New York: Holt, Rinehart and Winston, Inc., 1957), pp. 62-64.

servant to its master. The people have created it; the people, by common consent, permit its continual existence.

One of these duties of the State is that of caring for those of its citizens who find themselves the victims of such adverse circumstance as makes them unable to obtain even the necessities for mere existence without the aid of others. That responsibility is recognized by every civilized Nation.

... I assert that modern society, acting through its Government, owes the definite obligation to prevent the starvation or the dire [extreme] want of any of its fellow men and women who try to maintain themselves but cannot.

... [The] State [should take responsibility] when widespread economic conditions render large numbers of men and women incapable of supporting either themselves or their families because of circumstances beyond their control which make it impossible for them to find remunerative labor. To these unfortunate citizens aid must be extended by Government, not as a matter of charity, but as a matter of social duty.

It is true beyond question that aid must be and will be given in large measure through the agencies of private contributions; and in normal times these contributions should be regarded as sufficient to meet normal conditions. ...

I would not be appearing before you today if these were normal times. When, however, a condition arises which calls for measures of relief over and beyond the ability of private and local assistance to meet—even with the usual aid added by the State—it is time for the State itself to do its additional share.

A MESSAGE TO CONGRESS, 1935
The Federal government must and shall quit this business of relief.

I am not willing that the vitality of our people be further sapped by the giving of cash, of market baskets, of a few hours of weekly work cutting grass, raking leaves or picking up papers in the public parks. We must preserve not only the bodies of the unemployed from destitution [poverty] but also their self-respect, their self-reliance and courage and determination. This decision brings me to the problem of what the government should do with approximately five million unemployed now on the relief rolls [lists].

About one million and a half of these belong to the group which in the past was dependent upon local welfare efforts. Most of them are unable for one reason or another to maintain themselves independently—for the most part, through no fault of their own. Such people, in the days before the great depression, were cared

This message was delivered when Roosevelt dealt with the Depression as governor of New York.

"Remunerative labor" is work for which one is paid.

Franklin D. Roosevelt: Selected Speeches, Messages, Press Conferences, and Letters, edited by Basil Rauch, pp. 134-135.

President Roosevelt delivered this speech when the New Deal had been in effect for three years. He refers here to the emergency relief programs for giving people food and work.

for by local efforts—by states, by counties, by towns, by cities, by churches and by private welfare agencies. It is my thought that in the future they must be cared for as they were before. I stand ready through my own personal efforts, and through the public influence of the office that I hold, to help these local agencies to get the means necessary to assume this burden. . . .

There are however an additional three and one half million employable people who are on relief. With them the problem is different and the responsibility is different. This group was the victim of a nationwide depression caused by conditions which were not local but national. The Federal government is the only governmental agency with sufficient power and credit to meet this situation. We have assumed this task and we shall not shrink from it in the future. It is a duty dictated by every intelligent consideration of national policy to ask you to make it possible for the United States to give employment to all of these three and one half million employable people now on relief, pending their absorption in a rising tide of private employment.

FIRST INAUGURAL ADDRESS, 1933

. . . Our Constitution is so simple and practical that it is possible always to meet extraordinary needs by changes in emphasis and arrangement without loss of essential form. . . .

It is to be hoped that the normal balance of executive and legislative authority may be wholly adequate to meet the unprecedented task before us. But it may be that an unprecedented demand and need for undelayed action may call for temporary departure from that normal balance of public procedure.

I am prepared under my constitutional duty to recommend the measures that a stricken nation in the midst of a stricken world may require. These measures, or such other measures as the Congress may build out of its experience and wisdom, I shall seek, within my constitutional authority, to bring to speedy adoption.

But in the event that the Congress shall fail to take one of these two courses, and in the event that the national emergency is still critical, I shall not evade the clear course of duty that will then confront me. I shall ask Congress for the one remaining instrument to meet the crisis—broad Executive power to wage a war against the emergency, as great as the power that would be given to me if we were in fact invaded by a foreign foe. . . .

A CAMPAIGN SPEECH IN SAN FRANCISCO, 1932

Every man has a right to life; and this means that he has also a right to make a comfortable living. . . . We have no actual famine

Franklin D. Roosevelt: Selected Speeches, Messages, Press Conferences, and Letters, edited by Basil Rauch, p. 94.

Franklin D. Roosevelt: Selected Speeches, Messages, Press Conferences, and Letters, edited by Basil Rauch, pp. 83-85.

. . . our industrial and agricultural mechanism can produce enough and to spare. Our government . . . owes to every one an avenue to possess himself of a portion of that plenty sufficient for his needs, through his own work.

Every man has a right to his own property; which means a right to be assured . . . in the safety of his savings. By no other means can men carry the burdens of those parts of life which, in the nature of things, afford no chance of labor; childhood, sickness, old age. . . . If, in accord with this principle, we must restrict the operations of the speculator, the manipulator, even the financier, I believe we must accept the restriction as needful, not to hamper individualism but to protect it.

. . . [The] responsible heads of finance and industry . . . must, where necessary, sacrifice this or that private advantage; and . . . seek a general advantage. It is here that formal government—political government, if you choose, comes in. Whenever . . . the lone wolf, the unethical competitor, the reckless promoter . . . declines to join in achieving an end recognized as being for the public welfare . . . the government may properly be asked to apply restraint. Likewise, should the group ever use its collective power contrary to the public welfare, the government must be swift to enter and protect the public interest.

An "unethical" competitor is one who does not follow the principles of conduct governing the group with which he deals.

The government should assume the function of economic regulation only as a last resort, to be tried only when private initiative, inspired by high responsibility, with such assistance and balance as government can give, has finally failed. As yet there has been no final failure, because there has been no attempt; and I decline to assume that this nation is unable to meet the situation.

. . . We know that individual liberty and individual happiness mean nothing unless both are ordered in the sense that one man's meat is not another man's poison. . . . We know that liberty to do anything which deprives others of . . . elemental rights is outside the protection of any compact; and that government in this regard is the maintenance of a balance, within which every individual may find safety if he wishes it; in which every individual may attain such power as his ability permits, consistent with his assuming the accompanying responsibility. . . .

Faith in America, faith in our tradition of personal responsibility, faith in our institutions, faith in ourselves demands that we recognize the new terms of the old social [contract]. . . .

1. What did Hoover think the federal government should do to help Americans suffering from the Depression?

2. How does Roosevelt think the federal government should help?

3. How can you explain the differences in their approaches?

4. Why did Hoover fear Roosevelt's program?

5. Does Roosevelt answer any of Hoover's objections? Explain.

TWO APPROACHES: HOOVER AND ROOSEVELT

1. How different are the views of Hoover and Roosevelt? Are there any similarities between them?

2. What similarities or differences had you noticed between the programs of the two Presidents? How can you explain this?

3. What do the two men value, or consider important?

4. Whose ideas do you agree with, Roosevelt's or Hoover's? Why?

THE RESULTS

33. Statistics and the New Deal

Earlier you made a judgement about which program would have been more effective in combating the Depression. The following statistics will help you to reach a more definite conclusion. The statistics cover several economic aspects of the period just prior to the Depression and continuing through the 1940's.

THE GROSS NATIONAL PRODUCT*

YEAR	BILLIONS OF DOLLARS (Based on 1957 Dollars)
1925	91.3
1926	97.7
1927	96.3
1928	98.2
1929	104.1
1930	91.1
1931	76.3
1932	58.5
1933	56.0
1934	65.0
1935	72.5
1936	82.7
1937	90.8
1938	85.2
1939	91.6
1940	100.6

*The gross national product is the market value of all goods and services produced and performed in the country.

CONSUMER EXPENDITURES

YEAR	BILLIONS OF DOLLARS
1929	78.9
1930	70.9
1931	61.3
1932	49.3
1933	46.3
1934	51.8
1935	56.2
1936	62.6
1937	67.2
1938	64.6
1939	67.5
1940	71.8

EMPLOYMENT AND UNEMPLOYMENT

YEAR	MILLIONS EMPLOYED	MILLIONS UNEMPLOYED
1929	47.6	1.5
1930	45.5	4.3
1931	42.4	8.0
1932	38.9	12.1
1933	38.7	12.8
1934	40.9	11.3
1935	42.2	10.6
1936	44.4	9.0
1937	46.3	7.7
1938	44.2	10.3
1939	45.7	9.4
1940	47.5	8.1

FARM INCOME AND EMPLOYEE WAGES

YEAR	INCOME OF FARMS IN BILLIONS OF DOLLARS	WAGES PAID TO FARM EMPLOYEES IN DOLLARS PER MONTH (Without Board)
1929	—	51
1930	11.4	48
1931	8.3	38
1932	6.3	29
1933	7.0	25.50
1934	8.5	28
1935	9.6	30
1936	10.7	32
1937	11.3	36.50
1938	10.1	36
1939	10.5	36
1940	11.0	37.50

ELECTRIC POWER USERS

YEAR	% OF FARMERS	% OF NON-FARMERS
1930	10.4	84.8
1935	12.6	83.9
1940	32.6	90.8
1945	48.0	93.0

FEDERAL GOVERNMENT FINANCES IN BILLIONS OF DOLLARS

YEAR	RECEIPTS	EXPENDITURES	DEBT
1929a	4.1	3.2	16.9
1930	4.2	3.4	16.1
1931	3.1	3.6	16.8
1932	1.9	4.7	19.4
1933b	2.1	4.6	22.5
1934	3.1	6.7	27.0
1935	3.7	6.5	28.7
1936	4.1	8.5	33.7
1937	4.9	7.7	36.4
1938	5.6	6.8	37.1
1939c	4.9	8.8	40.4
1940	5.1	9.1	42.9
1941d	7.1	13.2	48.9
1942	12.5	34.1	72.4
1943	21.9	79.4	136.6
1944	43.6	95.1	201.0
1945e	44.5	98.4	258.6

a Depression starts in October.
b F.D.R. takes office in March.
c W W II begins in Europe.
d U.S. enters W W II.
e W W II ends in August.

BANK ASSETS

YEAR	BILLIONS OF DOLLARS
1929	72.3
1930	74.2
1931	70.0
1932	57.2
1933	51.3
1934	55.9
1935	59.9
1936	66.8
1937	68.4
1938	67.7
1939	73.1
1940	79.7

CIVILIAN EMPLOYEES OF THE FEDERAL GOVERNMENT

YEAR	NUMBER IN THOUSANDS
1929	579
1930	601
1931	609
1932	605
1933	603
1934	698
1935	780
1936	867
1937	895
1938	882
1939	953
1940	1,042

NUMBER OF FACTORIES

YEAR	NUMBER
1929	206,663
1931	171,450
1933	139,325
1935	167,916
1937	166,794
1939	173,802

1. According to these statistics, how effective were Hoover's measures? Explain.

2. According to these statistics, what problems of the Depression were affected by the New Deal? Did some problems remain unsolved?

3. Do these statistics confirm or contradict your ideas about the effectiveness of Hoover's and Roosevelt's programs?

THE DEBATE OVER THE NEW DEAL

34. Critics of the New Deal: The Liberty League and Others

During the New Deal, many people criticized the federal government for exercising powers that had previously belonged to state and local governments. They felt that the federal government was becoming too strong. Others criticized New Deal finances. To finance the New Deal, the government spent more money than it received from taxes. Consequently, the budget was unbalanced—that is, there was a debt, or deficit. This is called *deficit spending*. To obtain the money it needed, the government sold bonds: it borrowed from the people with a promise to pay back the price of the bonds plus interest. This is called *deficit financing*.

The labor policies of the New Deal also came under attack. In 1934, a group of industrialists and financiers who disliked the National Labor Relations Act formed the Liberty League to oppose the New Deal.

The following two readings are drawn from among the many criticisms of the New Deal. The first is by Samuel Pettengill, a congressman from Indiana. The second is by Carl Mote, a newspaper editor and lawyer from Indiana.

POINTS TO CONSIDER
How you would define "socialism."
How you would define "communism."
Whether the charges of these two authors are well-founded.

A SOCIALIST PROGRAM: SAMUEL PETTENGILL

Samuel B. Pettengill, Smoke Screen (New York: Southern Publishers, Inc., 1940), pp. 43-44.

The term National Socialism, here, does not refer to Nazism.
A "drone" is a male bee that does no work. He is completely supported by the others.

. . . As National Socialism marches on, we have legislation on the calendar of Congress to impose another billion a year for state medicine and a fifth of a billion a year for federal education. The worker bees are to be further taxed to support the drones. Those who go without to pay their doctor are to be taxed to pay the bills of those who spend six times their average annual doctor's bill for liquor, candy, cosmetics, amusements and gambling.

. . . [Excessive] taxation and the uncertainty of further increases, is making it difficult for free enterprise to expand, or even continue; . . . [It] discourages wealth creation and destroys jobs . . . .

. . . With the exception of the artist, poet, patriot or scientist, who labors for the joy of satisfying an inner hunger, there are, and have always been just two incentives for the creation of wealth, the hope of reward or the lash of the slave.

The hope of reward is the sparkplug of free enterprise. It is the principle of thrift. It is the desire of man to be a man, self-supporting and self-respecting . . . .

Because the Constitution of the United States is wrapped around this principle of reward for individual effort our form of government is the negation of National Socialism. The Federal government was given only specific powers, mostly to regulate and police. It was never intended by our fathers for the Federal Government to undertake business enterprise as such. That power was one of the great powers "reserved to the people."

An attack, therefore, upon the savings of honest thrift and the *principle of thrift,* is an attack upon the American form of government itself. . . .

A COMMUNIST PROGRAM: CARL MOTE

Carl H. Mote, The New Deal Goose Step (New York: Daniel Ryerson, Inc., 1939), pp. iii, vii, 227-228.

. . . [The purpose of] the New Deal [is] to attain a socialized state and the abolition of the private ownership of property. . . .

The similarities in the program of the Communists, as prescribed by Marx, Engels, Lenin and their disciples in America, and in the program of the New Deal have been pointed out again and again.

Lenin emphasized housing "workers" free and at half cost and the New Deal already has provided housing on a vast scale at half cost or even less . . .

Lenin stressed the sins of "monopoly" and the evils of "bigness" in business and industry. The New Deal's assault on business and industry began with the NRA and has continued with practically no breathing spells to the present moment. . . . The ceaseless assault by the New Deal bureaucracy on "monopolies," on "Capitalism," on Economic Royalists, on private business, on bankers, industrialists, public utility managers, physicians, lawyers, is merely an American adaptation of the Marxian formula for the promotion of the "class struggle. . . ."

The recreation and amusement sections of the WPA, the Federal theatre project of the WPA and the system evolved for feeding, clothing and housing the multitude, particularly just before elections, had their genesis [beginning] in the political economy of Greece and Rome in the last days when tyrants competed for the favor of the masses . . .

Karl Marx, Friedrich Engels, and Vladimir Lenin were the founders of modern communism.

The "Federal theatre project" gave employment to actors, directors, playwrights, and scene designers.

35. A Defense of the New Deal: James MacGregor Burns

James MacGregor Burns, chairman of the department of political science at William College, has written many books on the subject of political science. The following reading is from his book, *Roosevelt: The Lion and the Fox.*

The most agonized reply [to charges that the New Deal was socialistic] came from no New Dealer but from a tall handsome Socialist leader . . . The New Deal was socialism? cried Norman Thomas over the radio . . . Emphatically not. Roosevelt had not carried out the Socialist platform—except on a stretcher. One by one Thomas ticked off the New Deal reforms. The banks? Roosevelt had put them on their feet and turned them back to the bankers. Holding company legislation? True Socialists would nationalize holding companies, not try to break them up. Social security? The Roosevelt act was a weak imitation of a real program. The NRA? It was an elaborate scheme for stabilizing capitalism [making it steady] through associations of industries that could regulate production in order to maintain profits. The AAA? Essentially a capitalist scheme to subsidize scarcity. TVA? State capitalism. CCC? Forced labor.

James MacGregor Burns, **Roosevelt: The Lion and the Fox** (New York: Harcourt, Brace & World, Inc., 1956), pp. 242-243. © 1956 by James MacGregor Burns. Simplified and reprinted by permission of Harcourt, Brace & World, Inc.
Norman Thomas was the Socialist party candidate for President from 1924 to 1948.

A "holding company" is a company that holds stock in various corporations and thereby controls those corporations. It does not produce goods or services itself.

"To subsidize" something means to support it with a grant of money. Thomas refers here to the New Deal policy of paying farmers to keep their crops small. The government did this so that farm prices would go up. Socialists like Thomas believe that capitalism does not work. Thomas was arguing that the government was "subsidizing society" so that capitalism would appear to work.

701

Roosevelt's slogan was not the Socialist cry, "Workers of the world, unite," Thomas proclaimed. Roosevelt's cry was "Workers and small stockholders unite, clean up Wall Street." And that cry was at least as old as Andrew Jackson. . . .

. . . [As] ideological analysis, Thomas's answer was beyond dispute. If socialism had any coherent meaning, it meant the vesting of the ownership and control of capital, land, and industry in the whole community. With the exception of TVA, nothing important in the New Deal was of this description. . . .

Roosevelt, like major party leaders before him, had no compunction [regret] about plucking popular planks from the Socialist party platform—planks such as unemployment compensation and public housing. But he spurned [rejected] the central concept of socialization. . . . [In] 1933 he probably could have won congressional assent to the socialization of both banking and railroads, but he never tried. He wanted to reform capitalism, not destroy it. And in this sense he was a conservative. . . .

And the Communists? During Roosevelt's first two years they denounced his program as a capitalist ruse [trick], as fascism disguised in milk-and-water liberalism. "The 'New Deal' of Roosevelt," proclaimed a party resolution in 1934, "is the aggressive effort of the bankers and trusts to find a way out of the crisis at the expense of the million of toilers. . . ."

FEDERAL POWER AND FREEDOM

1. Compare Hoover's and Roosevelt's philosophies regarding the role of government in the lives of individuals. Do they have any similar goals? On what issues do they differ?
2. How do the values of Hoover and Roosevelt compare with the values of earlier Americans? Do you think either man departs from American values? Explain.
3. Is individual freedom in danger when the federal government assumes more power? Explain the basis of your answer. When forming your answer, did you consider the Constitution and the historical development of the federal government?
4. Might an individual be in danger when the federal government does not assume responsibility in some area? Explain. Can you cite any examples?
5. Formulate a hypothesis about the role of the federal government in protecting or endangering freedom of the individual. Explain the reasons for your statements.

BIBLIOGRAPHY

*ALLEN, FREDERICK LEWIS. ONLY YESTERDAY. New York: Harper & Row, Publishers, 1931; reissued 1957. †New York: Perennial Library, 1964.
A lively social history of the decade following World War I. The author vividly recalls not only the world of politics and fashion, but also the crazes and absurdities of the time.

THE AMERICAN HERITAGE HISTORY OF WORLD WAR I. New York: Simon and Schuster, Inc., 1964.
A colorful and detailed look at World War I. It describes and analyzes the origins, course, and immediate aftermath of the colossal conflict.

CONSIDINE, BOB, AND TED W. LAWSON. THIRTY SECONDS OVER TOKYO. New York: Random House, Inc., 1953.
A firsthand account of the bombing of Tokyo during World War II.

*FREIDEL, FRANK. THE SPLENDID LITTLE WAR. Boston: Little, Brown and Company, 1958.
Using the hundreds of pictures and drawings made on the spot, the author gives a pictorial history of the Spanish-American War. He also makes use of accounts by people who were there at the time.

GROFF, ROBERT, AND ROBERT EMMETT GINNA. FDR. New York: Harper & Row, Publishers, 1962.
A moving book that captures in words and pictures the personality of Franklin D. Roosevelt and evokes the mood of the times in which he was President of the United States.

HORAN, JAMES D. THE DESPERATE YEARS. New York: Crown Publishers, Inc., 1962.
Horan presents the story of the grim decade between 1929 and 1939. At the same time, he depicts the creativity and the sense of fun that sustained the American spirit.

PEARE, CATHERINE OWENS. THE FDR STORY. New York: Thomas Y. Crowell Company, 1962.
Peare writes an excellent biography of Franklin Roosevelt as a private and public figure, as well as a history of the time in which he lived.

*SULZBERGER, C. L. AND THE EDITORS OF AMERICAN HERITAGE. THE AMERICAN HERITAGE PICTURE HISTORY OF WORLD WAR II. New York: American Heritage Publishing Co., 1966.
A fine pictorial and narrative account of the major events of World War II.

*Denotes more advanced reading.
†Denotes paperback edition.

TIME LINE

	DOMESTIC EVENTS	FOREIGN EVENTS
1898	THE BATTLESHIP, *MAINE*, IS SUNK.	SPANISH-AMERICAN WAR IS FOUGHT.
1901	PRESIDENT McKINLEY IS ASSASSINATED. THEODORE ROOSEVELT BECOMES PRESIDENT.	
1902	END OF CUBAN OCCUPATION.	
1903	RECOGNITION OF PANAMA'S INDEPENDENCE. HAY-BUNAU-VARILLA TREATY.	PANAMA REVOLTS AGAINST COLOMBIA.
1904	ROOSEVELT COROLLARY.	
1907	U.S. NAVAL FLEET CRUISES AROUND THE WORLD FOR THE FIRST TIME.	

1911		REBELLION IN MEXICO.
1912	WOODROW WILSON IS ELECTED PRESIDENT.	BALKAN WAR.
1914		PANAMA CANAL IS OPENED. PANAMA CANAL TOLLS CONTROVERSY. WORLD WAR I BEGINS.
1915	MARINES LAND IN HAITI.	*LUSITANIA* IS SUNK.
1916	MILITARY OCCUPATION OF DOMINICAN REPUBLIC.	
1917	UNITED STATES ENTERS WORLD WAR I. VIRGIN ISLANDS PURCHASED.	ZIMMERMANN NOTE. GERMANS BEGIN UNRESTRICTED WARFARE. BOLSHEVIKS SEIZE POWER IN RUSSIA.
1918	WILSON ANNOUNCES HIS FOURTEEN POINTS.	RUSSIA MAKES SEPARATE PEACE TREATY WITH GERMANY. FIGHTING ENDS IN EUROPE.
1919	SENATE REJECTS PEACE TREATY.	WORLD WAR I OFFICIALLY ENDS WITH SIGNING OF THE TREATY OF VERSAILLES.
1920	NINETEENTH AMENDMENT GIVES WOMEN THE RIGHT TO VOTE. PROHIBITION BEGINS. WARREN HARDING IS ELECTED PRESIDENT.	LEAGUE OF NATIONS ESTABLISHED.
1923	HARDING DIES. CALVIN COOLIDGE BECOMES PRESIDENT.	
1928	HERBERT HOOVER IS ELECTED PRESIDENT.	
1929	STOCK MARKET CRASHES.	KELLOGG-BRIAND PACT SIGNED BY SIXTY-TWO NATIONS. RENOUNCES WAR AS A MEANS TO SETTLE PROBLEMS.
1932	FRANKLIN ROOSEVELT IS ELECTED PRESIDENT.	
1933	THE NEW DEAL BEGINS. PROHIBITION ENDS.	ADOLF HITLER BECOMES CHANCELLOR OF GERMANY. GERMANY QUITS THE LEAGUE OF NATIONS.
1935		LEAGUE OF NATIONS ENACTS SANCTIONS AGAINST ITALY FOR AGGRESSION IN ETHIOPIA.
1936	ROOSEVELT RE-ELECTED BY A LANDSLIDE.	SPANISH CIVIL WAR BEGINS. ITALY AND GERMANY FORM A MILITARY ALLIANCE.
1938		HITLER TAKES OVER AUSTRIA. GREAT BRITAIN, FRANCE, AND GERMANY SIGN THE MUNICH PACT GIVING GERMANY PART OF CZECHOSLOVAKIA.
1939	ROOSEVELT DECLARES A LIMITED NATIONAL EMERGENCY DUE TO WORLD CONDITIONS.	GERMANY INVADES POLAND. WORLD WAR II BEGINS. GERMANY, ITALY, AND JAPAN FORM AN ALLIANCE.
1940	ROOSEVELT RE-ELECTED FOR A THIRD TERM.	
1941	JAPANESE BOMB PEARL HARBOR. UNITED STATES DECLARES WAR.	
1944	ROOSEVELT RE-ELECTED.	D-DAY, ALLIES INVADE FRANCE.
1945	ROOSEVELT DIES. HARRY TRUMAN SUCCEEDS HIM AS PRESIDENT. ATOMIC BOMBS DROPPED ON JAPAN.	WORLD WAR II ENDS. UNITED NATIONS IS ORGANIZED.

704

unit IX
FACING
A NEW ERA 1945-

And so, my fellow Americans, ask not what your country can do for you: Ask what you can do for your country.

My fellow citizens of the world: Ask not what America will do for you, but what together we can do for the freedom of man.

JOHN F. KENNEDY
INAUGURAL ADDRESS, 1961

INTRODUCTION

This unit contains materials dealing with the post-World War II era in United States history. That is, it contains sources about the period from 1945 to the present. The first section explores the characteristics of the American people today. The second section is about the relationship between the federal government and state and local governments. The third section focuses on civil rights. Finally, there is a section which examines the problems of American foreign policy today. This section concludes with a study of some of the major issues about United States involvement in Vietnam.

At the end of the unit you will find a list of definitions of history. As you study them, determine which, if any, you would accept. Tell why you would accept or reject each. Then write your own definition of history. You may want to compare this definition with the one you wrote when you began your study of this course, or the one you wrote when you finished studying the exploration period in Unit I.

Unlike the other units in *Discovering American History,* this one includes no questions or "Points to Consider" along with the readings. Here it is up to you to think of the questions. By asking the right questions, you should be able to (1) criticize the documents, (2) determine if previous issues in American history re-emerged in the post-war era, and (3) interpret the information you find. Your job in this unit is thus very similar to the situation you will face when you read something outside of school. There, too, you will have no teacher or book to ask you questions. Your ability to use what you read will depend on your own ability to ask good questions.

Before you begin your study of Unit IX, you may find it useful to look at the following list. The questions in the list will help you to ask good questions about the documents in this unit and to evaluate your questions. Answer some of the questions you find here, such as numbers 1-5 and 7-8, right now. Keep the others in mind and refer to them later on.

ASKING QUESTIONS

1. What questions can you ask about the period from 1945 to the present *before* reading Unit IX?

2. Did your classmates ask similar questions? Different questions? If so, how can you account for this?

3. Would you ask these questions in every investigation? Why or why not?

4. Would someone from a different country or culture ask the same questions? Explain.

5. How, then, do you know you are asking the "right" questions?

6. After you examined the topics in this unit, how many of your questions were answered? What new questions can you now ask? Why didn't you ask them before? How do your new questions compare with those of your classmates? How can you account for this?

EVALUATING DOCUMENTS

7. What questions can you ask about the documents? Would you ask different questions about cartoons, charts, maps, paintings, time lines, primary sources, and secondary sources? If so, what?

8. Why should you ask these questions?

DETECTING PREVIOUS THEMES IN AMERICAN HISTORY

9. What issues that were important during the past are also major issues in this period? For example, is the role of government in a democratic society still a topic of controversy?

10. What specific problems or situations have caused these issues to reappear?

11. Do these problems and situations resemble events in previous periods of American history?

12. Review in your mind some of the events of earlier periods. Do these events suggest to you any additional questions about the period 1945 to the present?

INTERPRETING THIS PERIOD

13. How do you interpret this period in history?

14. Why do you interpret it that way?

I. The American Today

1. "Can I Have ...?"

Every spring during school vacations, large numbers of high school and college students descend on Fort Lauderdale in Florida. Their stay has at times been marked by riots.

"Pop, can I have four hundred dollars to go to Fort Lauderdale and run wild?"

2. The American Family Income

The chart below is based on figures compiled by the Bureau of the Census. The average family income in each year is known as the *median* income. Families with incomes below $3,000 are said to be in the "poverty bracket."

AMERICAN FAMILY INCOME, 1959–1964

FAMILY INCOME	1964	1963	1962	1961	1960	1959
UNDER $1,000	3.2%	3.8%	4.2%	5.0%	5.0%	5.1%
$1,000 TO $1,999	6.3%	6.8%	7.4%	7.7%	8.0%	8.3%
$2,000 TO $2,999	8.1%	7.9%	8.3%	8.7%	8.7%	9.3%
$3,000 TO $3,999	8.4%	8.7%	9.2%	9.4%	9.8%	10.1%
$4,000 TO $4,999	8.6%	9.0%	9.9%	10.5%	10.5%	11.7%
$5,000 TO $5,999	9.9%	11.1%	11.5%	11.7%	12.9%	13.2%
$6,000 TO $6,999	9.9%	10.2%	10.9%	10.2%	10.8%	11.0%
$7,000 TO $7,999	9.3%	9.1%	8.6%	9.1%	8.7%	8.4%
$8,000 TO $9,999	13.9%	13.4%	12.3%	11.6%	11.3%	10.6%
$10,000 TO $14,999	16.2%	14.5%	12.8%	11.3%	10.6%	9.1%
$15,000 TO $24,999	5.2%	4.4%	4.0%	3.6%	2.8%	2.4%
$25,000 AND OVER	1.1%	1.0%	0.9%	1.1%	0.9%	0.7%
MEDIAN FAMILY INCOME *	$6,569	$6,249	$5,956	$5,737	$5,620	$5,417
TOTAL NUMBER OF FAMILIES ...	47,835,000	47,436,000	46,998,000	46,341,000	45,435,000	45,062,000

*Median family income jumped 21.3% from 1959 to 1964. However, purchasing power increased only 4%.

COMPARISON OF WHITE AND NEGRO FAMILY INCOMES, 1964

	WHITE	NEGRO
MEDIAN FAMILY INCOME	$7,720	$5,184
PER CENT OF INCOMES BELOW $3,000	15.4%	37%
PER CENT OF INCOMES OVER $10,000		8.3%

3. Aspects of American Culture: John Steinbeck

John Steinbeck is a twentieth-century American writer. *Travels with Charley* is an account of Steinbeck's journey across the continent in a pickup truck, accompanied by his poodle, Charley. The first two passages below contain Steinbeck's reflections on certain features of American life. In the third selection, Steinbeck tells about a conversation he had with a garage mechanic and his wife who were living in a mobile home, or trailer.

Civilization

... I had neglected my own country too long. Civilization had made great strides in my absence. I remember when a coin in a slot would get you a stick of gum or a candy bar, but in these dining palaces were vending machines where various coins could deliver handkerchiefs, comb-and-nail-file sets, hair conditioners and cosmetics, first-aid kits, minor drugs such as aspirin ... pills to keep you awake. I found myself entranced with these gadgets. Suppose you want a soft drink; you pick your kind—Sungrape or Cooly Cola—press a button, insert the coin, and stand back.

John Steinbeck, **Travels With Charley, In Search of America** (New York: The Viking Press, Inc., 1961), pp. 82-83, 86, 91-92. Copyright © 1961, 1962 by The Curtis Publishing Company, copyright © 1962 by John Steinbeck. Reprinted by permission of The Viking Press, Inc.

A paper cup drops into place, the drink pours out and stops a quarter of an inch from the brim—a cold, refreshing drink guaranteed synthetic [artificial]. Coffee is even more interesting, for when the hot black fluid has ceased, a squirt of milk comes down and an envelope of sugar drops beside the cup. But of all, the hot-soup machine is the triumph. Choose among ten—pea, chicken noodle, beef and [vegetable], insert the coin. A rumbling hum comes from the giant and a sign lights up that reads "Heating." After a minute a red light flashes on and off until you open a little door and remove the paper cup of boiling-hot soup.

It is life at a peak of some kind of civilization. . . .

The Passing of Local Speech

By "localness," Steinbeck means the individuality of different places.

. . . It seemed to me [in my travels] that regional speech is in the process of disappearing, not gone but going. Forty years of radio and twenty years of television must have this impact. Communications must destroy localness, by a slow, inevitable process. I can remember a time when I could almost pinpoint a man's place of origin by his speech. That is growing more difficult now and will in some foreseeable future become impossible. It is a rare house or building that is not rigged with spiky combers of the air. Radio and television speech becomes standardized, perhaps better English than we have ever used. Just as our bread, mixed and baked, packaged and sold without benefit of accident or human frailty [weakness], is uniformly good and uniformly tasteless, so will our speech become one speech.

Roots: A Conversation with Trailer Residents

. . . [After] dinner . . . I brought up a question that had puzzled me. These were good, thoughtful, intelligent people. I said, "One of our most treasured feelings concerns roots, growing up rooted in some soil or some community." How did they feel about raising their children without roots? . . .

"Tuscany" is in northwestern Italy.

The father, a good-looking, fair-skinned man with dark eyes, answered me. "How many people today have what you are talking about? What roots are there in an apartment twelve floors up? What roots are in a housing development of hundreds and thousands of small dwellings almost exactly alike? My father came from Italy," he said. "He grew up in Tuscany in a house where his family had lived maybe a thousand years. That's roots for you, no running water, no toilet, and they cooked with charcoal or vine clippings. They had just two rooms, a kitchen and a bedroom where everybody slept, grandpa, father and all the

710

kids, no place to read, no place to be alone, and never had had. Was that better? I bet if you gave my old man the choice he'd cut his roots and live like this." He waved his hands at the comfortable room. "Fact is, he cut his roots away and came to America. Then he lived in a tenement in New York—just one room, walk-up, cold water and no heat. . . ."

"Don't you miss some kind of permanence?"

"Who's got permanence? Factory closes down, you move on. Good times and things opening up, you move on where it's better. You got roots you sit and starve. You take the pioneers in the history books. They were movers. Take up land, sell it, move on. I read in a book how Lincoln's family came to Illinois on a raft. They had some barrels of whisky for a bank account. How many kids in America stay in the place where they were born, if they can get out?"

" . . . [Suppose] the place I work goes broke. I got to move where there's a job. I get to my job in three minutes. You want I should drive twenty miles because I got roots?"

4. The American and Leisure

Business Week 1953

. . . [There] seems to be a major trend away from passive, crowd amusements toward active pursuits that people can carry on independently. . . .

Business Week, No. 1254 (1953), pp. 142, 145.

[The average man] can, in his spare time, dig in his garden [with a motorized tool], fly across the Atlantic, go swimming in a plastic pool, fish in the Adirondacks, ski in Sun Valley, winter in Florida, hear chamber music on his hi-fi phonograph, look at Cinerama, make a coffee table [with an electric saw], read a 35¢ edition of Shakespeare. The National Recreation [Association] distinguishes no less than 81 different organized activities offered by U.S. municipal parks. [One] hobby expert . . . has figured that there are some 200 recognizable "creative activities" in the U.S. today.

All of this has been wonderful for business, even if it does cut across an ingrained American puritanism that compels belief in work for work's sake.

"Puritanism" refers to values which were first brought to America by the Puritans. Since Puritans felt that idleness led to evil, they insisted that people keep busy with work almost all the time.

Russell Baker is a columnist whose comments often appear in *The New York Times.*

To "cajole" is to coax. To "badger" is to nag. To "blackguard" is to insult and scold.

"Ghost writers" are authors who write books, speeches, etc., for someone else. The ghost writer's name does not appear on his work.

RUSSELL BAKER, 1965

Every once in a while it is important to do nothing. . . .

Nothing is harder to do. Some puritan perversity [stubborn twist] in the American character makes us hate the nothing-doers of the world. A man quietly doing nothing is a challenge to the American system. He must be cajoled, badgered and, if necessary, blackguarded into purposeful living.

If a man inherits millions, it is thought disgraceful if he devotes them to a lifetime of doing nothing. He is expected to run for President. You see them all over the map, these wretched millionaires, wasting perfectly good fortunes on billboards, ghost writers and campaign planes, and slapping backs up and down the countryside. All because of the American hatred for doing nothing. Their wives work donut machines and nag people to give blood on their lunch hours. The tradition runs from top to bottom of the society. As the working stiff gets more and more leisure, he is urged to put it to hard use. On weekends, instead of dozing in a hammock, he will be found in his cellar doing cabinet carpentry, or perspiring through open fields trying to knock a ball into a hole in the ground.

The idea of using good time to do nothing offends the community. Go to a vacation spa [resort], ostensibly [apparently] devoted to the doing of nothing, and the social pressures to undertake strenuous activity are overwhelming. Tense gentlemen smelling of gymnasiums accost [approach] you over the hedge.

"What are you doing?"

"I am lying in the grass."

"Getting a suntan, eh?"

"No. When I laid [lay] down here, the hedge was shading me, but the sun has moved now and it's too much bother to get up."

"Just lying in the grass?" By this time, the inquisitor's voice will have taken on [a] slight edge of vicious hostility . . . "What are you lying in the grass for? . . . I see. Vacationing. Play golf?" And the interrogation [questioning] becomes uncomfortable. People who do not play golf are expected to play tennis or squash. Afternoons, they are expected to sail or churn around in motorboats. People who don't do any of these things are expected to fish. All these can be gratifying pastimes in their place, but they have nothing whatsoever to do with doing nothing. . . .

712

So, there you are, lying in the grass doing nothing but feeling the ants crawl up your cowlick or, at night, counting stars in the Milky Way, and word of it spreads all over the community. People call you up and offer to lend their tennis racquet, or drive by and suggest that you ought to go deep sea fishing with them and fight the big ones.

People lying in the grass doing nothing put the whole community on edge. All that idleness—it is like having an infection in the neighborhood. People talk about it. "Doesn't do anything at all, you say?"..."Must be some kind of nut...."

5. Our Younger Citizens

DRAWING BY BARNEY TOBEY; © 1967 THE NEW YORKER MAGAZINE, INC.

John Cogley, "All the Sad Young Men," **Commonweal**, Vol. LXII, no. 13 (1955), p. 326.

Commonweal is a weekly literary magazine.

6. The Youth of the 1950's

They know what they want and they are dogged [insistent] about getting it. They don't want either revolution or reaction. They want security and anyone who talks to them about security—whether it be economic, social or political—is sure to win their attention.

They might be the dullest generation in a long time and they have the faults of their qualities: the passion for security can lead to a creeping conformism [sameness]. But if you watch them playing with their babies in the suburbs or poring over the latest issue of *Fortune* [a business magazine] you realize that they are a wholesome, amazingly contented group—perhaps a bit too contented.

7. The College Student of the 1960's

The American Council on Education is composed of representatives of various educational institutions. One of its functions is to gather and organize information and opinions about educational problems. It also studies legislation affecting education. The following article, reporting the results of one of the council's studies, was written by Art Seidenbaum, a columnist.

Art Seidenbaum, " 'National Norm' succeeds Betty Coed, Joe College," Copyright 1967, Los Angeles Times. Reprinted by permission.

"National Norm" refers to the average student.

The American Council on Education went searching through the freshman classes of 252 schools last year in a relentless effort to identify National Norm by background, aspiration [goal], personality traits and private habits.

All the entering freshmen at all the participating colleges and universities were asked to reply to a questionnaire that included such public information as their high school grades and such private intelligence as whether they frequently try on clothes without buying them.

In many areas, the National Norms that emerge are wholly unsurprising. One is not supposed to be astonished that more than half of the [students questioned] earned B's (plus or minus) in high school, that 80 per cent of the freshmen attended public secondary schools, that most of them plan to do some form of graduate work toward an advanced degree.

The parents of the National Norms turn out to be a little poorer, a little less educated than one might have expected. For instance, nearly 60 per cent of the freshmen said their parents' total income was between $6000 and $15,000 a year. And 47 per cent of the students put their parents in a $4000 to $10,000 bracket.

Norm's mothers and fathers, most of them, graduated from high school. But only 28 per cent of the fathers and 20 per cent of the mothers completed college.

The questionnaire posed a list of 17 possible "objectives considered to be essential or very important." Four choices were selected by a majority of Norms: "Help others in difficulty," "Be an authority in my field," "Keep up with political affairs" and "Succeed in my own business."

Significantly, a mere 41 per cent of the Norms chose "be very well-off financially," apparently indicating that social concern and professional expertise are now the way students measure and describe themselves. Bank accounts are less important parts of the story. . . .

A mere 17.2 per cent participated in demonstrations of any kind.

A paltry [mere] 14.4 per cent smoked cigarets with frequency, which may be testimony to the growing effectiveness of medical warnings (or the trend toward new, more mysterious crutches in the emerging culture).

A modest 19.7 per cent confessed to having cribbed on an examination. Whether that means there's more honesty abroad in the land or more dishonesty in answering questionnaires is not clear.

National Norm isn't much of a drinker, gambler or even movie-goer (less than half of the freshmen allowed [admitted] to having attended films with frequency).

He does vote in student elections (73.3 per cent of him), does go to church and attends public concerts (in identical 69.9 per cent amounts).

Not such a bad guy, once you get to know him . . .

8. Political Opinions

OBSERVATIONS BY JOHN STEINBECK

I had been keen [eager] to hear what people thought politically. Those whom I had met did not talk about the subject, didn't seem to want to talk about it. It seemed to me partly caution and partly a lack of interest, but strong opinions were just not stated. One storekeeper did admit to me that he had to do business with both sides and could not permit himself the luxury of an opinion.

John Steinbeck, **Travels With Charley, In Search of America** (New York: The Viking Press, Inc., 1961), pp. 128-129. Copyright © 1961, 1962 by the Curtis Publishing Company, copyright © 1962 by John Steinbeck. Reprinted by permission of The Viking Press, Inc.

He was a graying man in a little gray store, a crossroads place where I stopped for a box of dog biscuits and a can of pipe tobacco. This man, this store might have been anywhere in the nation, but actually it was back in Minnesota. The man had a kind of gray wistful twinkle in his eyes as though he remembered humor when it was against the law, so that I dared go out on a limb. I said, "It looks then as though the natural contentiousness [argumentativeness] of people had died. But I don't believe that. It'll just take another channel. Can you think, sir, of what that channel might be? . . ."

I was not wrong, the twinkle was there, the precious, humorous twinkle. "Well, sir," he said, "we've got a murder now and then, or we can read about them. Then we've got the World Series. You can raise a wind any time over the Pirates or the Yankees, but I guess the best of all is we've got the Russians. . . ."

. . . Hardly a day goes by somebody doesn't take a belt at the Russians. . . ."

I asked, "Anybody know any Russians around here?"

And now he went all out and laughed. "Course not. That's why they're valuable. Nobody can find fault with you if you take out after the Russians."

"Because we're not doing business with them?"

He picked up a cheese knife from the counter and carefully ran his thumb along the edge and laid the knife down. "Maybe that's it. By George, maybe that's it. We're not doing business."

"You think then we might be using the Russians as an outlet for something else, for other things."

"I didn't think that at all, sir, but I bet I'm going to. Why I remember when people took everything out on Mr. Roosevelt. Andy Larsen got red in the face about Roosevelt one time when his hens got the croup. Yes, sir," he said with growing enthusiasm, "those Russians got quite a load to carry. Man has a fight with his wife, he belts the Russians."

"Maybe everybody needs Russians. I'll bet even in Russia they need Russians. Maybe they call it Americans."

He cut a sliver of cheese from a wheel and held it out to me on the knife blade. "You've given me something to think about in a sneaking kind of way.

". . . Know what I'm going to do? Next time Andy Larsen comes in red in the face, I'm going to see if the Russians are bothering his hens. It was a great loss to Andy when Mr. Roosevelt died."

DRAWING BY DONALD REILLY; © 1967 THE NEW YORKER MAGAZINE, INC.

"I'm afraid I have no opinion at the moment. All my journals of opinion have been late this week."

9. Conformism: Henry Steele Commager

Henry Steele Commager, a renowned twentieth-century historian, is a professor at Amherst College.

. . . [If] our democracy is to flourish it must have criticism, if our government is to function it must have dissent. Only totalitarian governments insist upon conformity and they—as we know— do so at their peril. Without criticism abuses will go unrebuked; without dissent our dynamic system will become static. The

Henry Steele Commager, "Who Is Loyal to America," **Harper's Magazine,** Vol. CXCV, no. 1168 (1947), pp. 198-199.
A "totalitarian" government is one led by a single party or group which attempts to prevent opposition from forming. The duties of the citizen to the state are stressed.

American people have a stake in the maintenance of the most thorough-going inquisition into American institutions. They have a stake in nonconformity, for they know that the American genius is nonconformist. They have a stake in experimentation of the most radical character, for they know that only those who prove [test] all things can hold fast that which is good.

It is easier to say what loyalty is not than to say what it is. It is not conformity. It is not passive acquiescence in [acceptance of] the status quo [the existing situation]. It is not preference for everything American over everything foreign. It is not an ostrich-like ignorance of other countries and other institutions. It is not the indulgence in ceremony—a flag salute, an oath of allegiance, a fervid [passionate] verbal declaration. It is not a particular creed, a particular version of history, a particular body of economic practices, a particular philosophy.

It is a tradition, an ideal, and a principle. It is a willingness to subordinate every private advantage for the larger good. It is an appreciation of the rich and diverse contributions that can come from the most varied sources. It is allegiance to the traditions that have guided our greatest statesmen and inspired our most eloquent poets—the traditions of freedom, equality, democracy, tolerance, the tradition of the higher law, of experimentation, cooperation, and pluralism. It is a realization that America was born of revolt, flourished on dissent, [and] became great through experimentation.

Independence was an act of revolution; republicanism was something new under the sun; the federal system was a vast experimental laboratory. Physically Americans were pioneers; in the realm of social and economic institutions, too, their tradition has been one of pioneering. From the beginning, intellectual and spiritual diversity have been as characteristic of America as racial and linguistic [differences]. . . . From the beginning Americans have known that there were new worlds to conquer, new truths to be discovered. Every effort to confine Americanism to a single pattern, to constrain it to a single formula, is disloyalty to everything that is valid in Americanism.

"Pluralism" exists when a society allows people with different backgrounds and beliefs to live together.

II. Federalism

10. A New Era?

In the United States, power is divided between the national government and the state governments. This system is known as federalism. The readings in this section deal with current debate about which tasks the national or federal government should assume, and which tasks should be left to the states.

"IT'S MORE THAN WE'VE PUT OUT BEFORE"

© 1966 HERBLOCK IN THE WASHINGTON POST

11. The War on Poverty: Lyndon Johnson

After the assassination of President John Kennedy in November 1963, Vice-President Lyndon Johnson succeeded to the Presidency. When Johnson had been in office for about a year, he declared that he would wage a "War on Poverty." The next two selections explain this program. The first is from Johnson's inaugural address of 1965. The second, which outlines the program, is from the 1964 State of the Union Message.

The New York Times, Jan. 21, 1965.

The New York Times, Jan. 9, 1964.

A LAND OF CONTRASTS

In a land of great wealth, families must not live in hopeless poverty. In a land rich in harvest, children just must not go hungry. In a land of healing miracles, neighbors must not suffer and die untended. In a great land of learning and scholars, young people must be taught to read and write.

THE NEED FOR A PROGRAM

... [This] Administration today, here and now, declares unconditional war on poverty in America ...

One thousand dollars invested in salvaging an unemployable youth today can return $40,000 or more in his lifetime.

Poverty is a national problem, requiring improved national organization and support. But this attack, to be effective, must also be organized at the state and the local level, and must be supported and directed by state and local efforts.

For the war against poverty will not be won here in Washington. It must be won in the field, in every private home, in every public office, from the courthouse to the White House.

The program I shall propose will emphasize this cooperative approach. To help that one-fifth of all American families with income too small to even meet their basic needs, our chief weapons in a more pinpointed attack will be better schools and better health and better homes and better training and better job opportunities to help more Americans, especially young Americans, escape from squalor and misery and unemployment rolls, where other citizens help to carry them.

Very often a lack of jobs and money is not the cause of poverty, but the symptom.

The cause may lie deeper in our failure to give our fellow citizens a fair chance to develop their own capacities, in a lack of education and training, in a lack of medical care and housing, in a lack of decent communities in which to live and bring up their children. ...

12. The Federal Government Must Do More: Hubert Humphrey

Hubert Humphrey wrote the following article when he was the Vice-Presidential candidate for the Democratic party in 1964.

720

The United States is a big country with big problems. We are enjoying the longest period of sustained economic growth in our history, but there is poverty, misery, and discontent. . . .

Hubert H. Humphrey, "My Case for the Democratic Party," **Saturday Review,** Vol. XLVII (Oct. 31, 1964), pp. 21-23. Reprinted by permission of the publisher and author.

[First, we must] face the [unemployment] problems brought about by automation and technological progress. The enormity of this problem is shown in the statistics: We shall soon face the need to provide 300,000 new jobs every month—more than the population of such cities as Omaha, Rochester, and Akron . . .

"Automation" is the process of replacing human labor with machine labor.

Public works can provide some of these jobs; others will come through the various levels of government and from the services and professions. But I am convinced that we must look to science and technology to generate new jobs . . .

The federal government devotes about $15 billion a year to research and development—some in government laboratories but mostly in industry and educational institutions. . . . We must develop more intermediate institutions between the laboratories and universities, where basic research takes place, and the existing and potential industries that can deploy it to make new products, develop new markets, and offer new jobs. . . .

To "deploy something" means to use it in an effective way.

One of our greatest needs is to create opportunities for our young people. Sixty-nine million children—more than a third of our present population—were born between 1946 and 1962. Most of these are now in grade school and high school. This flood tide of young people will begin to hit the colleges and the labor market next year. . . .

The central part of our domestic policy must be a greater new emphasis on education . . .

We added new jobs in our economy—2,500,000 of them in the past three years. But 2,000,000 of them were in the white collar sector and required educational qualifications. . . . As it is now, two out of every three Americans who are unemployed do not have a high school diploma. Unless we reverse the trend, this ratio will grow. Therefore we must keep millions of our young people in school longer and educate them better. . . .

"White collar" workers are office workers.

. . . The population pressure on our elementary and secondary schools is mounting day by day. In this decade elementary and secondary school enrollments are going to increase by 55 per cent—that is, by 23,000,000 students.

These schools must have more help. In addition to greater state and local effort, there will have to be some federal assistance.

721

The situations in our great cities are particularly critical and urgently need attention. The elementary and secondary schools of these areas are already suffering from an exodus of the well-to-do and a steady influx of the poor, from problems of desegregation, teacher shortages, building and equipment deterioration, and the need for new methods and equipment to deal with the difficult educational problems in these areas. These problems will get worse as more and more of our population crowds into giant cities. By 1980, when this country will have 250 million people, more than 75 per cent of that number—more than our entire population of today—will be living in the great urban centers.

Direct federal aid will have to come—not only for school construction and teacher salaries, but also for greater research at all levels on the problems of teaching our young. . . .

By attacking unemployment and inadequate education, we shall be striking at two of the main roots of poverty. The poor are not shiftless and lazy. They are, among others, marginal farmers, struggling along on $500 to $1,000 a year and unreached by the federal farm programs. They are migrant laborers. They are unskilled workers, discarded in the process of automation. They are residents of depressed areas like Appalachia, not only country people but a growing number from dying mining and industrial towns. They are people marooned among the exhausted mines of the Upper Great Lakes region. Ten to 15,000,000 of them are Negroes and Puerto Ricans, the last to be hired and the first to be fired. Eighteen million of them are elderly people—1,000,000 of them living in misery on less than $580 a year.

13. The Federal Government Must Do Less: Barry Goldwater

Barry Goldwater wrote the following article when he was the Republican candidate for President in 1964.

. . . [Today] we hear pleas for a new and concentrated "power to govern." Those who seek this concentration of power apparently reject the idea that the surest guarantee of individual freedom is the absence of concentration of power, whether it be governmental or economic power. . . .

Some of the current worship of powerful executives may come from those who admire strength and accomplishment of any sort.

"Marginal farmers" are farmers who produce just enough to live on and to cover their production costs.

Barry M. Goldwater, "My Case for the Republican Party," **Saturday Review,** Vol. XLVII (Oct. 17, 1964), pp. 21-23, 49-50. Reprinted by permission of the publisher and author.

Others hail the display of Presidential strength, or judicial strength, as the case may be, simply because they approve of the *result* reached by the use of power. This is nothing less than the totalitarian philosophy that the end justifies the means . . . If ever there was a philosophy of government totally at war with that of the Founding Fathers, it is this one. . . .

In recent decades . . . the ground has been shifting—seriously and significantly—beneath the structure of our American political system. One such shift has occurred at the level of state powers. These powers, the fuel of the federal system itself, have been siphoned [drained] off into the central government and away from the state capitals . . .

. . . [In] the structure of state power there has always been the guarantee that some minorities could preserve their dissident voices, in their local forums. . . .

"Dissidence" is disagreement or protest.

Or we might look upon the fifty states as fifty laboratories in which men, in their own and local ways, test and probe the modes [ways] of civil government, developing new tools and techniques, and, above all, developing their own skills. Those that develop well become available to the nation as a whole. Those that fail, or are warped in ways that make them unsuitable to the nation as a whole, can be buried in their own backyards. . . .

. . . [The Democrats] ask us to believe that all we have to consider when examining a proposed piece of legislation is whether it is desirable. According to this doctrine, anything that is desirable is, by that very fact, constitutional.

What the proponents of this doctrine seem never to ask themselves is: what of liberty? What will this legislation do to that balance of power between states and nation which is the genius of the entire system? They do not consider that legislation, otherwise desirable, becomes undesirable when it violates the principle upon which our whole federal form of government depends. . . .

The key question, then, is: How can this imbalance be redressed [corrected]? There are many ways, and I shall attempt to suggest only a few of them here.

One is for Congressmen and legislators to insist on a more positive role in policy-making. They can debate and decide fundamental questions, as well as details of program. They can, and should, submit legislative budgets on behalf of the nation or their state, as the case may be, and not rely solely upon the massive, often unarguable budget of the Executive branch. They can take care that all efforts to reform legislative procedures be calculated

723

to strengthen, and not weaken, the ability and responsibility of legislative branches to represent the people directly.

A second way is contained in the program that the Republican Party is offering to the people of America this year. The spirit, the underlying theme, of our program is the private man, the whole man—the man who stands in danger of becoming the forgotten man of our . . . times. Our Republican purpose is to end the erosion of his worth by a growing federal bureaucracy—and to end, as well, the erosion of the powers of those parts of our governmental system that are closest to the people; that is, the legislative branches and local governments. Thus, our domestic proposals are designed to provide an economic climate that nourishes private growth, that resists—and finally retards—the growth of federal power at the expense of the states and the individual. . . . [We] favor reform in the present complex system of programatic grants-in-aid which now keeps local officials under federal domination. There are today over a hundred such programs totaling more than $10 billion in federal spending and covering every major activity of state and local government. This country has, in effect, replaced its traditional three-layer horizontal government of federal, state, and local governments with a vertical organization composed of a centralized Executive in Washington issuing orders down the line to a series of administrative divisions and sections. Because of existing commitments we cannot of course re-do this undesirable and complex system overnight. But, with thought and care, we can gradually replace it with a much simpler and more sensible one. In addition, low-income states and cities could be helped further by a system of purely fiscal grants for general purposes.

A "fiscal grant" is a gift of money.

. . . [We] can, and must, find ways to reap the material fulfillment promised by advancing technology *without* sacrificing the fulfillment of mind and spirit characteristic of a free people. We must and can have progress *and freedom.* We must move forward *through* freedom.

Steven V. Roberts, "Instant Rehabilitation Proves Instant Success," **The New York Times,** April 14, 1967. © 1967 by The New York Times Company. Reprinted by permission.

14. A New Apartment in Two Days

Mrs. Willie May Grier's four children burst into their new apartment yesterday and their cries of delight echoed through the freshly painted halls of the ancient tenement.

They dashed from room to room turning on the bathroom-sink faucets, pulling open the refrigerator, sliding the closet doors back and forth.

724

"It's beautiful, lovely, gorgeous," said Mrs. Grier.

"I like it here," said 6-year-old Daniel. "There's a lot of room."

Forty-eight hours earlier the tenement at 633 East Fifth Street had been a decaying hulk of crumbling plaster, broken windows, leaky pipes and moldering [rotting] garbage.

But through a revolutionary engineering process called "instant rehabilitation" the building had been outfitted with entirely new walls, floors, window frames, appliances and electrical and plumbing systems.

"To rehabilitate" means to restore to useful condition.

The demonstration culminated a year of experimentation with materials and work methods on two adjoining tenements . . .

[A California engineering] concern directed the experiment with a $1-million grant from the Federal Department of Housing and Urban Affairs. The buildings are owned by the Carolyndale Foundation, which holds a $568,400 mortgage insured by the Federal Government. . . .

If there are not funds to cover the purchase of property, a "mortgage" is taken out. That is, money is borrowed and is paid back with interest over a period of time. If the payments cannot be met, the mortgaged piece becomes the property of the party who granted the loan.

The experiment began Tuesday morning when the 12 families occupying [one building] were moved to a hotel and their belongings were put into storage. . . .

Only the skeleton of floors, stairways, and a few walls were left by the evening. Three holes were cut in the roof and pre-assembled bathroom and kitchen units were lowered by a 250-foot crane as floodlights lit the scene.

On Wednesday, walls and floors were covered, electric and plumbing lines connected, and closets installed. By 8:30 P.M. painting had begun.

[Thursday] morning, 47 hours 52 minutes and 24 seconds after work had begun, some paint was still wet and the backyard was littered with refuse, but otherwise the building was ready for tenants to return.

Mr. Rice . . . said the cost should come to about $11,000 an apartment, compared with $13,000 for conventional rehabilitation and between $20,000 and $23,000 for new construction.

Rents . . . will go up . . . but the families . . . will pay only 25 per cent of their income for rent. The federal rent subsidy program will make up the rest.

Housing experts generally [agreed] . . . that the experiment has been useful in discovering new work methods to cut the time for rehabilitation. This virtually eliminates the problem of relocation, which has plagued every redevelopment project in the city.

They agreed also that valuable new products, such as highly durable [long-lasting] wall and floor coverings and expandable window frames, had been devised.

15. Running a Slum Building: A Private Experiment

Steven V. Roberts, "Civic Group Fails in Attempt to Make Slum Buildings Pay," **The New York Times**, March 9, 1967. © 1967 by The New York Times Company. Reprinted by permission.

[The] Citizens Housing and Planning Council started out to prove that private capital could make an annual profit of at least 8 per cent by renovating and running slum housing, Roger Starr, its executive director, said yesterday.

Last year, the council . . . lost $7,335 on . . . two buildings.

"It soon became clear that you couldn't make anything at all," Mr. Starr declared. "It simply costs more money to keep up your property than you collect from rents . . ."

The experiment indicates, Mr. Starr said, that city, state and Federal governments must provide huge subsidies to both landlords and tenants if the city's slums are ever going to be made habitable.

"Without subsidies rehabilitation is a snare and a delusion," Mr. Starr asserted. "No reasonable person would invest money to rehabilitate buildings like the ones we own."

The Citizens Housing and Planning Council is a nonprofit organization that has been concerned with the physical development of the city for 30 years. Its board of directors includes a broad range of civic leaders, businessmen and professional persons.

The council's findings contradict the growing belief in housing circles that massive private investment can, and should be attracted to slum areas to provide new housing and commercial facilities. . . .

The findings also differ with the widely held assumption that ownership of slum housing is a highly profitable business, even for landlords who spend money on repairs and maintenance.

Jason R. Nathan, the Administrator of Housing and Development, . . . said there was considerable evidence that rehabilitation could be feasible if done over a large area, and not just on scattered buildings.

The more sophisticated technology that is being developed would cut costs and make rehabilitation more profitable, Mr. Nathan added. . . .

Walking through the building yesterday, Mr. Starr pointed to broken windows, garbage a foot deep in the air shafts, defaced hallways and new mailboxes that already showed signs of being broken into, probably by narcotics addicts. . . .

The main reasons for the deficit, he said, were vandalism, the high costs of maintenance and materials, and the inability to charge rents that would meet these costs. . . .

Mr. Starr stressed that low-cost mortgages were not sufficient to attract private investment in the slums, and that some kind of outright grant was also needed. Large rent supplements would also be necessary to allow poor families to pay the rents the renovated buildings would require [in order for the buildings] to remain a workable proposition. . . .

Rehabilitation requires expert management that nonprofit groups cannot provide, he said. Moreover, nonprofit groups would tend to lose interest in a building after "the excitement of doing the work is over."

Another popular proposal—transferring renovated slum housing to the tenants themselves—also won't work, Mr. Starr said.

"Then you just give them all the headaches," he said.

III. Civil Rights

16. The Supreme Court and Segregation

During the 1960's there has been a strong movement in the United States to secure for Negroes *civil,* or civilian, *rights* equal to those enjoyed by white people. Two of the most important civil rights are the right to equal opportunity in education and the right to vote. Equally important is the right to take any job for which one is qualified. Civil rights also include the privilege of buying or renting any home that one is able to afford and the right to use public facilities like restaurants and parks.

The term *segregation* means separation of races. The Supreme Court has twice made major decisions about whether segregation was constitutional—whether or not it violated any of the rights granted to American citizens under the Constitution. In 1896, in the case of *Plessy* v. *Ferguson,* the Court ruled that a law requiring separate but equal railroad cars for white and Negro passengers was constitutional. In 1954, in the case of *Brown* v. *Board of Education of Topeka,* the Court ruled that segregation in the public schools was unconstitutional. This later decision on segregation overruled the earlier one.

PLESSY v. FERGUSON, 1896

Documents of American History, edited by Henry Steele Commager (Seventh edition; New York: Appleton-Century-Crofts, 1963), p. 629.

... If the two races [white and Negro] are to meet on terms of social equality, it must be the result of natural affinities [attractions], a mutual appreciation of each other's merits and a voluntary consent of individuals. . . . Legislation is powerless to eradicate [erase] racial instincts or to abolish distinctions based upon physical differences . . .

BROWN v. BOARD OF EDUCATION OF TOPEKA, 1954

Documents of American History, edited by Henry Steele Commager, pp. 621-622.

Today, education is perhaps the most important function of state and local governments. Compulsory school attendance laws and the great expenditures for education both demonstrate our recognition of the importance of education to our democratic society. It is required in the performance of our most basic public responsibilities, even service in the armed forces. It is the very foundation of good citizenship. Today, it is a principal instrument in awakening the child to cultural values, in preparing him for later professional training, and in helping him to adjust normally to his environment. In these days, it is doubtful that any child may reasonably be expected to succeed in life if he is denied the opportunity of an education. Such an opportunity, where the state has undertaken to provide it, is a right which must be made available to all on equal terms. . . .

A "plaintiff" is the one who initiates a lawsuit. In this case, Brown is the plaintiff.

We conclude that in the field of public education the doctrine of "separate but equal" has no place. Separate educational facilities are inherently [by nature] unequal. Therefore, we hold that the plaintiffs are, by reason of the segregation complained of, deprived of the equal protection of the laws guaranteed by the Fourteenth Amendment. This disposition makes unnecessary any discussion whether such segregation also violates the Due Process Clause of the Fourteenth Amendment.

17. A Southern Statement on School Integration, 1956

After the *Brown* v. *Board of Education of Topeka* case, ninety-six southern congressmen issued the following statement on integration in the schools. *Integration* is the process by which minority groups that have lived separately come to use the same schools, parks, and other facilities that the majority groups use.

Documents of American History, edited by Henry Steele Commager (Seventh edition; New York: Appleton-Century-Crofts, 1963), pp. 641-643.

We regard the decision of the Supreme Court in the school cases as clear abuse of judicial power. It climaxes a trend in the Federal judiciary undertaking to legislate, in [contempt] of the authority of

Congress, and to encroach upon the reserved rights of the states and the people.

The original Constitution does not mention education. Neither does the Fourteenth Amendment nor any other amendment. The debates preceding the submission of the Fourteenth Amendment clearly show that there was no intent that it should affect the systems of education maintained by the states.

The very Congress which proposed the amendment subsequently provided for segregated schools in the District of Columbia.

When the amendment was adopted in 1868, there were thirty-seven states of the Union. Every one of the twenty-six states that had any substantial racial differences among its people either approved the operation of segregated schools already [existing] or subsequently established such schools by action of the same law-making body which considered the Fourteenth Amendment. . . .

This unwarranted exercise of power by the court, contrary to the Constitution, is creating chaos and confusion in the states principally affected. It is destroying the amicable [friendly] relations between the white and Negro races that have been created through ninety years of patient effort by the good people of both races. It has planted hatred and suspicion where there has been heretofore friendship and understanding. . . .

With the gravest concern for the explosive and dangerous condition created by this decision and inflamed by outside meddlers:

We reaffirm our reliance on the Constitution as the fundamental law of the land.

We decry [strongly disapprove] the Supreme Court's encroachments on rights reserved to the states and to the people, contrary to established law and to the Constitution.

We commend the motives of those states which have declared the intention to resist forced integration by any lawful means. . . .

In this trying period, as we all seek to right this wrong, we appeal to our people not to be provoked by the agitators and trouble-makers invading our states and to scrupulously [carefully] refrain from disorder and lawless acts.

18. The Sit-Ins, 1960

The *sit-in* became popular early in 1960. In sit-ins, Negroes, and white people sympathetic to their cause, would sit at segregated lunch counters and ask to be served. If they were refused they would remain seated, thus blocking the normal flow of business. This technique was used to desegregate lunch counters in many cities. In the first of the next two selections, Merrill Proudfoot, a white Presbyterian minister and a professor at Knoxville College, describes a sit-in in Knoxville, Tennessee, in which he participated. He was accompanied by Robert Booker, a Negro who was president of the student body at Knoxville College. The Chattanooga, Tennessee, sit-in is described by *Newsweek* reporter Joseph B. Cumming, Jr.

KNOXVILLE

Merrill Proudfoot, **Diary of a Sit-In** (Chapel Hill, N. C.: The University of North Carolina Press, 1962), pp. 7-8. Reprinted by permission of the publisher.

. . . [We] walked up the street to the Todd & Armistead Drug Store. Robert and a Negro girl sat down at the rather small counter. I sat down next to the young lady. Immediately a waitress put up a cardboard sign on which was scrawled in crayon, "counter closed." The counter employees went into the back room and no one said anything to us.

Robert had taken a seat next to a white youth. This young man, looking down the counter at the Negro girl, muttered to Robert, "Say, do you think they are going to serve that—" The young man, belatedly noticing Robert's complexion, broke off in embarrassment.

Robert asked him testily, "What's the matter? You don't like sitting beside a Negro?"

Huffily, the fellow said, "I'm going to move!" and took the farthest seat at the end of the counter, because, as he muttered to another customer, he was determined to finish his hamburger. (I gleefully made a mental note to the effect that anyone who is more interested in a hamburger than in a protest is really on our side!) Immediately I slipped over onto the stool next to Robert on the other side so that the man would know that not all white people felt as he did. . . .

Shortly, an elderly white man came in, and although there were a number of vacant seats at the counter, chose to sit next to Robert on the stool the youth had vacated. He waited a long time for service. Finally Robert told him he thought the counter was closed. The old man protested, "But these other people are eating!" Robert explained, "Yes, but they were here before we came; you see this store doesn't serve Negroes." The old man couldn't understand such a ridiculous practice. Robert and he engaged in a conversation which was still going on when I slipped off to make a one o'clock engagement. . . .

CHATTANOOGA

Their mimeographed directions were explicit: "Dress well . . . no violence . . . no profanity . . . no weapons." By the time they started downtown, the Negro high-school students knew their orders by heart. They were neatly clad, and at first soft-spoken.

But the opposition was alerted. The first lunchrooms the Negroes tried to enter were already filled with hostile white students when they arrived. As the Negroes departed, the white students jumped up and raced them to wherever they headed next. Then, after a few failures, the Negroes outmaneuvered the whites and beat them to the long lunch counter of the big five-and-dime store between Market and Cherry Streets. They slid onto all the empty stools. For a few minutes they just sat there, catching their breath, fidgeting with the sugar and mustard, staring at the soda and sandwich posters. There were maybe 25 seated, and as many more standing behind them.

At the other end of the counter, the white youths gathered quickly. In a little while there were 150 or more, jeering at the Negroes, and shouting taunts. . . .

Soon, some of the Negroes, forgetting their mimeographed instructions, began answering back. The store's closing bell suddenly jangled out, although it was hardly past 4 p.m.

"They're closing an hour and a half ahead of time—just to keep us from sitting here," a Negro girl cried. Lights started flashing off. One of the policemen assigned to stand by said: "All right, let's get out."

No one could be sure just how it started—a stray punch, a jostle, an intentional trip-up—but within seconds the hostility exploded into a bloody free-for-all. The whites charged into the Negroes, fists flailed, cups and dishes hurtled through the air. A flowerpot brought blood gushing from a white combatant's head. A heavy object shattered a plate-glass door. A white boy leaped on the lunch counter and ran along it shouting: "Kill 'em."

The outnumbered Negroes were fighting a holding action as they retreated from the building. The battle tumbled out into Cherry Street. A Negro brandished a shovel, its blade broken into a sharp point. A white boy lashed about him with a toy bull whip, taken from a store counter. A Negro was arrested for petty larceny because he had a sugar jar, picked up, he said, as a defensive weapon. He was the only Negro arrested that day.

Within fifteen minutes, police had arrested eleven whites and

Newsweek, Vol. LV, Pt. 1(1960), pp. 29-30. Copyright 1960 by Newsweek, Inc. Reprinted by permission of the publisher.

"Petty larceny" is theft on a small scale.

herded the rest of the Negroes down Cherry Street toward Ninth, and their own district. The violence subsided like a summer storm, but the thunder kept reverberating [echoing] into the tense night.

19. Responses to the Sit-Ins, 1960

"Everywhere: Tension," **U.S. News & World Report,** Vol. XLVIII (March 21, 1960), pp. 74-75. Copyright 1960 U.S. News & World Report, Inc.

MONTGOMERY

Carl W. Bear, Building Contractor. People quite generally here feel that agitators from outside of Alabama are the principal troublemakers. We feel that the older and more substantial members of the Negro community are satisfied with the progress that has been made in racial relations. They don't even aspire to social integration. . . .

I don't know if Communists are behind it. But these agitators are following the pattern of trying to divide the country. It's the familiar principle of divide and conquer. If they are not Communists, they are pursuing the same tactics as Communists.

Rev. Arch L. McNair, Presbyterian Minister and President of the Montgomery Ministerial Association. The great majority of Southerners are people who wish well for the Negro. One of the worst things happening now is the forming of a chasm [great separation] between the white people and Negroes. The organizations leading the Negroes today have discouraged white people who would like to help.

The more the crisis grows, the less progress is made. All the progress at this time has been stopped by these demonstrations. . . .

Thomas B. Hill, Jr., Ex-President of the Alabama State Bar Association. The Negro cannot hope or expect to achieve the elimination of segregation in the South by force or violence.

The Southern white man will not be pushed around.

KNOXVILLE

. . . The "Good Will Committee" of white leaders . . . requested the merchants to desegregate their counters and the merchants . . . agreed! . . .

Merril Proudfoot, **Diary of a Sit-In** (Chapel Hill, N. C.: The University of North Carolina Press, 1962), pp. 150, 153, 181. Reprinted by permission of the publisher.

The Committee was appointed by the mayor and the Chamber of Commerce.

The negotiators had agreed on the following terms: The four variety stores and Walgreen's will begin serving Negroes next Monday, July 18. Included in the deal also will be Woolworth's two stores in suburban shopping centers. There will be a transition period of ten days during which no more than two Negroes will request service at a counter at the same time. Our organization has accepted responsibility to "police" the counters to see that no more than two try to eat at one time. There will be no restriction on the time of day Negroes can be served. At the end of ten days, the merchants and our negotiators will meet to decide whether the restrictions can be taken off. . . .

At the end of the ten-day "adjustment period" neither side contacted the other. The Associated Council simply quit sending supervisors, while the stores on their part continued serving everyone who came. Several outlying stores quietly advised Negro leaders that their people would be served. The manager who had served as the group chairman in the negotiations remarked a few weeks afterward, "I don't know why we didn't do this long before we did." This seems to typify the attitude of the merchants. The attitude of the Negroes was well expressed by a prominent Negro who is on the executive level with TVA: "I drop into Walgreen's every now and then to eat my lunch and they treat me as though I were a king; if I'd gone in there before July 18, I would have had the whole store in turmoil. . . ."

"TVA" is the Tennessee Valley Authority, a federal government agency.

20. A Northern Community and School Integration, 1964

There are two types of segregation. *De jure* segregation is segregation that is established and upheld by law. *De facto* segregation is segregation that just exists in fact. For example, a school might consist of all-white or all-Negro students simply because it is located in an all-white or all-Negro neighborhood. In the 1960's, attempts were made in many communities to end *de facto* segregation. One solution was to bus students to schools outside their neighborhoods.

In its campaign to end segregation in New York City's schools the Board of Education last spring decided to begin a program of school "pairing." Under this plan, a predominantly white school is linked with a predominantly Negro-Puerto Rican school—some grades attending one school and the remaining grades attending the other, thus achieving a racial mixture in both. This integration, proponents of the plan maintain, would end the "ghetto complex" that has held Negro children back. In some cases, a pairing scheme requires the busing of some children from their neighborhoods. A militant organization called Parents and Taxpayers has sprung

Peggy Streit, "Why They Fight for the P.A.T.," **The New York Times Magazine**, Sept. 20, 1964, pp. 20-21, 122-125. Reprinted by permission of the author.

A "ghetto" is a quarter of a city in which a minority group lives because of economic, political, or social pressure.

A "militant" group is aggressive and emphasizes action and well-disciplined organization.

up to fight the plan, however. This article records the views of members of one chapter...

"The way I see it, it's like this," said the taxi driver. "If I had kids of school age I'd join P.A.T. And I'd keep the kids out of school just as long as we white people didn't get our rights...."

... "[You] buy a house because you want your kid to go to a school nearby and the church is just around the corner. And then, here comes the government or school board and what do they say? They say, 'Mister, you can't send your kid to school near you. You got to bus him to school in a Negro neighborhood, 20 blocks away...' Now I ask you, is that right? And I say to you, no—that ain't right. We're losing our freedoms in this country. Next thing you know, they'll be telling you where to go to church...."

Stanley Smigiel, president of the South Richmond Hill-South Ozone Park P.A.T. and a grease monkey by trade, [spoke up at a meeting that evening]...

"When they told me, 'You got to do this and you got to do that,' that's when my dandruff went up," he said. "I lived in South Jamaica in a Negro area for 30 years. I don't have nothing against Negroes, but the only thing I care about is this: I don't want my child traveling no further than he has to to school. What if the bus breaks down? What about snowy days? What if he gets sick and it's an emergency and my wife can't get to him? And furthermore, I don't like him going into classes with a lot of slow readers who will pull down his I.Q. I was a drop-out in school and I learned my lesson. I don't want nothing going wrong with my son's education."

June Reynolds, a young, fresh-faced, bright-eyed, dedicated dynamo, doesn't have anything against Negroes either. "I went to school with Negroes when I was a girl," she said. "If I were a Negro, how would I see to it that my kids got a better education and a chance in the world?" She answered herself without hesitation. "I'd move into an interracial neighborhood. I wouldn't live in Harlem for anything in the world. I'd scrub floors. I'd take in laundry. I'd get any kind of job to get out of Harlem—and I know I'd succeed because I believe that in the United States anybody can do anything if he tries hard enough.

"Look at my father. Negroes can at least speak English, but when my father came here from Italy he had to learn the language, so he went to night school. Then he got a job as a wrapper in a

A "grease monkey" is a mechanic who primarily lubricates, or greases, machinery—often automobiles.

bakery. He worked there 47 years and was a supervisor when he retired. The way I see it," she added with finality, "if a Negro lives in Harlem, it's because he likes it there and because he doesn't want to work hard enough to get out of that environment."

Hannah Edell, a round, small, blond woman with soft pink cheeks and a troubled voice, was a little less dogmatic.

A "dogmatic" person asserts ideas without proof of their validity.

"Yes, I think the Negro has been discriminated against," she said, "and I think they should be helped along. But I don't think their problem is educational. It's social. I know that some Negroes think, 'Why should I bother to get an education if I can't get a job afterwards?'—and that's what I mean by a social problem. It's up to large corporations to give them jobs."

She acknowledged the obvious question with a long, hard sigh. "Yes, I know," she said. "Why *shouldn't* large corporations give their jobs to the best-educated—and they are usually white."

She paused then reflected sadly: "It's a vicious circle, isn't it? One hardly knows where to begin. But one thing I *do* know," she went on, gaining assurance. "They shouldn't begin with our children. Integration isn't a problem for children to solve—or their parents. It's up to the politicians, big corporations—other people. And the Board of Education. This problem has existed for a long time. Why didn't the board do something to improve Negro education a long time ago, so things wouldn't have got to this state?"

Joe Lamanna, project manager for a contractor, saw the problem differently. A large young man, dark-eyed, handsome, well-turned-out and the possessor of a college degree earned after five and a half years of night school, he is proud of his Italian ancestry, of his home in one of Ozone Park's more affluent districts and of a gigantic new car, which he won in a church raffle.

"This is most of all a moral issue," he said. "What right does any-body—*anybody*—have to tell me what to do? Where does it all end? I worked with Negroes on a construction job for seven years. They don't work hard or help their children in school or care about their families or keep their homes clean. But that's not the issue. I just won't tolerate anybody telling me I've got to send my son into another neighborhood to school."

His small, chic wife agreed. "I don't think I have a moral obliga-tion to anyone—to my family, my husband and child maybe, but no one else. If Negroes have been deprived of some rights, it's because they haven't worked for them. They don't deserve them.

735

And the only way they're finally going to get them is through hard work—not by having our children bused into their schools. . . ."

"People just aren't psychologically ready for all this—this mixing," she complained. "We're not bad people . . . We are decent, hard-working, churchgoing, law-abiding people—but we're bewildered. . . . Why do things have to change overnight? Why can't it be gradual? . . ."

Felicia Petosa, married to a cook, is a warm, ardent woman. . . . She has two children, the eldest of whom spent his first years in a school in East Brooklyn—an area 70 per cent Negro and Puerto Rican.

"Pathetic," began Mrs. Petosa, taking a deep breath. "The school had no hallway. You got to the second classroom by walking through the first, and the third by walking through the first two. P.T.A. meetings were held next to the boiler room. I could never get interested. Fights all day. When the kids finished fighting at school they fought at home. Just on our block there were over 75 kids. The Puerto Rican lady who lived next door had five and 15 people lived in four rooms. We paid our own exterminator bills, but finally the man said he wouldn't do our place no more because it wouldn't do no good unless the whole block got done. We lived upstairs and the landlord lived down and every day he'd complain about the noise my kids made and I'd say to him, 'Excuse me, I'll go put them in a freezer and take them out for supper.'

"Finally, my husband was getting along better in his business and we moved, and the first day my little boy went to school here his conduct improved so much I took his temperature. I don't have anything against Negroes," added Mrs. Petosa, "but I believe in the neighborhood-school system. Why do our children have to be inconvenienced, just to satisfy the Negroes' whims? . . ."

A woman paused on the street, a large, brown-paper shopping bag in her arms, and said: "What do they think they're going to accomplish with this pairing? . . .

"There's a little boy on our street," she went on, "who uses bad language and doesn't do his school work and won't behave. *He* goes to school with our kids but he doesn't change just because he sits next to a well-behaved child. He stays the way he is because that's the way his parents are. And as for raising the educational standards, give me one example—just one example—where mixing Negroes and whites hasn't pulled standards down to the Negro level rather than raising them to the white level. I don't know why the Negroes are behind. But they are, and I don't want them hurting my child's chances in school."

Farther down the street . . . an elderly lady sat on a camp chair in her front yard . . .

"If the Negroes come into our neighborhood schools, does that mean they will be *moving* in?" she asked with a worried frown. "Eight years ago we paid $12,000 for this house. We scraped together every penny we had and borrowed more. Now it's worth at least $16,000. My husband and me we worked so hard to get it and it's all we have. And now, if the Negroes start coming into the neighborhood it won't be worth a cent. . . ."

"I don't know what to think," said an elderly woman plaintively [sadly]. "Please come in and sit down." She settled onto an ancient divan covered with a green tasseled throw.

"My son comes home a couple of weeks ago and when I say I think it's shocking, the thought of busing our neighborhood children into Negro schools and Negro children into our schools, my son gets furious and he says, 'You're a bigot!' Then he says to me, 'Don't you know Negroes were slaves once and they have been discriminated against for 150 years? That people haven't given them decent jobs and have forced them to live in Negro ghettos? Can you imagine what that does to people psychologically?' he says to me. And I say, 'But look how dirty they are and how bad their morals are and would you want your children going to school with Negroes?' And he gets mad again and he says I ought to be ashamed. 'Don't you understand that if you don't give people a decent education, or home, or chance, they lose hope and don't bother to work or study or keep their homes clean? If you treat them inferior, they *act* inferior,' he says. And then he says, 'If a Negro and [a] white person asked you for a job and both were equally qualified, which would you choose?' I didn't know what to say, but finally I said I guessed the white person. And then"— and the old lady shook her head in distress and disbelief—"then he said, 'You're a bigot!' and he walked out."

A "bigot" is one who holds to an opinion or a belief to such an extent that he is intolerant.

21. Housing, 1957

What happens when a Negro family . . . moves into a Northern community that has always had an all-white population?

"When a Negro Family Moved into a White Community," **U.S. News & World Report**, Vol. XLIII, (August 30, 1957), pp. 29-32. Copyright 1957 U.S. News & World Report, Inc.

This sprawling development of 16,000 homes just north of Philadelphia is finding out the hard way. . . .

No Negroes had ever lived in Levittown until August. Then, 34-year-old William Myers, Jr., and his wife moved here from neighboring Bloomsdale Gardens, a racially integrated housing development. They are Negroes, parents of three small children. They bought a $12,100 house in the Dogwood Hollow section . . .

Nightly, crowds of as many as 500 persons gathered in the vicinity of the Myers house. One night someone threw stones which broke the big picture window in the living room.

Squads of local police, and state troopers ordered to the scene by Governor George M. Leader, ringed the area.

Police barricades went up at the entrance to the street on which the house is situated. Only neighborhood residents were permitted to pass.

Clashes between troopers and white residents have occurred. Police, trying to break up the crowds, used clubs. Rocks were thrown by people in the crowd at the police. Arrests for disorderly conduct were made, and a few persons were fined. Levittowners were warned that they faced possible jail terms if the disturbances continued. Residents complained of police brutality. After a week the violence simmered down, but the tension . . . lingered on. . . .

Lewis Wechsler [a machinist], who lives in the house next door, expresses one viewpoint. Of the Myerses he says: "They have a right to live here the same as any other Americans. . . ."

"We certainly have had a lot of trouble since they moved here," Mrs. McShea said of the Myerses. "I don't like to speak out against anybody, but you couldn't say I like colored people moving into the neighborhood. They seem like a nice family, well educated and clean, but what happens if others move in, too? You don't know.

"They don't have any children going to school right now, but they will have. A lot of people aren't going to like that, either. . . ."

"I really don't have any objections to colored people, but I don't think they ought to live in white neighborhoods," [George Bessam, a bachelor] says. "A lot of people moved into Levittown from Philadelphia and other places for just one reason—to get away from colored people in their old neighborhoods. . . .

"And I think all this police stuff is terrible—people getting hit over

738

the head by police clubs when they're just trying to see that they get their rights," adds Mr. Bessam....

On the opposite side of the fence are the civic groups like the Citizens' Committee for Levittown, headed by the Rev. Ray Harwick of Levittown's Evangelical and Reformed Church of the Reformation.

"An overwhelming majority of our neighbors," the committee reports, "have been calmly accepting the Myerses' move. . ."

... [Real] estate men say privately that Negroes never will be allowed in Levittown in any numbers. They point out that this community is one of low and medium-priced homes occupied for the most part by young couples just getting a start as homeowners. Such people, it is held, are touchy about things like property values, which they believe drop precipitately [steeply] when Negroes move into a neighborhood.

22. Equal Jobs

In 1963, *Newsweek* released the results of a poll testing white attitudes toward Negroes.

Equal employment, which is also the number-one priority for Negroes, seems ripe for a breakthrough. Nearly nine out of every ten whites—including eight out of every ten Southerners—feel that Negroes have the right to equal jobs. What is more, as another question in the poll revealed, a majority all over the country do not fear that Negroes will take their jobs away. Significantly, a solid majority (62 per cent) of whites favor a Federal law enforcing an end to discrimination on the job. However, white people are equally adamant that there should *not* be a strict 10 per cent quota for Negroes in job-hiring (rejected by over 4 to 1) or that Negroes should actually be given job preference over whites (turned down by a staggering 31 to 1 margin).

William Brink and Louis Harris, **The Negro Revolution in America** (New York: Simon and Schuster, Inc., 1964), pp. 148-149. Copyright © 1963 by Newsweek, Inc. Reprinted by permission of Simon & Schuster, Inc.

"Priority," here, means the most important request or demand.

"To be adamant" is to be immovable or unshakable in regard to something.

23. The Changing Mood of the Country

In the following reading, the terms "white backlash" and "black power" are used. "White backlash" refers to the reaction of white people who oppose further extension of civil rights for Negroes. In 1966, Negro leaders impatient with the slowness of civil rights progress proclaimed the doctrine of "black power." There is a great deal of disagreement over the meaning of the term. However, many Negro leaders have defined it as the organization of

739

the Negro community to win equality through such means as voting power and economic boycotts.

The New York Times, Oct. 2, 1966.

Nowadays, street marches command little attention, while riots make news across the nation ... But the risks of such a protest technique are great, and all over the country, they seem to have intensified "white backlash" and, thus far, have made it more difficult for politicians to get public support for massive attacks on Negro problems. ...

... [This] change in attitude ... has a number of causes. These include the increasing number of riots in urban areas, the emergence of "black power" and decline of non-violence in the civil rights movement, spread of the Negro revolution from the South to the North and prospects of integrated housing in areas where whites have been stanchly [firmly] opposed to it ...

In 1964, 1965, and 1966, Negroes rioted in many cities, including Chicago, Los Angeles, Omaha, Atlanta, and New York.

The "white backlash" already has become a factor in elections from one end of the country to another ... Among long-time civil rights leaders ... there was mounting fear ... that the days of wide national support for civil rights had come to at least a temporary end ...

24. Civil Rights Legislation

THE CIVIL RIGHTS ACT, 1964

The Vote

	For	Against
Senate	73	27
House of Representatives	289	126

Major Provisions
1. Forbids discrimination in voter registration.
2. Forbids discrimination in places of public accommodation.
3. Forbids discrimination in public facilities.
4. Forbids discrimination in public schools.
5. Extends the term of the Commission on Civil Rights for four years.
6. Forbids the use of federal funds in programs that practice discrimination.
7. Forbids discrimination in job hiring.
8. Orders a survey to be made of registration and voting statistics by race.

9. Allows more civil rights cases to go through federal rather than state courts. Permits the Attorney General to intervene in private suits of discrimination.
10. Authorizes the Community Relations Service to assist communities in solving racial problems.
11. Provides that the penalty for violation of the act will not exceed a $1,000 fine or 6 months imprisonment.

THE VOTING RIGHTS ACT, 1965

The Vote

	For	Against
Senate	79	18
House of Representatives	328	74

Major Provisions
1. Insures federal supervision and control of voter registration in areas of racial discrimination.
2. Prohibits anyone from depriving another of his right to vote or register to vote.
3. Directs the Attorney General of the United States to initiate a court case to test the validity of state poll taxes used as a device to deny voting rights.

THE CIVIL RIGHTS BILL, 1966

The Vote

	For	Against
House of Representatives (on bill)	259	157
Senate (on motion to end a filibuster against the bill)	41	52

Major Provisions
1. Forbids discrimination in the choice of jurors for federal or state juries.
2. Forbids discrimination in the sale, rental, leasing, or financing of housing.
3. Provides fines and prison terms for people using violence or intimidation to prevent others from exercising their civil rights.
4. Gives the Attorney General of the United States power to initiate action to prevent discrimination in the selection of state juries, housing, and the use of public schools, colleges, or other facilities.

IV. Foreign Affairs

COMMUNISM vs. DEMOCRACY

25. The Two Camps: President Harry Truman

Toward the conclusion of World War II, Russia and the other allies abandoned their policy of mutual support. In an atmosphere of growing suspicion, due to hostile actions on both sides, Russia erected an invisible "iron curtain" which divided Europe into a Western bloc and a Communist bloc. The Western bloc was made up of countries that favored the policies of the United States, while the Communist bloc favored Russia's policies. Historians and politicians mark this division as the beginning of the "Cold War." In 1949, early in the Cold War, President Harry S. Truman delivered the following inaugural address.

Inaugural Addresses of the Presidents of the United States (Washington, D.C.: United States Government Printing Office, 1961), pp. 252-253.

The American people stand firm in the faith which has inspired this Nation from the beginning. We believe that all men have a right to equal justice under law and equal opportunity to share in the common good. We believe that all men have the right to freedom of thought and expression. We believe that all men are created equal because they are created in the image of God.

From this faith we will not be moved.

The American people desire, and are determined to work for, a world in which all nations and all peoples are free to govern themselves as they see fit and to achieve a decent and satisfying life. Above all else, our people desire, and are determined to work for, peace on earth—a just and lasting peace—based on genuine agreement freely arrived at by equals.

In that pursuit of these aims, the United States and other like-minded nations find themselves directly opposed by a regime [communism] with contrary aims and a totally different concept of life. . . .

Communism is based on the belief that man is so weak and inadequate that he is unable to govern himself, and therefore requires the rule of strong masters.

Democracy is based on the conviction that man has the moral and intellectual capacity, as well as the inalienable right, to govern himself with reason and justice.

Communism subjects the individual to arrest without lawful cause, punishment without trial, and forced labor as the chattel [property] of the state. It decrees what information he shall receive, what art he shall produce, what leaders he shall follow, and what thoughts he shall think.

Democracy maintains that government is established for the bene-fit of the individual, and is charged with the responsibility of protecting the rights of the individual and his freedom in the exercise of his abilities.

Communism maintains that social wrongs can be corrected only by violence.

Democracy has proved that social justice can be achieved through peaceful change.

Communism holds that the world is so deeply divided into oppos-ing classes that war is inevitable.

Democracy holds that free nations can settle differences justly and maintain lasting peace.

26. The Soviet Threat: Adlai Stevenson

Adlai Stevenson was the Democratic party's Presidential candi-date in 1952 and 1956. He later became the United States ambas-sador to the United Nations, a post which he held until his death in 1965. Stevenson spoke about the origins of the Cold War in a speech before the United Nations Security Council in 1962.

Panorama of the Past: Readings in World History, edited by Louis L. Snyder, Marvin Perry, and Benjamin Mazen (Boston: Houghton Mifflin Company, 1966), Vol. II, pp. 211-212.

. . . In 1945, we were incomparably the greatest military power in the world. . . . If the American purpose had been world domina-tion, there could have been no more [favorable] moment to set out on such a course.

Instead . . . we dismantled the mightiest military force we had ever assembled. . . . Within two years after the end of the war, our defense spending had fallen by nearly 70 billion dollars. Our armed forces were slashed from more than twelve million to one and one-half million men. . . . We did not have a single military alliance anywhere in the world. History has not seen, I believe, a more complete and comprehensive demonstration of a great na-tion's hope for peace and amity.

Instead of using our monopoly of atomic energy to extend our national power, we offered in 1946 to transfer the control of atomic energy to the United Nations.

Instead of using our overwhelming economic strength to extend our national power, we contributed more than 2.6 billion dollars to the United Nations Relief and Rehabilitation Administration, much of which went to the relief of suffering in the Communist countries. And after 1948 we contributed many more billions to

A "puppet regime" is one whose actions are controlled by an outside group.

the economic restoration of Europe—and invited the Communist countries to participate as recipients of our assistance.

Instead of using our substance and strength to extend our national power, we supported the movement for independence which began to sweep through Asia and Africa. . . .

I have often wondered what the world would be like today if the situation at the end of the war had been reversed—if the United States had been ravaged and shattered by war and if the Soviet Union had emerged intact in exclusive possession of the atomic bomb and overwhelming military and economic might. Would it have followed the same path and devoted itself to realizing the world of the Charter?

Against the idea of diversity, communism asserts the idea of uniformity . . . against choice, compulsion . . . against tolerance, conformity. Its faith is that the iron laws of history will require every nation to traverse [travel] the same predestined [predetermined] path to the same predestined conclusion. Given this faith . . . the very existence of diversity is a threat to the Communist future.

I do not assert that communism must always remain a [crusading] faith. Like other fanaticisms of the past, it may in time . . . accept the diversity of human destiny. . . . [We] may all earnestly hope that [the Soviet rulers] . . . will renounce the dream of making the world over in the image of the Soviet Union. It must be the purpose of other nations to do what they can to hasten that day.

But that day has not yet arrived. . . .

The ink was hardly dry on the Charter before Moscow began its war against the world of the United Nations. The very first meeting of the Security Council—and I was there—was called to hear a complaint by Iran that Soviet troops had failed to withdraw from the northern part of that country on the date on which they had agreed to leave. Not only had they declined to go; they had installed a puppet regime on Iranian soil and had blocked Iranian troops from entering part of Iran's territory. . . . Eventually the United Nations forced a reluctant agreement from the Soviet Union to live up to its pledge.

This was only the beginning. At the time of the German surrender, the Red Army was in occupation of Romania, Bulgaria, Hungary, Poland, Eastern Germany, and most of Czechoslovakia. And there the Red Army stayed. . . . By 1948 five nations and half of a sixth, with a combined population of more than 90 million people, had been absorbed into the Communist empire. To this day the peoples of eastern Europe have never been permitted to exercise the Charter right of self-determination.

Before the suppression of eastern Europe was complete, the Soviet Union was fomenting guerrilla warfare and sabotaging economic recovery in Greece and Turkey. . . .

Nor were such activities confined to Europe. In Malaya [now Malaysia], in the Philippines, in Burma, in Indochina [now Cambodia, Laos, and Vietnam], the Communists encouraged and supported guerrilla uprisings against constituted governments.

In one event after another . . . the rejection in the United Nations of the American plan for the internationalization of atomic energy, the rejection of the Marshall Plan . . . the blockade of Berlin, and, finally, the invasion of South Korea—the Soviet Union assailed political independence, resisted the world of the Charter, and tried to impose its design of a Communist future. . . .

The Marshall Plan was a program aimed at putting Europe on its feet after World War II. In 1948, the Russian government blocked the flow of traffic between Berlin and West Germany. This is known as the "Berlin Blockade."

The Soviet government has signed treaties of nonaggression, as it did with the Baltic states and Finland—and then systematically invaded the countries whose integrity it had solemnly promised to respect.

At Yalta and in a succession of peace treaties, it pledged to the liberated countries of eastern Europe "the right of all peoples to choose the form of government under which they will live—the restoration of sovereign rights and self-government to those peoples who have been forcibly deprived of them"—and then it systematically denied those rights. . . .

In 1945 it signed a 30-year pact of mutual assistance and nonaggression with China . . . and violated that treaty almost before the Chinese negotiators had left Moscow.

At Potsdam it promised that "all democratic political parties with rights of assembly and of public discussion shall be allowed and encouraged throughout Germany"—and within its own zone promptly repudiated [went back on] that promise. At Geneva in 1954 it agreed not to introduce arms into Vietnam—and sent guns and ammunition to the Viet Minh.

The "Viet Minh" is the Communist-led independence league in Vietnam.

It denounced nuclear testing—and then violated the moratorium [suspension of testing] . . .

Within this Council it has thwarted the majority will 100 times by use of the veto.

The record is clear . . .

27. Major Events in Soviet Foreign Affairs, 1945-1967

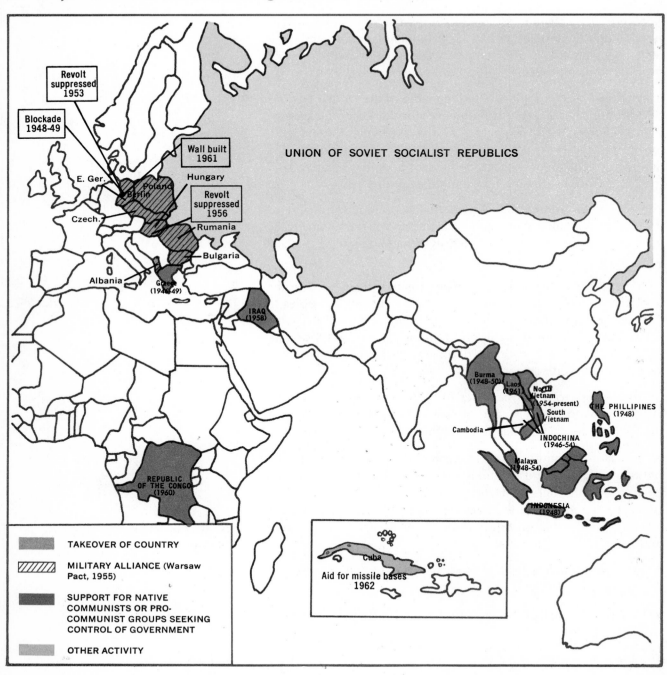

UNION OF SOVIET SOCIALIST REPUBLICS

Revolt suppressed 1953

Blockade 1948-49

Wall built 1961

E. Ger.
Berlin
Poland
Hungary

Revolt suppressed 1956

Czech.

Rumania

Albania

Bulgaria

Greece (1946-49)

IRAQ (1958)

Burma (1948-50)
Laos (1961)
North Vietnam (1954-present)
South Vietnam
Cambodia
INDOCHINA (1946-54)

THE PHILLIPINES (1948)

Malaya (1948-54)

INDONESIA (1948)

REPUBLIC OF THE CONGO (1960)

TAKEOVER OF COUNTRY

MILITARY ALLIANCE (Warsaw Pact, 1955)

SUPPORT FOR NATIVE COMMUNISTS OR PRO-COMMUNIST GROUPS SEEKING CONTROL OF GOVERNMENT

OTHER ACTIVITY

Cuba
Aid for missile bases 1962

746

28. The Threat of Communist China

In 1949, Mao Tse-tung and his followers established a Communist government on mainland China. His opponent, the Nationalist leader Chiang Kai-shek, retreated to the island of Formosa, or Taiwan, off the Chinese coast.

The Red Chinese government had very close ties at first with the Soviet Union. Early in the 1960's, however, friction began to develop. Today, the Soviet Union and China compete for the leadership of the Communist world. The Chinese advocate revolution to overthrow non-Communist governments. The Chinese often denounce the Russians for being too cooperative with the West. The following selection from *Newsweek* magazine presents several points bearing on the issue of whether China will become more peaceful in the future.

[In] an attempt to insure that China's younger generation will never make peace with capitalism, Mao has recently launched what is possibly the most thorough brainwashing campaign in human history. The method is to turn the writings and thoughts of Mao Tse-tung into a sort of divine gospel . . .

To a Westerner, such methods seem like mass enslavement, but . . . [the Chinese] for most of the past 2,000 years have been a heavily regimented people, taught that the individual can only find happiness by conforming to an ethic laid down by the state. . . .

. . . [The] prevailing theory in Washington [is] that the Chinese will eschew [avoid] war with the U.S. unless they are directly attacked. . . . It may well be true, but it appears to overlook . . . the fact that three times in the past fifteen years—in Korea, Tibet, and India—China has gone to war when its own territory was not directly threatened.

Behind the U.S. [military] containment policy lies the hope that the second or third generation of Chinese Communist leaders will be more moderate than the first one—as proved true in the Soviet Union. But most Sinologists [experts on China] see little assurance of this happening. . . . In talks with Westerners, [the men who are likely to succeed Mao] have shown themselves to be as tough as today's top leaders. And of the generation that will succeed them, little is known in the West.

Moreover . . . since the beginning of its history as a nation, China has called itself the Middle Kingdom. The meaning of that phrase is simple: China occupies the center of the world and all other nations are inferior to it. This deep-rooted notion prevails as strongly today as ever . . .

Newsweek, Vol. LXV (March 15, 1965), pp. 40, 45.

"Brainwashing" is a process of forced teaching to replace one set of political, social, and religious beliefs with another.

To be "regimented" is to be subject to rigid discipline.

An "ethic," here, is a set of moral principles or values.

The United States' "containment policy" is designed to contain, or hold, the Communist bloc within its present area by preventing additional countries from becoming Communist.

29. Major Events in Red Chinese Foreign Affairs, 1949-1967

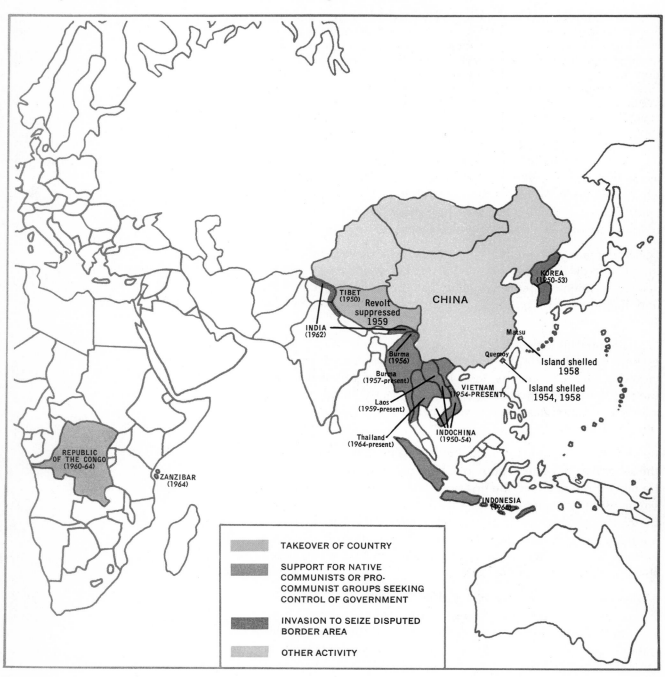

CHINA

KOREA
(1950-53)

TIBET
(1950)
Revolt
suppressed
1959

INDIA
(1962)

Burma
(1956)

Burma
(1957-present)

Laos
(1959-present)

Thailand
(1964-present)

VIETNAM
(1954-PRESENT)

INDOCHINA
(1950-54)

Matsu

Quemoy

Island shelled
1958

Island shelled
1954, 1958

INDONESIA
(1965)

REPUBLIC
OF THE CONGO
(1960-64)

ZANZIBAR
(1964)

TAKEOVER OF COUNTRY

SUPPORT FOR NATIVE
COMMUNISTS OR PRO-
COMMUNIST GROUPS SEEKING
CONTROL OF GOVERNMENT

INVASION TO SEIZE DISPUTED
BORDER AREA

OTHER ACTIVITY

30. Military Alliances and Bases

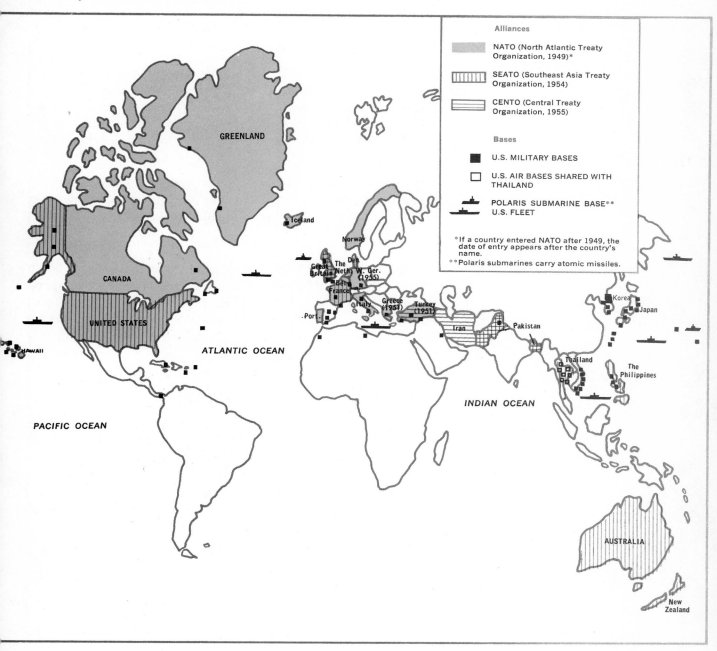

Alliances

- NATO (North Atlantic Treaty Organization, 1949)*
- SEATO (Southeast Asia Treaty Organization, 1954)
- CENTO (Central Treaty Organization, 1955)

Bases

- U.S. MILITARY BASES
- U.S. AIR BASES SHARED WITH THAILAND
- POLARIS SUBMARINE BASE**
  U.S. FLEET

*If a country entered NATO after 1949, the date of entry appears after the country's name.

**Polaris submarines carry atomic missiles.

GREENLAND

Iceland

Norway

Great Britain The Neth. Den. W. Ger. (1955)
Belg.
France

Port.

Italy Greece (1951) Turkey (1951)

Iran Pakistan

Korea Japan

Thailand

The Philippines

CANADA

UNITED STATES

HAWAII

ATLANTIC OCEAN

PACIFIC OCEAN

INDIAN OCEAN

AUSTRALIA

New Zealand

31. Main Events in United States Foreign Affairs, 1945-1967

1945–1947 UNRRA. The United States gives over $11 billion to the United Nations Relief and Rehabilitation Agency (UNRRA). The program distributes food in war-shattered Europe. Critics attack the large amount of relief sent to Communist eastern Europe.

1947–1950 Marshall Plan. To halt the march of communism and restore free Europe to economic health, Congress allots $12 billion for a three-and-a-half-year period.

1947 Truman Doctrine. To combat communism, Congress appropriates $400 million for military and economic aid to Greece and Turkey. President Truman says, "I believe that it must be the policy of the United States to support free peoples who are resisting attempted subjugation by armed minorities or by outside pressures."

1948 Berlin Airlift. The Soviet government blockades land traffic between Berlin and West Germany. The United States and Great Britain airlift food and coal to the blockaded area.

1949 NATO. The North Atlantic Treaty Organization is formed.

1950–1953 Korean War. North Korean Communists invade South Korea. The United States responds to a United Nations request and sends troops and supplies. Truman declares, "The attack upon Korea makes it plain . . . that Communism has passed beyond the use of subversion to conquer independent nations and will now use armed invasion and war. It has defied the orders of the Security Council of the United Nations . . ."

1954 SEATO. The Southeast Asia Treaty Organization is formed.

1954, 1958 Taiwan Straits. In 1954, the Red Chinese threaten to liquidate Taiwan, or Formosa. President Eisenhower announces that the U.S. Seventh Fleet will protect Formosa. Red China then bombards Quemoy, an island off the Chinese mainland. Congress passes a resolution stating that American forces will protect Formosa and the Pescadores, a group of islands off the Formosan coast. Chinese bombardments cease.

In 1958, Red China again bombards Quemoy, as well as Matsu, another island off the mainland. American ships escort Nationalist ships that supply the islands. Red China orders a cease-fire.

1956 Suez Crisis. In July 1956, Premier Nasser of Egypt accepts an offer of American aid to help build the Aswan Dam.

Shortly after, the United States withdraws the aid, partly because Egypt is buying arms from the Soviet bloc. In response, Nasser seizes the Suez Canal from the foreign company that owns it. He says he will use Canal profits to build the dam.

Three months later, in October, Israel invades Egyptian territory. Israel is angry over repeated terrorist raids from Egypt and Egyptian restrictions on Israeli shipping through the Suez Canal. France and Great Britain, whose trade depends heavily on the Suez Canal, join the Israeli attack. The United States votes with Russia at the United Nations in condemning the attack on Egypt. The Soviet Union provides Nasser with aid for building the Aswan Dam.

1956 Military Committee of the Baghdad Pact. Without becoming a full member of the Baghdad Pact, the United States joins its Military Committee. The Baghdad Pact was an alliance formed in 1954 to protect Turkey, Pakistan, Iraq, and Iran against the Soviet Union. Great Britain, which ruled many Middle Eastern countries as its colonies before World War II, was a member of the Pact. Egypt always criticized the Pact as a remnant of colonialism. So as not to offend Egypt, the United States never joined the Pact.

1957 Eisenhower Doctrine. In March 1957, President Eisenhower requests money for military aid to protect Middle Eastern countries against aggression from any country controlled by communism. The Senate provides $200 million to assist Middle Eastern countries in developing economic or military power.

1957 Jordan Crisis. The Prime Minister of Jordan places the Jordanian army under Egyptian command. He begins negotiating with the Soviet Union. In April 1957, Jordan's King Hussein dismisses his pro-Nasser, anti-Western Prime Minister for plotting to overthrow him.

King Hussein has been unpopular with many Jordanians and other Arabs for his friendliness toward western nations. Taking help from the West is often viewed as a return to colony status. Strong criticism of the king has come from Egypt and Syria, especially. In Syria, the two main parties are a pro-Nasser Socialist party and a pro-Russian Communist party.

Riots follow the Prime Minister's dismissal. The United States sends the Sixth Fleet to the eastern Mediterranean near Jordan, although the king has not requested that this be done. The United States also sends $10 million which the king has requested.

1958 Lebanon Crisis. In May 1958, pro-Nasser Lebanese rebel against the government of President Camille Chamoun. Many of the rebels have long favored the reunion of Lebanon with Syria. Syria, in February 1958, joined with Egypt to form the United Arab Republic (UAR). Chamoun accuses the UAR of provoking and aiding the rebellion.

Meanwhile, on July 14, pro-Nasser elements overthrow the government of Iraq. The Soviet Union applauds the coup and gives huge amounts of aid to the new government. Iraq drops out of the Baghdad Pact.

On July 15, Chamoun requests the support of American forces, and about fifteen thousand marines are sent to Lebanon.

1960–1964   Congo Crisis. In 1960, Belgium grants independence to her African colony, the Congo. Belgium has given the Congolese almost no training in self-government. Most people in the Congo feel more loyalty to their tribes than to the country. The tribes have long been hostile to each other, and violence soon breaks out. Meanwhile, the province of Katanga, which has rich copper mines, secedes.

UN troops are sent to restore order and to help put down the Katanga revolt. By 1963, Katanga surrenders. The UN troops stay for another year. The cost is almost half a billion dollars. The United States pays more than a third, while Russia refuses to pay its share.

When UN troops leave, rebellions erupt again. The United States helps the Congo government, while Russia and Red China aid the rebels. At one point, Communist-led rebels seize white people as hostages and massacre them. The United States supplies planes for a rescue mission.

1960   U-2 Incident. The Soviet Union announces that an American plane has been forced down inside Russia. The Russians claim the plane was taking photographs in order to collect military information. Six days later, after Russia announces that the pilot is alive and has confessed, President Eisenhower declares that he himself authorized the flight. Eisenhower says, "Here in our country anyone can buy maps and aerial photographs showing our cities, our dams, our plants, our highways—indeed, our whole industrial and economic complex. We know that Soviet attachés regularly collect this information. . . . Our thousands of . . . publications, our radio and television, all openly describe to all the world every aspect of our society.

"This is as it should be. We are proud of our freedom.

An "attaché" is a member of a diplomatic staff who is usually an expert in a particular area.

752

"Soviet distrust, however, does still remain. To allay these misgivings I offered five years ago to open our skies to Soviet reconnaissance aircraft on a reciprocal [mutual] basis. The Soviets refused. That offer is still open."

1961 Bay of Pigs Invasion. The United States Central Intelligence Agency equips and trains Cuban refugees, who invade Cuba in an attempt to overthrow Fidel Castro. The invasion fails.

1961 Berlin Crisis. In an attempt to squeeze the Western forces out of West Berlin and to make it a Communist city, the East German government builds a wall around West Berlin. President Kennedy calls for an increase in the draft and reactivation of reserve units. He declares, [West Berlin] ". . . is more than . . . an island of freedom in a Communist Sea. It is even more than a link with the free world, a beacon of hope behind the Iron Curtain, an escape hatch for refugees. . . .

"[It] has now become . . . the great testing place of Western courage and will. . . ."

1961 The Alliance for Progress. Congress appropriates $10 billion for a ten-year period to aid Latin American countries. The money is to be used to strengthen the economies of these countries and to help them improve their housing, medical, and school facilities. It is hoped that such improvements will strengthen resistance to communism. Supporters of Castro have been gaining followers in many Latin American countries.

1961 The Peace Corps. At President Kennedy's suggestion, a program is established to send American volunteer workers abroad. The volunteers, mostly young people, teach school, train people in practical skills, and help build new facilities. The volunteers go to countries that ask for their help.

1961–1962 The Laos Crisis. Communists are close to victory in a civil war in Laos. President Kennedy responds by sending American marines to nearby Thailand. Eventually both sides in the war agree to a plan drafted in Geneva which sets up a neutral government. Kennedy approves of this agreement.

1962 Cuban Missile Crisis. By use of aerial photographs, President Kennedy discovers that Russia is building missile bases in Cuba from which nuclear attacks can be launched against the eastern part of the United States and against nations around the Caribbean Sea. He demands that the bases be dismantled. He orders American ships to search ships going to Cuba for offensive weapons. Khrushchev promises to dismantle the missile bases.

1962 Vietnam War. In 1962, the United States sends troops to South Vietnam. The Americans act as military advisers to Vietnamese troops that are fighting the Vietcong, or Communist guerrillas. (See page 771.)

In 1965, American troops actively participate in the war for the first time.

Since 1963, Communist guerrillas have been active in Laos, in violation of the Geneva agreement. The Communists win control of large sections of the country. North Vietnam sends supplies to its forces in the South over the "Ho Chi Minh Trail" in eastern Laos.

1963, 1965 Dominican Crises. In 1963, Rafael Trujillo, long-time dictator of the Dominican Republic, is assassinated. For the first time in many years, the country holds free elections. Juan Bosch is elected president. Seven months later he is removed from office by an army coup. The generals behind the coup accuse Bosch of being "soft on communism." The United States takes no action.

In 1965, the same group of generals, or *junta,* who deposed Bosch stage another revolt, this time against the government of Donald Reid Cabral. A younger group of officers organizes a popular movement to restore Bosch. The Bosch rebels are close to victory when 22,000 United States troops arrive. President Johnson at first announces that the troops have been sent to protect American and foreign citizens. The American troops then support the military junta. To explain this action, the State Department releases a list of fifty-eight Communists who, it says, have seized control of the pro-Bosch revolt.

1966 Thailand. Thirty-five thousand United States troops are stationed in Thailand, which is used as a base for air strikes against North Vietnam and the Ho Chi Minh Trail. American helicopters, meanwhile, fly Thai police and troops to areas of Thailand where Communist guerillas are active.

1967 Middle East Crisis. At Nasser's request, U Thant, the Secretary General of the United Nations, withdraws United Nations peace-keeping forces from Egyptian-Israeli borders and the Sinai Peninsula. The forces were placed there after the fighting in 1956. Egyptian soldiers take over the UN positions, including a post overlooking the Straits of Tiran at the southern end of the Red Sea. Ships sailing to Elath, Israel's only non-Mediterranean port, must pass through the Straits. Egypt declares that the Straits are part of Egyptian territorial waters, and that she will bar Israeli ships and ships carrying strategic goods to Israel from going through the Straits. Israel, which receives much of her oil supply through Elath, declares that the blockade is an act of war. Israel recalls that she withdrew from Sinai in 1956 partly on condition that the United Nations would guarantee free passage through the Straits for all ships. She reminds the United States that it has also promised to guarantee free passage. Israel announces that unless these guarantees are backed up, she will be forced to open the Straits herself. Moscow announces that Russia will protect Arabs from Israeli aggression. Arab forces assemble on Israel's borders, and Arab leaders say that the time has come to destroy Israel. The United States Sixth Fleet begins cruising the Mediterranean. Soviet warships enter the Mediterranean and begin following American ships.

The United States pleads with Israel to await preparation of a statement by maritime nations that the Straits are international waters. Few nations seem willing to use force to guarantee the freedom of the Straits, however. France refuses to sign altogether. A few days later fighting breaks out. Americans and Russians re-assure each other by phone that they wish to avoid a confrontation. Israeli forces single-handedly defeat the armies of Jordan, Egypt, and Syria.

32. The Threat of Nuclear Weapons

In the 1930's and 1940's, the United States secretly developed an atomic bomb. It was tested in New Mexico in July 1945. On August 6, 1945, the United States dropped an atomic bomb on Hiroshima, Japan. Out of 343,000 people, 66,000 were killed and 69,000 were injured. Sixty-seven per cent of the city was destroyed or damaged. Three days later another bomb, dropped on Naga-saki, destroyed or damaged forty per cent of that city.

Russia exploded her first atomic bomb in 1949. With both the United States and Russia in possession of atomic weapons, the world was plunged into an arms race. Great Britain had nuclear weapons in 1957, France in 1960, and Communist China in 1964. Israel and Egypt may be developing such bombs by underground testing.

In 1952, the United States tested a stronger bomb, the hydrogen bomb. It can devastate nearly 150 square miles with its blast and cause serious damage to an area of about eight hundred square miles with its searing heat. Russia tested her first hydrogen bomb in 1953 and Communist China in 1967.

33. The Nuclear Test Ban Treaty, 1963

United States Arms Control and Disarmament Agency, **Review of International Negotiations on the Cessation of Nuclear Weapon Tests, September 1962-September 1965** (Washington, D.C.: U.S. Government Printing Office, 1966), Publication 32, pp. 101-103.

Formal Title: A Treaty Banning Nuclear Tests in the Atmosphere, in Outer Space and Under Water.

Preamble: The Governments of the United States of America, the United Kingdom of Great Britain and Northern Ireland, and the Union of Soviet Socialist Republics . . .

Proclaiming as their principal aim the speediest possible achievement of an agreement on general and complete disarmament under strict international control in accordance with the objectives of the United Nations which would put an end to the armaments race and eliminate the incentive to the production and testing of all kinds of weapons, including nuclear weapons, seeking to achieve the discontinuance of all test explosions of nuclear weapons for all time . . . and desiring to put an end to the contamination of man's environment by radioactive substances, have agreed as follows:

Article I. Each of the Parties to this Treaty undertakes to prohibit, to prevent, and not to carry out any nuclear weapon test explosion, or any other nuclear explosion, at any place under its jurisdiction or control . . . in the atmosphere; beyond its limits, including outer space; or under water, including territorial waters or high seas . . . .

Article III. This Treaty shall be open to all States for signature . . . .

Article IV. This Treaty shall be of unlimited duration.

Each party shall in exercising its national sovereignty have the right to withdraw from the Treaty if it decides that extraordinary events, related to the subject matter of this Treaty, have [endangered] the supreme interests of its country . . . .

Countries that originally signed the treaty: the United States, the United Kingdom, and the Soviet Union.

Countries that signed under the Article III provision: over one hundred nations.

Countries with atomic power that refused to sign: France, Red China.

756

OPINIONS AND RESPONSES

34. "A House Divided Against Itself..."

WOOD. COURTESY OF THE RICHMOND NEWS-LEADER

35. The McCarthy Era

On February 9, 1950, a little-known Republican senator from Wisconsin, Joseph R. McCarthy, made a speech in Wheeling, West Virginia, that brought him sudden fame. He produced a piece of paper which he described as a list of Communists working in the State Department. He claimed that the Secretary of State knew these people were Soviet agents. During McCarthy's brief career as a foe of Communist conspiracy, he accused many people of being Communist agents. None of his accusations were ever proven correct, but he nevertheless ruined many reputations and careers. On December 2, 1954, the Senate voted 67 to 22 to censure McCarthy for damaging the dignity of Congress. In the following selection, Richard Rovere, a writer for *The New Yorker* and author of a book about McCarthy, comments on the senator's popularity.

... [A] few months after the Wheeling speech he was known throughout the country and around the world, and he was a great power in American politics. ...

At home, he was greatly feared and greatly admired. From the President on down, no prudent [cautious] member of the Truman

Richard H. Rovere, "The Most Gifted and Successful Demagogue This Country Has Ever Known," **The New York Times Magazine,** April 30, 1967, pp. 23, 115, 117-118. © 1967 by The New York Times Company. Abridgement printed by permission of the author.

Administration in its last two years, or of the Eisenhower Administration in its first two, took any important decision without calculating the likely response of Joe McCarthy. After a bitter wrangle [fight] with McCarthy over the Senate's confirmation of Charles E. Bohlen . . . as Ambassador to the Soviet Union, Robert A. Taft, the leader of the Republican majority in the Senate, told President Eisenhower that he would not again do battle in behalf of anyone McCarthy opposed.

During the months in which the first Republican Administration in 20 years was setting itself up in business, McCarthy held a veto power over appointments.

Many of his colleagues in the Senate convinced themselves that he could determine the outcome of elections. On this the evidence was inconclusive; the chances are that his powers were somewhat overrated.

It was nevertheless a fact that in the elections of 1950 some Senators who had been critical of McCarthy lost their seats, and for the next four years there was scarcely any senatorial criticism of him. Few spoke well of him, but fewer still spoke ill of him—until at last the day came when the President of the United States decided that McCarthy threatened the morale of the United States Army and gave the first signal for resistance.

Whatever his impact on elections, he enjoyed, throughout this period, an astonishing and alarming amount of approbation [approval] in the country at large. . . . [It] was found by the Gallup Poll early in 1954 that 50 per cent of Americans held a "favorable opinion" of him, while only 29 per cent held an "unfavorable opinion. . . ."

McCarthy discovered the value of numbers. Had he said in Wheeling or at any point during his career that there was one Communist or two or even five or six, in this or that agency, his bluff could quite easily have been called. But he used large figures and kept changing them. After his Wheeling speech, of which no transcript was ever found, there was some dispute over the number of Communists he had said were on his "list"—it turned out not to be a list but a copy of an old letter from a former Secretary of State to a Congressman—but the highest figure he used was 205, the lowest 57. These were numbers with built-in safety. Showing him to be wrong about three or four of them proved little—what of the other 200 or so, what of the remaining 50-odd? . . .

McCarthy used, to great and at times quite amusing effect, many of the trappings of scholarship, of research. The bulging brief-case was his symbol. He was rarely seen without one. Inside were photostats, transcripts, clippings, copies of other people's corre-spondence, and assorted "documents." I met him for the first time a year or so before his rise to fame, and he was trying to persuade me of the soundness of the stand he was taking on a matter that had nothing to do with Communism. In his office, he produced for my enlightenment great stacks of papers. . . . It took me hours to learn . . . that he was passing off as "research" a mere mess of paper that he or someone else had stacked up so that its sheer . . . bulk looked impressive. In time, he was to con half the country as, for a time that day, he had conned me.

To "con" is to trick or deceive.

36. "Where To?"

SEIBEL. COURTESY RICHMOND TIMES-DISPATCH
A cartoon comment on the Truman Doctrine.

37. An Appraisal of American Asian Policy: Robert A. Taft, 1951

Senator Robert A. Taft of Ohio was a leading spokesman for the Republican party. He had opposed our entry into NATO and

Sources of The American Republic. A Documentary History of Politics, Society and Thought, edited by Marvin Meyers, Alexander Kern, John G. Cawelti (Chicago: Scott, Foresman and Company, 1961), p. 458.

A "reactionary" group opposes change and wants to preserve or return to the old order.

instead had called for further development and extension of our air power as a deterrent to Soviet advances. In 1951, Senator Taft, speaking for most Republicans, made the following remarks about President Truman's handling of our government's policy toward Asia. Specifically, Taft spoke about the failure of America to bomb Chinese military supply lines in Manchuria when the Communist Chinese entered the Korean War.

. . . I only insist that we apply to Asia the same basic policy which we apply to Europe. As I have said, that policy is to check communism at every possible point . . . within our capacity to do so.

Broadly speaking, my quarrel is with those who wish to go all-out in Europe, even beyond our capacity, and who at the same time refuse to apply our general program and strategy to the Far East. In Greece we moved in with overwhelming support for the Greek Government, even though it at first had strong reactionary tendencies. We gave it hundreds of millions of dollars to suppress Communists within the country. But in China we hampered the Nationalist Government. We tried to force it to take Communists into the Cabinet. The State Department spoke of Communists as agrarian reformers and cut off arms from the Nationalist Government at the most crucial time. Contrary to the whole theory of the containment of communism, where it could be done without serious cost or danger, the Administration proposed to surrender Formosa to the Communists and has constantly flirted with that idea.

Even though we were engaged in a bitter and dangerous war, the Administration refused to fight that war with all the means at its command, on the theory that we might incite Russia to start a third world war. But in Europe we have not hesitated to risk a third world war over and over again. When we moved into Greece to support the Government the Russians might have moved in to support the Communists. The building up of a Turkish Army and Air Force within easy reach of Moscow is far more of a threat to Russia than the bombing of Chinese supply lines in Manchuria. In Europe we have not hesitated to say to Russia, "If you cross certain lines and attack any one of eleven nations you will find yourself at war with the United States." We have laid down no such principle in Asia, except as to island nations. . . .

I think we have to recognize that the policy we have adopted of the containment of communism involves a constant danger that Russia may begin a third world war. But it is beyond our capacity to invade China with American soldiers, and such a program is not included in MacArthur's suggestions or anyone else's. There is no possible threat to Siberia, therefore, from anything we may do in China. On the other hand, in Europe the building up of a great army surrounding Russia from Norway to Turkey and Iran might produce a fear of the invasion of Russia or some of the satellite countries regarded by Russia as essential to the defense of Moscow. Certainly our program in Europe seems to me far more likely to produce war with Russia than anything we have done in the East. I am only asking for the same policy in the Far East as in Europe.

A "satellite" country is a political entity which is within the sphere of influence of a stronger entity. Poland, for example, is a Russian satellite.

38. Khrushchev Interprets the Cold War

In 1963, Premier Nikita Khrushchev of the Soviet Union stated the official Soviet view on the Cold War.

Soon after the Second World War ended, the influence of reactionary and militarist groups began to be increasingly evident in the policy of the United States of America, Britain, and France. Their desire to enforce their will on other countries by economic and political pressure, [by] threats and military provocation prevailed. This . . . "positions-of-strength" policy . . . reflects the aspiration of the most aggressive sections of present-day imperialism to win world supremacy, to suppress the working class and the democratic and national-liberation movements; it reflects their plans for military adventures against the Socialist camp.

The international atmosphere was poisoned by war hysteria. The arms race began to assume more and more monstrous dimensions. Many big United States military bases designed for use against the USSR and the People's Democracies were built in countries thousands of miles from the borders of the United States. Cold war was begun against the Socialist camp. International distrust was artificially kindled, and nations set against one another. A blood war was launched in Korea; the war in Indochina dragged on for years.

The inspirers of the cold war began to establish military blocs, and many countries found themselves, against the will of their peoples, involved in restricted aggressive alignments—the North Atlantic bloc [NATO], Western European Union, SEATO (military bloc for Southeast Asia), and the Baghdad Pact.

The organizers of military blocs allege that they have united for defense . . . against the "Communist threat." But that is sheer hypocrisy. We know from history that, when planning a redivision of the world, the imperialist powers have always lined up military blocs. . . . The new thing here is that the United States wants

Panorama of the Past: Readings in World History, edited by Louis L. Snyder, Marvin Perry, Benjamin Mazen (Boston: Houghton Mifflin Company, 1966), Vol. II, pp. 214-216.

A nation which follows a policy of "imperialism" tries to extend its power and authority over others.

"Hypocrisy" is pretending to do one thing, while in reality doing something else.

...to secure a dominant position in the capitalist world for itself...

The inspirers of the "positions-of-strength" policy assert that this policy makes another war impossible, because it insures a "balance of power" in the world arena. . . .

Can peace be promoted by an arms race? It would seem that it is simply absurd to pose such a question. Yet the adherents of the "positions-of-strength" policy offer the arms race as their main recipe for the preservation of peace! . . .

We see the obvious intention of . . . the imperialist powers to aggravate international tension, to continue the arms race for the enrichment of a handful of monopolists at the expense of millions of taxpayers, to intensify the cold war on the basis of the "policy of strength," to halt the disintegration of the colonial system of imperialism, and [to] strangle the national-liberation movement of the peoples for freedom and independence. The ruling circles of the imperialist countries are . . . trying to unite all the aggressive blocs such as NATO, the Baghdad Pact, and SEATO into a single aggressive military bloc led by the United States of America. Is not this policy of the present-day claimants to world domination reminiscent of that pursued by Hitler and Mussolini when they based their policy on strength and built the notorious anti-Comintern pact, the Berlin-Rome-Tokyo Axis?

"Comintern" is short for Communist International. It was the official policy-making body of the international Communist movement until 1943.

39. The Good Old Days

BY BARNEY TOBEY. COURTESY OF SATURDAY REVIEW

"War wasn't so bad in those days, was it?"

40. "We Shall Bear Any Burden": John F. Kennedy

These statements are part of the inaugural address delivered by President John F. Kennedy on January 20, 1961.

Let every nation know, whether it wishes us well or ill, that we shall pay any price, bear any burden, meet any hardship, support any friend, oppose any foe, in order to assure the survival and the success of liberty.

This much we pledge—and more.

To those old allies whose cultural and spiritual origins we share, we pledge the loyalty of faithful friends. United, there is little we cannot do in a host of cooperative ventures. Divided, there is little we can do—for we dare not meet a powerful challenge at odds and split asunder.

To those new states whom we welcome to the ranks of the free, we pledge our word that one form of colonial control shall not have passed away merely to be replaced by a far greater iron tyranny. We shall not always expect to find them supporting our view. But we shall always hope to find them strongly supporting their own freedom—and to remember that, in the past, those who foolishly sought power by riding the back of the tiger ended up inside.

To those peoples in the huts and villages across the globe struggling to break the bonds of mass misery, we pledge our best efforts to help them help themselves, for whatever period is required—not because the Communists may be doing it, not because we seek their votes, but because it is right. If a free society cannot help the many who are poor, it cannot save the few who are rich.

To our sister republics south of our border, we offer a special pledge—to convert our good words into deeds, in a new alliance for progress, to assist free men and free governments in casting off the chains of poverty. But this peaceful revolution of hope cannot become the prey [victim] of hostile powers. Let all our neighbors know that we shall join with them to oppose aggression or subversion anywhere in the Americas. And let every power know that this hemisphere intends to remain the master of its own house.

To that world assembly of sovereign states, the United Nations, our last best hope in an age where the instruments of war have

Inaugural Addresses of the Presidents of the United States (Washington, D.C.: United States Government Printing Office, 1961), pp. 268-269.

far outpaced the instruments of peace, we renew our pledge of support—to prevent it from becoming merely a forum for invective [destructive criticism]—to strengthen its shield of the new and the weak—and to enlarge the area in which its writ [authority] may run.

Finally, to those nations who would make themselves our adversary, we offer not a pledge but a request: that both sides begin anew the quest for peace, before the dark powers of destruction unleashed by science engulf all humanity in planned or accidental self-destruction.

We dare not tempt them with weakness. For only when our arms are sufficient beyond doubt can we be certain beyond doubt that they will never be employed.

But neither can two great and powerful groups of nations take comfort from our present course—both sides overburdened by the cost of modern weapons, both rightly alarmed by the steady spread of the deadly atom, yet both racing to alter that uncertain balance of terror that stays the hand of mankind's final war.

So let us begin anew—remembering on both sides that civility is not a sign of weakness, and sincerity is always subject to proof. *Let us never negotiate out of fear. But let us never fear to negotiate. . . .*

All this will not be finished in the first 100 days. Nor will it be finished in the first 1,000 days, nor in the life of the administration, nor even perhaps in our lifetime on this planet. But let us begin.

41. Why We Bear the Burden

"Why America Carries the World's Burden," **U.S. News & World Report,** Vol. LXII (March 6, 1967), pp. 35-37.

The American "presence" in the outside world will continue as the single stabilizing influence in areas where Soviet Russia and Red China . . . are to continue to stir trouble. [These areas include the] Middle East, the area of the Western Mediterranean, black Africa, [and] much of Asia . . .

The facts show . . . that the British—who, prior to World War II, were a leading power . . . are trying to draw into isolation on their little island, looking to the U.S. for protection. Japan . . . wants no part of the job of defense, either of itself or of the areas on which her trade depends.

France has given up its empire and is devoting itself to sniping at the U.S. The West Germans are preoccupied with reunification of their country . . .

The United States is left to take on the role of leadership. It is in that role, striving to counter expansion of Communist rule by subversion and military force, that Americans now are in Vietnam and have undertaken a number of military actions in the years since World War II.

It is the immense power that resides in today's America—as the single giant of the non-Communist world—that probably makes any escape from this role impossible.

The United States has only 7 per cent of the earth's surface, and less than 6 per cent of world population. And yet the U.S. has become, by all measures, the dominant power among nations. Some examples show the vast extent of U.S. superiority.

TOTAL OUTPUT
PRODUCTION OF ALL GOODS AND SERVICES, 1966:
$740 BILLION IN U.S., ONE THIRD OF THE WORLD TOTAL.
NATION NO. 2: SOVIET UNION, $340 BILLION.
NATION NO. 3: WEST GERMANY, $115 BILLION.

MILITARY MIGHT
U.S., DEFENDING NOT ONLY ITSELF BUT ALSO NEARLY ALL OF THE FREE WORLD, IS THE WORLD'S NO. 1 MILITARY POWER. THIS NATION HAS—
MORE MEN UNDER ARMS—3,335,000—THAN ANY OTHER NATION. RUSSIA HAS 3,165,000, RED CHINA 2,486,000.
THE WORLD'S GREATEST NAVY, WITH 934 COMMISSIONED SHIPS, INCLUDING THE ONLY MAJOR FLEET OF AIRCRAFT CARRIERS.
THE BEST-EQUIPPED AIR FORCE ON EARTH.
A LONG-RANGE MISSILE FORCE NEARLY FOUR TIMES AS LARGE AS THAT OF THE ONLY REAL RIVAL, RUSSIA.
ARMS OUTLAYS FAR BIGGER THAN THOSE OF ANY OTHER NATION.

PEOPLE'S INCOMES
INCOME PER PERSON IN 1966:
$2,950 IN U.S. NO OTHER COUNTRY IS EVEN NEAR THAT FIGURE.
NO. 2 NATION IS SWEDEN, WHERE AVERAGE INCOME IS JUST 60 PER CENT OF THAT IN U.S.
THE AVERAGE RUSSIAN GETS ONLY 40 PER CENT AS MUCH INCOME AS THE AVERAGE AMERICAN.

SOME OTHER MEASURES
INDUSTRY. U.S. HAS PRODUCTIVE POWER MORE THAN TWICE THAT OF SOVIET UNION, TURNS OUT TWICE AS MUCH AS ALL COMMON MARKET COUNTRIES AND BRITAIN COMBINED.
STEEL PRODUCTION. ONE FOURTH OF THE WORLD TOTAL.
AUTOS. U.S. HAS THREE FIFTHS OF ALL THE WORLD'S CARS.
TRUCKS. TWO OUT OF EVERY FIVE.
SURFACED ROADS. A THIRD OF THE WORLD TOTAL.
ELECTRICITY. U.S. USES ONE THIRD OF ALL ELECTRIC POWER PRODUCED ON EARTH.
RAILROAD FREIGHT. ONE QUARTER OF THE WORLD TOTAL.
CIVIL AVIATION. HALF THE WORLD MILEAGE.

42. The Wrong Approach

In his book, *The Futile Crusade,* author Sidney Lens argues that Americans, panicked by Communism, fail to see the best means for preventing its spread. He feels that our large-scale military assistance doesn't work and that we give our aid to the wrong people.

In the following excerpts from the book, Lens discusses nations, nationalism, and imperialism. A *nation* is a group of people with a common heritage who live together in one country. Usually, they have their own government. *Nationalism* is devotion to one's nation, the desire to advance its interests. *Imperialism,* which you read about earlier, refers to the policy of building an empire by taking over other countries. Many western nations were imperialistic between the sixteenth and nineteenth centuries. Countries like Spain, England, France, and Holland claimed parts of Asia, the Middle East, Africa, and Latin America as their colonies. After World War II, many of these non-European peoples began to clamor for their own independent governments. They also wanted to have for themselves the same high standard of living enjoyed by the Europeans. In other words, they became nationalistic.

Sidney Lens, **The Futile Crusade: Anti-Communism as American Credo** (Chicago: Quadrangle Books, 1964), pp. 20, 94-98, 130, 193-196. Reprinted by permission of the publisher.

. . . Is it possible . . . that "we are not being defeated in the Cold War by our communist adversaries [opponents]. We are defeating ourselves."? . . .

[At the end of World War II the] vast majority of people outside Western Europe and America lived . . . in geographic units that were sometimes called "nations," but were nothing of the sort. They were neither free, independent, united, nor economically viable [workable]. For centuries the people of these areas had tolerated their lot in hopeless stupor [dullness]; now they were ready to give their lives for nationalist goals. . . . [They wanted] independence, land reform, industrialization, and twentieth-century living standards . . . Anyone who would raise the banner of independence and land reform [in particular] would win their allegiance.

"Land reform" is a policy whereby the government takes large parcels of land from private owners and redistributes it to people who have no land. This policy is common in countries where almost all the land is owned by a very small minority of the population.

Herein lies the strength of communism . . . And therein lies the weakness of the United States . . .

. . . The communists embrace nationalism with fervor and seek to lead it . . .

A "radical" group is one that favors extreme change. Radical nationalists are people who want to make revolutionary changes in their countries so that the aims of nationalism can be fulfilled.

The United States, on the other hand, has never drawn close to radical nationalism. So far as we know, there is not a single instance of the United States actively supporting nationalists *before* they came to power. . . . Once certain revolutions succeeded, the United States policymakers *did* give succor [aid] in the form of grants and technical know-how. But it was done . . . to contain communism—and in the hopes finally of wooing the revolutionaries into America's military alliances, rather than . . . [to help] revolutionary nationalism. . . .

Thus the communists remain important factors in the lives of nations such as Indonesia, India, Burma, and many others, where they have blundered shamefully; while the United States has lost its original attractiveness, and is today lumped with Britain and France as part of "imperialism. . . ."

. . . America's best intentions are subverted [undercut] by its primary allegiance to Anti-Communism. Where it must choose between reform and a dictator who is "Anti-Communist," it chooses the latter, agrees to postpone the former. . . .

In Guatemala the dictator, Jorge Ubico, was ousted in 1944 and a democratic-minded former school teacher, Juan José Arevalo, was elected to office. Following his full six-year term, Jacobo Arbenz, a military officer with leftist leanings, became president. Under the two regimes, until Arbenz was ousted by a U.S.-sponsored coup, there were significant social reforms. All men eighteen years or over, whether literate or not, and all women of the same age, provided they could read and write, were granted the right to vote. Presidents were restricted . . . to a single six-year term, with no right to succeed themselves. Elections were held by secret ballot, and the freedom of assembly, expression, press, and the like, were . . . written into the constitution. Unions, never before legal, were given modern status . . . Wages in most sectors [parts of the economy] went up appreciably. During the short three-year Arbenz regime, some 85,000 peasant families were given plots of nationalized land, and in many areas peasants overran the farms of the [estate] owners and divided the acreage themselves. . . .

"Nationalized" means taken over by the nation.

. . . There is no question that many communists associated themselves with the Arbenz cause . . . and no doubt rose to prominent positions. This became a cause of concern in Washington . . . [However,] instead of . . . aiding [the] reforms [of the Arbenz regime] and drawing it away from communists, the Central Intelligence Agency assumed the task of overthrowing it. Under CIA tutelage, Colonel Carlos Castillo Armas outfitted a small force in neighboring Honduras and invaded his homeland. . . . [The] CIA and Castillo won an easy victory . . .

"Tutelage" means instruction or influence.

The first acts of Castillo's regime in 1954 were ominous. From

767

To do something with "impunity" means to do it with confidence that one cannot be harmed or punished.

June to November, thousands of workers and political leaders were arrested. Employers fired militant [active] unionists with impunity... All unions were disbanded because they were "political." The 85,000 parcels of land that had been given to Indian peasants were taken back and returned to the... owners.... In the next seven years, the Guatemala dictators distributed land to only 4,078 peasants—in a country where 70 per cent of the rural population is landless. The union movement was reduced to sixteen thousand members (from 107,000), no strikes were tolerated, and no wage increases granted—in a nation where 66 per cent of those employed earned less than $30 a month. Illiteracy, 72 per cent in 1954, remained at 72 per cent in 1961....

...Communism has won only in China, North Viet Nam, and Cuba, so far. But as the revolution continues and accelerates [moves faster], other nations will turn to communism, other nations will become more unfriendly to the United States.... Unless... we can convince the radical nationalists... that we are not interested in them primarily for military bases and spheres of investment, but because we truly want to help *them*, the pendulum will swing further away from us....

43. Crusaders of the World

The first of the following statements was made in 1966 by Walter Lippmann, a well-known columnist and political philosopher. The second was made by Henry Steele Commager in 1967 when he testified before the Senate Foreign Relations Committee. You read some of Commager's writings earlier in this unit (see pages 717–718.)

Viewpoints: U.S.A., edited by Bernard Feder and Jack Allen (New York: American Book Company, 1967), p. 320.

To "intoxicate," here, means to excite to frenzy.

WALTER LIPPMANN

A mature great power will make measured and limited use of its power. It will eschew [reject] the theory of a global and universal duty which not only commits it to unending wars of intervention but intoxicates its thinking with the illusion that it is a crusader for righteousness, that each war is a "war to end all war." Since in this generation we have become a great power, I am in favor of learning to behave like a great power, of getting rid of the globalism which would not only entangle us everywhere but is based on the totally vain notion that if we do not set the world in order, no matter what the price, we cannot live in the world safely.

HENRY STEELE COMMAGER

I do not think the United States is prepared to be a power everywhere—in the Western Hemisphere, in Europe, in Asia—nor do I think we should wish to exercise power everywhere.

"Excerpts From Commager Foreign Policy Statement to Senate Hearing," **The New York Times,** Feb. 21, 1967.

There have been, in the long course of history, many nations that regarded themselves, and always with some justification, as world powers, but there has never been a nation that could, in fact, exercise power everywhere on the globe. . . .

Because governments must of necessity use power, it does not follow that they are capable of using it everywhere, or using it absolutely. Our whole history, and our political philosophy, is a monument to the belief that power is limited, and that power should be limited. That is, in a sense, what the Revolution was about—a repudiation of the British claim, set forth in the Declaratory Act, that Parliament had the right to "bind the colonies and people of America in all cases whatsoever."

The American position was, quite simply, that no government had all power. That is part of the meaning of our written constitutions—documents that enumerate with greatest care the powers which governments may exercise. That is at the heart of our elaborate system of checks and balances—the determination to limit the authority and the power of government.

That is what the Bills of Rights, state and Federal, are about—limitations on government.

And as Americans have required, and provided, restraint on the domestic scene, so they are pledged to restraint in the international arena. Almost all our traditions here emphasize limitations on power. . . .

Although we used something like total power in the second World War, once victory had been achieved we contented ourselves with trying to put the broken fragments of the war-torn world together again. We used aid, we used influence, we used military power, but we did not use the ultimate power of the nuclear weapon, nor did we in fact attempt to order the affairs of Asia.

It has remained for the statesmen of this decade to insist that we are an Asian power, and have the same kind of responsibility for Asia that we have for Western Europe.

It is my feeling that we do not have the resources, material, intellectual, or moral, to be at once an American power, a European power, and an Asian power. Justice Holmes used to say that the first lesson a judge had to learn was that he was not God. It is a lesson every man has to learn and a lesson every nation has to learn. . . .

It is not our duty to keep peace throughout the globe, to put down aggression wherever it starts up, to stop the advance of Communism or other isms which we may not approve of. It is primarily the responsibility of the United Nations to keep the peace, to settle disputes, to discourage aggression, and if that organization is not strong enough to do the job we should perhaps bend our major energies to giving her the necessary authority and the tools.

One explanation of our obsession with Communism and more particularly, now, with "Communist aggression" in Asia is to be found, I think, in a deep and persistent trait of the American mind: the belief in Old World corruption and New World innocence. The men who won the independence of America from the mother country were convinced that the Old World was abandoned to tyranny, misery, ignorance, injustice and vice and the New World was innocent of these sins . . .

A "shibboleth" is a commonplace saying or idea.

The notion of an international Communist conspiracy, which a good many Americans still cling to, fits neatly into this shibboleth of Old World wickedness and New World virtue. And so, too, our habit of throwing a mantle of morality over our own wars. We tend, perhaps more than other nations, to transform our wars into crusades. The Mexican War was part of manifest destiny. The Spanish-American War was a crusade to free Cuba from Spanish tyranny. The First World War was a crusade to make the world safe for democracy. The Second World War did indeed have moral purposes, more clearly, I think, than almost any war of modern times.

Our current involvement in Vietnam is cast, increasingly, into a moral mold; it is, quite simply, a war to halt Communist aggression. . . .

Closely associated with the notion of New World virtue is the somewhat more activist notion of New World mission. This, too, is a familiar theme: Providence, or history, has put a special responsibility on the American people to spread the blessings of liberty, democracy, and equality to other peoples of the earth. . . .

THE VIETNAM DEBATE

44. The Background of War

The country of Vietnam was born from French Indochina. Indochina, composed of the present countries of Cambodia, Laos, and Vietnam, became a protectorate of France in 1884. At the end of World War II, most Indochinese wished to be independent of French rule. The Vietminh (Independence) League, headed by Ho Chi Minh, a Communist guerilla leader, emerged as the most important of many groups that hoped to secure independence for Vietnam. In 1945, Ho Chi Minh proclaimed the establishment of the Democratic Republic of Vietnam. Hanoi was designated as its capital.

The French did not want to give up their colony, so fighting began in 1946. The French-Indochinese War lasted until 1954. The Geneva Accords of 1954 ended the war and divided Vietnam into two zones. The North was placed under the Vietminh and the South under the French army and the State of Vietnam. The French pledged to withdraw their troops when requested to do so by the government of South Vietnam. French troops were withdrawn early in 1956. The Geneva Accords also provided that elections to decide the future government of the country were to take place in 1956.

In 1955, Ngo Dinh Diem, who was premier of a temporary government, proclaimed the southern zone a republic and became its first president. At that time, the United States took over the training of South Vietnam's army. In 1956, the South Vietnamese government declared that the elections specified by the Geneva Accords would not be held since it was impossible to hold free elections in the North. Privately, many South Vietnamese leaders feared that Ho Chi Minh would win the election. Guerilla fighting then broke out between the South Vietnamese forces and the Vietcong, Communist guerillas, aided by North Vietnam. The United States supplied aid and advice to the government of. South Vietnam.

In November 1963, the government of Ngo Dinh Diem was overthrown. Diem was killed during the revolt. Since that time, South Vietnam has had a succession of different governments. United States troops have participated actively in the fighting since June 1965.

771

45. The Reasons for American Policy: President Johnson

On March 15, 1967, President Johnson delivered a major address on American foreign policy before the Tennessee Legislature. In the following excerpt from his speech, headings that did not appear in the original have been added.

"Text of President Johnson's Nashville Address on U.S. Role in Vietnamese War," **The New York Times,** March 16, 1967.

It was two years ago that we were . . . forced to make a decision between major commitments in defense of South Vietnam or retreat . . .

We chose a course in keeping with American tradition, in keeping with the foreign policy of at least three Administrations, with the expressed will of the Congress of the United States, with our solemn obligations under the Southeast Asia Treaty and with the interests of 16 million South Vietnamese who had no wish to live under Communist domination. . . .

Our Basic Objectives

I think we have all reached broad agreement in our basic objectives in Vietnam. . . .

First, an honorable peace that will leave the people of South Vietnam free to fashion their own political and economic institutions without fear of terror or intimidation from the North.

Second, a Southeast Asia in which all countries, including a peaceful North Vietnam, apply their scarce resources to the real problems of their people, combating hunger and ignorance and disease. . . .

Third, a concrete demonstration that aggression across international frontiers and demarcation lines is no longer an acceptable means of political change.

There is also, I think, a general agreement among Americans on the things that we do not want in Vietnam.

We do not want permanent bases. . . .

We do not seek to impose our political beliefs upon South Vietnam. . . .

Our Military Situation

. . . Vietnam is aggression in a new guise as far removed from trench warfare as the rifle from the longbow. This is a war of infiltration, of subversion, of ambush; pitched battles are very rare and even more rarely are they decisive. . . .

Will the North Vietnamese change their tactics? Will there be less infiltration of main units? Will there be more of guerrilla warfare?

The actual truth is, we just don't know.

What we do know is that . . . our military situation has substantially improved, that our military success has permitted the ground work to be laid for a pacification program which is the long-run key to an independent South Vietnam.

The Reasons for Bombing

Since February, 1965, our military operations have included selective bombing of military targets in North Vietnam. Our purposes are three:

To back our fighting men by denying our enemy a sanctuary; to exact a penalty against North Vietnam for her flagrant violations of the Geneva accords of 1954 and 1962; to limit the flow or to substantially increase the cost of infiltration of men and material from North Vietnam. All of our intelligence confirms that we have been successful. . . .

[It] is not the position of the American Government that the bombing will be decisive in getting Hanoi to abandon aggression. It has, however, created very serious problems for them. The best indication of how substantial is the fact that they are working so hard, every day, with all their friends throughout the world, to try to get us to stop. . . . The strength of Communist main-force units in the South is clearly based on their infiltration from the North.

So I think it is simply unfair to our American soldiers, sailors and marines and our Vietnamese allies to ask them to face increased enemy personnel and firepower without making an effort to try to reduce that infiltration.

Now, as to bombing civilians, I would . . . say that we're making an effort that's unprecedented in the history of warfare to be sure that we do not. It is our policy to bomb military targets only. . . .

We hasten to add, however, that we recognize and we regret that some people, even after warning, are living and working in the vicinity of military targets, and they have suffered. . . .

Look for a moment at the record of the other side.

Any civilian casualties that result from our operations are inadvertent [unintentional] in stark contrast to the calculated Vietcong policy of systematic terror.

The aim of the "pacification program" is to help the South Vietnamese learn to improve their living conditions, their schools, and their local governments. It is hoped that such reforms will give the people a stake in supporting the Saigon government, rather than the Vietcong.

A "sanctuary" is a place of refuge and protection.

The Geneva Conference of 1962 established a neutralized status for Laos. Hanoi had placed its military strength behind the pro-Communist faction there.

773

Tens of thousands of innocent Vietnamese civilians have been killed and tortured and kidnapped by the Vietcong. There is no doubt about the deliberate nature of the Vietcong program. One need only note the frequency with which Vietcong victims are village leaders and teachers and health workers and others that are trying to carry out constructive programs for their people.

Yet the deeds of the Vietcong go largely unnoted in the public debate. And it is this moral double bookkeeping which makes us get sometimes very weary of our critics.

But there is another question that we should answer: Why don't we stop bombing to make it easier to begin negotiations? The answer is a simple one.

We stopped for 5 days and 20 hours in May, 1965. Representatives of Hanoi simply returned our message in a plain envelope.

We stopped bombing for 36 days and 15 hours in December, '65 and January, '66, and Hanoi only replied: "A political settlement of the Vietnam problem can be envisaged only when the United States Government has accepted the four-point stand of the Government of the Democratic Republic of Vietnam, has proved this by actual deeds, has stopped unconditionally and for good its air raids and all other acts of war against the Democratic Republic of Vietnam."

And only last month we stopped bombing for 5 days and 18 hours, after many prior weeks in which we had communicated to them several possible routes to peace, any one of which America was prepared to take. Their response, as you know, delivered to His Holiness the Pope, was this: The United States "must put an end to their aggression in Vietnam, end unconditionally and definitively the bombing and all other acts of war against the Democratic Republic of Vietnam, withdraw from South Vietnam all American and satellite troops, recognize the South Vietnamese National Front for Liberation, and let the Vietnamese people settle themselves their own affairs . . ."

We Are Ready to Negotiate
The problem is a very simple one. It takes two to negotiate at a peace table, and Hanoi has just simply refused to consider coming to a peace table. . . .

We are prepared to go more than half-way and to use any avenue possible to encourage such discussions, and we have done that at every opportunity.

We believe that the Geneva accords of 1954 and 1962 could serve as the central elements of a peaceful settlement. These accords provide in essence that both South and North Vietnam should be free from external interference, while at the same time they would be free independently to determine their positions on the question of reunification.

We also stand ready to advance toward a reduction of hostilities without prior agreement. The road to peace could go from deeds to discussions, or it could start with discussions and go to deeds. . . .

So let me conclude by saying this: I so much wish that it were within my power to assure that all those in Hanoi could hear one simple message—America is committed to the defense of South Vietnam until an honorable peace can be negotiated.

And if this one communication gets through and its rational implications are drawn, we should be at the table tomorrow. . . . Then hundreds of thousands of Americans as brave as any who ever took the field for their country could come back home . . .

And as these heroes come back to their homes, millions of Vietnamese could begin to make a decent life for themselves and their families without fear of terrorism, without fear of war or without fear of Communist enslavement. That is what we are working and what we are fighting for. And we must not, we shall not, we will not fail.

46. Aggression or a Civil War?

John Knight is publisher of the *Miami Herald*. Frank Church is a Democratic senator from Idaho and a member of the Senate Foreign Relations Committee.

JOHN KNIGHT

The situation in Vietnam has overtones of an indigenous civil war. . . . There are Communist overtones but the Vietcong are inspired more by feelings of nationalism. It was this feeling that put the Vietnamese against the Japanese, also the French. . . .

FRANK CHURCH

The concept of drawing a line against Communist aggression has little validity. In Europe, we were faced with Russian massed troops. We responded with NATO and a drawn line. But the countries there—with whom we share a common culture—had the

"Big New Base Behind A Dynamic Strategy; Cam Ranh Port," **Life,** Vol. LX (February 25, 1966), p. 58.

An "indigenous" war is one that grows out of native movements rather than one that is foreign-inspired.

Life, Feb. 25, 1966, pp. 58-59, 62.

internal cohesion [unity] and resistance to Communism to form a stable front. In Southeast Asia we are facing revolutionary wars, which are indigenous. Our failure to distinguish between aggression and revolution has been the most serious defect in our policy....

Communism won't take over the world ... It is much too poor a system. Its successes have usually been coincidental with the thrust of nationalism. It is our misfortune that in North Vietnam, the authentic vehicle of nationalism was a Communist. We are such prisoners of our own semantics [words] that we cannot see that, even in Communist lands, nationalist feelings of the people are governing.

This war is forcing Ho Chi Minh to his knees—not before Saigon but before Peking.

47. The Domino Theory

D. F. Fleming is a professor of international relations at Vanderbilt University and author of a history of the Cold War. Hans Morgenthau is a prominent critic of American foreign policy in Vietnam.

D. F. FLEMING

D. F. Fleming, "What Is Our Role In East Asia?" **The Western Political Quarterly,** Vol. XVIII, No. 1 (1965), pp. 79-80.

... [In] the last analysis our reason for being in South Vietnam ... is a belief that this peninsula is an extremely strategic spot and that if it "went" communist all Southeast Asia and beyond would turn Red.

This is the domino theory which has been used to justify every move in the cold war. In 1947 it was said that if Greece went communist so would Turkey, the Middle East, Iran and beyond. So, too, would Italy and France in the West. In 1950 the Korean War was justified in the same way. We have been taught likewise that if Formosa were lost the Chinese would soon take the Philippines, then Hawaii, then Catalina Island and our own Pacific coast.

Under this theory any American intervention anywhere in the world can be justified. If South Vietnam "goes," it is said, then a long set of standing dominoes will fall down through New Zealand to the South Polar continent, which fortunately has been neutralized. But would they? The Vietnamese are a tough and patriotic people. They were ruled by China for centuries and have no wish to be again. Nor is there any evidence that Red China has dominated North Vietnam or North Korea. On the contrary, she has helped them both to industrialize, from her own limited means. China hopes to cut a big figure politically throughout the vast under-developed southern hemisphere. Would she begin by making colonies out of her small neighbors? North Vietnam and China do need the surplus rice of South Vietnam, but would they take it without payment?

Of course it is unthinkable to us that South Korea or South Vietnam should become communist, but is that automatically involved in peace settlements which would neutralize both states by international agreements between the great powers including China?

HANS MORGENTHAU

[The domino theory] has not the slightest basis in history. . . . [Revolutions] succeed or fail because of local conditions, not on the basis of what happens in another country.

"Big New Base Behind A Dynamic Strategy; Cam Ranh Port," **Life,** Vol. LX (February 25, 1966), p. 59.

48. An Answer to Opponents of the War: June, 1966

The following article was written by Arnaud de Borchgrave, an editor of *Newsweek*.

The slogans about why the U.S. is in Vietnam—e.g., making South Vietnam safe for democracy . . . [tend] to obscure . . . the fundamental interest . . .

Arnaud Borchgrave, "A Dissent From the Dissenters," **Newsweek,** Vol. LXVII, Pt. 2 (June 6, 1966), pp. 32-33. Copyright 1966 by Newsweek, Inc. Condensed from **Newsweek** by permission.

The fundamental interest, quite simply, is to contain the expansion of Chinese Communist imperialism. . . .

[What] we are trying to do in Vietnam is to demonstrate that changes in Asia—and elsewhere in the world—are not to be precipitated [brought about] by "outside" force . . . What's at stake for the U.S. in Vietnam is not freedom and democracy for South Vietnam, though this might become a happy by-product. The key point at issue is whether the U.S. can successfully resist and subdue a war of "liberation. . . ."

In power politics—and that is still the name of the game—lines must be drawn somewhere, and if the U.S. doesn't draw them, who else in the Western world today would—or could? . . . What the U.S. is doing in Asia is no different, in basic principles, from what the U.S. helped the Europeans achieve during the past two decades: a line was drawn and Russia was contained and has now . . ."joined the ranks of those nations seeking peace in the world."

How long will it take to contain China . . . ? It could be another ten years or more. But evidence is accumulating that it might be shorter. I doubt whether Mao would be so obsessed [overly concerned] with the need to prevent the next generation from becoming "Khrushchevite revisionists" if it were not already happening. . . .

Two years after Premier Chou En-lai toured Black Africa as a liberating hero, one black African country after another is expelling Chinese [agents] and/or severing relations with Peking.

Captured documents have now produced the evidence that it was on instructions from Peking that the Communist party tried to seize power in Indonesia last fall [in 1965]. And the ensuing bloodbath of revenge against Communism has made the Vietnam war seem mild by comparison. Indonesia was a deadly blow to Peking's strategy in Southeast Asia; the largest Communist party in the non-Communist world lies destroyed. We now see Indonesia negotiating an end to its military confrontation with Malaysia.

Other Asian countries have drawn a lesson from China's failures in Africa and the Far East, and the American commitment in Vietnam has helped to convince them that China's brand of Communism is not necessarily the wave of the future. Indeed, there is a world of difference between what some Asian leaders say publicly and what they concede [admit] privately. One of India's highest government officials told me that "if you give up in Vietnam we will most probably have to double our military presence in the Himalayas." No sooner said than he added, "but for the record I will go on saying you must get out of Vietnam."

Burma is another case in point. In Rangoon [the capital] recently, Liu Shao-chi, the Chinese chief of state, could not get Burmese leaders, not noted for their pro-American sentiments, to sign a joint declaration condemning the U.S. for its actions in Vietnam.

For China . . . Vietnam is the crucial test of Mao's theories. It is also China's big chance to wreck America's entire position in Asia. If we hold our ground and Communist expansion is blocked . . . the Chinese will have suffered another major foreign policy setback. The dogmas will be shattered once and for all and we may at last look forward to change in Peking.

If we give in, what incentive will there be for China to change? We would probably have to start all over again two or three years hence, perhaps in Thailand, which is neither a better time nor a better place. . . .

The claim is often made that there is no practical alternative to the eventual takeover of South Vietnam by the Vietnamese Communists; that the NLF is truly a national movement in tune with the aspirations [aims] of the people; that we are still losing ground militarily; and that the South Vietnamese don't want us. . . .

"NLF" refers to the National Liberation Front, the political arm of the Vietcong.

If Communism is so popular, why has the Viet Cong felt it necessary to assassinate more than 20,000 local officials? Three leaders of the National Students Association of America have returned from Vietnam reporting they found no sympathy for the NLF among Vietnamese students. If the NLF is the embodiment of national aspirations and its victory is inevitable, how does one explain, as Buddhist leaders never tire of pointing out, that no one of prominence has joined the cause? If the NLF is indigenous to the South, how does one explain that it was created and is now controlled by Le Duan, after Ho Chi Minh the most powerful Communist leader in Hanoi?

If we are not doing immeasurably better militarily, how does one explain that Communist defectors [deserters] for the first time are now disclosing their unit locations and enabling U.S. forces to go in and hit them when they least expect it? . . . Or that both prisoners and defectors, taken in widely scattered parts of the country, say they are physically exhausted, always on the move, with no campfires allowed at night, little food and haphazard supplies? Or that a recent survey taken among 500 prisoners showed that only 30 per cent believed in a VC victory against 70 per cent a year ago? . . .

"VC" refers to the Vietcong.

. . . Premier Ky and his fellow generals (and some U.S. advisers), quite unwittingly [without meaning to], have helped the various religious groups to surface [emerge] as the true spokesmen for the people. This is basically a healthy development. The Buddhists (about 80 per cent of the population) are indeed an indigenous movement. They have no love for the West in general and the U.S. in particular—but they have no use for Peking or Hanoi either. Their leaders have said over and over again that no Communist party in Asia can live in harmony with other political parties. The last thing they want is for the U.S. to leave or stop fighting the Viet Cong until they are sure of a secure, independent, internationally guaranteed future. . . .

779

49. More Bombs? — May, 1967

Many critics have attacked the United States policy of *escalating,* or stepping up, the Vietnamese war by pouring in more men and dropping more bombs. The following selection appeared in *The New York Times.*

The News of the Week in Review, **The New York Times,** April 30, 1967. © 1967 by The New York Times Company. Reprinted by permission.

. . . [American officers in Saigon insist that] while air raids may for a time seem to weld the [North Vietnamese] population more closely together, the North Vietnamese . . . will some day begin to ask themselves why their government permits them to go on suffering, working longer hours for fewer rewards, and seeing the fruit of their labor destroyed. "When enough people begin asking that question," one expert said, "it will simply redouble the pressure on Hanoi to stop what they're doing. . . ."

The same reasoning applies to the escalation [of bombing] against industrial and communications targets. . . .

. . . No one in the American command denies that the North Vietnamese are tough and resilient [adaptable]. But, it is argued, everyone has a breaking point, and the bombing will go on until that point is reached.

But this analysis, though now the guiding one, is not accepted by all the experts on the American side, and those that oppose it point out that first Britain and then Germany withstood ferocious air assaults in World War II without buckling.

Furthermore, North Vietnam's most critically needed military supplies—planes, surface-to-air missiles, communications equipment, weapons and ammunition—come largely from the Soviet Union and China by way of the port of Haiphong and the railroad lines to the Chinese border.

The rail lines, though hit repeatedly, seem to be endlessly repairable, sometimes, according to reports, within a matter of hours. The same seems to be true of the infiltration and supply routes to the South. As for bombing Haiphong harbor in the absence of a declaration of war, that could destroy Soviet ships—not to mention those of friendly powers such as Britain and France—and lead to an international crisis.

Considering that the production of North Vietnam's immovable factories and utilities [light and power plants] is probably barely equal to that of a medium-sized American manufacturing city, one can look ahead to the day, perhaps within six months, when all these plants have been pretty much reduced to rubble. If Hanoi still doesn't crack, it is asked, what do you do for an encore?

50. The Question of Debate: General William Westmoreland

General William Westmoreland, commander of the United States troops in Vietnam, made the following remarks at a press luncheon in New York in April 1967.

The New York Times, April 25, 1967.

... I am mindful that the military war in South Vietnam is, from the enemy's point of view, only part of a protracted [long] and carefully coordinated attack, waged in the international arena. Regrettably, I see signs of enemy success in that world arena which he cannot match on the battlefield. He does not understand that American democracy is founded on debate, and he sees every protest as evidence of crumbling morale and diminishing resolve. Thus, discouraged by repeated military defeats but encouraged by what he believes to be popular opposition to our effort in Vietnam, he is determined to continue his aggression from the North. This, inevitably, will cost lives—American, Vietnamese and those of our other allies. . . .

The magnificent men and women I command in Vietnam have earned the unified support of the American people.

WHAT IS HISTORY?

Consider each of the following statements a hypothesis about history. Which of them would you accept? Tell why you would accept or reject each. Conclude your answers with a concise paragraph giving *your own* definition of history.

"[The job of history] is to show what actually happened. . . . The strict presentation of the facts . . . is undoubtedly the supreme law."

Leopold von Ranke, German historian, **Preface to Histories of the Latin and Germanic Nations from 1494-1514,** 1824.

"History is . . . the record of what one age finds worthy of note in another."

Jakob Burckhardt, (1818-1897) Swiss historian.

"[History is] . . . a fable agreed upon."

Attributed to Napoleon Bonaparte (1769-1821), French ruler.

"The history of the world is but the biography of great men."

Thomas Carlyle, English historian, **Heroes and Hero-Worship,** 1841.

"The subject of historians' study is the development of human societies in space and time."

Henri Pirenne, Belgian historian, "What are Historians Trying To Do?" 1931.

781

Hendrik Van Loon, American Journalist, **The Story of Mankind,** 1921.

"The history of the world is the record of man in quest of his daily bread and butter."

Prefatory Note, **The English Historical Review,** 1886.

"History [is] the record of human action, and of thought only in its direct influence upon action."

Fustel de Coulanges, French historian, Inaugural Lecture at the University of Strasbourg, 1862.

"The historian observes what changes, what is variable in man's soul—his beliefs . . . the trends and changes of his ideas—along with the things that are transformed with these ideas—i.e. laws, institutions, art, and science."

German Proverb.

"Ignorant heads read the past in history, wise ones read the future."

Frederick Jackson Turner, American historian, "The Significance of History," 1891.

"The aim of history is to know the . . . present by understanding what came into the present from the past."

Friedrich Meinecke, German historian, "Values and Casualties in History," 1928.

"[It] is values . . . that we win from history . . . Whole ages and generations can draw nourishment from the cultural values of a particular period in the past which is specifically related to them."

Albert Guerard, Franco-American historian, **France, A Modern History,** 1958.

"The . . . essential service of history is to restore to man, absorbed in his little concerns of the moment, a sense of due proportion . . ."

Carl Becker, American historian, "What Are Historical Facts?" 1955.

"Every man has some knowledge of past events, more or less accurate . . . [History] as we commonly think of it . . . is only an extension of memory . . . Its chief value, for the individual, is doubtless that it enables a man . . . to judge the acts and thoughts of men, his own included, on the basis of an experience less immediate and restricted. . . . [The] kind of history that has the most influence on . . . the course of events . . . is the history that common men carry around in their heads."

TIME LINE

1946 FIRST MEETING OF THE GENERAL ASSEMBLY OF THE UNITED NATIONS.

1947 TRUMAN DOCTRINE.

1947 MARSHALL PLAN.

1947 TAFT-HARTLEY ACT, AIMED AT REDUCING THE POWER OF ORGANIZED LABOR, PASSED.

1948 HARRY S. TRUMAN DEFEATS THOMAS E. DEWEY IN PRESIDENTIAL ELECTION.

1948 BERLIN AIRLIFT.

1948 THE ORGANIZATION OF AMERICAN STATES (OAS) FORMED TO IMPROVE THE EXCHANGE OF IDEAS, AID, AND DEFENSE AMONG AMERICAN COUNTRIES.

1949 NATO FORMED.

1950 NORTH KOREA INVADES SOUTH KOREA.

1951 TWENTY-SECOND AMENDMENT, LIMITING PRESIDENTS' TERMS OF OFFICE, ADOPTED.

1952 THE UNITED STATES EXPLODES ITS FIRST H-BOMB.

1952 DWIGHT D. EISENHOWER DEFEATS ADLAI E. STEVENSON IN PRESIDENTIAL ELECTION.

1954 *BROWN v. BOARD OF EDUCATION OF TOPEKA.*

1954 SEATO FORMED.

1954 SENATOR JOSEPH R. McCARTHY CENSURED BY THE SENATE.

1955 WARSAW PACT FORMED.

1956 EISENHOWER DEFEATS STEVENSON A SECOND TIME IN PRESIDENTIAL ELECTION.

1956 SUEZ CRISIS.

1957 EISENHOWER DOCTRINE.

1957 THE SOVIET UNION LAUNCHES THE FIRST MAN-MADE SPACE SATELLITE.

1960 JOHN F. KENNEDY DEFEATS RICHARD M. NIXON IN PRESIDENTIAL ELECTION.

1961 TWENTY-THIRD AMENDMENT, GRANTING RESIDENTS OF THE DISTRICT OF COLUMBIA THE RIGHT TO VOTE IN PRESIDENTIAL ELECTIONS, ADOPTED.

1961 THE BERLIN CRISIS.

1961 THE UNITED STATES SENDS ITS FIRST MAN INTO SPACE.

1961 BAY OF PIGS INVASION.

1961–65 UNITED STATES SENDS ADVISORY GROUPS TO SOUTH VIETNAM.

1962 CUBAN MISSILE CRISIS.

1963 PRESIDENT KENNEDY ASSASSINATED. LYNDON B. JOHNSON BECOMES PRESIDENT.

1964 TWENTY-FOURTH AMENDMENT, BARRING POLL TAX IN FEDERAL ELECTIONS, ADOPTED.

1964 LYNDON JOHNSON DEFEATS BARRY M. GOLDWATER IN PRESIDENTIAL ELECTION.

1964 CIVIL RIGHTS ACT PASSED.

1964 WAR ON POVERTY DECLARED.

1965 U.S. TROOPS INVOLVED IN COMBAT IN SOUTH VIETNAM.

1965 VOTING RIGHTS ACT PASSED.

1965 DEPARTMENT OF HOUSING AND URBAN DEVELOPMENT CREATED AND ITS HEAD MADE A CABINET OFFICER.

1966 MEDICARE, WHICH HELPS TAKE CARE OF THE MEDICAL EXPENSES OF PEOPLE OVER SIXTY-FIVE YEARS OF AGE, GOES INTO EFFECT AS PART OF SOCIAL SECURITY.

BIBLIOGRAPHY

GUNTHER, JOHN, and BERNARD QUINT. DAYS TO REMEMBER: AMERICA 1945 TO 1955. New York: Harper & Row, Publishers, 1956.
A pictorial history of one decade.

JOHNSON, GERALD W. AMERICA MOVES FORWARD: A HISTORY FOR PETER. New York: William Morrow and Company, Inc., 1960.
Johnson covers the crucial years from 1917 to 1960, giving illuminating accounts about the United Nations' role in the drama of nations and about the Truman administration.

*JOHNSON, LYNDON B. MY HOPE FOR AMERICA. New York: Random House, Inc., 1964.
President Johnson relates his visions for a Great Society at home and the hopes for world peace.

LEVINE, I. E. YOUNG MAN IN THE WHITE HOUSE: JOHN FITZGERALD KENNEDY. New York: Julian Messner, Inc., 1964.
A biography of President Kennedy which interestingly relates his early childhood, his World War II experiences, and his role as a political leader.

*MICHENER, JAMES A. THE BRIDGES AT TOKO-RI. New York: Random House, Inc., 1953. † New York: Bantam Books, Inc., 1955.

A novel which vividly depicts naval air operations during the Korean War, 1950–1953.

MOOS, MALCOLM. DWIGHT D. EISENHOWER. New York: Random House, Inc., 1965.

A biography of Eisenhower which describes his early life, college days, his role as Supreme Commander of the Allied Forces during World War II, and his two terms as President.

STEINBERG, ALFRED. HARRY S. TRUMAN. New York: G. P. Putnam's Sons, 1963.

A biography which depicts the former President's life, from his birth in 1884 through his eight years in office.

*WHITE, WILLIAM S. THE PROFESSIONAL: LYNDON B. JOHNSON. Boston: Houghton Mifflin Company, 1964. † Greenwich: Crest Books, 1964.

A study of President Johnson as the Chief Executive and his emergence as what many historians label a "professional."

* Denotes more advanced reading.
† Denotes paperback edition.

Index

PAGE NUMBERS FOR MAPS ARE PRINTED IN BOLD.